HOW TO USE THE SABIAN ORACLE

There are several ways to use this book:

• Shuffle the cards and look up the Symbol in the book.

• Think of a number between 1 and 360 and look up the relevant page number.

• Open the book at random.

• Look up the Symbols for your birthday in the Birthday Table.

• Using your Birthchart, investigate the Symbols for any planet or point in the chart.

As with all Oracles,

whichever answer you find is the one you need.

May the Symbols speak to you!

360 DEGREES
OF WISDOM

360 DEGREES OF WISDOM

CHARTING YOUR DESTINY WITH THE SABIAN ORACLE

Lynda Hill

A PLUME BOOK

PLUME
Published by the Penguin Group
Penguin Group (USA) Inc., 375 Hudson Street, New York, New York 10014, U.S.A.
Penguin Books Ltd, 80 Strand, London WC2R 0RL, England
Penguin Books Australia Ltd, 250 Camberwell Road, Camberwell, Victoria 3124, Australia
Penguin Books Canada Ltd, 10 Alcorn Avenue, Toronto, Ontario, Canada M4V 3B2
Penguin Books India (P) Ltd, 11 Community Centre, Panchsheel, New Delhi – 110 017, India
Penguin Books (NZ), cnr Airborne and Rosedale Roads, Albany, Auckland 1310, New Zealand
Penguin Books (South Africa) (Pty) Ltd, 24 Sturdee Avenue, Rosebank, Johannesburg 2196, South Africa

Penguin Books Ltd, Registered Offices: 80 Strand, London WC2R 0RL, England

First published in 1995 by Hill & Hill P/L.

First Edition, March 1995
Revised Edition, December 1995
Special Edition, May 2002
First Plume Printing, December 2004
10 9 8 7 6 5 4 3 2

The Ashleigh Brilliant Pot-Shots (Brilliant Thoughts) epigrams appearing on pages 38, 65, 74, 80, 115, 117, 122, 160, 164, 171, 178, 185, 194, 209, 246, 306, 333, 334 are protected by copyright, and are used here by permission. www.ashleighbrilliant.com

Excerpts from poems: "So Long, Marianne" © 1967 Leonard Cohen; "Sisters of Mercy" © 1967 Leonard Cohen: "The Traitor" © 1979 Leonard Cohen; "Dance Me to The End of Love" © 1984 Leonard Cohen; "Hallelujah" © 1984 Leonard Cohen; "The Captain" © 1984 Leonard Cohen; "Boogie Street" © 2001 Leonard Cohen; "You Have Loved Enough" © 2001 Leonard Cohen. Used by permission. All rights reserved.

 REGISTERED TRADEMARK—MARCA REGISTRADA

LIBRARY OF CONGRESS CATALOGING-IN-PUBLICATION DATA
Hill, Lynda.
360 degrees of wisdom : charting your destiny with the Sabian oracle / Lynda Hill.
p. cm.
ISBN 0-452-28541-0 (trade pbk.)
1. Divination cards. 2. Zodiac. I. Title: Three hundred sixty degrees of wisdom. II. Title:
Three hundred and sixty degrees of wisdom. III. Title.

BF1778.5.H55 2004
133.3'242—dc22   2004044779

Printed in the United States of America
Designed by Paul Smyth

BOOKS ARE AVAILABLE AT QUANTITY DISCOUNTS WHEN USED TO PROMOTE PRODUCTS OR SERVICES. FOR INFORMATION PLEASE WRITE TO PREMIUM MARKETING DIVISION, PENGUIN GROUP (USA) INC., 375 HUDSON STREET, NEW YORK, NEW YORK 10014.

This book is dedicated to Elsie Wheeler

ACKNOWLEDGMENTS

It has taken ten years for this book to evolve. I am incredibly grateful that I can stand on the shoulders of giants such as Marc Edmund Jones, Dane Rudhyar and Elsie Wheeler.

So many people have helped me on my journey. Thank you to all those who believed in the work, encouraged me or assisted me along the way.

Special thanks go to:

Richard Hill and his partner Sue Davis. Richard and I shared our lives for twenty years and continue to be supportive of each other as we enter an exciting new period of our lives.

My daughter Jess—my wonderful editor and sounding board in the writing of this book. Her brilliance has taught me many things; one of them being how to be a better writer.

My son Joel, the coolest person I know on the planet. He did more than his fair share of the cooking while I sat at the computer.

Deirdre Hill, for so many things.

My father Ken Rigby, who for many years was an astrologer and an Edgar Cayce healer.

Alice Kashuba and Dale O'Brien, wonderful students of the Sabian Symbols, who were there from the very beginning of my sojourns into the United States.

Gary Rabideau and Claudia Lapp for doing the Birthday Index and being great mates.

Elizabeth Paul Avedon for designing the Oracle cards, believing so strongly in my work and giving me the step up the ladder that I needed at just the right time.

Paul Smyth for doing the wonderful layout and design.

Philip Sedgwick for being so special—such an incredible mind and inspiration.

Graham Dawson and Stephanie Johnson—directors of Esoteric Technologies Pty Ltd., the company behind Australia's successful astrology software programs Solar Fire, Solar Maps, Solar Writer and Solar Spark—for their enthusiastic nudge that led me to write the Oracle.

Eben Weiss, Michael Lutin, Ray Merriman, Alan Oken, Georgina Haul, Judith Levy, Bob and Diana Zoller, Rick Levine, Scott Davis, Vicki and Dennis Spanogle, Janis Watson, Ananda Bagley, Linda Reid, Ben Cameron, Chrissie Eglem, Deborah Kennedy, Yasmin Boland, Jessica Adams, Ian Mortimer, Ada Cumming, Val and Frank Budny, Diana Hunter, Richard Giles and Susie, Randy and Brian Main, Rick and Angie Romero.

And all the special people who've touched my life.

CONTENTS

PREFACE

Introduction

More and more people in this new era are seeing how magical and mystical life can be. We are finding our ways into much broader, enriching and rewarding levels. So many of us are now exploring the spiritual aspects of our existence; observing our lives, and the effects we have on the people around us and on planet earth. Life today is increasingly complex, however, with so many decisions to make and puzzles to solve. We hunger for meaning and guidance and often want and need answers to life's many questions—here and now.

As many of us already know, there are tools for discovering what's going on, and why, which help us to find our path. Throughout history successive generations have created intuitive guidance tools that reflected the vibration of their culture and their times—the I Ching in ancient China; the Runes in Scandinavia; the Tarot in early Europe.

Oracles have been "read" from an incredible array of objects, including stones, bones, tea leaves, coins, sticks, the backs of tortoise shells and cards. The word "oracle" comes from the Latin word meaning "to pray." It is also connected to the word for mouth. An oracle is described in Webster's Dictionary as being "a divine announcement" and "the medium by which a god reveals hidden knowledge or makes known the divine purpose." Further, it is said to be "an authoritative or wise statement or prediction." In essence an oracle is a tool that allows a conversation with divine forces. They give us signposts and maps so that we can make better, more informed choices in life. In truth, we have the answers to the questions we ask inside of us; however we often need the answers to come through a vehicle outside of ourselves. Now we have the Sabian Oracle, which gives us a direct route into issues that reflect our modern era.

Based on the Sabian Symbols, first created in 1925, and consisting of 360 answers, the Sabian Oracle can be used to guide us through questions about our day-to-day lives: work, relationships, health, spirituality etc. Using the Sabian Oracle will help you to discover what's going on and why, leading to deeper self-awareness. You are able to make more informed choices and greatly enhance your life. It provides us with a psychic and spiritual tool for deep guidance, insight and the ability to see into the amazing occurrences and synchronicities that occur to us and happen around us. You can ask questions about what your future holds, how to go about doing something, what you need to know about a situation or the people involved, directions on your spiritual path, or you can use it to get a message for the day. They lead us out of the wilderness into a place of greater self-determination, fulfillment and enjoyment. Using them also widens and enlarges our psychic abilities and awareness and increases our attunement with our intuitive depths.

THE SABIAN SYMBOL STORY

What are the Sabian Symbols?

The ancients divided up the sky, just like any other circle, into 360 degrees. They assigned each of the 12 constellations (star signs or zodiac signs) 30 degrees each: 12 times 30 = 360. The Sabian Symbols are a set of 360 phrases of words that correspond with each of the 360 degrees of the wheel of the zodiac, from Aries 1 to Pisces 30. Consisting from as little as two words (Virgo 7: "A Harem") to as many as 21 words (Taurus 5: "A Youthful Widow, Fresh and Soul-Cleansed from Grief, Kneels at an Open Grave to Receive the Secret of Eternal Life"), each one of these Symbols holds both a story and a unique energy field of its own. These images hold meaning for those degrees of the signs. Although the Symbols have their foundations in astrology, absolutely no knowledge of astrology is needed to use them.

The Sabian Symbols were given birth in San Diego, California, in 1925 by Marc Edmund Jones, a noted American astrologer and spiritualist, and the gifted clairvoyant Elsie Wheeler. Jones was interested to find a set of word images to go with every degree of the zodiac. Elsie Wheeler was an extraordinary clairvoyant confined to a wheelchair for most of her life. Jones chose Elsie Wheeler as his partner in this "experiment" as she had a remarkable ability to "see" messages, images and symbols. She used this talent to help her clients, but was rather weary of the standard questions she received, such as "When will I be rich?" and "When will I meet the love of my life?" She was eager to take part as she believed that this was an opportunity to really contribute something to astrology.

How Elsie and Marc brought through the Symbols

One day in San Diego in 1925 (unfortunately the date was not recorded), not far from the harbor, astrologer Marc Edmund Jones assisted spiritualist-medium Elsie Wheeler into his car. Elsie was afflicted with severe arthritis, making any movement very difficult and most likely painful. Marc's car made its way from the house on India Avenue where Elsie lived up the sloping hills to Balboa Park. Exactly where in the park they worked is not known. Marc Edmund Jones wrote that they found a place where they could be surrounded by the vibrations of modern American life but would not be disturbed by passers-by. Also, as Elsie was unable to walk, they could not be moved from the car.

Marc Edmund Jones wrote in his book *The Sabian Symbols in Astrology* (first published in 1953), "Miss Elsie Wheeler was very anxious to start ... it was necessary to provide uninterrupted hours, with a problem of inevitable fatigue to be taken into account. She had to be carried, no others could be present and conditions in general had to enable her to function in her accustomed manner. Balboa Park in San Diego offered a spot where a driveway was a matter of a very few yards from one of the city's busiest traffic intersections, fortuitously meeting the necessity that work of this sort be done in the turmoil of some metropolitan center or other unusually dense aggregation of people active in the business of being. There was a screen of trees and bushes, and during the day no one would show any interest in a car parked here for a few hours."

Marc had a set of 360 3" x 5" cardboard cards that he had prepared. These were blank except for a small notation of the sign and number on one side (i.e., Aries 1, Aries 2, up to Pisces 30). Marc would shuffle the cards and place one in front of Elsie, neither of them knowing the sign or number on the card. Marc wrote about this: "One card was put face down before the medium, and she reported on the picture she saw by inward vision. This was noted hurriedly in pencil on the card itself." During the whole process, Marc kept shuffling the cards. Hence, the Sabian Oracle clairvoyantly came through Elsie's psychically attuned mind completely at random (i.e., not in zodiac order Aries 1, Aries 2, Aries 3, etc.) They did ninety Symbols, took a break, did another ninety, had lunch and a short drive, then did another ninety and finished the last ninety at the end of the day.

That the entire set of Sabian Symbols was visualized and recorded in one day is a truly extraordinary feat! If the process of visualizing and recording the Symbols took four hours in the morning and four hours in the afternoon, on average 45 Symbols would have to have been visualized per hour, or one every minute and a half. Elsie Wheeler was obviously tapping into another level of consciousness.

What they'd achieved on that day became clearer and clearer to Marc Edmund Jones over the following years. He had called the exercise an "experiment," but exactly what they had discovered is still emerging today through the minds of those who use the Symbols.

The magic behind the "experiment"

Marc Edmund Jones believed that Elsie Wheeler had tapped into what he called the "ancient mind matrix" of the Sabian alchemists of ancient Mesopotamia. Jones wrote that "...psychism seems to deal with [a] sort of group identity, or with an intelligence which is immortal in the fact that it can be revivified and consulted at will."

Marc said that there was a presence and cooperation "on the invisible side of life" of one of the Brothers of the ancient Sabian occult sect. At the end of the day, when the entire Oracle had been completed, Marc sensed something was wrong with one of the Symbols, and asked Elsie to do that particular one again. He felt this so strongly that it occurred to him that he was being guided by something, so he asked Elsie if "the Brother" was there. Upon hearing that he was, Marc asked her what he was doing, to which she responded that he was "standing with his arms folded." Marc then said, "Ask him why he didn't correct that." Elsie responded, "He says that is up to you." It appears that on all levels, a higher kind of "consciousness" or "intelligence" was operating.

Why the name "Sabian"?

The Sabian Symbol story is embedded in the ancient cultures of the Middle East. Marc Edmund Jones felt that there was an "unseen agency"—an external, esoteric mind-set at work in the birthing of the Sabian Symbols. Connection was made through a "Brother," a member of the ancient Mesopotamian brotherhood, the Sabian Brotherhood. He believed that they were the "voices" that were spiritually behind Elsie Wheeler, delivering the messages that became the Symbols.

The Sabian people were an ancient race of alchemists, living in Harran, a city on the banks of the Euphrates River in Mesopotamia, where astrology is said to have originated. Harran existed from the third millennium BC to the thirteenth century AD. It was the repository for the philosophy of the ancient Chaldeans, who were among the founders of astrology. The Sabians were alchemists who were into talismanic magic and hermeticism. Michael Baigent, in his book *From the Omens of Babylon,* describes talismanic magic as "the magic whereby a deity's power is attracted or coerced down to be concentrated into a physical object. It is, perhaps, analogous to a huge spiritual lens which might magnify and concentrate the powers from above."

In early Babylonia the moon-cult was the national religion: the name Chaldeans means "moon-worshippers." As the religion was gradually wiped out elsewhere, the Sabian people maintained and developed the tradition of Chaldean astrology. They built temples to planets and their rather sophisticated system of alchemy linked the seven planets (as were known then) with metals, colors and numbers. They worked with talismans, oracles and magic. The last temple that was left standing was a moon temple, destroyed by the Tartars in AD 1032. The sect itself disappeared during Mongol invasions of the thirteenth century, when its water supply was diverted to a neighboring town.

The visionaries behind the Oracle

Elsie Wheeler, the clairvoyant

Elsie May Wheeler was born on September 3, 1887, at 9:39 pm in Norris City, Illinois. Severely afflicted and crippled with arthritis, she spent her entire life in a wheelchair. Jones said of her, "She couldn't turn her head and could barely hold her hands." Her intuitive and visionary abilities were not impaired by her handicap. She was an extraordinary clairvoyant and said to be blessed with the ability to see images quickly and clearly.

In the 1920 Census, Elsie is listed as being at the Bethesda Hospital and Home for the Incurables in St. Louis, Missouri. She moved to San Diego some time in the early 1920s, living with her uncle Frank W. Baxter on India Street, on Washington and on Market Street at various times. In the 1930 Census, Frank was listed as being a barber and Elsie as a spiritualist medium. She spent many of her days at the San Diego Indoor Sports Club, a place disabled people have been socializing at since the early 1900s, and which is still in operation today.

Even though her Birthday Symbol is Virgo 12: "A Bride with Her Veil Snatched Away," Elsie never married nor had children. It seems that she was "wedded" to a higher spiritual purpose. Her "Veil" seems to be firmly in place as not much has been recorded or written about her, but the legacy she leaves behind lives on through the gift that is the Sabian Oracle. The beauty and grace with which she is said to have lived her life is enhanced by the gift she gave to the world. She died at the age of 51 in San Diego on the 26th of November 1938.

Marc Edmund Jones, the astrologer

Marc Edmund Jones was born on October 1, 1888, at 8:37 am in St. Louis, Missouri. He lived a colorful and varied life, being a Presbyterian minister, American Theosophist, occult philosopher and prolific scriptwriter for the film industry. Jones was an astrologer for over sixty years and is widely accredited with having made major contributions to the field of astrology. Not only did he create the Sabian Symbols, he devised a whole different approach to the understanding and teaching of astrology, assigning to it a more spiritual basis. He died on March 5, 1980, in Stanwood, Washington, at the age of 91.

What is the zodiac?

The zodiac is an imaginary band of sky that follows the sun's annual path as seen from earth. If we could observe the motion of the sun against the stars for an entire year, it would appear to trace out a large belt or circle in the sky that we call the "ecliptic." This circle also happens to be the plane of the earth's orbit around the Sun. The zodiac is a thin band of the sky on either side of the ecliptic. The word "zodiac" literally means "circle of life," or "circle of living beings," as most of the zodiac signs are animals or people. The band is divided into twelve equal parts, each containing a different astrological constellation. These are the sun signs or star signs of the zodiac.

The zodiac acts as the earth's aura. Just as a human being possesses an aura which surrounds and penetrates the physical body, so also is the earth planet clothed with the subtle matter of the zodiac. The physical plane is familiar ground to everyone, but not so the spheres that lie beyond it. These include the etheric, the astral, the mental, the spiritual and the higher spiritual. All of these dimensions affect us in many ways.

The earliest recorded mention of the zodiac we know of comes from the lands of ancient Mesopotamia, which is roughly the area of modern Iraq. The Mesopotamians, most particularly the people of Babylon, recorded astronomical events on clay tablets. These tablets show the first record of the use of the zodiac in the fifth century BC. Other evidence for a Mesopotamian origin for the zodiac exists in the types of animals chosen for the constellations (e.g., lions and scorpions).

What are zodiac signs?

The expressions "star sign," "sun sign" or "zodiac sign" all actually mean the same thing. When someone says "I'm an Aries," what they're really saying is they were born at the time of the year when the sun was in the zodiac sign of Aries. In other words, their sun sign is Aries. Because our calendar is designed to coincide with the motions of the Sun around the zodiac, the sun is in Aries at nearly the same time period each year (roughly March 21st to April 20th). Hence the 12 zodiac or sun signs are like months of a calendar based on the zodiac.

The zodiac is divided into 12 signs, each 30 degrees long. The zodiac signs start with Aries, which begins at the spot on the ecliptic where the sun is on the first day of spring in the northern hemisphere i.e., March 21. These 30-degree sections of the sky mark out the signs from Aries through to the last sign, Pisces. The 12 signs of the zodiac are Aries, Taurus, Gemini, Cancer, Leo, Virgo, Libra, Scorpio, Sagittarius, Capricorn, Aquarius and Pisces.

Some notes on symbolism

Symbolism is a catalyst or key to accessing our inner wisdom, our connection with the universal consciousness, our spirit or soul—what some call the higher self. This aspect of ourselves does not think in words, but in images, feelings, colors and sounds from a symbolic perspective. It is the abstract part of our psyche that our logical and rational society often does not accept as valid because it doesn't make literal sense: it requires interpretation into objective language, which is not always wholly adequate or accurate.

One of the major current effects that is occurring is a real need to reconnect with "the feminine" —the right brain, intuitive functions. More than ever, we are realizing that the left brain, the logical and reasoning mind, doesn't provide wholly adequate answers to the questions we are asking. We are finding more creative solutions that add meaning to our lives and moments of illumination than we previously thought possible. We are often surprised by images and situations that affect us far more deeply than is logically explicable. It is symbolism that creates a pathway to our deeper understandings and brings our deeper understandings into the conscious world. As Tom Chetwynd says in his book *Dictionary of Symbols*, "Symbols have always been treasured as a means of releasing sources of energy from the unconscious."

When we ask the Sabian Symbols a question, we must keep in mind the need to widen our vision. Looking at the answer through a narrow range of focus may lead to missing the many rewarding possibilities inherent in the answer we're given. For instance, a client asked about the romantic possibilities that were available to him as he was in the process of breaking up a long-term relationship. The answer he got was Leo 15: "A Street Pageant Moving along a Street Packed with People." After a minute looking at the Symbol, he realized the answer he was receiving was to get out into life, out where there are lots of people in order to increase his possibilities of meeting someone. The literal translation of the Symbol did not necessarily include that exact message for him; it was more about adapting the Symbol to his particular question. However, it is indeed possible that he may meet someone while at a street market, or bump into someone on the street, as these things are inherent in that Symbol.

Looking with an increased depth of view always helps when you're dealing with oracles.

Notes for astrologers

How does one use the Sabian Symbols in astrology?

When looking up the Symbol for a planet or placement in a chart, one must round up the degree to the next whole number i.e., if the planet is at 27.15 Pisces, you should read Pisces 28. This is because the zodiac starts at 00.00 Aries and the Symbols begin at Aries 1. So, even if the degree you're looking at is 27.00 Pisces, you would still read Pisces 28. Having said that, it should be emphasized that the Symbol for the degree before (i.e., Pisces 27) will shine a lot of light on the issue being investigated—the degree before indicates the "karmic" issues of the planet or placement, a talent that's been brought through or an issue that needs to be worked out and possibly let go of. Think of the interpretations applied to the moon's south node as a guide to the degree before. The degree after (Pisces 29) is also very illuminating.

These Symbols can be used in every aspect of astrology, including horary, mundane, electional and indeed for any of the zodiacal systems such as heliocentric, sidereal or draconic. A great exercise that helps one to see more into these Symbols is to look up the symbol for the sun at sunrise and watch what happens throughout the day. You can also tune into the degree of the new or full moon for clues to what's going on during that period.

The Symbols can be applied to any point in the zodiac. They will reveal, at times brilliantly and clearly, added layers of meaning to the degree of any of the planets, any asteroids that one might use, the angles—in fact anywhere there's a zodiacal degree.

My belief is that wherever one seeks meaning, one will find meaning.

As we move out of the Piscean age and into the Aquarian age, we are transmuting in many ways, with the vibration of our spiritual and intellectual minds moving into higher gears as we evolve. In such hectic times, we hunger for meaning and guidance, but often don't have the time or the patience to pause and reflect deeply on our situations. The Sabian Oracle opens the doorway between our inner feelings and intentions and our conscious minds. It does this by helping to put what is within us into words. Being provided with possibilities enables us to act positively and confidently, and think rationally.

Welcome to the wonderful, mystical, magical Sabian Oracle.

Recommended reading:

The Sabian Symbols in Astrology by Marc Edmond Jones, Sabian Publishing Society, 1976.
An Astrological Mandala by Dane Rudhyar, Vintage Books (Random House), 1973.
From the Omens of Babylon: Astrology and Ancient Mesopotamia by Michael Baigent, Arkana (Penguin) 1994.
The Sabian Assembly website: *www.sabian.org*
Lynda Hill's website: *www.sabiansymbols.com*

MY JOURNEY WITH THE SABIAN SYMBOLS

Finding and studying the Sabian Symbols has changed my life far more than I could have imagined. My life has been enormously enriched. The interest that people have in the Sabian Symbols has led me to travel the world for the last ten years, teaching and giving readings, and my articles have been published in magazines and journals all over the world. It feels like an honor to do this work.

These days, studying and spreading the message of the Sabian Symbols is an integral part of my life. In my youth I didn't understand why I was irresistibly drawn to certain places. From 1976 and over the course of twenty years I traveled to more than eighty countries. I was most touched with the depth and wisdom of civilizations of the past, particularly the Middle East. I now realize I have been guided and driven to take this journey—even from my early years.

I originally came across the Sabian Symbols in the late 1980s. I found them fascinating and very telling about a person's life and indeed their destiny. I used them here and there in my work and found them to be extraordinary in painting the stories that we live out. However, on my birthday in 1992, a clairvoyant friend of mine, Georgina, said that I had a mission to spread the word of something "special" in astrology. She told me that I would be invited to speak at conferences in Australia and around the world, particularly the United States. My instant response was, "Sure, Georgina, except when I stand up in front of a crowd to speak, I turn to jelly. I even cried once." I didn't feel filled with confidence on any level to do what she was saying I'd do. She continued, saying that I'd write books, one of which would be a big success. I would become known for teaching something special and I would gain the respect of my peers. I remember her words when I protested that I had nothing special to lecture or write about: "Well, I'm just telling you what I'm seeing."

Despite my reluctance, at first, to admit it, the things that Georgina said to me resonated with what I wanted. Two weeks later, in my office, I decided to "ask" for what she'd said. I stated what I wanted, holding the thought for a moment or two. I asked for something "special" to contribute to astrology, for the ability to be able to lecture and write, for the respect of my peers and to be able to travel with my work. Soon after, I picked up a copy of Dane Rudhyar's *An Astrological Mandala*, a book published in 1973 on the Sabian Symbols, and within weeks of asking for these things, I was tearing around the house like a woman possessed, researching and writing about them.

Within the next month I lectured for the first time in my life: I gave two lectures in Sydney and five months later delivered my first talk to an American audience at the Aquarian Revelation Conference in Lansing, Michigan. I also spoke on a panel at that conference in front of some three hundred people at the invitation of one of astrology's brightest stars, Alan Oken. In the thirteen years since then, I have given lectures, workshops and readings in the United States, England, Scotland, Wales, Ireland, Holland, South Africa, New Zealand and Australia. At the time of writing this, I've completed 19 lecture tours of the United States and three world tours. Every step of the way I've felt guided and supported.

It really all began at the age of 22. I felt compelled to travel to the Middle East, to walk on the soil and breathe the air. I felt particularly drawn to Iraq, Turkey and Jordan. On this particular trip, in 1976, I was interested in astrology, but didn't have any in-depth understanding of it; I certainly had no awareness of the Sabian Symbols.

I arrived in Tehran by myself to meet up with a bus tour that would take me through the Middle East, taking in Iran, Iraq, Jordan, Syria, Egypt, Israel, Turkey and then through Europe to London. It was an "overland expedition" that drew the young, alternative-minded travelers of the day. We were told that we were the second bus to be given permission to travel through Iraq after the borders opened up. I joined 36 Australian, British, New Zealand and U.S. nationals and careened off through the lands of Iran and Iraq. Here I was, 22 years old, in the cradle of civilization: Baghdad, Babylon, Ur, Ctesiphon, Petra, Aqaba, Jerusalem, etc., relishing the atmosphere and wondering, at times, what I was doing there. The trip left an indelible impression on me. I remember saying that I had photographs of the people of Iraq in my photo album, and pictures of them in my heart. When I'd say this, I'd wonder why I felt it so strongly.

During my visit to Petra, the ancient rose-red city in southern Jordan, I was sitting in the amphitheater and suddenly had an overwhelming sense of emotion engulf me. In completely alien surroundings, I felt I'd been brought home. I was even moved to say "thank you" to some higher being. I had never felt truly at home anywhere, and haven't felt the same in any of the 80 or so countries I've traveled to since.

In 1995, Robert Zoller, a New York medieval astrology scholar who translates ancient Latin astrological texts into English, was my tour guide around New York. I spoke of my fascination with the Middle East and particularly Petra. We were walking along the street when he pointed out that the Sabian alchemists' ancestors from Mesopotamia, an area which encompassed modern day Iraq, were the Nabateans, the people who built Petra. This aroused feelings in me that defy words or logic. How extraordinary that some twenty years before, Petra had felt so amazingly familiar.

These kinds of synchronicities really do defy words. It's an amazing journey, this journey we're on! Life is more amazing than we know and the Sabian Symbols help us realize its magic and mystery.

—Lynda Hill
January 2004
Avalon, Sydney

USING THE ORACLE CARDS

First—concentrate on your question or situation

The Sabian Oracle seems to work most effectively when your question is important to you and your concentration is undisturbed. This is true of most oracles. However, if you want guidance and are not sure which question to ask, you can ask "What do I need to know most?" or "What's coming up for me?" There are no rules, but the more focused you are, the more you will understand what the Oracle is telling you.

Pick a red card and a blue card

The simplest method is to pick two cards, one red and one blue. The red cards are marked with a sign and the blue ones with a number.

Look up the answer in the book

The end result (e.g., Aquarius 29) is then looked up in the book and the answer needs to be contemplated.

It really is as simple as that.

However, there are other ways of selecting a Symbol. Each page has been numbered from 1 to 360 so that you can simply choose a number in your mind or even a number that may come up in your surroundings. You can also randomly choose a sign and a number; or perhaps just open the book and see where your eyes fall. However, the thing to remember when using these other methods is after using them for some time you may affect the selection by preferring particular numbers or signs, or the book may open to the most often used pages. The best method by far is the card method. It ensures a true selection that the others may not.

The rule I use for accessing the wisdom of the Sabian Symbols is that there are no mistakes, even if you read the "wrong" interpretation, or find out later you've made some kind of mistake. There are no mistakes. We receive the message we're meant to receive when we're meant to.

If a card falls or jumps (as they sometimes do) out of the deck, attention should be paid to it. For instance, if you've just selected a red card and it's Aries and the number 18 falls out as you're shuffling, you should continue, select another blue card, but refer to Aries 18 as part of your answer.

Sometimes, the first answer outlines the actual situation, and gives advice about it. You may indeed need further guidance and consulting the Sabian Oracle again will provide deeper insight. There are no rules for how many times you should consult the Oracle about a particular question, but it must be remembered that time should be taken in considering what it is telling you. The first answer is most likely to contain the purest expression of the situation and any subsequent queries on the same matter will show added layers and descriptions. Unfortunately, continuing to pull the cards until you get the "right answer" is not a good way to go about it, as you can become confused and lose the wisdom that should really be helping you.

You can also make up your own spreads. For instance, you could pull three cards about an issue: one for the past, one for the present and one for the future. The possibilities are only limited by the imagination.

A magical tool we can all use

Remarkable things happen when we use the Sabian Symbols. Events can become unreal and multi-layered. Watching the Symbol come alive around you expands your sense of everything being interrelated, and events of synchronicity happen more and more often. Things that defy explanation often occur.

One such time was during a workshop in New Zealand. During the first part of my lecture, a woman at the back of the class asked if she could use numerology to come up with a Sabian Symbol. I replied that it didn't matter what system was used to come up with a Symbol, there would be meaning in it. With expressions of amazement she told the class that she'd added up the numbers for the letters in her name and it came to 35. She'd looked up the Sabian Symbol on page 35—Taurus 5: "A Youthful Widow, Fresh and Soul-Cleansed from Grief, Kneels at an Open Grave to Discover the Secret of Eternal Life." Her husband had built a coffin for her! The woman said that the coffin was stored in their garage and every time she drove in and out of the garage, she was confronted by it. She said it was to save money and added that he'd built one for himself; their two coffins stood on end, side-by-side in her garage.

The Sabian Symbols can have a sense of humor at times. I was speaking at an astrology conference in Moscow in 1996. A party was held for the speakers, both foreign and Russian, on Saturday night in the hostel room of a couple of the Russian academics. It was by no means luxurious; it was a cheap student hostel. One by one, the furniture in the room collapsed. First the table where I had put two bottles of wine; then we were warned not to sit on a particular chair and a different one collapsed and the bed collapsed into pieces as we tried to move it to make way for more people.

Amongst gales of laughter, somebody drew two cards to get a message for the moment. They drew Virgo 27: "Aristocratic Elderly Ladies Drinking Afternoon Tea in a Wealthy Home"—the Sabian Symbols revealing a great sense of humor, as this was the exact opposite of what was happening. The guy whose bed fell apart fell against the wall and slid down it, laughing. The Symbol was showing the sheer wealth of spirit and enjoyment.

Of course, many times the answer will reflect serious and important issues in your life. One client of mine selected the Symbol Virgo 22: "A Royal Coat of Arms Enriched with Precious Stones." Up until she pulled that Symbol she wasn't feeling very happy or regal at all. However, what she read surprised and encouraged her as she was directly descended from New Guinea royalty and the Symbol was reminding her of it. It told her to believe in herself and always hold her head up high.

Several years ago, our 14-year-old tabby cat, Bubbles, died. We were all very upset, especially my two children. The same day she died, my daughter Jess, who was about 12 at the time, asked me if we could ask the Sabian Oracle for a message about Bubbles. She picked two cards and the answer she received was at once enlightening and reassuring; Aquarius 14: "A Train Entering a Tunnel." We somehow knew that Bubbles was heading for the "light" and we sat and together cried tears of joy, feeling that she was moving somewhere toward the light. The following day, Jess asked if we could ask the Oracle again. I hesitated, wondering what on earth it could tell us, but knowing that the Oracle is always illuminating in some measure, I decided to take another look. The Symbol Jess got was Leo 27: "Daybreak—The Luminescence of Dawn in the Eastern Sky." That felt extraordinary! Reading the words I'd written about that Symbol was very healing for Jess: "You may feel that there is finally a chance for a new beginning. Things have been sacrificed and there may be a certain emptiness, but now you can see the light and move forward again. New ideas, new opportunities, new perspectives, new realizations are emerging." It seemed to us that Bubbles had reached the other side, indeed it felt that she was reincarnating!

Some things to remember

The "you" referred to in the wording of the text may refer to you, a friend, the situation you're in, etc. Read the text and look to see how it fits the particular situation you're inquiring about.

Sometimes the image of the Symbol opens up a dialogue between your intuitive awareness and conscious awareness, sometimes it is the text, sometimes just snippets of it, but the purpose of the Symbols is not only to instruct you, but also inspire you to recognize and realize your own understanding of the answer—the answer that is right for you.

There are a number of generally accepted meanings and archetypes to certain images. It is, however, important to remember that each individual must allow for their own personal response to a Symbol. The Symbols will have different meanings to different people at different times in different situations, although the nature of the Symbol will define the parameters of possibility

The more you expand your vision, the more you'll find layers and layers of meaning. There is always more to a Sabian Symbol than first meets the eye. If you take notice, you will see actual representations of the Symbol in the world around you. For instance, you may pull Aquarius 29: "A Butterfly Emerging from a Chrysalis" and see butterflies around you: perhaps you'll be walking outdoors and a butterfly floats past you, you go to lunch and your girlfriend turns up wearing a butterfly clip, you see a butterfly in an advertisement on the television. Clues can pop up everywhere, particularly if you leave your mind open and receptive to the impressions. Further, the more you open up to seeing the Symbol around you, the more you will expand your psychic awareness. Your intuition will reward you more and more with deeper insights and understanding.

What separates the Sabian Symbols from most other symbolic oracles is that the language is modern and reflects the images of today. A wonderful oracle like the I Ching is made difficult by the references to things that were relevant to the ancient Chinese culture. Things like princes, tigers and ox-carts. The Sabian Symbols talk about cars, trains and airplanes. In the symbolic context these images have clear and current meaning. The Car is symbolic of the individual; a Train speaks of the collective; Window Shopping speaks of desirable things that are out of reach; the Glass-Bottomed Boat shows observing things and viewing the emotions; Santa Claus brings gifts; and so on.

The Caution section at the bottom of each page is included to open your mind to the more difficult or confronting possibilities that you may need to be watchful for in your situation. Your intuition will soon tell you if the situation surrounding your question is more positive or negative.

The greatest barrier to understanding what the Symbol is telling you is not allowing your mind to switch to an intuitive way of thinking. It's best not to let the rational mind and your hopes and desires color your interpretation. Spend time and wait until you become aware of the answer that feels right—even if the answer is difficult. We tend to grow spiritually or emotionally through difficult experiences. The Sabian Oracle is here to give you a guiding hand. The answers truly lie inside you; the Oracle serves to make you consciously aware of them.

I advise people using the Sabian Symbols to use them as a tool for inspiration and guidance. Look at the words and allow your mind to become consciously aware of your situation. It is by taking control and ownership of your own experience that you make a tool like the Sabian Oracle so valuable.

To learn more about how to use the Sabian Symbols, and how to apply them in astrology, please visit *www.sabiansymbols.com.*

HOW TO PREPARE ORACLE CARDS

In case you misplace your cards, here is a method to create a replacement deck.

All you need are two packs of ordinary playing cards with different color (or style of) backing. Most commonly available are red and blue. You can use only one pack, but you will need to make some marking on the back or add a sticker to distinguish between the court cards and number cards.

Creating the 42 cards:

1. Separate the court cards from the number cards. (The Ace is a number card.)
2. Remove and discard the Spade number cards. (Ace–10)
3. Put the red-backed court cards with the blue-backed number cards. (You will then have a spare set of blue court cards and red number cards.)
4. Now you are ready to name the court cards and number the number cards.

Naming and numbering the cards:

The court cards represent the 12 sun signs and the number cards represent the 30 degrees. You now need to mark the cards. You can use an indelible pen or some other form of permanent marker. You can also use stickers that you can write on.

The correspondences:

Aries _____ K♥	**Libra** _____ K♠	1–10 _____ A♥–10♥
Taurus _____ Q♥	**Scorpio** _____ Q♠	
Gemini _____ J♥	**Sagittarius** ___ J♠	11–20_____ A♦–10♦
Cancer _____ K♦	**Capricorn** ___ K♣	
Leo _____ Q♦	**Aquarius** ____ Q♣	21–30_____ A♣–10♣
Virgo _____ J♦	**Pisces** _____ J♣	

Your cards are now ready!

USING THE BIRTHDAY TABLES

You can learn a lot about yourself by looking up the Sabian Symbol for your birthday (go to the Appendix for the Birthday Tables). For each day of the year, there are three Sabian Symbols listed. Each of these will all have an effect on your life in some way. Sometimes the message of a Symbol listed for a birthday will immediately stand out, other times the meaning may not be quite so obvious. The Sabian Symbols are played out through the way we express our personalities and by the events in our lives. Alternatively, you may see the Symbol demonstrated through the agency of someone else in your life: friends, parents, partners, etc. However, even in the case of seeing the Symbol expressed through somebody else, it is often that person mirroring something that you perhaps haven't noticed or learned about yourself.

It is also extremely useful to look up the Symbols for the date of an event, something that's happened, or indeed, something you're planning to do. If you are planning a wedding or a party, for instance, see what the Symbols are saying for that date.

Celebrity Birthday Symbol Examples

Princess Diana—July 1

Cancer 9: A Small Naked Girl Bends over a Sparkling Pond Trying to Catch a Fish

Diana was often photographed in her bathing costume, swimming in the ocean or relaxing by a pool. This Symbol also speaks of naïveté and innocence, qualities she was both known and admired for.

Cancer 10: A Large Diamond in the First Stages of the Cutting Process

When the first pictures of Diana appeared in the media, she was like a beautiful uncut diamond. As the years went by, we saw a beautiful woman emerge, well known for her penchant for fashion and beauty.

Cancer 11: A Clown Is Caricaturing Well-Known Personalities

The "Clown" is reflected in her need to put on a face for many occasions. It seems she was seldom really allowed to just "be herself."

Michael Jackson—August 29

Virgo 6: A Merry-Go-Round

The "Merry Go Round" reflects his life as more circus than reality. Indeed, he has merry go rounds at his own theme park/home, Neverland.

Virgo 7: A Harem

Among other things, the Harem Symbol speaks of his large family and his sizable entourage of people.

Virgo 8: A Girl Takes Her First Dancing Instruction

Jackson can easily take credit for changing the face of modern dance.

Christopher Reeve—September 25

Libra 2: The Light of the Sixth Race Transmuted to the Seventh

This Symbol speaks of his days as Superman, plus the "superhuman" qualities he expresses in his everyday life. In the movie *Superman*, he is portrayed as coming from a planet that is more highly evolved than Earth.

Libra 3: The Dawn of a New Day Reveals Everything Changed

One moment he was a vital, athletic and able man, the next minute he was in a totally new reality, facing life in a wheelchair. Reeve has also said that after the accident, every single time he woke up, he'd have to face the reality he was really in after having dreams that pictured him with full mobility.

Libra 4: A Group of Young People Sit in Spiritual Communion around a Campfire

Reeve has an uncanny ability to bring people together in a common cause—his work for the support of spinal research has developed worldwide awareness.

Hillary Clinton—October 26

Scorpio 2: A Broken Bottle and Spilled Perfume

Hillary had an amazing capacity to restrain her emotions during the scandals surrounding her husband. Even though the "contents" of her marriage and private life were "spilled" (so to speak!), she retained a high degree of dignity.

Scorpio 3: Neighbors Help in a House-Raising Party in a Small Village

Hillary is known for her community work. Indeed, she wrote a book titled *It Takes a Village.*

Scorpio 4: A Youth Holding a Lighted Candle in a Devotional Ritual Gains a Sense of the Great "Other World"

This Symbol speaks about Hillary's devotion, her causes and her career. Her speeches are often focused on talking about our hopes and fears, and about our children's futures.

Deepak Chopra—22 October

Libra 28: A Man Alone in Deep Gloom. Unnoticed, Angels Are Coming to His Aid

People all over the world claim that his philosophies have helped them through difficult periods of their lives.

Libra 29: Mankind's Vast and Enduring Effort to Reach for Knowledge Transferable from Generation to Generation

Chopra's books seem to have assumed a timeless quality, and an appeal to people of all ages.

Libra 30: Three Mounds of Knowledge on a Philosopher's Head

This is indicative of his finely tuned teachings and ideas.

Marilyn Monroe—June 1

Gemini 10: An Airplane Dives Toward the Earth as Though Falling

Through taking risks, her life often got out of hand. This Symbol also reflects the depressions she frequently experienced.

Gemini 11: Newly Opened Lands Offer the Pioneer New Opportunities for Experience

This Symbol paints the picture of how Norma Jean went off to Hollywood, starting a brand-new life.

Gemini 12: A Black Slave Girl Demands Her Rights of Her Mistress

Marilyn was underestimated by both her peers in the movie industry and her audience. People saw her as just a pretty face and didn't take her seriously.

Recently, I met a Pisces woman who was lamenting being married to an Aries man. She said she was tired of battling with him. I asked her what her birthdate was and she replied March 3. I told her that one of her Sabian Symbols was Pisces 13: "A Sword, Used in Many Battles, is now in a Museum." I explained to her that "battling" was not something she wanted to be doing anymore. This Symbol gives the advice "There may have been a lot learned in the "Battles" you've experienced, but one thing that's best learned is that continuing to fight may lead to a bitter end, with no one being a true winner." The Symbol for Pisces 14: "A Woman Wrapped in Fox Fur," contained clues to how she needs to use her feminine intelligence in order to get the most out of her relationship with her husband.

I asked what her husband's birthday was. Her reply was the 11th of April. One of the Symbols for his birthday is Aries 21: "A Boxer is Entering the Ring." She explained how he would take any opportunity to pick on her or to start a fight. This insight lead to some extraordinary insights into their situation and no doubt helped her to understand what was happening between the two of them. In order for him to gain the benefits of the other Sabian Symbol for his birthday—Aries 22: "The Gate Opens to the Garden of All Fulfilled Desires," he had to drop his "warring" attitude and accept his life for all the beauty and promise it contained without fighting or being defensive.

But enough about everybody else—it's time for you to look up your own Birthday Symbols!

360 DEGREES
OF WISDOM

A WOMAN HAS RISEN OUT OF THE OCEAN, A SEAL IS EMBRACING HER

Aries 1

Commentary: "A Woman Has Risen out of the Ocean." She is consciously aware of leaving the past behind in order to emerge into a whole new arena of existence and activity. The "Seal Embracing Her" symbolizes her being welcomed into this new arena. This degree is right on the cusp of Pisces and Aries, when the yearly astrological cycle begins again. It's like the beginning of a new year. In the northern hemisphere it marks the beginning of spring—the spring equinox. Long ago there was a belief that the spirits of those who had drowned at sea had the ability to enjoy life in the ocean in the form of "Seals." When they wished, the Selkies could, once per moon cycle, swim ashore, drop their sealskins and become mortals again.

Oracle: New understandings and awareness are coming to light. Whatever is emerging, either in you or around you needs to be accepted, welcomed and nurtured. It's best to resist the old familiar ways of being or relating as they can pull you back to outgrown and possibly unsatisfactory conditions. Maybe you feel you are not being acknowledged, don't have a voice or are not being heard. Take heart, as comfort and salvation are likely to be found in the most unexpected places. Despite any setbacks, be aware that you possess the power to make the necessary changes in your life. It is time to claim your place or make a mark in this new world. So much potential lies ahead of you. Welcome this new beginning and be fearless in the face of the changes that are coming. Accept the "Embrace" of those who welcome you into this new sphere. It is inevitable that you'll leave something behind as you move into this new territory. Enjoy the journey and give birth to self-love, self-worth and divine creativity. Let go of the past and emerge into life and love.

Keywords: Cycles starting. Beginnings. Emergence into concrete manifestation. Embracing and honoring the shadow. Recognizing our animal side. Tropical islands or lands. Rocky shores. Seals. Oceans and water. Shedding skins. Transmutation. The Selkie myth. Grounding one's energy. Stepping between the sea and the shore. Androgyny. Love and its embrace. Finding your feet and your voice. Mermaids.

The Caution: Using masculine power to overshadow emotions. Refusing to move on. Feeling held back by fears and old life patterns. Falling back into previous, unsatisfactory conditions. Dragging others backward. Immobilizing fear of the unknown. Being just another "fish in the sea."

What does this **SYMBOL** say to *you?*

Change starts when someone sees the next step.
William Drayton

But the beginning of things, of a world especially, is necessarily vague, tangled, chaotic, and exceedingly disturbing. How few of us ever emerge from such a beginning! How many souls perish in its tumult!
Kate Chopin

*Who would be
A merman bold,
Sitting alone
Singing alone
Under the sea,
With a crown of gold,
On a throne?*
Lord Alfred Tennyson

The journey of a thousand leagues begins from beneath your feet.
Lao Tzu

And forget not that the earth delights to feel your bare feet and the winds long to play with your hair.
Kahlil Gibran

Everything teaches transition, transference, metamorphosis: therein is human power, in transference, not in creation; and therein is human destiny, not in longevity but in removal we dive and reappear in new places.
Ralph Waldo Emerson

Aries 2

In the end, everything is a gag.
Charlie Chaplin

Sometimes when reading Goethe I have the paralyzing suspicion that he is trying to be funny.
Guy Davenport

The best way to cheer yourself up is to try to cheer somebody else up.
Mark Twain

To make mistakes is human; to stumble is commonplace; to be able to laugh at yourself is maturity.
William Arthur Ward

Not one shred of evidence supports the notion that life is serious.
Anonymous

A serious and good philosophical work could be written consisting entirely of jokes.
Ludwig Wittgenstein

Different taste in jokes is a great strain on the affections.
George Eliot

A COMEDIAN ENTERTAINING A GROUP OF FRIENDS

Commentary: "A Comedian Entertaining a Group of Friends" is seen. The function of the "Comedian" is to show that there's a need to have a lighter and more positive attitude toward ourselves, others and life in general. He's "Entertaining a Group of Friends" which promotes a feeling of coming together or sharing through laughter and fun. The talk may center on people, things or situations with the more amusing aspects brought out. An objective awareness of life can bring enjoyment to concerns as we see things in a different or wider perspective.

Oracle: We often need to be reminded that we are essentially human and share the same imperfections, frailties and shortcomings as the next person. Look for the fun in what's going on around you as light relief can often be found through seeing the humor and the funny side. In answer to your question this Symbol often shows that there's a need to let go of seriousness. Try looking at things with a smile on your face. Simple changes in attitude or approach can often free your mind and bring about a much better outcome. However, this can show somebody not taking life seriously enough or perhaps putting on a show to get attention or to be liked. Look at what's happening and evaluate it: is there any truth in what's being said or is it really just a joke? Although there is often pleasure in sharing fun, sometimes it is just masking the more serious aspects of the situation. The old saying, "Many a truth is told in jest," is often right. Things are often revealed by a slip of the tongue. Whatever, remember; it's good to be lighthearted—and other people's spirits will probably be raised at the same time.

Keywords: Seeing the funny side. Having insights. Always being on the "go" mentally. Putting on a show for others. Having presence and charisma. Being the life of the party. Banter. Cracking up with laughter. Ragging each other. Humorous interplay. Saying what the group wants to hear. Jokes. The buffoon. Inside jokes. The jester.

The Caution: Being silly or trivial to avoid reality and gain acceptance. Feeling separate because of different views. Not seeing the light side. Being a bore with many irrelevant things said. Being flippant and insincere. Not being amused. Demanding the spotlight. Feeling responsible for how others feel. Not knowing when to stop. Not having good boundaries.

What does this **SYMBOL** say to *you?*

A CAMEO SHOWS THE PROFILE OF A MAN THAT SUGGESTS THE OUTLINE OF HIS COUNTRY

Aries 3

Commentary: "A Cameo Profile" is a simple yet strong definition of an individual's character, shape, loyalties and role in life. The "Cameo" suggests the appearance of a growing objective awareness of how someone fits into the larger picture. You may find that you, or someone else, have a more important role than was previously thought; or that you are imprinting your mark; or possibly becoming a model of one's tradition, culture, thoughts or ideas.

Oracle: There's often a need to feel included or involved in the larger picture in order to feel "whole" or accepted. Taking the time to examine your place in society can bring about insights into just what the big picture is for you. Understanding and expanding your true place in the scheme of things can lead to actually having a much larger "Profile." This could be on any level, emotional, physical, mental or spiritual. The "Country" that this Symbol implies may not have national boundaries. There is the spiritual "country," the ideological "country," even past life "countries." There are some people who find their roots in a mixture of these places, or realities, and don't actually feel a belonging to their actual "homeland." The sense of having a place is often deep-seated and truly found in the individual's belonging to the essential self. How do you, and others, fit into this situation? Does your "Profile" define you in a different way from what you'd like, or are you happy with the outline of your image? Picture who you want to be or what you want out of life. Using a pen and paper, draw your "Cameo" or just picture what the outline of your "Country" should be, as it could be an interesting exercise. We are what we believe we are. What face are you showing to the world?

Keywords: Observing one's limitations. Living a life that is large. Atlases and maps. Standing by one's self. Allegiances with creed, religion, race or country. Nationhood. Brotherhood. The land. People in uniforms of any kind. The face of fighters who fought "the good fight." Borders and limitations to activity. Identification. Expatriates.

The Caution: Stereotyping one's self or others. Blindly following the dogma of parents, government or officials. Not seeing the true essence of one's self. Expecting to fit into some "shape" or model. Becoming identified with externals. Seeking recognition from others.

What does this **SYMBOL** say to *you?*

As a woman I have no country. As a woman my country is the whole world.
Virginia Woolf

He worked like hell in the country so he could live in the city, where he worked like hell so he could live in the country.
Don Marquis

A man's country is not a certain area of land, of mountains, rivers, and woods, but it is a principle; and patriotism is loyalty to that principle.
George William Curtis

Socrates said he was not an Athenian or a Greek, but a citizen of the world.
Plutarch

He who has an art has everywhere a part.
Romanian Proverb

I have never belonged wholeheartedly to a country, a state, or to a circle of friends, nor even to my own family.
Albert Einstein

All the world is a stage, and all the men and women merely players. They have their exits and entrances; each man in his time plays many parts.
William Shakespeare

Aries 4

Let there be spaces in your togetherness.
Kahlil Gibran

Whether joy or sorrowful, the heart needs a double, because a joy shared is doubled and a pain that is shared is divided.
Anonymous

The man who goes alone can start today; but he who travels with another must wait till the other is ready, and it may be a long time before they get off.
Henry David Thoreau

I was never less alone than when by myself.
Edward Gibbon

Far from the madding crowd's ignoble strife.
Thomas Gray

Love does not consist in gazing at each other, but in looking together in the same direction.
Antoine de Saint-Exupéry

TWO LOVERS ARE STROLLING THROUGH A SECLUDED WALK

Commentary: "Two Lovers" are shown "Strolling through a Secluded Walk." This image shows that there's sometimes a need to escape the realities of the world and touch the deeper feelings of one's heart. The "Secluded Walk" that the "Lovers" are taking pictures the need for private time, solitude or quiet romance. An actual "Secluded Walk" may not be necessary—what is important is the ability to exclude outside energies that interfere with the sharing of intimate time.

Oracle: This Symbol shows that some time should be taken away from the hustle and bustle of the everyday world, even if only for a short while. Sometimes a detour must be taken and the materialistic world put aside in order to share special moments with someone close to you. You may desire, or even *need* to exclude others or outside energies from your life at the moment. These things may be interfering with what needs to be said or done in order to solve relationship difficulties and to move forward in life. If you are by yourself in this situation, the solution may lie in taking time off and just being alone and rediscovering yourself. This can open the door to sharing more intimate dimensions of yourself with another person when you feel you're ready for it. This is especially true if your life has been hectic or confused recently. Sending out an invitation to someone special to share moments of your life may bring more rewards than are immediately apparent. Can you schedule things so that you can afford some time out?

Keywords: Walking love's path. Secret love affairs. Seeking shelter from others' eyes. Wanting or needing to be undisturbed. The young at heart. Being by one's self and wondering where the "other" is. Romance. Quiet moments. Seclusion and peace. Intimacy and sharing. Desired destinations. Walking and strolling together. "Keep Out" signs. Relationships that are solid and satisfying. Issues of seclusion, inclusion or exculsion. Privacy. Being self-sufficient.

The Caution: Being "selfish" by keeping one's partner or friend to one's self. Jealousy when others are around. Feeling "left out" and uninvited. Narrow-minded responses to people or things. Loneliness and/or the desire to be left alone. Denial of self and needs. Not wanting contact. Rejecting those who don't measure up. Seeing one's partner as a possession.

What does this **SYMBOL** say to *you?*

A WHITE TRIANGLE IS SEEN; IT HAS GOLDEN WINGS

Aries 5

Commentary: "A White Triangle" with "Golden Wings" is a spiritually uplifting image. It is hard to know exactly what the clairvoyant Elsie Wheeler saw when she received this image, but it could be that she saw the vision of a moth—the White Triangle Tortrix which has gold-colored wings. The Symbol implies the possibility of being able to raise yourself above the ordinary, using your natural gifts to find a new perspective into what's going on. What's needed is an uplifted view to expand your scope of awareness.

Oracle: This is a beautiful Symbol that indicates that you don't have to feel stuck in the present situation—you can rise above it to something more spiritual, beautiful and joyful. It can picture an eagerness for spiritual integration. At this time there may be a need not to ground your visions, but allow them the free flight of imagination. However, sometimes the drive for spiritual integration or the longing for ecstatic experiences can cause a feeling of being out of touch with reality. It is important to persevere through any feelings of disorientation until a new sense of balance is discovered—then the grounding of your vision (or situation) can take place naturally. Use your imagination and remember to integrate the three agencies: body, mind and spirit. "A White Triangle with Golden Wings" is a wonderful image or mandala for meditation. Drawing it on a piece of paper and hanging it up on the wall may well bring some amazing insights into the situation or the question that has brought you to the Oracle. Seeking harmony will cause things to move, sometimes in a very surprising way!

Keywords: Inspiration and zeal. Feeling elevated and inspired through spiritual or creative agencies. Flying to a greater perspective. Taking off. Purity of thought and expression. Angelic forms. Creative imagination. Self-transcendence. Finding new dimensions of experience. Illusions of sight. Visions. Untethered imaginations. Ascension. Ascended beings. Moths. Butterflies. Flying Machines.

The Caution: Not noticing your own down-to-earth needs or the needs of those around you. Losing the plot. Escapism. Forgetting about the requirements and desires of the body. Being ungrounded. The space cadet. Things that aren't based in reality.

You cannot depend on your eyes when your imagination is out of focus.
Mark Twain

Love and desire are the spirit's wings to great deeds.
Goethe

I know of no more encouraging fact than the unquestionable ability of man to elevate his life by conscious endeavor.
Henry David Thoreau

Scully: Another Bermuda Triangle?
Mulder: It's more like a wrinkle in time.
The X-Files

He who has imagination without learning has wings but no feet.
Horace

You see things as they are and ask "Why?"
I dream things as they never were and ask "Why not?"
George Bernard Shaw

And I said, oh that I had wings like a dove! For then would I fly away, and be at rest.
The Bible

What does this **SYMBOL** say to *you?*

Aries 6

Fresh activity is the only means of overcoming adversity.
Goethe

Conformity is the jailer of freedom and the enemy of growth.
John F. Kennedy

Within yourself deliverance must be searched for, because each man makes his own prison.
Sir Edwin Arnold

A man will be imprisoned in a room with a door that's unlocked and opens inwards, as long as it does not occur to him to pull rather than push.
Ludwig Wittgenstein

Room Service? Send up a larger room.
Groucho Marx

There comes a time in a man's life when to get where he has to go—if there are no doors or windows, he walks through a wall.
Bernard Malamud

Light can penetrate dark, but dark can't penetrate light.
Kryon

It's futile to gaze at the world through a car window.
Albert Einstein

A SQUARE BRIGHTLY LIGHTED ON ONE SIDE

Commentary: "A Square Brightly Lighted on One Side" is a Symbol of containment, walls and boundaries. A four-sided structure can lead to feeling contained, boxed in, trapped or claustrophobic in a place or situation. However, the "Square" of this Symbol is not completely walled in; it is being lit up "on One Side," which shows there are solutions and a way out. It indicates creative solutions are at hand, if one will turn their attention to that possibility.

Oracle: In the situation facing you there's a need to not concern yourself too much with one side of an issue, even though you may feel boxed in with little sign of resolution. Look around with a positive, problem–solving attitude, and apply simple, active solutions. There *is* a way out of your dilemma, although at first it may not be very obvious. It is important not to surrender to frustrations and limitations. As an exercise, try drawing an image of a square with one side not drawn in. Label each of the sides with a part of the problem that makes you feel trapped and constricted. What part of your problem, or the solution, could you write in the fourth, "Brightly Lighted" side? What are your possibilities for free movement in this situation? There is a "Lighted" illumination and a solution if you turn your attention to it. Moving toward that "Light" and refusing to be limited can lead to a sense of freedom and security to do what you need to do. Open a window, turn on a light or open the curtains. Relinquishing the experience of "bouncing off the walls" will most likely bring you to the place where you belong and the answers that you seek.

Keywords: Illuminated solutions that provide ways out of tight situations. Having to put up walls to protect or defend versus taking down the barriers. Putting all your eggs in one basket. Feeling fully contained. Walls and fences. Boxes. Understanding the borders of one's activities. Looking for stabilization. Lighting up dark corners. Sunshine. Stepping outside the square or feeling there is no square. Moving out. Windows and doors. Rubik's Cube.

The Caution: Surrendering, feeling trapped. Seeing only one side. Bouncing around, feeling like there's no way out. Internal struggles that prevent seeing solutions. Not acknowledging or expressing true feelings. Desperately wanting to escape tight situations. Fear of ambush. Fear of attack from behind. Claustrophobia. Padded cells. Painting oneself into a corner.

What does this **SYMBOL** say to *you?*

A MAN SUCCESSFULLY EXPRESSING HIMSELF IN TWO WORLDS AT ONCE

Aries 7

Commentary: "A Man Successfully Expressing Himself in Two Worlds at Once" shows someone having the ability to be versatile and adaptable. When operating in "Two Worlds," one's life may seem divided with divergent responsibilities, needs and urges. As this image implies that this person is "Successfully Expressing Himself," it shows that this is a time when it is possible, and probably necessary, to cope with separate or diverse areas of life.

Oracle: You have the ability, or the challenge, to shift your focus from one thing to another when it is necessary. There is also the drive, determination and focus not to run out of energy. However, there is a need to be careful not to scatter your energies, as this may lead to wasting time and losing valuable opportunities for growth. Remember to be versatile and adaptable. There is often the need for a form of balance between the emotional, spiritual and material arenas. It's through being clear and true to the difference between these two areas, these "Two Worlds," that great things can be achieved. For instance, one can have a "straight" job during the day, and be doing something really unusual during the rest of the time, or live between two homes, two cities, two relationships, etc. On another level, there could be a realization of operating on the physical, more everyday level of your life while having messages coming through from more spiritual realms. You can be successful in anything you undertake now, as long as you are happy with the compromises that may be asked of both you and others and the splitting up of areas of your life. Are you enjoying the best of both "Worlds?"

Keywords: Integrating the spiritual with the material. Balancing things. Doing juggling acts. Moving through people's lives and social stratas. Translations of words and thoughts from one area of life to another. Having separate family situations. Living a dual life. Being adaptable. Moonlighting. Alternate realities. Shifting focus when necessary. Versatility. Looking elsewhere.

The Caution: Fooling yourself that you can be all things to different people, but eventually failing in one or both. Exhaustion through trying to achieve too much. Deception, if allegiances are not clear. Infidelity and fickleness. Scattering of interests with little being achieved. Bigamy. Two-faced. Lies and masquerades. Feeling like one doesn't truly fit in anywhere. Not being able to stop.

What does this **SYMBOL** say to *you?*

Think like a man of action, and act like a man of thought.
Henri L. Bergson

I've been trying for some time to develop a lifestyle that doesn't require my presence.
Gary Trudeau

Any woman who has a career and a family automatically develops something in the way of two personalities, like two sides of a dollar bill, each different in design... her problem is to keep one from draining the life from the other.
Ivy Baker Priest

There are no elements so diverse that they cannot be joined in the heart of a man.
Jean Giraudoux

Communication is a continual balancing act, juggling the conflicting needs for intimacy and independence.
Deborah Tannen

It is the nature of ambition to make men liars and cheats, to hide the truth in their breasts, and show, like jugglers, another thing in their mouths.
Sallust

Aries 8

I am a feather for each wind that blows.
William Shakespeare

Our plans miscarry because they have no aim. When you don't know what harbor you're aiming for, no wind is the right wind.
Seneca

Like a kite cut from the string, lightly the soul of my youth has taken flight.
Ishikawa Takuboku

Distracted by what is far away, he does not see his nose.
Malagasy Proverb

If the winds of fortune are temporarily blowing against you, remember that you can harness them and make them carry you toward your definite purpose through the use of your imagination.
Napolean Hill

If you pay nervous attention to other people's opinions, maneuver to obtain their indulgence and to stand high in their esteem, you will be whisked about in their winds and you will lose yourself.
Jo Coubert

A great wind is blowing and that gives you either imagination or a headache.
Catherine II

A WOMAN'S HAT WITH STREAMERS BLOWN BY THE EAST WIND

Commentary: "A Woman's Hat with Streamers Blown by the East Wind." The "East Wind" often implies messages or forces coming in seemingly from out of the blue. These messages could be about spirit or spiritual teachings. There's a degree of gentleness here and adaptability to external forces. Eastern philosophies can come to mind as a way of thinking through this experience. Indeed, some of the oriental systems of thought may play a major part in this situation.

Oracle: In the situation facing you, you may feel as though you're being blown a little off course from what you originally set out to do. This can happen even more if you or someone you're dealing with can't make up their mind, or is constantly shifting their perspective. There's a need to adjust continually to the direction of outside forces. Shifts of mind and attitude may happen as a result or may, indeed, need to happen. Any changes are best greeted and considered playfully and lightly. Allow wisdom to lead you to new and different solutions, but be wary of acting superficially. Look to see if your mind keeps changing course and blowing you off center. If you do lose your way temporarily, be assured that you can be steered back onto the right course with just a little contemplation on the direction your life is meant to be taking you. Take your time, be patient and act with the feminine forces of gentility, grace and dignity. This Symbol indicates that you are somewhat protected from the more disturbing elements of your situation. Is someone running after something or someone trying to retrieve it while it just keeps being "Blown" further away? In what direction is this "Wind" blowing you?

Keywords: Attuning one's self through Eastern philosophies. Protective guidance. Balloons and hot-air ballooning. Compasses. Weather vanes and wind chimes. East meets west. Being adaptable to the moment. The winds of time and change. Shifts in the "Wind" bringing shifts in attitude or direction. Hats, scarves, streamers.

The Caution: Only accepting solutions that satisfy selfish or social needs. Insincere and easily blown around. Fickleness. Being tossed around by momentary patterns in the "weather." Conflicting ideals. Forgetting things in a moment. Being easily distracted. Changing course midstream. Being blown off the path, thereby losing one's center or way. Breezes that disturb one's equilibrium. Losing yourself in others' opinions.

What does this **SYMBOL** say to *you?*

A SEER GAZES INTENTLY INTO A CRYSTAL BALL BEFORE HIM

♈

Aries 9

Commentary: "A Seer Gazes Intently into a Crystal Ball before Him" shows the talent, the need and the tools for intense focus and concentration. The "Seer" sees many things as he "Gazes Intently," looking for clues through a narrow focus in the "Crystal Ball." Using a "Crystal Ball" is his method of receiving information from the world of spirit. By looking deeply into a situation, images can form and meaning can be revealed. This enhances the ability to observe things that others may miss.

Oracle: In your situation the whole picture is probably right before you but you may need help in interpreting its meaning. With a little concentrated effort, you will be able to see things more clearly. Find or retrieve information and clues by really looking at the structure of things. What are you doing and how are you focusing toward what you really want? The more you narrow your "Gaze," and the more you trust in your own intuition, the sharper and clearer the focus will become. What is your unconscious mind trying to tell you? Find something to focus on, something beautiful, illuminating or inspiring in some way. Consider what messages your psyche is trying to bring you. If you have a dream, write it down. Drawing this Symbol may show an ability to see things ahead of their time. Tools of divination such as crystal balls, tarot cards, the runes, the I Ching, the Sabian Symbols or anything you have at your disposal will help you find the answers. However, there may be a need for caution if you are constantly seeking answers from tarot cards, astrology, clairvoyants, etc. Perhaps you should know when to call a halt, examining your own goals rather than merely getting answers from other people. Whatever, be patient and have a good, long, insightful look. The steadier your "Gaze," the more will be revealed.

Keywords: Flashes of inspiration. Tuning in and looking within for answers. Creative visualizations. Aura readings. Cutting through irrelevant messages. Looking carefully at structure. Seeking perfection. Clairvoyance. Illumination and deep insights. Looking ahead to see the signs.

The Caution: Confused by literal meanings. Not seeing the symbolic message. Always looking this way and that, not at the center. Getting lost in the big picture. Daydreaming and ignoring what's really going on. Obsessing over what may happen. Needing to know what's coming up. Being impatient.

The only limits are, as always, those of vision.
James Broughton

We are always in search of the redeeming formula, the crystallizing thought.
Etty Hillesum

Everyone sees the unseen in proportion to the clarity of his heart, and that depends upon how much he has polished it. Whoever has polished it more sees more — more unseen forms become manifest to him.
Jalal-Uddin Rumi

Refrain from asking what is going to happen tomorrow, and every day that fortune grants you, count as gain.
Horace

It is said that the present is pregnant with the future.
Voltaire

The most pathetic person in the world is someone who has sight, but has no vision.
Helen Keller

What does this **SYMBOL** say to *you?*

Aries 10

It is better to fail in originality than to succeed in imitation.
Herman Melville

Originality does not consist in saying what no one has ever said before, but in saying exactly what you think yourself.
James Stephens

Adam was the only man who, when he said a good thing, knew that nobody had said it before him.
Mark Twain

It is the fate of new truths to begin as heresies and end as superstitions.
Thomas H. Huxley

Half my life is an act of revision.
John Irving

Civilization had too many rules for me, so I did my best to rewrite them.
Bill Cosby

Great innovators and original thinkers and artists attract the wrath of mediocrities as lightning rods draw the flashes.
Theodor Reik

A TEACHER GIVES NEW SYMBOLIC FORMS TO TRADITIONAL IMAGES

Commentary: "A Teacher Gives New Symbolic Forms to Traditional Images." This Symbol shows someone who can take a thing or a situation and transform and update it. The "Traditional Images" can be ideas, objects, icons, beliefs; things we are familiar with. That a "Teacher Gives New Symbolic Forms" shows the ability to restructure, reinterpret and present them in a way more in tune with the times. It indicates a need for a fresh and revitalized perspective on things. This is what Marc Edmund Jones and Elsie Wheeler did with the Sabian Symbol "experiment." This book has taken the Symbols a step further, giving them further depth and insight.

Oracle: In the situation facing you there's a need to analyze and perhaps rewrite what has been observed and learned in the traditional roles we live out. Things may need a new interpretation to bring them up to speed with today's thinking. Someone in this situation may have truly original ideas, but there's a possibility of holding these back, feeling it has all been done before. The message here is to allow yourself to be creative and look for modern answers, seeing things in a different light or from a different angle. This may lead to realizations you have never even considered or imagined. Bringing out something new will revitalize your situation and affect those around you. This can bring new understandings about people and the way things work. There could be a revisioning of how one sees something like marriage, work, relationships, education, etc. Sometimes this requires one to be daring, to "step outside the box." Be prepared to take a different stance or look at things from a new and fresh perspective. Don't stick to limitations, either your own or those others place on you. You may have to make a stand against those in a higher or more exalted position who think they know more than you—perhaps they don't.

Keywords: New dimensions breaking old thought forms or behavior. Quantum science. Innovation and re-creation. Working with educational tools. Finding new inspiration. Being "ahead of one's time." New-age consciousness. Ideas out of the past for the future. Sticking one's neck out. Rewriting the book.

The Caution: Rejecting old ideas because they are old instead of reforming them. Throwing things of worth out, without examining them. Having little respect for things that are really worthwhile or traditional. Sticking with the tried and true, no matter what. Thinking that no one will be interested in your ideas. Heresy. Dogma.

What does this **SYMBOL** say to *you?*

THE PRESIDENT OF THE REPUBLIC OR THE RULER OF ONE'S COUNTRY

Aries 11

Commentary: "The President" or "the Ruler" pictures a person who's in control, has a sense of authority and is called upon to do the right thing for his people, his "Country" and indeed, his position or office. This "President" or "Ruler" has the right, and the duty, to call the shots in their territory or sphere of operation.

Oracle: This Symbol says that it's time to take charge, and to expand your base of operations. There may be a need to take control and command respect from others by showing that you have the confidence to make your own decisions. This is your opportunity to prove that you have the integrity and the necessary energy to get things done. It's also a great time to bring a sense of order and discipline into your life—physically, spiritually or emotionally. It is important to grasp the boundaries of your influence and power as this will lead to a strong and renewed sense of self. Who's in charge of operations in this situation—is it you or another? What can you do to strengthen your position and show that you can be relied upon to get the job done? If someone is trying to take your sense of individuality and power away through being bossy and in control, what can be done to reclaim your authority? Giving your power away to someone can lead to being taken advantage of in many ways. The undermining of one's authority can lead to a loss of position and self-respect. Stay in a relationship only if it gives you a good sense of yourself. Whoever is involved in this situation should wield their power in a careful and thoughtful way. There may be a need to accept people's recognition of you as a person in control of your own life and destiny. Doing this with dignity can lead to a whole new sense of self, position and personal power.

Keywords: Developing willpower. Inner power, discipline and integrity. Discipline of thoughts, emotions and actions. Leadership, power and ability along with their responsibilities. Accepting responsibility for one's actions. "Calling the shots." Rulers, presidents, leaders. Taking charge. The need for loyal subjects. Being voted in. The democratic process.

The Caution: Taking control. Lording it over everyone. Being overbearing. Not allowing others to be in charge of their own lives, health or situation. Egotistical and self-centered. Undermining others through a lack of self-awareness or confidence. Being larger than life. Dictators and tyrants. Military Governments.

What does this **SYMBOL** say to *you?*

What government is the best? That which teaches us to govern ourselves.
Goethe

No man is free who is not a master of himself.
Epictetus

He is free ... who knows how to keep in his own hands the power to decide.
Salvador de Madriaga

To put the world in order, we must first put the nation in order; to put the nation in order, we must put the family in order; to put the family in order, we must cultivate our personal life; and to cultivate our personal life, we must first set our hearts right.
Confucius

He that would govern others first should be the master of himself.
Philip Massinger

He is not fit to command others that cannot command himself.
Proverb

I am, indeed, a king, for I know how to rule myself.
Pietro Aretino

It is a strange desire to seek power and to lose liberty.
Francis Bacon

Aries 12

Birds of a feather flock together.
Old Saying

There is a destiny that makes us brothers,
No one goes his way alone;
All that we send into the lives of others,
Comes back into our own.
Edwin Markham

I met a hundred men going to Delhi and every one is my brother.
Indian Saying

A goose flies by a chart which the Royal Geographical Society could not mend.
Oliver Wendell Holmes

Don't refuse to go on an occasional wild goose chase. That's what wild geese are made for.
Henry S. Haskins

Cross in a crowd and the crocodile won't eat you.
Malagasy Proverb

Likeness causes liking.
Romanian Proverb

Not the cry, but the flight of the wild duck, leads the flock to fly and follow.
Chinese Proverb

Why do you lead me a wild goose chase?
Miguel de Cervantes Saavedra

A FLOCK OF WILD GEESE

Commentary: The "Flock of Wild Geese" is a beautifully inspiring image of brotherhood and Aquarian ideals. Watching them fly can inspire feelings of group cohesion and the beauty of natural rhythms. The "Flock" shows the need to join with others in a journey or a quest. Remember to take your cue from the "Wild Geese"—when they fly in formation, they take turns in leading the way. Likewise, when one gets tired or sick, another takes the lead.

Oracle: While this is a Symbol of working together with others, be wary of losing your sense of individuality. There may be a feeling of wanting to leave behind previous life constraints, to be able to spread your wings, to seek freedom from difficulties. However, there's a need to take note of "seasonal" variations that are happening around you. Obviously there is a time to "fly" and a time to relax and recover. You can't always be on the go; you must look after your needs for nourishment and sleep. "Geese" are known for forming lifelong partnerships, so marriage or partnership may indeed be a consideration in this situation. However, it can sometimes be hard to "ground" relationships. This Symbol is very much about brotherhood, respect and getting along with others. Setting out with those of like mind can lead to an expanded view of life or indeed a whole new adventure. Still, continually taking off on tangents with others while you could be making more permanent and loyal commitments to the long term can really test relationships. Remember to be aware of your responsibilities, to both yourself and others in the group. Know that there is support out there for you; just ask.

Keywords: Aquarian ideals of brotherhood. Attunement to planetary rhythms. Spirit liberated from matter. Wanting to take off by one's self, but not being able to. Focused group activity and support. Group mentality, action and agreement. Intuition and telepathy. Choreography. Camaraderie. "Honking" to egg each other on. Flying in the slipstream. Responses to seasonal changes. Migrating at the right times. Traveling. Herds, gangs, broods. Flying in formation.

The Caution: Following the leader without knowing where one's going. Never knowing where to land, or where to ground one's self. Wild goose chases. Not recognizing the brotherhood in humanity. Losing a sense of individual identity. Going off in the wrong direction. Being lost in the crowd. Being one of a gaggle.

What does this **SYMBOL** say to *you?*

A BOMB WHICH FAILED TO EXPLODE IS NOW SAFELY HIDDEN FROM DISCOVERY

Aries 13

Commentary: "A Bomb Which Failed to Explode" shows potentially explosive energies are around which haven't gone off yet that may now be "Safely" defused. Things are "safe" from detection, but dangerous elements are possibly still within. Handling "a Bomb" needs to be done with extreme care and caution. That the "Bomb" is "Now Safely Hidden from Discovery" shows it's still potentially explosive, but has somehow been made safe. The duration of the apparent calm depends on whether the "defusing" is done with attention to all of the details involved, no matter how small.

Oracle: Has this situation been defused or is still likely to "Explode"? Unexploded "Bombs" can be like grenades—ready to go off at any moment, spraying everyone with shrapnel. The "Bomb" is often something of an emotional nature, but can also be the suppression of a truth that has emotional side effects. There may be time to eliminate the impending explosion before it is discovered, bringing relief and release. If, however, things remain charged up, the result could be depression or internal anger and calling in the "bomb squad" may be necessary. This could mean the help of friends, family and assistants. Calling in your own emotional, mental or spiritual "bomb squad" allows you to take control of your emotional nature. If a "Bomb" is "Discovered," it may point to the guilty party who will have to explain their behavior. Did you plant this "Bomb" or did someone else? Take time to reflect on rash emotional decisions or situations that, if "Exploded," could damage much more than was intended. Getting everything under control and safely out of the way will reveal how you can handle things. Act with integrity. People involved can learn a lot from how they react, especially when under pressure.

Keywords: Pressure valves. Getting away with something. Tantrums and frustration. Tempers that simmer. Explosive behavior. Bombs, explosions. Sudden and forceful events. Intelligence organizations, CIA, FBI, ASIO, etc. Valuable lessons of self-restraint. Relief from problems. Discharging nervous energy. Security checks. Last minute escapes.

The Caution: Suppressing stress or illness. Doing inappropriate things and thinking the secret safe. Repressing emotions. Undefined anger. Pressure cooker energy that needs to be released slowly. Explosions damaging more than expected. Activists. Deception behind one's back. Clash of ideals. Terrorism.

What does this **SYMBOL** say to *you?*

Anger will never disappear so long as thoughts of resentment are cherished in the mind. Anger will disappear just as soon as thoughts of resentment are forgotten.
Buddha

How much more grievous are the consequences of anger than the causes of it.
Marcus Aurelius

"I lose my temper, but it's all over in a minute," said the student. "So is the hydrogen bomb," I replied. "But think of the damage it produces!"
George Sweeting

I do not like this word "bomb." It is not a bomb. It is a device that is exploding.
Jacques le Blanc, French ambassador to New Zealand, on Greenpeace's Rainbow Warrior bombing

As in an explosion, I would erupt with all the wonderful things I saw and understood in this world.
Boris Pasternak

When the habitually even-tempered suddenly fly into a passion, that explosion is apt to be more impressive than the outburst of the most violent amongst us.
Margery Allingham

Aries 14

Religion has done love a great service by making it a sin.
Anatole France

It was from the rind of one apple tasted that the knowledge of good and evil as two twins cleaving together leaped forth into the world.
John Milton

This desire to govern a woman—it lies very deep, and men and women must fight it together before they shall enter the garden.
E. M. Forster

Forbidden fruit is sweet.
Traditional Proverb

Adam was human; he didn't want the apple for the apple's sake; he wanted it because it was forbidden.
Mark Twain

Adam and Eve had many advantages, but the principal one was that they escaped teething.
Mark Twain

There are several good protections against temptation, but the most popular is cowardice.
Mark Twain

Do not bite at the bait of pleasure until you know that there is no hook.
Thomas Jefferson

A SERPENT COILING NEAR A MAN AND A WOMAN

Commentary: "A Serpent Coiling Near a Man and a Woman" symbolizes the story of the "temptation" of Adam and Eve in the Garden of Eden. The "Serpent" offered Adam and Eve the gift of self-knowledge. However, this "knowledge" also revealed to them that they were naked and that this was sinful. The "Serpent" was said to have brought them both knowledge and guilt. The "snake" can be symbolic of anything that induces fear or negativity into a situation. On the other hand, what the "snake" symbolizes can bring a healing and a profound sense of, or need for, self-knowledge. This Symbol can show the celebration of the physical body and the enjoyment of another through all of the senses.

Oracle: Something or someone may be coming between two people. "A Serpent" is shown "Coiling Near a Man and a Woman"; this can be a third person or some kind of threat. It can bring jealousy, resentment, distrust or separation. What comes between people may be an idea or a belief system, such as the fear of God. It may be some insight or knowledge that has come to light; it may be another person or a lover. Temptation, fear and passion can all too easily get in the way of any relationship, old or new. It can sometimes be difficult to tell exactly what's coming between people; it could be an emotion, psychological condition or memory. The "Serpent" in this situation is not necessarily in a threatening pose, yet it can still induce a sense of fear or tension because of assumptions and prejudice. Snakes by their very nature don't have to do anything to be intimidating—they arouse fear, uneasiness and other, more extreme, reactions by their mere presence. Maybe one needs to let go of inhibitions in order to find new depths and ways of relating. If the fear of the "snake" were to disappear, would you then be able to return to your own "Garden of Eden"? Alone, or as a couple?

Keywords: Enticement. Allurement. Revealing archetypal knowledge that may not be "socially acceptable." Temptations. The Adam and Eve story. Jealousy. Sexual instincts. Life and death issues. Relating based on control. Kundalini energy. Realizing polarity. Individuation. Eating the Apple. The "knowledge of good and evil." Having one's eyes opened. Marking one's territory.

The Caution: Feeling guilty. Being afraid to express one's feelings. Basic instincts and sexual energy. The fear of knowledge, secret or otherwise. Using sexuality as a control device. Disgust or distrust of the body. Sexually transmitted diseases. Hiding nudity or sexuality. Being thrown out of paradise.

What does this **SYMBOL** say to *you?*

AN INDIAN WEAVING A BLANKET IN THE LIGHT OF THE SETTING SUN

Commentary: "An Indian Weaving a Blanket" shows that people need to take time out to do the things that aren't particularly exciting or rewarding on a large scale, but do, however, provide feelings of contentment, warmth, safety and security. In "Weaving the Blanket," the "Indian" not only creates something that is useful, but weaves into it images of their life and history. Often the patterns and pictures woven into it easily identify the tribe this "Blanket" comes from. Being "in the Light of the Setting Sun," there may be a feeling of the energy of the light, the "Sun," fading, leaving little time to achieve what needs to be done.

Oracle: By practicing our skills in an artful way there can be a celebration and remembrance of the experiences that led to this moment. Doing one's chores with enjoyment leads to inner contentment and a sense of self. In contemplation or meditation one can find peace, relaxation and a feeling of meaning and accomplishment. Taking time to do the job well is important, as is reverence for those things in your possession. Even small contributions in life are important and your integrity should not be compromised. A lot of effort goes into "Weaving a Blanket" and there may be no worthwhile shortcuts to its completion. Do you need to bring many strands from different areas or parts of your life together? What materials are available to you? It's best to relax into your activities. Take time to enjoy the tranquility of dusk, possibly catching sight of a sunset. Conditions will change with time and you can get back to more exciting ventures. Remember to "weave your dream."

Keywords: The fabric of one's being. Traditional pastimes and skills. Weaving security and independence. Patience and gentle handcrafting. Stories, especially those handed down. Tales and traditions. Consideration of one's unique history. Weaving, spinning looms. The warp and weft of life. One's life story—past and present. Being focused on one's tasks. Colors, dyes. Threads.

The Caution: Underestimating skills of self-expression in comparison with intellectual skills. Allowing dull routines to overcome. Feeling one hasn't got much to contribute. Inability to apply to routine and necessary tasks. Being too "full-time" about one's work. Feeling insecure no matter what the situation. Selling off one's integrity. Finding that it's too late in the day to get anything done. Not knowing when to stop.

What does this **SYMBOL** say to *you?*

Aries 15

Man was made for Joy and Woe,
And when this we rightly know,
Thro the World we safely go.
Joy and Woe are woven fine,
A clothing for the soul divine.
William Blake

We sleep, but the loom of life never stops and the pattern which was weaving when the sun went down is weaving when it comes up tomorrow.
Henry Ward Beecher

Humankind has not woven the web of life. We are but one thread within it. Whatever we do to the web, we do to ourselves. All things are bound together. All things connect.
Chief Seattle

For the American Indian, the ability of all creatures to share in the process of ongoing creation makes all things sacred.
Paula Gunn Allen

Life is what we make it, always has been, always will be.
Grandma Moses

America is woven of many strands. I would recognize them and let it so remain. Our fate is to become one, and yet many. This is not prophecy, but description.
Ralph Ellison

Aries 16

The worst thing about work in the house or home is that whatever you do is destroyed, laid waste or eaten within twenty-four hours.
Lady Kasluck

Housework is what a woman does that nobody notices unless she hasn't done it.
Evan Esar

Housekeeping ain't no joke.
Louisa May Alcott

Few tasks are more like the torture of Sisyphus than housework, with its endless repetition: the clean becomes soiled; the soiled is made clean, over and over, day after day.
Simone de Beauvoir

At worst, a house unkempt cannot be so distressing as a life unlived.
Rose Macaulay

For the elemental creatures go about my table to and fro.
William Butler Yeats

All of us, at certain moments of our lives, need to take advice and receive help from other people.
Alexis Carrel

To the man who himself strives earnestly, God also lends a helping hand.
Aeschylus

BRIGHTLY CLAD BROWNIES DANCING IN THE WARM DYING LIGHT

Commentary: "Brightly Clad Brownies Dancing in the Warm Dying Light" is a wonderful and rather mischievous image. "Brownies" are nature spirits that come to help us with our work. The concept of "Brownies" has existed in many cultures for a long time. They lived with humans and sometimes they were said to live in the attic. They often helped the humans in the kitchen; they got the fire going by blowing on it, took care of the humans' children and saw that the food was properly cooked. But nowadays, with the use of electric machines and lights, "Brownies" are disappearing more and more. However it is said some of them still try to stay around. Although mostly associated with housework, we can call on their help in many different ways. Nature spirits are often around us, particularly if we believe in them, welcome them and trust in their presence. They are "Dancing in the Warm Dying Light" inferring that while intuitive powers are at a real high, the available physical energy is not; it is sunset, and the close of the day.

Oracle: You may be feeling tired and in need of help to get everything, or even anything, done. Have faith, and call on any assistance you can as this Symbol implies that you will surely receive it. This Symbol shows that you are being guided and protected. Friends or people may arrive unexpectedly to help out at the "last moment." Sometimes the people who turn up to help are "strangers." Trust that things will be okay even if things feel "too late in the day." Of course, you could be a "Brownie" for someone else, assisting others when they need it. How about "Dancing"? It can refresh and revitalize the spirit and invite love and light into your life.

Keywords: Reveling in nature. Believing in guides. Fairies and nature spirits. The wonder and awe of nature. The setting sun. Last-minute preparations before evening. The psychic magic of dusk. Light that dances. Unseen guardians. Receiving guidance and help. Seeing the invisible. Help at the last minute. Fairy godmothers. Questions of: What is the "real" world?

The Caution: Self-delusions. Missing the true picture of what's happening in the "real world." Losing the plot. Relying on others, including angels, nature spirits, etc., instead of yourself. Neglecting responsibilities. Crying wolf. Using people.

What does this **SYMBOL** say to *you?*

TWO PRIM SPINSTERS SITTING TOGETHER IN SILENCE

Aries 17

Commentary: "Two Prim Spinsters" are shown "Sitting Together in Silence." This Symbol shows people who know and understand each other without the need for chatter. Feelings of contentment can come in time spent with a special friend, someone who you feel completely at ease with. A real sense of understanding of what the other is feeling and thinking can be a central quality of strong companionship. Of course, the "Two Spinsters" may not be together through choice, but rather through life situations.

Oracle: In the situation facing you, remember that it is easy to become socially isolated when you hold on to conservative, judgmental, or moral ideas. Ask yourself if there is a select, restricted group with whom you are associating. Look for any opportunities to open you up to deeper and further levels of communication. Be wary that a false sense of security doesn't isolate you from change and growth. People don't want to talk to each other if they feel their relationship has become boring, with nowhere to go and without much of a future. If people have nothing to say to each other should they spend their time together? Unresolved issues may be too difficult to discuss, they can lie beneath the surface causing fear, isolation and loneliness. "Silence" or quietness can conceal frustration or feelings of sacrifice and loss. If there are no children in their lives and they are said to be "Spinsters," unmarried women, is that an issue? There is an old-fashioned belief which says: It is important to our friends to believe that we are unreservedly frank or honest with them and important to friendship that we are not. That may have suited conditions in the past, but now we have to be more open, honest and communicative, with others and with ourselves.

Keywords: The need to loosen up emotional blockages. The struggle to hold onto one's original identity. Compromise because of social expectations. Meditations that communicate. Exclusive relationships. Relationships that have a quiet "knowing." Dignified silence. Inner withdrawal. Communicating through body language.

The Caution: Emotional isolation. Refusing to accept a relationship. Pretending to be someone whom one is not. Disapproval of younger, more vital energies. Being fussy and judgmental. Chattering that is not conducive to growth or true relating. Gossip. Difficulty in communicating. Being shut off, or shut down. The loss of joy and spontaneity.

What does this **SYMBOL** say to *you?*

Silence gives consent.
Pope Boniface VIII

Silence is one of the hardest arguments to refute.
Josh Billings

When you have nothing to say, say nothing.
Charles Caleb Colton

Wisdom is knowing when to speak your mind and when to mind your speech.
Evangel

The best mirror is an old friend.
Proverb

We are not amused.
Queen Victoria

For the friendship of two, the patience of one is required.
Indian Proverb

Good men are scarce.
Proverb

We are growing serious, and let me tell you, that's the next step to being dull.
Joseph Addison

The loneliest woman in the world is a woman without a close woman friend.
George Santayana

Aries 18

Stop and smell the roses.
Old Saying

It is better to wear out than to rust out.
Richard Cumberland

Sleep is that golden chain that ties health and our bodies together.
Thomas Dekker

Laziness may appear attractive but work gives satisfaction.
Anne Frank

If all the year were playing holidays, to sport would be as tedious as to work.
William Shakespeare

If you want your dreams to come true, don't sleep.
Yiddish Proverb

A change is as good as a holiday.
Old Saying

He that would thrive must rise at five; he that have thriven may lie till seven.
John Clarke

Laugh and the world laughs with you, snore and you sleep alone.
Anthony Burgess

AN EMPTY HAMMOCK HANGS BETWEEN TWO LOVELY TREES

Commentary: "An Empty Hammock" is shown hanging "between Two Lovely Trees." The image of the "Hammock" conjures up the allure of a peaceful and safe environment. It can bring memories of better days, and of restful periods when there was an opportunity to enjoy rest and relaxation. The "Empty Hammock" is an invitation to jump in, relax and take time out to enjoy nature. Time spent lounging in the garden or in nature can revitalize the senses. Often solutions to problems can come while lying in a hammock or enjoying the garden.

Oracle: You may have been too hard on yourself, or others, lately. It is not a crime to rest or take a short pause, and there should be no guilt in taking time out in order to regain strength. Emotions, minds and bodies need relaxation; time to let the weight of life's problems lift from our shoulders. You needn't sacrifice your opportunity to rest for something or someone else. Look at your situation and take note of whether you are always on the go. If so, how can you relax and enjoy your life? Invitations to take a holiday, or simply rest, are likely to come if you are thinking that is what you need right now. Has the "Hammock" been beckoning you for some years? By denying yourself rest you can forget how to enjoy a moment off, or even fool yourself into not being able to relax when you do get the opportunity. This Symbol is probably reminding you that there needs to be some rest right now in order to maintain harmony. On the other hand, it is possible that someone has actually been lounging around or goofing off a little too much lately. A lack of energy or mental or physical motivation can make the hours go by sometimes very slowly without getting anything truly productive done. Exercise is as necessary as rest. Keeping things in moderation is the key.

Keywords: Detachment. Abandonment. Having too much to do to be able to rest. Issues to do with sleep. Sleeping difficulties. Planning for days off or for retirement. Hustle and bustle. Memories of loved ones. Lounging or sitting under trees. Having permission to stop. Time out. Missing a lover. Beds, sheets, pillows, sofas. A favorite chair. Holidays. Trees and gardens.

The Caution: Deliberately pushing when in need of rest *or* not being involved in life's complexities. Dodging responsibilities. Having nowhere to rest or retire. Neglecting time for one's self. Too much work and no play. Areas of life which are not fulfilled. Having so much work there's no time for relationships. Always being on the go.

What does this **SYMBOL** say to *you?*

A MAGIC CARPET HOVERS OVER THE DEPRESSING REALITY OF EVERYDAY LIFE IN AN INDUSTRIAL AREA

♈

Aries 19

Commentary: "A Magic Carpet" is a wonderfully rich image of fantasy and escape. That it "Hovers over the Depressing Reality of Everyday Life in an Industrial Area" shows the contrast between life based on material production and consumption, with its resulting pollution, and the need for escape to the magic and beauty of life. The "Magic Carpet Hovers"—it observes ugliness, noise and hustle and bustle, without being touched by it.

Oracle: "A Magic Carpet" may be what's needed in your situation now. By lifting ourselves above the more "Depressing Realities" that are around us, we can get a better perspective or outcome about the more difficult issues in our lives. The "Magic Carpet" is actually a vehicle for your imagination and using your imagination can elevate your understanding, awareness and existence into the mystic, sometimes fantastic, realms. With this Symbol there is a clear message that you have the ability to get above, or even transcend, worry and strife. Things will be revealed to you if you allow creative and spiritual truths into your conscious awareness. Be wary not to underestimate the potential power in the most ordinary and mundane things; there can be signs of "Magic" in them. Perhaps you are being an "escapist" or dreaming of the impossible. Are you trying to use the "Magic Carpet" to see a greater truth? What new ideas can you materialize into your life in order to lift you out of where you are now? Try sitting on a special rug and allowing your imagination to fly!

Keywords: Practicing meditation. Finding a vehicle for transcendence. Elevated views and perspectives. Rising above problems. Astral travel. Meditation or levitation. Lateral thinking —"Magic Carpets" travel sideways. Rugs, carpets, the Middle East. Fantasy and fiction. Transcending worries. Escaping the depressing realities of the everyday world.

The Caution: Self-defeating detachment. Not being able to cope with the real world. Losing one's self completely in flights of fancy. The longing for escape. The lure of the exotic. Using drugs or alcohol in order to escape drudgery or difficulties. Smog. Filthy air. Feeling stuck. Pollution and muck. Industrial landscapes. Losing touch with the body and physical realities.

I'll need a magic carpet to get out of this one.
Donald Davis

If you surrendered to the air, you could ride it.
Toni Morrison

I'd like to get away from earth awhile
And then come back to it and begin over.
Robert Frost

If the winds of fortune are temporarily blowing against you, remember that you can harness them and make them carry you, through the use of your imagination.
Napolean Hill

Man's desires are limited by his perceptions; none can desire what he has not perceived.
William Blake

A field cannot well be seen from within the field.
Ralph Waldo Emerson

Imagination is a good horse to carry you over the ground — not a flying carpet to set you free from probability.
Robertson Davies

The power of thought—the magic of the mind!
Lord Byron

What does this **SYMBOL** say to *you?*

Aries 20

No act of kindness, no matter how small, is ever wasted.
Aesop

If you always give, you will always have.
Chinese Proverb

A kind and compassionate act is often its own reward.
William John Bennett

The greatest wealth consists in being charitable and the greatest happiness in having tranquility of mind ... And the best comrade is one that hath no desire.
Tibetan Doctrine

Simply give others a bit of yourself; a thoughtful act, a helpful idea, a word of appreciation, a lift over a rough spot ... You take something out of your mind, garnished in kindness out of your heart, and put it into the other fellow's mind and heart.
Charles H. Burr

Give a man a fish and you feed him for one day. Teach a man to fish and you feed him for a lifetime.
Chinese Proverb

What is food to one man may be fierce poison to others.
Lucretius

A YOUNG GIRL FEEDING BIRDS IN WINTER

Commentary: "A Young Girl Feeding Birds in Winter" is an image of care, innocence, nurturing and benevolence. She brings nourishment to those who need it—this can be physically, emotionally or spiritually. It is "Winter," which shows that times may be lean and food or resources scarce. The "Young Girl" shows that even when the cold winds are around us, we can find joy through sharing or doing things for others. Long talks with those in need, be they family, friends or, indeed, strangers, can bring a sense of nurturing, reassurance, satisfaction and love.

Oracle: It can be very rewarding to provide love, reassurance and nourishment to those who need it. Nonjudgmental help can lead others to trust and respond, while little acts of kindness can improve people's lives. Things done for others often have an unexpected spin-off: you can enjoy the sharing and giving, have fun and feel really good about what you've done. Nourishment can come in the form of food, water, words, advice, etc. There are, however, those who stubbornly resist moving on or changing their habits even if it is to their own detriment. Someone needs help, someone who may even be the cause of his or her own problems. Continued shows of love and dedication may be required, even when it may be tiring or time-consuming. What would really happen if you left or withdrew your time, resources or energy? Are you stepping out into the cold to help others? Be careful that what's being "fed" is in fact nourishing for those receiving it, and not just feeding codependence. There may be a need to be alone to do simple yet compassionate things. Try feeding birds outdoors or through open windows and see what feelings are triggered.

Keywords: Nurturing innocence. Feeding energy to situations that feel cold, hopeless and lost. Small efforts bringing their rewards. Codependent relationships. Nurturing. Helping those less fortunate or smaller. Taking time out for others. Doing things without thought of reward. Enjoying nature. Trying to find friends or company. Bread and water. Soup kitchens. Counseling. Hot vs. cold weather.

The Caution: Wanting to win approval. Creating dependence with others that has to be maintained. Feeling bleak, lost and alone. The need to continually rescue others. Doing anything in order to be liked. Finding it difficult to stop giving. Not being able to say "no." Feeling used and unrewarded.

What does this **SYMBOL** say to *you?*

A BOXER IS ENTERING THE RING

Commentary: "A Boxer" shows someone with the ability to stand up, fight or take on a challenge. This person is seen "Entering the Ring"—a place where they need to stand up for something, tackle an issue or a person; to prove themselves strong in some measure. Fighting can take many forms, it can be done obviously or subversively. One can throw punches on every level of consciousness: physically, spiritually, mentally and emotionally.

Oracle: It may be time to fight about some issue, but it should be done within the bounds of the "Ring"—heeding the rules and regulations of decency. Make sure you possess the skills and have earned the right to defend what you believe. Are "rules" being broken? Is there someone keen to battle? Are they causing problems? At times it may be appropriate or necessary to physically "fight," however signaling your readiness to fight may cause the other to back down. If you really need to go into the "Ring" be fully prepared for any consequences. Be aware that you may need to back off if you are losing ground. Standing up to something or someone can lead to a new level of self-confidence, but are you ready for the punches that might be thrown your way? Use your instincts and watch every movement carefully. Knowing where the next punch is coming from can help. Who is the likely victor? Emotionally there are no real winners when lovers or friends fight—both lose in one way or another. Also, it's often others who judge the real outcome or who's the "winner" in the end. Are you prepared to lose? It could be a situation of "may the best man win." "Boxing" is a sport that owes its pleasures to people's glory, bravery, pain and sometimes humiliation; however, standing up for yourself and your rights can lead to others taking you more seriously.

Keywords: Physical or psychological self-assertion and determination. Attack or defense? Fighting for emotional, psychological or physical space. Being seen as a person of strength. Throwing punches. Fighting on any level. Being prepared to take a swing at someone or something. Stepping up to the plate. Throwing down the gauntlet. Going after the title. Big vs. small egos.

The Caution: Using force or power to dominate people or those who challenge. Acting in a combative manner. Not displaying sportsmanship. Wanting to knock people out. Looking for combat. Throwing punches at anything. Belting, smacking, invading. Being punch-drunk.

Power is not revealed by striking hard or often, but by striking true.
Honoré de Balzac

In fighting and in everyday life you should be determined though calm. Meet the situation without tenseness yet not recklessly, your spirit settled yet unbiased. An elevated spirit is weak and a low spirit is weak. Do not let the enemy see your spirit.
Miyamoto Musashi

He that wrestles with us strengthens our nerves, and sharpens our skill. Our antagonist is our helper.
Edmund Burke

Never go to bed mad. Stay up and fight.
Phyllis Diller

He who fights and runs away may live to fight another day.
Proverb

If you cannot bite, never show your teeth.
Proverb

Fortune favors the brave.
Terence

What does this **SYMBOL** say to *you?*

Aries 22

Paradise is always where love dwells.
Jean Paul F. Richter

Pure love and suspicion cannot dwell together: at the door where the latter enters, the former makes its exit.
Alexandre Dumas

When one door closes another door opens; but we so often look so long and so regretfully upon the closed door, that we do not see the ones which open for us.
Alexander Graham Bell

If you haven't all the things you want, be grateful for the things you don't have that you wouldn't want.
James S. Hewett

Be an opener of doors.
Ralph Waldo Emerson

When the doors of perception are cleansed, Man will see things as they truly are, infinite.
William Blake

Straight is the gate and narrow is the way.
The Bible

Opportunities multiply as they are seized.
Sun Tzu

THE GATE OPENS TO THE GARDEN OF ALL FULFILLED DESIRES

Commentary: "The Gate Opens to the Garden of All Fulfilled Desires" is an image rich with future possibilities. This is such a promising Symbol—it seems limited only by the imagination. How exciting to think that one could be so close to having all of their "Desires" fulfilled. This new place or realm of activity sounds incredibly enticing on many levels. As the "Gate Opens to the Garden," it leads to potential for growth and rewards.

Oracle: What and where is the place you strive for? It seems that you have brought yourself to what you want, but there may still be obstacles. There may be fear about just what "All Fulfilled Desires" may actually represent. Maybe you already have everything you need—take a look around and ask yourself this. Are you ready and willing to accept the rewards? Perhaps you need to make the deliberate action of opening the "Gate," allowing entry to where you belong and where you want to be. It can often be difficult accepting or admitting what we really want, especially to ourselves. You may be used to (or addicted to) being in a difficult or unfulfilling situation or relationship. Can you cope with the more rewarding possibilities that lie beyond any barriers? As this "Gate" opens (in your mind, your emotions or literally) you'll find you've come to a new threshold, possibly a whole new beginning in life. Often there needs to be a pause, a reflection of how real or rewarding this new place is that you are about to enter. Perhaps you need to knock first, showing your clear intention of "wanting in." Then you can take that step toward what you want. Be prepared to tend to your "Garden of All Fulfilled Desires."

Keywords: Craving happiness. Gardens and their treasures. Trellises and flowing plants. Pathways to bliss. Gates and doors. Unlocking and opening gates and doors. Analyzing your heart's desires. The grass being greener on the other side. Rewards and treasures waiting. The allure of somewhere else. Initiations. Passages to a better life. Acquiring property. Sexual fulfillment. Opening up to life's possibilities and rewards.

The Caution: Feeling or being shut out. Denying yourself the right to just rewards. "Wild goose chases." Being afraid of losing everything. Having everything, but wanting more. Things not being as real as you imagined. Feeling unhinged. Not having the materials to make dreams come true. Issues of possession that separate. Your cup being half empty or half full.

What does this **SYMBOL** say to *you?*

A WOMAN IN PASTEL COLORS CARRYING A HEAVY AND VALUABLE BUT VEILED LOAD

Commentary: "A Woman in Pastel Colors Carrying a Heavy and Valuable But Veiled Load" shows someone having to carry, shoulder or put up with something that is weighing them down. Although the "Load" may not be comfortable, there is some kind of perceived reason or reward for hanging onto it. Often in trying to conceal problems or issues from others, things become more of a burden. The fact that she's dressed in "Pastel Colors" reveals that the "Woman" is a person who doesn't necessarily want to put on a dramatic show or draw attention to herself.

Oracle: The "Veiled Load" shows someone going to a great deal of effort to conceal or cover up something very important. There could be worry about being "revealed" if anyone (let alone everyone) found out what's being covered up. It may seem they have succeeded in keeping secrets to themself, but it is probably apparent to others that the burden is affecting their behavior. Carrying the "Load" may provide a convenient excuse for not participating in life. However, although it may be a "Heavy Load" it is also said to be "Valuable" in some measure. Others may benefit from hearing what needs to be said. Further, hanging on to upsets from the past can stop the enjoyment of life in the present. It may be time to share previously private stories, attitudes or beliefs with others. Enjoying all that one has in life right now can lift the spirits and release any burdens. To varying degrees everyone is carrying some sort of "Heavy Load" which they try to conceal. Going through the day expressing kindness and courtesy will leave behind a feeling of warmth and good cheer for others. Positive attitudes and behavior helps to lighten the "Load" of everyone struggling with their burdens.

Keywords: Privacy. Quiet determination to get on with the job. Mild manners. Carrying more than one's share, gratefully or grudgingly. Shouldering problems. Bad backs. Victim status —poor me! Secret pregnancies. Doing overtime. Heavy loads. Smiling against the odds. Pastel colors. Codes of silence.

The Caution: Covering something up. Trying to conceal distrust. Keeping one's thoughts and emotions locked in, creating ill health and disease. Fading into the background. Not being noticed or recognized. Feeling weighed down with shame, loss or humiliation. Wearing dark clothes. Dressing in order to cover up. Being the family scapegoat. Heavy karma.

What does this **SYMBOL** say to *you?*

Truth fears nothing but concealment.
Proverb

Conceal a flaw, and the world will imagine the worst.
Marcus Valerius Martial

Our lives begin to end the day we become silent about things that matter.
Martin Luther King, Jr.

The deeper the sorrow the less tongue it hath.
The Talmud

One stops being a child when one realizes that telling one's trouble does not make it any better.
Cesare Pavese

The mass of men lead lives of quiet desperation. What is called resignation is confirmed desperation ... a stereotyped but unconscious despair is concealed even under what are called the games and amusements of mankind.
Henry David Thoreau

And when a woman's will is as strong as the man's who wants to govern her, half her strength must be concealment.
George Eliot

Aries 24

Every separate thought takes shape and becomes visible in color and form.
Liu Hua-Yang

Wishes expand in direct proportion to the resources available for their gratification.
Robert Dato

The charitable give out the door and God puts it back through the window.
Proverb

When God closes a door He opens a window.
Anonymous

If opportunity doesn't knock, build a door.
Milton Berle

There is no one, says another, whom fortune does not visit once in his life; but when she does not find him ready to receive her, she walks in at the door, and flies out the window.
Charles Montesquieu

Certain winds will make one's temper bad.
George Eliot

AN OPEN WINDOW AND A NET CURTAIN BLOWING INTO THE SHAPE OF A CORNUCOPIA

Commentary: "An Open Window and a Net Curtain Blowing into the Shape of a Cornucopia" is a Symbol of abundance and prosperity. Abundantia was a Roman goddess of abundance, prosperity and good fortune. She has the "Cornucopia," the "horn of plenty," from which she distributes grain, money, fruits, flowers and food. In fact, all that one truly wants is represented as sitting in the "horn." The wind blows in the "Open Window" and reminds us of the beauty, joy and richness of life.

Oracle: We often long for what we want and this Symbol shows that something is most probably coming your way. "An Open Window and a Net Curtain" suggests that with the slightest change of direction in the wind, our fortunes can change. Quite possibly something is coming that has many promises. What actually arrives on your doorstep may or may not be exactly what was wished for, but it is very likely to be somehow rewarding. How wonderful and yet surprising would it be if what you wanted actually did manifest? This could be a time of the realization and enjoyment of layers of spiritual nourishment. The "Blowing" of wind often implies spiritual agencies coming in. "Open" your mind to the possibilities that are being "Blown" in from the realm of spirit. The rewards can be plentiful, full of promise and self-sustaining. Be wary, however, of merely drifting and imagining that the big jackpot is going to just fall out of the sky. Buying the ticket helps to win the lottery. Look for unusual or extraordinary opportunities in the signatures of things around. Picture what you want and project it out into the world with the full intention of it being fulfilled. What you want may just manifest itself in front of you.

Keywords: Imagination. Keeping your options open. The promise of fruition. The breath of life filled with inspiration. Realizing that in everyday life, one has it all. Windows of opportunity. Gain, abundance, riches. Spiritual energies pouring in. Concentrated energy. Seeing desires taking shape. Curtains and windows.

The Caution: Relying on spiritual ideas to provide material sustenance. Dreaming of things dropping into one's lap. Hoping that good luck will just "blow in." Shutting windows, keeping light and life out. Drawing curtains and withdrawing. Promises, promises.

What does this **SYMBOL** say to *you?*

A DOUBLE PROMISE REVEALS ITS INNER AND OUTER MEANINGS

Aries 25

Commentary: "A Double Promise Reveals Its Inner and Outer Meanings" implies that what may at first have appeared to be simple will probably end up being more complicated than was first imagined. Things may look great on the outside, but internally there could be complications that should be considered. There may need to be an honest appraisal of what was actually said, thought or "Promised," and what is actually possible in the real world.

Oracle: It may seem as though there are so many possibilities coming that could change your life on many levels, but "Promises" are often more complicated than we initially think. Is this a situation with integrity or is it laced with duplicity? Look carefully at any "Promises," or outcomes that were assured or perhaps assumed in this situation. Did you expect more than was actually delivered? One's rational understanding and emotional desires and responses can often conflict with each other. Consider the effects of the "Promise" on all levels of your being. What comprehension, thoughts and emotions do you have surrounding what was said or implied? This Symbol often indicates a choice that arises between the heart and doing what you want to do and social obligation and knowing what's right. There is much to be realized and learned from the situation that has led you to the Oracle. There may be a need to draw another Symbol to get further information, to clarify and refine your direction.

Keywords: Rewards, but what do they bring with them? The possible implications of or reasons for any promises. Something that may look good on the outside, but prove to be difficult. Looking for consensus. Possibilities and promises. The ins and outs of situations. Not turning up. The need to look at situations from all sides. Internal vs. external realities. Catch-22 situations. Contracts.

The Caution: Fickleness, insincerity and two-facedness in human relationships. Expectations without clarification. Reversals of decisions or promises. Duplicity. Manipulating people in order to achieve outcomes. Promising more than can be delivered. Endeavours or projects that are not worth the effort. Lies and misleading statements. Having a hidden agenda. Momentary pledges that are soon forgotten. Contracts that bind.

A wise man hears one word and understands two.
Yiddish Proverb

Danger and delight grow on one stalk.
Scottish Proverb

The reverse side also has a reverse side.
Japanese Proverb

What a difference there is between what we say and what we think.
Jean Racine

We must not promise what we ought not, lest we be called on to perform what we cannot.
Abraham Lincoln

What's important is promising something to the people, not actually keeping those promises. The people have always lived on hope alone.
Hermann Broch

All promise outruns performance.
Ralph Waldo Emerson

Words are words, explanations are explanations, promises are promises but only performance is reality.
Harold S. Geneen

What does this **SYMBOL** say to *you?*

Aries 26

A full cup must be carried steadily.
Old Saying

Everyone has inside himself a piece of good news! The good news is that you really don't know how great you can be, how much you can love, what you can accomplish, and what your potential is!
Anne Frank

A wise man will make more opportunities than he finds.
Francis Bacon

You must learn day by day, year by year, to broaden your horizon. The more things you love, the more you are interested in, the more you enjoy, the more you are indignant about, the more you have left when anything happens.
Ethel Barrymore

And the wild regrets and the bloody sweats
None knew so well as I:
For he who lives more lives than one, more deaths than one must die.
Oscar Wilde

He was one of those men who possess almost every gift, except the gift of the power to use them.
Charles Kingsley

A MAN POSSESSED OF MORE GIFTS THAN HE CAN HOLD

Commentary: "A Man Possessed of More Gifts Than He Can Hold" is an image of a wonderful abundance of gifts, talents or possessions. The words "More Than He Can Hold" imply that it's rather difficult to keep or contain all of these great things at once. Perhaps some things need to be let go of. In this Symbol "Gifts" can refer to talents, possessions, people, possibilities, status, etc.

Oracle: This Symbol is about gifts of all kinds. As it talks about "More Gifts Than He Can Hold," it suggests that we need to realize that sometimes we can't have and hold everything to ourselves. There may be so much to possess. We may need to let go of something in order to make space for new things in our lives. There are, however, a lot of good things that can be "Held." This Symbol implies being prepared to give up, or put aside something or someone, in order to pursue something else or to have a desired outcome. Having many great ideas and ambitions is wonderful, but it can keep us from really achieving anything; life can become unfocused or distracted by too many possibilities. Feeling weighed down by and keeping tabs on your possessions can be tiring. The best way to get things done is to do them one at a time. Recognize that you are surrounded by abundance, but you may be unable to experience it all at once. The aim is to appreciate those things you can do or achieve now and not feel bad about the things you can't. If you feel you don't have the ability to cope, look into your "storehouse." You will be surprised at what talents you have probably never used. Just remember that you can't do and have everything at once.

Keywords: Potentials and the obsessions they can bring. Obsessions about "having things" or achieving goals. Counting one's blessings. Jack-of-all-trades. Having to drop the bundle if one more thing is added. Being talented and blessed. Enormous responsibilities. Wanting to contain all possibilities. Storage. So many things to do—so little time.

The Caution: Not being able to focus on one issue at a time, or on ideas of real worth and therefore not really achieving anything. Inability to gain or contain everything that is desired. Ambition that knows no bounds. Greediness and insatiability. Being told that you can't have what you want. Things piling up. Juggling and dropping the ball. Feeling as though you will lose everything. Being overwhelmed with possibilities.

What does this **SYMBOL** say to *you?*

THROUGH IMAGINATION, A LOST OPPORTUNITY IS REGAINED

Aries 27

Commentary: "Through Imagination, a Lost Opportunity Is Regained" implies an opportunity to set something right that was thought to be gone or past any hope of recovery. The power of the mind and the imagination are the best tools to use to retrieve this issue. This Symbol shows that by using creative ideas, the very thing that was "Lost" can be brought back into reality.

Oracle: You will have to summon up your talent and energy to recapture what has been "Lost" to you. This can be about jobs, relationships, creative ideas, possesions, anything. Use your creative energy to revitalize an idea or opportunity, even if it seems to be hopeless. Even if you don't get exactly what you want, you will probably feel an incredible sense of relief as things are put back on track again. You need to believe that it is possible to recapture what you thought was gone. Create an image in your mind; imagine yourself with this "Lost Opportunity Regained" then you will most likely succeed in your objectives, at least on some level. Visualizing what you want, allowing time and watching for it to manifest can bring astounding results. Just about anything can be recovered when this Symbol is around, but you must put some energy into it, particularly using your "Imagination." Timing may be important in this situation and you might need the help of others along the way. Finding ways to get the results you want may take time, or it could indeed happen overnight. Listen to your imagination and intuition and let creative solutions to your problems rise up from within. Remember, though, that often our rewards are different from what we first imagined.

Keywords: Creative imagination and visualization. Hopes renewed when all seemed lost. Second chances. Last minute reprieves. Retracing your steps. Judging things to be positive when once they were thought to be negative. Being exonerated or forgiven. Pardons giving release. Imagineering. Retrieving things. Making up for lost ground or time. Changing your mind, therefore changing your outcome.

The Caution: Relying on self-pity. Denying the imagination to recover the situation. Not noticing solutions to problems. Letting chances for recovery disappear through inaction or laziness. Going over and over lost opportunities. Finding it impossible to let go. Staring at loss and not realizing what one has.

Just think how happy you would be if you lost everything you have right now, and then got it back again.
Frances Rodman

The ultimate function of prophecy is not to tell the future, but to make it.
Joel A. Barker

"There is no use trying," said Alice, "one can't believe impossible things."
"I dare say you haven't had much practice," said the Queen. "Why, sometimes I've believed as many as six impossible things before breakfast."
Lewis Carroll

Opportunities are never lost; they are taken by others.
Anonymous

In a minute there is a time for decisions and revisions which a minute will reverse.
T.S. Eliot

Lest he should wander irretrievably from the right path, he stands still.
William Hazlitt

A mind once stretched by a new idea never regains its original dimension.
Oliver Wendell Holmes

What does this **SYMBOL** say to *you?*

Aries 28

It is always better to fail in doing something than to excel in doing nothing.
Anonymous

There is luxury in self-reproach. When we blame ourselves, we feel no one else has a right to blame us.
Oscar Wilde

Nothing is enough for the man to whom enough is too little.
Epicurus

We are ever striving after what is forbidden, and coveting what is denied us.
Ovid

People ask for your criticism, but they only want praise.
W. Somerset Maugham

Plato was a bore.
Friedrich Nietzsche

Stupid TV. Be more funny.
Homer Simpson

The greatest mistake you can make in life is to be continually fearing you will make one.
Elbert Hubbard

A LARGE DISAPPOINTED AUDIENCE

Commentary: "A Large Disappointed Audience" implies that a performance of some kind or something that was done was not what was wanted or expected. People have witnessed or experienced something that was a "Disappointment" or a letdown. It's hard to know just what or how much the "Audience" was expecting, but it is clear that they weren't happy with the performance or outcome.

Oracle: You might feel as though you or someone else has failed and left others wanting. But how much is this because too much was expected in the first place? The "Audience" only remembers the last performance, so get up and try again, but this time be more realistic. Be aware that in drawing this Symbol you may be an observer (in the "Audience"), or you may even be your own "Audience." Does this picture a situation where you are living through the responses you receive from others? Do you feel that you've let yourself down? Sometimes it is necessary to acknowledge when an idea or action needs to be dropped or stopped to be able to cut your losses. Still, getting mentally and emotional psyched up for something enjoyable and worthy can bring rewards, especially if you lower the expectations of the end result. Quick realizations of things as they really are can bring a sense of hope for a better outcome next time. We need to remember that we often project our own thoughts and expectations onto others; perhaps we can actually learn something more from failure than from success. Watch your reactions to the situation facing you, and see what comes up. What can you learn from observing your and others' expectations? How strongly do you expect them to be fulfilled?

Keywords: Adjustments of expectations bringing realizations about what is really possible. Expecting the response of others. Walking out during a performance. Not listening to something through a lack of interest. Anticipating a different result from what is delivered. Relying on feedback. Lines and queues of people. Criticism. The need to inspire and enthuse.

The Caution: Feeling sad, sorry or let down because of defeat and frustration. A lot of people left feeling emotionally "wiped-out." Shattering of illusions. Fickleness. The attitude that one can't do anything. Everything being out of one's control. Watching what's going on and not participating. Being at the mercy of the whims and fancies of others. Judging and analyzing oneself or others. Too many people crammed into one spot. Not getting a seat. Refusal of entry. Booing and hissing.

What does this **SYMBOL** say to *you?*

THE MUSIC OF THE SPHERES

Commentary: "The Music of the Spheres" is a beautiful image of music and harmony. It implies harmonies in sounds of all kinds. In this Symbol, the words "the Spheres" refer to the planets in our solar system. The scholar Pythagoras observed that the pitch of notes or sounds depends on the rapidity of vibrations, and also that the planets move at varying rates of motion. He concluded that the sounds made by their movement vary according to these different rates of motion. Kepler said of this, "I grant you that no sounds are given forth, but I affirm . . . that the movements of the planets are modulated according to harmonic proportions." Since all things in nature are harmoniously made, different sounds can harmonize. The combination of these sounds he called "the Harmony of the Spheres."

Oracle: This is a particularly intuitive Symbol. It appears that it doesn't matter if things are going well or not, if you are in tune with your own inner voice, this can be a time of at-one-ment or attunement with your path. Listening to the "Music" around you can open up messages from your own inner voice. The beauty of cycles that go round and round, as seen through the lens of astronomy and astrology, can lead to an understanding of the rhythms of nature and the seasons. Natural cycles revolve, meshing precisely like the gears in a clock. We each have a musical voice, our unique sound. We join with others in harmony and the voices together create alchemy. Sing, ring a bell, play some music, use Tibetan bowls for their beautiful tones. Listen to the words of songs to receive messages that are relevant to you. Being in harmony with your surroundings can bring rewards both seen and unseen.

Keywords: Voices bringing messages. Attuning to the messages inherent in astrology. Harmonies, chords, keys, octaves, tones. Things heard. Natural harmony of life. The beauty of the planets. The measurement of time. Circadian rhythms. Dancing to the wind. The humming of bees. Days of the week. The sound of water over rocks or crystals. The planets speaking through or to you. Sending love. The atomic clock. Harmonics. Musical ratios. Numbers. Numerology. Sound healing.

The Caution: Inflating rational ideas. Delusion or enlightenment? Getting lost in abstractions. Rejecting what's obvious on an intuitive level in favor of more intellectual answers. Loving the sound of your own voice. Not listening to obvious messages.

Listen within yourself and look into the infinitude of Space and Time. There can be heard the songs of the Constellations, the voices of the Numbers, and the harmonies of the Spheres.
The Divine Pymander

There's music in the sighing of a reed; there's music in the gushing of a rill; there's music in all things, if men had ears: Their earth is but an echo of the spheres.
Lord Byron

The heavenly motions ... are nothing but a continuous song for several voices, perceived not by the ear but by the intellect, a figured music which sets landmarks in the immeasurable flow of time.
Johannes Kepler

Every action of our lives touches on some chord that will vibrate in eternity.
Edwin Hubbel Chapin

Among those whom the gods bless, high on the list are the music people, who tune into celestial vibe-brations and give mortals a taste of immortal sensations.
Ruby Dee

What does this **SYMBOL** say to *you?*

Aries 30

There are only two lasting bequests we can hope to give our children. One of these is roots, the other, wings.
Hodding Carter

Birds of a feather flock together.
Proverb

Where can a person be better than in the bosom of their family?
Marmontel Gretry

Always behave like a duck— keep calm and unruffled on the surface but paddle like the devil underneath.
Jacob Braude

A baby is an inestimable blessing and bother.
Mark Twain

Each thought that is welcomed and recorded is a nest egg by the side of which more will be laid.
Henry David Thoreau

God stirs up our comfortable nests, and pushes us over the edge of them, and we are forced to use our wings to save ourselves from fatal falling. Read your trials in this light, and see if your wings are being developed.
Hannah Whitall Smith

A DUCK POND AND ITS YOUNG BROOD

Commentary: "A Duck Pond and Its Young Brood" can indicate issues of belonging to a family, clan or tribe. The "Duck Pond" is a place where a family can live, forage for food, gather life's necessities and be safely together. The parents, or at least the mother "Duck," needs to look after the "Brood" to ensure that they are kept together, nourished and protected. Guidance and direction need to be given so the youngsters grow into mature and responsible adults.

Oracle: You may feel restricted and bound in by reality, but you probably also feel safe. Every day can hold some type of adventure, but it is always within limits. Family, friends and the environment around us often set these limits. The mother figure needs to be strong and vigilant to see that all is well with her "Young Brood." She needs to take great care in directing them in life so that they grow and flourish both as a family and out there in the real world as individuals. Is this "Duck Pond" inviting to others, or do some "Ducks" scare off others who try to come near? Who belongs and who doesn't? Who's invited to visit for a while, but then expected to leave when their time is up? It's quite natural to sometimes feel threatened when people who don't "belong" call or barge in unannounced, but an accommodating "Duck Pond" should be able to have differing types living in quiet safety together. Sometimes we need to remind ourselves of the comforting things around us and the people who really belong with us. Are you looking after those in your care?

Keywords: Nurturing family. Contentment. Realizing limitations. Reliability. The problems and joys in the responsibilities of having a brood to look after. Finding friends or family that enrich one's life. Psychoanalysis. Family patterns and analysis. Family support. The family sphere. Feeling safe in one's environs. Being the mother duck. Adoption and foster families. Communes and communities. Facing the music that you've composed.

The Caution: Denying your own needs for others in the "Brood." Narrow-minded attitudes. Not inviting others in. Feeling stuck. Not wanting to leave the nest, grow up or take risks in life. Feeling left out and alone. Smugness or exclusivity. All looking the same and no one standing out as individuals. Being lost in the crowd. Distrusting those who are "alien." Borders erected to keep out "foreigners."

What does this **SYMBOL** say to *you?*

A CLEAR MOUNTAIN STREAM FLOWS STEADILY DOWNSTREAM

Taurus 1

Commentary: "A Clear Mountain Stream Flows Steadily Downstream" in a path ultimately to the sea. The "Mountains" are the source of all the oceans and, like the "Stream," life is a process of change from the cradle to the grave. A "Stream" must follow its sure course even if it gets distracted from its goal, as can happen when the flow of water is diverted by something or someone. As it "Flows Steadily Downstream," nothing can really stop its ultimate direction. If it is stopped or dammed, it accumulates immense energy, and will practically burst to keep going. The water just goes on, over, under, around, forever onward.

Oracle: There may be a need to choose a course and then not deviate from it. This will help to nourish and inspire confidence in yourself and those around you. There is likely to be some type of tradition and strength behind you. Realize that many came before you and you are a part of their story. You can become fresh, vibrant and revitalized from your own spiritual source. Be wary of standing still in this situation as still water can become stagnant. Further, icy feelings and being alienated from others will invite trouble further down the line. Set a course and go with the flow. As you get closer to your objective you will probably find you have a growing supply of impetus and power. Keep moving toward your goal while remembering to cultivate warmth and acceptance with all that you meet along the way. However, this Symbol can also describe a person that refuses to do anything other than what they have in mind. Having tunnel vision about one's direction can alienate others. Performing your tasks with focused vitality will be positive and productive. Picture a "Stream" flowing downhill, going around any obstacles and finding its true course.

Keywords: Remaining fluid. Flowing energy. Pure sources, nourishment and refreshment. Sure sense of direction. "Untainted" blood lines. Purifying one's thoughts, ideas and beliefs. Things set in train from upstream. Water. Dams. Water as a resource. Purification. Cleaning and cleansing. Pipelines. The spiritual dimensions of water. Baptism. Elemental knowledge. Traffic. Flowing crowds of people. Going against the tide.

The Caution: Aimlessness. Aloofness. Feelings of physical, spiritual, racial or intellectual purity that can lead to smugness, bigotry or a false sense of superiority. Ice-cold feelings and responses. Not taking notice or being concerned about another's feelings. Cold ambition. Mud and sediment. Pollutants. Algae. Stagnant moments.

What does this **SYMBOL** say to *you?*

Everything flows and nothing abides; everything gives way and nothing stays fixed.
Heraclitus

You will live your life secure in that you are no longer manipulated by what other people want you to do and be, but are directed by your own inner desires.
H. Stanley Judd

You can never enter the same river twice.
Indian Proverb

No river can return to its source, yet all rivers must have a beginning.
Native American Proverb

Ideas are refined and multiplied in the commerce of minds. In their splendor, images affect a very simple communion of souls.
Gaston Bachelard

It isn't pollution that is hurting the environment; it's the impurities in our air and water that are doing it.
Dan Quayle

The fountains of sacred rivers flow upwards.
Euripides

Time is but the stream I go a-fishing in.
Henry David Thoreau

Taurus 2

Lightning is the shorthand of a storm, and tells of chaos.
Eric Mackay

The difficulties we experience always illuminate the lessons we need most.
Anonymous

The best lightning rod for your protection is your own spine.
Ralph Waldo Emerson

I'd rather be a lightning rod than a seismograph.
Ken Kesey

Knowledge does not come to us in details, but in flashes of light from heaven.
Henry David Thoreau

Nothing in life is more exciting and rewarding than the sudden flash of insight that leaves you a changed person—not only changed, but for the better.
Arthur Gordon

His intelligence seized on a subject, his genius embraced it, his eloquence illuminated it.
Velleius Paterculus

And God said: Let there be light: and there was light.
The Bible

Where God and Nature met in light.
Lord Alfred Tennyson

AN ELECTRICAL STORM ILLUMINATES THE HEAVENS AND THE FORESTS

Commentary: "An Electrical Storm" can really wake us up. Sometimes it comes out of the blue, when we're not expecting it. As it approaches there is a strong buildup of energy and things can become stuck and static. There is a feeling of something pending; the tension and promise of a breaking point occurring at any minute. As it "Illuminates the Heavens and the Forests," it sheds flashes of light on the environment or the immediate situation. It often happens that the cleansing promise of rain is held back momentarily while the "Electrical" power of the situation seems to take over everything.

Oracle: This situation will most likely change from what it first appeared to be. You may actually have little influence over what is being unleashed. In the meantime, there's a need to keep a cool head while observing everything around. Eventually the energy will dissipate and you will regain control: physically, mentally or emotionally. Lightning is a powerful "Electrical" energy, and brilliant flashes of intuition can come when it is unleashed. This Symbol says that the "Electrical Storm Illuminates the Heavens and the Forests"; with a sense of added awareness, it brings insight and "Illumination" to a high point of focus. Things that have not been obvious before are likely to become much clearer to you, sometimes crystal clear. Paths out of confusion can suddenly be revealed. Pay attention, as this can be in short grabs. Things will seem better if you feel safe in your environment and with the people around you. Keep your eyes wide open. Don't worry about losing control, as the "Electrical Storm" will pass relatively quickly, possibly leaving you in a better place and a fresh state of mind.

Keywords: Reverence for the forces of nature. Loud cracks, flashes, and bangs that clear the air. Flashes of insight. Tension and its release. Electrical conductors. The sense that all hell is going to break loose. Short circuits of mind or emotions. Electricity failures. Crackling emotions. Flashes in quick succession. Bursts of energy. Light changing. Psychic clearing. Hot flushes. Surges.

The Caution: Being frozen in fear just when one needs to spur to action. Losing control. Being distracted by surroundings. Not being completely aware of all the potential dangers. Worry that overtakes and engulfs. Chaos in the brain. Nervous reactions. Things changing quickly. Brilliance that is quickly or easily lost. Power blackouts.

What does this **SYMBOL** say to *you?*

NATURAL STEPS UP TO A LAWN BLOOMING WITH CLOVER

Commentary: "Natural Steps Up to a Lawn Blooming with Clover" implies "Steps" that are inviting, promising and easy to climb. It feels as though they're leading to the promise of beauty, greenery and repose. They are "Blooming with Clover," which shows there is a reward at hand when those "Steps" are taken. Bees love "Clover" and "Lawns Blooming" with it ensures that the bees will make honey and therefore life will be sweet. Clover has long been believed to mean good luck, prosperous circumstances and luxurious surroundings. Also, the expression "he's in clover" or "living in clover" comes from the belief that if you had plenty of "Clover" for your cows to eat, they would produce good milk, thereby providing nourishment for everyone.

Oracle: This Symbol shows that a time of fulfillment and completion is close, but there is still some small effort to be made to attain what you want or need. You must take the "Steps," even though they may be simple, to achieve what you want or to arrive where you want to be. There is definitely a need to put some effort into getting what you want but it's probably not going to be too difficult or hard going. Be on the alert for laziness and a "come what may" attitude. Regardless of what others are doing, keep going the way you are, following your natural intuition and you will find, or achieve, what you have in sight. Rewards can be just a few "Steps" away. It may be worth remembering that this landing in the "Clover" may only be temporary, as there will be new things to do and further things to strive for. You may not have found your "Pot of Gold at the End of the Rainbow" just yet, but you are most likely on the right path.

Keywords: Hopefulness. Inspirational possibilities. Gradually enlarging one's vision. Harmony. Seasonal changes. Running around on grass. Bare feet. The beauty of greenery and flowers. Stability on the path. Steps that invite one on to bigger and better things. Abundance, nourishment. Making small efforts that can lead to large returns. Places to spread out and relax. Having plenty of room to move. Gardens and parks.

The Caution: Looking for the easy way out. Not making the effort to find what is just a few steps away. Being lazy when one should be going for the objective. Temporary success. Expecting everything to be laid out before you. Weeds. Unkempt lawns. Neglected land.

What does this **SYMBOL** say to *you?*

Like the bee that now is blown honey-heavy on my hand, from his toppling tansy-throne, in the green tempestuous land—I'm in clover now, nor know who made honey long ago.
Edmund Blunden

Sweet scents of summer air breathing over fields of beans or clover; the perfume of wet leaves or moss; the life of waving trees, and shadows always changing.
Charles Dickens

The reason so many people never get anywhere in life is because when opportunity knocks, they are out in the backyard looking for four-leaf clovers.
Walter Chrysler

Talk to him of Jacob's Ladder and he would ask the number of the steps.
Douglas William Jerrold

*I like the man who faces what he must,
With steps triumphant and a heart of cheer;
Who fights the daily battle without fear.*
Sarah Knowles Bolton

What a miserable thing life is: you're living in clover, only the clover isn't good enough.
Bertolt Brecht

Taurus 4

*If I traveled to the end of the
rainbow, As Dame Fortune did
intend, Murphy would be there to
tell me, The pot's at the other end.*
Bert Whitney

*Ah, Hope! what would life be,
stripped of thy encouraging
smiles, that teach us to look
behind the dark clouds of today, for the golden beams that
are to gild the morrow.*
Susanna Moodie

*Pennies do not come from
heaven—they have to be
earned here on earth.*
Margaret Thatcher

*The foolish man seeks
happiness in the distance, the
wise grows it under his feet.*
Robert Oppenheim

*He felt like a man who, chasing
rainbows, has had one of them
suddenly turn and bite him in
the leg.*
P.G. Wodehouse

All is not gold that glitters.
David Garrick

*A golden key will open every
lock.*
Yiddish Proverb

*Every absurdity has a champion
to defend it.*
Oliver Goldsmith

THE POT OF GOLD AT THE END OF THE RAINBOW

Commentary: "The Pot of Gold at the End of the Rainbow" is a wonderful image. "Rainbows" are said to be a bridge to the Divine. They inspire awe as we gaze at their beauty and the sheer wonder of nature. They can represent boundless promise, and there is said to be a reward, a "Pot of Gold," to be found at its end. In folklore, elves, leprechauns and fairies are associated with the "Pot of Gold."

Oracle: The quest to find our "Pot of Gold" is very tempting but it can be forever elusive because it appears to move as we move or as we change our perspective. However, we all have our dreams and with a little concentrated effort we can reach our own version of the "Pot of Gold." It can imply riches and rewards on many levels, sometimes beyond our wildest dreams. There may be a need to reflect on just what exactly these "riches" are. The promise of the "Pot of Gold" entices us, but this can also be the cause of problems if we forget other more important things in life. Some people want material or spiritual riches without putting in any hard work. This way of thinking may lead one astray. Although some people can earn their way through life on a wing and a prayer, most have to put in a true effort to succeed. Often it is not the finding of the elusive "Pot of Gold" at the "Rainbow's End" that is the real reward, but the rewards found during the search and the wonder the "Rainbow" creates as it links heaven and earth. Perhaps there is a constant search for rewards without recognizing the riches that are already at hand. In this situation, many rewards can come from creative and spiritual efforts—just be a little wary of expecting too much. Picture a "Rainbow" in your mind, see "The Pot of Gold"; and hold it in your memory bank—this will sustain you and may indeed lead you to your reward.

Keywords: The promise of riches, in whatever forms these may take. Creative imagination. Goals and ambitions. Alchemy. Splashes of color. Rewards contained. The search for the treasure. Seeking communion with nature and life's bounty. Wealth derived from changing perspective. Talent and beauty. Fantasies. Illusions vs. reality. Fairylands.

The Caution: Seeking easy, tempting solutions. Thinking that rewards are always just "over the horizon." Thinking that one is never going to get near "it." Elusive success. Forgetting the more immediate things in life. Seeking perfection. Castles in the air. Pipe dreams. Fool's paradise.

What does this **SYMBOL** say to *you?*

A YOUTHFUL WIDOW, FRESH AND SOUL-CLEANSED FROM GRIEF, KNEELS AT AN OPEN GRAVE TO RECEIVE THE SECRET OF ETERNAL LIFE

Taurus 5

Commentary: "A Youthful Widow, Fresh and Soul-Cleansed from Grief, Kneels at an Open Grave to Receive the Secret of Eternal Life." She's learning some hard-won and valuable lessons through her loss. She is mourning at a grave and receiving meaningful insights into the purpose of life. However, the "Grave" is still "Open," which shows that in some respect she hasn't had the necessary time or hasn't been able to complete the mourning process and move on with her life. The "Grave" will only be filled in when she can sincerely say good-bye to the person or situation that has been lost. If she continues to stand at the "Open Grave" the "burial ritual" cannot be fully accomplished or completed.

Oracle: Looking at things that are gone or lost can stop people from accepting newer, more vital relationships and opportunities. Don't let loss make you give up and throw everything away. Gathering up one's energy and starting on a new path is often the key. Realizing that life must go on, we learn that we can recover our feet and move forward. However, it is very important to allow time to grieve. Letting go of the past and things that are worn out, and being accepting will bring release. The memory of the person, thing or situation that has passed from your life can bring tears of "Grief," but also tears of joy. Remember the gifts that have been given or left to you, and don't focus on the losses that you can't replace. How many times and for how long do you have to say good-bye to someone or something? Don't stand still, staring at loss, immobilized by fear. Imagine yourself walking away to a new chapter of your life. Take note of when it is time to fill in the "Grave" and complete the circle. Fill in the "Grave," bless the past and move on.

Keywords: Gradual realization of the illusion of matter. Letting go of that which no longer works. Purging and burning the past. Giving up past grievances. The passage of grief. Receiving the gifts that loss and separation can bring through time. Grief, divorce, loss. Redundancies. Near-death experiences. Inheritances.

The Caution: Wasting time staring at lost opportunities. Grudges and bad feelings that last much longer than needed. Staring at issues of loss and death. War and its horrors. The feeling that one has no future. People or events that just won't leave one's memory. Hanging on for fear of the future. Empty legacies.

What does this **SYMBOL** say to *you?*

The bitterest tears shed over graves are for words left unsaid and deeds left undone.
Harriet Beecher Stowe

We don't have an eternity to realize our dreams, only the time we are here.
Susan L. Taylor

If you're still hanging onto a dead dream of yesterday, laying flowers on its grave by the hour, you cannot be planting the seeds for a dream to grow today.
Joyce Chapman

Make the most of your regrets; never smother your sorrow, but tend and cherish it till it comes to have a separate and integral interest. To regret deeply is to live afresh.
Henry David Thoreau

Every time I think that I'm getting old, and going to the grave, something else happens.
Lillian Carter

The pain passes, but the beauty remains.
Pierre Auguste Renoir

The grave is but the threshold of eternity.
Robert Southey

Taurus 6

Faith is building on what you know is here, so you can reach what you know is there.
Cullen Hightower

Don't be afraid to take a big step when one is indicated. You can't cross a chasm in two small steps.
David Lloyd George

Being on the tightrope is living; everything else is waiting.
Karl Wallenda

We are told never to cross a bridge till we come to it, but this world is owned by men who have "crossed bridges" in their imagination far ahead of the crowd.
Anonymous

People are lonely because they build walls instead of bridges.
J. F. Newton

The hardest thing in life to learn is which bridge to cross and which to burn.
David Russell

Voyager, there are no bridges; one builds them as one walks.
Gloria Evangelina Anzaldua

Creativity is the power to connect the seemingly unconnected.
William Plomer

A BRIDGE BEING BUILT ACROSS A HIGH NARROW GORGE

Commentary: "A Bridge Being Built across a High Narrow Gorge" is about finding a creative and concrete solution to be able to cross to the other side of a separation or dilemma. There may be a separation or gulf, shown here by the "Gorge," between places, people or objectives. "Bridges" need to be built to overcome separate areas of activity and to link people and places together.

Oracle: There may seem to be no way of overcoming the distance between you and another, or the outcome or thing that's desired. Realizing the gulfs you face and doing something about any breaks in communications between you can lead to whole new possibilities. Building a "Bridge" takes time, energy and most often, the help of others. It may be best to start working toward "Building a Bridge" now. Once it is completed, the dangers that the "Bridge" spans are no longer of such great concern—that is, unless the "Bridge" is not secure. Failure to adequately span the gap may actually feel life threatening. Looking back or down may bring on a sense of danger or instability. However, with this Symbol, you can feel secure that the "Bridge" will be there for you when you need it. Imagine yourself coming to the brink and going straight ahead, but don't look down. With creative thought physical limitations can be overcome most of the time. Be careful not to get preoccupied or wound up worrying whether things are going to fail. Remember the saying, "Don't cross that bridge until you come to it." This basically indicates that you shouldn't concern yourself with difficulties until they arise. Don't place too much importance on the outcomes until you get to the other side. It may help to get some plans drawn up, in reality or in your imagination.

Keywords: Overcoming distance and separation. Endeavoring to build continuity. Solving problems with creative solutions. Bridging emotional chasms. Spanning gaps. Breaking down barriers. Structures spanning distances between places or people. Conquering time and space barriers. Physical limitations overcome. Taking one step at a time. Avoiding looking down.

The Caution: Taking the long way round to avoid asking for help. Using shortcuts to cut across the real issue. Only seeing the risks, not the solutions to problems. The fear of establishing connections. The pervading sense that it could all fall through at any moment. Extreme sports.

What does this **SYMBOL** say to *you?*

THE WOMAN OF SAMARIA COMES TO DRAW WATER FROM JACOB'S WELL

Taurus 7

Commentary: "The Woman of Samaria Comes to Draw Water from Jacob's Well" is a Symbol that comes from the Biblical story of Jesus meeting the "Woman of Samaria" at "Jacob's well." She, along with others, was taken by surprise that Jesus would actually speak to her, for she was a Samaritan and he was a Jew. The Jews and the Samaritans normally did not get along. She was also on the fringe of her own society as she was not married. As Jesus spoke to the "Woman," he revealed to her that he was the Messiah. This was a great blessing to her. The Buddhist tradition tells a very similar story of being accepted regardless of caste.

Oracle: This Symbol calls for universal love to be available to everyone. It speaks of the need to dispel prejudice, either given or received. With this Symbol, there can be the urge to seek and to find acceptance, love and redemption. If one's elders have passed down prejudices, be aware that they lived in a different time; living in the present may require the updating of ideas and opinions. If your heart is clogged up with old emotions or spent feelings, it is time to clear these. In doing so, address situations that hold people apart. Take action to restore any lost self-respect. Own up, express your concerns to that stranger within yourself, your shadow, and then let them go. It may be that someone else needs your help. If so, draw on your inner resources and take time out to assist them. No matter your situation, you will be blessed by "higher powers" if you give others respect and reverence. It is about discovering what you share with others, not what separates you. Similarities lie deep within us all. Imagine yourself drawing "Water" up from that special "Well," then find yourself refreshed and ready for a more rewarding, compassionate and confident life.

Keywords: Dipping into family ancestry. Past lives. New ideas being revealed about one's social and spiritual integrity. Going below the surface. Assimilation of divergent ideals. Feeling blessed. Life-altering experiences. The blessing of water. Freedom and respect for all. Stepping over social boundaries.

The Caution: Allowing social prejudice to rule decisions about one's self and others. Unacceptable behavior based on social conditioning. Feeling that one is from the "wrong tribe" and can't assimilate or contribute. Issues of being acceptable, worthy or a "local." Water disputes.

What does this **SYMBOL** say to *you?*

*"Is this one tribe or a stranger?"
is the calculation of the narrow-minded; but to those of a noble
disposition the world itself is
but one family.*
Hitopadesa Proverb

*We never know the worth of
water till the well is dry.*
English Proverb

*Your vision will become clear
only when you can look into
your own heart … Who looks
outside, dreams; who looks
inside awakes.*
Carl Gustav Jung

*It was … enough to suffer as a
woman, an individual, on one's
own account, without having to
suffer for the race as well. It was
brutality, and undeserved.*
Nella Larsen

*We need to feel the cheer and
inspiration of meeting each
other; we need to gain the
courage and fresh life that
comes from the mingling
of congenial souls, of those
working for the same ends.*
Josephine St. Pierre Ruffin

*Men can be attracted but not
forced to the faith. You may
drive people to baptism, but
you won't move them one step
further in religion.*
Alcuin

Taurus 8

I don't have any solution but I certainly admire the problem.
Ashleigh Brilliant

Not only is there no God, but try finding a plumber on Sunday.
Woody Allen

The poverty of our imagination is no measure of, say, the world's resources. Our posterity will no doubt get fuel in ways that we are unable to devise for them.
George Eliot

A creative economy is the fuel of magnificence.
Ralph Waldo Emerson

Confront the dark parts of yourself, and work to banish them with illumination and forgiveness. Your willingness to wrestle with your demons will cause your angels to sing. Use the pain as fuel, as a reminder of your strength.
August Wilson

No steam or gas ever drives anything until it is confined. No Niagara is ever turned into light and power until it is tunneled. No life ever grows until it is focused, dedicated, disciplined.
Harry Emerson Fosdick

Nothing is so difficult that diligence cannot master it.
Malagasy Proverb

A SLEIGH WITHOUT SNOW

Commentary: "A Sleigh without Snow" is a Symbol of something that has difficulty finding the means to get to its destination. A "Sleigh" can't go anywhere without "Snow," as it is the medium which supports the "Sleigh" in its movement, and without it the "Sleigh" isn't going anywhere. The "Sleigh" may be useful at other times, but now it is either ahead of its time or useless, redundant, or waiting for the right moment.

Oracle: It may seem that there isn't much that can be done with the fuel that is readily available. Regardless of the amount of desire or the need for progress or forward push, this "Sleigh" without "Snow" will not be going anywhere in a big hurry. This can symbolize a situation where someone is ahead of their time, but it can also show that someone has missed their time to go forward and they have to wait for future opportunities to show themselves. They may also have to wait for a healing, or for financial situations to resolve. Regardless of which is true, there is a sense here of having to wait until conditions and situations change to be able to achieve what it is that you want or to get where you want to go. Are you using up a lot of energy trying to make things work in very difficult conditions? You may have part of the problem solved (you at least have a vehicle for moving forward), but now you must have the patience to wait for the rest of the elements to fall into place. This Symbol is often about timing. You can often fuel your situation by really tapping into your imagination. The question is, what adjustments or improvisations can be made? You need to wait until the time is right, then you will have exactly what you need—the "fuel" and the right conditions which allow you to complete your mission.

Keywords: Independence from outer circumstances. Using the creative mind to work through momentary shortages or problems. Anticipating future conditions. Having the "vehicle," but not the time, energy or the "fuel." Improvising things so that they work better or ahead of their time. Gas, oil, fuel. Snow. The value of timing. Lack of resources. "Tires" that are missing or don't work. Being ahead or behind one's time.

The Caution: Forcing your ideas or feelings even though the time is not right. Lack of support from the environment. Missing connections. Running out of energy. Having the right thing in the wrong place. Ideas without the capital to make them reality. A lack of impetus or propulsion. Feeling stuck, unmoving. Traffic jams. Empty tanks.

What does this **SYMBOL** say to *you?*

A CHRISTMAS TREE IS DECORATED AND SHINES IN THE DARKNESS

Taurus 9

Commentary: "A Christmas Tree Is Decorated" is a Symbol that brings feelings of family, celebration and happiness. When the "Tree Is Decorated" it represents a sign of unity and that many of our family and celebrational needs are, or will be, met. The star placed on top of the "Tree" represents the star that led the wise men, the Magi astrologers, to the stable in Bethlehem where Jesus was born. As long as the spirit of Christmas is celebrated with thankfulness and joy, people will be happy and share both their love and their time. Often at Christmas it is cold outside. There is the sensation of snow on the ground and everything being rather bleak outside while inside there is love, shelter, food and warmth. There is also the beauty of the Christmas lights—the "Tree Is Decorated and Shines in the Darkness." The presents glint and a feeling of anticipation hangs in the air of what fun and rewards are yet to come. Giving and receiving while enjoying family and friends are the main elements behind the spirit of Christmas. The presents don't have to be big and expensive, it's the warmth and spirit of sharing that matters.

Oracle: This is an opportunity for enjoying or accepting family, for celebrations and appreciating cultural ties, and for taking time out to remember and honor these things. Activities with the group will bring joy to all those who are close enough to partake. Even if you don't know the people you are celebrating with, joy will be spread and celebrated—unless there are feelings of alienation, loneliness or loss. Do some elements of your situation shine more brightly in the cloak of the night than the clear light of day? If there are gifts you want to give, are you worried about how they will be received? Even if you arrive empty handed, the true gift is in the giving of yourself, not in the actual gift itself. Hopefully everybody realizes this. One of our presents to others is to be able to receive our gifts and each other joyfully without worry or judgment.

Keywords: Enjoying the fruits of one's culture. Warmth within while it may be cold outside. The rebirth of the spirit. Faith and the hope of happiness and goodwill of people to one another. Celebrations bringing people that once were parted together. Decorations. Things done with loving intent. The promise of good things. Colored lights. Gifts. Stars and angels.

The Caution: The pretense of happiness or success in a decorative show. Not allowing for others from different religions or social classes. Being excluded and left in the cold. Family cohesion on display belying the real situation. Commercialism. Family disappointments.

What does this **SYMBOL** say to *you?*

Remember, if Christmas isn't found in your heart, you won't find it under the tree.
Charlotte Carpenter

I bought my brother some gift-wrap for Christmas. I took it to the gift wrap department and told them to wrap it, but in a different print so he would know when to stop unwrapping.
Steven Wright

Rings and jewels are not gifts, but apologies for gifts, for the only [true] gift is a portion of thyself.
Ralph Waldo Emerson

And every gift, though it be small, is in reality great if given with affection.
Pindar

A good conscience is a continual Christmas.
Benjamin Franklin

Adults who [hang] gifts of a ready-made education on the Christmas tree of a child waiting outside the door to life do not realize how unreceptive they are making the children to everything that constitutes the true surprise of life.
Karl Kraus

Taurus 10

If you treat a sick child like an adult and a sick adult like a child, everything usually works out pretty well.
Black Hawk

I may be compelled to face danger, but never fear it, and while our soldiers can stand and fight, I can stand and feed and nurse them.
Clara Barton

Complain to one who can help you.
Yugoslav Proverb

When you are in trouble, people who call to sympathize are really looking for the particulars.
Ed Howe

The comforter's head never aches.
Proverb

A broken bone can heal, but the wound a word opens can fester forever.
Jessamyn West

God appoints our graces to be nurses to other men's weaknesses.
Henry Ward Beecher

If you want others to be happy, practice compassion. If you want to be happy, practice compassion.
Dalai Lama

A RED CROSS NURSE WITH WARM SYMPATHY

Commentary: "A Red Cross Nurse" is someone who can be called upon to help in an emergency. She is receptive to the emotional and physical needs of others. Reliable and caring, she brings healing and relief as she patches up what needs to be fixed. Making things better is her quest and her duty. Mostly, she carries out her duties without fuss or fanfare. That she does this "with Warm Sympathy" implies that the "Red Cross Nurse" is a kindly person, someone who can be relied upon for doing the right thing with care, attention to detail and the intention of healing. She needs to be attentive every time she is called upon, regardless of whether she is tired or has chores of her own to attend to.

Oracle: It seems that there is a lot you have to do, but first you will probably have to provide help to others. There can be a great deal of inner healing achieved when helping others. Through empathy and sympathy we often learn about aspects of ourselves. How willing and able are you to give your time to help another, either physically or emotionally? How can you be expected to cope if you have too much to do? Perhaps you are in need of some help yourself. Things may not be easy or enjoyable and you may have to cross over into the "dark side" in order to bring light and love to the situation. Things may call for a more personal touch, and approaching matters sympathetically rather than just clinically may be appropriate. Look at what's occurring, and take into consideration people's shortcomings. Sometimes others need care because they can't cope with even the smallest things. There may not be many apparent rewards but the sense of care and healing that is invoked is often its own reward. Through showing "Warm Sympathy" to those involved, a solution and a healing can be attained.

Keywords: Unconditional and compassionate understanding and caring. Breaking down the borders between self and others. Always having to find reserves of energy. Looking after people's physical, emotional, spiritual welfare. Giving and also receiving. Volunteer work. First aid kits. Bedside manners. Having a mission to fulfill. Having a shoulder to cry on.

The Caution: "Fussing" around and doing more than one needs to. Always butting in, even when it's not necessary or wanted. Being a doormat and doing more than your share. Not caring how others are coping, even when it's really necessary. Being officious and bossy. Feeling used.

What does this **SYMBOL** say to *you?*

A WOMAN SPRINKLING LONG ROWS OF FLOWERS

Taurus 11

Commentary: "A Woman Sprinkling Long Rows of Flowers" is a lovely picture of the rewards that come from tending a garden and being responsive to its needs. This takes perseverance and can be hard work as there are weeds or other unwanted elements to keep an eye out for. However, tending to the "Flowers" gives the "Woman" time to pause for a moment and breathe in the beauty of nature and her place in it. She can relax into nature and enjoy the moment as a lot of the hard work is finished; her garden has now come into bloom.

Oracle: This Symbol often speaks of the need to take time to nurture the physical self. Along with smaller, less able things that need care, your body needs water, sustenance and nourishment, too. Drinking plenty of water and nourishing yourself with good food is part of this. Hence there may be the need to pay attention to what your body is telling you. Sometimes the mind needs to take a rest, and the body needs to be allowed to come to bloom and bask a little in the sunlight. Now is the time to enjoy the fruits of one's work. Also, looking after younger and smaller things so they may grow to maturity and fullness brings its own type of reward. This might require patience and a determination to work at something. Keeping an eye on things that you are responsible for will ensure that they don't dry out and fade away ahead of, or before, their time. Weeding out undesirable factors is often a necessary part of this process. Taking time out to actually water plants or the garden may bring some wonderful realizations to your life. As fairies and nature spirits are said to live in gardens, meditating while "Sprinkling" the garden, potted plants may bring nourishing insights to the question that brought you to the Oracle.

Keywords: Having patience and care. Nurturing and fertilizing creativity. External evidence of internal beauty. Looking after small details to reap treasures later. The Tree of Life. Stopping to smell the roses. Paying attention to detail. Flower essences. Sprinkling love and sustenance. Watering and fertilizing. Tending the soil. Care and love.

The Caution: Giving superficial attention just to keep up appearances. Neglect of things once they're established. Giving up on projects halfway through. Dehydration and neglect. Droughts of energy, love or feeling. Neglecting things in favor of other priorities. Water restictions.

What does this **SYMBOL** say to *you?*

Cultivate more joy by arranging your life so that more joy will be likely.
George Witkin

Flowers always make people better, happier and more helpful; they are sunshine, food and medicine to the soul.
Luther Burbank

Would that the little flowers were born to live conscious of half the pleasure which they give.
Henry Wadsworth Longfellow

Cultivate peace first in the garden of your heart by removing the weeds of lust, hatred, greed, selfishness, and jealousy. Then only those who come in contact with you will be benefited by your vibrations of peace and harmony.
Sivananda

By cultivating the beautiful we scatter the seeds of heavenly flowers, as by doing good we cultivate those that belong to humanity.
Vernon Howard

For the benefit of the flowers, we water the thorns, too.
Egyptian Proverb

Some of the sweetest berries grow among the sharpest thorns.
Gaelic Proverb

Taurus 12

Joy is not in things, it is in us.
Richard Wagner

You can't have everything. Where would you put it?
Stephen Wright

Large desire is endless poverty.
Indian Proverb

We don't need to increase our goods nearly as much as scaling down our wants. Not wanting something is as good as possessing it.
Donald Horban

Advertising may be described as the science of arresting human intelligence long enough to get money from it.
Stephen Leacock

What really matters is what you do with what you have.
Shirley Lord

When we are not rich enough to be able to purchase happiness, we must not approach too near and gaze on it in shop windows.
Tristan Bernard

Marrying a man is like buying something you've been admiring for a long time in a shop window. You may love it when you get it home, but it doesn't always go with everything else in the house.
Jean Kerr

A YOUNG COUPLE WALKS DOWN MAIN STREET, WINDOW SHOPPING

Commentary: "A Young Couple" is walking down the "Main Street, Window Shopping." They may be looking with hopes for the future, or perhaps they are just seeking to while away the time together. Regardless, they are an image of youth and the expectations of bigger and better things. If this "Young Couple" has goals in common and a common path to share, all will be well and things will unfold naturally. It may be that in light of their social position or their financial possibilities, they can only "Window Shop" for the moment. Is this "Couple" really "Window Shopping" together, or is only one of them dreaming of what they could have and how things could be better? Are they "together" or do they really want different things out of life?

Oracle: Things are probably out of reach for you at the moment, including the stability of your domestic or emotional needs, but that shouldn't stop you looking or planning for the future. However, care may need to be taken, as jealousy and greed can rise up easily when there seems to be so much, so close and yet so far away. Enjoy the display and the quiet moments of togetherness without rush, and then get back to your real life. Realize that even though things feel far off in some way, things of inner worth are available to you, right now. Is there an issue concerning commitment to a relationship, or is this a situation of just having a look to see what might be possible for the future? Now is possibly not the right time to make any firm decisions, but rather to look at all your possibilities and options. "Window Shop" a little and share your dreams. See how they can turn into reality.

Keywords: The longing for "things." The allure of ownership. Consumerism. Trying to raise money. Worrying about the "cost" of things. Weddings and engagements. Credit cards. Finances that are shared. Shared dreams. The future and its possibilities. Young people. Planning. Shopping. The honeymoon period. So much so close and yet so far.

The Caution: Denying happiness because of material deficiency. "Keeping up with the Joneses." Not focusing on your partner/ friend. Unsure of where one stands. Being unwilling to commit to anything just yet. Avoiding the heart of one's relationship. Focusing on the financial side. Issues of "who pays for what." Arguments over money or possessions. Merely "Window Shopping," not committing. Overspending. Being in debt. Monetary distractions. Missed opportunities.

What does this **SYMBOL** say to *you?*

A PORTER CARRYING A MOUNTAIN OF HEAVY BAGGAGE

Taurus 13

Commentary: A "Porter," otherwise known as a baggage handler or bellboy, has a lot of work to do. He is performing a service for others and here he is seen having "a Mountain of Heavy Baggage" to move or "Carry." He needs to remain cheerful and not reveal how much this "Mountainous" load is weighing him down; otherwise he may not get the approval of those he is "Carrying" the load for. There would be no thanks and no "tips" if he were to complain, groan or grumble. "Porters" do a lot of hard work but don't often get much appreciation or attention. They are expected to just get on with the job, sometimes they become almost invisible. This Symbol can also be an expression of class-consciousness.

Oracle: There may be a load or a heavy burden to bear. It may be your own burdens or could indeed be other people's. Be careful that you are not doing too much for others as you may be carrying their burdens for them. You could end up just helping people to hang on to their extra "Baggage" through your desire to help out, be useful and share the load. This can be a problem, weighing them down when you are not available, and of course it can also weigh you down emotionally, as well as physically. It may be that others are expecting you to shoulder their responsibilities. Having so much to "Carry" can lead to bad posture, bad backs or a distorted infrastructure. Are you going from one burdening experience to another? For some people, to have the service of a "Porter" can be a pleasant and well-earned respite from their daily struggles. For others, there can be the expectation that someone else will always shoulder the load. That may be okay in a hotel or a train station, but how appropriate is it in everyday life? Don't let yourself be used to carry other people's "stuff."

Keywords: Self-reliance. Owning other people's "garbage." Shouldering baggage or weight. Being weighed-down. Feeling responsible for everything. Bad backs and posture. Carrying others. Counseling people, taking on their emotions. Bad backs, shoulders, knees, etc. Strain and wear. Bearing the family guilt. Luggage. Trolleys. Looking for tips.

The Caution: Being busy with other people's problems. Unable to work for your own benefit. Carrying other people's responsibilities. Being indispensable until the energy is all worn out. Not knowing when to say "no" to others' demands. The burden of debts. Being useful but unimportant.

What does this **SYMBOL** say to *you?*

Everyone thinks his own burden heavy.
French Proverb

The burden which is well borne becomes light.
Ovid

Do not free the camel of the burden of his hump; you may be freeing him from being a camel.
Gilbert K. Chesterton

No one is useless in this world who lightens the burden of it to anyone else.
Charles Dickens

Your body is the baggage you must carry through life. The more excess baggage, the shorter the trip.
Arnold H. Glasow

RESPONSIBILITY, n. A detachable burden easily shifted to the shoulders of God, Fate, Fortune, Luck or one's neighbor.
Ambrose Bierce

Almost everybody walks around with a vast burden of imaginary limitations inside his head. While the burden remains, personal success is as difficult to achieve as the conquest of Everest with a sack of rocks tied to your back.
J. H. Brennan

Taurus 14

In every outthrust headland, in every curving beach, in every grain of sand there is a story of the earth.
Rachel Carson

I seem to have been only like a boy playing on the seashore, and diverting myself in now and then finding a smoother pebble or a prettier shell than ordinary, whilst the great ocean of truth lay all undiscovered before me.
Isaac Newton

One cannot collect all the beautiful shells on the beach. One can collect only a few, and they are more beautiful if they are few.
Anne Morrow Lindbergh

To live and let live, without clamor for distinction or recognition ... to write truth first on the tablet of one's own heart—this is the sanity and perfection of living, and my human ideal.
Mary Baker Eddy

Sit in reverie and watch the changing color of the waves that break upon the idle seashore of the mind.
Henry Wadsworth Longfellow

ON THE BEACH, CHILDREN PLAY WHILE SHELLFISH GROPE AT THE EDGE OF THE WATER

Commentary: "On the Beach, Children Play While Shellfish Grope at the Edge of the Water" speaks of peaceful coexistence among beings on different levels of evolution. The "Children are Playing" while the "Shellfish" are feeding. Each is getting on with what they are doing in peaceful harmony. It shows the essential unity of all life, no matter how "evolved" each being is. Getting back to the basic elements, such as nature, with a sense of "Play" will help alleviate the seriousness of any problems or stress.

Oracle: Allow your instincts to guide you in the process facing you. Get on with your own activities, focus on these and enjoy them, regardless of what others are doing. Looking outside of your own sphere of operations may bring harm to others, as can happen when "Children" on the "Beach" take "Shellfish" and put them in buckets. The day and the experience will come to an end with the tide bringing another day and another episode in your life. Sometimes you can feel confident and settled with how your desires are being manifested in the world, while at other times you may feel out of your depth with the expectations that the world seems to have of you. In truth, you will find that most situations will be a combination of both. Just be yourself, lighten up and relax. The message is to enjoy those things that make sense and just allow time to teach you how to deal with those things you don't understand. Try indulging in some time out by the water and interact with nature. An insight into your problem is likely to be revealed with the coming and going of the tide.

Keywords: Being self-sufficient. Looking after one's own affairs. A sense of at-one-ment with all forms of life. Having a live-and-let-live attitude. Peripheral vision. Returning to the source. Feeling safe in a natural environment. Playing alongside nature. Building sand castles. Playing in pools or baths. Buckets and spades. Sun protection. Interacting without *really* interacting. Swimming. Sand, wind and sea. Rockpools. Shellfish, oysters, shrimp.

The Caution: Meddling in people's lives. Restriction of play. Being distracted. Sandcastles that will eventually get washed away. Not knowing how to loosen up with others and relax into a natural environment. Fussing that people aren't doing the "right thing." Sunburn and exposure to weather. Voyeurism.

What does this **SYMBOL** say to *you?*

A MAN WITH A SILK HAT, MUFFLED AGAINST THE COLD, BRAVES A STORM

Taurus 15

Commentary: "A Man" in this Symbol is shown "Muffled against the Cold." He is experiencing a time of hardship and discomfort, and is unable to avoid the difficulties that have arisen. He "Braves a Storm," yet he is wearing his "Silk Hat." The "Silk Hat" indicates that he may be somewhat of an expensive and stylish dresser. The fact that he's wearing it shows a somewhat "Brave," dignified and optimistic attitude of confidence and hope for the future. However, people often don't take others' difficulties seriously if they put on a brave and dignified attitude, dressing properly and presenting things as if they were really okay.

Oracle: Someone may not be admitting to what's really going on, or acting as if everything is just fine. There is a need to show determination, confidence and hope for the future, as this will encourage you and those around you. There may not be much that can really be done; it's just a difficult, "Stormy" time. It's the nature of life for things to turn around and improve. Forge ahead knowing that life will calm down and get easier. It is important to know whether the "Storm" is visible to everyone and not merely in someone's mind. The bad weather you perceive could be hidden from others. Presenting a brave face to all you meet and hoping for a better future often helps. However, it could lead to you not being taken seriously by others. "Brave the Storm" and eventually you will you be able to relax both your mind and body. Then you will be able to, once again, show your individual style and be appreciated.

Keywords: Inner poise being more important than outer appearances. Braving stormy weather. Plowing on through difficulties. Being willing to weather storms and take on the hard times. Having tasks or errands to perform when one would rather not. Hats, scarves and mufflers. Sudden change of circumstances.

The Caution: Not showing your true feelings. Superficial shows of strength. Not noticing things improving. Always battling the "elements." Complaining and whining instead of getting on with the task at hand. Wanting to be pampered and not have to face up to life's storms. Considering appearance before all else. Superficiality. Insufficient or inappropriate clothing or apparel. Refusing to protect one's self from cold or harm.

The measure of a man is the way he bears up under misfortune.
Plutarch

The sum of the whole is this: walk and be happy, walk and be healthy. The best way to lengthen out our days is to walk steadily and with a purpose.
Charles Dickens

There is many a good man to be found under a shabby hat.
Chinese Proverb

And all your future lies beneath your hat.
John Oldham

It is easy enough to be pleasant when life blows by like a song. But the man worthwhile is the one who will smile when everything goes dead wrong.
Ella Wheeler Wilcox

Patience serves as a protection against wrongs as clothes do against cold. For if you put on more clothes as the cold increases, it will have no power to hurt you.
Leonardo da Vinci

Never run after your own hat. Others will be delighted to do it. Why spoil their fun?
Mark Twain

What does this **SYMBOL** say to *you?*

Taurus 16

*A teacher affects eternity;
he can never tell where his
influence stops.*
Henry Brooks Adams

*Think like a wise man but
communicate in the language
of the people.*
William Butler Yeats

*The more abstract the truth
you want to teach, the more
thoroughly you must seduce
the senses to accept it.*
Friedrich Nietzsche

*I have learned silence from the
talkative, toleration from the
intolerant, and kindness from
the unkind; yet strange, I am
ungrateful to these teachers.*
Khalil Gibran

*When I was fourteen years
old, I was amazed at how
unintelligent my father was. By
the time I turned twenty-one, I
was astounded how much he
had learned in the last seven
years.*
Mark Twain

*You cannot teach a man
anything; you can only help
him to find it within himself.*
Galileo

*The man with a new idea is a
crank until the idea succeeds.*
Mark Twain

AN OLD MAN IS ATTEMPTING, WITH A DEGREE OF SUCCESS UNSUSPECTED BY HIM, TO REVEAL THE MYSTERIES TO A MOTLEY GROUP

Commentary: The "Old Man" is someone who understands many things. He is "Attempting to Reveal the Mysteries to a Motley Group" that doesn't seem to understand, or at least isn't readily showing that they do. This is "a Motley Group," which means it is made up of people who may be different from each other in appearance, background, interests, etc. However, he is succeeding in teaching them as he's accomplishing a "Degree of Success Unsuspected by Him." It is likely that the "Old Man," or the teacher, is the one who misunderstands what's going on with the "Group," or his students. He may see the superficial differences in the "Group" as a barrier to their ability to understand his message. It is more likely that they are actually quite focused, but each in their own distinct or unique way. By imparting his knowledge, "the Mysteries," the "Old Man" has unified the "Motley Group."

Oracle: It may seem that nobody is paying attention to the advice or wisdom that is being offered, but it is not the wisdom that is at fault. There may certainly be a need to alter the way information is delivered to make it more easily understood, however it is also important not to underestimate the capacity of the listeners to comprehend the messages that are being imparted. Take confidence in the knowledge being given, or received, and have less expectation of how people should behave, respond or look. Remember that "conventional wisdom" does not always overcome the human emotional issues of confidence and self esteem. Be confident that the message is valuable enough to hold the attention of those participating.

Keywords: The need to try a new approach. Challenging the status quo. Astrodrama. Being way ahead of one's time. Getting one's message across in an innovative and creative way. A teacher uniting diverse people in a common cause. Generation gaps. Wisdom given with expectation. Ideas bringing people together.

The Caution: Exaggerated opinion of one's understanding of the situation. The mistaken belief that others need to know something. Not being in touch with the "times." Feeling outdated. Preaching old, possibly outworn ideas. Insecure feelings based on conservative expectations of others.

What does this **SYMBOL** say to *you?*

A SYMBOLICAL BATTLE BETWEEN "SWORDS," THE DISCIPLES OF MIGHT, AND "TORCHES," THE DISCIPLES OF ENLIGHTENMENT

Taurus 17

Commentary: "A Symbolical Battle" is pictured here, between the "Swords and Torches." The "Swords" are pictured to be "the Disciples of Might" and the "Torches," "the Disciples of Enlightenment." The "Swords" show weapons and strong-arm tactics, whereas the "Torches" are instruments that bring truth and light. Arguments over ideals can easily lead to "Battles" and war. This suggests a split between using power and strength and using reason and intelligence.

Oracle: There is a struggle between practical needs and the underlying reasons for having those needs. It can be that someone has become so caught up in "what" they are trying to achieve that they have probably lost sight of "why." The endeavor to bring "Enlightenment" to people often meets with resistance, particularly when this "Enlightenment" will disrupt the usual process of things. One can see this in places where the media has a stranglehold on information. In some instances it is for political agendas and in others it is for commercial reasons, but the effect is the same: to achieve or to maintain a particular agenda by persuasive force. "Battles" are only truly worth fighting when the ideals behind them are clearly believed in or understood. To do this it is often important to pause and reassess why you are doing what you are doing. If fighting becomes a habit and loses its purpose, the spirit can become confused and therefore weakened. Any confusion inside you is an indicator that the power of the outer world needs to be reconsidered. How can things be transformed and brought into the light of acceptance and understanding so that the "Sword" can be dropped and peace reign?

Keywords: The battle of "might vs. light." The Spear of Destiny. Spiritual differences. Arguments. The story of Hitler. The Inquisition. The Crusades. Bringing love and light to war zones. The pen being mightier than the sword. Peace marches, candles, torches. Weapons. The might of the media.

The Caution: Controlling those around with rational or brute force rather than with inner enlightenment or knowledge. People arguing over ideals. Forcing opinions on each other. Religious conflicts. War rallies. Propaganda.

What does this **SYMBOL** say to *you?*

Let us have faith that right makes might.
Abraham Lincoln

A blow with a word strikes deeper than a blow with a sword.
Robert Burton

People who fight fire with fire usually end up with ashes.
Abigail Van Buren

Wisdom is always an overmatch for strength.
Phaedrus

Imagination is the one weapon in the war against reality.
Jules de Gaultier

Truth is a torch that shines through the fog without dispelling it.
Claude A. Helvétius

Bring on your tear gas; bring on your grenades, your new supplies of Mace, your state troopers and even your national guards. But let the record show we ain't going to be turned around.
Ralph Abernathy

War is hell.
General William Sherman

Taurus 18

Better keep yourself clean and bright; you are the window through which you must see the world.
George Bernard Shaw

God doesn't seek for golden vessels, and does not ask for silver ones, but He must have clean ones.
Dwight L. Moody

Cleanliness is next to godliness.
John Wesley

A new broom sweeps clean.
Romanian Proverb

It was not … that she was unaware of the frayed and ragged edges of life. She would merely iron them out with a firm hand and neatly hem them down.
P. D. James

A safe but sometimes chilly way of recalling the past is to force open a crammed drawer. If you are searching for anything in particular, you don't find it, but something falls out at the back that is often more interesting.
James Matthew Barrie

Cleanliness is next to impossible.
Saying

A WOMAN AIRING AN OLD BAG THROUGH A SUNNY WINDOW TO GIVE IT AIR AND SUNSHINE

Commentary: The "Woman" pictured here is "Airing an Old Bag through a Sunny Window to Give It Air and Sunshine." This shows the need to regularly clean out old and outworn habits, belongings and attitudes. Sometimes we accumulate so many bits and pieces, the vast majority being possessions from the past, that our lives can become clogged up and stagnant. Along with our physical world, this can also apply to our minds, emotions and memories.

Oracle: By holding onto everything old or outworn in your environment or, indeed, inside your self, you create clutter that restricts your well-being and your future. Consider discarding anything that doesn't measure up. Do you really need these possessions, habits or thoughts these days? Bringing these things to the outer world will enable you to see if they are still relevant or useful in the clear light of day. Taking time to clean up old habits and memories can change things for the better. What relevance do these things have for your future? It can be good to clean out your cupboards and drawers and get the dust out of all the corners. Washing sheets, towels and clothes can remove that old and moldy feeling. Doing this may inspire solutions to old problems. It is a good opportunity to move to sunnier conditions, wherever or whatever these may be. It is probably important to talk about things that are bothering you. It may be wise to talk through your thoughts and ideas with someone you trust. You will then be able to make better sense of what's going on. In the process you may learn a lot about yourself. Just be careful not to reveal too much to too many people. Act with discretion. Now is the time to seize the moment—bring light and air to everything you can, inside and out.

Keywords: Psychoanalysis. Past life regressions or memories. Doing domestic chores with a feeling of purpose. Work, shopping, ideas. Bringing light and freshness to old feelings. Renewal. Throwing out the old or outlived. Cleaning out rooms. Renovations. Letting the sunshine in.

The Caution: Expecting others to take responsibility for cleaning up and airing out. Hanging on to outworn things and memories. Airing one's "dirty laundry" in public. Rehashing old situations. Going over the same ground again and again. Bringing up issues when it's inappropriate. Depressed attitudes.

What does this **SYMBOL** say to *you?*

A NEW CONTINENT IS RISING OUT OF THE OCEAN

Commentary: The Symbol of a "New Continent Rising out of the Ocean" is a powerful image of new opportunities and a whole new sphere of operation. When a land mass emerges from the ocean—the "New Continent" that is "Rising"—there is usually some kind of eruption or disruption that precedes it. A whole field of activity is coming to light as a fresh, new arena of opportunity erupts.

Oracle: "A New Continent Is Rising out of the Ocean"; it might feel as though it is coming out of nowhere, or from somewhere you didn't expect, however things have probably been building up for some time. Perhaps you saw it coming, or maybe you weren't aware that the changes would go as far as they have. One thing's for sure: it is coming from somewhere deep within your emotional and spiritual development. There is a promise of rewards and brand new beginnings. However, this is probably only the beginning. There is much work to be done developing this possibility into something fertile and productive. Observe and learn from the things that are erupting into your conscious reality. You will (or will have to) find that extra spark to create a brand new, original opportunity. What is possible, and what is not, will become more obvious as time goes on. You may feel a little alienated in this new "Continent" or sphere of activity, but that's only relative to the conditions of what it is that you're leaving behind. There has probably been a recent period of throwing out things that haven't worked, or cluttered up your life and been in the way of your forward growth. What you've done or achieved in the past has led to this, but these new beginnings need to be met with a fresh sense of purpose, confidence and possibility.

Keywords: Enormous potentiality emerging. New trends and ways of being. Sudden eruptions of talent or fields of endeavor. The greenhouse effect. Global warming. Atlantis and other ancient underwater cities. Evolution. Patience. Developing slowly but surely. Emerging generations of people. New environments. Things feeling suddenly foreign. The birth of a nation. Migration. Land masses. Endeavouring to hold life together under the enormous pressure of the new.

The Caution: Continually seeking "new worlds" rather than finding a place in the existing one. No responsibility for the birth of the new. No respect for the old or established. Not shifting or evolving. Staying stuck in old realities.

What does this **SYMBOL** say to *you?*

One does not discover new continents without consenting to lose sight of the shore for a very long time.
Andre Gide

AUSTRALIA, n. A country lying in the South Sea, whose industrial and commercial development has been unspeakably retarded by an unfortunate dispute among geographers as to whether it is a continent or an island.
Ambrose Bierce

I know that Nature designs that this whole continent, not merely these thirty-six states, shall be, sooner or later, within the magic circle of the American union.
William Seward

Nay, be a Columbus to whole new continents and worlds within you, opening new channels, not of trade, but of thought.
Henry David Thoreau

There are continents and seas in the moral world, to which every man is an isthmus or inlet, yet unexplored by him.
Henry David Thoreau

Taurus 20

The golden moments in the stream of life rush past us, and we see nothing but sand; the angels come to visit us, and we only know them when they are gone.
George Eliot

Every event that a man would master must be mounted on the run, and no man ever caught the reins of a thought except as it galloped past him.
Oliver Wendell Holmes

I am not a speed-reader. I am a speed understander.
Isaac Asimov

All human joys are swift of wing, For heaven doth so allot it; That when you get an easy thing, You find you haven't got it.
Eugene Field

The cloud never comes in the quarter of the horizon from which we watch for it.
Elizabeth Gaskell

Every cloud has a silver lining.
Proverb

A great wind is blowing, and that gives you either imagination or a headache.
Catherine the Great

WISPS OF CLOUDS, LIKE WINGS, ARE STREAMING ACROSS THE SKY

Commentary: The "Wisps of Clouds" are "Like Wings Streaming across the Sky." This Symbol implies emotions or situations that are shifting and can feel as though they could change direction quickly. The "Wisps of Clouds" can indicate fleeting moments and conditions that aren't stable or do not have any longevity. Sometimes we look up at clouds, such as those shown here, in awe and wonder at how fast they are racing, and here they are seen "Streaming across the Sky."

Oracle: You may feel driven forward, almost out of your own control. In doing so you run the risk of either going past things too quickly, or tiring if you try to resist the momentum of forward push. It may be best to let the superficial excitement affect you and then be prepared to go back and sort out the details later. However, there can be a danger in making decisions and taking action too quickly, without enough consideration. You may find that you have no choice. You have an opportunity before you, and it could feel like it's now or never and you must seize the day. Another element of this Symbol is that there can be very little actually going on around you, but there is so much going on over your head. Your imagination is active, but perhaps you are not really aware of it. You may find that your mind is working out what to do in this situation and in the next day or so "the coin will drop." Enjoying the pleasant "weather" around you and allowing the natural energies to blow away the confusing aspects of your life will lead to things being sorted out before too long.

Keywords: Fleeting opportunities or inspiration. Feeling things "in the wind." Seeking a change in the weather. Thinking on your feet. Doing things at a fast pace. Placing too much importance on the fast movement of the issue at hand. Wasting energy on nonessentials. Things floating in the air. Going at full tilt. Skywriting. Vapor trails. Things, here one minute—gone the next. Messages read from clouds. Planes. The beauty of the sky.

The Caution: Resistance to the creative flow. Superficial excitement. Unstoppable progress. Destructive development. Forces beyond your control. Making unformed or uninformed decisions on a whim. Not thinking things through. Impatience. Continual impermanence. Lack of rest or sleep. Contrails. Weather control. Overcast skies.

What does this **SYMBOL** say to *you?*

A MOVING FINGER POINTS TO SIGNIFICANT PASSAGES IN A BOOK

Taurus 21

Commentary: "A Moving Finger" is said to be pointing to "Significant Passages in a Book." This speaks about information being sought through the written word. However, the "Moving Finger" can also be your own thoughts, suggestions from those around you, or inspirations from meditations or dreams. Whatever the "Book" may be, it will contain "Significant Passages." It will tell you something useful and necessary now. It can be a classic of literature, or it can be something as everyday as a street map or telephone book.

Oracle: In your situation, something needs to be researched, or looked up, in order to "Point to" what is relevant and what is not. When you realize what the "Significant Passages" are, the solution will become clear. Even if you feel you already know all about it (you have read the book) there is more information to be gleaned by going carefully through what's in front of you, missing nothing. Fine details may have been overlooked or not considered. Perhaps you need to check them out. However, do be discriminating about what really is "Significant" and useful. Be wary of relying purely on the written word. Strict applications of the written word can lead to a lack of innovation and fundamentalism. Going by the "Book" or the rules can be useful and all to the good, but information is often best applied to inspire creative and spontaneous solutions. Someone may be mentally or emotionally "keeping a book" of the things that have happened or have been done by others. If things are not quite right at the moment, maybe you need to read, or pay attention to, any instructions or lessons more carefully. Read the fine print and look carefully at any conclusions or contracts. Also, solutions can be found by flipping open a "Book" and placing a finger on a line or paragraph. This can lead to amazing insights into just what is bothering you.

Keywords: Finding the essential details of a situation and disregarding the rest. The cursor on the computer screen. Reading and writing books. Keeping records. Instruction manuals. Lawyers and the law. Editing. Reviewing. Reference books. Reading the Oracle. Memories. Quoting scripture. Testimony. Rules.

The Caution: Doing things because they need to be done and only going by the rules of the book. Automated responses. Religious fundamentalism. Only doing those things that are officially sanctioned. Not observing the entire picture. Keeping tallies. Flaunting the rules.

What does this **SYMBOL** say to *you?*

The telephone book is full of facts, but it doesn't contain a single idea.
Mortimer Adler

The man who does not read good books has no advantage over the man who cannot read them.
Mark Twain

Beware the man of one book.
St. Thomas Aquinas

The skilled theologian can wrest from any scripture that which will serve his purpose.
Bhagavad Gita

When I am attacked by gloomy thoughts, nothing helps me so much as running to my books. They quickly absorb me and banish the clouds from my mind.
Michel Eyquem de Montaigne

We sometimes get all the information, but we refuse to get the message.
Cullen Hightower

I hate quotations.
Ralph Waldo Emerson

Taurus 22

Peace can be reached through meditation on the knowledge which dreams give. Peace can also be reached through concentration upon that which is dearest to the heart.
Patanjali

Flying might not be all plain sailing, but the fun of it is worth the price.
Amelia Earhart

O Swallow, Swallow, flying, flying South,
Fly to her, and fall upon her gilded eaves,
And tell her, tell her, what I tell to thee.
Lord Alfred Tennyson

Whenever you have truth it must be given with love, or the message and the messenger will be rejected.
Mahatma Gandhi

Loose lips sink ships.
Saying

Oh that I had wings like a dove! For then I would fly away, and be at rest.
The Bible

I survived that trouble so likewise may I survive this one.
Anonymous

A WHITE DOVE FLYING STRAIGHT AND FEARLESSLY OVER TROUBLED WATERS

Commentary: The "White Dove" is a reassuring symbol of messages regarding peace, hope and redemption. That the "White Dove" is "Flying Straight and Fearlessly over Troubled Waters" shows a clear mission that needs to be fulfilled, without worrying about any personal consequences. Noah sent out a "White Dove" from the Ark. It flew "Straight and Fearlessly over Troubled Waters," bringing back an olive branch, a sign that landfall was near and redemption was at hand.

Oracle: This Symbol shows the need for hope and help to be delivered to those who need it. Although there may be trouble all around, you will be able to rise above it and find safe ground. Even though you may be lost from your loved ones' sight for a while and they may feel abandoned, you will eventually return to them safely. Alternatively, you may be guiding them to safety and reassurance, or they may be returning to you. Bringing hope, sustenance and comfort to others is a blessing to all involved. The "Dove" of this Symbol, by "Flying Straight and Fearlessly," brings the message to stay on course, go straight ahead and don't worry about what's happening around you. Soon there will be a signal of better times and relief from your concerns. Often it's not possible for us to see what is just beyond our sight, whether we're looking into the future or trying to understand the present. If things that are outside of your control or influence "Trouble" you, then you may need to ask for a message that will reassure you. The "Dove" is often portrayed as a symbol of the soul. Try sending out a "Dove" from your spiritual center, and ask for what you require in order to bring things back to safe ground again. Equally, you may need to send a message to those who are feeling left out and needing love and assistance.

Keywords: Transcending worries through spiritual awareness. Prophetic missions. Peace. Healing messages from the "other side." Overcoming phobias. Fearlessness. Feelings of immortality. Going straight for the objective. Calming troubled minds. Redemption and messages of hope. Couriers.

The Caution: Being too caught up in worries. Not accepting that things are getting better or accepting reassurance from others. Not being cautious of risks. Being daunted by an ominous task. Gossip. Spreading rumors.

What does this **SYMBOL** say to *you?*

A JEWELRY SHOP FILLED WITH THE MOST MAGNIFICENT JEWELS

Taurus 23

Commentary: "A Jewelry Shop Filled with the Most Magnificent Jewels" speaks of a high degree of integrity, talent and worth that is able to be valued, seen and appreciated. There can be great pleasure to be enjoyed in marking our achievement in life with enduring and satisfying symbols, such as gemstones, jewelry or crystals. Also, knowing how to recognize and appreciate talent, joy and beauty can be its own reward.

Oracle: This is a time to admire the achievements of others and allow yours to be admired too. Realize that what is needed is either at hand, or soon will be. Believing in yourself can bring a sense of reward, and can allow you to reach for higher aspirations. If you need help believing in yourself, try wearing a beautiful piece of jewelry that has a lot of meaning for you. This can bring a wonderful sense of self worth, pride and beauty into your life. Crystals and jewelry may be received, or somehow bring a message. It can be a testament to how talented, gracious and cultured our lives and achievements are. It is good to remember that sometimes our most precious possessions are rarely truly owned by us, they will most likely survive well beyond our time. It is partly this longevity and contribution to the future that makes them so precious. Having a piece of jewelry or crystal nearby can be a reminder of your self-worth, beauty and integrity. Sometimes buying a special piece, such as a crystal, a necklace, earrings, ring or brooch can lift your spirits.

Keywords: Great talent, wealth, rewards and gifts. Beauty that brings joy. Materialization of perfection. Judges of worth. Things that shine. Jewelry, stones, gold and silver. Shops, especially those that have beautiful displays. The rewards and bounty of the natural world. Treasure of any description. Purity. Genius. Crystals. Security guards. Window shopping. Personal Adornments. Things that glimmer.

The Caution: Wanting more than one's share of rewards and spoils, even if there is plenty to share. Things for looking at, not touching. Always wanting more. Being dazzled by possessions. Greed. Stealing or wanting other people's valuables. Superficial displays. The need for security. Jealousy. Theft. Beauty that covers up a lack of worth, talent or depth. Faking authenticity. Having to have bars on the windows. Longing for ownership. Objects of envy.

If you really put a small value upon yourself, rest assured that the world will not raise your price.
Anonymous

Your treasure house is within; it contains all you'll ever need.
Hui-Hai

The fortune, which nobody sees, makes a person happy and unenvied.
Francis Bacon

He does not posses wealth that allows it to possess him.
Benjamin Franklin

Who finds a faithful friend, finds a treasure.
Jewish Saying

Not on one strand are all life's jewels strung.
William Morris

The man who treasures his friends is usually solid gold himself.
Marjorie Holmes

Treasure your relationships, not your possessions.
Anthony J. D'Angelo

What does this **SYMBOL** say to *you?*

Taurus 24

To win without risk is to triumph without glory.
Pierre Corneille

There is no decent place to stand in a massacre.
Leonard Cohen

Do not throw the arrow which will return against you.
Kurdish Proverb

Anger will never disappear so long as thoughts of resentment are cherished in the mind. Anger will disappear just as soon as thoughts of resentment are forgotten.
Buddha

You win battles by knowing the enemy's timing, and using a timing which the enemy does not expect.
Miyamoto Musashi

Courage is being scared to death but saddling up anyway.
John Wayne

He that is not with me is against me.
The Bible

There are many humorous things in the world: among them the white man's notion that he is less savage than the other savages.
Mark Twain

AN INDIAN WARRIOR RIDING FIERCELY WITH HUMAN SCALPS HANGING AT HIS BELT

Commentary: "An Indian Warrior Riding Fiercely with Human Scalps Hanging at His Belt" is a Symbol of great force and conquest. "Scalping" is often associated with American Indians. Long ago, the English paid bounties for Irish scalps. The Indians actually learned the practice of "Scalping" from the Europeans, where it was a well-established tradition. The original Indian tradition was for the "Warrior" to steal something from the person conquered to show how strong his medicine was. Regardless, a vengeful heart creates only sadness for all concerned, and there are no real winners in the end.

Oracle: Someone may have been holding back from pursuing what they've wanted and is now going after all they can get. The "us or them" mentality can lead to disputes, and separations and the forgetting of a sense of other people's humanity. Perhaps you haven't been given a fair share of things by society, or these have literally been taken from you. As a chain reaction can be set off with this Symbol, there needs to be care taken that a real "war" is not started with people seeking revenge. Consider everyone's rights as this can point to the invasion of other people's space or territory. There may be a need for someone to mark their territory and claim their dues. Look to see if there are barriers up to prevent invasions of territory, yours or another's. Be wary of excessive competition, in the marketplace or the home, as this can scare people off—making the environment unsafe and unsound. Taken to its extreme, this Symbol can point to all-out feuds between people. Alternatively, with a level of controlled aggression and taking the necessary risks, you can be recognized for your abilities as a successful leader, prepared to face danger and succeed. Bravery and honor are often admired and respected by others.

Keywords: Race wars. Claiming one's soil. Trophies of conquest. Aggression. Basic instincts. Territoriality. Chain reactions. Tit-for-tat. Competitive natures. Risks for the clan or group. Trophies, medals and diplomas. Striving for recognition and respect, deserved or not. Blood and sacrifice. Tribes mourning their losses. Ritualistic behaviors. Marking victories. War crimes. Ticket scalpers.

The Caution: Conquering others without emotion. Showing off to intimidate others. Domination and ruthlessness. Taking things because one can. Violation of other's space. Testosterone. Feeling taken advantage of. Notches on the belt, or gun. Cycles of retribution. Vengeance. Taking scalps.

What does this **SYMBOL** say to *you?*

A LARGE WELL-KEPT PUBLIC PARK

Taurus 25

Commentary: "A Large Public Park" implies a big area of land that has been kept aside from development for the enjoyment of the "Public." The fact that it is "Well-Kept" shows that the "Park" has gardens and public amenities, is well looked after and clean of mess and rubbish. People are able to meet together, play ball, lie in the sun and, perhaps, walk their dog in safety. There's lots of room to move and things are in their rightful place. In many ways our society is a "Public Park" and we each play a part in its beauty and success, whether our contribution is by working on the gardens or enjoying the amenities.

Oracle: You are part of something important, but you are only a part. It is when everyone works together that we can create a useful and lasting result that will be of benefit to the whole community. However, in a controlled and interdependent situation there can be the perception of a lack of privacy and the inability to get completely away from others. Hence, you may need to be mindful of the fact that other people can always see what you are doing. The best thing is to work together to create the cooperation and consideration that will afford privacy for all areas of life. In this situation it is not only a right, but also a well-earned reward. "Parks" are for recreation, but are you aware of what recreation means to you? Are you in a balanced state of work and play? Your leisure time needs to be tended to and organized, as much as your work life. However, a lot of maintenance may be required just to keep the situation under control. Also, others may have a vested interest in taking over the space or using it for something that wasn't intended, such as property development. Every community needs an area for recreation and enjoyment and it should be protected, nourished and looked after.

Keywords: Paying attention to appearances. People living in peace. Space for everyone. People taking to the streets. Park benches, swings, slippery dips and sandpits. Charities and their work. Maintaining order. Gardens and gardening. Town planning. Work of the few for the pleasure of the many. Appearances kept immaculate. Golf and other sports. Picnics. Eating alfresco. Meeting others out in the open. Large plots of land. Acreage. Subdividing and development. Suburbia.

The Caution: Difficulty in finding privacy. People continually coming by. Having so much to look after without much help. Public possessions being sold off for the benefit of a few. Mugging and robberies. Littering and graffiti.

What does this **SYMBOL** say to *you?*

Civilization is the progress toward a society of privacy. The savage's whole existence is public, ruled by the laws of his tribe. Civilization is the process of setting man free from men.
Ayn Rand

The materials of city planning are: sky, space, trees, steel and cement, in that order and that hierarchy.
Le Corbusier

When you see the earth from space, you don't see any divisions of nation-states there. This may be the symbol of the new mythology to come; this is the country we will celebrate, and these are the people we are one with.
Joseph Campbell

He enjoys true leisure who has time to improve his soul's estate.
Henry David Thoreau

If you are losing your leisure, look out! You are losing your soul.
Logan Pearsall Smith

The primary purpose of a liberal education is to make one's mind a pleasant place in which to spend one's leisure.
Sydney J. Harris

Taurus 26

When love is not madness, it is not love.
Spanish Proverb

Flattery is like cologne water, to be smelt of, not swallowed.
Josh Billings

An ecstasy is a thing that will not go into words; it feels like music.
Mark Twain

If music be the food of love, play on.
William Shakespeare

Tell me about yourself—your struggles, your dreams, your telephone number.
Peter Arno

The first man to compare the cheeks of a young woman to a rose was obviously a poet; the first to repeat it was possibly an idiot.
Salvador Dali

Give her two red roses, each with a note. The first note says, "For the woman I love" and the second, "For my best friend."
Anonymous

A SPANIARD SERENADING HIS SENORITA

Commentary: "A Spaniard Serenading His Senorita" is a lovely image of singing, music, romance and love. The "Spaniard" pours his heart out to his beloved in the hope that she will listen and respond to his advances. Beautiful words and music can lift the spirits and we all need a little romance now and then! The "Spaniard" is "Serenading" his love, his "Senorita," who may or may not know the depth of his feelings. Whether she accepts his advances or rejects them, this need not stop him from celebrating his feelings in a show of emotion.

Oracle: In this situation there is no guarantee of getting your message across, but you must act if you expect any chance of success. It is by being brave and confident enough to put our feelings on public display that we can convince others of our sincerity. It is possible that the worst that could be damaged is your ego, so think positively and play your role with enthusiasm and passion. However, be wary of insincerity or coming on too strongly. This Symbol can also point to people covering up their real feelings because they are looking for a calculated response from another. This "Serenade" should not be like some kind of desperate act, but, instead, an act of devotion and love. True expressions of feeling can lead to grand actions and reactions. The situation around the question is full of emotion and passion. To say "I love you" or "I care for you" or "I believe in you" or "I trust you" to those who want to hear it makes it even more special and encouraging. The confirmation of deep feelings is rewarding to all involved.

Keywords: Looking through pretence. Shared feelings, love or passion. Spontaneity. Welling expressions of romance. Being in tune with another. Soul mates. Chivalry. Reverting back to old methods of relating. Spinning tales to get a response. Knowing what to say and when. Music, singing, crooning, talking. Instruments. The use of the voice. Foreign voices. Guitars. Getting one's message across.

The Caution: A ruse performed to achieve a goal by deception. Lies, deceit and propaganda. Not believing messages given by loved ones. Feeling like something is missing from a relationship. Superficial judgments of how things should look or be. Emotional manipulation. Selfish agendas. Things said merely to sway someone's feelings. Empty promises or declarations. Pouring out the heart to deaf ears.

What does this **SYMBOL** say to *you?*

AN OLD INDIAN WOMAN SELLING BEADS AND TRINKETS

Taurus 27

Commentary: "An Old Indian Woman" is "Selling Beads and Trinkets." She probably spends a great deal of her time selling these small products of her culture for very little reward or real monetary return. The modern, and somewhat foreign, world often shows little regard and doesn't respect the crafts and skills that are probably well respected within her tribe. Despite this lack of appreciation, the "Old Indian Woman" can still enjoy a deep understanding of her self-worth and the dignity of her identity and tribal origins. However, she may be capable of much more: that she is reduced to "Selling Beads and Trinkets" is a measure of the poor treatment this world gives to those who are less fortunate, older, or who have fewer resources for making a living.

Oracle: Do not underestimate yourself or restrict yourself to what you think others believe you are capable of. Everybody has talents and abilities, including you. You may be placing limitations on your capabilities and it is it these very limitations that can truly reveal to you hidden talents and skills that are sometimes taken for granted. Having belief in what you're doing will bring rewards at the end of the day. Sometimes it is necessary to do things that seem below your true station in life in order to survive, but true survival begins in your heart and your belief in yourself. Positive affirmations are useful at this time—have faith in yourself and the products of your culture. Don't wait for passers-by to stop and pay attention to you or what you have to offer. Regardless of their actual monetary value, these "Beads and Trinkets," whatever they may be, can be beautiful, worthwhile and useful souvenirs to both yourself and others.

Keywords: Older, wiser elements of society making offerings to the younger, less integrated. Small but worthy products. Adapting to changing conditions, particularly monetary or financial. Working hard for small returns and rewards. Battling against the odds. Selling the products of one's culture. Artifacts. Jewelry. Handicrafts. Retailing. Supplying the populace with beautiful things. Markets and stalls. Patience. Bartering and bargaining.

The Caution: Looking down on those that seem less fortunate. Loss of culture and traditional duties. Menial jobs. Devaluing things or overvaluing junk. Feeling that you have nothing to offer. Waiting for others to validate your worth. Bickering over money. Feeling "cursed" with one's lot in life. Lack of the respect for the arts. Being stuck in the marketplace. Sweat shops.

Accomplishment of purpose is better than making a profit.
Hausa Proverb

There are very honest people who do not think that they have had a bargain unless they have cheated a merchant.
Anatole France

Perhaps middle age is, or should be, a period of shedding shells: the shell of ambition, the shell of material accumulations and possessions, and the shell of the ego.
Anne Morrow Lindbergh

Business has only two basic functions—marketing and innovation.
Peter Drucker

Each man takes care that his neighbor shall not cheat him. But a day comes when he begins to care that he does not cheat his neighbor.
Ralph Waldo Emerson

By virtue of exchange, one man's prosperity is beneficial to all others.
Frederic Bastiat

What does this **SYMBOL** say to *you?*

Taurus 28

We do not grow absolutely, chronologically. We grow sometimes in one dimension, and not in another, unevenly. We grow partially. We are relative. We are mature in one realm, childish in another.
Anais Nin

Probably the happiest period in life most frequently is in middle age, when the eager passions of youth are cooled, and the infirmities of age not yet begun.
Thomas Arnold

We in middle age require adventure.
Amanda Cross

One of the many things nobody ever tells you about middle age is that it's such a nice change from being young.
Dorothy Canfield Fisher

To exist is to change, to change is to mature, to mature is to go on creating oneself endlessly.
Henri Bergson

Aging is not "lost youth" but a new stage of opportunity and strength.
Betty Friedan

A WOMAN IN MIDDLE LIFE STANDS IN RAPT SUDDEN REALIZATION OF FORGOTTEN CHARMS, IN UNEXPECTED RECOVERY OF ROMANCE

Commentary: The "Woman in Middle Life" has found an "Unexpected Recovery of Romance." She has realized that "Romance" is not something that is only for the young; there is no time limit on the possibility of love and passion. The "Woman" has found herself in "Rapt Sudden Realization" and her "Romantic" longings and feelings have come flooding back. On the physical level, there can be a rush of hormones that back up these feelings. This Symbol shows that a surprising "Realization" can lead to sudden and overpowering joy.

Oracle: Love and "Romance" can dawn on us "Suddenly." When we are confronted by love it can come as a surprise as passions rise again in our lives. No matter what your age, there can be the "Realization" that the "Charms" of life have not deserted you, and it is unwise to listen to those who try to suppress or judge. These feelings of love can be very strong as one is no longer flushed with the naiveté and innocence of youth. It can be even better now because you know the pitfalls and can value and make the most of what's happening. You know not to be falsely swept off your feet and misguided by overreaction. Also, this should not be a time of desperation where you have to take whatever love and attention you can get. With a mature attitude, you can have a deep understanding of what is possible and you can choose to become involved, or not, for all the right reasons. Even if the "Romance" fades, you will find a new lease on life through a reawakening to life's possibilities. However, "Romance" can indicate many things; it can be a new passion for cooking, gardening, painting, music, astrology—anything. Anything that lights the fires in the heart can be "Romantic"—so open your heart and enjoy. Enjoy life more and more. This positive shift can lead to many good things—one of them could be a new lease on life itself.

Keywords: Finding a renewal of love, knowledge and interest when it looked like all opportunities had passed. Second chances. Starting over. Menopause. Romance renewed. Awakening to life's promises. Flowering of love, life and joy. Sudden realizations.

The Caution: Believing love and romance long gone. Denying emotional expression because of social expectation. Losing heart and feeling unloved. Having no time for romance due to responsibilities. Being skeptical of love, thinking it not possible or realistic. Resenting the aged finding love. Fickleness.

What does this **SYMBOL** say to *you?*

TWO COBBLERS WORKING SIDE BY SIDE AT A TABLE

Taurus 29

Commentary: The "Two Cobblers" are "Working Side by Side at a Table." "Cobblers" make and repair shoes and shoes cover and protect the feet. In a spiritual context the feet are said to be the symbol of "understanding." The "Cobblers" are working together "Side by Side" and yet both are accomplished in their own unique way. Because there are "Two" of them, they may see things in quite contrasting ways, which can enrich any projects they undertake. Equal partnerships can bring a sense of greater accomplishment to projects or the tasks at hand. The "Cobblers" work together with cooperation and mutual respect, bringing their individual talents and tools to the "Table."

Oracle: In order to get the best results, you need to work cooperatively with someone who has skills that are equal or complementary to yours, along with a sharing of similar interests. A partnership that brings together talent and energy will achieve a lot more than any solo effort now. If someone has talents that you don't, this can lead to a greater sharing of knowledge, resources and materials. By sharing tasks without ego or competition the outcome is not only better, but also more harmonious and satisfying. It may be that you are looking for someone who can complement your work. This Symbol implies that such a person will materialize. Remember the importance of your part and what you contribute. It is also important not to allow jealousy to interfere with any working partnership. The rewards along with the toil need to be shared. Couples working successfully at a task or duty can end up learning more about each other and the world they inhabit. However, if working together closely is not exercised carefully, it may bring feelings of criticism and judgment. Equality and respect is important. Done successfully, this will ensure that people will want to continue working "Side by Side."

Keywords: People sharing quietly and persistently in their labor. Equal opportunities and equal responsibilities. Skills complementing one another. Sharing materials, tools and tasks. Repairs to the soul. Reflexology. Partnerships. Work benches. Demarcations of work. The marriage of minds.

The Caution: Attempting to complete a task with shared responsibilities and yet gain all the credit. Committing to tasks that don't bring real satisfaction or reward. Fighting over "who has to do what." Bickering. Feeling like one's work is not appreciated. Arguing over the use of appliances or tools. Codependance.

What does this **SYMBOL** say to *you?*

Taurus 30

*It is neither wealth nor splendor,
but tranquility and occupation
that give happiness.*
Thomas Jefferson

*He enjoys true leisure who has
time to improve his soul's estate.*
Henry David Thoreau

*A peacock who sits on his tail is
just another turkey.*
Proverb

*It is not only fine feathers that
make fine birds.*
Aesop

*The sparrow is sorry for the
peacock at the burden of his
tail.*
Rabindranath Tagore

*The house of everyone is to him
as his castle and fortress.*
Lord Edward Coke

*Genius and virtue are to be
more often found clothed in
gray than in peacock bright.*
Van Wyck Brooks

*As long as you're going to be
thinking anyway, think big.*
Donald J. Trump

*A rich man is nothing but a
poor man with money.*
W. C. Fields

*A heart in love with beauty
never grows old.*
Turkish Proverb

A PEACOCK PARADING ON THE TERRACE OF AN OLD CASTLE

Commentary: "A Peacock" is "Parading," showing off his fine feathers and beauty. Peacocks were often installed in regal palaces as a show of opulence or extravagance. This "Peacock" is "Parading on the Terrace of an Old Castle," which shows that he is in a place that has all of the trappings of wealth and tradition. The situation is probably well established, but as it is "Old," it is probably also slowly breaking apart and showing signs of crumbling. "Peacocks" can be a reminder of the "grand old days." They are very territorial and will remain in a place long after the people have gone. Because of the many eyes displayed on their feathers they are said to be forever awake. "Peacocks" are used in place of guard dogs in India because they make a shrieking noise when they perceive intrusion or danger.

Oracle: In this situation there is a need to maintain your grace and pride while also maintaining a sense of being the center of attention. Polite behavior and the correct presentation of form are of vital importance and pride in one's inheritance is to be admired, but not overdone. Too much pride, and elitism, can lead to a feeling of being alone and the roof collapsing in on what was possibly once a magnificent empire. Remember: pride comes before a fall. You may have to accept that your situation or location may one day change, even if you fear that much will be lost. The key is to enjoy the beauty that is around you every day and take your sense of beauty and elegance with you everywhere you go. This Symbol can also point to people showing off and thinking they're better than others because of social prestige. Is there any danger of invasion of some kind?

Keywords: Tradition feeding ego-centered attraction. Grace and dignity. Splendor. Etiquette. Gardening. Enjoying the environment for its nature and beauty. Peacocks as "the watchers" and the Argus. Parading beauty. Beautiful old buildings. Empires that require protection. Issues of belonging and being allowed in. Prominent families. Inherited values. Castles and rambling estates. Beautiful colors.

The Caution: Risking integrity to display success. Strutting one's stuff. Inviting envy from others. Believing that one is all things to many people. Overloading others. Showing off and demanding acknowledgment. Trying to convince others of something. Noisy displays of wealth. Neglected buildings.

What does this **SYMBOL** say to *you?*

A GLASS-BOTTOMED BOAT REVEALS UNDERSEA WONDERS

Gemini 1

Commentary: "A Glass-Bottomed Boat" pictures a vessel that enables people to see underwater. It "Reveals Undersea Wonders"; we can observe the marvels of this "other world" through the lens of the glass, while remaining safe, dry and at a distance. Without this particular type of "lens," the "Glass," it would be impossible to see so much or so clearly. The "Wonders" of a normally unobserved world are brought into clearer focus. What is being observed is something quite separate from the observer, and yet it feels so close, almost like one could reach out and touch it.

Oracle: This Symbol implies that you can look at issues to do with your situation from an uninvolved and yet observing, knowing, perspective. This may be because the situation is separated, or away, from your natural environment. Take some time out to calmly observe what's going on around you. Things previously unseen or not understood will become evident. A distant, possibly uninvolved position is probably much safer for you as you can observe from a calm and detached perspective. As you have a special lens at your disposal, like the "Glass-Bottomed Boat," you will see much more than you might at first think. Adopt an attitude of being able to see through superficial appearances to what is actually there and what is really happening. You can get beneath the surface with a little concentration, and there can be incredible rewards if you focus on the task at hand. There are likely to be insights revealed that you could only have imagined before. Things may be revealed in a clairvoyant or intuitive way, with images and thoughts streaming across your mind. Imagine yourself with a new set of glasses or goggles that enable you to see through the apparent surface of things, down into the depths. Marvelous things can be "Revealed" with just a little effort, concentration and focus.

Keywords: Being able to see "within" to forms that are not usually observed by others. Clairvoyance. Observance of psychic phenomena. Connecting with the collective unconscious. Spiritual gifts that enlarge one's perspective. Amusement and wonder at natural beauty. Glass, lenses, refractions of light. Panoramic views. Water. Boats. Vehicles of discovery.

The Caution: Putting up barriers of social safety to avoid involvement in deep emotions. Overemphasis on safety concerns. Watching things from a distance, leading to separation and estrangement. Looking in the wrong direction. Cool, detached attitudes.

What does this **SYMBOL** say to *you?*

There's none so blind as they that won't see.
Jonathan Swift

"Truth is naturally universal," said Akananda, "and shines into many different windows, though some of them are clouded."
Anya Seton

The eyes are the window to the soul.
Proverb

Seeing is believing.
Proverb

Meditation is the soul's perspective glass.
Owen Felltham

Nature is the glass reflecting God, as by the sea reflected is the sun, too glorious to be gazed on in its sphere.
Brigham Young

Our house is made of glass... and our lives are made of glass; and there is nothing we can do to protect ourselves.
Joyce Carol Oates

The world will never starve for want of wonders; but only for want of wonder.
Gilbert Keith Chesterton

Gemini 2

The greatest pleasure I have known is to do good action by stealth, and to have it found out by accident.
Charles Lamb

I stopped believing in Santa Claus when I was six. Mother took me to see him in a department store and he asked for my autograph.
Shirley Temple Black

'Twas the night before Christmas, when all through the house, not a creature was stirring, not even a mouse. The stockings were hung by the chimney with care, in the hope that St. Nicholas would soon be there.
Clement C. Moore

I never believed in Santa Claus because I knew no white dude would come into my neighborhood after dark.
Dick Gregory

I like to deliver more than I promise instead of the other way around. Which is just one of my many trade secrets.
Dorothy Uhnak

A NERVOUS GENTLEMAN, DRESSED IN AN ELABORATE SANTA CLAUS COSTUME, IS FILLING CHRISTMAS STOCKINGS SECRETLY

Commentary: "A Nervous Gentleman, Dressed in an Elaborate Santa Claus Costume, Is Filling Christmas Stockings Secretly." "Stockings" are hung by the chimney in the hope of getting good things from "Santa Claus," otherwise known as St. Nicholas. The story of "Santa Claus" and the "Christmas Stocking" tells us that, out of compassion, Santa tossed three coins down the chimney of the home of three poor sisters. Each coin fell neatly into each of the "Stockings" left drying by the hearth. We therefore leave our "Stocking" out in anticipation that a similar bit of good fortune will befall us. He appears to be "Nervous" and acting "Secretly"; sneaking around. He wants to get his job done before the household wakes and he is discovered doing his rounds.

Oracle: Someone may be tiptoeing around, like "Santa Claus" in an effort to give out gifts while no one is looking. Be gracious and let those carrying the gifts have the pleasure of your reaction. You may, however, draw this Symbol in a situation where you are suspicious of someone being up to something. This Symbol may be saying that your fears are possibly not only unfounded, but can actually be quite wrong. You need to believe that something good is happening, and trust those involved in this situation. It may be you who is trying to surprise someone with a gift. Perhaps the giver in this situation is you? It is not necessarily the gift, but more the thought that counts. What would happen if the lights were suddenly turned on? Would things suddenly be known and revealed that were not apparent or visible before?

Keywords: Wishes fulfilled. The longing for superficial gratification. Gifts being dispensed. Receiving from unknown sources. Giving for no particular reason or thought of reward for one's self. Rewards coming. Making surprise visits. Token gestures. Furtive acts. Charity. Philanthropy. Masturbation. Secret affairs. The need for quick getaways.

The Caution: Hiding true gestures behind futile pretense. Concealing true intentions with a façade of goodness. Trying to get away with something. Stealing, shoplifting. Intrusion. Giving others what they want in a sly and secretive manner. Sneaking around in the dark. Bribes. Self-gratification. Eavesdropping and voyeurism. Being nervous or easily startled.

What does this **SYMBOL** say to *you?*

THE CHARMING COURT LIFE AT THE GARDEN OF THE TUILERIES IN PARIS

Gemini 3

Commentary: "The Charming Court Life at the Garden of the Tuileries" is a picture of elegance, riches and many of the things that comprise the "good life." "The Garden of the Tuileries" was huge, magnificent, well manicured and was said to have had up to 20,000 gardeners and servants working in the grounds. There was most likely barely a leaf out of place. People came together in this opulence to discuss politics, to enjoy the rich ambiance and each other. It must have been a "Charming Court Life" indeed!

Oracle: This is a time to enjoy the rewards of beauty, order, self-confidence and authority that you and others have developed and achieved. There may be a need to remember, however, that this does not make you, or those in your situation, greater, better or more deserving than others. The work you've done simply entitles you to a little luxury. Over time it is possible to develop your surroundings, both in possessions and spirit, to reflect the experiences of your life. This Symbol asks you to enjoy what you have achieved as it is a true expression of your self and those around you. Are you relaxed and comfortable enough to feel that you can maintain it, enjoy it or, indeed, deserve it? Perhaps you need the help of others to attain or maintain this lifestyle. The "Garden" is not restricted only to those who create it with financial wealth; it is available to all who share in its day-to-day life. It is also beautiful if it reflects a sense of spiritual wealth. Do you appreciate the health, wealth and beauty that surrounds you? Envy and jealousy need to be put aside, as these can lead to emotional alienation. Diplomacy, tact and skill will enable you to move more toward the center of this "Charming Court Life." Be grateful for all that you have, strive for the best and many wonderful things can be yours.

Keywords: A love of form and tradition. Cultivation of beautiful places. Symmetry of form being shown at its best. Gardens and gardeners. Garden ornaments. Statues. Having hired help to keep things beautiful or under one's control. Taking time to work in the garden. Going first class. Being in the inner circle. Pots, plants. Wealth. Tradition. Affluence and influence. Big houses and rooms. Ample amenities.

The Caution: Behaving in an elitist fashion. Being bossy. Snobbishness that separates people from each other. Being spoiled and shallow. Having more than one truly needs. Treating people like underlings or servants. Expecting others to do everything. Class-consciousness.

What does this **SYMBOL** say to *you?*

Let us be grateful to people who make us happy; they are the charming gardeners who make our souls blossom.
Marcel Proust

To laugh often and much; to win the respect of intelligent people and the affection of children; to earn the appreciation of honest critics and endure the betrayal of false friends; to appreciate beauty; to find the best in others; to leave the world a bit better, whether by a healthy child, a garden patch or a redeemed social condition; to know even one life has breathed easier because you have lived. This is to have succeeded.
Ralph Waldo Emerson

Pleasure for one hour, a bottle of wine. Pleasure for one year, a marriage; but pleasure for a lifetime, a garden.
Chinese Proverb

We must never confuse elegance with snobbery.
Yves Saint Laurent

We are all born charming, fresh, and spontaneous and must be civilized before we are fit to participate in society.
Judith Martin

Gemini 4

The mistletoe hung in the castle hall, the holly-branch shone on the old oak wall.
Thomas Haynes Bayly

*The holly and the ivy
Are plants that are well known
Of all that grow in the woods
The holly bears the crown.*
Anonymous

*Love is like the wild rose-briar;
Friendship like the holly-tree.
The holly is dark when the rose-briar blooms, But which will bloom most constantly?*
Emily Bronte

A good conscience is a continual Christmas.
Benjamin Franklin

*At Christmas play and make good cheer,
For Christmas comes but once a year.*
Thomas Tusser

*Heap on the wood!
The wind is chill;
But let it whistle as it will,
We'll keep our Christmas merry still.*
Sir Walter Scott

HOLLY AND MISTLETOE BRING CHRISTMAS SPIRIT TO A HOME

Commentary: "Holly and Mistletoe Bring Christmas Spirit to a Home" is a wonderfully warm and inviting image. The ancient Druids of Britain regarded "Mistletoe" as sacred and believed it had both magical powers and medicinal properties. They referred to it as the "heal all," although now we know the berries can be poisonous, so care needs to be taken with them. "Kissing beneath the mistletoe" is a tradition that has developed over the years as we have built barriers to more spontaneous expressions of affection. It is almost as though the "Mistletoe" and the "Spirit of Christmas" have become an excuse for us to be able to show our feelings. We have developed these types of rituals to compensate for what has truly been lost. "Mistletoe" was so sacred to the Druids that if two enemies met beneath a tree on which "Mistletoe" was growing, they would lay down their weapons, exchange greetings and observe a 24-hour truce.

Oracle: "Christmas" represents a time when we can reconnect with loved ones, family, or, in a larger sense, humanity, to discover the strengths and joys in the cultural and religious bonds that hold families and people together. However, we don't have to wait until a special celebration such as "Christmas" to feel close to friends and family. The openness that the "Holly and Mistletoe" represent should be carried in our hearts always and not restricted merely to a few days of the year. Realizing how important those near and dear to us really are, we should put in the effort to reach out to others at any time. It is not just about acknowledging these bonds, but also affectionately embracing them. "Mistletoe" is said to represent regeneration and the restoration of family life. Perhaps it is time to bring that "Spirit" of peace and reconciliation into the home and the family, regardless of the time or the season.

Keywords: Social celebrations of the spirit. Returning to basic joys. Remembering past celebrations of family and social cohesion. Kissing under the mistletoe. Simple gestures that remind us of larger realities. Warmth, joy and anticipation. The festive season. The spirit of special occasions.

The Caution: The use of superficial tricks. Performances to achieve the appearance of happiness or familial ties. Neglecting family. Excluding others because of religious beliefs. Rituals that have no depth or true meaning. Loneliness. Not being in the spirit of things. Having too much to do. The silly season. Scrooge mentalities that don't want to know about family and celebrations.

What does this **SYMBOL** say to *you?*

A RADICAL MAGAZINE OR PUBLICATION, ASKING FOR ACTION, DISPLAYS A SENSATIONAL FRONT PAGE

Gemini 5

Commentary: "A Radical Magazine or Publication" is shown. It is "Asking for Action" and "Displays a Sensational Front Page." Sometimes, in order to be taken seriously or be noticed, people need to do or say something rousing, radical or out of the ordinary, especially when there is a need, or a desire, to change things. There are probably some strong feelings that "Action" needs to be taken—bear in mind, however, that the status quo can be very hard to awaken, change or shift. As this is a "Radical Magazine" it can lead to moves that are disruptive or even threatening to stability or security in some measure. Further, the "Action" that is being called for can lead to less than desirable outcomes. Events that unfold can be highly charged emotionally.

Oracle: You may be motivated for change, and getting the attention of those around you may require radical and even abrasive action. This Symbol can be seen equally from the opposite view; perhaps you are having difficulty with someone who is being noisy, disruptive, demanding or looking to cause change. Whichever, the issue is most likely overblown and exaggerated in some way. There may be a lot of dramatic "Action" and overreaction to what is said or done. Things may currently seem threatening, but are probably just reflections of moments in time and likely to pass before long. Someone may meet his or her match vocally. Attention seeking devices, such as the "Sensational Front Page" should be used very carefully and never against anyone. Once everyone is paying attention there may need to be an effort to publicize a more reasonable perspective. Sometimes we overuse terms like "you never" and "that's the last time I ever..." It is important to get past the exaggerated "Sensational" words and look at why such large statements are thought necessary in the first place.

Keywords: Speaking one's mind. Messages and news that awakes or shocks. The need for reform. Challenging outlooks. Breaking out of constraints. The media. Issues of propaganda. Headlines that promise more than they deliver. Revolutions. Social or emotional causes. Conspiracy theories. Printing presses. Publishing. Publicity. Gaining attention. Speaking one's truth without fear of consequences.

The Caution: Being argumentative. Arousing others for selfish reasons. Distortions of the truth. Misinformation and disinformation. Getting the whole picture wrong. Exploitation of situations. Overstating messages. Biased information. Old and outworn news.

What does this **SYMBOL** say to *you?*

Controversy equalizes fools and wise men and the fools know it.
Oliver Wendell Holmes

There is nothing more wonderful than freedom of speech.
Ilya G. Ehrenburg

My sources are unreliable, but their information is fascinating.
Ashleigh Brilliant

Freedom of opinion can only exist when the government thinks itself secure.
Bertrand Russell

The sports page records people's accomplishments; the front page usually records nothing but man's failures.
Earl Warren

All the news that's fit to print.
Motto of the New York Times since 1896

*But words are things,
And a small drop of ink,
Falling like dew,
Upon a thought,
Produces that which makes thousands,
Perhaps millions, think.*
George Gordon Byron

The power of the press is very great, but not so great as the power of suppress.
Lord Northcliffe

Gemini 6

In deep meditation the flow of concentration is continuous— like the flow of oil.
Patanjali

Few things are impossible to diligence and skill. Great works are performed, not by strength, but perseverance.
Samuel Johnson

Rockefeller once explained the secret of success. "Get up early, work late—and strike oil."
Joey Adams

The meek shall inherit the earth, but not the mineral rights.
J. Paul Getty

Of course we all have our limits, but how can you possibly find your boundaries unless you explore as far and as wide as you possibly can? I would rather fail in an attempt at something new and uncharted than safely succeed in a repeat of something I have done.
A. E. Hotchner

It is while you are patiently toiling at the little tasks of life that the meaning and shape of the great whole of life dawns on you.
Phillips Brooks

Life leaps like a geyser for those who drill through the rock of inertia.
Alexis Carrel

WORKMEN DRILLING FOR OIL

Commentary: "Workmen Drilling for Oil" is a Symbol of people working, endeavoring to find some treasure. Often this treasure, the "Oil," is buried deep and there must be significant effort made to bring it to the surface. Searching deeply into the depths often carries a certain amount of risk, and the "Workmen" need to have an incentive for doing the task. "Drilling for Oil" also shows a desire to get to the depths, or the bottom, of an issue, or to find the rewards that exist deep within something.

Oracle: The situation facing you will probably need hard work, concentration and commitment. The rewards you are seeking may be hidden way beneath the surface. The answers you want are often held within yourself, or others, and it can be just a simple matter of having, and keeping, faith in the search. You may need to explore your inner self for answers. Acting in cooperation with those who have the skills to assist you in such an exploration can bring to the surface things that you didn't even know were there. As true rewards are at times both difficult to find and unsuccessful, it is through employing continual perseverance and shying away from feelings of futility that you will find success. You may need to get used to operating in the dark or acting without a clear view of outcomes. Exposing yourself to risks is often necessary in order to gain rewards or wealth. You will need to stick with the task, while keeping an eye on what the real objective is. Trust your intuition and follow your heartfelt endeavors. Even if you don't actually strike "Oil," there can still be much learned during the exploration. Consider the value or the risk in "Drilling" for this potential reward. Keep a positive attitude; perseverance and hard work will pay off in some measure.

Keywords: Pursuit of material or spiritual wealth. Ambition. The drive to plumb the depths. Trying to get to the bottom of things. Opportunistic attitudes. Making a fortune through other's resources. Psychoanalysis and psychotherapy. Dream analysis. Explorations, past life or present. Dependence on wealth. Research. Exploring answers. Oil and oil wells. Drills and equipment. Searching for a reward.

The Caution: Putting a great deal of effort into risky activities for uncertain returns. Unceasing work. Hoping to just "strike it rich." Neglecting friends and loved ones. Focusing too deeply on a goal. Being opportunistic and looking for the "lucky strike." Relying on others to come up with the goods. Gold diggers and opportunists. Exploiting resources. Depression. Digging into people's private matters.

What does this **SYMBOL** say to *you?*

AN OLD-FASHIONED WELL WITH THE PUREST AND COLDEST OF WATERS

Gemini 7

Commentary: "An Old-Fashioned Well with the Purest and Coldest of Waters" pictures a reliable, sustainable and refreshing supply of the essence of all life—"Water." Over the years, the "Water" from the "Well" has been available to all who came to draw on it. This 'Well' can supply "Water" to a single person, a small family, or a big community. "Wells" symbolize sources of nourishment, the quenching of thirst, and can also show inner wisdom, and the depth of people, emotionally and spiritually. The people of old saw "Wells" as gateways to the spirit world where the veils between human existence and the greater spirit became thinner, and communications could take place with the gods and goddesses of the nature religions. That this "Old Well" has "the Purest and Coldest of Waters" shows that wisdom and nourishment has not diminished over time. There is always a plentiful supply for those who draw on the "Well" with the right attitude and with sincerity.

Oracle: You are able to access the "Well" through faith and self-confidence and the ability to respond to others on all levels, particularly emotionally. In order to partake of the benefits of the "Well," you will need to make the effort to draw the "Water" up from the "Well." There should be nothing to stop you. You probably don't need to employ your thoughts as much as your beliefs, compassion and love. You may, however, need a long rope and patience to reach into the depths. Imagine yourself with a big strong bucket that is being filled with what you need. The greatest barrier to partaking of these "Waters" is to disregard the value of the "Well" because it is "Old" or because it is not "on tap." Feeling like you can tap into the essence of a person, a situation or some knowledge can be very nourishing, rewarding and illuminating.

Keywords: Being nourished and satisfied. Feeling supported by the environment. Clarity of thought and perception. Drawing on deep resources. Links to the past. Deep and sustaining. Things you can rely upon. The pool of universal experience. Oasis. Believing in others. Ensuring water supplies. Cool, refreshing water. Plenty for everybody.

The Caution: Not trusting advice based on established ideas. Being blind to the sincerity and depth of others. Judging by appearances. Not recognizing inner values. Droughts, emotional and literal. The well drying up, leaving nothing to nourish. Muddying of issues that make them difficult or impossible to tap. Stagnant water. Poisons. Molds.

What does this **SYMBOL** say to *you?*

Few men during their lifetime come anywhere near exhausting the resources dwelling within them. There are deep wells of strength that are never used.
Richard E. Byrd

We never know the worth of water till the well is dry.
English Proverb

I worked for a menial's hire, Only to learn, dismayed, That any wage I had asked of Life, Life would have gladly paid.
Jessie Rittenhouse

How many times has the water you're drinking been drunk before?
Anonymous

American society is a sort of flat, fresh-water pond which absorbs silently, without reaction, anything which is thrown into it.
Henry Brooks Adams

And Noah, he often said to his wife when he sat down to dine, "I don't care where the water goes if it doesn't get into the wine."
G. K. Chesterton

I believe in getting into hot water. I think it keeps you clean.
G. K. Chesterton

Gemini 8

If you want creative workers, give them enough time to play.
John Cleese

In really hard times the rules of the game are altered. The inchoate mass begins to stir. It becomes potent, and when it strikes, ... it strikes with incredible emphasis.
Walter Lippmann

Man's biggest mistake is to believe that he's working for someone else.
Nashua Cavalier

Human beings are so made that the ones who do the crushing feel nothing; it is the person crushed who feels what is happening. Unless one has placed oneself on the side of the oppressed, to feel with them, one cannot understand.
Simone Weil

Strike while the iron is hot.
Proverb

We are so bound together that no man can labor for himself alone. Each blow he strikes in his own behalf helps to mold the universe.
Jerome K. Jerome

AROUSED STRIKERS SURROUND A FACTORY

Commentary: "Aroused Strikers Surround a Factory," they are obviously unhappy with their work, their pay or their conditions, and they are now on "Strike." In some measure, they are not putting up with what they're receiving for their efforts. For the moment, the disagreement has stopped anyone from benefiting from anything at all as events have come to a standstill. This Symbol pictures a dramatic type of power struggle or disagreement over how something of value is to be shared. It may be about work conditions, or the distribution of wealth that results from the work they are expected to do. What is their incentive for putting in the effort? The "Strikers" may be calm, but all hell could break loose, turning into a full-blown demonstration with placards, yelling and violence.

Oracle: What is really needed is a discussion of the need for one's rights to be heard and hopefully worked out. There is an obvious imbalance of power and it is time to consider what negotiations can be made. It may be difficult to find creative solutions, but that is probably what is important now. If you are in a situation where you have to stand up for your rights, or entitlements, or for those of a group, you will probably need the support of others. This could be your coworkers, friends or family. Try to enlist the help of those who feel the same as you, but at the same time take care to be sure that the cause is justified. There is an element of imbalance and emotion here. Is what's being said really being heard by those who need to hear? Are the "Strikers" asking too much? Justice can only come through negotiation, mutual consideration and a fair sharing of rewards. Once this is accomplished, everyone can come back together, working toward common goals in a more satisfying atmosphere.

Keywords: Bargaining to find more equitable solutions. Demanding better rights and conditions. Comradeship. Disruption of the normal flow. Not wanting to contribute or work. Taking time out to consider one's position. Taking action or refusing to act. Labor strikes and strikers. Demonstrations. Peace rallies. Standing up for others. Scab labor. Sweat shops. Slave labor. Strikes. Bosses. Workers. Placard waving.

The Caution: Being obsessed with what is desired. Refusing any compromises. Going without one's due in order to protest. Being locked out because of one's actions or attitude. Being left out in the street. Greedy behavior. Asking for more than one's share. Overworked and underpaid. Shutting down.

What does this **SYMBOL** say to *you?*

A MEDIEVAL ARCHER STANDS WITH THE EASE OF ONE WHOLLY SURE OF HIMSELF, BOW IN HAND, HIS QUIVER FILLED WITH ARROWS

Gemini 9

Commentary: The "Archer" has "His Quiver Filled with Arrows." He is someone who is "Wholly Sure of Himself," and he has his "Bow in Hand." The "Medieval Archer" was used in great numbers in open battles in England. They could fire as many as fifteen "Arrows" a minute. As the "Archer's Quiver" is "Filled with Arrows," it seems he may not have drawn "His Arrows" yet. There may be no immediate threat as the "Archer" stands with only "His Bow in Hand." By being alert, having the ammunition he needs can assist him to be true to himself, and with vigilance, he can remain "Wholly Sure of Himself."

Oracle: Your situation requires skill, courage, a true sense of confidence and the knowledge to get right to the heart of the matter facing you. You may need to examine just how prepared you are for a surprise situation. If you have some form of test coming up, are you armed with the knowledge and the ammunition you need? Can you face life with calm and a quiet assurance of the soundness of your position? Be careful not to rush into something unprepared. It is not enough to just hope for the best. This will only leave you feeling inadequate if you find yourself unable to cope. If you are on "the hunt" for something, are you prepared for the prize? Don't be distracted or led away from what needs to be done. Stay focused, armed and ready to go for the objective when it presents itself. Make a strategy, and hit the target. If you get stressed or confused, take a moment to compose yourself and remember that you have the ammunition of knowledge and the marksmanship that confidence and assurance provide. Using the symbol of an "Arrow," or a target, in some way can lead to surprising results.

Keywords: Being armed and ready. Having the aim and ammunition. Accuracy and strength. Getting to the point. The power of tension. Sending a message true and clear. Skills that create confidence and assurance. Focus. Bulls-eyes. Bows and arrows. Warriors. The determination to prevail.

The Caution: Going into battle unprepared. Overconfidence in one's mission. Being trigger-happy. Someone "cocksure" of themselves. Threatening postures of attack or defense. Always being on the alert for any opportunity to fight. The thug.

What does this **SYMBOL** say to *you?*

If you would hit the mark, you must aim a little above it; every arrow that flies feels the attraction of earth.
Henry Wadsworth Longfellow

Practice makes perfect.
Old Saying

You will soon break the bow if you keep it always stretched.
Phaedrus

None learned the art of archery from me who did not make me, in the end, the target.
Saadi of Shiraz

Talking without thinking is like shooting without taking aim.
Proverb

Next in importance to having a good aim is to recognize when to pull the trigger.
Elmer G. Letterman

If you shoot your arrows at stones, you will damage them.
Austrian Proverb

Do not throw the arrow which will return against you.
Kurdish Proverb

They couldn't hit an elephant at this distance.
General John Sedgwick

Gemini 10

*Life changed after that jump
...I'd suddenly stepped to the
highest level of daring, a level
above even that which airplane
pilots could attain.*
Charles A. Lindbergh

*Later, I realized that the mission
had to end in a letdown
because the real barrier wasn't
in the sky but in our knowledge
and experience of supersonic
flight.*
Chuck Yeager

*Lovers of air travel find it
exhilarating to hang poised
between the illusion of
immortality and the fact of
death.*
Alexander Chase

*More people are killed every
year from donkeys than from
airplane crashes.*
Trivia.net

A stumble may prevent a fall.
English Proverb

*The airplane stays up because
it doesn't have the time to fall.*
Orville Wright

*Nothing is more desirable than
to be released from affliction,
but nothing is more frightening
than to be divested of a crutch.*
James Baldwin

AN AIRPLANE DIVES TOWARD THE EARTH AS THOUGH FALLING

Commentary: "An Airplane Dives toward the Earth as Though Falling" pictures risks, daring and going against the odds. The nose "Dive" may look exciting, but things could really be heading for disaster. Onlookers may be unsure of what's really going on. Is the pilot of this "Airplane" just playing around by defying gravity or is he really in a life-threatening situation? If the one in control, the pilot, makes the slightest error of judgment, there could be a terrible outcome, with the "Airplane" crashing and burning. At the right moment someone, whether it is the pilot, or someone else who can take command, needs to pull out of the "Dive" and save the day. Everything will be fine, possibly exciting and even exhilarating, as long as everything is truly under control.

Oracle: Are things really going the way they should? Risk taking may pay off in a big way and may well be worth it, however, it may end up in a self-defeating crash-and-burn situation. Are you, or is someone else, actively working against their own best interests? Those around you may begin to panic; it may be necessary to reassure them that everything is going to be okay. Let go of things that aren't really necessary—you can't deal with too many things right now. It is important to try and keep distractions to a minimum, concentrating on this situation only, and rely solely on those you can trust. A sense of equilibrium needs to be reached or regained. Grabbing hold of the situation and facing it with composure and confidence can straighten things up. Imagine yourself pulling out of a nose "Dive" or repeat an affirmation of rising up and pulling through. This is certainly a time when courage is needed, but keep an eye on what's developing, as everyone may need to bail out to safety. Having a safety device, such as a parachute or a safe landing pad, may be necessary. The last thing you want to do is to crash and burn.

Keywords: Plunging into situations without considering the ramifications. Becoming conscious of what's happening. Being protected (and saved) at the last moment. Defying gravity. Facing consequences. Dangerous displays. Hitting the ground running. The art of smooth sailing. Daredevil stunts.

The Caution: Refusing to help yourself even when disaster is imminent. Free falls and defying the consequences. Shakeups. Things getting completely out of control. Overshooting the mark by aiming too high. Turbulence. Reckless behavior. Neglect of physical realities. Freaking out at crucial moments.

What does this **SYMBOL** say to *you?*

NEWLY OPENED LANDS OFFER THE PIONEER NEW OPPORTUNITIES FOR EXPERIENCE

Gemini 11

Commentary: The "Pioneer" in "Newly Opened Lands" shows someone who is ready to break away from old familiar ground and move into unknown and more exciting territory. This new sphere, these "Newly Opened Lands of New Opportunity" are open to "The Pioneer," someone who is prepared to venture into the unknown for the benefits that may be there. It is the "New Opportunities for Experience" that this Symbol is promising, a chance to explore the unexplored. Fear is often the greatest barrier to moving forward, but any fears must be put aside or faced and the familiar must be left behind for these new possibilities to occur.

Oracle: This situation is one that will fulfill its potential if you go forward, leaving the past and what's familiar behind, to seek out potential new "Experiences." Although it can take some time to adjust to a new place or space, different customs or unfamiliar conditions, striking out for what's possible can be rewarding in the long run. However, if someone is merely trying to manipulate the world to give them exactly what they want, or is just moving on in order to get more control, they may be sadly disappointed. Don't rush or expect too much but also don't accept too little from these "Newly Opened Lands." There may be some experiences that come your way that seem difficult, hard work or just plain undesirable, but that is often the result of venturing into new and unfamiliar environments. There may be a need to start life all over again in this new "Newly Opened Land." You could be starting from scratch. Be open to whatever comes your way. Take the time you need to adjust to this "New Opportunity" and enjoy the experience!

Keywords: Pioneering attitudes bringing rewards. Going off the beaten track. Coming up with new ideas. New spiritual realizations opening up vistas of hope and experiences. Opportunities to move on to new realms. Adjusting to new places. The Promised Lands. Being prepared to take risks. Moving out. New time zones. Foreign customs and languages.

The Caution: Clinging to the old and familiar when it is outworn and boring. Restricting growth and change. Not moving on. Invading other people's space. Claiming what's rightfully someone else's. Hanging on when it's time to let go. Running off to avoid involvement or responsibilities.

What does this **SYMBOL** say to *you?*

Explore thyself. Herein are demanded the eye and the nerve.
Henry David Thoreau

Explorers have to be ready to die lost.
Russell Hoban

Civilization no longer needs to open up wilderness; it needs wilderness to open up the still largely unexplored human mind.
David Rains Wallace

In my writing I am acting as a mapmaker, an explorer of psychic areas … a cosmonaut of inner space, and I see no point in exploring areas that have already been thoroughly surveyed.
William S. Burroughs

Take a chance! All life is a chance. The man who goes farthest is generally the one who is willing to do and dare.
Dale Carnegie

The Promised Land guarantees nothing. It is only an opportunity, not a deliverance.
Shelby Steele

In wisdom gathered over time I have found that every experience is a form of exploration.
Ansel Adams

Gemini 12

Freedom—to walk free and own no superior.
Walt Whitman

Freedom is the emancipation from the arbitrary rule of other men.
Mortimer Adler

Bit by bit ... she had claimed herself. Freeing yourself was one thing; claiming ownership of that freed self was another.
Toni Morrison

No man is good enough to govern another man without that other's consent.
Abraham Lincoln

We need to find the courage to say NO to the things and people that are not serving us if we want to rediscover ourselves and live our lives with authenticity.
Barbara De Angelis

To sin by silence when they should protest makes cowards of men.
Abraham Lincoln

The limits of tyrants are prescribed by the endurance of those whom they oppose.
Frederick Douglass

A BLACK SLAVE-GIRL DEMANDS HER RIGHTS OF HER MISTRESS

Commentary: The "Black Slave-Girl" who "Demands Her Rights of Her Mistress" is someone who wants to be taken seriously. She is tired of being treated like a "Slave" or dutiful underling. Like everyone else, she has "Rights" and she "Demands" that her needs be heard in order to improve her living conditions or situation. This can be difficult for the "Mistress" because it is not uncommon for those in dominant positions to fail to understand that everyone is entitled to their own freedoms. The "Mistress" may have assumed that everything was fine, as everything was okay at her end. Indeed, the "Slave-Girl" may not have realized that her position was something that needed changing or that she needed liberation from, until just recently.

Oracle: If you are in a situation where you are spoken to badly, or treated with less respect than you deserve, make a stand—don't just put up with it. It's time to break the pattern and move ahead with self-respect and self-determination. This will encourage others to show respect and acknowledge that you should be taken seriously. You can take responsibility for your own life and how it is lived. Whether you are the "Slave-Girl" or the "Mistress," it is important now to allow some changes or adjustments to the usual order and the established distribution of power. Nothing stays the same in a world of such broad experiences. It is how we react to others that measures our humanity. Parents can fall into this "Slave" trap and children sometimes need to show maturity by having sympathy for the dilemma their parents face in their own lives. State what you want clearly and simply and see how your situation improves. Keeping quiet can lead to illness and disgruntlement that simmers until it explodes. Whatever side of this situation you find yourself, it's better to act now.

Keywords: Rising above conditioning and limitations. Standing up for one's self. Demanding better treatment. Seeking recognition and self-respect. Being in charge of one's life. Breaking away from oppression. Wanting a raise in pay or conditions. The need for freedom. Desiring property and rewards. Rising up from an "underdog" position or situation. The quest for identity.

The Caution: Feeling hard done by. Being demanding. Blaming others. Bucking authority. Demanding to be recognized or noticed. Feeling used and abused. Oppression and slavery. Jealousy and envy. Exploitation.

What does this **SYMBOL** say to *you?*

A WORLD-FAMOUS PIANIST GIVING A CONCERT PERFORMANCE

Gemini 13

Commentary: "A World-Famous Pianist" is someone who, through years of rigorous practice, has learned their craft and knows how to show it so it can be shared, enjoyed and experienced by others. In this Symbol, the "Pianist" is "World Famous," and others come to watch the "Concert Performance." Perhaps he or she is performing in some distant place or foreign land. The audience has come to enjoy the melodies, emotions and dramas that are brought to their ears, minds and hearts. They come to see the person who embodies this talent. The "Pianist" has the ability to concentrate on the flow of the music and the actions of the body whilst being attentive to the audience. Rewards always come to those who are well rehearsed and prepared to share their talent.

Oracle: This Symbol shows the need to lay one's talent on the line, often in front of others, without fear of ridicule or rejection. It is not enough for someone talented to know how wonderful they are, the proof is in the expression of their skills in the real world, creating something as a result. It is important to remember that this "Performance" should spring from a love of what one is doing, whether it is music, performing, or some other type of artistic or creative expression. However, it may be that the enjoyment and passion have become overshadowed by the responsibility and difficulty of having to maintain high standards. It can be difficult to persist in practicing a learned talent if it is not a keen interest or passion. In order to revive these feelings it may help to present your skills, expertise and talent to others, or to the public. Know your audience and communicate with them. Show that you are skilled and practiced and you will earn the praise, attention and respect of others.

Keywords: Talent. Validations of social standing. Working hard at being special (or noticed). Reverence, respect and patronage of the arts. Feeling attracted to those with creative ability. Music, whether inspiring or tiring. Hands-on creativity. Feeling empowered by ability. Success. Practice makes perfect. Singing. Playing out front or in the band. Having an adoring public. Repertoires. Concerts.

The Caution: Relying on past success. Not putting in the day-to-day practice. The need for applause and acclaim to validate one's existence. Inflated egos demanding attention. Smugness about being talented, cultured, wealthy or privileged. Prima donnas. Cultural rewards for the privileged few. Conceit. Nerves that can ruin performance.

What does this **SYMBOL** say to *you?*

The only thing that separates successful people from the ones who aren't is the willingness to work very, very hard.
Helen Gurley Brown

The deepest principle in human nature is the craving to be appreciated.
William James

An acre of performance is worth a whole world of promise.
William Dean Howells

Never promise more than you can perform.
Publilius Syrus

The piano is the social instrument par excellence... drawing-room furniture, a sign of bourgeois prosperity, the most massive of the devices by which the young are tortured in the name of education and the grown-up in the name of entertainment.
Jacques Barzun

Please do not shoot the pianist. He is doing his best.
Oscar Wilde

Gemini 14

I think we dream so we don't have to be apart so long. If we're in each other's dreams, we can be together all the time.
Thomas Hobbes

Absence makes the heart grow fonder.
Proverb

Absence sharpens love, presence strengthens it.
Romanian Proverb

Separation secures manifest friendship.
Indian Proverb

Distance lends enchantment to the view.
Thomas Campbell

I waited and waited, and, when no message came, I knew it must be from you.
Ashleigh Brilliant

Love does not consist in gazing at each other, but in looking together in the same direction.
Antoine de Saint-Exupéry

To the query, "What is a friend?" his reply was "A single soul dwelling in two bodies."
Aristotle

Great minds think alike.
Proverb

TWO PEOPLE, AT WIDELY DIFFERENT POINTS, ARE IN CONVERSATION WITH EACH OTHER BY MEANS OF TELEPATHY

Commentary: The "Two People" are far apart—they are at "Widely Different Points." This can show that they are far apart in distance from each other, but it can also be that they live in very separate worlds or have very different viewpoints on life. Whatever, they are "in Conversation with Each Other by Means of Telepathy." This Symbol embodies the idea that we are never really separate from those with whom we truly belong, as long as we keep them in our minds and our hearts. It is not always necessary to be physically face-to-face with others to communicate in some manner.

Oracle: This Symbol shows that lines of communication can still be established if you can't be near a friend or loved one. It seems that you have bonds with another, perhaps with many people, that are unaffected by distance or frequency of communications or visits. When you are unable to be together, it is possible for you to remain connected through sending messages from your mind and heart. You could also be feeling as though you are receiving messages from or about them, but are afraid to pay attention to them. If you have been receiving clairvoyant flashes or premonitions, don't block them, as it is highly likely that they are trying to tell you something worth listening to. Society often frowns on things concerning psychic matters; but don't allow yourself to submit to other people's disapproval and opinions. Trust your intuition, both in the sending and receiving of messages. You may feel isolated or unable to physically bridge the gap between yourself and someone special. Try to set aside a time of the day or night when you can meditate on each other. Let your heart tell you that you are always in their company and there is no need to feel alone.

Keywords: Conquering space and time limitations. Psychic and mental communication. Sharing and thinking the same ideas. Knowing what is felt or thought by others. Feeling connected regardless of physical contact. Being on the same frequency. Mediumship. Telepathic communication. Conversation. Direct lines of communication. Mind reading.

The Caution: Blocking out sensitive awareness for the sake of social needs or expectations. Mind and thought control. Manipulating by subtle means. Losing contact. Not getting the message. Not seeing eye-to-eye. Barging into other people's space.

What does this **SYMBOL** say to *you?*

TWO DUTCH CHILDREN TALKING AND STUDYING THEIR LESSONS TOGETHER

Gemini 15

Commentary: "Two Dutch Children Talking and Studying Their Lessons Together" shows the need for clarity and for those of like mind to share and communicate spontaneous and creative ideas. The "Two Dutch Children" are discussing and sharing their thoughts, ideas and feelings about "Their Lessons." Every now and then they are likely to bring up side issues about their personal lives and to chatter about friends, etc. It may be that they are meant to be only "Studying Their Lessons," however they probably have the freedom to be able to relax and take things easily. The people around them probably won't be interested in what they are "Studying," although they may sometimes pretend to be. Some may feel left out because the level of conversation or the ways of communicating are so carefree, in-depth or inaccessible to others' minds.

Oracle: This Symbol shows people enjoying each other and sharing common goals. When a lot of the confusion of the day-to-day life is put aside, there can be an understanding of each other or those around you that is so strong it can feel like a soul connection. These are said to be "Dutch Children." Feeling cut off and isolated because of language or cultural separations can be frustrating, but if you have companionship with someone on your wavelength, it is much easier to bear. You should be able to relax and feel comfortable with your associates. Try not to look for or create any unnecessary complications. Get on with your job quietly and effectively with company that seeks the same things in life. Getting a grip on life's "Lessons" will enlighten and enrich everyone in this situation. Finding a friend to learn and be creative with could lead to some valuable lessons about friendships, relating and the world.

Keywords: Sharing of innocence and carefree thoughts and ideals. Exchanging views with like-minded individuals. Simplicity. Sense of companionship. Communication. Best friends. Having the right teacher. Learning and studying. Conversations that illuminate issues. Speaking many languages. Gossiping.

The Caution: Failing to communicate in depth. Unsophisticated viewpoints. Excluding others as "unworthy." Societal or racial prejudice. "Hearing voices" that don't make sense. Not hearing the opinions of others to further understand how the world works. Foreign languages that exclude others.

What does this **SYMBOL** say to *you?*

The language of friendship is not words but meanings.
Henry David Thoreau

Friendship is a single soul dwelling in two bodies.
Aristotle

A friend is a present you give to yourself.
Robert Louis Stevenson

The pleasure of reading is doubled when one lives with another who shares the same books.
Katherine Mansfield

Whenever two good people argue over principles, both are always right.
Marie von Ebner-Eschenbach

A different language is a different vision of life.
Federico Fellini

In studying the way, realizing it is hard; once you have realized it, preserving it is hard. When you can preserve it, putting it into practice is hard.
Zen Proverb

Gemini 16

The only cure for grief is action.
George Henry Lewes

Words are potent weapons for all causes, good or bad.
Manly Hall

It is always brave to say what everyone thinks.
Georges Duhamel

To sin by silence when they should protest makes cowards of men.
Abraham Lincoln

The last struggle for our rights, the battle for our civilization is entirely with ourselves.
William Wells Brown

Violence in the voice is often only the death rattle of reason in the throat.
John F. Boyes

Cautious, careful people, always casting about to preserve their reputations ... can never affect a reform.
Susan B. Anthony

A sufficient measure of civilization is the influence of good women.
Ralph Waldo Emerson

A revolution is not a dinner party.
Mao Zedong

A WOMAN ACTIVIST ON A PLATFORM GIVING AN EMOTIONAL SPEECH DRAMATIZING HER CAUSE

Commentary: "A Woman Activist" is "on a Platform Dramatizing Her Cause." There is a "Platform," that she is standing on and a message that she wants others to hear and understand. Although she stands up for what she feels, she may strike resistance. She may feel misunderstood and disadvantaged simply because of her gender, status or experience. This may be due to the ignorance of others but she must press her case or the status quo will remain.

Oracle: There's something that must be said or announced. If the cause is worthy or timely and your communications are clear, you will be heard by those who resonate with your message and your influence will spread. Think things through before speaking and the message will be a whole lot clearer. If emotions or energies get out of control it can lead to hysterics and tantrums. People are likely to switch off in some way. Similarly, when someone is saying something somewhat confronting it is likely to arouse people's emotions, or it can literally get their physical bodies responding—by moving about and fidgeting. What's being expressed may be too emotional and dramatic for some, but this may be what is necessary to shift stubbornness or to wake people up. This situation is quite possibly about inequality and the efforts that will need to be taken to find a fairer outcome, sometimes for many people. Who is listening and who is not? Are those who are not listening creating frustration? Is this causing a disturbance? Everyone making an effort to listen and show kindness and patience may solve any problems.

Keywords: Stating one's case. Revealing social passions. Being a mouthpiece for the emotions of the collective. The desire to be heard. Having a platform or stage. The need for rational emotional points to be made. Being the "underdog." Many things running through the mind. The battle between the masculine and the feminine. Taking it to the streets. Announcements. Fighting for a cause. Having to shoulder too many things.

The Caution: Pressing opinions on the unwilling and disinterested. Feeling that no one listens or cares. Rational or political structures overriding one's life. Going over the top trying to get a message across. Feeling like the "Woman" who is never listened to. Controlling the agenda. Hormonal swings. Male chauvinism blocking female progress. Justifying one's self. Silly ideas.

What does this **SYMBOL** say to *you?*

THE HEAD OF A ROBUST YOUTH CHANGES INTO THAT OF A MATURE THINKER

Gemini 17

Commentary: "The Head of a Robust Youth Changes into That of a Mature Thinker" shows that the young male energy in us has to grow up sooner or later. The various stages of life's experience are often marked by the changing appearance of our face as we age and the lines and gray hair appear. Life can only be lived in the fast lane for so long. It may have been appropriate to be somewhat young and reckless, but now it is time to stop "tearing around," to be more responsive to life and aware of its limitations and the consequences of one's actions. Growing up and taking a more "Mature" attitude will bring a new understanding of the world and how it works.

Oracle: Regardless of age, it's time for a more "Mature" attitude. The old ways of solving things will no longer work because this situation requires a more mature response, which will lead to another level of wisdom. There is only so much that one can do with youthful force—now it's time to use your intuition and intellect. Look to what's being learned and allow wisdom to shine through. Even though there may be some level of pain in adjusting to a life with more responsibilities, let the situation help bring about any necessary changes, even if they are hard to bear at first. Once we mature in life it is rare to go backward. Feel and acknowledge the "Youthful" mindset that is now changing, evolving and growing. Think things through and look to the consequences of your actions. More respect will, or at least should, be shown toward people as they "Mature" and take on a more thinking attitude. Getting to know yourself and your responses to the environment will produce a more "Mature," grounded and empowered you.

Keywords: Thinking with the higher mind. Gaining maturity. Making wise decisions. Using the system to get what one wants. Growing up "overnight." Having to change whether one likes it or not. Learning the lessons that come with age. Initiations into adulthood. Life changing events. Thinking, pondering. Finding a state of calm. Refined thinking. Facing reality.

The Caution: Suddenly becoming old. Losing innocence and energy. Clinging to the illusions of childhood. Peter Pan attitudes. "Never growing up." Feeling old when one could, or should, be feeling young. Hormones taking over and dictating behavior. Reacting with the lower emotional nature. Forever adolescent.

What does this **SYMBOL** say to *you?*

To live lightheartedly but not recklessly; to be gay without being boisterous; to be courageous without being bold; to show trust and cheerful resignation without fatalism—this is the art of living.
Jean de La Fontaine

Are you green and growing or ripe and rotting?
Ray Kroc

If youth but had the knowledge and old age the strength.
French Proverb

The old believe everything; the middle-aged suspect everything; the young know everything.
Oscar Wilde

If youth knew; if age could.
Henri Estienne

You're only young once, but you can be immature forever.
John Greier

Be wise with speed, for a youth at 40 is a fool indeed.
Edward Young

Don't trust anyone over 30 who used to say "Don't trust anyone over 30."
Anonymous

It takes a long time to bring excellence to maturity.
Titus Livy

Stupid is forever.
Anonymous

Gemini 18

The time to stop talking is when the other person nods his head affirmatively but says nothing.
Anonymous

It was Greek to me.
William Shakespeare

What a delightful thing is the conversation of specialists! One understands absolutely nothing and it's charming.
Edgar Degas

I believe they talked of me, for they laughed consumedly.
George Farquhar

A thousand cups of wine do not suffice when true friends meet, but half a sentence is too much when there is no meeting of minds.
Chinese Proverb

A different language is a different vision of life.
Federico Fellini

Great minds think alike.
Proverb

I speak Esperanto like a native.
Spike Milligan

TWO CHINESE MEN SPEAKING CHINESE IN A WESTERN CROWD

Commentary: The "Two Chinese Men" are "Speaking Chinese in a Western Crowd." Even though these "Chinese Men" may be able to speak English very well, it may not necessarily be their native tongue or their preferred language. In a "Western Crowd" they are foreigners. However, as there are "Two" of them, they have somebody who shares a common language, thoughts and ideas, and they may feel totally at home. This Symbol shows that even in complex groups there is an attraction toward people who have cultural or mindset similarities to ours. This could be about looks, nationality, ideas, language or even social status.

Oracle: No matter how adept one is at learning the ways of different people, there is still much greater ease and comfort in speaking our native tongue or speaking a language that more truly reflects our attitudes and beliefs. By finding someone of like mind we can feel more comfortable and secure. Sharing mutual thoughts can transcend feelings of alienation and lead to new understanding. It can, however, be frustrating and confusing to be in a situation where few can understand what someone is saying and thinking. Misunderstandings sometimes occur when we hear a few isolated words and don't get the true picture of what's actually really being said. This can be even worse if there is also some level of prejudice or criticism shown toward you or others. There is a need to not judge others just because they are different from one's self. If there's a feeling of not quite fitting in, don't be concerned—someone will turn up to share your experience. Indeed, there can be a strong feeling that there is only one other person, or very few special people, with whom you can share thoughts, plans and ideas. Having someone you can communicate with on the same level will dispel any feelings of alienation.

Keywords: Finding those of like mind. Leaving the "Western Crowd" behind. People having a specialized language that doesn't communicate with the larger population. Exclusivity in communication. Interpreting or misinterpreting tones of voice. People being drawn to each other. "Chinese whispers."

The Caution: Reluctance to adapt. Being with people who don't share the same philosophies or understandings. No one to communicate with on the same level. Stories that get out of control. Depending on others to mirror one's self. Being in alien territory. Schizophrenia. Hearing voices. Racism.

What does this **SYMBOL** say to *you?*

IN A MUSEUM A LARGE ARCHAIC VOLUME REVEALS A TRADITIONAL WISDOM

Gemini 19

Commentary: The "Large Archaic Volume Reveals a Traditional Wisdom." It is in a "Museum" where it is safe and secure, and available to all who pass by and appreciate it. "Traditional Wisdom" is nowadays often taken for granted or ignored. In this Symbol this "Wisdom" is locked away in a "Museum" like some kind of curiosity that is somehow revered, but possibly no longer relevant. The "Museum" may literally be a building, but it may also be information or knowledge hidden deep within yourself or the elders of your community. This "Wisdom" is held within all of us and needs to be tapped to be truly understood.

Oracle: Some effort needs to be made to discover this "Large Archaic Volume" and to allow the "Traditional Wisdom" within it to inspire your actions in present-day situations. You may experience intuitive "Wisdom" that seems to be generated outside your own experience. In a progressive world we look so often for new ideas and new solutions. "Traditional" knowledge can seem to be irrelevant to the present, but in truth it is something we often need in our lives. The knowledge behind those beliefs or rituals can be as relevant today as it has always been. Reading and studying this "Archaic Wisdom" can bring a sense of pride in our ancestors and those who went before us. It is, however, often important to update the way we view and use "Traditional Wisdom." This may be what is needed in this situation. Confidence in your actions will come from foundations that have a history or a strong sense of the past. Learn to take the best from the past, as it is useful for providing answers and clues to modern life problems. However, let go of any old and outworn beliefs that are holding you back.

Keywords: Reading and learning. Collective knowledge coming from ancient sources. Enormous potential to be tapped. The Akashic records. Astrology. The Bible. Learning from the victories and mistakes of the past. Old stories that come out of the past or are hard to forget. Shamanic knowledge. Learning from heritage. The roots of civilization. Books. Ancient sources of information. The mysteries. Being in the public domain.

The Caution: Not understanding wise messages or advice. Being caught up in accepting only what tradition dictates. Old fashioned rules of "the book." Old and outdated laws.

What does this **SYMBOL** say to *you?*

The books we read should be chosen with great care, that they may be, as an Egyptian king wrote over his library, "The medicines of the soul."
E. Paxton Hood

To me the charm of an encyclopedia is that it knows and I needn't.
Francis Yeats Brown

The Bible remained for me a book of books, still divine—but divine in the sense that all great books are divine which teach men how to live righteously.
Sir Arthur Keith

There are worse crimes than burning books. One of them is not reading them.
Joseph Brodsky

The worst thing about new books is that they keep us from reading the old ones.
Joseph Joubert

In science, read by preference the newest works. In literature, read the oldest. The classics are always modern.
Lord Edward Lytton

Gemini 20

The whole world is our dining room, but be careful: it is also our garbage can.
Ashleigh Brilliant

There are people who so arrange their lives as to only feed themselves on side dishes.
José Ortega y Gassett

He looked at me as if I was a side dish he hadn't ordered.
Ring Lardner

At a dinner party one should eat wisely but not too well, and talk well but not too wisely.
William Somerset Maugham

Appetite comes with eating; the more one has, the more one would have.
French Proverb

There are many of us who cannot but feel dismal about the future of various cultures. Often it is hard not to agree that we are becoming culinary nitwits, dependent upon fast foods and mass kitchens and megavitamins for our basically rotten nourishment.
M.F.K. Fisher

A CAFETERIA WITH AN ABUNDANCE OF CHOICES

Commentary: "A Cafeteria" is shown which has "an Abundance of Choices." We are very lucky in this modern age that everything is laid out for us so easily and so temptingly. There are all sorts of foods available, and we have only to reach out and take them. There are sometimes so many choices that it can be hard to make up one's mind. Also, each has its price. The "Cafeteria" is different from the a-la-carte restaurant—everything that is on display is available instantly. This can mean that what is available is not necessarily the best quality, but it is ready for use and consumption straight away. There is no time lost in preparing food—it's all there in front of you.

Oracle: Although everything looks so near and so convenient, be careful of your choices. Each will nourish you and fill you up to some extent, but some things are more nourishing or beneficial than others. Some things are downright bad for your health and should be avoided like the plague! However, we have a lot of free choice in our modern society; if you don't like your first choice, you can go back for something else—that is, if you can afford it. This Symbol is telling you that you may not need the special a-la-carte options of life right now. There are plenty of things immediately available that will do just fine. In fact you probably don't have the time or the opportunity to be too fussy. You may have to just take advantage of what is available. Take what you need, use it quickly and effectively so that you can clear those issues and get on with the more difficult situations later when there is time for more planning and patience.

Keywords: Overwhelming alternatives in modern society. Satiation. Everything provided for. Self-service. Issues of indulgence and one's needs satisfied. Salivating over what's on display. The incredible number of "choices" in a technological society. Too many choices (food, lovers, jobs, opportunities)—so little time. Instant gratification. Takeaway food. Buffet-style meals. Obesity. Chef's surprises. The need to be discerning. Mechanized systems that don't require much thought.

The Caution: Taking everything you can simply because it is available, regardless of needs. The inability to make life's decisions. Things so near, yet so far. The inability to satisfy no matter how much one has. Feeling that one has to eat because it's there. Indulgence beyond reason. Indigestion. Waste. Obsession with food. Using up people one by one.

What does this **SYMBOL** say to *you?*

A TUMULTUOUS LABOR DEMONSTRATION

Gemini 21

Commentary: "A Tumultuous Labor Demonstration" is shown. It seems there are many people who are unhappy and who feel that they are not getting their fair share. "Labor Demonstrations" can cause work to come to a standstill as people make their point. There is an injustice that needs righting and a spontaneous group reaction may be what is needed to wake up those in charge. Sometimes there's a need to lift one's voice or make a huge fuss otherwise nothing will be done; things are not likely to change by themselves. Sometimes it is only by rallying many people together in a common cause that you can be heard, or be taken seriously. Indeed, grinding things to a halt may be the appropriate thing to do at this time.

Oracle: This Symbol is suggesting that there are probably others who are involved or sympathetic to your situation. However, if there is a feeling of being alone and powerless, it is important to find out what level of support you actually have. Responses to this situation can cause emotions, and therefore actions, to get out of control. On the other hand, if you are the one trying to take advantage of someone else because you think they haven't got the power to defy you, you may be unleashing a reaction that will involve many other people. Whatever the situation, never underestimate the power of the collective, whether the people be blue collar or corporate. Indeed, the level of one's status plays a somewhat diminished role when it comes to the power and might of the majority. It is important to speak up for your rights and when the issues are important there is good reason to seek out support. You will be surprised how much support for the cause is out there. Stand up for what you want and see what happens.

Keywords: Pushing for change to the status quo. Feeling hard done by or taken advantage of. Seeking a better share of the profits. Protest about having too much to do. Standing up for yourself. Issues being trivialized. Overreaction. Melodramatic approaches to serious issues. Voting for change. Periodic blowing up. The rights of democracy. People in the street. Peace rallies.

The Caution: Using the group to accomplish a personal agenda. Asking for more than one's share, or not being able to ask for one's share. Protests that can lead to riots. Resisting change. Feeling that one's vote or voice doesn't count. Emotions that get completely out of hand. Refusing to cooperate or to be productive. Brutality and violence.

A riot is the language of the unheard.
Martin Luther King, Jr.

In union there is strength.
Aesop

Whenever you find yourself on the side of the majority, it's time to pause and reflect.
Mark Twain

If we don't stand for something, we may fall for anything.
Malcolm X

We are one, our cause is one, and we must help each other if we are to succeed.
Frederick Douglass

Those who sit at the feast will continue to enjoy themselves even though the veil that separates them from the world of toiling reality below has been lifted by mass revolts and critics.
Mary Ritter Beard

We must develop huge demonstrations because the world is used to big dramatic affairs. They think in terms of hundreds and millions and billions … Billions of dollars are appropriated at the twinkling of an eye. Nothing little counts.
A. Philip Randolph

What does this **SYMBOL** say to *you?*

Gemini 22

Life is a festival only to the wise.
Ralph Waldo Emerson

Wives are people who feel they don't dance enough.
Groucho Marx

If in February there be no rain, 'tis neight good for hay nor grain.
Proverb

Not what we have but what we enjoy constitutes our abundance.
John Petit-Senn

Plant a kernel of wheat and you reap a pint; plant a pint and you reap a bushel. Always the law works to give you back more than you give.
Anthony Norvell

Earth is here so kind, that just tickle her with a hoe and she laughs with a harvest.
Douglas Jerrold

Out of the abundance of the heart the mouth speaketh.
Romanian Proverb

Take rest; a field that has rested gives a bountiful crop.
Ovid

DANCING COUPLES CROWD THE BARN IN A HARVEST FESTIVAL

Commentary: "Dancing Couples Crowd the Barn in a Harvest Festival." Successful achievements have been accomplished, such as the "Harvest," and efforts have come to a fruitful conclusion and now it is time to gather together with others to celebrate. Everyone should share the pleasure that comes from a successful "Harvest." The hard work is put behind them and they reap the rewards of the benefits available to them in their leisure time. As "the Barn" is "Crowded," many people from the community come together to enjoy each other and the music and to dance. By gathering together and celebrating, a sense of community spirit can develop where there is always something worthwhile to be celebrated, even if it is not your own success.

Oracle: This Symbol shows the need to be in tune with seasonal rhythms and the natural flow of life. The "Harvest" may mean many things. It can be the actual bringing in of a "Harvest," the birth of a baby, the first performance at school, a religious ceremony, such as a communion or bar mitzvah, or a job well done. It is wonderful when people come together and warmly and sincerely congratulate someone who has good news without nagging feelings of jealousy or resentment. There is a need to get back to a simpler, conservative level of enjoyment where each and every person's achievement is everybody's pleasure. This can lead to an increased understanding and concern for the individuals within our community. It is also possible for one person's pain to become everyone's care. Whatever, the feeling of a healthy heart and a healthy mind, while taking a break from the struggles of providing, is what gives us the strength for the battles of life. Perhaps it's time to kick up your heels and dance. See if you can take some time out to enjoy your environment, the gifts of nature and the people around you.

Keywords: Celebrating the warmth and providence of the earth. The joy of nature's harvest. Joining with others to celebrate. The reality of rhythmical or seasonal adjustments. Agriculture. Good, old-time values. Issues of pride in one's place. Going out, having fun, listening and dancing to music. Square dancing, ballroom dancing, etc. Barns and dance halls.

The Caution: Being the wallflower and not participating. Waiting for a special invitation rather than responding to the possibilities available. Resentment. Isolation. Going alone. False displays of community. Shallowness. Attention paid to only those who are important.

What does this **SYMBOL** say to *you?*

THREE FLEDGLINGS IN A NEST HIGH UP IN A TREE

Gemini 23

Commentary: The "Fledglings in a Nest" are not yet able to fly properly as they haven't developed the feathers for flying. They are in their "Nest High up in a Tree." The "Three Fledglings" should feel warm and supported in their "Nest" and safe and at home in their environment. Although there is sometimes a feeling of being left alone and neglected, there is, hopefully, still a sense of safety in their isolation. This reflects a time of dependency on others to provide food and shelter. It may be too soon for them to move out on their own, but, after more nourishment, their time will come.

Oracle: The situation facing you is full of promise for the future. The "Fledglings" are not yet ready to fly and are still in need of the "mother" to sustain, protect, nourish and educate them. The universe flows in a pattern, and this pattern includes taking time to grow, mature and learn how to fly off into our own lives under our own steam. This period in the "Nest" gives us a time to be dependant and nurtured. Knowing that you will be able to rise up on your own and leave the security and safety of the "Nest" is the motivation to focus on while growing and developing your inner self. There may be a need to resist feelings of frustration. Arguments and contests with siblings can arise, especially if you feel "cooped up" together. Perhaps you have to stay when you really would prefer to leave because of others you may feel somewhat responsible for. Perhaps there would be more room available for everyone if someone left the "Nest." Whether you are one of the "Fledglings" or one of the "parents" who have to protect and nurture, don't worry—your opportunity for independence and free flight will come. Integration of spirit, soul and body will lead to you being able to fly on your own in good time.

Keywords: Discovering a whole new sense of being. Teaching. Safety. Living in small spaces. Wanting room to move. Privacy. Staying in the "Nest" vs. leaving it. Resisting change. Providing room and board for others. Sharing flats and houses. The battle for survival. Being different, therefore breaking the mold. Brothers and sisters. Expecting to be looked after and fed. Growing spirituality. Sibling rivalry.

The Caution: Wanting to leave home before one's ready. Wondering if one's needs will be met. Arguments about the pecking order. Psychological immaturity. Feeling dependent on external influences for survival. Feeling trapped by circumstance. Insecurity. Feeling exposed to danger. Codependence. Not knowing or realizing one's place. Falling out. Bickering over space.

What does this **SYMBOL** say to *you?*

The greatest gifts you can give your children are the roots of responsibility and the wings of independence.
Denis Waitley

Fledgling: 1. A young bird that has recently acquired its flight feathers. 2. A young or inexperienced person.
American Heritage Dictionary

In a broken nest there are few whole eggs.
Chinese Proverb

Birds in their little nest agree; and 'tis a shameful sight, when children of one family fall out, and chide, and fight.
Isaac Watts

"Come to the edge," He said. They said, "We are afraid." "Come to the edge," He said. They came. He pushed them … and they flew.
Guillaume Apollinaire

God stirs up our comfortable nests and pushes us over the edge of them, and we are forced to use our wings to save ourselves from fatal falling. Read your trials in this light, and see if your wings are being developed.
Hannah Whitall Smith

Gemini 24

The thinner the ice, the more anxious is everyone to see whether it will bear.
Josh Billings

Children are curious and are risk takers. They have lots of courage. They venture out into a world that is immense and dangerous. A child initially trusts life and the processes of life.
John Bradshaw

A man learns to skate by staggering about making a fool of himself; indeed, he progresses in all things by making a fool of himself.
George Bernard Shaw

In skating over thin ice, our safety is in our speed.
Ralph Waldo Emerson

We live amid surfaces, and the true art is to skate well on them.
Ralph Waldo Emerson

In the depth of winter I finally learned that there was in me an invincible summer.
Albert Camus

CAREFREE CHILDREN SKATING ON ICE

Commentary: "Carefree Children Skating on Ice" symbolizes the freedom and pleasure of "Children" enjoying themselves outdoors, even though it's winter and cold outside. It also reflects the general lack of concern they have for issues of personal danger. "Children" learn at an early age to "Skate" over difficulties. Being "Carefree" and unconcerned, they will often take risks when they play, unaware of the true realities and possible dangers in life. They keep "Skating" and playing, but need to be carefully aware of what's going on around them; otherwise the game could fall apart. There is the possibility of losing the pleasure they are experiencing as cracks form in the "Ice"—their joy and pleasure becomes more risky.

Oracle: If your situation is "on thin ice," it may be challenging, but it may be that most of the challenge comes from the fears and concerns that adulthood brings. Sharpen up your senses and your reflexes so that you can cope with any sudden surprises. Even if you have a positive attitude you may sense that everything could collapse at any moment. Listen for subtle changes in the environment that tell you whether you are still "safe" in your surroundings. If you don't acknowledge these fears and adjust yourself accordingly, then you may be put at a disadvantage. Perhaps an avenue of escape should be set up in case cracks in the "Ice" start to appear. Dangerous situations can lead to a heightened sense of awareness and fun, but how long can one feel safe taking such risks? Sooner or later the cracks will widen. What will happen then? Similar to the "Children," you may not even be aware of the risk in your situation. Be wary not to blindly rush into anything, as you may get to the point where you can't safely return to where you began. Watch out for the weak spots and listen carefully for clues to how to maneuver through difficulties.

Keywords: Getting around difficult situations by making the most of them (or evading them). Skating over problems. Finding creative and childlike solutions. Testing the boundaries. Considering consequences. Tiptoeing around problems with family. Responding quickly to every type of situation. Knowing how to maneuver in tight situations. Observing one's center of gravity. Being keenly aware. Testing the waters. Being alert.

The Caution: Rushing before checking that it is safe to do so. Living for momentary pleasures, without thought of ramifications. Getting away with things through acting naively and childishly. Taking risks that put others' lives on the line. Going too far too fast. Lack of warm clothing. Frozen atmospheres.

What does this **SYMBOL** say to *you?*

A GARDENER TRIMMING LARGE PALM TREES

Gemini 25

Commentary: "A Gardener Trimming" shows someone clipping dead fronds off "Large Palm Trees." He is working at getting rid of the old foliage that looks messy and unkempt. His job is to take notice of the things that other people may find irritating or cluttering, but don't have the time or the tools to take care of themselves. By "Trimming" the lower fronds from the "Palm Trees," he reveals their beauty more and more as he works.

Oracle: This Symbol shows a clearing away of the evidence of the past in order to give a fresh, clean image. There may need to be a special effort to make your creations or situations looks their best. But how much of your work only ends up making little difference to the overall picture? Sometimes we like to have our past experiences on display, be they good or bad. This can elicit admiration or, sometimes, sympathy. The truth about your life, however, is gained from what you have learned and how it is taking you forward. "Palm Trees" always grow from the top of the head, from their crown. If you cut the crown out of a "Palm" it will die. The same applies to us. It is important to let the powerful energies within rise up and grow toward the heavens. What is past is past and once it has revealed its purpose, it is time to carefully and lovingly "Trim" any unnecessary elements away. It may certainly feel as though you are leaving yourself open and without protection from the lower, basic elements, but every now and then the "Gardener" has to do his job. There is a time when our past does indeed create some protection, and there is a time when we must listen to our intuition and know when it is time to let go. Learn what to say and when, and also what is and what isn't important.

Keywords: Trimming off nonessentials to get to the bare reality. Caring for one's possessions. Doing the work simply because it needs to be done. Getting rid of rubbish. Gardening and landscaping. Editing words, thoughts, emotions—superfluous things. Weeding out the unnecessary. Looking after cosmetic appearances. Tidying up. Tools. Trips to the dump.

The Caution: Doing the work because of routine, rather than need. Spending time doing things because of appearances. Neglecting the real issues at hand, which may include good nourishment, watering, and caring for physical realities. Doing menial jobs when one could be doing much bigger better ones. Not knowing when to stop. Leaving a mess.

What does this **SYMBOL** say to *you?*

Good thoughts bear good fruit, bad thoughts bear bad fruit— and man is his own gardener.
James Allen

Gather the flowers, but spare the buds.
Andrew Marvell

Choosing goals that are important to you is one of the most essential things you can do in order to live your dreams.
Les Brown

And add to these retired leisure, that in trim gardens takes his pleasure.
John Milton

'Tis in ourselves that we are thus or thus. Our bodies are our gardens to which our wills are gardeners.
William Shakespeare

Besides the noble art of getting things done, there is the noble art of leaving things undone. The wisdom of life consists in the elimination of nonessentials.
Lin Yu-t'ang

If I write four words, I shall strike out three.
Anonymous

Gemini 26

Lord, how the day passes! It is like a life, so quickly when we don't watch it, and so slowly if we do.
John Steinbeck

No winter lasts forever; no spring skips its turn.
Hal Borland

If we had no winter, the spring would not be so pleasant; if we did not sometimes taste of adversity, prosperity would not be so welcome.
Anne Bradstreet

I prefer winter and fall, when you feel the bone structure of the landscape—the loneliness of it—the dead feeling of winter. Something waits beneath it—the whole story doesn't show.
Andrew Wyeth

Let us learn to appreciate there will be times when the trees will be bare, and look forward to the time when we may pick the fruit.
Anton Chekhov

Let us love winter, for it is the spring of genius.
Pietro Aretino

Therefore my age is as a lusty winter, frosty, but kindly.
William Shakespeare

WINTER FROST IN THE WOODS

Commentary: "Winter Frost in the Woods" shows things being in a dormant stage. In the woods, winter is a time when energy is being used to reinforce the roots, to strengthen the support system and to build up the nourishment that's needed for the coming seasonal growth and the fruits of spring and summer. There is no point trying to force growth now, it is not possible, nor is it useful. This is not to say that this is not a valuable time. It is. It can be very easy to lose sight of the importance of each "season."

Oracle: In the situation facing you, it may be wise to prepare for more vibrant and expansive times by using this period to ensure that you get rest and recharge your batteries—on every level. Plans you've got for accomplishing things now may not work. There may be delays, equipment failures, etc. This can be frustrating. This Symbol says three things: there has been a time of fruitfulness which has passed; this is a time of withdrawal and inner growth; and a time of new beginnings or fresh developments is surely coming. Patience is needed for the time being. The "Frost" slows everything down as the temperature drops. Emotions can become dull and you may feel less responsive and decisions may be difficult to make because the future seems less certain. You may feel sluggish or find it difficult to get going because your emotions or your body are in need of a recharge. Use this time to make plans for the future and to test possibilities. It is a good time to pull back and observe how others are coping and consider how to help them or have them help you. Imagine spring coming, with all its warmth and growth—this will give you a sense of hope and confidence in the future.

Keywords: The calm before the dawn. The silence inherent in cold, barren times. Barren and cold feelings. Refrigeration and freezing. Serenity. Surviving cold conditions. Feeling like one's on the outside. Being lost in the wilderness. Beautiful surrounds. Lack of fertility. Things freezing up. The need to bundle up. Hibernation. Icicles. Battling through hard times. Depression. Growth that is halted or held up. The inevitability of change.

The Caution: Denying the natural flow of the season by trying to rush things. Feeling "frozen out," lost and neglected. Feeling dead lost and buried. Chills in the air. Keeping one's feelings on ice. Immobility. Not knowing where to find warmth or nourishment. Losing faith. Infertility. Frigid responses. Stagnation. Loss of love and light. Stunted growth.

What does this **SYMBOL** say to *you?*

A YOUNG GYPSY EMERGING FROM THE WOODS GAZES AT FAR CITIES

Gemini 27

Commentary: "A Young Gypsy Emerging from the Woods Gazes at Far Cities" shows someone who is preparing to leave their home, their family and what is familiar to them and move out into a new world. Only so much can be achieved living in the "Woods" and there's the need, or the desire, to move to "Far Cities." The "Gypsy" is somehow "different," having things about their background or upbringing that have kept them away from the mainstream. The "Gypsy" also brings to mind music, dancing, the gift of prophecy and a sense of the vibrancy and joy of life.

Oracle: This Symbol shows the desire to attempt or achieve something that currently seems out of your reach or distant in some way. You may be trying to participate with others or in a new arena of life or work, and finding it difficult because you don't command enough acceptance or respect. If you have to deal with rejection, dust yourself off and take another stab at it. A positive side of this Symbol is that an "outsider," or someone alien to a situation, can bring new qualities to the establishment; things that the conservatives may never have thought of, or tried. With this "Emergence," it is possible that you may not feel comfortable in any particular place, the "Woods" or the "Cities," for a while. The "Gypsy" may be the youth who is choosing to shift into the corporate and commercial world; it may be the housewife who seeks to break out; or it may be the dreamer who chooses to put their dreams into practice and makes a killing in business. There can be the worry of not having much in the way of financial resources or conventional accreditation. Although one's gut instincts can see things through, hard work and changes of perspective are probably needed in order to actually reach the "Far Cities" and to function there successfully. Feeling assured that you belong, no matter where you are, is likely to lead others to take you more seriously.

Keywords: Dreaming of becoming part of something far-off. Streetwise lessons. New perspectives arising from larger realities. The steps from bohemian to corporate and vice versa. Learning about credentials, using them to advantage. Things that are far off and distant. Ambition. Prophesy, astrology and tarot. Clairvoyance. Gypsies. Leaving family. Moving out on one's own.

The Caution: Dissatisfaction and always looking elsewhere. A feeling of being "cast out." Feeling alienated even among friends. Finding yourself a long way from home. Difficulty turning back. Being in limbo with a lack of ambition. Not having a family to turn to.

What does this **SYMBOL** say to *you?*

A nomad I will remain for life, in love with distant and uncharted places.
Isabelle Eberhardt

I have become a queer mixture of the East and the West, out of place everywhere, at home nowhere.
Jawaharlal Nehru

He had the uneasy manner of a man who is not among his own kind, and who has not seen enough of the world to feel that all people are in some sense his own kind.
Willa Cather

Ah, take the Cash in hand and waive the rest; Oh, the brave music of a distant drum!
Edward Fitzgerald

The biggest mistake people make in life is not trying to make a living at doing what they most enjoy.
Malcolm S. Forbes

I wish I were with some of the wild people that run in the woods, and know nothing about accomplishments!
Joanna Baillie

Gemini 28

The worst bankrupt in the world is the person who has lost his enthusiasm.
H. W. Arnold

It takes twenty years to build a reputation … and five minutes to ruin it.
Anonymous

The three things most difficult are: to keep a secret, to forget an injury, and to make good use of leisure.
Chilo

Making a life comes before making a living.
Anonymous

He is rich who owes nothing.
French Proverb

It is no disgrace to start all over. It is usually an opportunity.
George Matthew Adams

A man's judgment is best when he can forget himself and any reputation he may have acquired and can concentrate wholly on making the right decisions.
Raymond A. Spruance

Justice and judgment lie often a world apart.
Emmeline Pankhurst

SOCIETY GRANTING BANKRUPTCY TO HIM, A MAN LEAVES THE COURT WITH MIXED FEELINGS

Commentary: "Society Granting Bankruptcy to Him, a Man Leaves the Court with Mixed Feelings." The "Man" has had some moral or social judgment made, or placed upon him and now he must consider where the next phase of his life is going to take him. For some reason, who he is or what he's done has had to be considered and judged by others, and probably himself. To reach such a difficult position could be bitterly disappointing, but there is the possibility of a new life ahead. All is not lost.

Oracle: This Symbol rarely describes "Bankruptcy" in the literal sense. There may be "Feelings" of failure along with the need to have the slate wiped clean, to be able to "Leave the Court" and have a chance to start over again. When you actually reach rock bottom there are not many choices as to the way out. There's a need to grab hold of hope and let go of fear. The group, or society, can sometimes accept the responsibility for problems that people create, and give the individual a second chance. This Symbol can also show those who feel abandoned because someone has not lived up to their responsibilities. Alternatively, one may be prepared to give up everything and move on to a new and better life. The most important thing about "Bankruptcy" is that it should be undertaken without leaving feelings of guilt and loss. Forgiving and forgetting are both necessary. New truths will be learned and life will turn around with a feeling of release from the regrets of the past as life becomes lighter and better. Things will surely pick up again on many levels. One has to let go of things and be prepared to move into a new attitude or way of life. The mistakes of the past become the lessons that make for a better future.

Keywords: Protection. Being let off the hook and set free to get on with a new life. Starting back at square one. Renewal. Sacrifice. The need to remain optimistic about the future. Release of pressure. Facing judgment on one's worth. Booms and busts. Playing with money. Taking risks in the quest for money. Issues of deserving respect. Leaving the scene. Feeling sad and relieved at the same time.

The Caution: Feeling let off the hook and able to commit the same mistakes. Running full tilt and risking everything. Not learning the lessons of how to operate in a structured society. Shifting responsibility onto others. Going "off duty" regardless of how others feel. Moral bankruptcy. Being kicked out. Using other people's resources. Dejected and deserted.

What does this **SYMBOL** say to *you?*

THE FIRST MOCKINGBIRD OF SPRING SINGS FROM THE TREETOP

Gemini 29

Commentary: "The First Mockingbird of Spring Sings from the Treetop." The "Mockingbird" is usually thought of as copying others and therefore not particularly original. However, although the "Mockingbird" copies the sounds of other birds, it uses the best of those sounds to create a very unique call of its own. Some say that the "Mockingbird's" call is the sweetest of all, especially if it's "the First Mockingbird of Spring." It is heralding the new season; which signifies new life, new growth, warmth and fertility. Being "the First" shows that the "Mockingbird" is ready to spring to action when it is the right time. It is useful to be like the "Mockingbird" in many circumstances.

Oracle: The trick with this Symbol is to take the best of what's available, make sense of it and to then improve it. There can be a great deal of skill involved in this, but there are always those who will respond with scorn or jealousy, especially if a success of some type is involved. Knowing what to discard or leave out when you have a number of options is a valuable skill and may need to be employed now. If you are not good at these sorts of decisions then perhaps you need to employ the services of a good "Mockingbird." It may be important to listen to and see what "song" "the Mockingbird Sings." Are the thoughts original and unique or are they borrowed from others without any sense of a filter of personal authenticity? The new "song" that is created can be an announcement or signal of new beginnings. This can also show the mimicking of "sounds" to bring joy to those who need to hear the right thing. Sometimes it is better to tell someone what they would like to hear than to confront him or her with a harsh reality or something new and unfamiliar. It will still be, however, uniquely put together by the "Mockingbird" and should leave anyone who hears the message happy.

Keywords: Enormous creative potential and talent. Integrating sounds to find a new melody. Being the first to see potential. Music and musicians. Interpretation. Pleasing others. Getting the story out first. Seeing and telling things ahead of their time. Being an innovator. Passing on messages. Tunes, songs. Positive vibrations.

The Caution: Taking from others and claiming the credit. Being noisy. Announcing new possibilities or just sounding off? Mimicking others. Not coming up with one's own creative ideas. Having to always get in first. Making a noise and expecting others to respond. Stretching the truth. Revving up a story to get an effect.

What does this **SYMBOL** say to *you?*

No bird has ever uttered a note
That was not in some first bird's throat,
Since Eden's freshness and man's fall,
No rose has been original.
Thomas Bailey Aldrich

Every man is a borrower and a mimic, life is theatrical and literature a quotation.
Ralph Waldo Emerson

Use what talent you possess: the woods would be very silent if no birds sang except those that sang best.
Henry Van Dyke

The bird is known by his note, the man by his words.
Romanian Proverb

If I keep a green bough in my heart, the singing bird will come.
Chinese Proverb

The birds I heard today sang as freshly as if it had been the first morning of creation.
Henry David Thoreau

Until spring comes, nightingales do not sing.
Azerbaijani Proverb

The early bird catches the worm.
Proverb

Gemini 30

Beauty is in the heart of the beholder.
Al Bernstein

Beauty in things exists in the mind which contemplates them.
David Hume

That which is striking and beautiful is not always good; but that which is good is always beautiful.
Ninon De L'Enclos

You must look into people, as well as at them.
Lord Chesterfield

I'm tired of all this nonsense about beauty being only skin-deep. That's deep enough. What do you want—an adorable pancreas?
Jean Kerr

Sunburn is very becoming, but only when it is even. One must be careful not to look like a mixed grill.
Noel Coward

Beauty is everywhere a welcome guest.
Goethe

The ideal has many names, and beauty is but one of them.
W. Somerset Maugham

A PARADE OF BATHING BEAUTIES BEFORE LARGE BEACH CROWDS

Commentary: The "Parade of Bathing Beauties before Large Beach Crowds" is reminiscent of the Miss America pageant, where the women line up in their bikinis and their finest dresses. They present themselves beautifully and work hard to make an impact with their looks and grace. Their bodies and their fresh smiling faces are not only to be admired, but also judged by others.

Oracle: In this situation you may feel as though you are only being appreciated for your superficial attractions and beauty without appreciation of your deeper purpose. However, this is what is often needed in order to gain the attention of others, particularly if they are strangers. Be aware that you are getting a lot of attention, so it is important to put on your best face and to present it with confidence as there is a potential audience that may be used to your advantage. It is not really the superficiality of the "Bathing Beauties," but really of the "Crowds" that is revealed here. Those putting themselves on display are doing so by choice and with some knowledge of the fact that they are trying to gain the attention, admiration and appreciation of the people watching. It is the "Crowd" that is having basic responses which may vary from seeking simple entertainment to voyeurism. Displays of beauty and physical fitness can bring joy and stimulation from others, or jealousy and derision, so be careful of what's being revealed and whom you are revealing it to. After the process of display and attention has been achieved, there will be opportunities to relate on a deeper level. When you are able to bring the situation to a more personal and one-to-one basis some real value can be gained. Something must begin the process, and being noticed, for whatever reason, is a good start.

Keywords: Being on show. Sheer attraction of beauty. Seeking praise. Displaying in order to get people to observe and/or evaluate. Beauty pageants. Bathing costumes and skimpy clothing. Beaches. Lifeguards. Beauty judges. Nudist beaches. Breast sizes. The mysteries of the feminine. Playing dressups. Gatherings of goddesses. Mermaids converging. The water element. Recognizing superficiality and shallow behavior. Water nymphs.

The Caution: Using superficialities to win support. Giving importance to the issues of appearance. Neglecting the "beauty within." Too much makeup. Flaunting one's body. Not employing intellect. Leering, jeering. Lusting after the unattainable. Feeling like merchandise. Making superficial judgments.

What does this **SYMBOL** say to *you?*

ON A SHIP SAILORS LOWER AN OLD FLAG AND RAISE A NEW ONE

Cancer 1

Commentary: "On a Ship Sailors Lower an Old Flag and Raise a New One" signals a real turning point. A "Flag" is symbolic of ideals and it represents an allegiance or loyalty to those ideals. That the "Sailors Lower an Old Flag and Raise a New One" shows a symbolic expression of a change of loyalties or alliances. Although this may not be a decision made by every one of those "on the Ship," those in charge seem sure of what they're doing. What was important before is no longer relevant.

Oracle: There is, or there soon will be, a momentous change in the works. Something that once stood as part of your life is changing, whether this is something you desire, or not. As we grow and change there are many things both big and small which, like signposts, show or signal our position and beliefs. The changes could be of clothing, style, work, one's primary relationship, sexuality, country or even friends. Some people may be very pleased with this new shift, while others may feel neglected or shut out. Indeed, some may be shocked at this seemingly sudden change, even if it's been coming for a while. Those who have been really observant of what's been unfolding may not be surprised at all. The important point is that it is not enough to just go through change as we journey through the emotional seas of life; we also need to make commitments of some kind and give obvious signs of where we stand, who we stand with and what we stand for. Something is changing, possibly dramatically, and this transformation should be taken seriously. What signals are you sending out or displaying? It might be a good idea to run any new ideas or plans up the "flagpole" to see if anybody salutes them. Making affirmations of what is wanted may be a useful gesture to yourself and those involved.

Keywords: Changing loyalties. Turning points in one's obligations or duties. Announcing new standards. Turning a corner. Getting rid of the old guard. Letting go of old allegiances and taking up new ones. Giving up old ways. Changing bad habits. Taking the helm. Switching sexual preferences. Sailors. Ships. Flags. Divorces. Marriages. Change of shifts.

The Caution: Rejecting the old just for the sake of change. Fickleness. Not sticking with one thing for long enough to realize the rewards of loyalty. Being a traitor. Religious quarreling. Going only where the "good action" is. Piracy. Mutiny. Treason. Abandoning former priorities.

What does this **SYMBOL** say to *you?*

The world is in everlasting conflict between the new idea and the old allegiances, new arts and new inventions against the old establishment.
Joyce Cary

Times change and we change with them.
Anonymous

It is said that I am against change. I am not against change. I am in favor of change in the right circumstances. And those circumstances are when it can no longer be resisted.
The Duke of Cambridge

If you want a symbolic gesture, don't burn the flag, wash it.
Norman Thomas

If you are ashamed to stand by your colors, you had better seek another flag.
Anonymous

From the death of the old the new proceeds,
And the life of truth from the death of creeds.
John Greenleaf Whittier

All changes, even the most longed for, have their melancholy; for what we leave behind is a part of ourselves; we must die to one life before we can enter into another!
Gail Sheehy

Cancer 2

A field cannot well be seen from within the field.
Ralph Waldo Emerson

Imagination is more important than knowledge.
Albert Einstein

What if everything is an illusion and nothing exists? In that case, I definitely overpaid for my carpet.
Woody Allen

I know of no more encouraging fact than the unquestionable ability of man to elevate his life by conscious endeavor.
Henry David Thoreau

Caution: Cape does not enable user to fly.
Batman costume warning label

*'Tis distance lends
   enchantment to the view,
And robes the mountain in its
   azure hue.*
Thomas Campbell

*Let him who elevates himself above humanity...say,
if he pleases, "I will never compromise"; but let no one who is not above the frailties of our common nature disdain compromise.*
Henry Clay

A MAN ON A MAGIC CARPET OBSERVES VAST VISTAS BELOW

Commentary: "A Man on a Magic Carpet Observes Vast Vistas Below" is an image straight out of the "Arabian Nights" stories. King Solomon would tell the wind where he wanted to go, and the carpet would rise in the air, landing him in the place he designated. In this Symbol, the "Magic Carpet" can elevate the "Man" above everything going on in his life, making it possible for him to escape problems and fly above and away from them. He is able to see what's going on from a calm, possibly detached and rather creative state, with his imagination working strongly.

Oracle: Even though you may feel that there are many possibilities open to you, you may be unable to proceed with realistic or grounded plans, leaving you in a state of limbo. It's important to make sure that you are not somehow disconnected from reality. It may be that some of the "Vast Vistas" that are "Observed" are really only fantasy, imagination or wishful thinking. There may be more inspiration in your mind's eye than can be translated into real life. On the other hand, you are probably in a state of heightened awareness and have a broad overview of the situation, which can give you an opportunity to plan for future action. Try to accept any positive opportunities that are offered, but allow your self time to put these opportunities into perspective. What is really possible now? There may be feelings of isolation. Perhaps you're running away from the truth or feeling that you're the only one who can truly see the whole picture. It is probably best not to rush into anything permanent now. This is something that you have to work through slowly and carefully. Remember the privilege of being given the opportunity of such an elevated view. Take some time, look around, but remember to come back to reality when it's time!

Keywords: Elevated observations and heightened feelings. Having faith in the good things of life. Not wanting to see the ugly truth of reality. UFOs and aliens. Escapism. Perspective and imagination. Out of body experiences. Dreams. Seeking transcendence. Astral projection. The dream of far destinations. Film and video.

The Caution: Feeling above everything and unaffected by situations. Losing touch with reality. Missing the point. Trying to avoid what's going on. Peter Pan attitudes. Not feeling responsible for anything. Longing for something "magic" to happen. Bugging devices. Living in a fantasy world.

What does this **SYMBOL** say to *you?*

AN ARCTIC EXPLORER LEADS A REINDEER THROUGH ICY CANYONS

Cancer 3

Commentary: "An Arctic Explorer Leads a Reindeer through Icy Canyons" shows a situation of risk and hard work to get to a destination. There are two elements here: the "Arctic Explorer" who is prepared to seek out new possibilities even at great risk to his life, and the "Reindeer" which may have been quite content where it was, but does not have the possibility (or the imagination) to find new pastures or the will to assert its own desires. They have somehow become dependent upon each other for mutual success and survival. There is no way of knowing exactly what is going to happen or if they will, indeed, reach their objective. The "Reindeer" may regret being roped into this endeavor, but what has been started can't be abandoned or stopped mid-journey. However, it is actually the "Reindeer" that is naturally suited to these conditions, enabling it to push onward if the "Explorer" finds it too difficult.

Oracle: It is through adapting to changing needs in the environment and being constantly aware of the difficulties involved that success can be achieved. You need to persevere and progress slowly. There is probably no going back; there may be little value in retracing your steps. Further, there is probably no possibility of stopping as the situation could freeze up in an instant. You may be surprised by "icy" feelings and cold responses from yourself, or others. However, these "cold winds" may indeed have been building up for some time. Although you may have help from those around you, it is more a time of struggling through an unusual difficulty than worrying about creating any proper appearance. Be prepared to use warmth and love, as this will bring more light and joy. Keep going—indeed it may be your only option.

Keywords: Using animal instincts to get through tough times. Facing bad weather and hardship. Following the leader without knowing where one's going. Unfamiliar surroundings. The point of no return. Being in a cul-de-sac. Being led around by the hand (or the nose). Treading carefully. Icebergs. Glaciers. Snow and ice. Risky ventures. The *Titanic* story.

The Caution: Taking those unfamiliar to the situation and unwittingly heading towards danger. Putting one's self through hard times when it's avoidable. Restrictive outlooks on life. Frozen responses. Frigidity. Feeling lost, alone, frozen with fear or forsaken. Willingly going the hard way. Lack of provisions.

What does this **SYMBOL** say to *you?*

It is easier to sail many thousand miles through cold and storm and cannibals, in a government ship with five hundred men and boys to assist one, than it is to explore the private sea, the Atlantic and Pacific Ocean of one's being alone.
Henry David Thoreau

Patience serves as a protection against wrongs as clothes do against cold. For if you put on more clothes as the cold increases, it will have no power to hurt you.
Leonardo da Vinci

If you're going through hell, keep going.
Winston Churchill

A man never reaches that dizzy height of wisdom that he can no longer be led by the nose.
Mark Twain

The state with the highest percentage of people who walk to work is Alaska.
Trivia.net

Friends are as companions on a journey, who ought to aid each other to persevere in the road to a happier life.
Pythagoras

Cancer 4

When the cat's away the mouse will play.
Proverb

It's not the size of the dog in the fight; it's the size of the fight in the dog.
Mark Twain

When the mouse laughs at the cat there is a hole nearby.
Nigerian Proverb

The cat in gloves catches no mice.
Benjamin Franklin

When Goliath came against the Israelites, the soldiers all thought, "He's so big we can never kill him." But David looked at the same giant and thought, "He's so big, I can't miss."
Ode to Joy

Kitty heaven is mousy hell.
Anonymous

The lion and the calf will lay down together, but the calf won't get much sleep.
Woody Allen

The mouse is a magician with only one trick: it can cast an illusion that it is as big as an elephant.
Jessica MacBeth

A CAT ARGUING WITH A MOUSE

Commentary: The Symbol of "A Cat Arguing with a Mouse" brings to mind feelings of unfair play all the way to downright bullying. The "Cat" may be planning to eventually eat the "Mouse," but he may also just be throwing it around for his own enjoyment. There is an imbalance at work here. It seems that someone or something is trying to gain unfair advantage against a weaker opponent. How long can someone expect to get away with treating someone as their victim? The situation may feel life threatening, but could turn out to be more of a game. The "Cat" may get bored with the whole thing, or become distracted, if the "Mouse" is lucky!

Oracle: Along with bullying, this Symbol can show bickering, which ultimately is time consuming and often doesn't lead to anything. Trying to influence another's thoughts by constantly repeating or going over things is not acceptable, especially if it feels like harassment. If you feel shell-shocked from being "tossed around," physically or emotionally, there may be a need to retire to somewhere inaccessible while you regain your breath and your confidence. If someone is tormenting you, why don't you become the "mouse that roared"? Just because you are in a weak or submissive position doesn't mean you have to sit there and just take it. Grab any opportunity you can to turn the situation to your advantage. However, no matter which side you are on, whether you're the "Cat" or the "Mouse," there are probably no true "winners" in this predicament. Also, this Symbol can imply a lot of "Arguing" going on inside your own mind, which can lead to feeling disempowered. How long can you engage in this game when the outcome is assuredly a useless waste of time and energy? Are you man or mouse?

Keywords: Aggressively and actively taking advantage of situations or people. Hide and go seek games. Aggression vs. innocence. Harassment. Standing up for one's self. The David and Goliath story. Questioning established power structures. Looking out for one's best interests. Shock and fear. Cats. Mice. Hiding. Waiting.

The Caution: Time-wasting arguments and bickering. Being aggressive because one can. Picking on those smaller. Fighting dirty. Being patronizing. Power trips. Hiding away to avoid being targeted. Feeling like someone's prey. Feeling victimized and bullied. Antagonism. Unfair battles. Those who think they know more. Mental, physical or emotional torment. Beating yourself up.

What does this **SYMBOL** say to *you?*

AT A RAILROAD CROSSING, AN AUTOMOBILE IS WRECKED BY A TRAIN

Cancer 5

Commentary: "At a Railroad Crossing, an Automobile is Wrecked by a Train." This image sounds rather ominous, however the only way that an "Automobile" can get "Wrecked at a Railroad Crossing" is if it gets in the path of the "Train." The car in this Symbol represents the free will of the individual, having the ability to go in the direction the driver chooses, and the "Train" represents a carriage for many people, the collective. The "Train" can only go on its tracks; it has no ability to maneuver tricky situations or to change direction quickly.

Oracle: Although this Symbol sounds worse that it often really is, there is a need for caution. The individual's ideas or actions will not easily survive in a collision with the more powerful collective, especially if they are reckless or not carefully thought through. Even with the best of intentions, this may not be a good time to be insisting bravely that you or your needs be considered. The collective has so much momentum; it will not stop its course to think about what's happening to a single individual. If someone pits themselves and their energies against a group or society, there is a good chance that they will lose, at least in some way. Be careful how much you take on in this situation. This Symbol was prevalent in the life and death of Princess Diana. She was endeavoring to "outrun" the media on the night of her tragic accident. It seems sure that she was fed up with compromising herself to the needs of the media, her driver speeding in an attempt to outrun them. One can only speed for so long in life before one becomes an accident victim or some other kind of statistic. If you examine what risks are being taken in your situation you may realize the need to slow down or drop the need to "win" or "outrun." Done carefully however, you can indeed challenge the "big guys," winning and coming out on top.

Keywords: Not looking to the consequences of actions. Recklessly going for an objective. Not considering the ramifications. Lots of people causing problems with scheduling. Having the guts to go against society. Cars, trains. Individual rights. Rebelling. Crossroads. The need for good timing.

The Caution: Recklessness. Sacrificing individuals for larger gains. Working until one drops. Not looking left or right for possible trouble. Going in the wrong direction. Working at cross-purposes. Not nourishing one's self. Putting the desire for gain before one's more basic personal needs. Valuing possessions before people. Talking so no one gets a word in. Going off the rails. Upsetting or obstructing others. Wreckage. Emotional panic. Spinning out of control.

What does this **SYMBOL** say to *you?*

Haste makes waste.
Saying

They're funny things, accidents. You never have them till you're having them.
Eeyore, Winnie the Pooh

Cover me, I'm changing lanes.
Bumper Sticker

It takes 8,460 bolts to assemble an automobile, and one nut to scatter it all over the road.
Bumper Sticker

Everything is energy in motion.
Pir Vilayat Inayat Khan

I couldn't repair your brakes, so I made your horn louder.
Bumper Sticker

Even if you're on the right track, you'll get run over if you just sit there.
Will Rogers

There is more to life than increasing its speed.
Mahatma Gandhi

The major cause of auto wrecks is a screw loose in the nut behind the wheel.
Bumper Sticker

Decisions are like switch points on a railroad track. They determine where you will end up in life.
Elder Richard G. Scott

Cancer 6

It is an ill bird that fouls its own nest.
Romanian Proverb

Every bird likes his own nest best.
Romanian Proverb

However well organized the foundations of life may be, life must always be full of risks.
Havelock Ellis

If you have built castles in the air, your work need not be lost; that is where they should be. Now put the foundations under them.
Henry David Thoreau

Some people are making such thorough plans for rainy days that they aren't enjoying today's sunshine.
William Feather

Conscience is the nest where all good is hatched.
Welsh Proverb

Birds in their little nest agree; and 'tis a shameful sight, when children of one family fall out, and chide, and fight.
Isaac Watts

IN SPRING GAME BIRDS ARE FEATHERING THEIR NESTS

Commentary: The "Game Birds" in this Symbol can picture the desire for security in the midst of a rather unstable situation. "Birds Feather Their Nests" in readiness for a new life and new beginnings. These are "Game Birds," which can symbolize an unknown future, or danger or threat in the environment. Even though there is an optimistic feeling about the future and the prospect of a new life beginning, there is the danger of being expendable in some way.

Oracle: In your situation, endeavor to feel comfortable and right at home, however, remember that security may only be temporary. Be careful not to become too complacent, but ensure that you aren't frightened at any sudden surprises or moves. You may have to relinquish what you've built up or worked for and have to move on at some stage. If you are entirely safe and stable in this situation, you will most probably be able to build a bigger and better "Nest" as time goes by. From another perspective, this can symbolize situations where the "parents" need to nurture and protect the "kids." This may be in personal relationships or even a business situation. Also be careful that someone is not trying to kick you, or somebody else, out of a space that should rightfully be yours. Invasions from other "Birds" can lead to one's home being endangered, if not completely taken over by strangers. As human beings we have distanced ourselves from the "eat or be eaten" world of nature. However, we have created other dangers for ourselves and hence the need for different strategies and survival techniques. Where can you find a place of security? This Symbol can remind us that we may be able to do things in comfort and apparent safety, however, if others are controlling our environment there are still concerns that may have to be dealt with.

Keywords: Instinctive dedication. Laying the groundwork for those to come. Creating a base to feel safe. Nurturing. Endangered habitat. Raising money. Making yourself or someone else comfortable. Interior decoration. Preparation. Home building. Landlords and tenants. Noisy or nosy neighbors. Renting vs. owning. Watching for danger. The nesting instinct. Renovations. Babies' rooms. Working to pay the mortgage or rent.

The Caution: Being unnecessarily afraid to venture out on "one's own." Taking over other people's territory. Feeling unwanted. Danger. Fussing over small details. Over-preparation. Not knowing how long one can hold out in a situation. Being vulnerable to change. Being at the mercy of others. Endless housework.

What does this **SYMBOL** say to *you?*

TWO FAIRIES (NATURE SPIRITS) DANCING ON A MOONLIT NIGHT

Commentary: "Two Fairies (Nature Spirits) Dancing on a Moonlit Night" is a beautiful image of lightness, fun and carefree joy. The fact that they are "Fairies" or "Nature Spirits" shows wonderful energy that can be enjoyed and marveled at. That they are "Dancing on a Moonlit Night" brings an element of fantasy and beauty—however, there can be a lack of reality. The relationship of the "Two Fairies" can be wonderful for special occasions, particularly during romantic moments on a "Moonlit Night," but when daylight comes they may have to return to the real world.

Oracle: Your intuition and imagination may be heightened now, with a stronger sense of your spiritual or emotional centers. Allow your creativity to flow without worrying about its usefulness. Finding a friend, or friends, to share things with will enhance your experience. Some caution, though, is necessary. One can get lost in abstractions and fantasies that can lead away from the truth that should really be faced. For now, life may seem wonderful, perhaps idyllic and romantic, but how do, or will, things measure up in the clear light of day? What will happen if you forget being rational and just enjoy what's happening? What is really going on? Are you truly communicating and understanding each other, or just playing around because it feels good, or somehow familiar? This Symbol certainly shows the need for some fun or emotional release. At the end of the day; we all need a release of the inner spirit. Reality may appear slightly hazy at the moment, like everything could slip away in a minute. However, you can reap rewards by letting your dreams wander into the realms of "Fairies and Nature Spirits." Before you go to sleep, try thinking of this Symbol and watch for messages in your dreams.

Keywords: Usually invisible astral realms. Reconnecting with the feminine. Dancing. Avoiding harsh reality. Slipping away somewhere unnoticed. Seeing what's usually hidden. Romances that have difficulty in the real world. Dreams and fantasies. Sharing common ground. Full moon celebrations. Moonlight. Sunlight. Couples inspirited. Women celebrating. Other realms. Invoking fantasies. Moon dances.

The Caution: Losing one's self in emotional dreaming. Not seeing the reality of the other you're "dancing" with. Lacking responsibility. Escapist attitudes vs. serious decisions. Relationships with no earthly reality or substance. Something too good to be true. Finding it hard to connect with others.

What does this **SYMBOL** say to *you?*

The loveliest of faces are to be seen by moonlight, when one sees half with the eye and half with the fancy.
Persian Proverb

Exuberance is beauty.
William Blake

Dreams are true while they last, and do we not live in dreams.
Lord Alfred Tennyson

If one is lucky, a solitary fantasy can totally transform one million realities.
Maya Angelou

The moon develops the imagination, as chemicals develop photographic images.
Sheila Ballantyne

They dined on mince, and slices of quince,
Which they ate with a runcible spoon;
And hand in hand, on the edge of the sand,
They danced by the light of the moon.
Edward Lear

Look for me by moonlight;
Watch for me by moonlight;
I'll come to thee by moonlight,
Though Hell should bar the way!
Alfred Noyes

Cancer 8

You can fool too many of the people too much of the time.
James Thurber

Those who do not study are only cattle dressed up in men's clothes.
Chinese Proverb

Lying to ourselves is more deeply ingrained than lying to others.
Fyodor Dostoevsky

There's no labor a man can do that's undignified—if he does it right.
Bill Cosby

A graduation ceremony is an event where the commencement speaker tells thousands of students dressed in identical caps and gowns that "individuality" is the key to success.
Robert Orben

A man is known by the books he reads, by the company he keeps, by the praise he gives, by his dress, by his tastes, by his distastes, by the stories he tells, by his gait, by the notion in his eye.
Ralph Waldo Emerson

A GROUP OF RABBITS DRESSED IN CLOTHES AND ON DIGNIFIED PARADE

Commentary: "A Group of Rabbits Dressed in Clothes" can represent people who may be trying to be more, or act like they are more, than they really are. The fact that they are "on Dignified Parade" means that they are working to put on a good show and to stand up for themselves. Our outer garments and demeanor act to both show and disguise who we truly are and what we really feel about ourselves. It's difficult to completely disguise the attempt, but the effort of trying to advance themselves may be appreciated and rewarded with people taking them more seriously. The "Rabbits" are still "Rabbits" after all.

Oracle: Your abilities can take a leap ahead of normal development, simply by making an attempt to be or to do more. This Symbol pictures the process of projecting into the future a higher sense of being or thinking forward into a more intelligent, more successful level of life. Another aspect of this Symbol speaks of wanting to cover up one's sexuality with an outer display of dignity and conservatism. This may be a necessity in some more conservative social circles. Through a sense of inferiority, there may be a need to take on another's role or personality. By wearing elaborate or unusual clothes, gowns, wigs, crowns, etc., we can influence or change how others perceive us. Clothing and costumes can either elevate or degrade one's status. Imagine yourself clothed elegantly and having a "Dignified" stance as this can lead others to think more of you. Project yourself with a sense of confidence and dignity. Don't be restricted by class, or status—excel other's expectations, and don't let anyone "pigeonhole" you.

Keywords: Emulation of higher forms. Procreation and having babies. Dressing up. Modeling shapes and forms. Parading and being on parade. Attempts to overcome class barriers. Popularity competitions. Groups with a particular agenda. Uniforms. Religious garments. Lifeforms posing as humans. Outfits that project a particular agenda, regardless of reality. Identification parade and identikit photos.

The Caution: Pretending to be what one is not. Sublimating one's instinctual (or animal) needs to maintain a dignified, straight front. Deception. Strutting one's stuff. Showing off. Demanding attention. Appropriating an office or sense of authority. Sociopaths. Losing respect. Criticism of those just starting out.

What does this **SYMBOL** say to *you?*

A SMALL NAKED GIRL BENDS OVER A SPARKLING POND TRYING TO CATCH A FISH

Cancer 9

Commentary: The "Small Naked Girl" represents an innocent naïveté and spontaneous fun. The fact that she's "Small and Naked" shows that society's demands and pressures do not yet restrain her. She "Bends over a Sparkling Pond Trying to Catch a Fish." What the "Girl" is trying to catch may be elusive, continually moving and difficult to grab hold of, or really grasp, physically, emotionally or mentally. Still, it seems if she just keeps trying, she may very well succeed.

Oracle: You may be unable to grasp the meaning or the true promise of your situation, but still fascinated with what is happening. Your position is relatively innocent and your perceptions may be limited, however lessons will eventually be learned about what is and what isn't possible. This Symbol can indicate the pure thrill of the chase without considering the consequences of what would happen if one actually caught something (the reward of the "Fish" in this Symbol). Keeping a sense of delight and fun while going after what you want will ultimately lead to fulfillment on some level. However, be wary of doing it for too long if you find that what you're trying to accomplish is not working. Naïveté and wonder may fade over time through experience and deeper investigations, but it is a wonderful place to start from. If frustration sets in, remember that you're supposed to be having fun when this Symbol is around. Keeping a lighthearted approach will ensure that something good comes from the experience. It is by innocently reaching out for life, and its wonder and beauty, that we expand ourselves and remain open to the many possibilities in life.

Keywords: Curiosity. Infantile cravings. Fascination with illusions. Grasping at abstract ideas. Longing for things. Going for the elusive. Taking advantage of the young and innocent. Objects that cannot be held or captured, only dreamed about. Fun found in simple activities. Childhood games. Communing with nature. Nakedness. Inexperienced sexuality. Splashing around.

The Caution: Being distracted by simple irrelevancies or abstractions. The frustration of not getting what one wants. Grappling more than grasping. Always going after the "sparkling and shining" things, no matter how based in reality. Sexual taboos regarding young people. Seeking revenge. Chasing the unattainable. Frustration and annoyance. Slippery people or objectives. Gullibility.

What does this **SYMBOL** say to *you?*

Chance is always powerful. Let your hook be always cast; in the pool where you least expect it, there will be a fish.
Ovid

Grown men can learn from very little children for the hearts of little children are pure. Therefore, the Great Spirit may show to them many things which older people miss.
Black Elk

There is always one moment in childhood when the door opens and lets the future in.
Graham Greene

Don't bargain for fish which are still in the water.
Indian Proverb

To climb a tree to catch a fish is talking much and doing nothing.
Chinese Proverb

The cat would eat fish, but would not wet her feet.
Proverb

We have sat on the riverbank and caught catfish with pin hooks. The time has come to harpoon a whale.
John Hope

Hope is nature's way of hiding truth's nakedness.
Alfred Nobel

Cancer 10

*The gem cannot be polished
without friction, nor man
perfected without trials.*
Confucius

*Life is a grindstone. Whether it
grinds us down or polishes us
up depends on us.*
Thomas L. Holdcroft

*He was always smoothing and
polishing himself, and in the
end he became blunt before he
was sharp.*
G. C. Lichtenberg

*Better a diamond with a flaw
than a pebble without one.*
Chinese Proverb

*The absence of flaw in beauty is
itself a flaw.*
Havelock Ellis

*I began to have an idea of my
life, not as the slow shaping
of achievement to fit my
preconceived purposes, but
as the gradual discovery and
growth of a purpose which I did
not know.*
Joanna Field

*The hues of the opal, the light of
the diamond, are not seen if the
eye is too near.*
Ralph Waldo Emerson

*There are three things extremely
hard: steel, a diamond, and to
know one's self.*
Benjamin Franklin

A LARGE DIAMOND IN THE FIRST STAGES OF THE CUTTING PROCESS

Commentary: "A Large Diamond in the First Stages of the Cutting Process" implies a person or situation that has the potential for perfection, talent, beauty and considerable wealth. The process of cutting, grinding and shaping a "Diamond" takes skill, care and time. As one continues to polish and grind away, a more refined and beautiful object will emerge. The facets of the gem become more and more beautiful as the "old bits of rock" are chipped off. However, care and accuracy are needed in order to shape and mold it, or all the work that's been done could easily be spoiled.

Oracle: The situation facing you has probably taken a long time to quietly develop. Something has been building up and becoming increasingly solid and real. However, it still needs to be somehow refined and have the rough edges cut away. Hacking away at things in one fell swoop could lead to disaster and shatter any hopes. Striving for perfection, however, can result in enormous rewards. This can be some kind of "gift" or beauty that keeps getting better and better. If someone or something is a bit unformed or "unevolved," try to remember that just a little more polishing may reveal a beautiful gem. Too much importance placed on outer looks or appearances alone can lead to continual searches for perfection. Look to the inside where true beauty may reside. However, even beautiful exteriors can have many flaws, and eventually the whole process may prove to be rather disappointing. Perhaps there's a need to relax around this situation—you've probably only seen the first stages of the final product. With more work comes perfection. Hard work and pressure will pay off, in the end. A useful thing to do is to imagine the enormous beauty that's emerging, regardless of any flaws—on the inside or the outside.

Keywords: Coming to terms with inner worth. Emerging perfection. Beauty that is still a bit "rough around the edges." Naïveté. Beauty that is within, even if it has flaws. Potential. Chopping and grinding away to get to the essential. Being almost, but not completely, perfect. Reserving judgment. Self-development courses. Knowing where to start or finish. Craftsmanship. Finding the best in everything.

The Caution: Leaving an important job unfinished. Seeing the flaws, not the inherent beauty. Being afraid to take the first stab at something. Being overwhelmed by importance and value. Being overprotective or insecure. Not seeing the whole picture. Things unformed and incomplete. A "diamond in the rough," someone lacking social polish.

What does this **SYMBOL** say to *you?*

A CLOWN IS CARICATURING WELL-KNOWN PERSONALITIES

Cancer 11

Commentary: "A Clown Caricaturing Well-Known Personalities" symbolizes someone clowning around, doing impersonations (or taking on other personalities), and putting on a mask. There can be role playing here, where someone is putting on an archetypal "face" and performing because one must, for some reason. The entire act can be masking what is really going on within them. This can end up obscuring who one truly is on the inside. This can be because it is difficult, or compromising, to let one's real emotions or thoughts be known. Perhaps there are secrets or information that it's best for others not to know. The "Caricaturing" can take up time while things, or conditions, change for the better.

Oracle: Laughter is often said to be the best medicine and "many things said in jest" may be a useful thing to remember as you relax and get things back on the right track. Perhaps someone is not being real, using masks and play acting in order to hide what their true emotions, needs or objectives are. Or, they can just be playing the fool when the situation needs a more serious response. This can be acceptable for a while, but, sooner or later, this kind of behavior can end up being both annoying and frustrating. This can also be about the need to see things objectively or from someone else's point of view. Things may seem exaggerated and blown out of proportion. "Chameleons," people who act differently around different people, are somewhat hard to take seriously. Are people being true to themselves in this situation? What is really behind the facial expressions and masks?

Keywords: Exaggerated responses. Wanting to entertain. Show business. Trying to be something or someone that one's not. Putting on a face. Comic performances. Parodies of personalities. Making fun of someone. Clowns and clowning. Life imitating art. Always performing. Irony. Satire. Objective observance. Criticism. Laughter. Caricatures. Cartoons. Lampooning. Voice impressions.

The Caution: Being foolish in the face of positive potential. Trying to cover up reality through buffoonery. Being constantly "on stage." Living vicariously. Inauthentic behavior. Not having the courage to display one's true self. Putting on a face to manipulate or fool others. Irritating behavior that wears thin after a while. Being the laughing stock. Overblown impressions. Loss of true identity.

What does this **SYMBOL** say to *you?*

He's a fool that cannot conceal his wisdom.
Benjamin Franklin

Clown and guru are a single identity: the satiric and sublime side of the same higher vision of life.
Theodore Rozak

We take greater pains to persuade others that we are happy than in endeavoring to think so ourselves.
Confucius

There are no greater wretches in the world than many of those whom people in general take to be happy.
Seneca

Art must discover and reveal the beauty which prejudice and caricature have overlaid.
Alain Locke

There is hardly any mental misery worse than that of having our own serious phrases, our own rooted beliefs, caricatured by a charlatan or a hireling.
George Eliot

Being a funny person does an awful lot of things to you. You feel that you mustn't get serious with people. They don't expect it from you, and they don't want to see it. You're not entitled to be serious, you're a clown.
Fanny Brice

Cancer 12

Every man is a divinity in disguise.
Ralph Waldo Emerson

The promise to all men that God may take birth within their souls.
Dane Rudhyar

He whose face gives no light shall never become a star.
William Blake

We hear about the birth of a child and ask questions like, "What did she have? How much did it weigh?" and "Does it have any hair?" The Athabaskan Indians hear of a birth and ask, "Who came?"
Lisa Delpit

A man is a god in ruins.
Ralph Waldo Emerson

Grown men can learn from very little children for the hearts of little children are pure. Therefore, the Great Spirit may show to them many things which older people miss.
Black Elk

Where children are, there is the golden age.
Novalis

Where are you searching for me, friend? Look! Here am I right within you. Not in temple, nor in mosque, not in Kaaba nor Kailas, but here right within you am I.
Kabir

A CHINESE WOMAN NURSING A BABY WHOSE AURA REVEALS HIM TO BE THE REINCARNATION OF A GREAT TEACHER

Commentary: The "Chinese Woman" senses something "Great" in the "Baby" she is "Nursing." The fact that she is "Chinese" is significant, as the "Chinese" have had a long tradition of seeking the spiritual layers of life. The "Woman" is sensing and seeing something in the young person that other nannies may not. She's aware that he holds great talent and gifts for the future. His "Aura Reveals Him to be the Reincarnation of a Great Teacher." Being able to see reverence in young people that appear to be "old" or "evolved" souls is an expression of a strong intuitive sensitivity. The "Woman" sees that this child, this "Baby," has a unique and special talent that can be of benefit to the world in some way. The "Child" needs to be nurtured, nourished and cared for so he can reach his full potential.

Oracle: Messages of hope for the future are coming through younger and more vital elements. There may be an opportunity to learn important lessons from younger beings. The feeling that someone is an "old soul" can be felt but can be rather hard to explain; it seems to come with a special kind of "knowing." While taking the time to try and make sense of it, the benefit or insight may be lost. The joy and power of young people is fleeting and may require close attention to truly appreciate. This Symbol shows seeing the greatness in others, and this may be speaking about you, regardless of your age. Good nourishment and care increases everybody's ability to make the most of their potential. Nurturing and caring for any small, but nonetheless significant, talents can allow things to blossom into something beyond present expectations. Are you a "Great Teacher"? Do you have largely untapped talents?

Keywords: Nurturing innocence and its rewards. Reincarnation and past lives. Charisma and presence. Channeling entities. Tibetan mysteries. Monks and the Dalai Lama. Ancient knowledge. Child prodigies. Seeing greatness ahead of its time. Indigo children. Discovering latent talent. Visions. Holistic perceptions. Potential. Nurses. Nannies. Finding "the one." Auras. Special people.

The Caution: Not seeing the beauty of youngsters. Being overcome with complexity. Demanding to be recognized. Missing inherent greatness. Under- or over-estimating the potential of youth. Pushy and demanding. Precocious behaviour.

What does this **SYMBOL** say to *you?*

A HAND, WHICH IS HELD OUT RECEPTIVELY, IS REMARKABLE FOR THE SUGGESTION OF CHARACTER IN ITS PROMINENT THUMB

Cancer 13

Commentary: "A Hand, Which Is Held out Receptively" implies reaching out to others. The "Prominent Thumb" implies a strong will. This image infers a "handshake" of some kind. A "handshake" can bridge differences and gaps between people, bring them closer together and also show that one doesn't have (or shouldn't have!) a hidden agenda. The person reaches out to others showing their strong "Character." Palmists say the "Thumb" shows the predisposition of a person's future and state of health.

Oracle: Although a degree of flexibility needs to exist in this situation, it will, inevitably, be strength of "Character" and a willingness to extend one's self to others that will enable you to succeed. Being in control of one's self and one's environment is an effective and lasting expression of power. It is also important to note that this Symbol is about strength of will and character, and that being receptive does not weaken this. In fact, it is by being receptive that we can truly be powerful and have a positive influence on those around us. The "Prominent Thumb" can show a strong sense of determination and a desire to impress others. However, if this sense of strong determination does not come accompanied by the ability to compromise and listen, it will only create the potential for problems. This can also apply to groups of people and also to elements of your inner self. Reaching out and extending your "Hand" "Receptively" to others may be what's required. Show that you are approachable and caring, and you'll most likely see the situation resolve itself naturally. When the time is right you will be able to "grasp" what is needed.

Keywords: Openness and willingness to extend oneself to others. The handshake and the need for it. Being approachable and friendly. Palmistry and palm reading. Having a firm will. Introductions. Strong character. Flexible behavior. Hitchhiking.

The Caution: An aggressiveness and overbearing nature. Feeling that one is better, or stronger, than others. The smooth handshake that manipulates to impress one's personality. Unbending and dominant behavior. Taking over situations regardless of what others want. Defensive, insecure, unsure, introverted. Blocking human exchanges.

You can't shake hands with a clenched fist.
Indira Gandhi

It is easier to point the finger than to offer a helping hand.
Anonymous

The lonely one offers his hand too quickly to whomever he encounters.
Friedrich Nietzsche

The world can only be grasped by action, not by contemplation. The hand is the cutting edge of the mind.
Jacob Bronowski

Nothing up my sleeve!
Magician's Saying

Spiritual love is a position of standing with one hand extended into the universe and one hand extended into the world, letting ourselves be a conduit for passing energy.
Christina Baldwin

I hate the giving of the hand unless the whole man accompanies it.
Ralph Waldo Emerson

If my hands are fully occupied in holding onto something, I can neither give nor receive.
Dorothee Solle

What does this **SYMBOL** say to *you?*

Cancer 14

Every country has the government it deserves.
Joseph Marie de Maistre

A man is a very small thing, and the night is very large and full of wonders.
Lord Dunsany

He whose face gives no light can never become a star.
William Blake

The greatest thing in the world is not so much where we stand as in what direction we are moving.
Goethe

I never saw a man who looked with such a wistful eye upon that little tent of blue which prisoners call the sky.
Oscar Wilde

Interestingly, according to modern astronomers, space is finite. This is a very comforting thought—particularly for people who can never remember where they have left things.
Woody Allen

There's none so blind as those who won't see.
Old Saying

A VERY OLD MAN FACING A VAST DARK SPACE TO THE NORTHEAST

Commentary: "A Very Old Man" is "Facing a Vast Dark Space to the Northeast." He may be feeling old, lost and in need of guidance. Washington, D.C., the capital of America, from the majority of the country is in the "Northeast." This is the Symbol of America's sun sign, the fourth of July. It speaks of looking toward that place. This is also the degree of the fixed star Sirius, the star many have looked to for spiritual direction. The "Vast Dark Space" may feel like alien or foreign territory. The "Very Old Man" looks to the "Northeast" for guidance; perhaps he is looking at a particular star or merely "staring into a void." Can he find salvation there? Answers? Or does he feel lost and deserted? People overwhelmed by "big brother," commercialism and the battle to "keep up" can feel "Old" in some way. However, direction may be found in this "Vast Dark Space."

Oracle: Guidance may be needed, but it can be hard to come by; faith may be the only light to guide you through. As we grow and age, we can choose to become more enlightened, with a greater ability to see spiritual truth. However, you could be feeling that even faith is difficult to keep hold of at the moment. You may feel let down by people—friends, family, or lovers, right through to authorities or the government. There needs to be both trust and courage that one's inner wisdom is in touch with some higher truth. We need this especially when we don't know where we're going and feel like we have to take things one day at a time. Once we have completed our journey in this life, there is still the mystery of the next life. Venturing into the unknown when you think you have seen it all can be a reminder of the thrill of life. Take some time to look to to the sky at night; this may bring encouragement and some kind of realization or fulfillment.

Keywords: American Indians and other native peoples who have been left in the dark. Losing faith in the future. The dying out of cultures or languages. Washington, D.C. Staring into a void. Blindness. Searching for answers. Sirius—the Dog Star. Magnetic shifts. Compass directions. Stargazing. Navigation. Faith. The earth's poles. Astronomy. Vast dark arenas. Wisdom that comes with age. Feeling old before one's time. Seeking purpose and direction.

The Caution: Seeing nothing. A lack of purpose. Abandonment, rejection, loss and darkness. The exploitation and abandonment of native people. Myopia. Voids. Emptiness.

What does this **SYMBOL** say to *you?*

A GROUP OF PEOPLE WHO HAVE OVEREATEN AND ENJOYED IT

Cancer 15

Commentary: "A Group of People Who Have Overeaten and Enjoyed It" is an image of people consuming to their fill and having a good time of it. It seems they had big appetites and have overindulged themselves, and are now feeling satisfied. They have taken time out to satisfy their hunger and "Enjoy" the leisure of catching up with what's going on with others. There is a certain measure of pleasure and satisfaction, but it is probably only temporary, and they may need to return to work. This can be difficult, as overeating can lead to dulled senses and an inability to make intelligent decisions. People become energetically bound up in digesting what they've "consumed," while the body is preoccupied with handling the load. This can make the mind and body slow and, sometimes, lazy. This Symbol can picture enjoying "consuming" anything, not only "eating." They probably enjoy many of the good things in life.

Oracle: It may be that you, or someone else, has overindulged in material objects or success. For now, enjoy your good fortune. Beware, however, as sometimes "feeding frenzies" can turn into issues that need to be sorted out later. Problems can be experienced through overspending, overeating, putting on weight, etc. Constantly overeating or overspending in an attempt to feel better can lead to issues of self-worth, greed and debt. There is possibly a need to curb this indulging. Realize when it's time to return to work, and to be productive instead of just swallowing, or "consuming," more and more. In fact, there may be a need for "tightening the belt." Commodities, like food, etc., may run short now due to extravagance or excess. Remember to say Grace in thanks for the good fortune you have.

Keywords: Consumerism. Communal cohesion through indulging in the senses. Satisfied hunger. Commercialism and longing to own things. Eating disorders. The right of everyone to enjoy food and nourishment. Big business. Success. Enjoying "the good life." Having plenty. Abundance. Temporary fulfillment.

The Caution: Self-indulgence through the senses. The "haves" and the "have nots." People going without so that others can have more. Monopolization. Bloating. Feeling that one deserves everything on a platter. Overweight. Bad nourishment. Eating binges. Indigestion. Obsession with ownership. Deprivation. Exploiting resources. Overspending. Gluttony.

Appetite comes with eating; the more one has, the more one would have.
French Proverb

The lunches of fifty-seven years had caused his chest to slip down to the mezzanine floor.
P. G. Wodehouse

A fool bolts pleasure, then complains of moral indigestion.
Minna Thomas Antrim

I saw few die of hunger; of eating, a hundred thousand.
Benjamin Franklin

Never eat anything at one sitting that you can't lift.
Miss Piggy, Muppet Character

True enjoyment comes from activity of the mind and exercise of the body; the two are ever united.
Wilhelm von Humboldt

Gluttony is not a secret vice.
Orson Wells

Subdue your appetites, my dears, and you've conquered human nature.
Charles Dickens

Never eat anything bigger than your head.
Kliban

What does this **SYMBOL** say to *you?*

Cancer 16

We are called to be architects of the future, not its victims.
Buckminster Fuller

Can't nothing make your life work if you ain't the architect.
Terry McMillan

I have an existential map; it has "you are here" written all over it.
Steven Wright

Oh well, back to the drawing board.
Old Saying

But how shall I get ideas? Keep your wits open! Observe! Observe! Study! Study! But above all, Think! Think! And when a noble image is indelibly impressed upon the mind—Act!
Orison Swett Marden

A structure becomes architectural, and not sculptural, when its elements no longer have their justification in nature.
Guillaume Apollinaire

All my best thoughts were stolen by the ancients.
Ralph Waldo Emerson

Ancient laws remain in force long after the people have the power to change them.
Aristotle

A MAN STUDYING A MANDALA IN FRONT OF HIM, WITH THE HELP OF A VERY ANCIENT BOOK

Commentary: The Symbol "A Man Studying a Mandala in Front of Him" shows someone intent on gaining insight and meaning through "Study." He is "Studying a Mandala" which may be in the form of a picture, design or structure. This can be anything from an astrology chart to an architectural drawing to a sacred image, etc. The "Mandala" is often a collection of ideas and possibilities, experiences and lessons, and history and mythology. These things can be presented as a kind of tapestry. He is "Studying" this "with the Help of a Very Ancient Book"; it has clues and answers from ages past. Looking to the "secret mysteries" can reveal answers to life's questions, and how best to proceed.

Oracle: You may be attempting to understand what these "secret mysteries," mentioned above, may mean in the current context and applying them to the relevance of today. You may be puzzled by the deeper meanings of the subject you're "Studying" or trying to unravel. Reverting to traditional answers is not always easy in the present day. The key to deciphering these mysteries is in traditional knowledge and wisdom. Adopting a plan or a strategy is a good idea, as is following "the rules of the book." With devices like the Internet and television, the quicker options are usually chosen. These methods have their merits, but they can be enhanced further when teamed up with the older, more tried and true, answers. Perhaps you feel "boxed in" by your situation. You must seek what is already known in order to understand what's happening. If a plan is adopted, make sure it is based on sound principles and everything should work out. Patience, research and respect for the past are all vital elements here. A teacher is likely to appear. Much will be learned and revealed.

Keywords: Concentration. Overcoming obstacles by gaining control of one's inner and outer life. Architecture and strategic planning. Lessons to be learned from history. Astrology, numerology, tarot. Systems of thought that are laid out. Maps. The rules of warfare—anything with a strategy. Drawing strength and inspiration from squares and circles. Inward attention. Mandalas.

The Caution: Ignoring the old wisdom for modern rational systems. Lack of imagination. Going into a situation unorganized and without a plan. Trying to gain the better of others by outstrategizing them. Not wanting to put in the work.

What does this **SYMBOL** say to *you?*

THE SEED GROWS INTO KNOWLEDGE AND LIFE

Cancer 17

Commentary: "The Seed Grows into Knowledge and Life." The process of the germination of the "Seed" is slow and progressive, and must start from the very beginning. This "Seed" may be an idea, a relationship, a process, a job or a course of study, etc. From the germination of the "Seed" comes "Knowledge and Life." Remember the maxim: Think a thought and sow a seed; sow a seed and do a deed. Do a deed, create a habit, create a lifestyle.

Oracle: The important thing to realize is that something of value has the opportunity to develop, but will need nurturing, attention, fertilization, care and hope. Things grow and, with time and nourishment, flourish, eventually providing further "Seeds" for the future. However, at first you may feel as though you are not growing or developing properly, or fast enough. Maybe there is dissatisfaction regarding your perceived progress. Perhaps you feel that everything will take too long if you start at the beginning. There are no shortcuts with nature—things have to grow at their own pace and in their own time. It is important to start small and let things develop from there. Even if you feel as though there is no time to "baby" along the situation, in the long run it will be for the best. Sacrifices may be necessary to ensure the development is complete. This can indicate pregnancy or the inception of a new idea. In a broader context, there may emerge a whole new and inspiring approach to, or participation in, life. It could eventually lead to the birth or the growth of something. A hobby or interest could turn into a money earning project. The time is fertile for the process of growth to begin.

Keywords: Small and careful beginnings leading to a beautiful flowering. Seeding things. New ideas bringing fulfillment. Pregnancy, childbirth and growing up. The growth of knowledge. Embryonic cells. Giving and receiving lessons. The urge to grow. Germination. Reaching toward light. Fertilization. Nourishment. Tender care. Genetic engineering. Transmutations. Teachers and students. The tree of knowledge. The Kabbalah. Enjoying each step of the process.

The Caution: Rushing and missing vital parts. Arrogance about how much one knows. Being afraid to start a project because of time constraints. Not giving small things the reverence they deserve. Grabbing the fast dollar. Things that get out of hand.

The true purpose of education is to cherish and unfold the seed of immortality already sown within us; to develop, to their fullest extent, the capacities of every kind with which the God who made us has endowed us.
Anna Brownell Jameson

The seed of God is in us. Given an intelligent and hard working farmer, it will thrive and grow up to God, whose seed it is; and accordingly its fruits will be God-nature. Pear seeds grow into pear trees, nut seeds into nut trees, and God seed into God.
Meister Eckhart

Is life worth living? This is a question for an embryo, not for a man.
Samuel Butler

With every deed you are sowing a seed, though the harvest you may not see.
Ella Wheeler Wilcox

We can see a thousand miracles around us every day. What is more supernatural than an egg yolk turning into a chicken?
Rutherford Platt

In creating, the only hard thing is to begin: a grass blade's no easier to make than an oak.
James Russell Lowell

What does this **SYMBOL** say to *you?*

Cancer 18

The heart is the household divinity which, discharging its function, nourishes, cherishes, quickens the whole body, and is indeed the foundation of life, the source of all action.
William Harvey

An atmosphere of trust, love and humor can nourish extraordinary human capacity. One key is authenticity: parents acting as people, not as roles.
Marilyn Ferguson

My father had always said there are four things a child needs: plenty of love, nourishing food, regular sleep, and lots of soap and water. After that, what he needs most is some intelligent neglect.
Ivy Baker Priest

Sometimes you struggle so hard to feed your family one way, you forget to feed them the other way, with spiritual nourishment. Everybody needs that.
James Brown

A mother never realizes that her children are no longer children.
James Agee

To nourish children and raise them against odds is in any time, any place, more valuable than to fix bolts in cars or design nuclear weapons.
Marilyn French

A HEN IS SCRATCHING FOR HER CHICKS

Commentary: "A Hen Is Scratching for Her Chicks." The essential need for nourishment must be satisfied in order to proceed in life. There is no guarantee that she will find food where she is "Scratching," but a wise "mother" knows where nourishment is likely to be found. It is for her offspring, for herself or for others that she is searching and "Scratching." "Scratching" the ground is the instinctive, traditional way that "a Hen" looks for food. For a mother "Hen" this process has an inherent element of sacrifice, or at the least concern for others ahead of her own needs.

Oracle: This Symbol is about motherhood and its inherent responsibilities. This Symbol is encouraging you to take action to find nourishment, protection and the other things necessary for the well-being of both yourself and those in your care. It is not just about being caring and vigilant, it also means getting down to business and finding what is needed for those less able than yourself, regardless of how difficult or time consuming it may be. This is also showing that there are those around who are dependent on others to provide nourishment. When those you care about have what they need, you will have the opportunity to look after yourself. However, you may be the mother hen, or you may be the "Chick." This nourishment can mean both the literal, i.e., food, and the symbolic—spiritual caring and guidance. You are being asked to understand and accept the responsibilities of caring for and looking after others. If you are in the position to nurture, however, be cautious not to be overprotective or fuss over your brood.

Keywords: Searching for sustenance. Being devoted to nurturing small beginnings. Concern for the essential, small details. Repetitive cycles of things that have to be done. Being the "breadwinner." Doing one's duty. Being loaded with responsibility. Children. Progeny. Feeding others. Catering. Seeding ideas. Latch-key children. Working long hours.

The Caution: Pointless searching where there is no nourishment. Fussing too much. Not letting people grow up. Neglecting to nourish those who need it. Acting like a mother hen. No life of one's own. Becoming a martyr for others. Self-sacrifice. "Scratching" for tiny rewards. Codependence. Tiring responsibilities. Scratching and picking. Paying the bills for others. Expecting to be looked after.

What does this **SYMBOL** say to *you?*

A FRAGILE MISS, REPRESENTATIVE OF PROUD OLD BLOOD, IS WED IN A MARRIAGE CEREMONY BY A PRIEST TO AN EAGER YOUTH OF THE NEW ORDER

Cancer 19

Commentary: "A Fragile Miss, Representative of Proud Old Blood, is Wed in a Marriage Ceremony by a Priest to an Eager Youth of the New Order." The "Fragility" and respectability of the past is energized with the "eagerness" of the new. The two people marry, even though they come from quite different backgrounds. The "Old" and conservative is "married" to the "New" and "Eager."

Oracle: A "Marriage" of any kind can bring people together and produce wonderful things as a result. There comes a time when the "Old" ways, ideas or behaviors need to be renewed with fresh "Blood." But the old ways should not be merely replaced by updated methods, but rather blended to attain the best of both worlds. The important thing is what this union can produce. This is the birth of something with the potential for change, new ideas and new growth. There may be some problems in the early stages, as others may object to this "Marriage." The "Eager Youth" may not immediately fit the stereotype of the "Fragile Miss" family. Sometimes there's the fear of upsetting family by introducing new people or even new ideas. Every type of "Marriage" needs to go through its ups and downs. Bridging generation gaps, altering prejudices, updating "Old" ideas and breaking social rules can come as a result of any successful union. Simple expressions of our heart and mind may be acknowledged in ritual performances or a "Ceremony" of some kind. This may require a sanctification, or blessing, from a higher power or authority.

Keywords: Wedding ceremonies. Sanctified unity. Expressions of loyalty and allegiance. Making sacred vows. Commitment to a person or project. New ventures involving a lowering of accepted standards. Breaking social norms. Integration of heart and mind. Bridging generation gaps. Marriage guidance. Contracts signed and honored. Hand claspings. Hatch, match and dispatch ceremonies. Celebrants.

The Caution: Rigidly following established rules at the expense of new ways that may have greater personal relevance. Forcing people to come together. Bondage to social expectations. Arranged marriages. Taking risks with partners. Conforming to the expectations of the others.

What does this **SYMBOL** say to *you?*

'Tis not the many oaths that make the truth;
But the plain single vow, that is vow'd true.
William Shakespeare

I dreamed of a wedding of elaborate elegance; a church filled with flowers and friends. I asked him what kind of wedding he wished for; he said one that would make me his wife.
Anonymous

Marriage is our last, best chance to grow up.
Joseph Barth

The curse which lies upon marriage is that too often the individuals are joined in their weakness rather than in their strength—each asking from the other instead of finding pleasure in giving.
Simone de Beauvoir

MARRIAGE, n. The state or condition of a community consisting of a master, a mistress, and two slaves, making in all, two.
Ambrose Bierce

Marriage is a great institution, but I'm not ready for an institution.
Mae West

A good marriage is like a good trade. Each thinks he got the better deal.
Ivern Ball

Cancer 20

If music be the food of life, play on.
William Shakespeare

Anything that is too stupid to be spoken is sung.
Voltaire

Love is like a violin; the music may stop now and then, but the strings will remain forever.
Anonymous

The French are true romantics. They feel the only difference between a man of forty and one of seventy is thirty years of experience.
Maurice Chevalier

If you describe things as better than they are, you are considered to be a romantic; if you describe things as worse than they are, you will be called a realist; and if you describe things exactly as they are, you will be thought of as a satirist.
Quentin Crisp

Beware of over-great pleasure in being popular or even beloved.
Margaret Fuller

He must have a truly romantic nature, for he weeps when there is nothing at all to weep about.
Oscar Wilde

VENETIAN GONDOLIERS IN A SERENADE

Commentary: "Venetian Gondoliers in a Serenade" is a Symbol that speaks of the ideals of romantic fantasy. Although it can sometimes sound like an old cliché, the "Gondoliers Serenading" is the sort of fantasy or special event that many people long for or desire. To be pampered, cared for and transported to a place of romance can be just what is needed, though there may be a need for caution if the romance is really just a fairytale.

Oracle: This Symbol encourages the breaking away from any restriction or expectation and letting yourself float on the pleasure of romance. Someone may be a little frustrated or bored, and looking to find ways to satisfy their emotional needs. Although this is not the time for seriousness, don't be fooled by any insincere charades. You may need to develop trust in those around you to be able to surrender to your feelings spontaneously. If the circumstances are right, surrendering to romance should be enjoyed to the hilt. Don't let doubts get in the way of love or passion; but do be cautious that you're not being used for someone's imaginary or idealistic life. Look to see if you are ignoring the truth of a relationship in order to satisfy someone else's needs. Read between the lines of what's truly being said, or the emotions that are conveyed. Look for anything misleading or overblown. Someone may try to convince others of how good they are, or compete with others for love. Be wary of reacting to others who have recently come into the picture, especially those that are vying for affections. Those working hard at winning others over can lead to not being taken seriously. In the end, people get found out for who they really are. Seek out honesty and truth and love will fill your life.

Keywords: Romantic fantasy. Singing and music. Performance. Public speaking. Impressing people with joy, romance, fun and the wonder of life. Venusian displays. Issues of the truth. Ease of communicating. Working to win people over. Appealing to the beloved. Elegance. Floating on the emotions. Festive atmospheres. Nostalgia. Boats. Water.

The Caution: Insincere charades. Retreating into one's self. Saying whatever it takes to get what one wants. Superficial displays. The delusion of being beyond criticism. Emotional manipulation. Sucking up to others. Misplaced trust. Competing for affections or attention. Losing one's self.

What does this **SYMBOL** say to *you?*

A PRIMA DONNA SINGING

Commentary: "A Prima Donna" is the principal female singer in an opera. The expression "Prima Donna" is Italian for "first lady." This can be a double-edged image. The positive reality of the "Prima Donna" is someone whose talents allow, or cause, them to stand out from the crowd. Here the "Prima Donna" is pictured "Singing," which means that her talent is being shared and hopefully enjoyed by all. Her voice, song and words resonate with many and bring messages from the stories or the myths of our lives and society. On a more negative level, the "Prima Donna" can be the fussy, demanding type who expects special and unreasonable consideration for her talents or her position in society. Many adore such people, while others can become completely bored, especially if the "Prima Donna" doesn't know how or when to stop "performing."

Oracle: This Symbol can indicate that someone's abilities, talents or limits will be tested. To fully win in this situation, one must open up their heart and let go of inhibitions, while others should drop their judgments. This will please some that are listening and allow people to feel fulfilled. Even where there are a lot of voices, there will be one that will be most listened to. Is this your voice or someone else's? Sometimes the "Prima Donna" demands more attention than she truly deserves. Having a loud voice can be annoying and create an imbalance that destroys the harmony or balance of the group. However, lifting your voice to convey messages that are powerful and moving can be very rewarding. The thing to remember is that we all have talent that distinguishes us from others in some way. Sometimes it is not so obvious, but it is within us all in some description.

Keywords: Powerful voice. Emotional dramatizations. Talent. Taking center stage. Messages that need to be heard for social reasons. Playing out the myths of society. Makeup, hairstyles, wigs and costumes. Feeling important and special. Singing and performing. Opera and drama. Fame and fortune. Charisma and presence. Commanding attention. Having control and good timing. Flowers or brickbats. Years and years of training or improvising on the spot.

The Caution: Overplaying one's role. Displaying noisily. Driving people to distraction. Refusing to keep quiet. Demanding to be heard. Wanting everyone to listen. Overreacting. Throwing tantrums. Not knowing when to stop. Passions worn on the sleeve. Showing off.

What does this **SYMBOL** say to *you?*

Cancer 21

We respond to a drama to that extent to which it corresponds to our dream life.
David Mamet

A singer starts by having his instrument as a gift from God ...When you have been given something in a moment of grace, it is sacrilegious to be greedy.
Marian Anderson

Every accent, every emphasis, every modulation of voice, was so perfectly well turned and well placed, that, without being interested in the subject, one could not help being pleased with the discourse.
Benjamin Franklin

My voice has been raised not only in song, but to make the big world outside through me, understand something of the spirit of my beloved country.
Dame Nellie Melba

I sometimes wonder which would be nicer—an opera without an interval, or an interval without an opera.
Ernest Newman

Cancer 22

We love to expect, and when expectation is either disappointed or gratified, we want to be again expecting.
Samuel Johnson

The real voyage of discovery consists not in seeking new landscapes, but in having new eyes.
Marcel Proust

You can't cross the sea merely by standing and staring at the water. Don't let yourself indulge in vain wishes.
Rabindranath Tagore

How much of human life is lost in waiting.
Ralph Waldo Emerson

If your ship doesn't come in, swim out to it!
Jonathan Winters

Fortune brings in some boats that are not steered.
William Shakespeare

Every ship is a romantic object, except that which we sail in.
Ralph Waldo Emerson

Everything you want is out there waiting for you to ask. Everything you want also wants you. But you have to take action to get it.
Jack Canfield

A YOUNG WOMAN AWAITING A SAILBOAT

Commentary: "A Young Woman" is seen "Awaiting a Sailboat." She has hopes in mind that something special will either arrive or happen in some way. There is a strong sense that some ideal she's hoping for will come to her if she waits long enough. Often there is delight in looking forward to a particular pleasure or event. However, sometimes it feels like one's "ship" will never come in. The "Young Woman" can be left waiting for a long time. She may miss other aspects of her life by not paying attention to what's readily available. Viewed positively, the "Waiting" can lead to a pleasurable anticipation of what, or who, may arrive. Sometimes we actually vicariously enjoy it in advance, dreaming of what rewards may come.

Oracle: You may need to be patient, and confident that what you want will come to you. However, there is a warning not to become dependent on an unreliable outcome. Also, if you are constantly looking out, then you are probably not spending enough time looking back or inward at the things you already possess or have ready access to. People dream of the perfect partner suddenly appearing, or the big win in the lottery that will rescue them from their problems or dull lives. The outcome may prove to be less than imagined. Often, the more we look forward to something, the less we enjoy it when it actually arrives. Bearing that in mind, we should draw to ourselves the things we truly desire through positive affirmations and a determined focus on a desired outcome. Clean the barnacles off your "Sailboat"—the remnants of the past—so that new life, love and spirit can come to you. It is the level of confidence that supports our "Waiting" that can determine the success of the outcome. When the tide changes, your "ship" may very well come in. Make sure you are rowing your own boat and steering your own course.

Keywords: Waiting for one's ship to come in. Escapist fantasies that rob everyday life. Travel and the longing for escape. Living in the future vs. being in the here-and-now. Nervous anticipation. Leaving things to chance. Believing that things will come eventually. Opportunism. Rocking someone's boat. Expectant waiting. Constant looking to the horizon. Boats. Tides. Creating a safe harbor.

The Caution: The bubble bursting. Waiting for Mr. or Ms. "Perfect." Ignoring what's readily available. Longing for that which may never come. Missing opportunities. Always looking over one's shoulder, seeking better things. Boredom with one's life. Escapism. Possibilities that are never "good enough." Pining for the unattainable. Not taking life on. Delusions of grandeur. Things always being better tomorrow.

What does this **SYMBOL** say to *you?*

THE MEETING OF A STUDY GROUP OR LITERARY SOCIETY

Cancer 23

Commentary: "A Study Group" or a "Literary Society" pictures people coming together to share opinions and ideas. The "Society" can symbolize any situation where people get together to discuss and share their thoughts; from a board or committee meeting to a gathering of people with common goals or interests. With modern communications, such as the Internet and large-scale publishing, efforts can reach right out to the masses and the collective. Finding the best way to analyze, direct or describe something creates better understanding for others.

Oracle: Situations or creative ideas can be given an objective, critical analysis or review in order to see what's really going on and what can be shared with others. However, the "Meetings" are best served in the search for greater meaning in order to enrich people, the group or the populace. There may be the need to have patience and an "ear" for what the whole "Group" has to say, instead of allowing people to just push their own beliefs, desires or agenda. This being said, however, individuals need to have the opportunity to have their visions and thoughts aired. They can hold useful, creative or new ideas, which may promote better outcomes. If you, or someone else, have something to say, say it. People will listen, even if some act as though they're not really interested. Is everyone having their say in this situation or are some merely "hogging the floor"? Who's in charge here? Are they doing the job honestly and sharing with others? Is this "Meeting" being run with everyone considered on an equal basis? Be careful that these "Meetings" don't turn out to be all talk and no action. What is the agenda?

Keywords: Shared higher knowledge. Print media, libraries. The written word. Committees. The movie *Dead Poet's Society*. Workshopping and brainstorming. Critics and criticism. Diaries, records and minutes of meetings. Newspapers and news media. Consulting with learned people. Talk radio. Sharing beliefs and ideas. The mirrors of society. Discussions. Letters to the editor. The meeting of the minds. Reviews.

The Caution: Falsifying of ideas. Propaganda spread by the media. Intellectual smugness. Excluding anything nonestablishment. Chatting instead of doing. Intellectual bickering. Analyzing every piece of information until it loses its inherent message. Being told only what's safe to reveal. Disinformation.

What does this **SYMBOL** say to *you?*

Great minds discuss ideas; average minds discuss events; small minds discuss people.
Eleanor Roosevelt

Let me never fall into the vulgar mistake of dreaming that I am persecuted whenever I am contradicted.
Ralph Waldo Emerson

Insanity in individuals is something rare—but in groups, parties, nations and epochs, it is the rule.
Friedrich Nietzsche

Half of the American people never read a newspaper. Half never voted for President. One hopes it is the same half.
Gore Vidal

Those who write clearly have readers; those who write obscurely have commentators.
Albert Camus

The well bred contradict other people. The wise contradict themselves.
Oscar Wilde

An element of exaggeration clings to the popular judgment: great vices are made greater, great virtues greater also; interesting incidents are made more interesting, softer legends more soft.
Walter Bagehot

Cancer 24

Paradise is always where love dwells.
Paul F. Richter

Anyone must see at a glance that if men and women marry those whom they do not love, they must love those whom they do not marry.
Harriet Martineau

Successful marriage is always a triangle: a man, a woman, and God.
T. Cecil Myers

There were three of us in our marriage, so it was a bit crowded.
Diana, Princess of Wales

Don't look now, but there's one too many in this room and I think it's you.
Groucho Marx

Of all human powers operating in the affairs of mankind, none is greater than that of competition.
Henry Clay

Do not put your spoon into the pot that does not boil for you.
Romanian Proverb

In married life, three is company and two none.
Oscar Wilde

A WOMAN AND TWO MEN (OR A MAN AND TWO WOMEN) CAST AWAY ON A SMALL ISLAND

Commentary: "A Woman and Two Men (or a Man and Two Women) Cast Away on a Small Island" is an image of people being or living in close proximity. They are "Castaways" and are somehow "stuck" with one another for the time being. They could be thrown together by circumstances or by choice. Regardless, being on a "Small Island" leaves no way of concealing behavior or keeping secrets and things get found out, sooner or later. It can reflect situations that are out of balance with the normal harmony of relationships. Things need to be dealt with carefully and sensitively.

Oracle: The people seen here may be "locked in" to some situation, environment or relationship. Their desires may be vacillating from one extreme to the other. There could be a desire to get away from those who have conflicting views or are trying to confuse things. There may be uncomfortable and even impossible choices to be made. At this time, however, removing one's self from the situation may not be possible. The value of this experience is to attempt to create new understandings and standards in order to turn the imbalance to everyone's advantage in whatever way possible. It may be impossible, but it is necessary to try. This Symbol can also reflect personality issues and confusions that are happening on an inner level. Symptoms of ill health, unhappiness, mood swings and temper tantrums can be an indication of an inner battle. This may be because of a change in relationships, beliefs or ideals. It may be a hidden memory or inner childhood issue that is rising to the surface and now manifesting in split relationships or similar problems. Take some care to work with the issue, as battling it out can lead to problems. Working out each person's position in the situation will help you to decipher what's really going on and who belongs with whom.

Keywords: Feelings of being fenced in. Too little room to move. Lack of privacy. Relationship triangles. Claustrophobia. Isolation. Love affairs. Too many people or having no one. Having to schedule people's needs. Competition and rivalry. Polygamy.

The Caution: Not seeing the whole picture. Fighting over one's "territory." The specter of "someone else." Jealousy. Sexual infidelity. Misleading relationships. Being shut out of a relationship. Fickleness. Not being able to choose. Having too many people to consider.

What does this **SYMBOL** say to *you?*

A LEADER OF MEN WRAPPED IN AN INVISIBLE CLOAK OF POWER

Cancer 25

Commentary: "A Leader of Men Wrapped in an Invisible Cloak of Power" is an image of someone who has the charisma, leadership or position that implies great authority and responsibility. Often these things need to be handled carefully; having a lot of "Power" can lead to corruption and abuse of privileges. As this pictures a "Leader of Men," this person must work for the good of the whole—not purely for personal advantage.

Oracle: There comes a time for most of us when we have to rise to the occasion as someone in charge or as a decision maker. Whatever the situation, there is a need to accept that you, or someone else, has this level of "Power," and this must be used and wielded wisely. You have an unavoidable obligation to accept responsibility and respond rationally. It may be that you have not sought out this "Power" or position of "Leadership." It can feel as though it has been thrust upon you, but you have been placed in this position and you need to understand and accept the consequences. This Symbol can also mean the abdication or giving away of your power to others—people who seem stronger or more in charge than yourself. The responsibility of it can be refused and handed on. Alternatively, if someone is abusing their authority, others can be roused to remove this "Cloak" or "mantle," thereby stripping them of their authority or control. Positively, the "Invisible Cloak of Power" can be something that lands in one's lap, and must be responded to with responsibility and acceptance. We can all be our own "gurus"—taking on our own sense of strength and ability. Sometimes we can find this out through the agency of someone else. Don't wait for somebody to tell you of your ability—believe in your "Power" and act on it. Wearing a special shawl or "Cloak" can work wonders to attract power and energy.

Keywords: Leadership and its honors and responsibilities. Powerful descent of energies taking over one's being. Feeling invincible—one can do nothing wrong. Hugging and being hugged. Sore shoulders. Shawls and cloaks that empower or coverup. Gurus. Quiet, unassuming strength. Charisma, strength and presence. Beautiful coats. Furs. Huge personalities.

The Caution: Shows of superiority. Presuming oneself to be more than one is. Megalomania. Abuse of power. Not owning one's magnificence. Having the weight of the world on your shoulders. People on power trips. Lording it over others. Being pushy.

What does this **SYMBOL** say to *you?*

Great hearts steadily send forth the secret forces that incessantly draw great events.
Ralph Waldo Emerson

Leadership is practiced not so much in words as in attitude and in actions.
Harold S. Geneen

A leader is best when people barely know he exists.
Lao Tzu

Nearly all men can stand adversity, but if you want to test a man's character, give him power.
Abraham Lincoln

A person wrapped up in himself makes a small package.
Harry Emerson Fosdick

It is better to be violent, if there is violence in our hearts, than to put on the cloak of nonviolence to cover impotence.
Mahatma Gandhi

A man who lives right, and is right, has more power in his silence than another has by his words.
Phillips Brooks

All I want is a warm bed and a kind word, and unlimited power.
Ashleigh Brilliant

Cancer 26

A house is not a home unless it contains food and fire for the mind as well as the body.
Margaret Fuller

A room without books is like a body without a soul.
Marcus T. Cicero

The man who does not read good books has no advantage over the man who can't read them.
Mark Twain

Never lend books, for no one ever returns them. The only books I have in my library are books that other folks have lent me.
Anatole France

Books like friends should be few and well chosen.
Samuel Paterson

War and Peace must wait for the leisure of retirement, which never really comes: meanwhile it helps to furnish the living room. Blockbusting fiction is bought as furniture.
Anthony Burgess

The richest minds need not large libraries.
Amos Bronson Alcott

GUESTS ARE READING IN THE LIBRARY OF A LUXURIOUS HOME

Commentary: The Symbol "Guests Are Reading in the Library of a Luxurious Home" pictures people taking an opportunity to relax and enjoy themselves in comfortable surroundings. It is a time to catch up on the thoughts of others, whether by reading books, magazines or newspapers, or having quiet moments in conversation with people without feeling any pressure to return to work. If one feels at home in this situation, there will be feelings of release and relaxation. There is the opportunity to do some reading, a few crossword puzzles, perhaps some researching or learning, etc. There does, however, need to be caution against self-indulgence, or just sitting around, as this could lead to laziness and a lack of motivation to get going with life. The "Luxurious Home" illustrates the fact that the opportunity to take time out to read, or learn is really a "Luxury" for many people.

Oracle: If you feel that everything is too confusing and complicated, you should go somewhere that allows for quiet times and informed reflection. We all lead busy lives, but finding time for "Reading" or other leisure activities should not have to be difficult. Remember that life consists of more than work. Play as much as you can—don't live life dreading the weekdays and longing for weekends. Nowadays, you don't even have to leave home to enjoy others and exchange thoughts; the Internet can bring both people and huge libraries of information to you, saving you the effort of physically going out and searching for them. We are able to have access to a wide range of information, comment and imagination without the restrictions of having to be wealthy—both in the luxury of time and the availability of valuable material. Don't cut yourself off from other people, though, as this could lead to loneliness.

Keywords: Sharing of thoughts and ideas in an environment of social privilege. Social protocol that says what one should be digesting emotionally, intellectually or physically. Libraries. Hotel reading rooms. Chatting quietly. Books, magazines. Quiet, knowing atmosphere. Learning and sharing ideas. Having friends over. Relaxing. Taking time off. Study groups.

The Caution: Relating on a superficial level or not being able to relate at all because of social expectations. Being told to "keep quiet." Not saying what one really feels. Focusing on the mind, not the heart. Not being invited to the inner circle. Special privileges for the few.

What does this **SYMBOL** say to *you?*

A VIOLENT STORM IN A RESIDENTIAL CANYON FILLED WITH VALUABLE HOMES

Cancer 27

Commentary: "A Violent Storm in a Canyon Filled with Valuable Homes" shows that a "Storm" has released its fury on those in its path. The weather that has been unleashed can reflect actual weather, or psychological or emotional conditions. The "Homes" need not be expensive, but are places that are "Valuable" to the occupants. They usually feel protected and safe. Somehow, a "Storm" has raged through. Exactly what will happen next may be rather uncertain.

Oracle: You may find yourself much deeper in a situation than you may have imagined, and now you are caged by the "walls" around you. There is probably no immediate escape from the turbulence that is happening. You may have had some forewarning that this "Storm" was coming; with pressure piling up, threatening to explode at any moment. You may have had no intention or made no particular movements to invoke this "Storm," however it's out of hand in your environment nonetheless. The best thing to do is to wait it out and protect yourself, and those around you. Although this may have been building for days, or years, many are often taken by surprise at the sudden turn of events or the intensity of what's being unleashed. An event or something that was said can let loose a torrent of emotional and physical energy that may be hard to contain. In fact, endeavoring to contain it may result in more damage. Things probably need to blow themselves out naturally. A positive outcome may not come to light for awhile, but things will fall back where they are meant to, in the end. Look back to see what you've contributed, as it may help to see a way out, or at least reconcile what's happened. It's likely that a number of people have been affected. It may be a disaster, or it may end up being a blessing in some way. See if you can rebuild your community—some people may have to be left out of your life, however.

Keywords: Arguments and emotional confrontations. The "pressure cooker" environments of modern-day living. Psychic energy unleashed. Furious emotions. Changing the status quo. Bad weather and its consequences. Rebuilding from the foundations. Living in canyons. Being surrounded by mountainous peaks. The awesome power of nature.

The Caution: Wrongly believing that you are in control of the uncontrollable. Enjoyment of emotional storms and turmoil. Lots of noise that erupts out of nowhere. Whipping things up. Life-threatening behavior. Confrontations. Stormfronts. Social upheavals. Disturbing or violent reactions. Domestic violence.

What does this **SYMBOL** say to *you?*

Try to relax and enjoy the crisis.
Ashleigh Brilliant

A man is sometimes lost in the dust of his own raising.
David Ruggles

It is your business when the wall next door catches fire.
Horace

Rain does not fall on one roof alone.
Cameroon Proverb

You don't develop courage by being happy in your relationships every day. You develop it by surviving difficult times and challenging adversity.
Barbara De Angelis

"I lose my temper, but it's all over in a minute," said the student. "So is the hydrogen bomb," I replied. "But think of the damage it produces!"
George Sweeting

There is a great deal of unmapped country within us which would have to be taken into account in an explanation of our gusts and storms.
George Eliot

Cancer 28

For that reason, if no other,
Would I wed the fair Dacotah,
That our tribes might be united,
That old feuds might be
forgotten,
And old wounds be healed
forever.
Henry Wadsworth Longfellow

It is a common enough case,
that of a man being suddenly
captivated by a woman nearly
the opposite of his ideal.
George Eliot

It is the mark of an educated
mind to be able to entertain a
thought without accepting it.
Aristotle

Differences challenge
assumptions.
Anne Wilson Schaef

Honest differences are often
a healthy sign of progress.
Mahatma Gandhi

Ideological differences are no
excuse for rudeness.
Judith Martin

What sets worlds in motion is
the interplay of differences, their
attractions and repulsions; life
is plurality, death is uniformity.
Octavio Paz

AN INDIAN GIRL INTRODUCES HER COLLEGE BOYFRIEND TO HER ASSEMBLED TRIBE

Commentary: "An Indian Girl Introduces Her College Boyfriend to Her Assembled Tribe" is an image of the spanning of cultures, languages or belief systems through love and acceptance. The people in this Symbol are bridging the gap between people or situations that are usually foreign to each other. They may come from completely different "sides of the tracks." However, it is the deeply felt understanding of both camps, intellectual and tribal, and the respect with which these people are held that makes their mutual acceptance possible. It may be that having an education creates a gap between those that have formal training and those that haven't. This Symbol can also refer to generation gaps. Despite any differences in the way a family or close group may see the world, there should always be the essential elements of family, respect and pride shown to those who come.

Oracle: It is by "Introducing" new people, those who are outside our usual intimate circle, whether it be family, community (or tribe) or even our business world, that the potential of our lives is expanded. The motivation for this change, or challenge, to the status quo is love and the willingness to accept things that are normally foreign to us. There may be all kinds of intellectual disputes or stubborn resistance to new people or ways of life, but these will be welcomed when the there is a motivation for acceptance. It is in both the giving and seeking of acceptance that we show a wise heart, even in the face of surface or social difficulties. If there are hurdles or barriers around you, persevere. These can, and will, evaporate with time as people's ideas soften through becoming familiar with each other. With persistent love and openness, barriers can be overcome.

Keywords: Challenging or going against the status quo. Bringing in a new, more intellectual, element or bringing in a more natural, earth-based attitude. Being the odd one out. Revealing strange, foreign situations or truths to others. Accepting people without judgment. Being welcoming and loving. Clans. Tribes.

The Caution: Deliberately upsetting the group. Unconventional or alternative behavior. Choosing friends or mates that could never fit in with one's family, friends or social expectations. Using prejudice to keep people apart. Judging people by social standards. People misunderstanding each other. Hidden motives. Rebellion for the sake of being different. Ignoring tradition.

What does this **SYMBOL** say to *you?*

A GREEK MUSE WEIGHING NEWBORN TWINS IN GOLDEN SCALES

Cancer 29

Commentary: "A Greek Muse Weighing Newborn Twins in Golden Scales." The "Muses" were Greek deities of the arts and sciences. Artists and scientists alike would invoke the wisdom and inspiration of the "Muses" before any creative or intellectual work was begun. In Greek mythology there are nine "Muses" who specialize in different aspects of thought and creativity.

Oracle: In the situation facing you, you may be pressed into making judgments and decisions in a creative or intuitive way. As the "Greek Muse" is "Weighing Newborn Twins," the elements of your judgment are likely to be, in many ways, very similar. The choices are confusing because they essentially lead to the same result. This situation is probably brand new. It may be that the answer lies in taking an intuitive "punt," or guess, or perhaps you need to wait for more information for the solutions to become more clear cut. Either way it is by consulting universal wisdom that you can focus on the best answer. Are you consulting the right "Muse"? Are you considering the issue from the best perspective? This is, overall, a very fortunate Symbol—it indicates that your choices are equally beneficial, or at least, equally balanced. Whatever you decide will most likely be a good decision. This Symbol can also indicate a very quick mind that can make decisions very quickly due to a natural mechanism that can be called on.

Keywords: Comparisons and similarities. Weighing things up. The law and lawyers. The Scales of Justice. First communion. The value of new beginnings. Grand gestures. Ceremonies. Looking for subtle aspects. Balances. Using intuition. Weighing pros and cons. Hesitating before making decisions. Subtle discriminations of differences. Measured responses. Inspiration. The gift of prophecy. Patrons of the arts. Ponder. Fairness. Equality. Meticulous attention to detail. Evaluations.

The Caution: Expressing judgmental opinions about things that are essentially equal. Being picky. The scales tipped. Everything getting off balance. Constantly weighing things up instead of just accepting them. Not being able to move forward with plans or ideas because of a feeling of being stuck. Excessive arguments for or against. Continual wavering. Being persnickety. Tipping the scales.

Perfection is reached not when there is no longer anything to add, but when there is no longer anything to take away.
Antoine de Saint Exupéry

It is in your moments of decision that your destiny is shaped.
Anthony Robbins

A mind that questions everything, unless strong enough to bear the weight of its ignorance, risks questioning itself and being engulfed in doubt.
Emile Durkheim

He is no lawyer who cannot take two sides.
Charles Lamb

The wise weigh their words on a scale with gold.
The Bible

If there was two birds sitting on a fence, he would bet you which one would fly first.
Mark Twain

Spend time every day listening to what your muse is trying to tell you.
Saint Bartholomew

Choice—It is always your next move.
Napoleon Hill

What does this **SYMBOL** say to *you?*

Cancer 30

The greatest glory of a freeborn people is to transmit that freedom to their children.
William Harvard

The hand that rocks the cradle rules the nation and its destiny.
South African Proverb

A citizen of America will cross the ocean to fight for democracy, but won't cross the street to vote in a national election.
Bill Vaughan

Dear Mr. President,
There are too many states nowadays. Please eliminate three.
P.S. I am not a crackpot.
Abraham Simpson

It is easy to take liberty for granted when you have never had it taken from you.
M. Grundler

They want to be free and they do not know how to be just.
Abbe Sieyes

Seek not to change the world, but choose to change your mind about the world.
A Course In Miracles

A DAUGHTER OF THE AMERICAN REVOLUTION

Commentary: "A Daughter of the American Revolution" is an image of someone who stands for and is a product of change. She has promoted and adopted the changes that the "Revolution" sought to achieve. "The American Revolution" was a full-scale militant revolt against tradition, and the monarchy behind it. The "Daughters'" forefathers fought for independence and took the "feudal system" head on. The "Daughers" stand for maintaining what has been won. They need to continue working and, although the war has largely been won, there are many more "peaceful" battles that must be waged to keep victories the "Revolution" was fought for. They are not necessarily engaged in direct political or military activity, but offer their support to the powers that be.

Oracle: A "Revolution" is just the shakeup; it is the "Daughters" (and sons) of the "Revolution" who bring new ways into the world. The person pictured here is said to be a "Daughter" because the way of continuing the revolution is with the feminine ways of communication, example and teaching. The ways of the "sons," those of war and fighting, should be over and done with. That is, unless a battle needs to be fought to secure freedom from external forces once again. You may find yourself having to stand up for an ideal or a situation that demands your involvement. The difficulty is that these traditions are now predictable, conservative values. Despite any inner feelings of modern freedom, this is not how the situation now appears. However, although this image can be very conservative, there can be an element of the "radical" within it. There still may be much yet to be achieved even though there have been major breakthroughs already.

Keywords: Being bound by social conditioning or leading the charge to break down the barriers of tradition. Putting in the time to change social conditions for the betterment of all. The feminist movement. Sacrificing personal conviction to ambition. Sacrificing philosophy to a relationship that builds the ego. Inherited values. Being the rebel in the family.

The Caution: Supporting battles that have already been fought. False feelings of superiority. Having to be "in the club" to be accepted. Narrow-minded conservatism. Glorifying the past. Relying on old traditions that were, in their day, radical and transforming. Rejecting one's inheritance.

What does this **SYMBOL** say to *you?*

A MAN IS UNDER EMOTIONAL STRESS AND BLOOD RUSHES TO HIS HEAD

Commentary: "Under Emotional Stress, Blood Rushes to a Man's Head" is what happens when a situation arises which fires up one's mind and emotions quickly and suddenly. This can lead to anger, but it can also lead to being stuck in a sequence of emotional reactions. If this "Emotional Stress" proves to be embarrassing, it can lead to blushing, which can be hard to conceal.

Oracle: There may be nothing that can be done at the moment. It's like being immobilized with neither mental nor physical control. Resistance may just make the situation worse. Don't panic, though—this will not last forever. When emotions or ambitions take over there is a need to put extra energy into thinking everything through with a calm frame of mind. However, when you're under "Stress" it is often difficult, if not impossible, to settle down and think rationally. When temper erupts it works against the mind settling down. If you restrict or ignore your frustrations and anxieties your situation could blow out of control. It is important to recognize whether you're reacting to a situation because it bothers you, or whether it's because you're generally going through a stressful time. Be careful not to explode every time you are under some kind of duress, as this can create a "cranky" type of person who is unbearable unless circumstances are smooth and calm. At the very least it is important to notice what the underlying problems are that are bringing things to a head. What is the real problem? If someone explodes every time there is some emotional stress, it can become a habit. Consequently, family and friends tiptoe around in an effort to keep things calm. This leads to everyone internalizing their anger and frustration, and the problem is projected onto those around. Try to not to take things, or yourself, too seriously. It may take some time to take the energy out of the charge. Meditation or "getting away from it all" could be a solution.

Keywords: Ambition. Becoming fired-up. Charging off in all directions at once. Dizziness and disorientation. Nervous breakdowns. Not acting like one's usual self. Events coming to a head. Feeling like one will explode at any moment. Too many obligations to live up to. Feeling incapable of action. Too much excitement to contain safely. Headaches. Blood pressure. Erections. Animal passions.

The Caution: Becoming ill through emotional suppression. Losing one's cool. Going off the deep end. Lack of self-restraint. Taking things too seriously. Grumpiness and irritability. Not knowing how to act or respond. Difficulty containing emotional reactions. Unable to make accurate decisions due to irrational thoughts. Sunburn.

What does this **SYMBOL** say to *you?*

Leo 1

It doesn't pay to say too much when you are mad enough to choke. For the word that stings the deepest is the word that is never spoke. Let the other fellow wrangle till the storm has blown away, then he'll do a heap of thinking about the things you didn't say.
James Whitcomb Riley

When anger rises, think of the consequences.
Confucius

Anger is a short madness.
Romanian Proverb

Perhaps there is only one cardinal sin: impatience. Because of impatience we are driven out of Paradise; because of impatience we cannot return.
Franz Kafka

It's been lovely but I have to scream now.
Bumper Sticker

The ruling passion, be it what it will, the ruling passion conquers reason still.
Alexander Pope

How forcible are right words! But what doth your arguing reprove?
The Bible

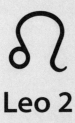

Leo 2

Ninety-nine per cent of the people in the world are fools and the rest of us are in great danger of contagion.
Thornton Wilder

Scandal: gossip made tedious by morality.
Oscar Wilde

My sources are unreliable, but their information is fascinating.
Ashleigh Brilliant

We are more apt to catch the vices of others than their virtues, as disease is far more contagious than health.
Charles Caleb Colton

Good, the more communicated, more abundant grows.
John Milton

A lie can run around the world before the truth can get its boots on.
James Watt

Life is a disease; and the only difference between one man and another is the stage of the disease at which he lives. You are always at the crisis: I am always in the convalescent stage.
George Bernard Shaw

AN EPIDEMIC OF MUMPS

Commentary: "An Epidemic of Mumps" can indicate a situation, illness or event that is affecting a number of people. An "Epidemic" is something contagious, like an illness that is racing throughout the populace or raging through a chain of friends or family. Although it can affect people on a large scale, it may have started with just one person. The disease "Mumps" can lead to sexual impotence in men and a feeling of being ineffectual and useless. As it is an "Epidemic," it will pay to nip it in the bud. It may, however, have to run its course.

Oracle: In the situation facing you, this Symbol can talk about the literal spread of disease, but it can also symbolize news or gossip, e.g., a story that's gotten completely out of control. This "infecting influence" could be affecting you or someone else in the group, and it is likely to be spreading regardless of whether anybody wants it to. This situation, or "disease," needs to be harnessed as soon as possible, as this "Epidemic" may spread fear or upset to all those involved and those further afield. The situation may indeed get worse before it gets better. Finding the origin of the "infection," or the extent of its spread or how far it has reached will go a long way toward resolving the situation. It can at least act to slow it down so it can lose energy and dissipate. Therefore it can be important to discover the facts about how or when it started, or perhaps how best to stop it. There may be a need for some kind of separation or isolation, and then some time for recovery. Remember that laughter can be infectious. Spread joy and love instead of fear and worry!

Keywords: Hysterical feelings. Ideas of immunity. Things getting out of control. Common threads that link people and places. Infectious diseases. Medicine and cures. Discovering the truth of a situation and acting accordingly. Viruses and bacterial infections spreading. Rumors. Colds. Flu. Fear in general. The cat let out of the bag. The need for "immunization." The need for hygeine. Isolating causes of problems. Vaccinations. Outbreaks. Blood tests. Tumors. Measles. Chicken pox.

The Caution: Fear of bad health. Hypochondria. Rampaging gossip. Widespread fear or upset. Stories that get out of control. Rashes and skin problems. Deprivation. Hiding one's self away for fear of contagion. Fear of sharing one's self with others. Obsession with health. Embarrassment. Impotence. Contagious thoughts. Negative thinking and compulsive actions. The complications of disease. Media frenzies. Problems that multiply with alarming speed.

What does this **SYMBOL** say to *you?*

A MATURE WOMAN, KEEPING UP WITH THE TIMES, HAVING HER HAIR BOBBED

Leo 3

Commentary: "A Mature Woman" here is "Keeping up with the Times" through having a modern hairstyle; she's "Having Her Hair Bobbed." She doesn't want to be out of touch with fashion and considered old-fashioned. Getting her "Hair Bobbed" helps her to present an image of being modern and in tune with what's current in the world. As she's said to be a "Mature Woman," the hairstyle may be her way of making the statement that with the changes that are happening in her life she's feeling somewhat different about herself. When the Symbols were brought through in 1925, it was, indeed, thought rather radical to cut your hair in a "Bob" if you were a woman.

Oracle: Although we cannot really become different by changing our appearance, feeling good about the image we display does radiate both inward and outward. This might be just what is needed in the situation that brought you to the Oracle. However, as comforting and rejuvenating as an external change may be, remember that it is your inner self that is the essence of your persona, not the mask you wear. Altering your appearance just for the sake of being trendy may be detrimental to your self-esteem or confidence; you may feel as though you are constantly following the crowd. "Keeping up with the Times" can sometimes become an obsession. Be sure that you are not making these cosmetic changes to replace something lacking inside. Having said that, asserting your right to present your own style and feeling confident about yourself can be invaluable for self-esteem and can lead to others appreciating you for your true qualities.

Keywords: Making an effort to keep up with trends. Asserting one's independence from social constraints. Wanting to shrug off the years. Adopting a younger attitude. Following the herd. Going along with the fashions. Plastic surgery. Changing appearances. Hairdressers and hairstyles. Gray hair. Hats and scarves. Meeting the challenges of age. Radiating sexuality. Bad hair days. Midlife crisis. Being a trendsetter.

The Caution: Relying on external fashion to disguise inner emptiness. Cosmetic changes that are transitory. Making superficial but not meaningful alterations. Fashion slaves. The illusion of keeping up with the times. Giving up on one's appearance. Battling society's glorification of youth. Mutton dressed up as lamb.

What does this **SYMBOL** say to *you?*

Women's fashion is a euphemism for fashion created by men for women.
Andrea Dworkin

Every generation laughs at the old fashions, but follows religiously the new.
Henry David Thoreau

When a woman ceases to alter the fashion of her hair, you guess that she has passed the crisis of her experience.
Mary Austin

By common consent gray hairs are a crown of glory; the only object of respect that can never excite envy.
George Bancroft

I base most of my fashion taste on what doesn't itch.
Gilda Radner

A truth looks freshest in the fashions of the day.
Lord Alfred Tennyson

Some never choose an opinion. They just wear whatever happens to be in fashion.
Leo Tolstoy

Leo 4

DUEL, n. A formal ceremony preliminary to reconciliation of two enemies. Great skill is necessary to its satisfactory observance; if awkwardly performed ... deplorable consequences sometimes ensue. A long time ago a man lost his life.
Ambrose Bierce

There's always something about your success that displeases even your best friends.
Mark Twain

One nice thing about egotists: they don't talk about other people.
Lucille S. Harper

I don't deserve this award, but I have arthritis, and I don't deserve that, either.
Jack Benny

He who doesn't risk never gets to drink champagne.
Russian Proverb

A sportsman is a man who, every now and then, simply has to get out and kill something.
Stephen Leacock

The English country gentleman galloping after a fox—the unspeakable in full pursuit of the uneatable.
Oscar Wilde

A MAN FORMALLY DRESSED STANDS NEAR TROPHIES HE BROUGHT BACK FROM A HUNTING EXPEDITION

Commentary: "A Man Formally Dressed Stands Near Trophies" is an image of someone putting on their best attire and showing something that's seen by himself and others as being a reward for achieving success in a male-dominated arena. These are "Trophies He Brought Back from a Hunting Expedition" and they are his to display or show off. It can be something he's found, fought, shot or "bagged" in some way. It's safe to assume that he's very proud of his success and he may have had to endure incredible stress and dangers to acquire it. Whatever the "Trophies" are, it is one thing to achieve them and another to then display these achievements for all to see.

Oracle: This Symbol shows that there may be the urge, or the need, to impress others. There should always be some form of recognition or reward for a job well done. Being proud and having a sense of satisfaction for accomplishing something should be rewarded and congratulated. But just what are the rewards and spoils that you're after? Some people will be pleased with the display, but there's the possibility of some being uninterested and, further, others could be distinctly unimpressed. Think carefully of the effects before you do anything, as others may feel jealous or try to shoot you down for showing off. The "Trophies" can be diplomas and awards for performing well on any level. Have you truly accomplished something? If so you should be acknowledged and congratulated. Or are they just "things" that you can claim for yourself without considering where they've come from or caring about what had to be done to achieve them?

Keywords: Trophies of conquest. The desire to show one's self. Proving one's animal instincts for the benefit of social position. Displays of manliness. The spoils of daring and courage. Notches on the belt. Victories over another. Trophies awarded for one's club, social standing or country. Looking for pats on the back. Diplomas. Guns, rifles, ammunition. Academy Awards. Animal liberationists.

The Caution: Dominating nature with power. Showing off. Warfare and the ravages of it. Keeping tabs on one's conquests. Boasting of masculine prowess. Living in the past. Arrogance. Seeing things as objects to conquer. Testosterone overloads. Compromises made to attain social acceptance. Envious responses to success.

What does this **SYMBOL** say to *you?*

ROCK FORMATIONS TOWERING OVER A DEEP CANYON

Leo 5

Commentary: "Rock Formations Towering over a Deep Canyon" is an image of large prominences of rock forming a steep precipice over a canyon, valley or gorge. The landscape can be very formidable, awe-inspiring and rather off-putting, making one feel very small and somehow insignificant when observing it. We are reminded of the enormity of nature and how small we truly are in the grand scheme of things.

Oracle: Things may have been smooth sailing for some time, but now you could be finding yourself trapped between a rock and a hard place. It's likely that the natural structure of your situation has carefully grown and developed over time. There is a history here, but this is only recognizable by the obvious emotional and physical effects that are shown around you in the world. The soft spots have been worn away; and many of the hard edges have been smoothed under the weight of the weather and experience. Right now progress is at a precipice, with the structures of the past pressing from behind. There seems to be no going back—forward is probably the only way out. There may be a feeling of being unable to cope out in the wilderness. The best, or possibly only, solution may be to "jump into the void." It may be a lonely journey, but you will find new depths of experience that you could only have imagined before now. Be wary though, another side to this Symbol can indicate instability—the "Rock Formations" that "Tower over the Deep Canyon" are not going to be stable forever. They are at the mercy of the elements; we can't rely on these formations forever. The situation may look rock solid, but time may tell a different story.

Keywords: Old structures and deep hazards. The choice: taking chances or standing still. Walking very close to the edge. Extreme sports. Risk taking. New takes on old situations. Additions to things long established. Masada. Mountains. Valleys and gorges. Fortifications. Isolation. The grandeur of nature. The forces of evolution. Rock. Geology. Layers of permanence. Landscapes. Canyons. Vertigo. No going back. Stability behind—the unknown in front. Great heights. Monuments.

The Caution: Painting oneself into a corner. Not being able to retrace one's steps. Instability. Erosion. Jumping into the void without a safety net. Cracks appearing. Doing a "Geronimo." Being right on the edge. Feeling like life is impossibly hard.

What does this **SYMBOL** say to *you?*

When you look long into an abyss, the abyss looks into you.
Friedrich Nietzsche

Do the thing you fear and the death of fear is certain.
Ralph Waldo Emerson

Look twice before you leap.
Charlotte Bronte

When one must, one can.
Yiddish Proverb

The greatest mistake a man can make is to be afraid of making one.
Elbert Hubbard

Man can learn nothing except by going from the known to the unknown.
Claude Bernard

When you fall into a pit, you either you get out or die.
Chinese Proverb

A journey of a thousand miles starts in front of your feet. A tower nine stories high is built from a small heap of earth.
Lao-Tzu

Drive a rat into a corner, and he'll jump at you.
Proverb

Leo 6

To live lightheartedly but not recklessly; to be gay without being boisterous; to be courageous without being bold; to show trust and cheerful resignation without fatalism— this is the art of living.
Jean de La Fontaine

I used to be with "it," but then they changed what "it" was. Now what I'm with isn't "it" anymore and what's "it" seems weird and scary.
Abraham Simpson

No idea is so antiquated that it was not once modern; no idea is so modern that it will not someday be antiquated.
Ellen Glasgow

The virtue of some people consists wholly in condemning the vices in others.
Herbert Samuel

It is only the modern that ever becomes old-fashioned.
Oscar Wilde

Women dress alike all over the world: they dress to be annoying to other women.
Elsa Schiaparelli

AN OLD-FASHIONED, CONSERVATIVE WOMAN IS CONFRONTED BY AN UP-TO-DATE GIRL

Commentary: "An Old-Fashioned, Conservative Woman Is Confronted by an Up-to-Date Girl." They have somehow been brought together by a situation or circumstance and are now face-to-face with each other. The "Old-Fashioned, Conservative Woman" may feel somehow "Confronted" or challenged by the presence or the very existence of the "Up-to-Date Girl." The "Girl" may remind her of how she used to be, or how she always wanted to be. The "Up-to-Date Girl" may be confronted by the "Conservative Woman"—she may have her own sense of inferiority, or even superiority, and many things may run through her mind as she sees herself reflected in the older woman. One of the scariest things to young people is the thought of aging. They like to believe they will remain young and bright forever.

Oracle: This Symbol often shows issues of the aging process being a positive experience, rather than the negative image people generally have of it. The "Old-Fashioned Woman" or the "Up-to-Date Girl" do not have to stick to their stereotypes; they can, indeed, bring the best of both worlds together. In fact, their roles may be reversed with the "Older" woman being less "Conservative" than the younger one. You may find yourself faced with a choice between tried-and-true established ways and the modern or innovative. It is most likely that the best qualities of both attitudes is the proper compromise. There may be a need to be mindful of other people's mindsets and generational differences. However, you can't please everyone all the time. Also, remember that what bothers people about someone else is often a reflection of their own issues.

Keywords: Conservatism challenged by changing, energetic forms. Learning to let one's hair down. Letting go and having a good time. Issues of age and what one's capable of. Ideas challenged. Learning experiences. Renovations. Business takeovers. Different capabilities and talents. People acting or working together regardless of their differences. Generation gaps. Concentrating. Face-to-face meetings.

The Caution: Denying the duality within. Being afraid to get out there. Jealousy between people on different levels of being or different ages. Paying no attention to change/being afraid of it. Difficult combinations of people. Projection of the shadow. Standoffs. Criticism. Derision, envy, fear, jealousy. Age overriding feelings.

What does this **SYMBOL** say to *you?*

THE WONDER OF THE CONSTELLATIONS OF STARS IN THE NIGHT SKY

Leo 7

Commentary: "The Wonder of the Constellations of Stars in the Night Sky" brings to mind the amazing sense of beauty that can be felt when observing the heavens. Just as our ancestors saw pictures in the "Stars," a "Constellation" is an expression of how our imagination can see designs and symbols in things that we usually take for granted. "The Night Sky" can create images that inspire us to greater awareness. Questions such as "What am I here for?" "What is life really about?" and "What difference do I (or can I) make to this world?", etc., can come up as we gaze at the heavens. The clearer the sky and the darker the night, the more we can feel drawn to that vast space and are held in awe of it. Nature can often show us how "small" we are in the universe, and yet how important we are to "the whole."

Oracle: The bigger questions are likely to be in your mind at the moment. Simple issues will be viewed against a backdrop of something greater. This helps to keep your life in perspective. This Symbol is about the need to see the patterns in what is going on around you. Rather than looking at each thing separately, step back and see the wider view—allow your imagination and intuition to create an inspiring vision that gives answers and direction to your life. Sometimes individual events have no more importance than to act as cogs in a wheel of a broader, more inspirational message. Looking at the sky can induce wonder at life's possibilities. The "Stars" are so far away, yet they feel large and close when the sky is clear and dark. Try to get out and observe the "Night Sky." This can help to bring a sense of wonder and awe into your life and remind you of the beauty of our universe.

Keywords: Reminders of the patterns, integration and enormity of nature. The big picture. Observing signatures. A determination to "be somebody." The Stars and Stripes. Feeling like a tiny fleck against the backdrop of the vault of the sky. Space travel and its wonders. Signs from the heavens. Answers sought through astrology. Astronomy. Being a shining star. Enormous people or personalities.

The Caution: Ignoring down-to-earth issues. Missing the small details. Only being amazed by huge things and not seeing wonder in the small things in life. Being starstruck and not seeing the true picture.

What does this **SYMBOL** say to *you?*

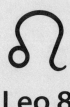

Leo 8

If you don't stand for something, you will fall for anything.
Chinese Proverb

A man may be poorly dressed and penniless, yet his burning desire can bring him the opportunity of his lifetime.
E. Barnes

There is nothing more difficult to take in hand, more perilous to conduct or more uncertain in its success than to take the lead in the introduction of a new order of things.
Niccolo Machiavelli

The people must fight for their laws as for their walls.
Heraclitus

The first duty of a revolutionist is to get away with it.
Abbie Hoffman

I hate the idea of causes, and if I had to choose between betraying my country and betraying my friend, I hope I should have the guts to betray my country.
E. M. Forster

A man is sometimes lost in the dust of his own raising.
David Ruggles

All movements go too far.
Bertrand Russell

AN ACTIVIST IS STIRRING UP DISCONTENT BY SPREADING HIS REVOLUTIONARY IDEALS

Commentary: "An Activist Is Stirring up Discontent by Spreading His Revolutionary Ideals." He has had some enlightening or disturbing insight into what's going on in society. He wants people to listen to his message and, probably, to influence or change their way of thinking. The "Activist" feels that he has the answers to how life should really be and what rights people are entitled to. To some people, his beliefs, or his radical ways, may be somewhat confronting and threatening to their everyday lives. To others, his "Ideals" may fit with what they've wanted in their own lives; he can be a beacon calling out for action. His message can be challenging, stirring or misleading.

Oracle: Society often looks down on those who have bright and burning ideas of "Revolution," when in reality they should perhaps be thanked for having the vision, or foresight, to see the need for it. On the other hand, somebody may be forcing their ideas on others—what one person thinks is not always right for others. And, of course, "Activists" are not always spreading useful, or practical, ideas. They can be extremist and unrealistic. Striving for the ideals of equality for all tends to be more relevant to those in a disadvantaged position. Those who live safely within the comfort of society rarely rebel against what's happening; however, there are exceptions to this. There may indeed be the need for a change to the status quo. This must come from someone who is prepared to sacrifice personal comfort in order to remain true to his or her ideals fighting for the common good. You may feel that you have had enough of the situation and that you have no power. If so, you probably need to enlist the support of others if you wish to succeed. It is through the promise of equality that power will be won.

Keywords: Unwavering and unbending intellect. Burning passions. Revolutionary ideals. Change for the sake of change. Making one's ideas and passions known. Standing on a soapbox. Greenpeace and other radical groups. Anti-capitalism. Entrepreneurs. Working hard to wake others up. Challenging authority. Demonstrations. Placards. Rejecting oppression. Soapboxes.

The Caution: Political brainwashing. Finding things to be dissatisfied with. Extremism. Religious fundamentalists. Street preachers. Cult leaders. Terrorism. Breeding hate. Challenging powerful institutions. Propaganda. Animosity.

What does this **SYMBOL** say to *you?*

GLASS BLOWERS SHAPE BEAUTIFUL FORMS WITH THEIR CONTROLLED BREATHING

Leo 9

Commentary: "Glass Blowers" are shaping "Beautiful Forms with Their Controlled Breathing." They have to be craftsmen of their art in order to be able to make the forms "Beautiful." They must take care and work with precision to have their "Glass" objects take shape and be pleasing to the eye. When Venetian "Glass Blowers" made a mistake in creating fine bottles, they called them a fiasco. "Their Controlled Breathing" can almost be like a meditation, with every "Breath" and every movement being important to the final result.

Oracle: This Symbol is about understanding the spiritual flow involved in creativity. It is also about the wonderful things that can be done when one has a great depth of understanding of what one wants to achieve. It can also signify the things we might leave behind that symbolize or act as reminders of significant moments of our lives. These memories are fragile and dependent upon how well they are cared for. Your inner spiritual energies can shape your situation into something worthwhile now. It is only with the controlled use of these energies that you will actually be able to craft this situation correctly. It is important, however, for you to let go of any fears that what you do may not last. It is the act of creating something beautiful, from the heart and soul, that is the point of our participation in life. Be careful not to let your imagination get out of control; the mind can be responsible for warping reality to fit our thoughts. Connecting with the unknown depths of unconscious experience is often reliant upon the control of "Breath." Practicing breathing meditations and learning about diaphragm control can take one's whole existence onto a new level of being. Watching what you breathe life into can be very illuminating. Focus on what you're creating with your life. Are you "Shaping Beautiful Forms" with your creations?

Keywords: Being able to create beautiful forms out of nothing. Prana. Singing, performing. Buteyko breathing method. Sculpture. Beauty. Breath meditations. Artisans. Rebirthing. Extreme care and detail. Lungs. Respiration = creation and inspiration. Pouring life into creative visions. Smoke rings. Didgeridoos. Smoking pipes and implements.

The Caution: Failing to take proper care. Lapses of concentration. Distortions of the truth. Hyperventilation. Lung troubles. Asthma. Smoking too much.

What does this **SYMBOL** say to *you?*

As the same fire assumes different shapes, when it consumes objects differing in shape, so does the one self take the shape of every creature in whom he is present.
Upanishads

Anger is an acid that can do more harm to the vessel in which it is stored than to anything on which it is poured.
Anonymous

The breath becomes a stone; the stone, a plant; the plant, an animal; the animal, a man, a spirit; and the spirit, a god.
H. P. Blavatsky

Courage is a matter of the red corpuscle. It is oxygen that makes every attack; without oxygen in his blood to back him, a man attacks nothing— not even a pie, much less a blank canvas.
Elbert Hubbard

The artist is nothing without the gift, but the gift is nothing without work.
Emile Zola

Every artist dips his brush in his own soul, and paints his own nature into his picture.
Henry Ward Beecher

Leo 10

The darkest hour is just before dawn.
Thomas Fuller

Let your life lightly dance on the edges of Time like dew on the tip of a leaf.
Rabindranath Tagore

There was never a night or a problem that could defeat sunrise or hope.
Bern Williams

On life's journey faith is nourishment, virtuous deeds are a shelter, wisdom is the light by day and right mindfulness is the protection by night. If a man lives a pure life, nothing can destroy him.
Buddha

In the real dark night of the soul it is always three o'clock in the morning.
F. Scott Fitzgerald

Do not anticipate trouble, or worry about what may never happen. Keep in the sunlight.
Benjamin Franklin

There are twelve hours in the day, and above fifty in the night.
Marie de Rabutin-Chantal

The morning pouring everywhere, its golden glory on the air.
Henry Wadsworth Longfellow

EARLY MORNING DEW SALUTES THE SUNLIGHT

Commentary: "Early Morning Dew Salutes the Sunlight" gives the feeling of freshness in the air as the sun comes up in the "Morning." The warmth of the Sun is yet to create the vibrancy of the new day, but the promise is there. This is a time of limbo, when the stillness and the darkness of night are washed away as the day progresses into light and activity. However, this Symbol can signify a time known as the "dark night of the soul." St. John of the Cross used this term to describe the experience of mystics who feel depressed and isolated from the world and even from God. This was often prior to the attainment of mystical transcendence—when the "Sunlight" breaks through and a healing takes place. This is a time of freshness where the "air" (the newly awakened mind) is crisp and the "ground" (the refreshed and renewed body) readies itself for a new round of activity. The birds are stirring and there is a buzzing in the air as all the creatures start moving about.

Oracle: There are times in our life when we wonder if we can persevere to the end of some ordeal. After a cold and difficult time, you may now be close to the end of your troubles and sensing that the resolution to your problems is imminent. The reward of relief may prove to be transitory, so enjoy it before you move on with the activity of the new day. You may still have some of the same issues to face, but now there is probably more insight into what changes and shifts in attitude can be made. Awakening energies are signaling new beginnings. Taking your shoes off and walking on the grass in the early morning is said to be very good for the soul.

Keywords: Refreshment after "the dark night of the soul." Dawn meditations bringing new starts and new inspiration. Dew. Water dripping from trees. The dawning of a new day and the relief that it can bring. Changing of the guard. Natural progression. Inheritances. Exhalted feelings of release. Droplets on spiderwebs.

The Caution: Not letting go of difficult situations. Persisting with problems that could have been solved. Feeling that the worst is going to happen, even though things are lightening up. Being afraid of the night. Staying up all night, being upset or unable to sleep. Gloominess. Staying in bed well into the day. Leaving the light on all night.

What does this **SYMBOL** say to *you?*

CHILDREN ON A SWING IN THE SAFETY OF A HUGE OAK TREE

Leo 11

Commentary: "Children on a Swing in the Safety of a Huge Oak Tree" brings to mind images of "Children" playing, having fun together and being protected by the big branches of the "Huge Oak Tree." "Oak Trees" infer enormous strength. The "Oak's" strength, the hardness and durability of the timber, and its long life give the "Oak" a special significance. In England, the oak has been referred to as the "Monarch of the Forest." Cowthorpe Oak in Yorkshire can hold 70 people in its hollow. It is said to be over 1,600 years old. The Ellerslie Oak, near Paisley, is reported to have sheltered Sir William Wallace and 300 of his men. Honour Oak, Whitchurch, Tavistock, was the place where money was left in exchange for food during the cholera epidemic of 1832.

Oracle: It is easier to enjoy carefree, childlike play when one's "Safety" and care is assured. Protective environments are the places where playgrounds can be created. In this Symbol it is the very structure of the things around you or even your particular location that provides the "Safety" that's needed. By the very nature of things, safe surroundings can take care of everyone. Institutions like the Social Security system are similar to the "Oak Tree." Religions and social organizations can also provide this protected environment for people. In general, it is security and protection that needs to be afforded to us for us to follow our true path. Look for the stability and strength in your situation, and expand your wishes and dreams into that protected environment. This Symbol can indicate being relieved from responsibility. This is a good time to relax into playing with others. Feel "Safe" in the knowledge that everything will remain secure. Keep in touch with the innocence and openness of youthful play.

Keywords: Creativity in safe surroundings. Being protected and privileged. Social security and other forms of governmental protection. Agencies that bring food, education and basic needs to children in difficult circumstances. Children, trees, grass, swings, parks. Amusement parks. Childhood memories. Climbing trees. Spontaneous activity. Humanitarian agencies. Security coming through family. Safe confines.

The Caution: Expecting others to take all the responsibility while one just plays. Children not being looked after. Disadvantaged people. Desertion by government and big business. Not wanting to grow up. Always relying on others to provide fun, safety or shelter.

What does this **SYMBOL** say to *you?*

I sit beneath your leaves, old oak,
You mighty one of all the trees;
Within whose hollow trunk a
* man*
Could stable his big horse with
* ease.*
W. H. Davies

One that would have the fruit
must climb the tree.
Thomas Fuller

Woodman, spare that tree!
Touch not a single bough! In
youth it sheltered me, and I'll
protect it now.
George Pope Morris

The forest laments in order that
Mr. Gladstone may perspire.
Sir Randolph Churchill

One generation plants the trees;
another gets the shade.
Chinese Proverb

Train up a fig tree in the way it
should go, and when you are old
sit under the shade of it.
Charles Dickens

Cut not the bough that thou
standest upon.
Romanian Proverb

The public good is in nothing
more essentially interested
than in the protection of every
individual's private rights.
William Blackstone

Leo 12

If I shall sell both my forenoons and afternoons to society, as most appear to do, I'm sure that, for me, there would be nothing left worth living for.
Henry David Thoreau

Ever notice that Soup for One is eight aisles away from the party mix?
Elayne Boosler

There is only one thing in the world worse than being talked about, and that is not being talked about.
Oscar Wilde

Giving parties is a trivial avocation, but it pays the dues for my union card in humanity.
Elsa Maxwell

Existence is a party. You join after it's started and you leave before it's finished.
Elsa Maxwell

Living in New York is like being at some terrible late-night party. You're tired, you've had a headache since you arrived, but you can't leave because then you'd miss the party.
Simon Hoggart

The cocktail party is easily the worst invention since castor oil.
Elsa Maxwell

AN EVENING GARDEN PARTY OF ADULTS

Commentary: "An Evening Garden Party of Adults" is an image of people relaxing, chatting and getting to know each other. Enjoying time spent with friends, family or neighbors can bring new depths to relationships and community. It can also lead to meeting new people and the networking of ideas. Gossip often comes up at "An Evening Garden Party." People talk about each other, swapping tales of their own and other people's lives. As long as it is not harmful or malicious, gossip can be a valuable part of the weaving of society. Talking together about one's life, each other and, indeed, those not present, can lead to a deeper understanding of our lives and provides the chance to catch up on what people have been doing. Socializing and chatting is part of the way we keep in contact with the news of the day.

Oracle: This Symbol signifies taking a much-needed break from work. Give the rigors of your work routine a rest. Relaxation among your peers, where there is no need for exuberant pretense, can do nothing but good. Remember to live in the moment, enjoying this time out from care and trouble. It's important to give time and energy to your social life as it can refresh you and lead to new friendships and contacts. However, too much ambition, or trying to compete with others on a social level can make it hard to relax and truly enjoy yourself and can alienate others. If you don't feel that you fit in with the group, remain composed and wait it out. You may have to put on a socially acceptable or brave face and go along with whatever's expected. If this is the case, fulfill your role for the time being. It won't be long before you're back in your own space again. Whatever, fill your cup, have a bite to eat and relax with friends.

Keywords: Rising above superficiality into receptivity and peace with others. People mixing in a social setting. Sedate and conservative celebrations. Formal events vs. impromptu gatherings. Gossip. Leisure time. Political correctness. Enjoying socializing. Being a good conversationalist. Drinks and food on platters. Knowing who to invite.

The Caution: A sense of superficiality where things are known but not said out loud. Appearance and social standing taking on too much importance. Ignoring real and immediate issues. Not knowing how to act with the "adults." Malicious gossip. Having to face those you don't want to see. Getting drunk and "out of bounds." False fronts.

What does this **SYMBOL** say to *you?*

AN OLD SEA CAPTAIN ROCKING ON THE PORCH OF HIS COTTAGE

Leo 13

Commentary: "An Old Sea Captain" is "Rocking on the Porch of His Cottage." This Symbol is an image of someone who has put a lot of time and energy into his life's work. He has now reached the point where he can take time out to rest and relax. However, being an "Old Sea Captain," the love of the sea and adventure will be with him forever. He may or may not be retired; whatever, he is taking a break. He has a chance to get on with more domestic matters and to seek peace and quiet "on the Porch of His Cottage."

Oracle: There is a need for quiet reflection, to look back at past experiences, especially those times that may have seemed threatening. Take some time for a little solitude and to contemplate the overall picture before you. When you are back into the business of life, you will be more relaxed and have a better idea of how you fit into the big picture. Feeling tired and reluctant to get on with work can lead to feelings of failure and missed opportunities. You may need to take time out to contemplate your home and environment and how you fit in. Perhaps jotting down your memoirs can bring the missed and more dramatic moments back into you mind. Even if things seem quiet now, it is probably only you holding yourself back from more exciting adventures. The minute you feel like getting back to it, do it. You'll be surprised by how easy it can be to get back into the swing of things. For now, enjoying the "Porch" or the garden of your home can lead to inner calm and quiet after many years of work, struggles or difficulty.

Keywords: Retreating into one's self. Reflecting. Quiet confidence. Knowing that one can conquer life's storms and come out wiser. Observing life from afar. Wanting to opt out. Retirement, pensions and pension plans. Being dismissed from one's job. Redundancy. The story of one's life. Memoirs. Rocking chairs and verandas. Contemplation. Gardening. Longing for calmer days. Letters, diaries, photographs. Houses, cottages. Taking a break from society.

The Caution: Ignoring what is happening in favor of memories. Inability to get going. Disconnecting from reality. Feeling lazy. The world owes you a living. Feeling jaded and worn out. Envying those who are "out there" in the world. Wanting others to look after you. Complacency. Giving in and giving up. Hangovers. Forgetfulness. Feeling impotent. Being uninvolved. Opting out before one's time.

What does this **SYMBOL** say to *you?*

Millions long for immortality but do not know what to do with themselves on a rainy Sunday afternoon.
Susan Ertz

Praise the sea; on shore remain.
John Florio

Would you learn the secret of the sea? Only those who brave its dangers comprehend its mystery!
Henry Wadsworth Longfellow

Absence of occupation is not rest. A mind quite vacant is a mind distressed.
William Cowper

I pant for retirement and leisure, but am doomed to inexpressible and almost unsupportable hurry.
Sarah Siddons

People are always asking me when I'm going to retire. Why should I? I've got it two ways— I'm still making movies, and I'm a senior citizen, so I can see myself at half price.
George Burns

Alone, alone, all, all alone, alone on a wide, wide sea!
Samuel Taylor Coleridge

Leo 14

Let us be silent, that we may hear the whispers of the gods.
Ralph Waldo Emerson

In prayer, it is better to have a heart without words than words without heart.
Mahatma Gandhi

It is the still, small voice that the soul heeds, not the deafening blasts of doom.
William Dean Howells

What I like in a good author isn't what he says, but what he whispers.
Logan Pearsall Smith

The strongest muscle in the body is the tongue.
Trivia.net

Let not thy will roar when thy power can but whisper.
Thomas Fuller

The urge for self-actualization.
Dane Rudhyar

When hearts listen, angels sing.
Anonymous

You called me, you shouted to me, you broke past my defenses.
St. Augustine

CHERUB-LIKE, A HUMAN SOUL WHISPERS INTO EVERY RECEPTIVE EAR, SEEKING TO MANIFEST

Commentary: "Cherub-Like, a Human Soul Whispers into Every Receptive Ear, Seeking to Manifest" is a Symbol of the desire to be heard and taken seriously. This "Human Soul" is trying to find a "Receptive Ear," someone who will listen to or understand what's being said, perhaps to spur others to take some kind of action. Something that has been waiting to be "Manifested," said, heard or realized could come out quite suddenly.

Oracle: There is likely to be a deep realization that will transform your life on some level. The time may not be quite right, but it is coming soon. Your creative or spiritual talents are attempting to come through into conscious expression. Listening to your inner voice, and heeding messages from others, can lead you to the next level of your life. On the spiritual level, this Symbol shows the movement of the "Soul" to new possibilities and opportunities. On the more everyday level, it can imply that in order to find those who wish to join our process or task, ideas need to be communicated in a quiet and suggestive manner, rather than being loud and demanding. Often when there's a new idea in the air, many people seemingly come up with it at the same time. This can be rather astounding; it's time for this new thing to "Manifest" and those who are "Receptive" to the message will hear and respond. However, if the messages coming through are not clear, intelligent or useful, it may lead to wild goose chases and extremes of behavior. Parts of the mind can come tearing out—wishing to make themselves heard or known. Discriminate between what's important and what's not. Listen to messages; something is seeking expression and needs a vehicle to be able to "Manifest." Are you the "vehicle"?

Keywords: New realizations and impulses. Seeking to have one's voice heard. Messages from the other side. Reincarnation. Channeling information. Spirit descending, wishing to make itself known. Whispering. Passing on news and messages. Seeking embodiment. Transpersonal urges. Cherubs and spirits. Ears and hearing. The urge to accomplish something. Compassion. Manifesting intention.

The Caution: Confusing voices. Signs of instability or madness. Feeling that if one isn't heard, they will miss out. A need to be noticed and acknowledged. Not feeling like one can speak up. Shouting and making a spectacle. Trying to convince others of something. Misleading statements.

What does this **SYMBOL** say to *you?*

A STREET PAGEANT MOVING ALONG A STREET PACKED WITH PEOPLE

♌ Leo 15

Commentary: The "Street Pageant" is seen "Moving along a Street Packed with People." People really enjoy a "Street Pageant" or a carnival, they get together to celebrate their community, even if they aren't directly involved in what's being celebrated. Just watching the "Street Pageant" can inspire fun, joy and even a sense of pride as people come out to watch and enjoy.

Oracle: It may be a great achievement, or an anniversary event, that has spurred this "Street Pageant." A large celebration can bring the community together and create some type of recognition for what has been accomplished. Most people will contribute to and support this display and share in the festivities. However, there will always be those who grumble about something: a lack of parking, too much noise or garbage being strewn about. Ignore the grumblers and go for it, you and others deserve the fun and the rewards. You are either in the "Pageant" or watching it—what does it feel like to you? Are you celebrating and enjoying the fun? Are you feeling a little out of your depth and at the mercy of the people around you? Is there disagreement over the values of what's being celebrated? If things get out of hand in this situation, you may feel like you're pressed in and can't get out. There can be a feeling of being walled in by people. Whatever is true, put on a happy and expressive face and go out and enjoy what's going on. If people let down their barriers, they will find it easier to relate to others they may have never seen or interacted with before. This can create a wonderful feeling of unity as people join in and come together as one.

Keywords: Demonstrations of joy. Spectacular shows of solidarity. Ticker-tape parades. Community celebrations of victory or faith. Food and drink stalls. Mardi gras and gay pride parades. Being a participant or an observer. Having a following. Gaiety and spectacle. Performers, musicians, magicians. Street stalls. Traffic management. The mob. Lots of people. Cul de sacs. Carnivals.

The Caution: Egocentric displays. Blowing one's trumpet. Closing off some areas of life, overplaying others. Problems with neighbors or people. Displays with little warmth or genuine communal feelings. Feeling like sardines in a can. Noisy neighborhoods. Loud music that annoys. Disruptive behavior. Hooligans and louts. Looting. Lack of privacy and quiet. Garbage on the street. Barriers between people.

What does this **SYMBOL** say to *you?*

You see someone on the street, and essentially what you notice about them is the flaw.
Diane Arbus

Industrial societies turn their citizens into image-junkies; it is the most irresistible form of mental pollution. Poignant longings for beauty, for an end to probing below the surface, for a redemption and celebration of the body of the world.
Susan Sontag

The parade was here, but it disappeared around a corner.
Mason Cooley

I live in a one-way dead-end street.
Bumper Sticker

Every crowd has a silver lining.
P. T. Barnum

We learn about one another's culture the same way we learn about sex: in the streets.
Ishmael Reed

Everything being a constant carnival, there is no carnival left.
Victor Hugo

Leo 16

If we had no winter, the spring would not be so pleasant. If we did not sometimes taste of adversity, prosperity would not be so welcome.
Anne Bradstreet

Most of the shadows of this life are caused by standing in one's own sunshine.
Ralph Waldo Emerson

Where there is sunshine, there is also shade.
Kashmiri Proverb

The world goes up and the world goes down,
And the sunshine follows the rain;
And yesterday's sneer and yesterday's frown,
Can never come over again.
Charles Kingsley

The hopeful man sees success where others see failure, sunshine where others see shadows and storm.
Orison Swett Marsden

All sunshine makes the desert.
Saudi Arabian Proverb

The wise man in the storm prays to God, not for safety from danger, but for deliverance from fear.
Ralph Waldo Emerson

BRILLIANT SUNSHINE JUST AFTER A STORM

Commentary: "Brilliant Sunshine Just after a Storm" shows the relief and joy that can result after a "Storm" has come through, sweeping away many of the elements that have been clogging the environment. "After a Storm" the "Sunshine" can appear more "Brilliant" than it usually does. In fact, the light can appear to be rather mystical and eerie. The moisture still in the air acts to amplify and intensify light, hence, everything around looks more vivid and beautiful especially compared to how it seemed during the "Storm." Things that felt threatening or charged up can dissolve and disappear, sometimes very quickly. The remaining "mist" of an emotional "Storm" can cause intense, positive emotions as the weather and the atmosphere clear up and the birds start to sing again and life gets back to normal.

Oracle: This Symbol indicates a clearing of the air and the resolving of issues that have been building up. The "Sunshine" shows that the worst is probably over and at last the situation can resolve and recovery begin. There is probably still work to be done, but for now enjoy the release and the pleasure of renewal. Bask in the sunlight a little and then get on with the work of mopping or cleaning up the remnants. Another aspect of this Symbol can show a situation that goes to and fro in extremes, finding it hard to strike a happy medium. Perhaps you need to try to avoid such extremes, and work on achieving a more constant state of well-being. Sometimes we need sadness to fully appreciate happiness and, vice versa. Enjoy the "Sunshine"—you've come through the "Storm."

Keywords: The warmth of renewal. Things glistening with raindrops. Extremes. Recovery. Hallucinogenic drugs. Extreme weather, e.g., El Niño. Religious experiences. Brighter worlds. Optimistic feelings after hopes dashed. Relief and joy. The sun breaking through clouds. Overcoming crisis. The longing for rain to quench dryness. Floods of emotion. Negative ions bringing relief. Rainbows. Brilliant light that brings joy.

The Caution: Assuming that the storm will soon return. Being stuck in fear. Manic depression. Distorted viewpoints. Bouncing around from one emotion to another. Invoking arguments because of the reward of "making up." Enjoyment of conflict. Plumbing problems. Refusing to move into the sunlight. Bipolar behavior. On-off behavior.

What does this **SYMBOL** say to *you?*

VOLUNTEER CHURCH CHOIR MAKES SOCIAL EVENT OF A REHEARSAL

Leo 17

Commentary: The "Volunteer Church Choir" is pictured here. They come together to make a "Social Event of a Rehearsal." Although their voices will often hit the right pitch, sometimes they won't. As they are a "Volunteer Church Choir," the issue is not the quality of people's voices or being able to hold a tune, but more the sharing of voices and the enjoyment that such gatherings can bring. Criticism of how folks "sing" should be left at the door. Each and every person should be encouraged to contribute what they can, to raise his or her voice in a celebration of spiritual unity and the enjoyment of life.

Oracle: You may feel the need to be with those of like mind, feelings and aspirations. Take the opportunity to share in their expression of spiritual joy and shared faith. Unified voices need to be heard, and can uplift all who hear them. Coming together to contribute to the community without thought of more tangible rewards will bring a sense of belonging and fellowship on many levels. Bringing even the smallest tokens and gifts to the gathering will be appreciated in some way. Helpers may be required to come to the aid of others. There may be a need to test things out to see if they stand up to reality. Whether you receive rewards or are paid for the work you do or not, there may be a need to inject more fun and lightheartedness. Ultimately, if everyone is comfortable and friendly with each other, communication and the quality of work will improve. Even a gesture such as drinks after work can bring people closer together. Overall, everybody should feel happy to be around people of like mind; not pressured to put in a top-rate performance.

Keywords: Making the most of any situation. Feelings of togetherness. Rehearsing without worrying about what might happen. Doing things without thought of reward. Sharing community. Catching up on what others are doing. Busking and street singing. Learning to open up the throat. Charity work. Volunteers. Sharing food and drink. Small gifts for others. Dedication to ideals. Extending yourself by mixing in. Gatherings. Church or school halls.

The Caution: Trivializing the purpose of gatherings. Being afraid or reticent to lift up one's voice. Standing in the background because of the belief that one is not "good" enough to join in. Criticizing others for not contributing enough. Feeling ripped off. Issues of being "in the club."

What does this **SYMBOL** say to *you?*

We do not exist for ourselves.
Thomas Merton

You give but little when you give of your possessions. It is when you give of yourself that you truly give.
Kahlil Gibran

Poor is the church without music.
Irish Saying

The first time I sang in the church choir, two hundred people changed their religion.
Fred Allen

Time is important to me because I want to sing long enough to leave a message. I'm used to singing in churches where nobody would dare stop me until the Lord arrives!
Mahalia Jackson

Please do not shoot the piano player; he's doing the best that he can.
Anonymous

The choir always tittered and whispered all through the service. There was once a church choir that was not ill-bred, but I have forgotten where it was.
Mark Twain

Leo 18

Observation is a passive science, experimentation an active science.
Claude Bernard

Everybody's a mad scientist, and life is their lab. We're all trying to experiment to find a way to live, to solve problems, to fend off madness and chaos.
David Cronenberg

A theory can be proved by experiment; but no path leads from experiment to the birth of a theory.
Albert Einstein

I have nothing new to teach the world. Truth and nonviolence are as old as the hills. All I have done is to try experiments in both on as vast a scale as I could.
Mahatma Gandhi

I have not failed. I've just found 10,000 ways that won't work.
Thomas Alva Edison

The true scientist never loses the faculty of amusement. It is the essence of his being.
J. Robert Oppenheimer

The fatal futility of fact.
Henry James

A CHEMIST CONDUCTS AN EXPERIMENT FOR HIS STUDENTS

Commentary: A "Chemist" is shown "Conducting an Experiment for His Students." Chemistry is the manipulation of elements of nature to create better or more valuable things. It is through our consciousness that we manipulate our environment. Through these efforts and the "accidents" that can happen, we come closer to an understanding of creation and perhaps an experience of God. The "Chemist" requires the right ingredients and equipment and his "Students" need to pay attention to what he does. Still, mistakes and miscalculations may occur. On a day-to-day basis, we use tools such as our minds to create awareness. By teaching people what we know, we change our understanding of the nature of our environment. It is likely that the "Chemist" has conducted this particular "Experiment" many times; still, each time it can inspire amazement and awe.

Oracle: The "Chemist" can be someone who is interested in trying something new. Even with all the appropriate credentials and experience, there may be a feeling of being unsure of the actual outcome. However, the "Chemist" may be someone who is not prepared to take any risks and is performing the exact same mix of ingredients, again and again. The creative "Chemist" knows that a mix of new ingredients can lead to new creations, solutions, observations and discoveries. You may find yourself discovering new things in an authoritative or observant position. The message for you in either situation, whether you are the "Chemist" or a "Student," is to pay attention to the small as well as the large details. Be prepared to take a few calculated risks with this situation, it may lead to new and satisfying solutions. Something unexpected and exciting may happen!

Keywords: Alchemy. Stepping out of the usual rules and taking a risk. New and untried procedures. Syllabi and education. Wisdom being passed on. Putting things "to the test." Throwing out what doesn't stand up. Ingredients. Bunsen burners. Test tubes. Microscopes. Seeking rational answers. Science and chemistry. Leading by example. The thrill of discovery.

The Caution: Always going "by the rules of the book," leading to inertia and suppression of creative ideas. Being afraid to take a chance because the situation may get out of control. Refusing to reveal one's formula, lest it be copied. Narrow viewpoints. Skepticism. Being a stickler for conservative science. Not trusting others' abilities. Chemicals that pollute and distort.

What does this **SYMBOL** say to *you?*

A HOUSEBOAT PARTY CROWDED WITH REVELERS; THE WATER REFLECTS ITS LIGHTS

Leo 19

Commentary: A "Houseboat Party" is shown. It is "Crowded with Revelers" and "the Water Reflects Its Lights." This pictures a need for lightening up, relaxing and spending time with like-minded individuals. This "Party" can represent a situation where people come together, eat, drink and share their thoughts and have a good time. The partygoers, the "Revelers," may all be enjoying themselves and having a great time, but it may seem rather short-lived, unstable or unreal.

Oracle: Although you are probably in a situation of definite structure and form, you may find that it needs to be changed from the normal routine and infused with unusual and unorthodox possibilities. However, one problem with "Houseboat Parties" is the inability to leave when you please. When you're socializing, seeing a crowd of friendly faces is comforting when you have no choice but to stay. If you are not enjoying what's going on, it may be that you're stuck with people you'd really rather not associate with. Who's steering or in charge of the "Boat" you're on? How long is this journey, and where will the "Houseboat Party" end up? You may feel a long way from home, and that you want to get off. If you can relax about the situation you're in, you may find yourself with fabulous friends and in great surroundings. This is often easier said than done—some people are not able to mix with people they're not familiar with, especially if they feel unsure about the circumstances they find themselves in. On a "Houseboat," this can be especially true. This being said, one does have to take risks every now and then. Enjoy the situation to its fullest, but remember that sooner or later you will have to get back to a more everyday, anchored life.

Keywords: Emotive social pleasure. Joining with others in an adventurous spirit. Cleopatra-style parties. The issue of knowing where one's going. Claustrophobia. Being cast adrift. Delicate social balances. Moored in water or on ground. Leisure times that are fun and free floating. People getting "out of it."

The Caution: Trapping people into ideals of pleasure. Self-indulgence. Not knowing "where" the party is going to be or finish up. Not being anchored in reality. Feeling "unmoored" and unable to disembark. Nowhere to permanently dock. Unknown destinations. Feeling trapped. Choppy seas. No one at the wheel. Springing a leak. Wanting to bail out. Tipping the boat.

What does this **SYMBOL** say to *you?*

These three take crooked ways: carts, boats, and musicians.
Hindu Proverb

We may have all come on different ships, but we're in the same boat now.
Martin Luther King, Jr.

Are we having fun yet?
Modern Saying

Are we there yet?
Modern Saying

There are some sluggish men who are improved by drinking; as there are fruits that are not good until they are rotten.
Samuel Johnson

So let's fill up our heads with ping-pong balls and go out and shoot the moon.
Paul Smyth

Here we are, going down the river like Antony and Cleopatra on that barge.
The African Queen

Let's have one other gaudy night: call to me all my sad captains; fill our bowls once more; let's mock the midnight bell.
William Shakespeare

Leo 20

Life is a pure flame, and we live by an invisible sun within us.
Thomas Browne

What is to give light must endure burning.
Viktor Frankl

The beauty of the world and the orderly arrangement of everything celestial makes us confess that there is an excellent and eternal nature, which ought to be worshipped and admired by all mankind.
Marcus Tullius Cicero

Hide not your talents, they for use were made. What's a sundial in the shade?
Benjamin Franklin

Be glad of life because it gives you a chance to love and to work and to play and to look up at stars.
Henry Van Dyke

An odd thing occurs in the minds of Americans when Indian civilization in mentioned: little or nothing.
Paula Gunn Allen

AMERICAN INDIANS PERFORM A RITUAL TO THE SUN

Commentary: "American Indians" are pictured here "Performing a Ritual to the Sun." Twice a year, each tribe performs a sun dance, a sacred ritual that is held over four days and honors grandfather sun and the four directions. The people respect and revere both their society and the natural environment. The warriors of the tribe endure trials of pain and endurance to prove their strength, stamina and ability to protect those in their care. They gather together with kindred spirits to pay homage to the natural elements that sustain them in their lives. They do this to get back to the natural elements; they respond with their intuitive feelings rather than logic. In our everyday modern lives there's a tendency to forget to take time out to "Perform" grounding "Rituals."

Oracle: The "Sun" in this "Ritual" can relate to one's sense of selfhood, identity and ego. A good, healthy sense of self and ego is wonderful and should be celebrated. There can be a feeling of belonging to a culture with shared visions, regardless of whether you actually come from it. However, it is possible that someone in this situation has been caught up in the glamor of "Ritual," ignoring the true purpose of it. Perhaps there is a need to draw the ego back into perspective, especially if it has become over-inflated. Traditional "Rituals," or ceremonies, can inspire people to action. They often bring renewal and relief to people, and solutions to situations. Tools like affirmations and meditation are useful to clarify goals and ambitions. It is important, however, not to merely rely on "Rituals" to magically produce what we want. Use these methods to enhance and contribute meaning to your life. Take a moment to remember your relationships with the earth and her people.

Keywords: Restoring spirit. Rituals and worship. The desire to return to nature. Shining through one's life, not through social credentials. Sweat lodges. Drum-beating. Celebrating a unique heritage. Participation with nature's cycles. Eclipses. Smudging. Reveling in the larger picture leading to belonging and oneness. Fire, passion, spontaneity, sacrifice. Restoring sacredness. American Indian traditions. Vision quests. Fasting. Courage. Conquering bad habits and attitudes. The truth of conviction. Prayer. Eagle feathers. Baptisms of fire.

The Caution: Egoistic responses to life situations leading to narrow responses. Relying on rituals to manifest magic. Losing sight of the meaning of ceremony. Holding on to tradition without intuiting new and modern truths. Living in the past. Cult worship. Losing identity in one's own culture. Sunstroke.

What does this **SYMBOL** say to *you?*

INTOXICATED CHICKENS DIZZILY FLAP THEIR WINGS TRYING TO FLY

Commentary: "Intoxicated Chickens Dizzily Flap Their Wings Trying to Fly" is a rather amusing image. The "Intoxicated Chickens" have been fired up by something, or eaten some seed that has become fermented. Having been "Intoxicated," they are "Dizzily Flapping Their Wings Trying to Fly." They have forgotten their true limitations and are trying to do more than they are usually physically capable of. This Symbol can indicate things such as giddiness, mistakes, headaches and regrets from ill-conceived projects.

Oracle: This Symbol can indicate somebody actually losing their sense of reality, or their sensible mind. One's first attempts at a new experience may prove less than elegant or skillful. There is possibly an attempt to do too much too soon. Perhaps you have not thoroughly planned what you want to achieve. Trying to accomplish something a little too eagerly and before the proper training has been completed can get you nowhere, no matter how much energy and enthusiasm is expended. Making a list of long and short-term goals will help to clarify your ideas. Soon things will improve and you can laugh about the mishaps and mistakes that were made when you started out. Being confused, or "Intoxicated," can be solved relatively easily, with some constraint. Further, it can be drink or drugs that caused this "Intoxication," or it can be unrestrained happiness and enthusiasm. Moderate any or all of these factors and you will gain a clearer vision and have a deeper focus on your situation. Either way, try not to worry about how much is actually being achieved. Right now, find enjoyment in this "Intoxication," but remember to come back to earth when the feelings diminish.

Keywords: False courage. Inexperience. Trying to do something beyond the bounds of experience or possibility. Getting "out of it" in order to escape something. Getting all worked up over tiny or illusive prospects. Alcohol and drugs and the allure of escapism. Drinking binges. Ecstasy. Hangovers. Attempting to do the impossible.

The Caution: Giddiness, lightheadedness, unwanted side effects. Getting nowhere. Inability to ground things in reality. Making a fool of one's self. Intoxication that inhibits seeing what's really possible. Alcoholism and drug habits. Losing reality. Mindlessness that confuses or misleads. Going too far too fast. Forgetting who or where you are.

What does this **SYMBOL** say to *you?*

The very best addictive drugs are produced by our bodies when we're in romantic/erotic love.
Barbara Sher

I like liquor—its taste and its effects—and that is just the reason why I never drink it.
Stonewall Jackson

When the wine is in, the wit is out.
Thomas Becon

We never really know what stupidity is until we have experimented on ourselves.
Paul Gauguin

When a man is intoxicated by alcohol, he can recover, but when intoxicated by power, he seldom recovers.
James F. Byrnes

The young are permanently in a state resembling intoxication; for youth is sweet and they are growing.
Aristotle

The aim of life is to live, and to live means to be aware, joyously, drunkenly, serenely, divinely aware.
Henry Miller

Leo 22

Here is the test to find whether your mission on earth is finished: If you're alive, it isn't.
Richard Bach

That's one small step for man, one giant leap for mankind.
Neil Armstrong

I got the message. All of us get the message, sooner or later. If you get it before it's too late or before you're too old, you'll pull through all right.
Nat King Cole

Whenever you have truth it must be given with love, or the message and the messenger will be rejected.
Mahatma Gandhi

When you discover your mission, you will feel its demand. It will fill you with enthusiasm and a burning desire to get to work on it.
W. Clement Stone

Don't shoot the messenger.
Old Saying

A CARRIER PIGEON FULFILLING ITS MISSION

Commentary: "A Carrier Pigeon Fulfilling Its Mission" shows the completion of a task—delivering a message or completing a voyage or "Mission." There is a clear sense of purpose and direction, even a sense of some divine guidance. "Carrier Pigeons" have a magnetic compass that allows them to know where they are and where they are going. They can pinpoint their destination exactly. Knowing and finding the route to their destination is a natural part of the "Pigeon's" life.

Oracle: This Symbol shows that you may have to let your natural relationship with the environment guide you intuitively and instinctively. We are most naturally inclined to follow a meaningful path if we just allow ourselves to respond to our inner guidance. It often feels strange to release control or inhibitions and to just "go with the flow," but this is not a meaningless and directionless destination. As this "Pigeon" is "Fulfilling Its Mission" you know that the end is in sight, and there is a prize to be won for bringing a message to those who need it. The reward can be financial, emotional, or otherwise somehow personally gratifying. The "Carrier Pigeon" needs to deliver a message or bridge distances between people. However, this "Mission" may not necessarily be positive or personally rewarding. The message being conveyed may be harmful or malicious gossip or merely useless information. In that case, the outcome may be less than desirable. This Symbol shows the importance of messages getting through to those who need to hear them. A special job that one must fulfill can lead to having a sense of duty or place. Whatever the "Mission" is, this Symbol indicates that done well, with love and awareness, it will be "Fulfilled" and carried out successfully.

Keywords: Bringer of good tidings and news. Creating lines of communication. Completing tasks. Feeling like one is on a mission. Finding out what's truly going on. Having a sense of destiny. Receiving orders from a higher authority. Being magnetically aligned. Pigeons, doves. Not being put off the track no matter what. Mail. Flying home.

The Caution: Gossip. Messages that are not useful to anyone or are outworn and old. Needing recognition and applause for doing simple things. Useless information. Putting a lot of effort into something that is not worth it. "Stool pigeons." Working until one drops from exhaustion. Being so one-pointed that you forget other parts of your life.

What does this **SYMBOL** say to *you?*

A BAREBACK RIDER IN A CIRCUS DISPLAYS HER DANGEROUS SKILL

Commentary: "A Bareback Rider in a Circus Displays Her Dangerous Skill." She puts herself in the middle of the action, taking risks that are second nature to her. Training has prepared her to perform tricks and maneuvers that seem awe inspiring, well timed and carefully planned. She is so well rehearsed that even the most dangerous stunts are done with ease. These things, however, can be so daring or dangerous that others would have trouble even imagining doing them, let alone actually attempting to do them. She has an amazing sense of balance and belief in her center of gravity.

Oracle: You may believe passionately in what you are doing, but in order to prove yourself to others you need to present your abilities and feelings boldly and skillfully. You may need to be fully prepared to rush into the "ring" and show what you're capable of. This done correctly will impress others, and may cause others to be in awe of your talent and the risks and dangers involved. However, remember to be wary of "running into the ring" unrehearsed, unprepared or in the wrong frame of mind. A sense of timing and the knowledge of what you're doing is critical, as is being unruffled that others may be watching to see how well you succeed. If you have confidence in your abilities, there's a good chance that you won't be "bucked" or "thrown off." You will have the ability to complete your mission and be applauded by others for your achievement. If, however, you are scared stiff of taking on this challenge, do you think you should chance it? If you are merely looking for applause, acclaim or recognition from others, without being sure of what you're doing, this may indeed be a dangerous and foolhardy stunt. Do you feel you have the balance, skills and courage to do what is necessary?

Keywords: Defying gravity. Controlling one's animal instincts. Courage and mastery over one's energies. Shows of strength. Situations where one might get "bucked." Rushing in where angels fear to tread. Being shown in the media. The allure of drama and danger. Life as a circus or carnival. Amazing displays of skill. Superheroes. Comic book characters. Impressing people with well-rehearsed skills.

The Caution: "Showing off," losing control and falling. Demanding attention. Looking for applause. Fooling with nature's energies. Arousing or controlling animal passions. Acting wildly and not thinking about the consequences.

What does this **SYMBOL** say to *you?*

He who rides a tiger is afraid to dismount.
Chinese Proverb

Being on the tightrope is living; everything else is waiting.
Karl Wallenda

I sit astride life like a bad rider on a horse. I only owe it to the horse's good nature that I am not thrown off at this very moment.
Ludwig Wittgenstein

CIRCUS, n. A place where horses, ponies and elephants are permitted to see men, women and children acting the fool.
Ambrose Bierce

I get enough exercise just pushing my luck.
Bumper Sticker

If you can't ride two horses at once, you shouldn't be in the circus.
Proverb

Better ride on an ass that carries me than a horse that throws me.
Romanian Proverb

Will is to grace as the horse is to the rider.
Saint Augustine

No one reaches a high position without daring.
Publilius Syrus

Leo 24

The man whose whole activity is diverted to inner meditation becomes insensible to all his surroundings. His passions are mere appearances, being sterile. They are dissipated in futile imaginings, producing nothing external to themselves.
Emile Durkheim

Self-loving is not so vile a sin, my liege, as self-neglecting.
William Shakespeare

I've never met a healthy person who worried much about his health or a good person who worried much about his soul.
John B. S. Haldane

Meditation has been defined as "the cessation of active external thought."
H. P. Blavatsky

If a man watches three football games in a row, he should be declared legally dead.
Erma Bombeck

Be careless in your dress if you must, but keep a tidy soul.
Mark Twain

In our era, the road to holiness necessarily passes through the world of action.
Dag Hammarskjold

He who conceals his disease cannot expect to be cured.
Proverb

TOTALLY CONCENTRATED UPON INNER SPIRITUAL ATTAINMENT, A MAN IS SITTING IN A STATE OF NEGLECT OF HIS BODY

Commentary: "Totally Concentrated upon Inner Spiritual Attainment, a Man Is Sitting in a State of Neglect of His Body." This brings to mind the Hindu yogi. The yogi can be so focused on his inner state of being that he doesn't notice his more earthly physical needs. He may be able to sit in one position for a very long time, or to use his body in ways that would make others uncomfortable. He may not eat or drink for days. The "Body" may, or may not, actually be "Neglected," but there may be a desire to put the body's needs on hold while he concentrates on more important or immediate spiritual or mental needs and values.

Oracle: There can be a feeling of imbalance at the moment. Some aspects of your life may be put on hold in favor of one central issue that has taken over. This can lead to a loss of holistic balance and, possibly, being misunderstood by others. Being so committed to spiritual or emotional concerns can lead to losing touch with more immediate, physical matters, but it can lead to a higher state of spiritual being. Although spiritual concerns are very important during our lifetime, remember that we also have a physical life to lead. This Symbol can show the opposite polarity: obsession with the body and physical fitness. As human beings, however, we are not supposed to concentrate solely on one or the other. We must strive to live equally in both. Our "Bodies," minds, hearts and spirits are gifts to us, and should be treated with care. When this Symbol is around, it can also indicate people getting a high from not eating, through fasting, etc. It can lead to many physical problems such as eating disorders, etc. However, physical fitness can be achieved by directing the body to do things using willpower and focus. A sense of equilibrium is the key.

Keywords: Issues of how we view and value our bodies. Fixation on exercise and nutrition at the expense of more spiritual or emotional issues. Eating disorders. Gymnasiums and physical fitness issues. Spiritual gurus. Yoga and yogis. Living for the future. Extreme states of meditation. Total concentration. Breatharians.

The Caution: Not enough attention to the body or physical needs. A lack of focus on more immediate issues such as food and exercise or forgetting spiritual, emotional or mental concerns through a focus on the body or physical aspects. Too many things on one's mind. Obsessions leading to imbalance. Not eating or drinking.

What does this **SYMBOL** say to *you?*

A LARGE CAMEL CROSSING A VAST AND FORBIDDING DESERT

Leo 25

Commentary: "A Large Camel Crossing a Vast and Forbidding Desert" is an image of endurance, strength and determination. The "Camel" has the ability to overcome challenges and obstacles to complete a "Vast and Forbidding" journey. The "Large Camel" doesn't realize how amazing and noteworthy this feat of endurance is; he's merely getting on with what he must do. It's part of his nature. Human beings, on the other hand, find going so far on so little reserves in such "Forbidding" conditions very challenging. Further, the "Camel" may also have a rider or a heavy load to carry. It can feel like something almost impossible or too much to ask of somebody.

Oracle: Your situation may already feel like an arduous journey, but there is still probably further to go. Be confident that you have the reserves to survive and the endurance to succeed. It may be that the source of this energy or confidence is stored in someone else. Expecting someone to be there to provide sustenance and revitalization can be a lot to ask of them. It can be a great sacrifice or burden, and it is often a family member or very close friend who will fulfill this duty. The important thing to remember is that this is a long and difficult journey, but whoever is doing it is purposely built for it and capable of achieving it. Issues to do with self-sufficiency may arise. Mental and emotional self-control are very necessary. Another perspective could show someone who's totally comfortable doing the "hard yards." It may look daunting and impossible to others, but to them it is familiar and perhaps even comforting. As the "Camel" is prepared for long stretches in the "Desert," so too are you for the task before you. Make sure you have what you need with you.

Keywords: Completing a journey. Protecting one's self from spiritual "sunstroke." Tests of karma. Taking on daunting tasks. Taking one step at a time. Feeling totally at home. Provisions that nurture and satisfy. Camels, caravans, oases, mirages, water, deserts. Stamina and fortitude. Crossing to the other side. Endurance. Thirst. Survival against the odds. Transport. Bad backs. Back packs. Cargo. Saddling up.

The Caution: Not preparing properly and running out of reserves. Feeling weighed down and in danger of not making it through. Not seeing the big picture. Lack of sustenance. Big plans with no back up. Taking on huge tasks when one shouldn't. Being daunted by huge projects. Mirages that confuse objectives.

What does this **SYMBOL** say to *you?*

What makes the desert beautiful is that somewhere it hides a well.
Antoine de Saint Exupéry

The Promised Land always lies on the other side of a wilderness.
Havelock Ellis

The man who goes alone can start today; but he who travels with another must wait till that other is ready.
Henry David Thoreau

My ancestors wandered lost in the wilderness for forty years because even in biblical times, men would not stop to ask for directions.
Elayne Boosler

Trust in God—but tie your camel tight.
Persian Proverb

Much has been written about the beauty, the stillness, the terror of the desert but little about its flies.
Belle Livingstone

Leo 26

Rain, rain, and sun! A rainbow in the sky!
Lord Alfred Tennyson

Be thou the rainbow to the storms of life, the evening beam that smiles the clouds away, and tints tomorrow with prophetic ray!
Lord Byron

We live in a rainbow of chaos.
Paul Cezanne

Our days and nights Have sorrows woven with delights.
François de Malherbe

Walk on a rainbow trail; walk on a trail of song, and all about you will be beauty. There is a way out of every dark mist, over a rainbow trail.
Navajo Song

The rainbow would be even more beautiful if the show was not for free.
Antilles Proverb

The soul would have no rainbow had the eyes no tears.
John Vance Cheney

AFTER A HEAVY STORM, A RAINBOW APPEARS

Commentary: "After a Heavy Storm, a Rainbow" shows the promise of relief, sunshine and beauty after a difficult passage. The "Rainbow" is a reminder of God's covenant that was made with every living creature of the earth; the promise that He would never flood the world again. The "Storm" may have been difficult to endure with deluges, threatening claps of thunder and lightning and difficult, torrid times. There can be great shocks, but as there is the promise of the "Rainbow," you can be certain that the end result will be okay.

Oracle: Although great obstacles to recovery often arise, for the moment you need to be reassured by signs of better times coming. This can be difficult to believe at first, it can be hard to trust that the "Storm" is not going to swing back around again. Take a look around, when you can, and assess what actual damage has been done by the "Storm." The "Heavy Storm" can inflict such damage and violence that it is hard to imagine things the way they were before it hit. There's a need to focus on hope to help you out of this dilemma, although it can be a struggle to persevere in these situations, and the possibility of a "Rainbow" at the end can seem almost laughable. However, keep in mind that although everyone has to go through the "Storms" and darkness that life throws at us they are rarely permanent. After the difficulties have passed, the calm that follows has a beautiful and "relieved" quality to it. Also, we are far more inclined to appreciate the happy times after we've been through the tempest. It may be time to "smell the roses." Try wearing colorful clothes, opening the windows and getting out into the fresh air. Appreciate the good things that are available right now. Remember, without the "Storm" there would be no possibility of the blessing of the "Rainbow."

Keywords: Release from stressful situations. The light of spirit returning to infuse with energy. Euphoria. Rushes of endorphins. Relief. The sun coming out while dark clouds are still in the air. The joy of survival. Rainbows and light. Piercing through darkness. Reminders of the good things in life. Peace restored.

The Caution: Having selfish thoughts about the rewards inherent in every external sign or "pot of gold." Seeking storms or arguments and trouble to stir things up. Enjoyment and promotion of conflict. Violence and destruction. Carnage. Not seeing the beauty around. Blocked drains and emotions.

What does this **SYMBOL** say to *you?*

DAYBREAK—THE LUMINESCENCE OF DAWN IN THE EASTERN SKY

Leo 27

Commentary: "Daybreak—the Luminescence of Dawn in the Eastern Sky" is a wonderful image of renewal, hope and possibility for the future. This Symbol beautifully illustrates the emergence of light from night to day—there is a "Luminescence in the Eastern Sky." It is the time when night and day both seem to exist at the same time. There is a little of both as the stars are still visible while the light of the sun slowly intensifies and claims the earth.

Oracle: This is a time for making plans, resolutions or meditating on any new tasks that are ahead. It seems there is finally a chance for a new beginning—to start over. Imagination can be strong with expectations and enthusiasm running high. These things can put us in the perfect frame of mind and give us the energy for the "Day" ahead. In regard to your situation, things have been sacrificed and there may be a certain emptiness. Regardless, you must see the light and move forward again. It is now time to stop operating in the dark. New ideas, new opportunities, new perspectives, new realizations are emerging. Don't dwell on what has passed away or what is yet to be. In order to fully realize the potential of this Symbol, try performing some morning rituals. Things like meditation, yoga, tai chi or going for a walk can prepare one's mind and body for the day ahead. These can really awaken both body and spirit. How do you feel when you wake up? This may help you to understand what's lying before you. Recognize the coming of this "Daybreak," this new day, and listen to the birds, watch the beauty of the morning sky and soak up the environment at "Dawn." Something is likely to have changed, even if it is just your perspective.

Keywords: Gradual realization of opportunities. New cycles beginning. Feeling that one can leave the past behind, finally. Transitions between darkness and light. Meditation and yoga. Scenes of awe and amazement. Things slowly being revealed. Dawning awareness. Light from the east. Awakening. Looking to the future. Luminescent light.

The Caution: Being fearful and distrusting new experiences or situations. Thinking that everything will be okay "tomorrow" (i.e., not today). Closing things down when they should be opening up. Feeling like one's asleep and can't wake up. Staying in bed and missing out on new opportunities. Not moving on when it's necessary.

What does this **SYMBOL** say to *you?*

Keep your face to the sunshine and you cannot see the shadows.
Helen Keller

Faith is the bird that feels the light when the dawn is still dark.
Rabindranath Tagore

Only that day dawns to which we are awake. There is more day to dawn. The sun is but a morning star.
Henry David Thoreau

In saffron-colored mantle, from the tides of ocean rose the morning to bring light to gods and men.
Homer

More light!
Goethe—last words

Dawn does not come twice to awaken a man.
Saudi Arabian Proverb

If every day is an awakening, you will never grow old. You will just keep growing.
Gail Sheehy

The sun puts on a wonderful show at daybreak, yet most people in the audience go on sleeping.
Ada Teixeira

Leo 28

The higher you go, the wider the spread of the network of communication that will make or break you. It extends not only to more people below, but to new levels above. And it extends all around, to endless other departments and interests interacting with yours.
Donald Walton

After all is said and done, more is said than done.
American Proverb

All of our operators are busy. Your call is important to us and will be answered by the first available operator.
The constant recurring message of business

The eagle suffers little birds to sing and is not careful what they mean thereby.
William Shakespeare

Gossip is nature's telephone.
Sholom Aleichem

If the first person who answers the phone cannot answer your question it's a bureaucracy. If the first person can answer your question, it's a miracle.
Gerald F. Lieberman

MANY LITTLE BIRDS CHIRPING ON THE LIMB OF A LARGE TREE

Commentary: "Many Little Birds Chirping on the Limb of a Large Tree" is an image of fluttering and chirping, movement and song. The "Tree" can seem packed with chattering and movement and yet the "Birds" can be quite invisible. "Birds" gathering, to chatter is common, particularly at the end of the day. The Symbol can reflect things like advertising, political campaigns, egotistical prattling and even children chatting and playing together.

Oracle: The common element in this Symbol is the attempt to have one's voice heard above all the noise and din of the everyday world. It can be hard to gain the attention of others when there's so much competition around. This also can be true when trying to listen to your own inner voice. It can feel like your needs, or your voice, are just one of so many, with little prospect or ability to have your ideas, opinions or plans heard. Perhaps you have a viewpoint or a project such as a book that you want to get "out there." There may seem to be too many points of view, opinions or options now. Although the overall situation is probably secure and stable, there are still some confusions to be resolved. There may be many people or personalities that one has to deal with or look after. Further, you may be vulnerable to lots of chatter going on in your mind. It can sometimes sound like a cacophony of sound, where the intuitive voice of wisdom is drowned out by noise from the emotional world inside. When this happens it is useful to use a tool, such as the Sabian Symbols, to help you focus on your true objective. Try to relax and gain some perspective until things become a little more settled.

Keywords: Gathering with people of like mind. Sharing ideas. Huge structures where people can get lost in the crowd. Big business, government and bureaucracy. Multilevel marketing. Databases. The Internet and chat groups. Books, tapes and CDs. Publishing houses. Competition. Telephone switchboards. Trying to gain attention.

The Caution: Many voices—some heard, some not. Being confused or immobilized by too much advice or information. Too many sounds. Having trouble hearing the essential truth. A scattering of energies. Not getting a word in edgewise. Everybody talking and nobody listening. Being one of many. Noise and distraction. Staying with the mediocre. The masses. Being invisible. Useless chattering or noise.

What does this **SYMBOL** say to *you?*

A MERMAID HAS CLIMBED TO THE ROCKY SHORE OF A BLEAK COAST; SHE AWAITS THE PRINCE WHO WILL BRING HER IMMORTALITY

Leo 29

Commentary: The "Mermaid Has Climbed to the Rocky Shore of a Bleak Coast," shows a woman who has previously merely existed in the waters of life and is now ready to emerge into a more conscious existence as an individual in her own right. She is willing to "Climb the Rocky Shore" no matter how "Bleak" the "Coast" may be. She may have to leave her home and past behind in order to move into a new life, a new relationship or new beginning of some kind. She will learn to better communicate her emotions, thoughts and ideas. In being able to more fully verbalize and express herself and to "walk her talk," she can find her place and sense of purpose: the "Immortality" that can be achieved in this new reality.

Oracle: You must have belief in your ability to cope as an individual emerging into new arenas. "The Prince Who Will Bring Her Immortality" can show the seeking of perfection in one's self through relationships. Be careful not to project too much authority onto your partner. This can lead to feelings of insecurity and being out of one's depth. You may be expecting others to acknowledge your existence, possibly feeling invisible until they do. However, other people, and probably someone in particular, may bring you insights into your capabilities, talents and attributes so that you can become more of what you're meant to become. The female/mermaid, male/prince doesn't necessarily always translate into these gender definitions. The "Mermaid" may indeed be male, waiting for his "princess" to come to make his life complete. Whichever, how will the partner cope when the "Mermaid" truly gains her own feet and voice? With this new sense of belonging, ideas can be brought into reality in a new world of experience.

Keywords: Coming into conscious form. New ways of being. Transformation. New forms emerging out of the past. Needing, and probably expecting, recognition. Feeling different from the crowd. Learning to stand on your own two feet. Problems with feet and legs. Longing to make an impression.

The Caution: Focusing on social or rational aspects before being ready. Naïveté. Being thrown in the deep end. Relying on relationships too much. Looking to the other for validation of one's existence. Codependent behavior.

What does this **SYMBOL** say to *you?*

I feel my immortality over sweep all pains, all tears, all time, all fears—and peal, like the eternal thunders of the deep, into my ears, this truth; thou livest forever!
Lord Byron

Hope is the expectation that something outside of ourselves, something or someone external, is going to come to our rescue and we will live happily ever after.
Dr. Robert Anthony

Higher than the question of our duration is the question of our deserving. Immortality will come to such as are fit for it, and he would be a great soul in future must be a great soul now.
Ralph Waldo Emerson

I don't want to achieve immortality through my work ... I want to achieve it through not dying.
Woody Allen

If a man carefully examines his thoughts he will be surprised to find how much he lives in the future. His wellbeing is always ahead. Such a creature is probably immortal.
Ralph Waldo Emerson

Leo 30

Please excuse the length of this letter; I do not have time to be brief.
Anonymous

Better than a thousand useless words is one single word that gives peace. Better than a thousand useless verses is one single verse that gives peace. Better than a hundred useless poems is one single poem that gives peace.
The Dhammapada

Afraid lest he be caught up in a net of words, tripped up, bewildered and so defeated— thrown aside—a man hesitates to write down his innermost convictions.
William Carlos Williams

It is wise to disclose what cannot be concealed.
Johann Friedrich Von Schiller

A writer is dear and necessary for us only in the measure of which he reveals to us the inner workings of his very soul.
Count Leo Tolstoy

Never write a letter while you are angry.
Chinese Proverb

A secret is like a dove: when it leaves my hand it takes wing.
Arabian Proverb

AN UNSEALED LETTER HAS VITAL AND CONFIDENTIAL INFORMATION

Commentary: "An Unsealed Letter" is an image of words or thoughts, letters, notes or messages. They have been written, but as the "Letter" is "Unsealed," they have not been "Sealed" in an envelope. "Vital and Confidential Information" implies that important messages and information may need to be concealed from others. Being "Unsealed" shows that it is possible that others would want to peek at (or be shown) what's been said or written. There could be important papers lying around, or perhaps they are lost among other papers and proving difficult to find. It is possible that this "Information" could be seen by the wrong eyes.

Oracle: Getting your thoughts down on paper can lead to greater understandings about people and situations. If there is a message that you wish to spread, you will be able to do it as long as you make the effort to put it into reality. When this is done out in the open anyone can, and will, benefit from it. Communicating in a trusting, carefree way leads to doubts being dispelled. However, are your ideas, thoughts and emotions feeling exposed because you have been too trusting and "worn your heart on your sleeve"? Pausing to reflect can be advantageous. Sometimes we have very strong feelings about a person or a situation, but caution is called for as these can change with time. You may regret someone having seen or learned what's been on your mind. The "Information" in the "Unsealed Letter" can be messages, thoughts or ideas that have been thought through and are now being translated to the written word. This also shows writing books, articles, e-mails along with verbal messages of all kinds. The "Vital and Confidential Information" is obviously something important. Should it be shared with all or only a few? Remember to employ integrity in all that is said and thought.

Keywords: Wearing your heart on your sleeve. Shared thoughts and feelings. Declaring what needs to be said. "Dear John" letters. Laying one's self on the line through writing things down. Diaries. Letters. Penmanship. Messages of intent. Things said out loud. Confidences.

The Caution: Playing games with information. Pretending to conceal for the purposes of deceit. Blurting things out. Not giving any indication of what's being thought. Being upset about having things out in the open. Passing on the secrets of others. Revealing things that shouldn't be revealed.

What does this **SYMBOL** say to *you?*

IN A PORTRAIT, THE BEST OF A MAN'S TRAITS AND CHARACTER ARE IDEALIZED

Virgo 1

Commentary: "In a Portrait, the Best of a Man's Traits and Character Are Idealized" is an image of a person shown, or portrayed, in a painting, drawing, story or photograph; with the good features highlighted and the negative factors left out. This may be a positive thing, or it may miss the true characteristics of the person. Our face is nature's "name tag"; it tells something about our personality, our temperament and race. Having features that make one stand out in the crowd can be a good or a negative thing, depending on one's situation, viewpoint or beliefs.

Oracle: You may need to remind yourself of the true features of the situation before you. Is the "true picture"—the "Man's Traits"—allowing true beauty to be seen? If so, someone is presenting him- or herself with integrity and distinction. However, we sometimes analyze others based on a superficial or "Idealized" image we have of them. This can distort the truth. When we do this, we are often really just projecting our own thoughts, or desires, on to them. If someone is "good looking," do we appraise them differently from others whom we think are not? If people have facial disfigurations, do we consider that they are somehow "lesser"? Be wary of "judging a book by its cover." However, it may be necessary to look for the best in a situation or person, and avoid the more undesirable factors. What lies within may be different from what's apparent on the surface. Studying someone's face, or how they look, for visual clues to who they are can lead to accurate conclusions, if you know how to look for the "right" things. Sometimes we make up stories or have fantasies about people so that we can justify thinking better or worse of them. What is the picture of the situation facing you? Do you feel it is an honest representation of what's going on, or is something being covered up?

Keywords: Projection of beauty. Drawings, paintings, photographs, etc. Art, cosmetics, beauty salons. Hairstyles. Elevated thoughts or memories. Taking someone at face value. Visual senses and clues. Recognition. Caricatures of people. Highlighting features. "Identikit" drawings. Visual prototypes. Profiles. Face reading. Written reviews and references. Viewpoints.

The Caution: Not truly assessing people. Vanity. Superficial judgments. Propaganda. Misleading appearances. Tagging people with labels. Misidentifications. Taking someone the wrong way. Seeing only the best, or the worst. Preconceived beliefs. Feeling misunderstood. Prejudice. Projections.

What does this **SYMBOL** say to *you?*

Every artist dips his brush in his own soul, and paints his own nature into his pictures.
Henry Ward Beecher

A man finds room in the few square inches of the face for the traits of all his ancestors, for the expression of all his history, and his wants.
Ralph Waldo Emerson

Did you ever see a portrait of a great man without perceiving strong traits of pain and anxiety?
John Adams

A man must be strong enough to mold the peculiarity of his imperfections into the perfection of his peculiarities.
Walter Rathenau

Throughout the centuries, man has considered himself beautiful. I rather suppose that man only believes in his own beauty out of pride; that he is not really beautiful and he suspects this himself; for why does he look on the face of his fellow man with such scorn?
Isidore Ducasse Lautreamont

The true ideal is not opposed to the real but lies in it; and blessed are the eyes that find it.
James Russell Lowell

Virgo 2

The anguish of the neurotic individual is the same as that of the saint. The neurotic and the saint are engaged in the same battle. Their blood flows from similar wounds. But the first one gasps and the other one gives.
Georges Bataille

The heresies we should fear are those which can be confused with orthodoxy.
Jorge Luis Borges

Victims suggest innocence. And innocence, by the inexorable logic that governs all relational terms, suggests guilt.
Susan Sontag

Martyrdom has always been a proof of the intensity, never of the correctness of a belief.
Arthur Schnitzler

If you bear the cross willingly, it will bear you.
Thomas A. Kempis

Forgive me my nonsense as I forgive the nonsense of those who think they talk sense.
Anonymous

Christ was crucified for saying "the Kingdom is within you."
Joseph Campbell

Greater love hath no man than this, that a man lay down his life for his friends.
Jesus Christ

A LARGE WHITE CROSS, DOMINATING THE LANDSCAPE, STANDS ALONE ON TOP OF A HIGH HILL

Commentary: "A Large White Cross, Dominating the Landscape, Stands Alone on Top of a High Hill" is a symbol of suffering and loss and the hope of faith and salvation. Symbols such as the "Cross" have long had a deep, meaningful and powerful influence. That the "Cross" is "Standing Alone" depicts a sense of desertion, perhaps of one's faith or life circumstances. This can bring a sense of isolation. The idea, or belief, that suffering and giving up one's personal desires as a means to salvation has special significance for many people, but what does it really mean? True religion is supposed to unite people in many ways. Dogmatic expressions of faith can either unite or divide, even in what should be seen as a common cause. People need symbols of faith to rally around and inspire them.

Oracle: Feelings of loneliness or loss can be healed with signs of hope and faith for a brighter future. A religious experience can change one's life and lead to spiritual fulfillment and the highest sense of joy. However, these experiences can also lead to throwing one's life away. There can be too much emphasis on spiritual and "other worldly" values, which can lead people to lose their day-to-day lives. Some may feel that they are being treated like a scapegoat, "hung out to dry"; punished for doing something or being different or special in some way. Instead of having a "cross to bear," we can work at realigning ourselves with our true desires and allegiances. We can ground our selves and our lives by creating a balanced set of circumstances in our life: money, relationships, family, career, etc. This can lead to a stronger sense of purpose and spirituality, dissipating feelings of sacrifice, separation or loneliness.

Keywords: Religious ideals dominating. The fear or the wonder of God. Following a mystic path. The need to find a savior. Being alone and forgotten. Monuments to pain and suffering. Tributes to or memories of those lost or gone before. Reminders of salvation. Images of redemption. The Church. Christianity and other religions. Martyrdom. The Inquisition.

The Caution: Aloneness and/or sacrifice or the yearning for it. Dogmatism. Scapegoating. Days in the wilderness alone. Religion dictating against one's desires or needs. Symbols that inspire guilt and anguish instead of love, acceptance and forgiveness. Institutions disregarding individual rights. Lording it over others. Bullying under the guise of religion. Imposing figures.

What does this **SYMBOL** say to *you?*

TWO GUARDIAN ANGELS BRINGING PROTECTION

Commentary: "Two Guardian Angels Bringing Protection" is a beautiful Symbol that brings to mind images of salvation, release and protection. Being there for us, "Guardian Angels" are believed to look out for our best interests, especially when we most need them. This is particularly true when we feel we are about to stumble or fall in some way. Our "Guardian Angels" are with us even if we don't have a conscious awareness of their existence or presence, although if we do consciously evoke them, they are likely to be more "present" or obvious to us, in whatever form.

Oracle: This Symbol reminds us that no matter what we do, where we are, how difficult our struggles or how successful our activities, our "Angels" are always with us. "Guardian Angels" appear in many forms—as strangers, friends, family members, even as events, etc. They can come to us in moments of deep despair, when all seems lost and we feel abandoned and alone. Their messages and actions can signal a turning point, a feeling that life is well worth the struggles and torments we have to sometimes endure. With this Symbol, there is reassurance that you are not alone, lost or forgotten in a situation, at least not for very long. There is a strong sense that protection, guidance and direction are around. Hold a feeling close to your mind and heart; the belief that invisible, or visible, help is coming. This will ensure that help and relief will, indeed, become available. Remember that friends and family can often help, especially in the role of acting as sounding boards or counselors. Once things are back on track, it is likely you will find the true path that you must follow. Feeling good about your direction and being protected builds a sense of inner strength. You are never alone when you draw this Symbol. Open up to the "Protection" being offered to you; don't resist it.

Keywords: Connection with a sense of inner guidance. Visible or invisible protection. People appearing when they're needed. Being saved in the nick of time. Creative solutions to problems that seemed hopeless and lost. Counseling and guidance. Angels. Security systems. Salvation. Social workers.

The Caution: Feeling lost and alone without help. Losing faith in the goodness of life. Expecting that fate, or others, will pick up the pieces without putting in any effort. Resisting help in order to hang onto your "wounds." Too much reliance on outside forces. Not acting to change things. Victim status.

What does this **SYMBOL** say to *you?*

Virgo 3

Angels around us, angels beside us, angels within us. Angels are watching over you when times are good or stressed. Their wings wrap gently around you, whispering you are loved and blessed.
Anonymous

There are only two ways to live your life. One is as though nothing is a miracle. The other is as though everything is a miracle.
Albert Einstein

Make friends with the angels, who though invisible are always with you ... Often invoke them, constantly praise them, and make good use of their help and assistance in all your temporal and spiritual affairs.
Saint Francis de Sales

We forget to pray for the angels and the angels forget to pray for us.
Leonard Cohen

We are like children, who stand in need of masters to enlighten us and direct us; and God has provided for this, by appointing his angels to be our teachers and guides.
Saint Thomas Aquinas

Virgo 4

Somehow our devils are never quite what we expect when we meet them face to face.
Nelson DeMille

I destroy my enemy when I make him my friend.
Abraham Lincoln

It's never to late to give up your prejudices.
Henry David Thoreau

Prejudice is the child of ignorance.
William Hazlitt

Though shalt love thy neighbor as thyself.
The Bible

The imposition of stigma is the commonest form of violence used in democratic societies.
R. A. Pinker

You cannot contribute anything to the ideal condition of mind and heart known as Brotherhood, however much you preach, posture, or agree, unless you live it.
Faith Baldwin

If you judge people you have no time to love them.
Mother Teresa

BLACK AND WHITE CHILDREN PLAYING HAPPILY TOGETHER

Commentary: "Black and White Children Playing Happily Together" is a Symbol of racial and social integration that brings enrichment and joy to all who participate. That they are said to be "Black and White" can, of course, imply that there are racial differences between them. However, it can also symbolize many other differences in background, religion, belief systems, social or economic, and professional levels. Essentially, it can represent anything based on social perceptions or prejudices that can keep people apart from each other. As these "Children" are said to be "Playing Happily Together," any feelings of prejudice are dispelled because of their overriding concerns of "Play" and the enjoyment of each other. The "Children" share an element of innocence, fun and creativity. Their only desire, here, is to be "Playing" with others. When these attitudes are adopted, it is easy to see that skin color or any other differences fade into insignificance.

Oracle: The situation facing you may have a lot of seemingly opposite elements, but this is probably only an illusion or social perception. In reality, it is the blending of people and their individual traits and talents that allows things to be resolved and to move forward. Accepting everyone as equal will dispel thoughts and attitudes that can bring about separation and suspicion. There may be a need to remember to "Play Happily Together," as this may have been forgotten recently. People who have been estranged from each other can drop their differences and come together in a fresh new light. However, if you're forced to be with people whose company you don't enjoy, this can lead to suppression of your own wants and desires. Finding joy in the pleasure of simply being with others or seeking out those who want to share your time can rejuvenate life and inspire creativity. When drawing this Symbol, it is important to consider where happiness and equality lie in your list of priorities.

Keywords: Universal brotherhood. Overcoming prejudices and boundaries that separate people. Knocking down social barriers to relate freely. Being able to let go, relax and have fun with people from anywhere. Adopted siblings. Foster homes. Affirmative action. Trust and joy. Play that unites people.

The Caution: Morality that is swayed by public opinion. Not adjusting psychologically to situations that require creative responses. Racial and social prejudice. Seeing things in black-and-white terms. Social demarcations that separate people or situations. Apartheid. Illusions based on the separative perceptions of society.

What does this **SYMBOL** say to *you?*

A MAN BECOMING AWARE OF NATURE SPIRITS AND NORMALLY UNSEEN SPIRITUAL ENERGIES

Virgo 5

Commentary: "A Man Becoming Aware of Nature Spirits and Normally Unseen Spiritual Energies" shows the rational mind of someone being overshadowed by supernatural and intuitive images, thoughts and feelings. Equipped to see the invisible, this person has started to penetrate into the deeper and more mystical levels of the unconscious.

Oracle: There may be strong feelings of other levels of awareness happening and these may be growing stronger by the moment. The imagination is showing a clearer path to some understanding, even though, along the way, there may be confusion. Look for insights and messages in the things that you see and hear around you. Try bringing these insights back into your everyday consciousness, as they can expand your feelings about your self and life. Remembering a strong sense of who you are while allowing messages to come through from "the other side" can lead to a heightened feeling of aliveness and an increased "Awareness" of the magic and mystery of life. Getting in touch with "Nature Spirits and Normally Unseen Spiritual Energies" can be incredibly enriching and miracles can happen in your life. Indeed, there can be the revelation of being close to God. Your senses can come alive on many levels, with things revealed that you may have only imagined before. By contrast, the ordinary, everyday world may seem boring, lifeless and shallow. You can have surprising perceptions of existence on another level—but will it be useful or just lead you astray? Remember to stay grounded in your experiences as it can bring you considerable joy. Losing touch with reality, however, can lead to losing the plot to the point where it is difficult to discern what is real and what is not. "Becoming More Aware" of other levels of existence can be enriching in many ways.

Keywords: Creative fantasies. Attuned minds perceiving subtle phenomena. Fairy tales. Seeing things or imagining them. Fantasizing. Seeing entities. Mental institutions. Halloween. Fairies, nature spirits. Seeing the normally unseen.

The Caution: Confusion. Lack of true perspective. Time wasted in escapes from reality. Imagining things. Losing the plot. Dreaming to the point of insanity. Making up things in order to be noticed or feel somehow special. Delusions. Dreaming of possibilities that disappear upon waking. Schizophrenia.

What does this **SYMBOL** say to *you?*

The universe is full of magical things patiently waiting for our wits to grow sharper.
Eden Phillpotts

Today there are no fairytales for us to believe in, and this is possibly a reason for the universal prevalence of mental crackup. Yes, if we were childish in the past, I wish we could be children once again.
Anita Loos

Don't ask questions of fairytales.
Jewish Proverb

Reality is merely an illusion, albeit a very persistent one.
Albert Einstein

There are nine orders of angels, to wit, angels, archangels, virtues, powers, principalities, dominations, thrones, cherubim, and seraphim.
Pope Gregory the Great

Reality is that which, when you stop believing in it, doesn't go away.
Philip K. Dick

Every time a child says, "I don't believe in fairies," there is a fairy somewhere that falls down dead.
James Matthew Barrie

Virgo 6

The wheel goes round and round, some are up and some are on the down, and still the wheel goes round.
Josephine Pollard

We dance round in a ring and suppose, but the Secret sits in the middle and knows.
Robert Frost

Life is a roller coaster.
Modern Saying

If only bad habits could be broken as easily as hearts!
Christopher Spranger

It's not true that life is one damn thing after another—it's the same damn thing over and over.
Edna St. Vincent Millay

Few tasks are more like the torture of Sisyphus than housework, with its endless repetition: the clean becomes soiled; the soiled is made clean, over and over, day after day.
Simone de Beauvoir

An umeboshi plum is a little Japanese salt plum. The best thing for motion sickness is to take one of these plums ... and tape it to your belly button. I'm not kidding you. This really, really works.
Marilu Henner

A MERRY-GO-ROUND

Commentary: A "Merry-Go-Round" is a Symbol that arouses memories of fairgrounds, carnivals, playgrounds and childhood fun and games. The blaringly loud music, the children looking around at each other and watching the faces and the squeals of the others were all part of the fun. The thrill of going around and around was the objective. This can be great fun for children and big kids alike, who enjoy this type of activity without tiring or getting bored. It can, however, be another story when we're older. It can be tiring going around in circles without finding any real outcome or having a clear sense of an objective to strive for.

Oracle: There's a need to see definite possibilities and evidence of advancement in life and to feel as though we are making progress toward a goal or a clear outcome. This image can relate to any situation where we feel stuck in repetitive or unprogressive ruts. Relationships, marriages, jobs and everyday chores or habits can have you running around in circles landing you right back in the same place. This can lead you to wonder if you should just hold on tight, wait to see if the thing will ever eventually stop or jump off. Jumping off while things are still in motion can actually feel life-threatening. The desire, longing or even addiction to things, people, places, substances, etc., can put a hold on your life to the point where you can't see a way out. Just when you may think you've seen a way to get off, or out, you're back in the same situation, emotion or location. However, each time you return to what feels like the same place, if you've been watchful, you've had the opportunity to look at other alternatives, answers or possibilities. At some stage, though, there will need to be a decision made: do you want to keep going round and round, or do you want to stop repetitive situations or reactions and get off?

Keywords: Repeating circles of activity. Looking for a park. Driving around and around. Motion sickness. Childhood fun and joy. Yo-yoing and oscillating backward and forward. Emotional polarization. Once you're on it, you want to get off. The ups and downs and the ins and outs. Habits that are hard to break. Carnivals. Lights. Noise. Music.

The Caution: Repeating the same mistakes. Bouncing around from one thing to another and not getting anywhere. Feeling like there's no end in sight. Addictive behavior. Feeling dizzy. Not being able to focus on one point. Manic depression. Getting nowhere. Seeking only pleasure. Seemingly endless treadmills. Motion sickness.

What does this **SYMBOL** say to *you?*

A HAREM

Commentary: "A Harem" is a Symbol of women being, living and working together. They are often dictated to by the needs of just one person or authority. Sometimes the women are happy with fulfilling the needs and desires of the "master"; sometimes they're not. Women in a "Harem" often enjoy each other's company more than they enjoy "the man." Among the women in a "Harem," there is at least one person who acts as the "leader," someone whom the others look up to. Even though they need to get along and function together as a team, there are still their individual personalities, qualities and gifts to consider.

Oracle: This Symbol can indicate too many people in a relationship or finding happiness through women friends and the sacrifices that may have to be accepted to achieve this. As this is "a Harem," there may be a feeling of being dominated or being part of a group where people compete for whatever small benefits are available. Some women want to have their women friends all to themselves, and of course men sometimes do this with each other, as well. In a "Harem," sometimes the men believe they are in charge, when in reality it is the women calling the shots! You may find it hard to be taken seriously, to be appreciated for your individuality or be noticed apart from the crowd. Have faith; you can use your charm and the appealing aspects of your nature to succeed. A greater sense of security can come when life is protected, the finances covered, and one's relationship needs are satisfied. However, the desire for protection can lead to the decision to give up other things in life. When we feel secure and just hang out with each other, we can be more creative, carefree and empathetic to the needs and desires of others. Remember, we all have a unique role.

Keywords: Rising above jealousy, arrogance and passion. Waiting to be bestowed with the gift of being "chosen." Women's circles, sometimes closed. Women's groups. Working together. Sharing feminine rituals and stories. Egyptian tales. One person calling the shots. Beauty salons. Seduction of the senses. Having one's needs serviced. Women pampering each other. People who serve. Adoring the other. Sultans. Polygamy.

The Caution: Being just one of "the mob." Not having a sense of personal importance. Mistrust of other women. Seeing people as competition. The spread of socially unacceptable diseases. Locked doors. Sexual infidelity. Needing the love of many. Eunuchs. Assuming the right to dominate others.

What does this **SYMBOL** say to *you?*

Virgo 7

A woman who is loved always has success.
Vicki Baum

Woman must not depend upon the protection of man, but must be taught to protect herself.
Susan B. Anthony

The dogma of woman's complete historical subjection to men must be rated as one of the most fantastic myths ever created by the human mind.
Mary Ritter Beard

Many abolitionists have yet to learn the ABCs of women's rights.
Susan B. Anthony

For what is done or learned by one class of women becomes, by virtue of their common womanhood, the property of all women.
Emily Blackwell

I can't say that the college-bred woman is the most contented woman. The broader her mind the more she understands the unequal conditions between men and women, the more she chafes under a government that tolerates it.
Susan B. Anthony

We are his, to serve him nobly in the common cause, true to the death, but not to be his slaves.
William Cowper

Virgo 8

Fine dancing, I believe, like virtue, must be its own reward.
Jane Austen

Dance is the hidden language of the soul.
Martha Graham

If you be a lover of instruction, you will be well instructed.
Isocrates

I don't try to dance better than anyone else. I only try to dance better than myself.
Mikhail Baryshnikov

Remember, Ginger Rogers did everything Fred Astaire did, but she did it backwards and in high heels.
Anonymous

How inimitably graceful children are before they learn to dance.
Samuel Taylor Coleridge

Will you, won't you
Will you, won't you
Will you join the dance?
Lewis Carroll

A child ... must feel the flush of victory and the heart-sinking of disappointment before he takes with a will to the tasks distasteful to him and resolves to dance his way through a dull routine of textbooks.
Helen Keller

A GIRL TAKES HER FIRST DANCING INSTRUCTION

Commentary: "A Girl Takes Her First Dancing Instruction" is a Symbol of youth, innocence and naïveté. The young "Girl" needs to show respect and reverence for the "teacher," as this person may hold the key to her future, in some way. The "Girl" must listen to her "Instructor" or teacher; otherwise she may miss the rewards and opportunities available in the lesson she's taking. She also has to listen to and become one with the music. Along with the need to accept "Instruction," she must learn the steps and the "rules." How well she gets along with the "teacher" will add to how well the lessons succeed.

Oracle: You may find yourself in a situation that is brand new to you and you need to "learn the ropes." You have the potential to do well, but initially you may be unsure of what to do or how to act (or react), or what "steps" to take. Even though you may know a lot about many things, in regard to the situation facing you, you may not have had much experience. There may be a lot to take in, absorb and learn at the moment but one day you'll probably look back and see that it was actually easy, like learning to ride a bike. After the steps to the "dance" have been learned, you will be able to display more maturity and grace. Eventually, people can stop telling you how to perform. However, no matter how much we know, we go on learning throughout our entire life. For now you have to listen, respond and learn—that is, unless you are the "teacher." Pay attention to what is being taught and what, indeed, can be learned, and you will continue to learn and go far in life. Music and "Dance" can lift your life; indeed they can transform it.

Keywords: Practice makes perfect. Higher talents being developed. Learning discipline, self-control and concentration. Taking on something new. Listening to and following instructions. Moving into a new sense of being. Losing innocence. Learning the steps without thinking. Music and dance. Following the rhythm. Progressing from one thing to the next. Instructors and students.

The Caution: Difficulty understanding lessons. Continually returning to the beginning. Not trusting the teacher or instruction. Having to learn things against one's desires. Believing that one knows everything already. Fears of being seen as a beginner or clumsy. Having two left feet. Not paying attention to life's lessons. Naïveté.

What does this **SYMBOL** say to *you?*

AN EXPRESSIONIST PAINTER MAKING A FUTURISTIC DRAWING

Commentary: "An Expressionist Painter" is "Making a Futuristic Drawing." As he's an "Expressionist Painter," he's probably an artist ahead of his time, or at least has a different perspective on life from most people. The "Painter" may be focused and concentrating on his task to the exclusion of all else in his life. The "Painter" paints, draws or makes plans with his thoughts, feelings and emotions; he responds to his creations in the moment. The "Futuristic Drawing" can be schemes, "Drawings" or plans of things that may or may not eventually come into reality.

Oracle: Individuality and originality seem to be the uppermost requirements to get the most out of the situation facing you. Even against the pressures for a more traditional or socially acceptable response, it is your individual creativity that is needed now. Try to look at things in a different light; picture how things will look in the "Future" if you take the steps you're contemplating. Will things work out as planned? What is your interpretation of the "Future"? Who and what does it include? Many different elements go into creating what's possible in our lives. One thing is having the vision—everyone has to have a vision. Another thing is having the drive, energy and a positive affirmation to see the vision turn into reality. The vision without the drive is useless. Maintain both aspects and your chances of success in the "Future" will undoubtedly improve. However, always thinking that things will be much better in the "Future" can lead to the loss of enjoying life in the present.

Keywords: Creativity projected into the future. Seeing things ahead of their time. Taking chances. Having the dreamer's disease. Talent. Seeing things in a different way. Being unrestricted by reality. Time machines and time travel. Artists, architects and engineers. Plans, schemes, blueprints. "When I win the lottery..." Forecasting and prediction. Genius. Sketches. Abstract art.

The Caution: Focusing on tomorrow not today. Not seeing the complete picture. Plans that often come to nothing. Being unrealistic. Losing touch with the real world. Losing enthusiasm. Thinking the worst will happen. Making things up that don't reflect reality. Being stuck on one version of the future. Distorted reality. Getting lost in abstract thought. Being divorced from the real world.

What does this **SYMBOL** say to *you?*

Virgo 9

I like dreams of the future better than the history of the past.
Thomas Jefferson

We worry about what a child will be tomorrow, yet we forget that he is someone today.
Stacia Tauscher

See things as you would have them be instead of as they are.
Robert Collier

Great minds have purposes, others have wishes.
Washington Irving

We are what we think. All that we are arises with our thoughts. With our thoughts, we make our world.
Buddha

Know what I'm looking forward to? The future.
Carl, The Simpsons

Every one is the architect of his own fortune.
Mathurin Regnier

You'll see it when you believe it.
Wayne Dyer

Well, back to the drawing board.
Peter Arno

Life is a great big canvas, and you should throw all the paint on it you can.
Danny Kaye

Virgo 10

Hearing both sides brings enlightenment. Believing only one side brings obscurity.
Vincent Wei Chang

Keep your face to the sunshine and you cannot see the shadows.
Helen Keller

I don't understand you. You don't understand me. What else do we have in common?
Ashleigh Brilliant

Do I contradict myself? Very well; I contradict myself.
Walt Whitman

Doubts are more cruel than the worst of truths.
Anonymous

The optimist proclaims that we live in the best of all possible worlds, and the pessimist fears this is true.
James Branch Cabell

That which we call sin in others, is experiment for us.
Ralph Waldo Emerson

We don't see things as they are. We see them as we are.
Anais Nin

Know that you are your own greatest enemy, but also your greatest friend.
Jeremy Taylor

TWO HEADS LOOKING OUT AND BEYOND THE SHADOWS

Commentary: "Two Heads Looking out and beyond the Shadows" is a Symbol of duality of thought and observation. This Symbol shows people looking at each other from a "Shadowy," hidden perspective, as though they are checking each other out. The "Two Heads" can illustrate groups of people having different perspectives, or occupying different camps, "Looking Out" and trying to understand, or investigate, what the "other" is doing.

Oracle: At the moment you may need to be able to see things from more than one side. While what's happening may not be entirely visible or obvious, it is necessary to look beyond the "Shadows" and into the light. If you feel stuck in a situation because the details of what's really happening are not clear, try making some type of plan. Mapping out what alternatives there are and the outcomes of possible scenarios will be beneficial. The right plan of action can lead to light being shed and things being revealed. As there are "Two Heads" pictured here, two people observing exactly the same thing can come to very different conclusions. There may be arguments, bickering and stalemates if they find it hard to agree with each other. Their observations can be quite different, but this can lead to interesting and useful solutions, especially if they take the time to listen to each other. The "Two Heads" duality can also exist in one person's thoughts. Seeing both sides of a situation can result in difficulty in making up one's mind. Losing the ability to make firm decisions and the loss of faith can open the door to fear. Regardless of potential confusion, it is beneficial in some respect to look at every possible aspect of the situation you are in. This may provide an understanding of just how another person may feel or react.

Keywords: Duality of observation or thought. Being able to see both sides of a situation. Fear being the opposite of faith. People peering and peeking. Secret service and government agencies. Gunfights of the old west. Trench warfare. The media, the press, paparazzi, spies, private detectives. Conspiracy theories. Crossed eyes. Eavesdropping. Voyeurism.

The Caution: Confused by duality of thought. Failing to see the integration and cohesion of more than one perspective. Schizophrenia. Fear freezing up positive attitudes. Debates. Stalemates. Making assumptions without the relevant information. Quarrelling. Not seeing the light. Inability to agree. Bickering with others or with one's self.

What does this **SYMBOL** say to *you?*

A BOY MOLDED IN HIS MOTHER'S ASPIRATIONS FOR HIM

Virgo 11

Commentary: "A Boy Molded in His Mother's Aspirations for Him" is a Symbol of someone having to live up to the expectations of parents or others. The "Mother," or other authority figure, often misses the point of the true potential of her offspring and may be projecting her own unlived life. Can the "Boy" live up to "His Mother's Aspirations"? Probably not, at least not all the time.

Oracle: Sometimes it's fine to be "Molded" by our parents, but often this is not a true reflection of who we truly are or of our own creative potentials. This being said, we still need to be aware of what others expect from us—what ideals do people expect us to embody and to live out? Once we've identified what "Mold" we have allowed ourselves to be persuaded or projected into, we can learn why we do certain things, often for others, and what truly needs to be done in order to be faithful to our own inner needs. It can be useful to know how and where the "Mold" one's been poured into is appropriate and where it isn't. The "Mother" that has the "Aspirations" can represent the expectations of a single individual or it can show groups of individuals. Indeed, society puts its own set of ideals and expectations on everyone, at least in some way. This can go all the way from family, spouse and friends, right through to other authority figures, such as the government or the dictates of one's country. The "Mother" "out there" may smother our true feelings of what we want to do, often for reasons of social respectability and prestige. However, if the "Aspirations" are worth striving for, this can lead to a great outcome, with people being proud of the person that one is becoming.

Keywords: Being directed on the journey or shaped against one's free will. Plastic or cosmetic surgery. Building the physical or emotional shape. Finding one's way or destiny. Predetermined destinies. Looking like one's mother or father. The challenge of individuality. DNA. Parents as patterns. Allowing others to dictate who you are. Inherited values. Following in the family's footsteps.

The Caution: Remaining tied to the apron strings of mother or others. Conforming to social expectations. Not having a clear sense of what one wants to be. Being a reflection of what somebody else wants. Being a "mama's boy." Not having the free will of one's own. Living the unlived life of the parents. Squashed individuality. Letting down the side.

What does this **SYMBOL** say to *you?*

Nothing has a stronger influence psychologically on their environment and especially on their children than the unlived life of the parent.
Carl Jung

My mother said to me, "If you become a soldier you'll be a general; if you become a monk you'll end up as the pope." Instead, I became a painter and wound up as Picasso.
Pablo Picasso

A child may have too much of his mother's blessing.
Proverb

I blame Rousseau, myself. "Man is born free," indeed. Man is not born free; he is born attached to his mother by a cord and is not capable of looking after himself for at least seven years (seventy in some cases).
Katharine Whitehorn

For a man to achieve all that is demanded of him he must regard himself as greater than he is.
Goethe

He that has no children brings them up well.
Traditional Proverb

Virgo 12

There was the Door to which I found no key;
There was the Veil through which I might not see.
Omar Khayyam

Beware of all enterprises that require new clothes.
Henry David Thoreau

Grief walks upon the heels of pleasure; married in haste, we repent at leisure.
William Congreve

When a husband is embraced without affection, there must be some reason for it.
Hitopadesa

Ah, to think how thin the veil that lies
Between the pain of hell and Paradise.
George William Russell

Personally, I hold that a man who deliberately and intelligently takes a pledge and then breaks it, forfeits his manhood.
Mahatma Gandhi

A man in love is incomplete until he is married. Then he is finished.
Zsa Zsa Gabor

No one worth possessing can be quite possessed.
Sara Teasdale

A BRIDE WITH HER VEIL SNATCHED AWAY

Commentary: A "Bride with Her Veil Snatched Away" is an image of revelation, unveiling and discovery. Traditionally, "Brides" have been thought to be particularly vulnerable to evil spirits and the "Veil" was thought to be able to outwit malevolent spirits. In some countries the groom is not allowed to see the "Bride's" face until after the ceremony. No matter what her situation, the "Bride" is now faced with the moment of moving into a new life and a new sense of identity.

Oracle: This speaks of "taking the plunge" and making a commitment to someone or something. It pictures a situation where the past and the future collide. One cannot continue to exist in limbo; the future has a stronger call than the past. This Symbol can also indicate that you must show your true face or you will be forced to reveal it. There may be a feeling that somebody is not quite ready to give themselves completely to the situation. However, as they've made some form of commitment to what they are doing, they don't really have much choice. Being unable to hide behind "Veils," illusions, or pretense any longer means that something will happen to break any resistance that may remain. If one doesn't go willingly, they may be pushed forward. Having to act, or relate, regardless of excuses or hesitation, puts the pressure on to move forward and to accept or reject the situation they find themselves in, regardless of reservations. Those who "Snatch the Veil Away" may not be acting in order to dominate or overpower, but just trying to remove barriers in the way of relating. It may be hesitation that is creating problems. Look to your motives and those of others around you; be sure of why they are doing what they do. Letting down your guard can open up whole new worlds.

Keywords: Secret motives being revealed. Unveiling or changing identity. Proving oneself with no excuses and no pretense. Breaking down walls. Relating on a deep level. "Honeymoon periods." Being true to one's self and others. Marriage rituals. Dropping pretense. Divorce. Veils. Vows. The veil between the conscious and unconscious.

The Caution: Stubbornly refusing to accept new directions. Failing to commit. Not coming up with what one promised. Feelings of violation. Not ready to give up fantasies or illusions. Being used or exposed. Harsh realities. Mysteries that may be best left that way. Withdrawal.

What does this **SYMBOL** say to *you?*

A POWERFUL STATESMAN OVERCOMES A STATE OF POLITICAL HYSTERIA

Virgo 13

To put the world in order, we must first put the nation in order; to put the nation in order, we must put the family in order; to put the family in order, we must cultivate our personal life; and to cultivate our personal life, we must first set our hearts right.
Confucius

A government is like fire, a handy servant, but a dangerous master.
George Washington

The worst tyrants are those which establish themselves in our own breasts.
William Ellery Channing

A fool gives full vent to his anger, but a wise man keeps himself under control.
Proverb

Political oratory is an art in which nothing you say reveals the fact that you're saying nothing.
Anonymous

Commentary: "A Powerful Statesman Overcomes a State of Political Hysteria" pictures someone being able to take charge or reign in energies that have gotten out of control. Indeed, as there is some "Hysteria" involved, something could have blown out of all proportion to reality. The "Powerful Statesman" may be someone who is strong, charismatic and energetic, having a powerful place in society or a position of strength. They have a sense of authority, and others will listen to what they have to say. A word from them can turn situations around with very little apparent effort.

Oracle: You may find that your situation is whipped up as people get carried away with the energy that's around. There is a need to get the upper hand to bring about a stabilized outcome—to "Overcome" the "Hysteria." It is through the "Power" of the personality of the "Powerful Statesman" that things can be resolved and brought to a state of equilibrium. Regaining control of one's thoughts, psyche and emotions can ease tensions and bring the situation back to normal. Changing one's mind about an issue that may have been overpowering can enable a whole new view of your position in life to crystallize. Employing discipline and control helps on a physical, mental or spiritual level. Looking after the small problems as they arise can stop them turning into issues that are larger, and more difficult to control. It is always better to notice when things are beginning to get out of hand or out of shape, not waiting until things are overwhelmingly messy. After all, an ounce of prevention is worth a pound of cure. Call on an your higher nature to regain control and bring the situation back to normality.

Keywords: The power to sway the mob. Having the charisma and talent to turn situations around. Elements of personality that get out of control and take over. Pulling the rope tight. Mind control. Political savvy. Knowing what to say and when to say it. Keeping your mouth shut and ears open. Rhetoric. Putting out spot fires. Being motivated. Issues of success.

The Caution: Conscious emotional manipulation and bullying. Misusing energy. Swaying others to personal advantage. Being aggressive, demanding and overbearing. Hypnotic persuasion. Propaganda. Misinformation. Using "political speak" to control. Emotional repression.

What does this **SYMBOL** say to *you?*

Virgo 14

Every time a baby is born, so is a grandmother.
Anonymous

To "be" means to be related.
Alfred Korzybski

Call it a clan, call it a network, call it a tribe, call it a family: Whatever you call it, whoever you are, you need one.
Jane Howard

Be tolerant of the human race. Your whole family belongs to it—and some of your spouse's family does too.
Anonymous

If you don't believe in ghosts, you've never been to a family reunion.
Ashleigh Brilliant

It is of no consequence of what parents a man is born, so he be a man of merit.
Horace

Everyone has something ancestral, even if it is nothing more than a disease.
Ed Howe

Remember, as far as anyone knows, we're a nice normal family.
Homer Simpson

FINELY LETTERED NAMES AND MYSTERIOUS LINES ARE SEEN; IT IS A FAMILY TREE

Commentary: "Finely Lettered Names and Mysterious Lines Are Seen; It Is a Family Tree." This Symbol gives the impression that the "Family Tree" is beautifully designed and mapped out. The "Tree" has branches with names connecting to more and more names as it goes back through the family history. There is often a sense of nostalgia and grandeur with "Family Trees." Many people are fascinated, and sometimes amazed, by looking back to their forefathers; where they came from, and who their close relations were. Some members of the "Family" will see the relevance and importance of the history and the "Mystery" of the "Family" lineage; meanwhile others may not even bother to look.

Oracle: There is a need to call upon the deeper and inherent knowledge within. What's been learned from past experience, possibly from one's ancestral roots, will help you allocate your greatest strength. This Symbol implies the need to feel links to a "Family" heritage or the desire for the sense of security that it can bring. If there is no strong sense of one's own biological "Family," this can be found through associations with people of like mind, or with those who share a common purpose in life. How do you see your place in the grand scheme of things? Both physically and spiritually, you carry the blood of all those who went before you. How attached are you to your "Family" and your origins? Where have you come from? How do you feel about the role you have in your "Family"? Do you feel involved, wanted and loved? Proving yourself and your bloodline can lead to a stronger sense of self, belonging and an understanding of how you fit in.

Keywords: Strength in tradition. Belonging to a lineage. The story of where one comes from. Issues of pride of heritage. The importance of parents and family. Branches in databases. Having strong and secure roots. Origins and their relevance to today's life. Ancestors. Calligraphy. Fine pens. Filling in the gaps. Adoptions. Step families. Pedigrees. Kin. Genealogy. Inheritance. Family Bibles.

The Caution: Disassociation or disconnection from family history. Exclusivity or snobbery. Feeling like an alien. Feeling, or being, a stranger in a strange world. Orphans. Not knowing where one came from. Being stuck with people you don't know. Examining roots. Missing identities. Skeletons in the closet.

What does this **SYMBOL** say to *you?*

A FINE LACE ORNAMENTAL HANDKERCHIEF

Commentary: "A Fine Lace Ornamental Handkerchief" is a beautiful, soft, lacy image. A "Lace Handkerchief" is an extremely feminine and personal possession associated with perfume, tears and matters of the heart. Since medieval times, women have given their loved ones this small token of their love and commitment before they went into battle or traveled abroad. The scent of the "fabric" and the care and loving that have gone into the crafting of it give a sense of security and being remembered and loved. We are often amazed by how much attention to detail, care and thought goes into making something so beautiful, small and delicate. Even small gifts can bring a sense of love and care; they can become very sentimental. The smallest tokens of our past can bring us a sense of security and joy.

Oracle: At the moment you may be feeling the want for love and the need for someone in your life. You need to relax a little in order to invite others in. The feeling of being lost and left behind can be relieved with the touch of fabric, a whiff of perfume, etc.; these can be a reminder of people or events past. Warm, sentimental feelings can be expressed, or poured out, showing tenderness and care. Carrying a beautiful lace handkerchief might be a nice way to remind yourself of your true sense of worth and beauty. However, this type of "Handkerchief," being made of "Lace," is not really suited for too many tears, as it can be more of an ornament that a true "Handkerchief." Hence, there can be a sense of false emotion evident with this Symbol. Sometimes we get upset about things that needn't really upset us, or we put on an emotional show because we feel it's expected of us. Being wound up and constantly "upset" or demanding emotional attention can put people off. Staying true to your emotions and remembering your self-worth may be very important now.

Keywords: Delicacy of feeling. Attention to detail. Winning awards through valor. Hypersensitivity. Looking but not touching. Overdressing. Appearing too delicate to truly enjoy life. Make-up and accessories. Fragility. Old things of lace and beauty. Refinement. Small gifts given with deep feeling.

The Caution: The artificial sob story. False sympathy. Asking for love when in reality one doesn't really want it. Impractical belongings. Things that get shunted aside as irrelevant, unworthy or unusable. Things of little use in today's world. Mass manufacturing. Things made in sweatshops.

What does this **SYMBOL** say to *you?*

Virgo 15

If you are not too long, I will wait here for you all my life.
Oscar Wilde

HANDKERCHIEF, n. A small square of silk or linen, used in various ignoble offices about the face and especially serviceable at funerals to conceal the lack of tears.
Ambrose Bierce

Where a blood relation sobs, an intimate friend should choke up, a distant acquaintance should sigh, a stranger should merely fumble sympathetically with his handkerchief.
Mark Twain

A little sincerity is a dangerous thing, and a great deal of it is absolutely fatal.
Oscar Wilde

Fame is the perfume of heroic deeds.
Socrates

So, as you go into battle, remember your ancestors and remember your descendants.
Publius Cornelius Tacitus

No duty is more urgent than that of returning thanks.
St. Ambrose

The better part of valor is discretion.
William Shakespeare

Virgo 16

There are 193 living species of monkeys and apes. 192 of them are covered with hair. The exception is a naked ape, self-named homo sapiens.
Desmond Morris

The city is not a concrete jungle, it is a human zoo.
Desmond Morris

Be tolerant of the human race. Your whole family belongs to it—and some of your spouse's family does too.
Anonymous

I am a creationist; I refuse to believe that I could have evolved from humans.
Anonymous

To be human is to keep rattling the bars of the cage of existence hollering, "What's it for?"
Robert Fulghum

Man must realize his own unimportance before he can appreciate his importance.
R. M. Baumgardy

If an animal does something, we call it instinct; if we do the same thing for the same reason, we call it intelligence.
Will Cuppy

I confess freely to you, I could never look long upon a monkey without very mortifying reflections.
William Congreve

DELIGHTED CHILDREN CROWD AROUND THE ORANGUTAN CAGE IN A ZOO

Commentary: "Delighted Children Crowd around the Orangutan Cage in a Zoo," pictures young people pressing together to observe intriguing and wonderful animals that are unusual to them. They don't have a chance to see these animals in their everyday life. Grown "Orangutans" are very similar to "Children": they are said to have a similar mental capacity to that of a five-year-old. "Children" have great fun watching their antics. The "Orangutan" can also be seen observing the "Children." The responses of wonder and curiosity are obviously evident in the "Delighted Children," but may well be what the "Orangutan" are also experiencing. The "Children" watch to see what will happen and they take pleasure in the things they can relate to.

Oracle: This Symbol expresses the desire to relate across gulfs of differences that are very obvious between different species. Observing the life of an "Orangutan" is like looking into an evolutionary mirror. We are able to see where we have been, how differently we relate to the world, and how we have chosen to deal with our environment. It is not a matter of the human species being better. Indeed, one comes to realize the degree of similarity. Sometimes people we encounter in life seem to be from a different species (or planet!) and have a totally opposite perspective of life, leading to completely different ways of acting and reacting. It can, at times, lead to a feeling of separation, but there is value in remaining aware of and appreciating the similarities and common ground along with the differences. There may need to be a "primitive," or "Childlike" response. It is also by facing the baser instincts that you can realize a fresh, new approach to those around you.

Keywords: Karmic confrontations between the creatively integrated and the unevolved. Objects of derision, fascination or worship. Showing off or acting to get a reaction from others. Trying to relate to others who don't understand. Feeling like one is in a zoo. Observing others. Curiosity. Crowding around. Everyone wanting to have a look. Going by instincts. Television shows such as *Jerry Springer*. News networks. The media. Lack of social inhibition.

The Caution: Egoistic feelings of being better or in a higher state of evolution. Having no place for privacy. Gaping at others. Taunting people. Daring others to do something outrageous or animal-like. Making fun of people. Building cages. Hiding from view. Fences and barriers. The intrusion of the media (beating up stories). Eliciting sick behavior from others.

What does this **SYMBOL** say to *you?*

A VOLCANIC ERUPTION BRINGING DUST CLOUDS, FLOWING LAVA, EARTH RUMBLINGS

Virgo 17

Commentary: "A Volcanic Eruption" is "Bringing Dust Clouds, Flowing Lava and Earth Rumblings." The "Volcano" may have been threatening to erupt for some time, but now it's actually doing it. The "Earth Rumblings" imply possible threats of further, perhaps more life-changing, even catastrophic, blasts. Only time will tell.

Oracle: Somebody or something may have been holding things inside until a powerful force has built up to the point where there can be no more resistance and everything is thrown, spewed or forced out. This "Eruption" could be expressed as anger, but also in the explosive form of ideas, beliefs, goals and insights. It is often best just to let it blow; resisting the urge can cause enormous pressure to build which can be harmful in many ways. However, one needs to keep a watchful eye on the situation so things don't get out of control, leading to hysteria and dramatic reactions. Things can get out of control very quickly. This often leaves "rubble," or mess, everywhere to be cleaned up. Watch out for overreactions. Is the force of emotions really related to the current situation? Having or regaining complete control is possibly out of the question until things settle down and the danger is past. There can be a sense of relief when the realization of surviving such a situation sinks in. Sometimes, after we've been through a major shakeup and rattling in our lives, we can feel a sense of gratitude and calm and peace is restored. You may find yourself in a whole new place or having extraordinary experiences on every level—physical, emotional, spiritual or mental. Whatever has erupted may have been building up for years. There can be fertile soil after the "Lava" has flowed—soil that can contain nutrients and riches from deep down inside your mind and body. What is coming out from within? What transformations can come from this?

Keywords: Thoughts or ideas pouring out. Torrents of thought or emotion. Anger that needs expression. Eruptions that are quickly overcome. Pressure cooker environments. Aftershocks. Waiting for the dust to settle. Cathartic release. Volcanoes. Earthquakes. Earth tremors. Rumblings. Earth changes. Dust.

The Caution: Suppression of anger or energy to the point of explosive disaster. Tantrums. Choking the air with sulfurous dust clouds. Holding things inside. Overreactions. Spewing one's insides. Flipping out. Events that throw out shocking news or emotions.

What does this **SYMBOL** say to *you?*

You can have anything you want if you want it desperately enough. You must want it with an inner exuberance that erupts through the skin and joins the energy that created the world.
Sheilah Graham

When the habitually even-tempered suddenly fly into a passion, that explosion is apt to be more impressive than the outburst of the most violent amongst us.
Margery Allingham

If you go in for argument, take care of your temper. Your logic, if you have any, will take care of itself.
Joseph Farrell

Californians are good at planning for the earthquake, while simultaneously denying it will happen.
Sheila Ballantyne

The human race likes to give itself airs. One good volcano can produce more greenhouse gases in a year than the human race has in its entire history.
Ray Bradbury

Virgo 18

*If I waited to be right before I
spoke, I would be sending little
cryptic messages on the Ouija
board, complaints from the
other side.*
Audre Lorde

*Imagination is the outreaching
of mind ... the bombardment of
the conscious mind with ideas,
impulses, images and every sort
of psychic phenomena welling
up from the preconscious. It is
the capacity to dream dreams
and see visions.*
Rollo May

*People need hard times and
oppression to develop psychic
muscles.*
Frank Herbert

*In my writing I am acting as
a map maker, an explorer of
psychic areas ... a cosmonaut
of inner space, and I see no
point in exploring areas that
have already been thoroughly
surveyed.*
William S. Burroughs

Is there a spirit present?
**Standard Ouija Board
Question**

*You must pray carefully and
for the very essence of your
desire or you will be caught up
in many musings of things you
may not want for your own
experience.*
Ouija Message

TWO GIRLS PLAYING WITH A OUIJA BOARD

Commentary: "Two Girls Playing with a Ouija Board." The "Girls" are curious to see what will happen if they contact spirits on the "other side." Indeed, it is said that it was "Two Girls" who popularized the Ouija board in 1848. They were sisters from Hydesville, New York. They became instant celebrities and sparked a national obsession that spread all across the United States and Europe, signaling the birth of modern spiritualism.

Oracle: Here, the "Two Girls" show that there may be a need to share your thoughts, explorations, dreams and ideas with another. They are "Playing with a Ouija Board"—there is a desire to contact a deeper wisdom, possibly by the use of some kind of divinational tool. You may need some form of assistance to help you focus on any messages that are coming through. This "tool" can be many things; a Ouija board, the Sabian Symbols, the I Ching, the tarot, etc. Wisdom and knowledge may come with time, serious intent and effort. At first, there may be rather youthful and naïve attempts to discover the deeper meaning of life. Things may become a little strange; there can be little control over what is coming through from "the other side." You may have to just sit and observe. Sometimes there's a need to explore these realms with others and there is often something scary about them. What is likely to happen if you leave yourself open and vulnerable? This Symbol can suggest the need to be with someone who shares the same beliefs and interests in life, and to have the curiosity to find out things that may not be immediately apparent. If someone you are in partnership with is reluctant to see things from a similar spiritual or esoteric perspective as you, you might find the relationship breaking down. One partner may be more "straight," the other more eager to take a chance and explore.

Keywords: Immature curiosity leading to messages and inner guidance. Listening devices. Tuning into possible meanings. Ouija boards. Séances. Clairvoyant abilities. Spirits of the departed. Contact with the "other side." Messages coming through from unknown sources. Spiritualism. Ectoplasms. Concentrated attention. Poltergeists. Haunted houses. Cold energies. Bringing spirit through. Moving furniture. Phenomena. Weird and spooky. Seeing ghosts. Being a channel.

The Caution: Dealing with situations beyond one's maturity. Looking for information instead of getting on with life. Naive playing with potentially dangerous elements. Seeking easy answers to avoid responsibility. Fooling around. Superstitious responses to natural phenomena.

What does this **SYMBOL** say to *you?*

A SWIMMING RACE

Commentary: A "Swimming Race" is an image of people competing against each other in order to win some award, medal, recognition or goal. Each has to win their own "Race" and go as hard as they possibly can for the objective. Rules and regulations have to be followed, otherwise they face the possibility of being "disqualified" from participating.

Oracle: You may find yourself in competition with others or working your way through conflicting emotions and hoping to win, or come out on top. It is through hard work, practice and the control of your self and emotions that success can be achieved. The lessons learned through your training must be called on now. Have faith in yourself and your abilities that you can win. You may be working hard at achieving the win for rewards in the larger picture (for club, school, country) or winning the race with purely personal gains in mind. If it's an intellectual or emotional "Race" that you're competing in, it may at times be easier to let the other "win." Although winning can be really wonderful, a feeling of constant competition and the desire to come out on top can wear you and others down, and take the joy and spontaneity out of life. Plus, there are no real winners when people compete emotionally. Is the situation facing you worth the effort you must put in? If it is, take a deep breath and go for it with all your might. If someone is just trying to outdo you, you might decide to pull out and let him or her go for it. People can't win against you if you're not competing against them and a refusal to compete may take the wind out of their sails. The best way to win is to run your own race, compete against yourself and always do your best. Looking sideways at others to see how they're doing can slow you down and weaken your performance. Look ahead and go for your own objectives. Doing the best you can is the best you can do, after all!

Keywords: Looking sideways to see how others are coping with the strain of competition. Competing with one's emotions. Capitalism. The striving for first place or greatness. Swimming, sports, competition. Wanting to be first at everything. Learning how fit one is. Concentrating on the goal. Medals and awards. Training and practice. Showing your abilities in front of others.

The Caution: Allowing the competitive spirit to dominate emotional sensitivity. Always going for "the win." Trying to outdo each other. Being on the go all the time. Bad sportsmanship. Not knowing how to lose. Wanting always to conquer others. Always seeing others as competitors.

What does this **SYMBOL** say to *you?*

Virgo 19

In between goals is a thing called life, that has to be lived and enjoyed.
Sid Caesar

Picture yourself vividly as winning, and that alone will contribute immeasurably to success.
Harry Emerson Fosdick

The battles that count aren't the ones for gold medals. The struggles within yourself—the invisible, inevitable battles inside all of us—that's where it's at.
Jesse Owens

When you are content to be simply yourself and don't compare or compete, everybody will respect you.
Lao-Tzu

The difference between a hero and an also-ran is the guy who hangs on for one last gasp.
Paul Dietzel

Of all human powers operating on the affairs of mankind, none is greater than that of competition.
Henry Clay

Live daringly, boldly, fearlessly. Taste the relish to be found in competition—in having put forth the best within you.
Henry J. Kaiser

Virgo 20

Wherever you go, go with all your heart.
Confucius

Go for it now. The future is promised to no one.
Wayne Dyer

Hitch your wagon to a star.
Ralph Waldo Emerson

Those who say you can't take it with you never saw a car packed for a vacation trip.
Anonymous

It is a curious thing that every creed promises a paradise which will be absolutely uninhabitable for anyone of civilized taste.
Evelyn Waugh

For where does one run to when he's already in the Promised Land?
Claude Brown

A nomad I will remain for life, in love with distant and uncharted places.
Isabelle Eberhardt

The Promised Land guarantees nothing. It is only an opportunity, not a deliverance.
Shelby Steele

A CARAVAN OF CARS HEADED FOR PROMISED LANDS

Commentary: "A Caravan of Cars Headed for Promised Lands" shows a group of people setting out on a journey to a better place or a better way of life. They've probably heard word that life is more promising in some distant place and they're packed up and moving in that direction. The "Promised Lands" can literally mean the west coast of America; however, in general terms it means a land that contains some reward, a new way of living.

Oracle: There is a feeling of the need to move on to new thoughts, new ways of doing things, possibly even a new way of life, but you are unlikely to be alone. As this is "a Caravan of Cars" there are probably several others who share the same desires and impulses. Setting out on a new venture can feel very exciting, especially if friends, family or colleagues are as enthusiastic as you are. It may not be a matter of whether these "Promised Lands" have real guarantees of satisfaction or reward. There's the need, or desire, to explore these fresh opportunities for the potentials they may hold. The simple act of moving to overcome stagnant lifestyles can create the possibility of some kind of "Promise." Making a commitment to overcome dull routines and leave the past behind with those who share a like mind and intention may be all that is necessary to open the path to a new reality. Heading for the future with a keen sense of excitement and anticipation can open you up to all sorts of possibilities and hope. Some kind of new "Land" or opportunity is an inevitable outcome of this change. Indeed, it can lead to a whole new life. This being said, one should stop for a moment and ponder the reasons for moving on. Do you have to leave loved ones behind in this quest? Is this quest based in reality, or is it something that has more "Promise" than reality?

Keywords: Venturing into life with like-minded companions. The support of others in a quest for the future. Seeking new territory. Rallies and caravans of cars. Exchanging money. Commerce. Buses, caravans, trucks, etc. Leaving behind the known for the unknown. Gypsies. Hollywood. California. "Boom" towns. The "magic bus." Conferences.

The Caution: Forsaking the individual path in favor of a more secure, common one. Perpetuating restlessness. Constantly seeking the "pot of gold." Far-off lands. Inability to settle anywhere. Being a rolling stone. Forsaking lasting relationships. Wild goose chases. Running away from problems. Fear of flying.

What does this **SYMBOL** say to *you?*

A GIRLS' BASKETBALL TEAM

Virgo 21

Commentary: "A Girls' Basketball Team" is pictured. The girls may be lighthearted about their game, enjoying the fun, the friendship, and the sportsmanship. Whether this is a professional or amateur game, there is a need to cooperate with others and to play by the rules of the game to achieve the "Team's" goals. Some on the "Team" however, may take the outcome very seriously, like it's a "life and death" situation. Playing the game to the best of their ability is necessary, as they will be judged by the others in the team, their coach and those on the sidelines. Popularity is often a factor, with some on the "Team" being star players and trendsetters and others merely making up the numbers, there to close the gaps and pass the ball.

Oracle: In the situation facing you, working with friends and those with similar interests will enable you to join together to achieve a mutually desired end. Which role do you play in the "game"? Are you happy with your status on the "Team"? Do you get recognition for the part you play or for what you do, or do you blend into the crowd, not standing out in any way? Regardless of outcomes, there's a need to enjoy the game and encourage group cohesion. Are people hogging the ball, or are they being fair and passing it when necessary? Are enough people getting to really play the game? Are people passing the ball to each other fairly? Is this a social game or are the stakes much higher? Do outcomes seem very serious? Whatever, respecting each other and giving each other a fair crack at having a moment of glory is the best for all concerned. Do you want to be a star player or be in a "Team" of stars? Without team effort no one will get to be on a star "Team" because it takes "teamwork" to shine and win. Look at how you and others play the game.

Keywords: The give and take of unity and equality. Everyone getting to play the game. Joyful participation. Friendship and sport. Fast footwork. Winning and losing. Being in the team. Playing fair and square. Coaching and practice. The need for a level playing ground. Uniforms. Codes of behavior and play. Locker-room antics.

The Caution: Forcing others to compete on the same level without regard for differences. Finding it difficult to play by the rules or cooperate. Bitchiness and rivalry taking the fun out of playing. Petulance and spitting the pacifier. Some being stars while others are merely drones. Taking things too seriously. Tantrums. The desire to win at all costs.

What does this **SYMBOL** say to *you?*

Please don't ask me what the score is; I'm not even sure what the game is.
Ashleigh Brilliant

A particular shot or way of moving the ball can be a player's personal signature, but efficiency of performance is what wins the game for the team.
Pat Riley

A team should never practice on a field that is not lined. Your players have to become aware of the field's boundaries.
John Madden

If a team is to reach its potential, each player must be willing to subordinate his personal goals to the good of the team.
Bud Wilkinson

Individual commitment to a group effort—that is what makes a team work, a company work, a society work, a civilization work.
Vince Lombardi

One man can be a crucial ingredient on a team, but one man cannot make a team.
Kareem Abdul-Jabbar

Life begins when you get out of the grandstand and into the game.
P. L. Debevoise

Virgo 22

Every king springs from a race of slaves, and every slave has had kings among his ancestors.
Plato

Dignity is not negotiable. Dignity is the honor of the family.
Vartan Gregorian

When I want a peerage, I shall buy one like an honest man.
Lord Northcliffe

Nobility has its obligations.
Saying

We are not a family, we're a firm.
King George VI

It is indeed a desirable thing to be well descended, but the glory belongs to our ancestors.
Plutarch

My mother told me I was blessed, and I have always taken her word for it. Being born of—or reincarnated from—royalty is nothing like being blessed. Royalty is inherited from another human being; blessedness comes from God.
Duke Ellington

Honor wears different coats to different eyes.
Barbara Tuchman

A ROYAL COAT OF ARMS ENRICHED WITH PRECIOUS STONES

Commentary: A "Royal Coat of Arms Enriched with Precious Stones" is shown. The term "a Coat of Arms," refers to the custom of the eleventh to fifteenth centuries, in England, of knights displaying their "Arms" on a tunic or coat worn over armor for identification. Royalty bestowed the "Royal Coat of Arms." The design of individual "Coats of Arms" varies, but all include things such as animals, words and colors. Along with people, towns, regions and countries can have "Coats of Arms."

Oracle: There is a strong connection to heritage, one's lineage and ancestors. This can give rise to feelings or pride and honor. There are things to stand up for and to represent. Being true to your heritage or beliefs will empower you with strength and stability. There can be the appearance, or the impression, of wealth, no matter what the actual financial status. There is a need to project a sense of nobility of character, pride and confidence as adopting these strengths will see you through this situation. Sometimes someone believes that they're "above" everyone else and they lord it over others believing they have a "God-given right" to be in charge, bully or call the shots. In situations of trouble, difficulty or betrayal (in fact any challenging emotion), falling back on a belief of your own "royalty," combined with a good sense of self-worth and who you are will help you get through with grace and without incurring bad blood or enemies or letting yourself down. Displaying markings of noble status and bearing, even if this is just in your behavior, can lead others to see and believe in your beauty, talent and worth.

Keywords: A long lineage standing behind. Social stratas. Royalty. Issues of social standing and identity. Having a regal bearing. Aristocratic status. Nobility. Coats of Arms. Strength of association. Pure blood. Ancestors of worth or note. Hereditary lines. Having rights and prestige. Pageantry. Knights jousting. Inheritances. Wealthy lineage. Displays of grace and honor. Beauty and wealth no matter what the status. Tartans. Precious stones. Shields. Inscriptions.

The Caution: Superficial judgment on one's ancestry. Believing in privileges for the select few. Seeing others as not being worthy. Class consciousness. Snobbery. Having "slaves" to do everything. Being "in the club." Elite school snobbery. Bastardizing others. Feeling above everyone because of lineage.

What does this **SYMBOL** say to *you?*

A LION TAMER RUSHES FEARLESSLY INTO THE CIRCUS ARENA

Virgo 23

Commentary: "A Lion Tamer" is seen. He "Rushes Fearlessly into the Circus Arena." The "Lion Tamer" needs to really know what he's doing; if he does not, he could be putting his life on the line. Not only does he have to be completely professional, he also has to be sure of his skill and display a complete lack of fear. Weakness of any description can have disastrous consequences.

Oracle: With this Symbol, there's a need for self-discipline and mastery. Being prepared to take on things that are "unknown" or risky may lead to excitement, but how much is being risked in order to accept the challenge? One has to be cautious with every move, as there's the need to anticipate every type of outcome or eventuality. In order to survive or "win" in this situation, there's a need to bite the bullet and to put fears behind you. It is not that you need to extinguish powerful emotions and energies, but skillfully manipulate things, so that the outcome will be that you are the one in charge. As long as you're aware of all the possible consequences, things should turn out okay. However, with this Symbol, there is a question of to what degree the risks are real and to what degree they are imagined. It is common for the lions to be well fed by the "Lion Tamer" before he ventures into the arena, reducing the risk of danger. The audience, oblivious of the methods the "Lion Tamer" utilizes or undertakes, are gripped by their own fears or the way they believe they would act if they were in his place. Hence, this Symbol can reflect that you are allowing others to think you are braver, and taking more risks than you really are. This can give you an advantage over others for a while, but the audience can easily become disillusioned if the truth becomes known. Whatever, how prepared are you for what may happen? Once you're out there in the "Circus Arena", you're committed to it, with no easy turning back.

Keywords: Having faith and courage in your abilities. Sublimating animal instincts. Control. Fearlessness. Professionalism. Extremism. Adrenaline rushes. Dangerous spectacles. Training and conditioned responses. Restrained passion. Coordination and skill. Superheroes. Holding the whip.

The Caution: Needing to be in control. Believing that things are dependent on your direction. Showing off and boasting. Plunging into situations, physically or emotionally, that are inherently dangerous without regard for the consequences. Overplaying one's abilities. Dominant attitudes. Taking on anything and anyone.

What does this **SYMBOL** say to *you?*

A great part of courage is the courage of having done the thing before.
Ralph Waldo Emerson

CIRCUS, n. A place where horses, ponies and elephants are permitted to see men, women and children acting the fool.
Ambrose Bierce

Nothing noble is done without risk.
Andre Gide

The wicked flee when no one pursues, but the righteous are bold as a lion.
Traditional Proverb

Half the failures of this world arise from pulling in one's horse as he is leaping.
Augustus W. Hare

Love is the only force capable of transforming an enemy into a friend.
Martin Luther King, Jr.

Mankind are animals that make bargains; no other animal does this.
Adam Smith

Virgo 24

Manifest plainness,
Embrace simplicity,
Reduce selfishness,
Have few desires.
Lao-Tzu

There are perhaps no days
of our childhood we lived so
fully as those we spent with a
favorite book.
Marcel Proust

A man's action is only a picture
book of his creed.
Ralph Waldo Emerson

The only gift is a portion of
thyself ... the poet brings his
poem; the shepherd his lamb.
Ralph Waldo Emerson

So much perfection argues
rottenness somewhere.
Beatrice Webb

Mary had a little lamb,
Its fleece was white as snow;
And everywhere that Mary
*   went*
The lamb was sure to go.
Nursery Rhyme

Mary had a little lamb.
The doctor was surprised.
Urban Joke

A loving heart is the truest
wisdom.
Charles Dickens

MARY AND HER WHITE LAMB

Commentary: "Mary and Her White Lamb" is a Symbol reflecting innocence and purity. It is derived from an old nursery rhyme; "Mary's White Lamb" followed "Mary" wherever she might go. They had a very strong bond between them. The "Lamb" seemed to be very taken by "Mary" as was "Mary" by the "Lamb." There is a need to be watchful for dependent or codependent behavior with others. This story shows a strong sense of attachment and dependence.

Oracle: Is someone following someone else around, or acting like a doe-eyed lamb? Maybe they are constantly checking on the other, wanting to know their every move. Are they trying to monopolize someone, while excluding others? If one were to leave the scene, how would the other react? Sometimes, what seems to be "codependent" behavior is someone merely looking out for your best interests, so don't assume the worst right away. Look at their motives, or your own, for that matter, for any clingy behavior and assess why they are behaving the way they are. Having a belief in the integrity of people and the purity of their motives can bring joy and a sense of belonging. There is usually a strong feeling of kindness and softness with this Symbol. Keeping a sense of innocence, purity and honesty in the situation will lift you up and out of any problems. Being kind and yet firm, loving and yet a separate individual and sharing without losing your boundaries can lead to a wonderful, pure experience of love and friendship. There's a need for imagination mixed with simplicity. However, there can be a feeling of being "lost" in the wilderness when there's no support or reassurance from others. In terms of relationships, there can be an imbalance where one person looks up to the other. Be watchful to see if anyone is giving away their power in this situation.

Keywords: Simple childlike innocence or pure escapism. Naïveté. The Mary and Jesus story. Dependence. Kindness. Friendship. Bonds between pets and owners. Believing in the essential goodness of others. Hanging out with people. Looking out for someone. Cuteness. The urge to prove something. Dislike of dirt or grime. Being "addicted" to someone or something.

The Caution: Naïveté. Avoiding real issues. Stalking. Overprotection. Doubting motives. Paranoia that someone is following you. Feeling lost without the other. Doe-eyed attraction. Clinging to people. Arousing jealousy through favoritism. Not leaving people alone. Checking people's whereabouts. Not growing up. Being the black sheep.

What does this **SYMBOL** say to *you?*

A FLAG AT HALF-MAST IN FRONT OF A PUBLIC BUILDING

Virgo 25

The monument of a great man is not of granite or marble or bronze. It consists of his goodness, his deeds, his love and his compassion.
Alfred A. Montapert

A life spent in constant labor is a life wasted, save a man be such a fool as to regard a fulsome obituary notice as ample reward.
George Jean Nathan

To be remembered after we are dead is but poor recompense for being treated with contempt while we are living.
William Hazlitt

If I have done any deed worthy of remembrance, that deed will be my monument. If not, no monument can preserve my memory.
Agesilaus II

If your contribution has been vital there will always be somebody to pick up where you left off, and that will be your claim to immortality.
Walter Gropius

It matters not how a man dies, but how he lives.
Samuel Johnson

The past is utterly indifferent to its worshippers.
William Winter

Commentary: "A Flag at Half-Mast in Front of a Public Building" is a Symbol of accomplishment and achievement coupled with the loss or mourning for someone or something that has died, been completed or been abandoned in some way. It can picture carrying a task through to completion. Now it is time for recognition of what's been accomplished during the life that's been lived. This Symbol can sometimes produce a feeling of loss, like something has passed from one's life.

Oracle: This Symbol reflects the need for the acknowledgment or public display of something that has passed on or disappeared from your life. It may be important to let others know that there has been a change of some kind or a passing on. This may be a lonely passage or it may involve many others. The display should not be noisy or overt, but a show of respect and accepted as a normal part of life. This means that you don't have to hide or pretend that nothing has happened. Others may prefer to have a simple and respectful sign that brings the loss to their attention. This allows for understanding without the embarrassment of saying or doing the wrong thing in what may be a sensitive and emotional time for both yourself and others. The fact that this "Flag" is "in Front of a Public Building" implies that this passing away may have importance to many in the community. People or groups wearing black armbands are similar to the flag at "Half-Mast." Grieving may be a necessary part of the process, but this is also a time for assimilating what it took to get you where you are.

Keywords: Public tribute and recognition. Political affairs. The desire to leave a legacy to society. Having the power to sway the masses or authorities. Signs for all to see. Destinies fulfilled. Coming together as a community or nation to share loss. Judgment on one's life. Appraisal of deeds and character. Public holidays. Obituaries. Taking the time to grieve. Black armbands. Institutions that are closed. Mourning the loss of somebody greatly admired.

The Caution: Feeling an obligation to carry on without taking time to sort out issues from the past or mourn any loss. Devastation and mourning. The burning desire to leave behind something no matter what the cost. Things coming to a standstill. Crocodile tears for what's passed away. Hypocritical mourning for the chosen few.

What does this **SYMBOL** say to *you?*

Virgo 26

A man who pays respect to the great paves the way for his own greatness.
Chinese Proverb

Freedom—to walk free and own no superior.
Walt Whitman

I don't know what your destiny will be, but one thing I know: the only ones among you who will be really happy are those who have sought and found how to serve.
Albert Schweitzer

Everybody can be great… because anybody can serve. You don't have to have a college degree to serve. You don't have to make your subject and verb agree to serve. You only need a heart full of grace. A soul generated by love.
Martin Luther King, Jr.

The surest way to corrupt a youth is to instruct him to hold in higher regard those who think alike than those who think differently.
Friedrich Nietzche

It is amazing what you can accomplish if you do not care who gets the credit.
Harry S. Truman

A BOY WITH A CENSER SERVES NEAR THE PRIEST AT THE ALTAR

Commentary: "A Boy" is shown with a "Censer." He "Serves near the Priest at the Altar." The "Boy" doesn't have the experience or social position of the "Priest," but that shouldn't put him off his duties. His position and responsibilities are still important. In a Catholic church service, wine is drunk as a symbol of the blood of Christ. Wafers are placed on the tongues of the believers as the representation of the body of Christ. How the "Boy" reacts to the ritual or ceremony will depend on his upbringing, beliefs or temperament. He could be rapt with fascination at what is being played out or he could be indifferent, bored and really preferring to go home. It is unclear whether the "Boy" wants to eventually take the position of the older "Priest," or colleague, or not. He may grow up to do other things, but right now he's got his position or duty to fulfill. This may be less than he's actually able to do or is truly "qualified" to do.

Oracle: Be cautious of feeling that what you are doing is inconsequential; even the smallest contribution is an important part of the whole and we all play our part in some measure. Sometimes there's the need to wait things out until one is more mature, practiced or prepared to be in charge. Right now you may be someone's "right-hand man" and not in charge of proceedings. A more exalted position will be attained, given time. Give reverence and respect to your everyday routines, no matter how insignificant they seem and you will find your sense of hope renewed. However, watch out for any feelings of jealousy that someone is bigger, better, more experienced or more respected than the other. Measuring one's self by the successes of others can be useful, except when it degrades your belief in yourself, or in others. In your situation who is the "Priest" and who is the "Boy"?

Keywords: Youthful attitudes. Doing what's simple, with silence and devotion. Participating in the toil but not the glory. Altars and shrines. Incense. Burning candles. Passing down wisdom and knowledge. Looking up to those in power. Work experience. Apprenticeships. Feelings of awe and respect. Religious and social ceremonies. Issues of authority and the abuse of it.

The Caution: Being dominated by spiritual hierarchy that is devised by human rationalism. Doing "lesser things" to avoid responsibility. Not taking a place of authority when one could or should. Feeling not good enough because of inexperience. Someone always hanging around. Incompetence. Refusal to take instruction. Sexual abuse. Betrayal of beliefs. The church overpowering one's life.

What does this **SYMBOL** say to *you?*

ARISTOCRATIC ELDERLY LADIES DRINKING AFTERNOON TEA IN A WEALTHY HOME

Commentary: "Aristocratic Elderly Ladies Drinking Afternoon Tea in a Wealthy Home" is a Symbol of people meeting to share a drink, something to eat, and a little chatter or gossip. The fact that they are "Aristocratic" and "Elderly" implies that they have everything they need, and quite possibly more. It also shows that they have an air of "Wealth" and grace about them, regardless of how "Wealthy" they actually are.

Oracle: In the situation facing you, regardless of your actual financial situation, there's a need to face things with elegant composure. This will attract the respect of others. There is no need to hurry and rush, however, being punctual and on time is probably important. Sharing your time with people who quietly know and understand each other can bring peace of mind and the opportunity to relax and take time off. Sometimes, however, issues that really should be discussed are "masked" and covered up in an effort to keep things looking respectable. Sharing stories and gossiping can be rather healthy, as long as things are kept within the bounds of friendship and decency. Others can feel excluded sometimes, particularly younger people and men. They may feel that they don't fit in or measure up. Is everybody having a relaxing "Afternoon Tea," or are they trying to outdo each other in some measure?

Keywords: Quite knowing atmosphere. Enjoying the company of others. Special privileges. Taking time off to relax, confident that all is okay. The elite vs. the masses. The appreciation of culture. Beauty and wealth. Gossip and chatter. Afternoon teas, brunches and lunches. Charity drives. Being in the group. Exclusivity vs. open-armed acceptance. Ladies at the club. Girls having fun. Knowing how to entertain. Joy in social communion. Servants. Fine furnishings. Fine china. Silver cutlery. Candles. Bridge games. Toasting abundance. Tea, coffee, cake and biscuits. Afternoon sources. Soirees.

The Caution: Snobbery and elitism. Always having to go to others or have them come to you. People expecting others to do all the work while they just sit around and chat. Mindless talk. Indulgent behavior. Having little to think about or do. Exclusion of others as not being worthy. Loneliness. Being rowdy and unkempt. Uncouth behaviour. "Hitting the bottle."

What does this **SYMBOL** say to *you?*

There are chapters in every life which are seldom read and certainly not aloud.
Carol Shields

To a philosopher all news, as it is called, is gossip, and they who edit and read it are old women over their tea.
Henry David Thoreau

Where there are friends there is wealth.
Titus Maccius Plautus

Don't take up a man's time talking about the smartness of your children; he wants to talk to you about the smartness of his children.
Ed Howe

Thank God for tea! What would the world do without tea? How did it exist? I am glad I was not born before tea.
Sydney Smith

I have measured out my life with coffee spoons.
T. S. Eliot

Frequently the more trifling the subject, the more animated and protracted the discussion.
Franklin Pierce

'Tis the privilege of friendship to talk nonsense, and have her nonsense respected.
Charles Lamb

Virgo 28

All I want is a warm bed and a kind word, and unlimited power.
Ashleigh Brilliant

All violence, all that is dreary and repels, is not power, but the absence of power.
Ralph Waldo Emerson

I have never been able to conceive how any rational being could propose happiness to himself from the exercise of power over others.
Thomas Jefferson

No person is your friend who demands your silence, or denies your right to grow.
Alice Walker

Never get angry. Never make a threat. Reason with people.
Mario Puzo, from The Godfather

Never strike your wife, even with a flower.
Hindu Proverb

Power tends to corrupt, and absolute power corrupts absolutely.
Lord Acton

A BALD-HEADED MAN IN UNIFORM HAS SEIZED POWER

Commentary: "A Bald-Headed Man in Uniform Has Seized Power." This pictures a situation where male power is dominant. The fact that this person is pictured as being "Bald-Headed" doesn't literally have to mean that he is "Bald." Baldness has long been associated with macho strength and testosterone. The fact that he's seen as being "in Uniform" shows that this person has, or needs to be given, a position of authority or "Power." However, this "Uniform" may give him more of this perceived "Power" than perhaps he should have or deserves to have.

Oracle: This may be the time to "Seize Power" and to push forward with decisions that need to be realized and grounded now. Someone may need to take a stand and direct the course of action. It is most likely by force of will that the best solution will be found, but one must be careful to temper the situation, as strong displays of masculinity could get out of hand very quickly. Somebody may be pushing their agenda a little too hard, taking over and showing control issues. There are times when someone has to take charge—the question in this situation is, are they doing it wisely and kindly? Is love guiding their decisions or are they just being pushy and forceful? If someone is being over the top and bossy, this may be because of feelings of inferiority that they are trying to mask or cover up, especially if they feel that life has passed them by. Reigning in the many facets of one's personality into a single focus of action can work wonders now.

Keywords: Dominating others' mental space. Male hormones running rampant. Issues to do with hair. Ponytails. The story of Samson and his hair. Taking positions of power. Uniforms. Demanding others follow one's lead. Strutting one's stuff. "Wearing the pants in the family." The ability to direct and organize many people. Letting others express their opinions or have a say. Domination. The government. The military. Decisions based on logic. Taking action or control.

The Caution: Pushing too hard or fast. Ramming one's convictions. Being unkind and bossy. Putting on a show because one's in uniform. Power tripping. Being cruel and domineering. Lording it over others. Being opportunistic. Corruption. Misuse of power. Bullying. Big business calling the shots. Domestic violence. Taking charge because one can. Strict rules to live your life by. Taking over. Not listening to what others have to say.

What does this **SYMBOL** say to *you?*

A MAN IS GAINING SECRET KNOWLEDGE FROM AN ANCIENT SCROLL HE IS READING

Virgo 29

Commentary: "A Man is Gaining Secret Knowledge from an Ancient Scroll He Is Reading." He's learning insights and things that will most likely further him in life and his quest for knowledge. The "Ancient Scroll" obviously contains some very important information. In order to really gain this "Secret Knowledge," he needs to pay attention to every detail and not overlook anything. The clues he is gathering may help him lead a fuller, more spiritual life, or they may assist him in his hobby or profession.

Oracle: This "Ancient Scroll" that the "Man Is Gaining Secret Knowledge" from can literally refer to written material, but it can also mean unwritten things, the myths and stories that are the base elements of our humanity. It is, however, the ability to translate this "Knowledge" into a practical set of lessons for our day-to-day life that assists our progress as we grow and mature. Stories from the past and from mythology are the verbalization of our inner archetypes. An oracle is something that reveals "Secret Knowledge"; our own inner wisdom can be revealed by the inspiration of an oracle. The most seemingly insignificant information can often turn out to be valuable for future understanding or for our experiences. There may be the feeling of not knowing what to do, or of not knowing what is going on. To gain a sense of clarity in your situation, go back to the basic or essential truths of the matter. This may indeed be the inner wisdom of the ages. Modern solutions may not be of use at this time. Understanding will come through patient, steady work and illuminating inspiration.

Keywords: Learning from ancient mysteries. Looking for answers. Study and its rewards. Reading between the lines. Finding clues from the past and applying them to the present. Being privileged to look into something special. Alchemy. The Bible, the Torah and the Koran. Manuscripts. Scrolls. Ancient writings. Akashic records. Classified documents. Secret papers. Scribes.

The Caution: Failing to acknowledge old wisdom or refusing the new. Losing one's common sense. Losing touch with reality. Reading importance into things that are not real or useful. Conspiracy theories. Religious zealotry. Feeling gifted over the rest. Finding nothing interesting in the everyday, modern world. Being single-minded.

What does this **SYMBOL** say to *you?*

On leaf of palm, on sedge-wrought roll, on plastic clay and leathern scroll, man wrote his thoughts; the ages passed, and lo! The Press was found at last!
John Greenleaf Whittier

History is the unrolled scroll of prophecy.
James A. Garfield

To furnish the means of acquiring knowledge is ...the greatest benefit that can be conferred upon mankind. It prolongs life itself and enlarges the sphere of existence.
John Quincy Adams

All men by nature desire knowledge.
Aristotle

All human knowledge takes the form of interpretation.
Walter Benjamin

Through zeal knowledge is gotten, through lack of zeal knowledge is lost.
Buddha

Memory is the scribe of the soul.
Aristotle

There is nothing new except that which has become antiquated.
Lycee Rose Bertin

Virgo 30

I love deadlines. I especially like the whooshing sound they make as they go flying by.
Douglas Adams

While we are postponing, life speeds by.
Seneca

For all sad words of tongue and pen, the saddest are these: It might have been.
John Greenleaf Whittier

It is not enough to be industrious; so are the ants. What are you industrious about?
Henry David Thoreau

The person who says it can't be done should not interrupt the person doing it.
Chinese Proverb

Until you value yourself, you will not value your time. Until you value your time, you will not do anything with it.
M. Scott Peck

There is not any memory with less satisfaction than the memory of some temptation we resisted.
James Branch Cabell

Every man who possibly can should force himself to a holiday of a full month in a year, whether he feels like taking it or not.
William James

HAVING AN URGENT TASK TO COMPLETE, A MAN DOESN'T LOOK TO ANY DISTRACTIONS

Commentary: "Having an Urgent Task to Complete, a Man Doesn't Look to Any Distractions" shows the need for an undisturbed focus in application and not allowing "Distractions" to interfere. The person pictured here has got something that needs to be done and completed, and he doesn't let anything "Distract" him from it.

Oracle: There is a need to pay complete attention to the job at hand as this is necessary now in order to get things done. Pushing through with the work and avoiding temptations regardless of what's going on around you will hasten the rewards of completion. However, sometimes friends, lovers, partners or children require our assistance, and we have to drop what we'd rather be doing. If these intrusions happen time and time again, we can feel loaded down with responsibilities that aren't ours, and can be weighed down by not getting on with what we really need to achieve. We must remember to put time and effort into what we want to accomplish, and not allow ourselves to be led astray. Alternatively, you may be allowing these intrusions as a way to solve boredom, or as an excuse to procrastinate. If this describes your situation, ask yourself how much you actually want what you are trying to do. An exercise to improve clarity is keeping a goals list. Write down everything you need to do, no matter how small, in order to realize your objectives. Every time you tick something off, you are that much closer to reaching your goals. On the other hand, one can become bogged down in the attempt to complete something and actually accomplish nothing. If this is so, a closer focus on what it is that you really need to achieve would help.

Keywords: Staying true to yourself and remaining on the path or on the job. One-pointedness. Meditation. Blocking out the external world in order to achieve complete focus on a situation or state of mind. Religious experiences. Maintaining one direction. Seeing something through to completion. Taking the phone off the hook. One-eyed behavior.

The Caution: Paying attention to outside influences. Letting the slightest excuse take one away from what needs to be done. Rigidity of thought or action leading to missed creative or intuitive opportunities. Obsession. Indulgences. Workaholics. Addictions and destructive behavior. Superficial distractions.

What does this **SYMBOL** say to *you?*

A BUTTERFLY PRESERVED AND MADE PERFECT WITH A DART THROUGH IT

Libra 1

Commentary: "A Butterfly Preserved and Made Perfect with a Dart through It" is an image of beauty captured and preserved for it to be admired and appreciated. People such as Marilyn Monroe, James Dean, J.F.K. and Princess Diana can appear like the "Butterfly" that is "Preserved and Made Perfect." They inspire awe and beauty in us; they represent something we aspire to and long for. No matter how old they were when they died, their deaths feel somewhat like a sacrifice; they left us far too soon. However, like the "Butterfly," they will remain forever beautiful and unchanging in our minds and culture. Their "Butterfly" is "Preserved and Made Perfect" by being kept forever in this "Perfect" unchanging state.

Oracle: Beauty in shape or form has been frozen in one moment, denying the natural processes of decay. An archetypal death is symbolized and perhaps a type of "Perfection" is enshrined through a sacrifice. As inspiring as this process can be, it can show difficulties in shifting or moving on. This Symbol can also picture an event that is frozen in time, like something that we just can't forget or let go of. Feelings of being stuck and immobilized, whether real or imagined, won't help at the moment. Perhaps there's a feeling that you, or someone else, are being used for something that you don't agree with or can't really benefit from. A movie may be playing in your mind, over and over, like it's somehow pinned on a "Dart." Whatever the situation, is there progress being made or is this a situation of capture, sacrifice and death? Is something being postponed because of an inability to move? What sacrifices are being asked? Is sacrifice really necessary, or is someone being used as a martyr, tied to a situation or an ideal? Are judgments being made on outer beauty rather than inner depth? Are issues from the past pinning you down and stopping you from forward movement?

Keywords: Perfection and beauty made immortal. Holding onto things or events from the past. Unchanging realities. Moments frozen in time. Superficiality. External beauty that's lacking animation. Pinning things up so they can be admired. The "handiwork" of creation on display. Transfiguration. Suspension in time. Posters.

The Caution: Impinging others' growth for selfish needs. Surrender and immobilization. Pinned down and unable to move. The attempt to freeze things from growing naturally. Placing importance on preserving appearances at the expense of all else. Staying far too long. Seeing no future. Having no past. Not letting go.

What does this **SYMBOL** say to *you?*

Life is short. Time is fleeting. Realize the self. Purity of the heart is the gateway to God. Aspire. Renounce. Meditate. Be good; do good. Be kind; be compassionate. Inquire, know thyself.
Sivananda

The butterfly counts not months but moments, and has time enough.
Rabindranath Tagore

A thing is right when it tends to preserve the integrity, stability, and beauty of the biotic community. It is wrong when it tends otherwise.
Aldo Leopold

LIFE, n. A spiritual pickle preserving the body from decay. We live in daily apprehension of its loss; yet when lost it is not missed.
Ambrose Bierce

It is necessary to write, if the days are not to slip emptily by. How else, indeed, to clap the net over the butterfly of the moment? For the moment passes, it is forgotten; the mood is gone; life itself is gone.
Vita Sackville-West

Love is like a butterfly, hold it too tight, it'll crush; hold it too loose, it'll fly.
Anonymous

Libra 2

It is not the strongest of the species that survive, nor the most intelligent, but the one most responsive to change.
Charles Darwin

All that is human must retrograde if it does not advance.
Edward Gibbon

Postmodernism represents a moment of suspension before the batteries are recharged for the new millennium, an acknowledgment that preceding the future is a strange and hybrid interregnum that might be called the last gasp of the past.
Gilbert Adair

There is nothing more innately human than the tendency to transmute what has become customary into what has been divinely ordained.
Suzanne LaFollette

Evolution ever climbing after some ideal good and reversion ever dragging evolution in the mud.
Lord Alfred Tennyson

THE LIGHT OF THE SIXTH RACE TRANSMUTED TO THE SEVENTH

Commentary: The "Light of the Sixth Race Transmuted to the Seventh." This may be a time of new beginnings—the implementation of a whole new order. A feeling of ascension is present here, with people approaching an entirely new level of living and operating. There's a need to be with or communicate with people who have shared visions and hopes for the future. We have a choice: the fruits of past experience can bring either light or dark to the present.

Oracle: This Symbol can show a leap ahead in consciousness, so much so that the old ways of functioning and living are no longer satisfying, or even possible. Sometimes the old codes for living are actually somewhat unsustainable or unbearable. It's best to respect the value of what is waning and leaving your life, taking all the best qualities of the past with you. Many things that were important before have now lost their imperative. The objectives that one wants to aim for are, or have, changed radically in the realization of this new age. The aspects of modern society are often left behind for a higher, more "evolved" state. This Symbol often shows someone who is within reach of their ultimate potential. A "new order" needs to be implemented and the time has come for it to happen. There are likely to be many who share the same aspirations as you, people who are on the same road and see the same signs. Join with those who are working at something truly worthwhile, as this will see you moving further and further toward a chosen future, rather than one that is just foisted on you by society. Some may not want to join you in your journey, though. Regardless of this progression and ascension, there is a need to remain rooted in the reality of practicality. Otherwise, you, or someone else, may lose the way in the glamour or "fog" that these new, sometimes deeply spiritual, realities can bring.

Keywords: Younger or more vital elements taking over from the elders. The fruits of the new age. Theosophy—Blavatsky's theories. Finding kindred spirits. Sharing visions. Ascension and evolution. Inheritances that move one forward. Growing older and wiser. UFOs and aliens. Music that lifts one's spirits. Gurus and avatars. Demarcations of evolution. Transmutations. Indigo children. Evolving.

The Caution: Losing touch with practical survival. Can be racial (or other) discrimination. Feeling that one is from a "higher" order (or more evolved) than other people. Leaving others behind.

What does this **SYMBOL** say to *you?*

THE DAWN OF A NEW DAY REVEALS EVERYTHING CHANGED

Libra 3

Commentary: "The Dawn of a New Day Reveals Everything Changed" pictures new beginnings that can be sudden and unexpected. It's like a new awakening; something new is taking shape and form and emerging into a "New Day" and this "Reveals Everything Changed." What was happening or evident just recently, even just the "Day" before, has "Changed" through an event or some shift of the mind or heart. Things are "Changed"; things are "New," they are somehow different.

Oracle: This "New Day" may not have "Dawned" yet, but it is definitely on its way. It's hard to believe at first, but eventually it will "Dawn" on you that many facets of your situation are different in the light of this "New Day." Life may have been difficult, or things unsure, and you may feel like you've been through a long night, or a period of darkness. Perhaps someone has been too comfortable in their habits, or in their complacency, and has let things just go on and on. There may need to be major changes in attitude with the new situation or information before you, and sometimes these changes are hard to adjust to, especially if what's happening hasn't been your idea or your desired outcome. Take heart, realize that the darkness is abating, and gradually let go of what went before. Realize that it's come time to let go of the old conditions and move on. This is an opportunity to "seize the day"; to see that there is light all around you. A change of scene can affect how you feel and how things appear. How does, or how will, this "New Day" affect you? Only you can know. However, getting up and seeing the "Dawn" can bring spiritual messages about the direction you are moving toward. It can infuse you with hope and energy for the future.

Keywords: New perspectives and realizations. Waking up to a whole new consciousness or sense of reality. Emerging from depression. Huge changes that erase things that mattered before. Radical shifts. Major life experiences. Being reborn. Events out of nowhere. Changes of fortune. Revitalized perspectives. Coming out of a sleep.

The Caution: Holding on despite all evidence and reason to move on. Refusing to believe that things are getting better. Waking up and not knowing where one is. Fickleness. Change for the sake of change. Sticking with the old. Having to adjust continually to changing circumstances. Unstable behavior.

There is nothing in this world constant, but inconstancy.
Jonathan Swift

Times change, and we change with them.
Anonymous

Things do not change, we change.
Henry Thoreau

One should count each day a separate life.
Seneca

A day is a miniature eternity.
Ralph Waldo Emerson

Finish each day and be done with it. You have done what you could; some blunders and absurdities have crept in; forget them as soon as you can. Tomorrow is a new day; you shall begin it serenely and with too high a spirit to be encumbered with your old nonsense.
Ralph Waldo Emerson

This is the highest wisdom that I own; freedom and life are earned by those alone who conquer them each day anew.
Goethe

What does this **SYMBOL** say to *you?*

Libra 4

In everyone's life, at some time, our inner fire goes out. It is then burst into flame by an encounter with another human being. We should all be thankful for those people who rekindle the inner spirit.
Albert Schweitzer

They eat, they drink, and in communion sweet Quaff immortality and joy.
John Milton

Even in a time of elephantine vanity and greed, one never has to look far to see the campfires of gentle people.
Garrison Keillor

Civilization no longer needs to open up wilderness; it needs wilderness to open up the still largely unexplored human mind.
David Rains Wallace

The hand of God is with the group.
Saudi Arabian Proverb

Double, double, toil and trouble; Fire burn and cauldron bubble.
William Shakespeare

An agreeable companion on a journey is as good as a carriage.
Publilius Syrus

A GROUP OF YOUNG PEOPLE SIT IN SPIRITUAL COMMUNION AROUND A CAMPFIRE

Commentary: A "Group of Young People Sit in Spiritual Communion Around a Campfire" symbolizes the need for connecting with others who have similar feelings and shared beliefs. The "Group of Young People" are connected not only through their sense of generation; they "Sit in Spiritual Communion" and are linked through their interests, beliefs and stories. Something they believe in has drawn them together and this can bring a sense of "Spiritual Communion" to each of them. They can each have a common focus that opens them up to creative and receptive responses.

Oracle: In the situation facing you, there is bound to be a central issue—the "Campfire"—that can bring many people, possibly everyone, together. There may be a feeling of being "out there," in the "wilderness," but remember that you are not alone. Whether physically, spiritually, mentally or emotionally, others are with you in some sense. Look to the "center," the "Campfire" that draws you together, to see who or what this is. It can be a belief, a religion, or a reunion of some kind. It can indeed be something as obvious as a "Fire," or it can be something technological, such as the Internet; anything that brings people together in "a circle," with a central focus. Loneliness and isolation can be overcome with a little concentrated attention, through joining with others in some kind of "Communion." Lighting a fire, even lighting a candle, can bring joy, pleasure and a sense of "Spiritual Communion." Rekindling energy can lead to a deep sense of bonding and understanding. However, there can be a concern, or fear, that if one's friends and fellows were to leave the "campsite" (whatever it is that brought you together), one could feel lost, alone and abandoned to life and the elements. The "Fire" can almost become addictive, and lure you away from other things in your life. This can lead to dependency and sometimes codependency on others. Be sure to recognize your individuality in the situation, and claim your power as an independent, but integral, part of the group.

Keywords: Material concerns left behind. Pioneering with like-minded others. Sweat lodges. Walks in the woods. Girl and Boy Scouts. Men's groups, women's groups. ESP. Kindred spirits. Soul mates. Unity. Fellowship. Campfires. Camping. Friends and companions. Spiritual circles.

The Caution: Being dependent on others. Feeling left out. Having to fend for one's self. Being lost in the wilderness. Obsession with objectives.

What does this **SYMBOL** say to *you?*

A MAN TEACHING THE TRUE INNER KNOWLEDGE OF THE NEW WORLD TO HIS STUDENTS

Libra 5

When the pupil is ready, the Master appears.
Confucius

I called the New World into existence to redress the balance of the Old.
George Canning

This precept descended from heaven: know thyself.
Juvenal

He knoweth the universe, and himself he knoweth not.
Jean de la Fontaine

Learning is finding out what we already know. Doing is demonstrating that you know it. Teaching is reminding others that they know just as well as you. You are all learners, doers and teachers.
Richard Bach

Why does life keep teaching me lessons I have no desire to learn?
Ashleigh Brilliant

May those whose holy task it is, To guide impulsive youth, Fail not to cherish in their souls A reverence for truth; For teachings which the lips impart Must have their source within the heart...
Charlotte Forten Grimke

Commentary: "A Man Teaching the True Inner Knowledge of the New World to His Students" pictures somebody "Teaching," instructing or passing on pure "Knowledge," insights and meaning about "the New World" and the new age they live in. What he is "Teaching" is somehow very important, valuable and expansive to "His Students." The more conventional certifications of "Knowledge," such as diplomas, are not necessarily what's important here. It's the "Knowledge" and awareness that is being brought through, taught and realized that's important.

Oracle: Information and understanding is coming to you or through you. Insight, knowledge and expertise are available or present, or at least they need to be. True "Inner Knowledge" is available to all, no matter how "educated" one may be. If everyone is coming from a true sense of this "Inner Knowledge," there can be whole "New Worlds" built, with the foundations being passed down from the "Teacher" to the "Students." Does everyone involved have the mindset and the "ears" to listen to what's being taught? Is the "Teacher" radiating a pure sense of integrity regarding how he teaches the ways of this "New World"? If so, this can picture a "True Teacher," someone who can lead others on to a brighter and better future. However, sometimes there can be feelings of superiority, that someone "knows it all." Their ideas can be rather uninspiring, yet they still try to foist them on anyone who'll listen. The "Students" who are truly learning are those who will be the pioneers of the "New World." How are you feeling about your "Teachings" and your lessons? What needs to be learned on an "Inner" level? What can be passed on to others so they might learn, and improve their lives?

Keywords: Guidance and protection on the path. Being a guiding light for others. Imparting knowledge. Wisdom. Looking for truth. Seeking answers to complicated questions. Listening and learning. Turning to others to receive guidance. Speaking one's truth. Instinctual knowledge. Pioneers on the path. Teachers and students. Secrets of the new age.

The Caution: Dogmatism. Feeling that one person has the only true answer. Feelings of being highly "evolved" and holding it over other people's heads. Arrogance. Evangelism. Telling others "how it is," regardless of how they feel. Gurus and cult dogma. The blind leading the blind.

What does this **SYMBOL** say to *you?*

Libra 6

When an idea exclusively occupies the mind, it is transformed into an actual physical or mental state.
Sivananda

The pure impulse of dynamic creation is formless; and being formless, the creation it gives rise to can assume any and every form.
Kabbalah

The desire accomplished is sweet to the soul.
The Bible

Determine that the thing can and shall be done, and then we shall find the way.
Abraham Lincoln

Plant the seed of desire in your mind and it forms a nucleus with power to attract to itself everything needed for its fulfillment.
Robert Collier

Speak of the devil and he appears.
Arabic Proverb

It would not be better if things happened to men just as they wish.
Heraclitus

Nature is a revelation of god; art is a revelation of man.
Henry Wadsworth Longfellow

A MAN WATCHES HIS IDEALS TAKING A CONCRETE FORM BEFORE HIS INNER VISION

Commentary: "A Man Watches His Ideals Taking a Concrete Form before His Inner Vision." This person has had the knowledge or insight to know what he wants, or what he wishes to accomplish, and it is now materializing in front of him—it is "Taking a Concrete Form before His Inner Vision." As the "Vision" unfolds, so do the things that he's wanted. He will see, realize and understand that dreaming of and working on future possibilities often does indeed, in time, bring them into current realities.

Oracle: This is a good time to visualize your needs, wants, thoughts and feelings. In the situation facing you, what are the "Ideals" that need to be made real? Something that we're learning in this new and exciting age of human progress is that conscious concrete manifestation is entirely possible, especially when we feel aligned to our core purpose. When you decide what it is that you truly want, allowing the energy of it to be focused through the power of the mind will allow it to manifest. Here, something new is being formed, even if it is only in its preliminary stage or early days. If these "Ideals" are really meant to be brought into "Concrete Form," focusing intently on them will bring them into reality. By doing this, you will make it possible for your creative ideas to be projected out into the real world. However, one must be truly thoughtful about what one wants to create. You may find that your hopes and dreams are not only brought into the light of reality, but are truly being put to the test. Be careful what you wish for. The mind is very powerful, and, if your focus is not used correctly, difficult situations can emerge. Concentrate carefully on what it is that you want and "Watch" what happens. Think positively as this Symbol can create wonderful magic in your life.

Keywords: Vivid confrontations with one's objectives. Creative visualizations. Imagining things. Meditations and affirmations. Ideas crystallized. Putting things out into the universe. Making things happen. Seeing things take shape and form. Clairvoyance. Filmmaking. Writing and getting published. The power of manifestation. Solidification. Builders. Sculptures. Dreams.

The Caution: Being dissatisfied with what was thought to be the true ideal. Feeling that things are "written in stone" and can't be changed. Calcified situations or emotions. Neurosis. Focusing on the negative thereby bringing the negative.

What does this **SYMBOL** say to *you?*

A WOMAN FEEDING CHICKENS AND PROTECTING THEM FROM THE HAWKS

Libra 7

Commentary: "A Woman Feeding Chickens and Protecting Them from the Hawks" is an image of maternal care and having a sharp eye to watch that everyone who needs "Protection" is protected. The "Hawks" are predators, and "Chickens" can be like sitting ducks, to be picked off. The "Woman" is responsible for the well-being of the "Chickens" and has to ensure their safety. With "Hawks" around, she could find it difficult to relax. There is the perception that one's guard can't be let down without someone, or something, taking advantage.

Oracle: There is a need to look after those in your care, whether they are people, things or ideas. If you put yourself in the position of being the caretaker, you must take responsibility for their care, nurturing and well-being, together with other necessary tasks. The "Woman," who has become the "Chickens'" caretaker, has not only to "Feed" them, but "Protect" them from any dangers. There are possibly dangers that no one else seems to be taking seriously. Making sure that safeguards are in place and working well will ensure that things don't go wrong. However, those in a position of caregiving need to recognize the fine line between protection and overprotection. There is always more to responsibility than meets the eye. Oversheltering can lead to alienation from the caretaker. A statement often associated with this is "I only did it to protect you." This can apply in another sense; it can indicate keeping people in the dark and not letting them know what's really going on—for their own good." This Symbol can show taking responsibility for things that are not normally yours. Any efforts directed toward protecting and nourishing will be rewarded in the future.

Keywords: Nurture, protection and guardianship. Being on the lookout for changes in the atmosphere. Spotting problems that nobody else notices. Shielding innocents from "bad guys." Motherhood and the stress of it. Predators. Being firm with outsiders. Asylum. Places of residence.

The Caution: Overprotection. Unable to cope with everyday problems. Taking over with the pretense of the need for protection. Not allowing others to grow up. Always being on the lookout for problems. Neurotic worrying about what may happen. Seeing the world as a big, scary place. Being picked on. Taking advantage of the innocent. Protection money. Attacking others.

What does this **SYMBOL** say to *you?*

I gave my beauty and my youth to men. I am going to give my wisdom and experience to animals.
Brigitte Bardot

Power always protects the good of some at the expense of all others.
Thomas Merton

The best protection any woman can have …is courage.
Elizabeth Cady Stanton

The raven sees its chicks as falcons.
Turkish Proverb

My father had always said there are four things a child needs: plenty of love, nourishing food, regular sleep, and lots of soap and water. After that, what he needs most is some intelligent neglect.
Ivy Baker Priest

Woman must not depend upon the protection of man, but must be taught to protect herself.
Susan B. Anthony

The mere apprehension of a coming evil has put many into a situation of the utmost danger.
Marcus Annaeus Lucan

Libra 8

Home is where there's one to love us.
Charles Swain

East, west, home's best.
Proverb

… And the still deeper secret of the secret: The land that is nowhere, that is the true home…
Chang Po-tuan

Since the house is on fire let us warm ourselves.
Italian Proverb

One may have a blazing hearth in one's soul and yet no one ever come to sit by it. Passersby see only a wisp of smoke from the chimney and continue on the way.
Vincent van Gogh

Figure it out. Work a lifetime to pay off a house. You finally own it and there's no one to live in it.
Arthur Miller

Men resemble great deserted palaces: the owner occupies only a few rooms and has closed-off wings where he never ventures.
François Mauriac

A BLAZING FIREPLACE IN A DESERTED HOME

Commentary: "A Blazing Fireplace in a Deserted Home" gives an impression of warmth, security and love. The "Blazing Fireplace" conjures up images of coziness and comfort, and can provide a feeling of being surrounded by the secure and good things in life. Even when no one is there to provide the warmth, there can be feelings of positive energy, containment and safety.

Oracle: Even in times of real loneliness, when you are separated from everyone or everything, there is a constant, sometimes unseen, sustaining energy ready to welcome you "Home," whether it be the "Fire" of your own spiritual center, the warmth and familiarity of family and kin, or the certainty that one is sustained by humanity at large. The "Home" may be "Deserted" through having no parent or no one living there, having someone moving out or having no furniture or few of the usual comforts. Everybody should have a place of refuge and safety and sometimes we have to be reminded that the warmth of the "flame" is always there for us, and that we just need to acknowledge it and accept it. A "Home" can be a symbol of love—even when it is left behind or "Deserted" it can remain warm and ready for your return. This can be the love within family, marriage or a group of close friends. This love should never really diminish or lose its warmth. Also, a "Home" can radiate warmth and protection by its very nature. Something simple like turning on the lights can make a home warm, comfortable and inviting to others. Placing a candle in the window or turning on a light in the hall can work wonders, lifting your spirits and inviting love in.

Keywords: Security and comfort left behind. A fire left blazing inside to reassure. Wood for burning. Gas, electricity connections. Holiday homes, or homes that are rarely visited. Homes filled with love, if not people or possessions. The warmth of the heart. Holding a candle for someone who's gone. Fertility issues. Heart and hearth. Fireplaces. The place to which one returns.

The Caution: A sense of isolation, separation, abandonment and bitterness. Sabotage by, or of, loved ones and family. Being forced out of the home, possibly for social reasons. Desertion and decay of love. Never being at home because of work concerns and commitments. Separation. Divorce. Latchkey children. Feeling alone and out in the cold. The light being on, but no one being at home. Lack of domestic supplies.

What does this **SYMBOL** say to *you?*

THREE OLD MASTERS HANGING IN A SPECIAL ROOM IN AN ART GALLERY— SOMETIMES THEY SEEM TO SPEAK TO EACH OTHER

Libra 9

Commentary: "Three Old Masters" are "Hanging in a Special Room in an Art Gallery." Being "Masters," they are very valuable, especially as they are "in a Special Room." The paintings are timeless, and can be so lifelike that "Sometimes They Seem to Speak to Each Other." Time often doesn't seem to exist in this realm. "Rooms" that are empty except for artworks on the walls can feel like something is going on at another level. Even when there's nobody actually there, it can seem as though conversations are being held. The eyes of the paintings can appear to be watching what goes on around them. It can even feel like the eyes actually follow you around the room.

Oracle: Communication here is at a completely different level than is normally experienced. It can be unspoken, and include subtle messages that are enduring and valuable. Going deeply into understanding truths about art, our cultural inheritance and its significance can bring about realizations and revelations that expand one's mind and life. This Symbol can picture speaking to others about abstract concepts on a higher level. Everyday chatter that doesn't go deep or explore life's beauties can become mindless and mundane. Go deeper into your situation. Find solutions as different parts of your personality and psyche give you clues or tell you what you should be doing or where you should be. Focus during quiet times, times of introspection when people aren't around to distract. The solution may rest in balancing the three agencies: spiritual, physical and mental.

Keywords: Truth in the image. Intuitive vision. Reverence for art, form and tradition. Images bringing messages. Art collections and collecting art. Photographs. Capturing life in a work of art. Furniture of a period. The art of placement. Beautiful images. Wisdom speaking. Crowded galleries or empty rooms. Images that speak volumes. The Sabian Symbols as images. Minds that don't shut down. Animations.

The Caution: Undue reliance on conservative values. Too much importance placed on appearance instead of substance. Snobbery caused by elevated feelings of importance. Art's rarefied atmosphere that excludes others as unworthy or uneducated. Serious faces.

One picture is worth a thousand words.
Proverb

Nature is a revelation of God; Art a revelation of man.
Henry Wadsworth Longfellow

Art is the lie that makes us realize the truth.
Pablo Picasso

Fine art is that in which the hand, the head, and the heart of man go together.
John Ruskin

Art is unquestionably one of the purest and highest elements in human happiness. It trains the mind through the eye, and the eye through the mind. As the sun colors flowers, so does art color life.
John Lubbock

Art has no enemy but ignorance.
Romanian Proverb

A painting in a museum probably hears more foolish remarks than anything else in the world.
Edmond Jules Goncour

What does this **SYMBOL** say to *you?*

Libra 10

God promises a safe landing but not a calm passage.
Bulgarian Proverb

The winds and waves are always on the side of the ablest navigators.
Edward Gibbon

I said here's the river I want to flow on, here's the direction I want to go, and put my boat in. I was ready for the river to take unexpected turns and present obstacles.
Nancy Woodhull

The man who is swimming against the stream knows the strength of it.
Woodrow Wilson

In this world there is always danger for those who are afraid of it.
George Bernard Shaw

Do the thing you fear most and the death of fear is certain.
Mark Twain

I am driven into a desperate strait and cannot steer a middle course.
Philip Massinger

Call on God, but row away from the rocks.
Indian Proverb

I can't change the direction of the wind, but I can adjust my sails to always reach my destination.
Anonymous

A CANOE IS APPROACHING SAFETY THROUGH DANGEROUS WATERS

Commentary: "A Canoe Is Approaching Safety" implies a time of calm and reassurance ahead. It is coming to "Safety through Dangerous Waters." The way ahead is showing itself and there is an assurance that one is reaching one's destination after a difficult or even life-threatening time. The person in the "Canoe" has probably been through a hair-raising or rough experience, having to shoot the rapids and having to be very adaptable to changing conditions.

Oracle: In the situation facing you, your "Canoe Is Approaching Safety," however, it is not quite there yet, and it may be that the hard times are not completely through. You are, most likely, not quite where you'd like to be. You may be experiencing "Dangerous Waters," but there is a guarantee of safety and "smooth sailing" in the near future. Things are moving into a new state of equilibrium. Although there is relief in sight, be sure not to switch off your attention to the difficulties or dangers that you are still experiencing. The last battles can be the ones that beat you. Even if you are the type who thrives on the thrill of danger, it's important to respect the times of calm to reflect on the lessons that have come from the recent dangers or difficulties. The difficulties in your situation are likely to have been quite arduous, and yet valuable in terms of your resistance against difficult times to come. Neglecting to take advantage of the placid waters (the "Safety" that is promised) is a waste of a valuable opportunity and may lead to being unprepared if the "Dangerous Waters" come again. The coming calm is an opportunity to review what has passed, and prepare for whatever is yet to come. Before long you'll realize that you've come through difficult straits and the worst of it is over.

Keywords: The calm after the storm. Navigating difficult straits and coming out okay. Whitewater rafting. Skydiving and other risky activities. Rough waters vs. plain sailing. Recovery. Remission. Light at the end of the tunnel. Personal initiations. Trials of test and defeat. Being stoic. Retaining dignity and graciousness. Exercising care and restraint. Avoiding overexaggerated enthusiasm. Deliverance on many levels. Salvation. Staying on track.

The Caution: Neglecting to take a time to rest. Taking foolhardy risks, believing that all will be okay. Pre-empting situations without completing things in the present. Thinking that "lightning never strikes in the same place twice." Shooting more rapids. Freezing up and not moving.

What does this **SYMBOL** say to *you?*

A PROFESSOR PEERING OVER HIS GLASSES AT HIS STUDENTS

Libra 11

Commentary: "A Professor" is "Peering over His Glasses at His Students." His eyes have been strained over the years from doing close-up work with books and papers and now he needs "Glasses" for reading and studying. The rational mind requires a different kind of "lens" to that of the emotion or intuition. When the "Professor" moves his gaze or attention to "His Students," he needs to use a different focus. He "Peers Over His Glasses" to look at them and to see them as they truly are. If he observes them through the same intellectual "lenses" he uses for his study, he may neglect to see them as individuals with their own abilities and needs, and their human attributes will get lost in the process.

Oracle: You may need to interrupt your rational, linear, skeptical concentration to realize that people, together with your intuitive ideas, are all around you, and they are valuable assets of your life and development. Are you, or is someone else, really looking at things with the right "Glasses"? Do you have "old eyes" or "new eyes" to see? Is there a projection of something, a thought or an attitude, onto others in this situation that isn't really appropriate or doesn't really belong to them? Someone is, or needs to, notice what's going on, or take a minute to observe people in their true light. There may be a need to remember that being "clever" or "intellectual" does not mean that someone is better or above everyone else. Although, of course, being in a position of some kind of authority can lend weight when there's a need for giving kindly advice. There may be an issue of telling people what to do and how they should act. Are you the "Professor" or are you a "Student"? Regardless of which one you are, keeping in mind that people are to be viewed kindly, seriously and with respect will help.

Keywords: Lenses of perception. Seeing that others get the message. Intellectual snobbery. Photography. Lenses as shields or barriers between people or things. Observing others. Examining one's self. Understanding where you're looking. Giving advice. Teachers. Professors. The ability to "read others." Motivations or talents of others seen and appreciated.

The Caution: Assuming a superior position. Thinking others have a lesser position or intelligence. Reading endless self-help books and not noticing real life. Bossing others. Not seeing, or caring to notice, one's own faults and limitations. Feeling separate from what's being said or taught. Distortions of perception or observation. Condescending behavior. Seeing people as interruptions.

What does this **SYMBOL** say to *you?*

We must look at the lens through which we see the world, as well as the world we see, and understand that the lens itself shapes how we interpret the world.
Stephen Covey

The mind is for seeing, the heart is for hearing.
Saudi Arabian Proverb

Every closed eye is not sleeping, and every open eye is not seeing.
Anonymous

Question and answer is not a civilized form of conversation.
Patrick O'Brian

A cynic is a man who looks at the world with a monocle in his mind's eye.
Carolyn Wells

The task of the educator lies in seeing that the child does not confound good with immobility and evil with activity.
Maria Montessori

A suppressed resolve will betray itself in the eyes.
George Eliot

Libra 12

The depth of darkness to which you can descend and still live is an exact measure of the height to which you can aspire to reach.
Laurens Van der Post

To me every hour of light and dark is a miracle. Every cubic inch of space is a miracle.
Walt Whitman

For many children, joy comes as the result of mining something unique and wondrous about themselves from some inner shaft.
Thomas J. Cottle

Underground issues from one relationship or context invariably fuel our fires in another.
Harriet Lerner

In isolation I ruthlessly plow the deep silences, seeking my opportunities like a miner seeking veins of treasures. In what shallow glimmering space shall I find what glimmering glory?
Jamaica Kincaid

Beauty is also to be found in a day's work.
Mamie Sypert Burns

Free men freely work: whoever fears god, fears to sit at ease.
Elizabeth Barrett Browning

MINERS ARE EMERGING FROM A DEEP COAL MINE

Commentary: "Miners Are Emerging From a Deep Coal Mine." They've been working hard, and now the siren has sounded and their shift is finished. Coming back to the surface, they can take a deep breath and feel themselves infused with fresh energy. Even if the Sun is going down at the end of the day, it and fresh air can bring a new awareness and wonder at being alive. The "Miners" are free for now and finished with the day's work.

Oracle: It may feel as though you've been operating in the dark, or in some kind of underworld. When we've been submerged in work, deep issues or spaces for a long time, we often end up feeling suppressed and worn out. Thoughts and emotions can be clouded with doubt and fear, making them difficult to plumb or discover. You may even feel like you have been in some kind of hell; perhaps you've had to go into the depths in the search for something. A feeling of breathlessness can erupt from not being able to understand what's happening. Take a deep breath and learn to relax! Delving deeply can bring messages from the subconscious that reveal some surprising things. However, it is often not enough to merely find the message; there's also a need to bring any realizations into the clear light of day so that you, and others, can benefit from this passage and learn to breathe more freely. Imagine coming back to the surface, taking a deep breath and feeling yourself infused with the energy of fresh air and sunshine. Look carefully at situations, for it may take time for your eyes to adjust to the new light. Even if you need to go back within, into the "Deep Coal Mine," in the near future, having faith and the acceptance of being able to operate and see in "the dark" will assist you with any problems you may encounter. If you are "Emerging" with others, this can lead to a "Deep" sense of camaraderie, as people realize that they've been through the same straights and have come out okay.

Keywords: Release from arduous labor. Stopping work. Coming into the light. Deep subconscious healing. Hypnotherapy. Going into dark places. Claustrophobia. Memories from the past or out of nowhere. Things dark and "gothic." Lung and breathing problems. Persephone emerging. The labyrinth of the mind. The mind flooding. Tunnel vision. Caves. Mines. Digging for answers. Relief and time off. Ghost stories. Being the "canary" in the mine. Work.

The Caution: Gloomy outlooks. Not seeing potentials. Emerging with a "blackened face." Difficulty breathing. Earning a living being a life and death situation. Working hard for small rewards. Emotional loops. Things hard to escape. Fear of confinement or capture.

What does this **SYMBOL** say to *you?*

CHILDREN BLOWING SOAP BUBBLES

Libra 13

Commentary: "Children Blowing Soap Bubbles" is a wonderful image of playfulness and fun. The "Children" are having fun "Blowing Soap Bubbles," they love to watch how big they can make them, how long they can last and how high they can go. The swirling colors of the "Soap" along with the fact that the bubbles can pop at any moment adds to the fun and the fascination.

Oracle: It is through fantasy, simplicity and imagination that you will find the best solution. Saying things for the sake of saying them, doing things for the sake of doing them, or doing things with no real thought of the outcome is fun, and perhaps what's needed to lighten things up—as long as nobody is offended, led astray or hurt in the process. This is not a time to be too deep and meaningful, for it will be in fleeting moments of pleasurable wonder that you will find the answer to what's needed. However, this can also show someone not being "real," not taking things seriously and not wanting to take the responsibility for any outcomes. Perhaps there's a feeling that the things that are being said aren't substantial—more like mere cartoon captions. Fantasy can intrude on reality and what's being said can sometimes be forgotten in a minute. It's almost like these issues didn't ever exist. Sometimes, however, something said in a fleeting moment, a mere throwaway line, can have a positive or permanent effect on others. While there is likely to be fun and joy, there may need to be consideration of whether it will produce anything substantial, permanent or real. If this situation is one of short-term rewards and enjoyment, it may be wonderful, but relying on anything long lasting may be unrealistic and disappointing. Whatever, enjoy the moment and the display of fun while it lasts.

Keywords: Spending time being creative with children. Drama. Being carefree or superficial. Finding joy in pure abstractions. Captions in cartoons. Pollyanna attitudes that can lead to fun or nowhere. Not caring about the future, only the moment. Rediscovering the simple joys of life. Toys and playing. Soap and bubbles. Comic book heroes. Being easily amused. Fun. Playing with friends.

The Caution: Never growing up. Frivolousness. Daydreaming. Resenting people who don't have serious work. Upset over the loss of things that don't have lasting substance. Not meaning what's said. Making light of the serious. Moving on without completing anything of lasting value. Dislike of chitchat. Gullibility. Impractical behavior. Not knowing when to stop talking.

What does this **SYMBOL** say to *you?*

Man is most nearly himself when he achieves the seriousness of a child at play.
Heraclitus

It's fun being a kid.
Anonymous

Children have neither past nor future; and that which seldom happens to us, they rejoice in the present.
Jean de la Bruyere

One of the most obvious facts about grownups to a child is that they have forgotten what it is like to be a child.
Randall Jarrell

My soul, what's lighter than a feather? Wind. Than wind? The fire. And what than fire? The mind. What's lighter than the mind? A thought. Than thought? This bubble world. What than this bubble? Nought.
Francis Quarles

Always tell the truth. That way, you don't have to remember what you said.
Mark Twain

Where there is joy there is creation. Where there is no joy there is no creation: know the nature of joy.
Upanishads

It isn't the great big pleasures that count the most; it's making a great deal out of the little ones.
Jean Webster

Libra 14

One should rest when it is time to rest and act when it is time to act.
Anonymous

Wasting time is an important part of living.
Anonymous

Sometimes the most urgent and vital thing you can possibly do is take a complete rest.
Ashleigh Brilliant

Take a rest; a field that has rested gives a beautiful crop.
Ovid

In Japan, employees occasionally work themselves to death. It's called Karoshi. I don't want that to happen to anybody in my department. The trick is to take a break as soon as you see a bright light and hear dead relatives beckon.
Scott Addams

I like work: it fascinates me. I can sit and look at it for hours. I love to keep it by me: the idea of getting rid of it nearly breaks my heart.
Jerome K. Jerome

Follow effective action with quiet reflection. From the quiet reflection will come even more effective action.
James Levin

IN THE HEAT OF THE NOON, A MAN TAKES A SIESTA

Commentary: "In the Heat of the Noon, a Man Takes a Siesta" points to the need to take some time off, even when one is in the middle of accomplishing some task or doing work. The "Man" knows that if he takes an hour or two off during the middle of the day, taking "a siesta," when he gets back to work he will have a clearer mind and more strength to get through what needs to be done.

Oracle: In the situation facing you, relaxing and recuperating will serve to give you greater reserves of strength to complete the tasks at hand. Sometimes we just have to stop and refresh our batteries—this is probably just such a time. Also, it's good to guard against working one's self into a lather and getting exhausted. This can have long-term effects and mistakes are easily made through tiredness, stress or boredom with the job or chore. A nap, a change of atmosphere or taking some time out can lead to new solutions about work and how to get things done. By the same token, you may need to ignore judgments from others who think that they know what you should be doing, how often and when. On the other hand, this Symbol can point to somebody taking time off when they should actually be getting things completed. A "Siesta" should not translate into neglecting your duties—if something needs completing, a "Siesta" may not be appropriate or possible. Take a break and think about the situation, as long as it is appropriate. When you get back on the job your renewed energy will help you get through everything. You may find the solution you've been searching so hard for just pops into your mind.

Keywords: Meditation. The need to take time out. Sleep apnea and other sleep disorders. Midday rushes. Recuperating or laziness. Hammocks. Long lunch hours. Rejuvenation. Knowing when to call a halt. Taking breaks. Looking after one's health. Tiredness and yawning. Hot and demanding days leading to inertia or exhaustion. Dreams and fantasies.

The Caution: Wasting time. Being disinterested in things. Losing energy or interest when one should be at the peak of activity or achievement. Refusing to take a break. Going past the bounds of what should be done. Working so hard that one is forced to stop through exhaustion or ill health. Always being on the go while others sit back and enjoy. Losing one's grip on reality. Unwinding after toil or trouble. Withdrawal.

What does this **SYMBOL** say to *you?*

CIRCULAR PATHS

Commentary: "Circular Paths" symbolize a situation where there is a continual coming around back to the same place. It can picture a pattern of going around and around, with no real outcome and no sense of a final destination. In some instances, this can be good, as it can be rather meditative but it can also prove to be a very real waste of time.

Oracle: You may feel as though you are back where you started, like you've been through this whole thing before. However, it's best to consolidate, remember and appreciate the experience and learn what you have gained on your way to where you are now. When you are returning to what appears to be where you started, you always have some level of new experience and new skills. Sometimes life seems to be a continuously repetitive journey and there can be the need to break the chains that bind you. It can feel like a karmic wheel. This theme of "Circular Paths" may be experienced in school, at work or at home where routines can become boring, repetitive and neverending. Indeed, it can feel like there's no possibility of escape. But every experience is an opportunity and every opportunity is an experience—no matter how many times it has been done before. That is, unless you're really losing ground or time is slipping away to complete something. Procrastination can be like treading water or being stuck on these "Circular Paths." Do you keep telling yourself that you're going to stop one day? Take heart and realize that everything is always in motion and there's the possibility of stepping off this treadmill when the time is right. If you take the trouble to look at the real details of your experience rather than just experiencing dull repetition, something new and inspiring can always be found.

Keywords: Going round and round. The orbits of the planets. Cosmic rhythms and cycles. The cycles of life. Things we feel we can trust. The secure path that never really leads anywhere. Crop circles. Realizing mistakes and learning from them. The wheels of progress. Merry-go-rounds. Circular machinery. Mazes and labyrinths. Chaos theory. Learning through repetition. Looking for somewhere to park.

The Caution: Being lost in abstractions or small details. Losing perspective from going around and around. Addictive cycles that are hard to get rid of. Boredom. Episodes that repeat themselves. Repeating the same actions or mistakes. Treadmills. Habits that are self-defeating.

What does this **SYMBOL** say to *you?*

Libra 15

History is simply one damned thing after another.
Winston Churchill

The air is full of our cries. But habit is a great deadener.
Samuel Beckett

Dangers bring fears, and fears more dangers bring.
Richard Baxter

We are what we repeatedly do. Excellence, then, is not an act, but a habit.
Aristotle

Search for meaning, eat, sleep. Search for meaning, eat, sleep. Die, search for meaning, search for meaning, search for meaning.
Doug Horton

When in danger or in doubt, run in circles, scream and shout.
Bumper Sticker

The great thing in the world is not so much where we stand, as in what direction we are moving.
Oliver Wendell Holmes

As people are walking all the time, in the same spot, a path appears.
Lu Xun

Men have become the tools of their tools.
Henry David Thoreau

Libra 16

Character builds slowly, but it can be torn down with incredible swiftness.
Faith Baldwin

Each man's task is his life preserver.
George B. Emerson

It takes a real storm in the average person's life to make him realize how much worrying he has done over the squalls.
Anonymous

A lot of people ask me if I were shipwrecked, and could only have one book, what would it be? I always say How to Build a Boat.
Steven Wright

What is the appropriate behavior for a man or a woman in the midst of this world, where each person is clinging to his piece of debris? What's the proper salutation between people as they pass each other in this flood?
Leonard Cohen

I inhabit a weak, frail, decayed tenement battered by the winds and broken in on by the storms, and, from all I can learn, the landlord does not intend to repair.
John Quincy Adams

Be an optimist—at least until they start moving animals in pairs to Cape Kennedy.
Anonymous

AFTER THE STORMS OF WINTER, A BOAT LANDING STANDS IN NEED OF RECONSTRUCTION

Commentary: "After the Storms of Winter, a Boat Landing Stands in Need of Reconstruction." A "Storm" has swept through and damaged, or ruined, some usually secure part of life. The "Boats" cannot dock at the "Boat Landing" if it is destroyed or shaky or insecure. Situations, possessions and people may be compromised, or even ruined. Our foundations can be rocked almost to the point of complete destruction. Now there's the need for "Reconstruction."

Oracle: In the situation facing you, there needs to be a plan put into action to get things repaired so that life can move on. Even situations built on solid foundations can quickly be swept away by the tidal forces of emotion or life's circumstances. "After the Storms of Winter" implies that there is a need to take stock of what's happened. Rebuilding and restructuring is timely and probably very necessary. When there is "nowhere to dock" your life or emotions, it can take time to recover your feet and get things back under control. You may have to "Reconstruct" some usually secure part of your life, but in the future you'll be wiser and you'll build something stronger. Rebuilding some area of your life will require patience, commitment, faith and a sense of security and purpose. Sometimes, through facing devastation, we can truly come to grips with our own power. Without positive attitudes, and a reinforced attitude, the "Reconstruction" may, at best, be shaky or temporary. You may ask whether "the Storms of Winter" have really finished and warmer conditions can be expected or trusted. Picking yourself up and rebuilding after some harrowing or dangerous collision with reality can lead to a better, stronger and safer sense of where you can feel safe and harbored.

Keywords: Temporary loss. Emotional repair. Tools to repair damage and build a new life. Having faith that the worst is over and recovery can begin. Calling in the experts. Taking time to put the pieces back together. Working to ensure the safety of the community. Insurance claims. The fragility of man's world in the face of nature. Returning to work.

The Caution: Making excuses instead of fixing things. Feeling emotionally swamped and powerless. Being torn apart. Leaving things a mess. Feeling shot to pieces. Letting things wear down to the point of collapse. Having nowhere to dock. Arguments and violence.

What does this **SYMBOL** say to *you?*

A RETIRED SEA CAPTAIN WATCHES SHIPS ENTERING AND LEAVING THE HARBOR

Libra 17

Commentary: "A Retired Sea Captain Watches Ships Entering and Leaving the Harbor" pictures an image of calmness, quiet and an inner knowledge that's come from years and years of going "out to sea." The "Sea Captain" has taken on the elements again and again and has survived some very dangerous situations. As he is now "Retired," it is a time for the type of quiet recollection and reflection that is usually only afforded to someone who has "been there, done that." His part for now is to observe life and its trials rather than participating directly in them.

Oracle: You may feel that the stormy, unpredictable emotional life is something you can leave behind. In your situation, like the "Sea Captain," however, there will always be frustration experienced in the desire to return to the arena where the action is. Right now an objective and calm understanding of life's experiences is the true goal, along with rest, relaxation and nourishing the body and spirit. However, there's a need to be wary of merely looking out at the world from a confined perspective and feeling like you've got no choice but to sit, observe and reflect. It is quite possible that there are still a lot of new experiences out there for you. This may be about some measure of "retirement," but it is certainly not likely to be the end of life. This time could be an interim period, with time spent contemplating your next move. Reflecting on the past shouldn't dominate your possibilities, opportunities or desires for new experiences. Rather, this is a time to sit and contemplate and to make plans for what is yet to come. A whole new arena of activity is quite likely to open up after a period of recharging your batteries.

Keywords: Memories and peaceful contemplation. Disconnection from the past. Concentrating on more immediate circumstances. Fatigue and the need for rest. Being a spectator rather than a participant. Being part of an audience. Voyeurism. Turning to domestic pursuits. Writing one's memoirs. Nostalgia. Safe ports or harbors. Retiring from public life.

The Caution: A cop-out. Escaping from reality. Relying on past experiences. A need to defend one's shoreline. Losing faith in life. Staring at lost opportunities and times gone by. Not wanting to contribute any more. Losing interest in the struggle. Disillusionment. Frustration. Boredom.

What does this **SYMBOL** say to *you?*

Too often man handles life as he does the bad weather; he whiles away the time as he waits for it to stop.
Alfred Polgar

Be not simply good; be good for something.
Henry David Thoreau

I must go down to the seas again,
To the lonely sea and the sky.
And all I want is a tall ship,
And a star to steer her by.
John Masefield

A ship in the harbor is safe, but that is not what ships are built for.
Proverb

There is no pleasure in having nothing to do. The fun is in having lots to do and not doing it.
Mary Little

Give wind and tide a chance to change.
Richard E. Byrd

The stately ship is seen no more,
The fragile skiff attains the shore;
And while the great and wise decay,
And all their trophies pass away,
Some sudden thought, some careless rhyme,
Still floats above the wrecks of Time.
William Edward Hartpole Lecky

What is this life if, full of care, we have no time to stand and stare?
William Henry Davies

Libra 18

To accuse others for one's misfortunes is a sign of want of education. To accuse oneself shows that one's education has begun. To accuse neither oneself nor others shows one's education is complete.
Epictetus

Many promising reconciliations have broken down because, while both parties came prepared to forgive, neither party came prepared to be forgiven.
Charles Williams

Most of us can forgive and forget; we just don't want the other person to forget that we forgave.
Ivern Ball

The robbed that smiles steals something from the thief.
William Shakespeare

No! No! Sentence first—verdict afterwards.
Lewis Carroll

Crime expands according to our willingness to put up with it.
Barry Farber

Little thieves are hanged, but great ones escape.
Proverb

TWO MEN PLACED UNDER ARREST GIVE AN ACCOUNTING FOR THEIR ACTS BEFORE THE TRIBUNAL OF SOCIETY

Commentary: "Two Men" are "Placed under Arrest." They have to "Give an Accounting for Their Acts before the Tribunal of Society." They are standing before some representative or authority and speaking about how they have acted against the rules and codes of "Society." The fact that they are "Placed under Arrest" doesn't have to mean that they are literally taken away by the police. It can be that they are held back by circumstances, people or experiences and they feel stuck, unable to move or stripped of their freedom. This can be rather compromising to one's integrity, ideals and strength of character.

Oracle: People's ideas or actions may be under criticism or examination, to the point of feeling that someone has offended social responsibility and acceptability. They may have to justify or explain themselves, and relationships can be held in limbo until all the facts come to light. There may be a need to be thoughtful about the situation, because there may be nothing but suspicion at this point. The "case" could well be dismissed, with people forgiven or let off the hook, but with suspicion in the air, what permanent damage has already been done? Often a sense of trust and belief in the goodness of people is necessary. An attitude of forgiveness may be really important to move through this situation with one's sense of pride intact. Being charged with an offense can drive people apart, with each trying to save their own neck. How long can someone be "handcuffed," either to themselves or to another? Imagining the removal of "the cuffs" could lead to a turnaround in the situation. People in positions of power, physical or emotional, should show mercy so others can also forgive and forget and get on with their lives. Ultimately, the goal must lead to freedom.

Keywords: Having to plead one's case. The need for "legal help." Unacceptable principles. Blowing the whistle. Pointing at others to get off charges. People unable to relate. The Romeo and Juliet story. Feeling caught. Restrictions. Karma to be worked out. Being framed. Circumstances out of control. People in handcuffs. Identification parades. Police. The law. Lawyers. Judges. Juries. Tribunals. Police states. Breaking laws.

The Caution: Refusing to conform. Sabotage of relationship values. Feeling stuck, unable to move. Staying in relationships when one should go. Deadening emotions. Shutting off to cope. Not having one's point of view heard. Losing one's authority. Being bound karmically. Being tied up and limited.

What does this **SYMBOL** say to *you?*

A GANG OF ROBBERS IN HIDING

Libra 19

Commentary: "A Gang of Robbers in Hiding" is an image of people, possibly hidden in the shadows, waiting to take advantage of someone or something. The "Robbers" are watching and waiting for the appropriate time to come out into the light of day, or it just might feel as though they are.

Oracle: In your situation, you may feel that you have been wronged or something has been taken from you. At the moment, however, because the "Robbers Are in Hiding," there is probably little or no way of finding out who or what is the cause. Check if you are exposing yourself to being taken advantage of or attacked in some way. Be careful not to get confused between reality and paranoia. You could spend your time searching for the real perpetrators, however a better solution may be to get on with your life, while being mindful that something could go awry. Perhaps an "authority" of some kind needs to come into play, to sort things through, to ensure future safety and get life back on track. This person can be an external party who's in charge and powerful in some way, or it can be your own sense of authority that needs to sort out the facts of what's really going on. Whatever happens in this situation, things will most probably come to light at a later time. This Symbol can point to delusions of someone's thought processes. Make sure that there is no undermining of faith in others by indulging in suspicions that are ungrounded in reality. Locking out life can lead to feelings of being a prisoner or result in alienation from others. Sometimes one has to "break a window" to allow the light to get in. The solution may lie in taking control of your emotional, mental and physical realities. If you merely react in a vulnerable and defenseless way, what is there to deter the "Robbers" from taking advantage of you?

Keywords: Gaining unfair advantage. Robbers and thieves. Spying. The cold war. Big business ripping off the "little guy." People appearing to be something that they are not. Con-men mentality. Holding up proceedings. Mental attitudes that sabotage, restrict or control. The need for light. Voyeurism. Gangs. Private detectives. Ambushes.

The Caution: Gaining unfair advantage at someone else's expense. Finding it hard to trust anything. Difficult hidden energy that may erupt into consciousness. Feeling that someone is going to "get" you. Hiding in the shadows. Locks and shutters that prevent true relationships. Unbalanced mental states. Paranoia. Distrusting life.

What does this **SYMBOL** say to *you?*

The robbed that smiles steals something from the thief.
William Shakespeare

In this world there is always danger for those who are afraid of it.
George Bernard Shaw

The man who trusts men will make fewer mistakes than he who distrusts them.
Camillo di Cavour

Our doubts are our traitors.
William Shakespeare

Don't hold to anger, hurt or pain. They steal your energy and keep you from love.
Leo Buscaglia

All stealing is comparative. If you come to absolutes, pray who does not steal?
Ralph Waldo Emerson

If you steal from one author, it's plagiarism; if you steal from many, it's research.
Wilson Mizner

Libra 20

Piety and holiness of life will propitiate the gods.
Cicero

I call that mind free which jealously guards its intellectual rights and powers, which calls no man master, which does not content itself with a passive or hereditary faith, and receives new truth as an angel from Heaven.
William Ellery Channing

Look for the good, not the evil, in the conduct of members of the family.
Jewish Proverb

All sorts of spiritual gifts come through privations, if they are accepted.
Janet Erskine Stuart

Any ritual is an opportunity for transformation.
Starhawk

Impart as much as you can of your spiritual being to those who are on the road with you, and accept as something precious what comes back to you from them.
Albert Schweitzer

A JEWISH RABBI IN A TINY ROOM FULL OF MANUSCRIPTS AND BOOKS, PERFORMING HIS DUTY

Commentary: "A Jewish Rabbi in a Tiny Room Full of Manuscripts and Books" shows a man of religion in a constant state of learning, interpreting and reinterpreting text. His job is to translate spiritual teachings and administer them on behalf of the community that he represents. The fact that the Old Testament, the Talmud, and other religious writings have changing relevance in different cultures signifies that we need to be aware of our established wisdom, but remain open-minded to the way we apply that wisdom to your modern day-to-day life. In order to have freedom of thought, the "Rabbi" needs to have a thorough knowledge of the history of the foundations of the society he represents.

Oracle: There is age-old wisdom and established tradition which has survived to this day. These teachings can give rise to rituals and initiations that are essential to our wellbeing at important landmarks in our lives such as births, weddings, funerals, etc. However, how relevant are some of the laws that pertain to these in today's world? Although they should be delivered and accepted with reverence, taking things literally from ancient texts is probably not always going to provide you with what is needed for modern solutions. Instead, take heed of the ethics and morals behind them, and translate them to become relevant to your life and times. You may need to access this knowledge though instruction or through an inner search in order to deal with your situation. Sometimes we feel a huge resistance to having to do things that we must perform, but if these are tried and true things, then they can lead us onward and upward by complying with society's needs and mores. Remind yourself of why there is a need to "Perform" these "Duties." This may help to keep you motivated when you're feeling doubtful.

Keywords: Connection with ancient sources of truth and understanding. Faith in abiding laws. Inherited wisdom. Ancient books. Fundamentalism. Rituals, social and otherwise. Initiation ceremonies. Book work. Studying and worshipping. Doing deeds on behalf of the community. Religious services. Writings that reveal rules for living. Lawyers. Advocates. Hidden knowledge.

The Caution: Religious dogmatism. Following the rules of "the book." Sticking to what convention says. Losing one's sense of individuality. Overinflated sense of self. Distrust or hate of different religions, backgrounds or ethnic origins. Restrictive rules.

What does this **SYMBOL** say to *you?*

A CROWD UPON A BEACH

Commentary: "A Crowd upon a Beach" pictures people coming together to enjoy the fresh air, the sunshine and the water. They leave behind the worries of their everyday lives as they take time out to enjoy the freedom and the freshness of the environment. Some will be swimming, some building castles in the sand, while others may be talking or reading or soaking up the sun and the ocean breeze. There can be a feeling of being blessed or lucky, as many people would like to be able to take this time out to enjoy the elements without worrying about money, work or responsibilities. People often stop and talk to each other, whether they have met before or not. Chance meetings with friends can be great fun, as can making new friends.

Oracle: You may feel a need to get back in touch with your emotions by relaxing and taking things easy. Joining with others of like mind in a natural setting and feeling the release that can come from reminding yourself of the joys and wonders of nature can be like taking a holiday. People love the feeling of the sun, the ocean air and the sand between their toes. Whether they are on the "Beach," or not, this Symbol implies that people can relax together, even if they don't know each other, and revive their spirits through taking time off. The feelings of guilt or worry about being "at work," or doing what one should be doing, shouldn't be entertained as this is a time for leisure, whether alone or among others. Is there a problem in revealing your body and being seen in a swimsuit or some other scant clothing? These issues really need to be dropped as most people really aren't concerned with how others look in this environment. There is quite possibly a need to get back in touch with your emotions and to join with others for some light recreation.

Keywords: Simple gatherings and sharing in natural values. Watching people swim, run, skip and play. People getting loose and revealing their bodies. Remembering the basic elements of life. Marveling at nature. Getting back to the basics of life. Enjoyment. Relaxing social constraints. Picnic hampers, towels, sunblock. Wanting a tan. Queues and lines. Swimming in the collective unconsciousness. Leisure times.

The Caution: Avoiding close interaction with others. Being just one of many who desire their moment in the sun. Drowning— with others or alone. Sunburn. Sunstroke. Feeling like just one of the many. Dehydration. Traffic that hampers flow. Loneliness.

In every outthrust headland, in every curving beach, in every grain of sand there is a story of the earth.
Rachel Carson

Miami Beach is where neon goes to die.
Lenny Bruce

The sea does not reward those who are too anxious, too greedy, or too impatient. One should lie empty, open, choiceless as a beach—waiting for a gift from the sea.
Anne Morrow Lindbergh

A crowd is not company, and faces are but a gallery of pictures.
Francis Bacon

The lives of happy people are dense with their own doings — crowded, active, thick ... But the sorrowing are nomads, on a plain with few landmarks and no boundaries; sorrow's horizons are vague and its demands are few.
Larry McMurtry

Among them, but not of them.
Lord Byron

What does this **SYMBOL** say to *you?*

Libra 22

To cultivate kindness is a valuable part of the business of life.
Samuel Johnson

A child is a quicksilver fountain Spilling over with tomorrows and tomorrows And that is why She is richer than you and I.
Tom Bradley

Love and kindness are never wasted. They always make a difference. They bless the one who receives them, and they bless you, the giver.
Barbara De Angelis

Practice random acts of kindness.
Modern Saying

Constant kindness can accomplish much. As the sun makes ice melt, kindness causes misunderstanding, mistrust, and hostility to evaporate.
Albert Schweitzer

He who sows courtesy reaps friendship, and he who plants kindness gathers love.
Saint Basil

Life is made up, not of great sacrifices or duties, but of little things, in which smiles and kindness, and small obligations win and preserve the heart.
Sir Humphrey Davy

A CHILD GIVING BIRDS A DRINK AT A FOUNTAIN

Commentary: "A Child" is seen "Giving Birds a Drink at a Fountain." The "Child" is carefree and enjoying the freshness of the outdoors and the thrill of watching the "Birds" having and enjoying the "Drink at the Fountain." The interaction of the "Child" and the "Birds" can bring joy and wonder. "Birds" represent spiritual messages, the "Child" is the physical presence of innocence, naïveté and fun, and the water represents the flow and empathy of emotional energy. This also symbolizes the joy and trust of innocence as it is a "Child" who holds the "Fountain" open for the "Birds." This does not mean that an adult is unable to be trusted. Instead, it shows that we must maintain the innocence and openness of a "Child" in order to be connected to and aware of simple, momentary and more spiritual energies.

Oracle: "Children" demonstrate a generosity of spirit and take delight in giving to beings less able than themselves. They give freely and unconditionally. This Symbol shows that we must assume the shaping and caring of a "Child" in order to be connected to and aware of, the needs and worries of others. The problem that can come out of adulthood is the expectation of return, the "what's in it for me" routine. It is when an experience is its own true reward that we achieve openness and joy in responding to the energies that surround us everyday. Someone's needs, hopes and wishes are in need of sustenance or refreshment. Whether this is you or someone else, simple gestures can revitalize situations beyond your expectations. If you or another have the resources to nourish or to help someone or something, the effort required will be minimal, but the rewards may be well worth it. Show some unconditional generosity and enjoy the resulting experience.

Keywords: Enjoyment experienced in nourishing simple souls. The need for water. Simple pleasures. Innocence. Birdbaths. Fountains. Water. Innocent reaching out to others. Taking time out for others. Spontaneous gifts. Moments of innocence, spontaneity and fun. Putting aside your own needs. Stopping to help others in need. Enjoying interactions with people, birds or animals.

The Caution: Looking for recognition for small deeds. Being condescending to others. Always feeling like you have to look after others, whether they are big or small. Interfering with nature. Being naïve. Feeling that one is the font of everything.

What does this **SYMBOL** say to *you?*

CHANTICLEER'S VOICE HERALDS THE RISING SUN WITH ENTHUSIASTIC TONES

Libra 23

Commentary: "Chanticleer's Voice Heralds the Rising Sun with Enthusiastic Tones." The word "Chanticleer" is from the French *chanter clair* meaning to sing clearly. He "Heralds the Rising Sun with Enthusiastic Tones." As this "Chanticleer" is quite clearly the symbol of a rooster, it's most likely he sings loudly as well. It is also said that the cock crows loudly in order to scare away evil spirits. The cock was dedicated to Apollo in ancient mythology because he gives notice of "the Rising Sun." Just like the cock, some people are heralds of the new day or the new age, and they notice and give voice to this emergence, often ahead of time. Most often the "Voice" that is heard is enthusiastically received, but there are times that what is said is rejected, ignored or reviled or it's perceived as loud and irritating.

Oracle: In this situation, someone may feel that they are the driving force behind what's happening. There may be a strong need, or desire, to draw attention to themself. This may be someone in the public eye, or someone who feels that they should be listened to, or that things cannot continue without them. Rightly or wrongly, there's often a claiming of responsibility for things. There is always a need to learn to listen, rather than just crowing about one's self, one's ideas or life. The sound of someone's voice can become grating and annoying when they don't know when, or how, to stop. It can be that the "Chanticleer with Enthusiastic Tones" overstates his role somewhat and there can be a blurring of the concept as to whether the cock causes or simply heralds the new day. Done correctly, however, "Enthusiastic Tones Heralding the Rising Sun" can be wonderfully stirring and can move people to new beginnings and realizations that they've not had before.

Keywords: Anticipating new opportunities. Waking early. Being a morning person. Having a clear, beautiful or loud voice. Speaking up when it's needed. Heralding the new age. Seeing things ahead of their time. Being attuned to cosmic forces. Change or renewal. Always being on the go. Being eternally vigilant. Alarms that spur to action.

The Caution: Overstating ones role, talents or abilities. Needing a wake-up call (literally and symbolically). Crowing about things—disturbing others. Being noisy when others are trying to sleep. Being loud and irritating.

What does this **SYMBOL** say to *you?*

Faith is the bird that feels the light when the dawn is still dark.
Rabindranath Tagore

Said a Rooster, "I'd have you all know
I am nearly the whole of the show;
Why, the Sun every morn
Gets up with the dawn,
For the purpose of hearing me crow!"
Ethel Watts Mumford

Dawn does not come twice to awaken a man.
Saudi Arabian Proverb

Great braggers, little doers.
Romanian Proverb

One filled with joy preaches without preaching.
Mother Teresa

It takes a person who is wide awake to make his dream come true.
Roger Babson

The sun sets without thy assistance.
The Talmud

She understood how much louder a cock can crow in its own farmyard than elsewhere.
Anthony Trollope

Noise proves nothing. Often a hen who has merely laid an egg cackles as if she had laid an asteroid.
Mark Twain

Libra 24

I'd give my right arm to be ambidextrous.
Yogi Berra

Handicaps are really to be used another way to benefit yourself and others.
Stevie Wonder

I thank God for my handicaps, for through them, I have found myself, my work and my God.
Helen Keller

Everything in moderation.
Proverb

You can have too much of a good thing.
Proverb

Too much of a good thing is wonderful.
Mae West

A THIRD WING ON THE LEFT SIDE OF A BUTTERFLY

Commentary: "A Third Wing on the Left Side of a Butterfly" is an image of imbalance and distortion combined with beauty and grace. A butterfly with three wings would be a beautiful thing to see. However, having a "Third Wing" may look lovely, but it would make it very difficult to fly. While we may marvel at such an oddity, it would prove to be very difficult for the "Butterfly" itself. It may look curiously beautiful, but in reality it can be difficult surviving in the physical world with such a difficulty or handicap. In French, *gauche* literally means "left," and it has the extended meanings "awkward" and "clumsy." In fact, "awkward" itself comes from the Middle English *awke,* meaning "turned the wrong way" or "lefthanded." On the other hand, "adroit" and "dexterity" have their roots in words meaning "right" or "on the right side." We see this fragility in creative people like van Gogh, Robin Williams or Spike Milligan.

Oracle: Understanding and accepting fragility and differences in others can give us greater empathy for those who have difficulty operating efficiently in this world. Emotional breakdowns, fears and phobias can be symptoms of being too sensitive, not necessarily as a fault, but as a response to an unforgiving and tough world. When the transformation into full potential occurs it is a wonderful thing but you may feel that you are unnaturally developed in the emotive, intuitive realms. Instinct may be swamping logic, and while this can be very creative, it would be a good idea to try to regain some balance. This can point to threesomes of any kind and, just as threesomes are considered to be an unbalanced relationship, "a Third Wing" can imply imbalance and an inability to get anywhere. A "Butterfly" can be someone who is bright when conditions are favorable, but is "done for" when the clouds gather. This Symbol can also indicate lopsidedness on the physical level, such as having one side of the body imbalanced in some way. Balance is difficult to achieve with this Symbol, but is something that needs to be strived for.

Keywords: Creative overbalance. Bodily impairments and handicaps. Being light, flippant and fluttering from thing to thing. Oversensitivities. Oddities. Beautiful imperfections. Idiot savants. Imbalances. One side of the body being more perfect than the other. Wings, arms, legs, feet.

The Caution: Unrealistic reliance on being different. Obsession with strange things. Feeling useless and out of place. Flapping around and not getting anywhere. Restlessness and nervousness. Lopsidedness. Impatience.

What does this **SYMBOL** say to *you?*

THE SIGHT OF AN AUTUMN LEAF BRINGS TO A PILGRIM THE SUDDEN REVELATION OF THE MYSTERY OF LIFE AND DEATH

Libra 25

Commentary: "The Sight of an Autumn Leaf Brings to a Pilgrim the Sudden Revelation of the Mystery of Life and Death" is an image of having the ability to see much more in the simple things than most people ever notice. A "Pilgrim" is a traveler, a voyager—someone who's on a journey. Often the "Pilgrim's" journey is a spiritual trek or a trip to increase the level of experience and understanding. The "Sudden Revelation of the Mystery of Life and Death" shows that the person on the journey is able to look at the smallest and sometimes most fleeting things and find layers and layers of meaning that others wouldn't.

Oracle: This Symbol can indicate an insight into something that can change the course of one's life. The "Autumn Leaf" in this Symbol brings to the "Pilgrim" the "Sudden" understanding of the cycle of life, death and rebirth. The "Mystery of Life" seems to unfold before the "Pilgrim's" inner vision. The "Pilgrim" can see that the seed has grown into a tree and the tree's leaves have now fallen with the change of the seasons, ready for the new birth in the spring. The "Autumn Leaf" becomes the composted material that nourishes the new seeds and fosters and nourishes new growth. Often we go through our lives without noticing the information that can be gained from looking at small or seemingly insignificant things. The "Revelation" that is experience can change one's life, if time is taken to stop long enough to really look into it. At this point, you may feel that you've learned much but have grown tired of seeking information for life's meaning through more conventional channels. Look for the answer to your problem in simple, everyday moments. They are fleeting, but they are around you. Look for the signs, they can have profound effects.

Keywords: Seasonal adjustments. Fleeting inspiration. Seeing things in their own time. Spiritual revelations. Conversations with God. Feeling blessed. The beauty and timelessness of nature. Contacts with nature spirits. Angelic visions. Photography and having a photographic mind. Being here now. Pilgrims and their journeys. The Hadj pilgrimage. Solving problems. Quick and deep minds. Snapshots in time.

The Caution: Focusing on things that have no lasting value or are no longer relevant. Looking for answers in everything, therefore missing out on the big picture that's right in front of you. Making a big deal out of insignificant or everyday occurrences.

What does this **SYMBOL** say to *you?*

To see the world in a grain of sand,
And a heaven in a wild flower;
Hold infinity in the palm of your
hand,
And eternity in an hour.
William Blake

A traveler without observation is
a bird without wings.
Moslih Eddin Saadi

Perpetual inspiration is as
necessary to the life of goodness,
holiness and happiness
as perpetual respiration is
necessary to animal life.
Andrew Bonar Law

To see a hillside white with
dogwood bloom is to know a
particular ecstasy of beauty, but
to walk the gray winter woods
and find the buds which will
resurrect that beauty in another
May is to partake of continuity.
Hal Borland

A man should hear a little music,
read a little poetry, and see a
fine picture every day of his
life, in order that worldly cares
may not obliterate the sense
of the beautiful which God has
implanted in the human soul.
Goethe

Nature will bear the closest
inspection. She invites us to lay
our eye level with her smallest
leaf, and take an insect view of
its plain.
Henry David Thoreau

Libra 26

For hatred does not cease by hatred at any time: hatred ceases by love—this is an old rule.
The Dhammapada

Censure pardons the ravens but rebukes the doves.
Latin Proverb

We must combine the toughness of the serpent with the softness of the dove, a tough mind and a tender heart.
Martin Luther King, Jr.

We are going to have peace even if we have to fight for it.
Dwight D. Eisenhower

"Oh, wise one!" said the eagle, while he sank, in deeper and ever deep'ning thought—"Oh Wisdom! like a dove thou speakest!"
Goethe

The eagle suffers little birds to sing, and is not careful what they mean thereby.
William Shakespeare

Shall eagles not be eagles? Wrens be wrens?
Lord Alfred Tennyson

The real and lasting victories are those of peace, and not war.
Ralph Waldo Emerson

AN EAGLE AND A LARGE WHITE DOVE TURNING CONSTANTLY INTO EACH OTHER

Commentary: The images of "an Eagle and a Large White Dove" are represented in many facets of our lives. Their symbols can be found in several religions, most notably Christianity, heraldry and hermeticsm. They represent opposite sides of the same spectrum. The "Eagle" is symbolic of strength, stamina and skyward flight. It is a bird of prey and can be seen as aggressive and domineering. It is also considered to be the king of the birds. The "Dove" is a symbol of peace, tenderness, innocence and gentleness. When they are "Turning Constantly into Each Other" we are able to embody a strong sense of grounding in one's own power and at the same time be aware of and awake to love and the wonderful messages that come from the emotional and spiritual realms.

Oracle: In the situation facing you, there is most likely a need to mix, and integrate, the principle of the will with the principle of the emotions. This symbolizes having the will and the strength to love and to do so with energetic conviction. It is the ideals of being strong, but not aggressive; firm without being overly assertive; and confident without being oppressive that creates a sense of peace. Equally, it is a sense of peace and love that can energize your convictions into action. However, there may be some confusion around whether to use force or love in this situation. This Symbol may also indicate that somebody's behavior is unpredictable and sometimes off-putting. Someone may be rather schizoid and flounder around from one response to another, leading others to wonder what sort of response they are likely to receive at any given time. This could be a result of a chemical imbalance, the use of drugs or alcohol, or merely their personality. Using moderation and the alternation of these responses will probably lead to a solution—being firm and yet kind.

Keywords: Tempering one's will with love and bolstering up one's emotional responses with strength. Cooperation of mind, will, spirit and heart. Schizophrenia. Eagles and doves. Being strong and soft at the same time. Adopting the attitudes of spirit, power and love.

The Caution: Being "all over the place" with reactions. Being changeable. Not acting for the purpose of a definite outcome. Confusing others with conflicting behavior. Not knowing what to expect next. On one minute, off the next.

What does this **SYMBOL** say to *you?*

AN AIRPLANE SAILS HIGH IN THE BRIGHT CLEAR SKY

Libra 27

Flying might not be all plain sailing, but the fun of it is worth the price.
Amelia Earhart

Words have no wings but they can fly many thousands of miles.
Korean Proverb

There are no signposts in the sky to show a man has passed that way before. There are no channels marked. The flier breaks each second into new uncharted seas.
Anne Morrow Lindbergh

The airplane stays up because it doesn't have the time to fall.
Orville Wright

*Twinkle, twinkle, little bat!
How I wonder what you're at!
Up above the world you fly!
Like a tea tray in the sky.*
Lewis Carroll

Faith without works is like a bird without wings; though she may hop with her companions on earth, yet she will never fly with them to heaven.
Francis Beaumont

Commentary: "An Airplane Sails High in the Bright Clear Sky" is an image of flight and escape and gives the feeling of unfettered freedom. It can symbolize being carefree and not bound to the everyday, grounded realities that most people are caught up in. Being in the "Airplane" can bring a sense of being above everything, an observer and somewhat detached. We all need moments of clear, focused detachment and the enjoyment of life's pleasures.

Oracle: There may be some people in this situation that need to be recognized, embraced or noticed in some way. Maybe it is you that has to do this, or to receive it. You, or another, may feel that they are somehow "above" or beyond the situation, but how long can one go on flying so high? Somebody in this situation is probably avoiding the reality of what's going on, or they may be avoiding having close, intimate interactions with people around them. How long can there continue to be "Bright Clear Sky"? We all need to come down to earth after some incredible or gravity-defying experience, even if we don't want to—or don't feel ready to. For now, there may be the feeling that you are above the situation and are being carried beyond this time or place to something completely new. There is probably a need for calm objective observation. "Sailing" above difficulties, and people, may bring new information to light; things that you weren't able to "see," or know, previously. For the moment, "Sailing" on and enjoying both the experience and the view may be what's needed. However, sooner or later you're going to have to land back in reality. Are you prepared not only for the flight but also for the landing? What are the real, down-to-earth needs that are being shown and that need attention?

Keywords: Transcending difficulties or escape from reality. Optimism that knows no bounds. A bird's eye view of things. Detachment. Objectivity. Chemical influences. Freedom from life's routine. Pilots and planes. Clear air turbulence. Roller coaster rides. Awareness of up and down, left and right, in and out. Sense of destination. Decreasing gravity. Acceleration of time. Fish-eye lens. The need for navigation.

The Caution: Difficulty in seeing the true details of what's going on. Escape from reality. Running out of fuel. Egoism. Playing with gravity. Disconnection from the everyday world.

What does this **SYMBOL** say to *you?*

Libra 28

We can easily forgive a child who is afraid of the dark; the real tragedy of life is when men are afraid of the light.
Plato

Confront the dark parts of yourself, and work to banish them with illumination and forgiveness. Your willingness to wrestle with your demons will cause your angels to sing. Use the pain as fuel, as a reminder of your strength.
August Wilson

As soon as your consciousness is right, God is there. He is not hiding from you, you are hiding from Him.
Paramahamsa Yogananda

Angels can fly because they take themselves lightly.
G. K. Chesterton

For fools rush in where angels fear to tread.
Alexander Pope

Make friends with the angels, who though invisible are always with you ... Often invoke them, constantly praise them, and make good use of their help and assistance in all your temporal and spiritual affairs.
Saint Francois de Sales

A MAN ALONE IN DEEP GLOOM. UNNOTICED, ANGELS ARE COMING TO HIS AID

Commentary: "A Man Alone in Deep Gloom," is an image of someone who's feeling very depressed, alone and somehow forsaken. As he's in "Deep Gloom," it seems that he's hit rock bottom and wonders if things can ever or will ever improve. He may have just about given up hope when "Unnoticed, Angels Are Coming to His Aid."

Oracle: This Symbol is very much about letting go and trusting. Just when someone needs rescue and salvation the most, it will often appear as if from out of nowhere. So often "Gloom" is brought about by depression, not knowing what is going to happen or assuming that something bad is about to happen. It may be that "Gloom" is disabling any ability to see one's "Angels" or accept any support that is being offered. It is not always necessary to "Notice" your "Angels," but this Symbol is asking you to open up to them and to allow them to help in some way. Whether the "Man," and this could be you or another, realizes it or not, things are somehow going to improve. This Symbol shows that it's been a difficult time, but it is just beginning to dawn on you that you are being "helped" as the "Angels Come to Aid" in some way. There will be a slow, but sure, realization that things are getting better. If you continue to see the "Gloom" and wallow, you will put up a subconscious, or conscious, resistance to help and may continue on a downward spiral. Look at the big picture and evaluate just how serious the situation is. If it can be mended, let it mend. Don't get stuck in misery. The "Angels" that come to help can be people, but it can also be your higher mind that brings this "Aid." Hope, faith and trust will help to move this situation on. Work on changing your attitude to your situation and watch the "light" returning.

Keywords: Feelings of not being alone. Awareness of spiritual help in times of need. Salvation vs. depression. Feeling like one's luck is about to change. Improvements in the pipeline. Changes in the "weather." Helpers arriving just when they're needed. Brightening influences. Angels and spiritual forces for good. Guardian angels.

The Caution: Unrealistic reliance on spiritual agencies or help from others. Feeling like no one cares or that no one is listening. Being alone and forgotten. Losing faith in things getting better. Refusing help. Misery and gloom and doom.

What does this **SYMBOL** say to *you?*

MANKIND'S VAST ENDURING EFFORT TO REACH FOR KNOWLEDGE TRANSFERABLE FROM GENERATION TO GENERATION

Libra 29

Commentary: "Mankind's Vast Enduring Effort to Reach for Knowledge Transferable from Generation to Generation" shows the handing down of learning or "Knowledge" from mothers and fathers to daughters and sons. By instruction, by observation and by acceptance, we pass information to the next "Generation," as this allows for the process to continue and develop from "Generation to Generation."

Oracle: This Symbol is about conscious awareness and how we use this capacity to know and to "Transfer" information from our mind to another mind through communication. This communication can be in the spoken word, the written word or through dance, body language or our deeds. We pass on the biological nature of "Knowledge" through our genes, our conscious "Knowledge" by teaching, our social "Knowledge" by example and training. Genetic memory is another way that things can be passed down from "Generation to Generation." It can be said that the "Knowledge" of the universe is within us, but bringing this out into our consciousness is something that occurs over time and through effort. The most likely "students" are those who are constantly around us, can relate to our activities and are inspired by our history and love—this often being our friends and family. However, students, as well as teachers, can pop up anywhere, especially when there's a need for the information to be "Transferred." With this Symbol, there can be an outreaching to others through awareness along with a desire to teach, as well as to learn. There is more to wisdom than just knowing. In the end, it's what is done with this "Knowledge" that creates wisdom. It is through knowledge and understanding that we can bridge the gap between ourselves and others.

Keywords: Interpreting and conveying beliefs and ideas. The desire to pass on something to others. Handing down possessions or knowledge. Knowledge being changed, modified or updated. Teaching by example. The wisdom of the ancestors. Research into history. Striving for answers. Books and the spoken word. Encyclopedias and reference books. The gift of knowledge.

The Caution: A belief that one knows it all. Information, knowledge or riches inherited by only the select few. Reliance on tradition. Fundamentalism. Doing what's always been done, regardless of the reason.

What does this **SYMBOL** say to *you?*

Children wish fathers looked but with their eyes; fathers that children with their judgment looked; and either may be wrong.
William Shakespeare

Employ your time in improving yourself by other men's writings so that you shall come easily by what others have labored hard for.
Socrates

That must be wonderful; I have no idea of what it means.
Jean-Baptiste Moliere

Education is the transmission of civilization.
Ariel Durant

Today's children are required to learn what most people in former times were forbidden to know.
Ashleigh Brilliant

We are the people our parents warned us about.
Anonymous

By the time a man realizes that maybe his father was right, he usually has a son who thinks he's wrong.
Charles Wadsworth

Ideas cross mountains, borders, and seas. They go anywhere a man can go…
Walter Goodstein

Libra 30

And still they gazed, and still the wonder grew, that one small head could carry all he knew.
Oliver Goldsmith

What if everything is an illusion and nothing exists? In that case, I definitely overpaid for my carpet.
Woody Allen

What if nothing exists and we're all in somebody's dream? Or what's worse, what if only that fat guy in the third row exists?
Woody Allen

I don't know why we are here.
Ludwig Wittgenstein

Philosophers have merely interpreted the world. The point is to change it.
Karl Marx

Plato was a bore.
Friedrich Nietzsche

I have tried too in my time to be a philosopher but, I don't know how, cheerfulness was always breaking in.
Oliver Edwards

The point of philosophy is to start with something so simple as to seem not worth stating, and to end with something so paradoxical that no one will believe it.
Bertrand Russell

THREE MOUNDS OF KNOWLEDGE ON A PHILOSOPHER'S HEAD

Commentary: "Three Mounds of Knowledge on a Philosopher's Head" brings to mind the science of phrenology, which is the study of the psychological implications of the bumps and irregularities on the surface of the skull. This Symbol is also about the signs that are evident in our physical being which reflect our inner wisdom. We can often identify people who are learned by merely looking at the way they present themselves, through their demeanor. Wisdom can also be reflected in the clarity of the eyes, a peaceful nature, and calmness in the event of difficulty. The face may have signs of wisdom in the lack of stress lines, or the strength of thought lines. A face may show the experience of life and the wisdom derived from it. Essentially, if we look, it is possible to see those who are wise and understand life.

Oracle: There is an ability here to read spiritual understandings into concrete, everyday objects. Several different aspects can be combined to result in a truly wise outcome. There's the ability to be able to pierce through appearances to see the inherent truth of a situation and bring abstract truths into reality. It can show concentration on questions of a philosophical nature. There may be the need to be cautious, however, of always "living in one's head." Constant thinking and talking about philosophical ideas or intellectualism can cause a strain in relationships when the partner may want to concentrate on simpler, more emotional or everyday thoughts. After all, as Voltaire said, "Four thousand volumes of metaphysics will not teach us what the soul is."

Keywords: Looking at the signs. Wisdom that transcends book knowledge. Philosophy. Having a knowledgeable demeanor. Being an impressive figure. Making wise decisions regardless of hard-line opinion. The head, skull or cranium. Knowledge directed to intellectual or spiritual goals. Predicting the future. An appearance that shows obvious intelligence. Wit. Style. Seeing potential in others. Receding hairlines.

The Caution: Analyzing things too much and reliance on intellect. Being a "know it all." Having a bossy attitude. Thinking that doesn't clarify issues but muddies them. Taking things far too seriously. People with "highbrow" attitudes. Feeling weighed down by intellectual concerns.

What does this **SYMBOL** say to *you?*

A SIGHT-SEEING BUS FILLED WITH TOURISTS

Commentary: "A Sight-Seeing Bus Filled with Tourists" is an image of people touring around, seeing the sights, taking in the atmosphere and learning about people and places that are new or foreign to them. There can be a feeling of knowing one's destination, having a map or guide, but not really knowing what it is actually like. There can be the feeling of being an observer, but also being observed by others yourself.

Oracle: Sometimes we find ourselves in situations where we don't understand the customs or the language of those around us. You may need a tour guide to help you acclimate or to make the most of this journey. If you are traveling with others, there may be a need to be punctual at all times as others could leave without you in their eagerness for getting on with things. New friendships can be made, while others are lost. Take in as much information as possible through sight, sound, touch and smells, as this will enable you to learn from your experiences. Pictures, postcards, leaflets and souvenirs from your journey may be useful reminders. Keep an eye on your belongings, especially if there are people you don't know or trust journeying with you on the "Bus." Remember that "belongings" may manifest on every level: the physical, mental, emotional and spiritual. This also applies to anything that proves your unique identity. Being in an unknown place without identification can be time-wasting and confusing and can lead to a sense of alienation or abandonment. Also, trying to communicate with people who don't understand can lead to feeling misunderstood, disconnected and shut out. None of this is necessary, of course, as long as you're awake and conscious. Maybe it's time to stop being a "spectator" in life and to become more of a participant. Whatever is happening, enjoy the ride, learn from the journey and take in all that is possible.

Keywords: Observing life. Feeling disconnected from reality. UFOs and aliens. Seeing how other people live. Watching from afar. Tourists, traveling, buses. Suitcases and luggage. Cameras, pictures, souvenirs. Tour guides. Timing and being on time. The untried and untrodden or the same old road. Getting lost in something for hours. Foreign territories. New ways of seeing.

The Caution: Feelings of naïveté and gullibility. Feeling like an alien even in familiar surroundings. Making assumptions about others' lives. Not fitting in. Expecting things without any personal expenditure or effort. Getting out of one's depth. Having difficulty calling one's own agenda. Separation anxiety. Inability to concentrate.

What does this **SYMBOL** say to *you?*

Scorpio 1

Though we travel the world over to find the beautiful, we must carry it with us or we find it not.
Ralph Waldo Emerson

If a man be gracious and courteous to strangers, it shows he is a citizen of the world.
Francis Bacon

If you want to understand democracy, spend less time in the library with Plato and more time in the buses with people.
Simeon Strunsky

At six one morning, Will went out in jeans and frayed sweater to buy a quart of milk. A tourist bus went by. The megaphone was directed at him. "There's one," it said. That was in the 1960s. Ever since, he's wondered. There's one what?
Renata Adler

The more I traveled the more I realized that fear makes strangers of people who should be friends.
Shirley MacLaine

The voyage of discovery is not in seeking new landscapes but in having new eyes.
Marcel Proust

The innocents abroad.
Mark Twain

Scorpio 2

By starving emotions we become humorless, rigid and stereotyped; by repressing them we become literal, reformatory and holier-than-thou; encouraged, they perfume life; discouraged, they poison it.
Joseph Collins

If you drink much from a bottle marked "poison," it is almost certain to disagree with you, sooner or later.
Lewis Carroll

A single event can awaken within us a stranger totally unknown to us.
Antoine de Saint-Exupéry

I looked into that empty bottle and I saw myself.
Grace Metalious

Forgiveness is the scent that the violet bestows upon the heel that crushed it.
Mark Twain

All the perfumes of Arabia will not sweeten this little hand.
William Shakespeare

Sabean odours from the spicy shore of arabic the blest.
John Milton

Each loss has its compensation, There is healing for every pain, But the bird with a broken pinion, Never soars so high again.
Hezekiah Butterworth

A BROKEN BOTTLE AND SPILLED PERFUME

Commentary: "A Broken Bottle and Spilled Perfume" is an emotionally evocative image. Something that was once beautiful, whole, precious and contained now lies "Broken." Its contents have "Spilled" in some way and it is now lost and shattered. "Perfume" can have a beautiful scent—it can transport our hearts and minds—or it can be rather cheap and nasty, almost giving us a headache. Regardless of how it actually smells, it can cause quite strong reactions, particularly on an emotional level. Scents can bring up memories of people or events from the past; they can even remind us of things that have been long forgotten. The smell of "Perfume" can release memories of love, longing and desire, but also anger, hurt and jealousy.

Oracle: Just as "Perfume" is something in a very concentrated form, you may feel that you've been holding in or building up your emotions. Now something has cracked and everything has suddenly been let out, "Spilled" or wasted. There is probably little that can be done about the initial outburst, but now there is a need to be careful of how you handle the situation, what you say and what you do as you sort things out. It's important to remember that sometimes things need to be "Broken" so that their contents can be released or revealed and fully appreciated. There can be a feeling of being completely overwhelmed with emotion when this Symbol is around. Perhaps you actually want to "Spill" your thoughts and feelings, your "insides," to let everything go, but feel stiff, unyielding and all "Bottled" up or contained. Not knowing how to think or react can lead to overblown reactions. It can feel as though everything is completely lost or destroyed. Take heart, though, things can be mended—it just takes time and clear intention.

Keywords: The memory of things lingering on. Scents or smells that evoke reactions. The "cat let out of the bag." The "genie let out of the bottle." Dizziness. Passing out. Smelling salts. Liquids spilled. Anything broken or shattered. Accidents. The loss of something precious. Alcoholism. Biological and chemical weapons of all kinds. Being emotionally charged. Cracking up to crack open. The sound of breaking glass.

The Caution: Things looking good on the outside, but the contents disappointing. Spilling one's guts. Things erupting suddenly. Injured or broken necks or backs. Envy and jealousy. Broken bones. Smelly remnants.

What does this **SYMBOL** say to *you?*

NEIGHBORS HELP IN A HOUSE-RAISING PARTY IN A SMALL VILLAGE

Scorpio 3

Light is the task where many share the toil.
Homer

Rome wasn't built in a day.
Proverb

Alone we can do so little; together we can do so much.
Helen Keller

If you build it, they will come.
Field Of Dreams

If a house be divided against itself, that house cannot stand.
The Bible

Regard your neighbor's gain as your own gain, and your neighbor's loss as your own loss.
Tai Shang Kan Ying P'ien

The hands that help are better far than the lips that pray.
Robert G. Ingersoll

A city is a large community where people are lonesome together.
Herbert Prochnow

There are no passengers on Spaceship Earth. Everybody's crew.
Marshall McLuhan

Commentary: "Neighbors Help in a House-Raising Party in a Small Village." They come together to help each other out and to get to know each other better. By acting as a community, rather than as separate individuals, small, large or even very difficult projects can be undertaken and completed more quickly and efficiently. People bring their individual talents and expertise with them. The sharing of these experiences will build community values and friendships. However, there needs to be a careful watch on how some people contribute as unskilled labor can end up costing both time and money.

Oracle: In this situation, great things can be achieved if everyone works together. Any efforts directed toward giving value and stability to one's community will be rewarded in some measure. Friends and those close to you can help you in any endeavor, big or small. Having faith in those around you can help bring a sense of belonging and relationship to your life. Sometimes a home or a community needs to be built or renovated in some way, with people coming together and everyone putting in their share of dedication, commitment and hard labor. There can be a feeling that there is so much to do on the domestic scene that other considerations have to be put on hold for the time being. People must all have a higher sense of purpose, otherwise some may work at cross-purposes, undermining people or even entire families. Is there a need for people to assist you because someone in your life has left behind their responsibilities? If you are in need of "Help," making a wish for assistance to arrive may bring a bigger response than you expected!

Keywords: Cooperation. Real estate deals. Community concerns. Buying or building houses. Renting apartments and homes. Needing help to find shelter. The agreement of neighbors to maintain community harmony. "Raising the roof." Parties. Dormitories. Having to consider the needs of lots of people. Matchmaking. Community halls. Understanding what it takes to make a village of people. Communal governance or being blocked by rules, laws and regulations of bureaucracy. Homeless shelters. Tools. Building expertise. Helping hands.

The Caution: Taking advantage of generosity. Refusing to cooperate in group endeavors. Building bigger and better things. Bickering over who does what. Not trusting people's input.

What does this **SYMBOL** say to *you?*

Scorpio 4

♏↗

Better to light a candle than to curse the darkness.
Chinese Proverb

If you have knowledge, let others light their candles in it.
Margaret Fuller

Thousands of candles can be lighted from a single candle, and the life of the candle will not be shortened. Happiness never decreases by being shared.
Buddha

Go within every day and find the inner strength so that the world will not blow your candle out.
Katherine Dunham

My candle burns at both ends; It will not last the night; But, ah, my foes, and oh, my friends— It gives a lovely light.
Edna St. Vincent Millay

We must view young people not as empty bottles to be filled, but as candles to be lit.
Robert H. Shaffer

How far that little candle throws his beams! So shines a good deed in a naughty world.
William Shakespeare

Curiosity is the wick in the candle of learning.
William A. Ward

A YOUTH HOLDING A LIGHTED CANDLE IN A DEVOTIONAL RITUAL GAINS A SENSE OF THE GREAT "OTHER WORLD"

Commentary: "A Youth Holding a Lighted Candle in a Devotional Ritual Gains a Sense of the Great 'Other World'." The "Candle" depicts the light that illuminates one's path and consciousness, and "a Youth" implies a devotee or aspirant on the path. He gains "a Sense of the Great 'Other World'," and there's a feeling of reverence, possibly awe and ceremony. He may feel that 'Great Other Worlds' are opening up to him.

Oracle: Your situation may require a fresh attitude in order to create room for new developments and a renewed sense of vitality. You may be feeling a sense of loneliness and alienation. Any form of light, perhaps a "Candle" or a torch, needs to be shed on the dark corners of one's mind. Try to focus on those things that bring you a sense of love and fulfillment. A simple ceremony performed with reverence and respect can bring wonderful results. Simple rays of hope, such as things like a "Candle" can bring, will remind you of or give you spiritual and moral strength. Try lighting a candle and affirming your intentions with a youthful attitude and watch things change for the better. Indeed, you may find yourself entering realms that you have only imagined or not truly dreamed possible. You may be "Gaining a Sense of the Great 'Other World'." Proclaiming a level of devotion to a person, situation or task can reaffirm that commitment and take it to deeper levels. If you feel that you are burdened by responsibilities in this situation, take heart and adopt a sincere and uncomplicated attitude to what you have to do. There's purity of heart and motive available to you.

Keywords: Simple ideals. Ceremonies that are pure and uncomplicated. Affirming intention to the path. The light of consciousness. Shining a light that brings understanding of things on the spiritual level. Spiritualist meetings. Feeling overwhelmed. Enlightenment. Wide-eyed innocence and wonder. Sexual experiments leading to transcendence. Potency. Devotion to ritual. Expansion of psychic talents.

The Caution: Naïve reliance on insincere promises. Feeling like someone is too young to be of any worth. False feelings of reverence and enlightenment. Placebos. Hallucinogens.

What does this **SYMBOL** say to *you?*

A MASSIVE, UNCHANGING ROCKY SHORE RESISTS THE POUNDING OF THE SEA

Scorpio 5

Commentary: "A Massive, Unchanging Rocky Shore Resists the Pounding of the Sea." This Symbol shows how strong the "Rocky Shore" is, or needs to be, to "Resist" the relentless "Pounding of the Sea." The "Rockiness" of the "Shore" is the slowly built result of millions of storms that have gone before. The storms have gone without much of a trace, but the beach remains, its contours changing very slowly.

Oracle: The elements of this situation are rock solid and any efforts to change them may take a long time and a lot of energy. With this Symbol one can feel under assault from a larger and crueler reality, but there is a degree of strength available with which you can resist. You're possibly dealing with trying to change the face of the rock-hard and established reality of life. You may find that you are under emotional assault, however you are probably strong enough to take it. How can you really make any difference in this situation, especially if "the Pounding" has been happening for so long? Sometimes it looks like the old and established is going to give way, but then stubbornness or resistance sets in and nothing changes—all remains the same. This can be good or difficult, depending on which side of this situation you are placed. If you want to keep things as they are, there's a good chance that when the storm is over everything will go back to being much the same as it was before. That's fine, if that's what you want, but if you're trying to make changes, that's a different and much harder story. "Rocks" will only wear down after a very long period of "Pounding" and battering. However, persistence can lead to the achievement of difficult outcomes and objectives. Perhaps love and compassion need to be employed. How long can things continue with the same energy? How long can people endure without changing? Consider your chances for success. You may be "Pounding" the wrong shore. Wait for the "Seas" to calm and look at your true emotional motivations. How long can one keep doing this?

Keywords: Relentless, unchanging reality. The establishment. Feeling battered and bruised. The need to hold onto reality in difficult situations. Sticking with something no matter what the cost or how long it takes. Chinese water torture. Evolution. Endurance. Pounding waves, rocks and sand.

The Caution: Stubborn acts leading to inertia, not growth. Tedious negotiations. Shooting yourself in the foot. Teenage rebellion. Fighting the elements.

What does this **SYMBOL** say to *you?*

The drops of rain make a hole in the stone, not by violence, but by oft falling.
Lucretius

The sea complains upon a thousand shores.
Alexander Smith

It struck me while I was sitting here; everything changes but the sea.
The X-Files

Life leaps like a geyser for those who drill through the rock of inertia.
Alexis Carrel

When much dispute has past, we find our tenets just the same as last.
Alexander Pope

In the confrontation between the stream and the rock, the stream always wins—not through strength, but by perseverance.
H. Jackson Brown

Constant dripping wears away a stone.
Proverb

Deep in the sea are riches beyond compare. But if you seek safety, it is on the shore.
Saadi of Shiraz

Scorpio 6

Security is not the meaning of my life. Great opportunities are worth the risk.
Shirley Hufstedler

Gold will be slave or master.
Horace

I kept on digging the hole deeper and deeper looking for the treasure chest until I finally lifted my head, looked up and realized that I had dug my own grave.
Dominic De Guzman

Although gold dust is precious, when it gets in your eyes it obstructs your vision.
Hsi-Tang

He is rich or poor according to what he is, not according to what he has.
Henry Ward Beecher

Often the search proves more profitable than the goal.
E.L. Konigsburg

Biggest profits mean gravest risks.
Chinese Proverb

That glittering hope is immemorial and beckons many men to their undoing.
Euripides

A GOLD RUSH TEARS PEOPLE AWAY FROM THEIR NATIVE SOIL

Commentary: "A Gold Rush Tears People away from Their Native Soil." The "Gold Rush" brings the temptation to chase the promise of riches, wherever they may be. There have been many "Gold Rushes" throughout history, and people often gamble their resources and their sense of security to chase the possibility of discovering treasures or rewards.

Oracle: The actual promise of abundance and fulfillment from the "Gold Rush" is only really available for a few, although this depends very much on the "Gold" that is being pursued. If the "Gold" is worth the journey and the search, particularly on an internal level, this could be a very rewarding journey that may lead to a better life. Before you set out, you need to make sure you have an adequate "map" of the new territory that you're exploring. The choice is often between an established, fairly stable situation and an unstable, temporary or risky situation. You may indeed strike "Gold" or you may just find yourself exhausted and a long way from home. Learning to discriminate just what is and what is not possible will enhance your judgment of what's worth pursuing. Feelings of excitement and hysteria can be infectious and you can find yourself heading off toward something that's not all it was cracked up to be. The desire to make easy money, to "strike it rich," or the grab for fame can easily overtake people if ambitions get out of hand. Long-term relationships may become unpredictable and unstable when this Symbol is around, as one, or possibly even both of you, are likely to run off for parts unknown just when you seem to be settling into an everyday sense of life. If you're both after the same treasure, however, this can be an incredibly exciting experience. Whatever the outcome, the trick is to enjoy the journey.

Keywords: Strong desires to move on. The longing and the search for the easy fulfillment of hopes and dreams. Leaving one's native soil. Having a cause or mission to pursue. Leaving home, people, family. Dropping everything to chase a project. Pilgrimages. The search for riches. Immigration and migration. Listening to clues. The search for the Holy Grail. Pursuing a better life.

The Caution: Chasing the impossible dream. Losing everything. Being unrealistic or opportunistic. Not being content with what one's got. The grass being greener elsewhere. Lusting after rewards that may be unreal or transitory. Risking what one has for what one could have. Wild goose chases.

What does this **SYMBOL** say to *you?*

DEEP-SEA DIVERS WITH SPECIAL MACHINERY

Commentary: "Deep-Sea Divers" are shown. They have "Special Machinery" which enables them to plumb and explore the depths, to see what they need to see, and to accomplish what they've set out to achieve. One certainly has to be brave and courageous to be a "Deep-Sea Diver," with the skills to be able to survive in unknown, unfamiliar and often risky territory. With their "Machinery" they have the ability to scan, look at and investigate what's usually not seen by many. There has to be a strong level of trust in their own physical and emotional abilities and that their "Special Machinery" will not fail them. "Deep-Sea Divers" go where others fear to tread, and to places that others wouldn't even dream of going. Some people may think the risks taken are foolish or that the journey into "the depths" is a mere fantasy or a waste of time.

Oracle: In the situation facing you, you may need to get deep below the surface to find out what's really going on. It is down within your subconscious and intuitive wisdom that you must search for solutions. Letting go of the intellect and allowing yourself to take a deep plunge into your inner self can reveal talents and wonders that you may have only imagined were there. If you feel out of your depth, there may be a sense of having no light to see what's going on or no oxygen for drawing a breath. You may feel a huge pressure from the world you have dived into. If you are feeling overwhelmed in some way, as if there's the possibility of drowning at any moment, imagine yourself being able to pierce through the darkness to see, and take a deep breath. You can handle the pressure as long as you are not pushing against it, or by changing your perceptions of that pressure. A feeling of awe and wonder can sweep over you as you realize you're in new territory, with a new awareness and so much promise. Remember, you have "Special Machinery" which can help you in this other world.

Keywords: Studying unconscious energies. Uncovering wonders. Breath meditations and techniques. Plunging in. Seeing things that others don't. Having the special insights, talents or technology to affect healings on deep levels. New levels of experience seen and felt. Atlantis and Lemuria. Breathing apparatus. Getting "the bends" and cramping up. Inner space. Highly tuned senses.

The Caution: Pretending to plumb the depths, but only for show. Escapism. Going over the top emotionally. Being unreachable by shutting off to the outside world. Feeling gloomy. No light, no oxygen. Losing touch with reality or the real world. Feeling like you're in a bubble. Isolation and dark thoughts. Not seeing the full picture.

What does this **SYMBOL** say to *you?*

Scorpio 7

Don't you believe that there is in man a deep so profound as to be hidden even to him in whom it is?
St. Augustine

Which is strongest—the reality out of which the illusion is created, the celluloid illusion itself, or the need for illusion? Do we hold the mirror up and dive in? And if we do, what are the consequences?
Marjorie Rosen

Throw a lucky man into the sea, and he will come up with a fish in his mouth.
Arabian Proverb

Sponges grow in the ocean. This bothers me. How deep would it be if they didn't?
Steven Wright

Working on navy sonar systems, we knew that sound propagates approximately four times faster in water than in air. Now here's an interesting image. When exploring the depths of the seas—symbolic of soulful emotions—acoustic images (as in hearing) arrive four times as fast. The suggestion is that with seeking out the greater depths, hearing, both audible and nonaudible, happens substantially faster. Perceptual abilities increase several fold.
Philip Sedgwick

Scorpio 8

We don't see things as they are; we see them as we are.
Anais Nin

A loving person lives in a loving world. A hostile person lives in a hostile world: Everyone you meet is your mirror.
Ken Keyes, Jr.

A lake is the landscape's most beautiful and expressive feature. It is earth's eye; looking into which the beholder measures the depth of his own nature.
Henry David Thoreau

There are some people who live in a dream world, and there are some who face reality; and then there are those who turn one into the other.
Desiderius Erasmus

There is one art of which man should be master; the art of reflection.
Samuel Coleridge

LUNARIAN, n. An inhabitant of the moon, as distinguished from Lunatic, one whom the moon inhabits.
Ambrose Bierce

Beauty is eternity gazing at itself in the mirror.
Kahlil Gibran

Life is the mirror of king and slave.
Madeline Bridges

THE SILVERY MOON SHINING ACROSS A BEAUTIFUL GEM OF A LAKE

Commentary: "The Silvery Moon Shining across a Beautiful Gem of a Lake" is a romantic, reflective and beautiful image. It evokes many emotional responses as we imagine the beauty of the surrounding landscape and the stillness of the "Lake." As this is a "Beautiful Gem of a Lake," its waters will be highly reflective of the moonbeams that "Shine" across it. The "Lake" may convey feelings of depth and the mysteries, or it could be so reflective of the Moon's beams that it seems to look like a mirror, having no feeling of depth at all.

Oracle: In your situation, whether there is a feeling of hidden depths or not, there may be a strong sense of things being "reflected." The image of the "Silvery Moon" or a "Lake" is very much like that of a mirror. What is it about your situation that may need more "reflection"? Is there a need to really take a good, close look inside yourself or another? Or are things being evaluated from a merely superficial level with everything being a mere reflection of someone or something else? It may be wise to remember that still waters run deep and things may not be as they seem on the surface. This image can bring beauty into your life and the need to remember the grace of nature. It's an opportunity to quietly reflect on the feminine aspects of your life and feel the gentle warmth of the Goddess.

Keywords: Reflections. Mirrors. Things mystical and alluring. The Narcissus story. Picturesque scenes. Picture postcard images. Peace and beauty. Halloween and magic. Escapism. Placid emotions. Peace and quiet. Contemplation and meditation. Having a reflective nature. Photographs. Psychic abilities. Hypnotic charm or manipulation. Beaming faces. Projections based on appearances. Beautiful landscapes. Stillness. Stairways to heaven.

The Caution: Acting out of moodiness. Losing the plot. Projecting one's self onto others. Narcissism. Looking at one's self and others as if in a mirror. Not wanting to see the whole picture. Being superficial. A lack of depth. Seeing everything as a reflection of one's self. Relationships that have ideals that aren't based in reality. Lack of everything. Codependent relationships. Superficial responses.

What does this **SYMBOL** say to *you?*

A DENTIST IS HARD AT WORK

Scorpio 9

Commentary: "A Dentist Is Hard at Work." His work involves finding out what's wrong in a situation and fixing it up so that things can work smoothly and efficiently once again. Our "chewing ability" is important as our teeth make it possible to break down nourishment to its smaller elements or to a more digestible consistency so that we can integrate these into our wellbeing. He concentrates on fixing damage that has probably occurred over a long period of time. The "patients" that the "Dentist Works" on may be nervous and restless, and looking forward to the whole thing being finished. Although he has a very important or valuable job to do, many in society don't fully appreciate his "Work."

Oracle: It is important to have healthy teeth as well as bodies and minds. All these factors go into making up our wellbeing and they need checks, balances and maintenance work done on a regular basis to ensure smooth functioning. It is also important for us to take responsibility for their efficient functioning to continue. We need to make sure that we supply our bodies and minds with good nourishment and hygiene, not just indulge in band-aid treatments and cover ups. "Dentists," doctors and other physicians are needed in society in order to fix up the problems that occur in our lives. Society needs to invent a way of repairing the somehow inevitable but probably largely unnecessary damage. On another level, however, there are people who feel it is their duty to continually point out where they think things need to be "fixed," and this can be painful in itself to endure. These people sometimes need to know when to back off; we should be able to assess and fix up our own mistakes. Whatever the situation, you may need help at this time to cope with some of the difficulties that might arise in this period e.g. finance, health, stress, etc.

Keywords: Repairing damage. Drilling at something. Plugging up situations. Being the responsible one who always has to fix things. Not being able to relax. Causing pain to erase pain. Tooth decay and bad breath. Medical equipment. Therapists. Treatments. Social comment to invoke a cure. Flossing and oral care. Attention to detail.

The Caution: Getting further into a hole by using more and more social solutions. Causing more pollution and damage when one should be honoring and fixing things. The fear of pain. Making wrong judgments and causing harm. Big dentist bills because of neglect. Always having to come up with solutions to problems. Always being "on duty." Nagging away at things.

What does this **SYMBOL** say to *you?*

It is very vulgar to talk like a dentist when one isn't a dentist. It produces a false impression.
Oscar Wilde

For years I have let dentists ride roughshod over my teeth: I have been sawed, hacked, chopped, whittled, bewitched, bewildered, tattooed, and signed on again; but this is cuspid's last stand.
S. J. Perelman

The electric chair was invented by a dentist!
Trivia.net

DENTIST, n. A Prestidigitator who, putting metal in one's mouth, pulls coins out of one's pockets.
Ambrose Bierce

A little neglect may breed mischief…for want of a nail the shoe was lost; for want of a shoe the horse was lost; and for want of a horse the rider was lost.
Benjamin Franklin

It is after you have lost your teeth that you can afford to buy steaks.
Pierre Auguste Renoir

The first thing I do in the morning is brush my teeth and sharpen my tongue.
Oscar Levant

Scorpio 10

Friendships develop over food and wine.
Prince Nicholas Romanoff

With true friends ... even water drunk together is sweet enough.
Chinese Proverb

If Jesus Christ were to come today, people would not crucify him. They would ask him to dinner, and hear what he had to say, and make fun of it.
Thomas Carlyle

Strange to see how a good dinner and feasting reconciles everybody.
Samuel Pepys

Every parting is a form of death, as every reunion is a type of heaven.
Tryon Edwards

Man cannot live by bread alone.
Romanian Proverb

We look like a road company of the Last Supper.
Dorothy Parker

Madam, I have been looking for a person who disliked gravy all my life; let us swear eternal friendship.
Rev. Sydney Smith

Better fare hard with good men than feast it with bad.
Thomas Paine

A FELLOWSHIP SUPPER REUNITES OLD COMRADES

Commentary: "A Fellowship Supper Reunites Old Comrades." Circumstances have bought people together and they are sharing "Supper" while reliving old memories. Getting together with people with shared visions or history can be very rewarding and renewing. Stories from the past come up, old friendships are remembered and memories are jogged. This can point to a get-together or a meeting, perhaps over dinner, and finding a special bond between people that feels like it stretches way back into history.

Oracle: In the situation facing you there is a chance to eat, drink and be merry with "Old Comrades." Reunions and gatherings of people who haven't seen each other for a long time can be very rewarding and can remind you of cherished days long gone. Stories from each one's past can be brought up as well as sharing present time realities. This Symbol can also indicate the feeling of having met or having known someone before, even if you haven't literally met each other previously. That this "Supper Reunites Old Comrades" shows there can be the sense that you've somehow shared past life experiences. Feelings or realizations of togetherness can come from "breaking bread," drinking and socializing with others. These feelings can be very strong and can bring up all sorts of reactions and emotions. True friendship and fraternity are likely to result from this meeting and bring a sweet sense of nostalgia. If there's a situation where you feel alienated from someone you'd like to reconnect with, try sharing a meal and see how this "breaks the ice." There may be some old issues that need to be worked through. Have you been avoiding socializing with like-minded people lately?

Keywords: Renewing bonds with those you've shared struggles with. Past life connections. Feeling like you've known someone for lifetimes. Reaching out to others. Having a million and one things to talk about. Reunions and memories. Talking about the past. Sharing meals. Drinking wine. The Last Supper. Partaking in the gifts of special relationships. Fated meetings.

The Caution: Only feeling comfortable with the past. Resisting joining with others. Feeling like a loner, with no one to share the good things in life. Being uneasy about having to face old comrades or adversaries. Secrets being revealed. Gossip that belittles others. Breaking the ice.

What does this **SYMBOL** say to *you?*

A DROWNING MAN IS BEING RESCUED

Scorpio 11

Commentary: "A Drowning Man Is Being Rescued" is a symbol of difficulties, relief, rescue and resuscitation. The "Drowning Man" often indicates someone who's fallen into something that is out of his or her control and who is out of their depth. They can feel like they're being overpowered by their inability to cope with life. This can manifest on any level, emotionally, physically or spiritually. Here, he is shown as "Being Rescued," and help is, or soon will be, nearby.

Oracle: We can feel like we are suffocated by our marriage, job, friendships, life path, etc., or through the lack of these things. Although this Symbol speaks of a "Rescuing," and this may indeed be at hand, sometimes it's essential that we admit to the fact that we are losing control or "Drowning" before a "Rescue" can even begin to take place. People will often lend a hand and spontaneously arrive on the scene to help others out, but they need to know the depths of the situation that's occurring. As the "Man" in this Symbol is "Being Rescued," it shows that the "Drowning" has been noticed and that "Rescue" or relief is imminent. People may indeed turn up to help out or this may be a more lonely passage, with you having to rely on yourself. However, continuing to struggle on alone may not solve anything—indeed, struggling can make things worse. This Symbol can also point to codependent types of relationships where there is a continual need to be available, to be on hand and to be reliable. This can be a tiring responsibility for the "Rescuer" as well as for the "Drowning" person. A true "Rescue" is often found when we look after our own needs, even if it entails a hand up from someone else along the way. Concentrate on the shore, even if it feels as though it's miles away from you. Reconnect with what's possible and real, ground yourself and know that help is at hand, even if it's your higher self that is performing the "Rescue." Soon you'll be able to "breathe" easily again.

Keywords: Resuscitation. Regaining one's breath. Finding life renewed. Asthma, bronchitis, breathing difficulties. Finding help in moments of crisis. Needing a hand. Being rescued. Salvation on any level. Ventilators. Breathing equipment. Oxygen. Dependence. Last minute reprieves. Born-again experiences. Help.

The Caution: Panicking in order to draw help rather than learning how to cope. Constantly finding reasons for losing control of situations. Getting into deep water on a regular basis.

What does this **SYMBOL** say to *you?*

The salvation of the world consists in the salvation of the individual soul.
C.G. Jung

Each man's task is his life preserver.
George B. Emerson

The drowning man will clutch at a straw.
Proverb

Anxiety is love's greatest killer. It makes one feel as you might when a drowning person holds on to you. You want to save him, but you know he will strangle you in his panic.
Anais Nin

You don't drown by falling in the water; you drown by staying there.
Edwin Louis Cole

If a man is destined to drown, he will drown even in a spoonful of water.
Yiddish Proverb

As long as you keep a person down, some part of you has to be down there to hold him down, so it means you cannot soar as you otherwise might.
Marian Anderson

♏↗

Scorpio 12

You can get through life with bad manners, but it's easier with good manners.
Lillian Gish

POLITENESS, n. The most acceptable hypocrisy.
Ambrose Bierce

Etiquette can be at the same time a means of approaching people and of staying clear of them.
David Riesman

You can't be truly rude until you understand good manners.
Rita Mae Brown

Never speak disrespectfully of society. Only people who can't get into it do that.
Oscar Wilde

It is sometimes necessary to lie damnably in the interests of the nation.
Hilaire Belloc

It is very vulgar to talk about one's business. Only people like stockbrokers do that, and then merely at dinner parties.
Oscar Wilde

The true definition of a snob is one who craves for what separates men rather than for what unites them.
John Buchan

A BRILLIANT ASSEMBLY OF DIGNITARIES AT AN OFFICIAL EMBASSY BALL

Commentary: "A Brilliant Assembly of Dignitaries" is shown at an "Official Embassy Ball." Everyone is expected to be dressed up, have good manners and follow certain established codes of behavior. As it is a "Brilliant Assembly of Dignitaries," we can be sure that some of the people have worked long and hard at getting themselves into a position of power and prestige. They must really be "someone" in order to be invited. If they weren't special in some way—powerful, political, influential or somehow well connected, they probably wouldn't be at the "Ball." Those who are invited range from the jaded consulate of some country, who's tired of the social whirl, all the way down to someone who's "on their way up." The younger and possibly more naïve are probably excited about participating in the splendor and finery. To be invited to the "Official Embassy Ball" is quite important or special to some, while others will take it for granted. Others wouldn't care to go if their life depended on it because of the perceived stuffiness and formality of the occasion.

Oracle: This Symbol speaks of a pleasant, almost partylike atmosphere, but one that is often caged in somewhat strict protocol and rules of behavior. The rules and manners of society can be rather limiting, but there are often good reasons for them. Without codes of ethics and manners, societies, business dealings and relationships can fall apart. Look at yourself and observe whether you are being true to your sense of self. Do you have to put on a false show in order to belong? Do you have to put on "airs" and impress people in order to be accepted? Would you rather be in a less formal atmosphere? Listen and learn from those around you; interesting and useful information can come to light. Put on your best face and behavior as connections with "the right people" can be made.

Keywords: Political game-playing. Manners and protocol. Dressing and looking right. Who knows who and what it's worth. Social and political standing. The Cinderella story. Sparkling occasions. Knowing etiquette. Looking for social connections and outcomes that are not necessarily immediate. International relations. "My Fair Lady." Social engineering. Speaking the right language.

The Caution: The habit of role-playing. Not being taught how to behave in "polite society." Having to learn how to fit in without having instruction. Dining, drinking and enjoying life while others can "eat cake." Diplomatic standoffs. Gate crashing. Feeling out of one's depth. Political point scoring that ignores the human dimension.

What does this **SYMBOL** say to *you?*

AN INVENTOR PERFORMS A LABORATORY EXPERIMENT

Scorpio 13

Commentary: "An Inventor" is seen "Performing a Laboratory Experiment." It's hard to know from this Symbol whether he is alone or working with others. Regardless of the circumstances, he has to take responsibility for the outcome. The "Inventor" has to imagine what is possible, gather the necessary ingredients and be willing to take a risk on whether things will work out or not. His "Experiment" may prove to be successful, scary or downright dangerous and risky. If the "Inventor" is doing something new and untried, he must be prepared to step out into unknown territory, and be prepared for the whole thing to blow up in his face. However, "Experiments" don't really fail; although he may have to start all over again with a new set of plans, something is always gained.

Oracle: If things are not working at the moment you probably need to "Experiment," trying different combinations and possibilities. In doing so you will not only most likely find the solution to the situation, but you will also learn a lot from any errors that are made along the way. Look for creative solutions to the situation facing you. A lot of amazing discoveries can be made simply by having a go at something or creating the right mix of ingredients. As the situation unfolds, you'll learn clues as to what should be the next thing to do, the tasks that are worth performing or the risks that you are prepared to take. Be prepared to be inventive and make things up as you go along. Sometimes we have to just "go for it" and do what we feel needs to be done without knowing what the outcome is going to be. Take a few calculated risks and along the way you just might discover something unexpected.

Keywords: Creating one's vision. Thinking quickly and making momentary decisions. Being prepared to risk failure. Bringing different mixes of things and/or people together. Taking calculated risks to see what will happen. Seeing if things live up to expectations. Looking for answers. The "mad professor." Mixing chemicals. Measuring and weighing. Going by one's gut reactions. Inventions and experiments. Discovery. Laboratories. Research.

The Caution: Becoming obscured by pointless goals. Making things up. Being one-eyed and focused to the exclusion of all else. Not fully understanding the consequences of actions. Always taking risks. Not taking adequate cautions. Not keeping track of what you're doing. Ignoring warning signs. Being a "mad professor."

What does this **SYMBOL** say to *you?*

Westheimer's Discovery:
A couple of months in the laboratory can frequently save a couple of hours in the library.
Anonymous

Discovery is seeing what everyone else has seen and thinking what no one else has thought.
Albert von Szent-Gyorgi

Science is the tool of the Western mind and with it more doors can be opened than with bare hands. It is part and parcel of our knowledge and obscures our insight only when it holds that the understanding given by it is the only kind there is.
C. G. Jung

If you shoot for the stars and hit the moon, it's okay. But you've got to shoot for something. A lot of people don't even shoot.
Robert Townsend

Name the greatest of all the inventors. Accident.
Mark Twain

Attempt the end and never stand to doubt; nothing's so hard, but search will find it out.
Robert Herrick

The man who makes no mistakes does not usually make anything.
Edward J. Phelps

Scorpio 14

If the first person who answers the phone cannot answer your question it's a bureaucracy. If the first person can answer your question, it's a miracle.
Gerald F. Lieberman

That's an amazing invention [the telephone], but who would ever want to use one of them?
Rutherford B. Hayes

Well if this is the wrong number, why did you answer it?
James Thurber

In the business world an executive knows something about everything, a technician knows everything about something—and the switchboard operator knows everything.
Harold Coffin

Gossip is nature's telephone.
Sholom Aleichem

Middle age is when you're sitting at home on Saturday night and the telephone rings and you hope it isn't for you.
Ogden Nash

TELEPHONE LINEMEN AT WORK INSTALLING NEW CONNECTIONS

Commentary: "Telephone Linemen at Work Installing New Connections" shows people working and concentrating on laying the "Lines" for "Connections" so that people may communicate with each other easily and effectively. They are laying cables to allow for the smooth functioning of the "Telephone" system. They have a clear understanding of how the equipment works and how necessary and valuable it is to enable people to link up with each other.

Oracle: This Symbol reflects an increase in the forms of communication that you can have access to, or in the amount of communications coming to you. You may find that there has been a failure in communicating your thoughts, ideas or emotions lately. Something is being (or needs to be) done or laid down, in order to solve, repair or patch up the situation. There is nothing to be achieved by worrying about any recent "connection" failures, however something should be done to set about making or repairing the necessary "Lines" of communication. Sometimes advice and help must be called on for all to be resolved. This may need to be expert advice, but it can also be gathered from your own common sense. This can symbolize expansion into areas like the Internet, faxes or business lines. It can also represent the spiritual connection to the "other side," even channeling. Sometimes, however, in the "Installing of New Connections," problems of crossed lines occur. It's important to listen for the real truth in the communications that are being made, not to all the faint chitchat that surrounds what's being said. Networking and new lines of communications often open up after this Symbol is revealed.

Keywords: Acupuncture and other therapies that work on the body's meridians. The nervous system. The Internet. Forming new lines of communication. New connections taking place. Linking people up. Making sure that messages get through. Mobile phones, faxes, email. Networks and networking. Switchboards. Satellites. Wires. The ability to reach far distances. Getting on other peoples' wavelengths. Contacts. Hooking up with the system. UFO experiences. Mobile phones.

The Caution: Failing to see the necessity for repairs to personal communication. Becoming involved in other people's lives. Gossip. News, thoughts and ideas spreading rapidly and getting out of control. Constant chatting. Being fickle. Sabotage. Engaged signals.

What does this **SYMBOL** say to *you?*

CHILDREN PLAYING AROUND FIVE MOUNDS OF SAND

Scorpio 15

Commentary: "Children Playing around Five Mounds of Sand" shows "Children" playing, enjoying themselves and each other in a safe, natural setting. The "Five Mounds" often represents the pentacle, or pentagram. A pentacle is a five-pointed star, often held to have magical or mystical significance. It is a symbol often associated with and used in Wicca and pagan rites. The "Sand" is symbolic of impermanence; it can disperse over time, leaving only a passing impression. The "Children" symbolize innocence and, in this case, almost a lack of awareness of the more serious or crucial factors in their lives. Here the "Children Play" in and around the pentacle with little consideration of whether there may be some other deeper or ritualistic purpose.

Oracle: You may feel that you have the potential for greater things, but don't understand what they are. Development takes time and it is the first experience of "Playing" with latent talent that leads to greater knowledge. You will be able to fulfill your potential, but maybe you need to start at the beginning. Nowadays, the true art of "Play" has largely been lost. We have the apparent need for more and more complicated machinery and gadgets in order to bring joy. Much can be learned from letting go and allowing yourself to experience joy naturally found in the company of others. Indeed, if "Playing" is seen as sacred and special, it can be particularly healing. Things such as walking in the desert, doing sweat lodges and enjoying spiritual gatherings with others. Interacting with others brings our "humanness" to life. It will be necessary to be conscious of their needs, as some may get lost in this situation, losing sight of the others as they disappear behind the "Mounds of Sand." Taking things lightheartedly and enjoying the company of other people, particularly those who are creative and intelligent, can move this situation forward.

Keywords: Creative integration of new ideals. Five being the number of mankind. The value of play in getting to know one another. Playgrounds. Crop circles. The desert. Throwing caution to the wind. Playing hide and seek. Shifting sands. Rituals. American Indian rites. The love of the physical world. The five senses. Carefree and happy playgrounds and laughter. Pentacles. Witchcraft. Solomon's Seal.

The Caution: Being too serious to see life's lighthearted side. Mourning over or regretting childhood lost. The inability to take life seriously. Brooding and hiding.

What does this **SYMBOL** say to *you?*

We must teach our children to dream with their eyes open.
Harry Edwards

The only moral lesson which is suited for a child, the most important lesson for every time of life, is this: "Never hurt anybody."
Denis Breeze

There are children playing in the street who could solve some of my top problems in physics, because they have modes of sensory perception that I lost long ago.
Julius Robert Oppenheimer

The soul is healed by being with children.
Fyodor Dostoevsky

The world is your playground. Why aren't you playing?
Ellie Katz

And on her head, lest spirits should invade, a pentacle, for more assurance, laid.
Orlando Furioso

Young fellows will be young fellows.
Isaac Bickerstaff

Scorpio 16

One should have a general attitude of welcoming to everybody.
Bertrand Russell

Enthusiasm...the sustaining power of all great action.
Samuel Smiles

Smile at each other, smile at your wife, smile at your husband, smile at your children, smile at each other—it doesn't matter who it is—and that will help you to grow up in greater love for each other.
Mother Teresa

Beauty is power; a smile is its sword.
Charles Reade

Your day will go the way the corners of your mouth turn.
Proverb

Flattery is from the teeth out. Sincere appreciation is from the heart out.
Dale Carnegie

Fake it, fake it until you make it (until you laugh).
Anonymous

Most folks are as happy as they make their minds up to be.
Abraham Lincoln

A tender smile, our sorrows' only balm.
Edward Young

A GIRL'S FACE BREAKING INTO A SMILE

Commentary: "A Girl's Face" is shown "Breaking into a Smile." She may have been facing a dilemma, or seriously contemplating something. Now, there has been a breakthrough, and her "Face Breaks into a Smile." By the mere change of her facial expression, her whole demeanor has shifted. We "Break into a Smile" when we choose to invite others to come closer to us. If we can't see another's "Face," we make all kinds of assumptions about what's going on in their minds—most often the wrong kind—often based on our own mindset. Road rage and e-mail misunderstandings happen because we're not able to read each other's "Faces." People bumping into each other in the street when walking don't become nearly as enraged as they do when they are driving cars. This is largely because people exchange looks of apology and forgiveness, and all is forgiven or forgotten.

Oracle: There may be a need to lighten up. "Smiling" not only makes us feel better, it makes others feel good as well. As happiness boosts the immune system, things are bound to turn around through showing a positive attitude. Many things can be gained through "Smiling," including getting your own way. There's the "Smile" we have when we're genuinely happy, or the "Smile" we have when the "penny drops" and something is realized or understood. A "Smile" may show a quiet, inner knowing, such as when you know more than what is being said or when you have an intuitive sense of what someone really means. True "Smiling" can be infectious, with others responding in the same way. If you are inviting a relationship, or trying to heal one, a "Smile" can be a great icebreaker. Others want to see you happy, calm, accepting or welcoming. In this context the "Smile" is a response to others and shows evidence of your empathy and desire to find a positive, warm, friendly outcome. Try doing it more and see how you feel.

Keywords: Breaking the ice. Drawing others. Radiating happiness. Facial expressions. Changing one's expression or demeanor. Facial feedback. Making positive eye contact. Transferring feelings that lift others. Releasing stress, worry and anger. Distances bridged between people. Being face-to-face. Teeth, lips, gums, dimples, eyes. Facial lines. Dental work. Beauty that radiates.

The Caution: False happiness to satisfy others' needs. Covering up how one's really feeling through putting on a show of happiness. Lack of sincerity. Rigidity of responses. Sour faces. Feeling sad and lonely. Keeping people on the sidelines and the periphery of one's life. Grumpy attitudes. Refusal to communicate.

What does this **SYMBOL** say to *you?*

A WOMAN, FILLED WITH HER OWN SPIRIT, IS THE FATHER OF HER OWN CHILD

Scorpio 17

Commentary: "A Woman, Filled with Her Own Father of Her Own Child." She radiates a sense of certainty and self-sufficiency about who she is. There is the feeling that she could accomplish almost anything, as she is "Filled with Her Own Spirit." This Symbol indicates the ability one has to be able to cope with being on their own, looking after the details of life without another's help. The "Woman" can look after the everyday needs of her own life along with those of her family.

Oracle: This situation may reveal the sense or the reality that you need to be totally self-sufficient at the moment, regardless of those around you and their input into your life. Alternatively, there can be the feeling of having been "left with the baby." It can indicate single parenthood or bringing up the young without outside help. This Symbol can indicate the loss of the males in one's life, such as the husband or father. However, it can also indicate the feeling that one's life is full enough as it is and the path ahead doesn't seem to include the desire or the need to have children. Be wary of isolationist and prohibitive emotions, though. Is there a situation here where others are not being invited to share or be included in your life? How are you coping with the more complicated tasks and chores that you have to get on with in life? Try to remember to include others respectfully, however. Although we are all blessed with our own unique and individual qualities, it is often the combination of ourselves with others that helps to create greater balance and depth in life. Confidence in the future and "Filling" yourself up "with Your Own Spirit" can lead to wonderful possibilities. Creative projects can be birthed more fully when one has an infinite and total connection with what one wants to produce.

Keywords: Single parenthood. Being proud of one's individuality. Feeling capable of anything. Spiritual experiences that fill one with one's own spirit. Self-reliance. The lack of a father figure. In-vitro fertilization. The complications of adoption. Self-sufficiency. Facing the world feeling whole. Having the right to determine one's future. The story of the conception of Jesus.

The Caution: Uncompromising feminism or chauvinism. Feeling like one has to be responsible for everything. Unrealistic independence. Being left alone and abandoned. Having no one to turn to for support. Being an adult before one's time.

What does this **SYMBOL** say to *you?*

I don't need anyone to rectify my existence. The most profound relationship we will ever have is the one with ourselves.
Shirley MacLaine

The consuming desire of most human beings is deliberately to plant their whole life in the hands of some other person.
Quentin Crisp

At work, you think of the children you have left at home. At home, you think of the work you've left unfinished. Such a struggle is unleashed within yourself. Your heart is rent.
Golda Meir

There are times when parenthood seems nothing but feeding the mouth that bites you.
Peter De Vries

It is easier for a father to have children than for children to have a real father.
Pope John XXIII

If one is not going to take the necessary precautions to avoid having parents one must undertake to bring them up.
Quentin Crisp

Scorpio 18

Unless a tree has borne blossoms in spring, you will vainly look for fruit on it in autumn.
Charles Hare

The clearest way into the universe is through a forest wilderness.
John Muir

Youth is like spring, an over-praised season more remarkable for biting winds than genial breezes. Autumn is the mellower season, and what we lose in flowers we more than gain in fruits.
Samuel Butler

Two roads diverged in a wood, and I took the one less traveled by, and that has made all the difference.
Robert Frost

How beautifully leaves grow old. How full of light and color are their last days.
John Burroughs

So many gods, so many creeds, So many paths that wind and wind, While just the art of being kind Is all the sad world needs.
Ella Wheeler Wilcox

Ah! Well away! Seasons flower and fade.
Lord Alfred Tennyson

A QUIET PATH THROUGH WOODS BRILLIANT IN AUTUMN COLORING

Commentary: "A Quiet Path through Woods Brilliant in Autumn Coloring." The "Quiet Path" is the "Path" that one should (or perhaps must) take, in order to finish something or accomplish some mission. The "Autumn" leaves are a symbol of change—the energy of the recent growth is returned to the earth in preparation for the next growing season. There is a feeling of transition as the leaves decay into the vegetation. Quiet walks can reconnect one with nature.

Oracle: In the situation facing you, fruitful success is now behind you. It is the dramatic preparation for change that has resulted from the fruits of your labor that surrounds you now. It is now either at (or just after) harvest time and everything is changing. Take a deep breath and infuse yourself with nature's gifts. This Symbol can also represent the opportunity to consider and reflect on the success of your recent activities. If there hasn't been enough success or productivity there is nothing more that can be done for the time being as the "season for harvest" has now finished. Winter is coming and with it the need to recuperate and restore energy. It is time to let the past go and prepare for making new plans. Whether your "harvest" has been successful or not, there will be many lessons and benefits from what has occurred. This Symbol is about the opportunity and maybe even the need to take time to quietly appreciate this shift of energy.

Keywords: Rewards of plenty. Transformations through the different seasons of one's life. Overcoming battles and disappointments. Finding peace. Layers of personality issues flaking off with maturity. Gardens, sometimes off the beaten path. Taking time out to reflect on nature. The feeling of change in the air. Mature and elegant responses. Rich colors. Memories and memoirs. Taking life one day at a time. Overcoming loss through positive attitudes. Warm responses. A calm knowingness. Reverence and respect. Having a "been there, done that" attitude.

The Caution: Being too late for the harvest. Concentrating on the past. Being oblivious to nature's beauty. Resisting the flow of the seasons. Feeling that winter is upon you with no way out. Issues of growing old. Being alone in one's "autumn years."

What does this **SYMBOL** say to *you?*

A PARROT LISTENING AND THEN TALKING, REPEATS A CONVERSATION HE HAS OVERHEARD

Scorpio 19

Commentary: "A Parrot" is shown "Listening and Then Talking." He "Repeats a Conversation He Has Overheard." The "Parrot" has the ability to mimic what's being said and the various sounds that surround him. In esoteric symbolism, birds often symbolize spiritual forces.

Oracle: This Symbol often infers some level of spiritual channeling, as thoughts and words can sometimes appear to course through a person, especially if the "messages" seem to come from somewhere else. It can show someone who is receptive to the thoughts and ideas that are around, or in the environment, and who can process the information to the point where it becomes their own. The ability to convey the facts or a message accurately and responsibly will be very important to the outcome. However, there is a need for caution with this Symbol. It can imply messages, talk or gossip that loses its integrity once it reaches someone who operates on an unconscious level. Translating things into different languages or repeating them can lead to things being either more or less understood. One needs to be accurate about what was actually said, and what was meant, before any misunderstandings take place. Look to the source of the information in this situation; is it reliable and was the original message understood in its entirety? Is this a "conscious" retelling of the story? Is what's being said coming from the heart, or is it really not worth listening to? Also, this Symbol can show someone who expects instructions or orders to be followed without question.

Keywords: Transmitting information or knowledge. The need to integrate things into consciousness. Recorded messages. Answering and fax machines. Mumbling. Translators, birds, parrots, news reporters, stool pigeons. Telephone operators. Messages from strange places. Automated responses. New languages. Talking to animals. Talk radio.

The Caution: Rote responses that are ill considered. "Towing the party line" without having any opinion of your own. Going over the same territory. Losing true meaning through repetition. Repeating without knowing the real meaning or purpose. Meaningless banter. Tunnel vision. Gossiping. Missing the essence of what's being said. Not having a mind of one's own. Brainwashing. Reruns of the same old line. Broken records.

What does this **SYMBOL** say to *you?*

INTERPRETER, n. One who enables two persons of different languages to understand each other by repeating to each other what it would have been to the interpreter's advantage for the other to have said.
Ambrose Biere

Accept your genius and say what you think.
Ralph Waldo Emerson

You have the right to remain silent. Anything you say will be misquoted then used against you.
Anonymous

When you talk, you repeat what you already know; when you listen, you often learn something.
Jared Sparks

The real menace in dealing with a five-year-old is that in no time at all you begin to sound like a five-year-old.
Jean Kerr

Children seldom misquote you. In fact, they usually repeat word for word what you shouldn't have said.
Anonymous

The best time to hold your tongue is the time you feel you must say something or bust.
Josh Billings

♏ Scorpio 20

*All is mystery; but he is a
slave who will not struggle
to penetrate the dark veil.*
Benjamin Disraeli

*Blow the dust off the clock. Your
watches are behind the times.
Throw open the heavy curtains
which are so dear to you—you
do not even suspect that the
day has already dawned
outside.*
Alexander Solzhenitsyn

*Who's not sat tense before his
own heart's curtain?*
Rainer Maria Rilke

*The first step toward change is
awareness. The second step is
acceptance.*
Nathaniel Branden

*Of what use is the veil if you are
going to dance?*
Hindu Proverb

*Happiness is nothing but
everyday living seen through
a veil.*
Zora Neale Hurston

*There was a door to which I
found no key: There was the veil
through which I might not see.*
Omar Khayyam

*Dance me through the curtains
that our kisses have outworn.*
Leonard Cohen

A WOMAN DRAWING ASIDE TWO DARK CURTAINS THAT CLOSED THE ENTRANCE TO A SACRED PATHWAY

Commentary: "A Woman" is "Drawing aside Two Dark Curtains That Closed the Entrance to a Sacred Pathway." She is revealing a way forward, a "Pathway" that has previously been closed off or completely unknown or unexplored. Perhaps she has just discovered this "Sacred Pathway" herself, or she could be revealing it for others so that they may explore new realms for themselves. "Drawing Aside the Dark Curtains" can allow light to flood "Dark" corners.

Oracle: You may sense the need to venture down new "Pathways" or to investigate new possibilities. You will have to muster intuitive faith and overcome any fears in order to truly enter into these new realms. Having or showing courage, being inquisitive and expressing strong desires may also be prerequisites for success in this new arena of experience. Your sphere of action and operation are likely to become vastly enlarged with the new perspectives that are opening up to you. All sorts of new possibilities and opportunities are before you. These can be felt on the physical level, on the more mystical planes, or in a sexual way. "Pulling back the curtains" to reveal what needs to be shown will lead to answers to this question. Look at your situation, what exactly is this "Sacred Pathway" and where is it leading you? Is it a place that has been dreamed about for some time, but until now there hasn't been a guide or a traveling companion to show the way or to share the journey? Whatever the case may be, it appears that help will soon be at hand in sorting out the mystery that stands before you. Be receptive, be loving and take the step into the unknown.

Keywords: Mysteries revealed, sometimes after a long wait. Feminine mysteries laid out before you. Woman's reproductive organs, especially the vagina. The mysteries of the Goddesses. Getting past things that are cloaked or shielded from entry or view. Sexual mysteries. Open Sesame. Clairvoyant readings that reveal the "Path." Invitations to the unknown. Drawing aside inhibitions. Following through on things. Undressing.

The Caution: Being seduced into dark and sinister things or being led astray. Not being shown the true picture or the truth. Frigidity and closing off sexual responses. Being, or feeling, shut out. Dark rooms with little sign of life.

What does this **SYMBOL** say to *you?*

OBEYING HIS CONSCIENCE, A SOLDIER RESISTS ORDERS

Commentary: "Obeying His Conscience, a Solder Resists Orders" is an image of someone coming to terms with the fact that he can't perform the duty that is expected of him because it goes against the grain of who he truly is, what he truly stands for and what it is that he wants out of life. He needs to "Obey His Conscience" and "Resist Orders." Doing things that go against the very fabric of his being may mean he may never be able to live with himself. Indeed, he may have to go AWOL and completely leave what he's been expected or, indeed, trained to do.

Oracle: We sometimes find that society has drawn up rules and regulations for us to live by that are inappropriate for our inner world. When this happens, we find ourselves compromised if we are expected to follow through or act on them. This Symbol speaks of the need to occasionally "disobey" the structures of society and what is expected. You may find yourself in a situation where expectations put on you go directly against your values. There is often the difficult choice between allegiance (to a relationship, a job, a country, etc.) and your own inner beliefs, truths, objectives and ambitions. True freedom can only be found within when one faces these situations with a sense of integrity and a full understanding of the consequences that are possible. Are you aware of and prepared for any consequences that may come from a refusal to comply or conform to what others want? What "punishments" may come from refusing to "Obey Orders"? What are the "Orders," who makes them and who is responsible for them when they're carried out? There can be confusion around relationships, resulting in difficulties in following what society says should be done. Is it a longing for a return to a pure state of love that freezes you? Are you prepared to stand your ground and uphold your values?

Keywords: Personal morality. Doing what one's conscience dictates. Going against the status quo. Doing the unexpected. Going by the promptings of the inner voice. The consequences of having a conscience. Not coming home. People clinging to each other. Love that restrains.

The Caution: Displaying cowardice or a lack of courage to act. Not doing what one is expected to do. "Going over the top" in a wild and crazy way. Going AWOL. Being the one who lets everyone down. Court martials. Antisocial behavior. Anarchists. Being "uncommitted" or "unavailable." Choosing play instead of duty. Goofing off.

What does this **SYMBOL** say to *you?*

Scorpio 21

A man must consider what rich realm he abdicates when he becomes a conformist.
Ralph Waldo Emerson

I've been trying for some time to develop a lifestyle that doesn't require my presence.
Gary Trudeau

He who learns and runs away, lives to learn another day.
Edward Lee Thorndike

I was court martialed in my absence, and sentenced to death in my absence, so I said they could shoot me in my absence.
Brendan F. Behan

So daily I renew my duty; I touch her here and there, I know my place; I kiss her open mouth, I praise her beauty and people call me traitor to my face.
Leonard Cohen

Theirs is not to reason why. Theirs is but to do or die.
Lord Alfred Tennyson

I had examined myself pretty thoroughly and discovered that I was unfit for military service.
Joseph Heller, Catch 22

The first duty of a soldier is obedience.
G.J. Whyte-Melville

A guilty conscience needs no accuser.
Proverb

Scorpio 22

When a man wants to murder a tiger he calls it sport; when a tiger wants to murder him, he calls it ferocity.
George Bernard Shaw

There are many humorous things in the world: among them the white man's notion that he is less savage than the other savages.
Mark Twain

Always behave like a duck— keep calm and unruffled on the surface but paddle like the devil underneath.
Jacob Braude

The coward threatens when he is safe.
Goethe

What constitutes a real, live human being is more of a mystery than ever these days, and men—each one of whom is a valuable, unique experiment on the part of nature—are shot down wholesale.
Hermann Hesse

Have a heart that never hardens, and a temper that never tires, and a touch that never hurts.
Charles Dickens

There is no decent place to stand in a massacre, but if a woman takes your hand, then go and stand with her.
Leonard Cohen

HUNTERS PROTECTED BY HEAVY CLOTHING ARE SHOOTING WILD DUCKS

Commentary: "Hunters Protected by Heavy Clothing Are Shooting Wild Ducks" is an image that brings to mind people taking unfair advantage of smaller beings. The "Hunters' Heavy Clothing" implies that they are wearing camouflage in order to hide from the "Ducks," or they are somehow protected by their "garb" as they are "Hunting" their prey. This "Protective Clothing" can make their prey an easy target. If the "Hunters" are "Shooting Wild Ducks" in order to make a living or to be able to eat, then the "Shooting" seems to be more justified, or acceptable, than if they are just doing it for sport.

Oracle: Sometimes there is the need for an outlet for aggressive emotions. Doing so in groups gives this some sense of acceptability, but is it ever really socially acceptable? If there is a clear cut reason for this "shooting party," such as survival or food, this action may be seen as a necessary part of life. However, this often shows innocent people or those not able to protect themselves being picked on, or their lives being threatened. Bullying can take many forms, as can violence. It doesn't have to manifest as actual physical violence, but can be done on a mental or emotional level. Be careful not to get into the line of fire in this situation, as things might get out of control quickly, leaving you, and possibly others, in a vulnerable position. The "Heavy Clothing" can imply that being rather invisible protects the "Hunters." They may wear some type of masking apparel or be protected by screens such as having an important job or role in society. Perhaps they are in the armed forces and commit atrocities in the name of war. Their "Heavy Clothing" can camouflage the fact that they are picking on people who are in defenseless positions; indeed they may get away with it successfully. Protecting yourself and others with a barrier of white light may serve to take the charge out of what's going on.

Keywords: Satiating one's aggressive desires. Being able to hit the mark. Putting up with violence in one's life, whether physical, mental, spiritual or emotional. Road, and other, types of rage. The armed services and their responsibilities. War. Terrorism in its many forms. Camouflage. Being an armed force. Armaments.

The Caution: Exploitation of those who are more vulnerable. Taking unfair advantage of the innocent or the less experienced. Feeling like a sitting duck. Nowhere to run or hide. Hormones running rampant. Mindless violence. War crimes tribunals. Gang warfare. Indiscriminate actions.

What does this **SYMBOL** say to *you?*

A RABBIT METAMORPHOSED INTO A NATURE SPIRIT

Scorpio 23

Commentary: "A Rabbit Metamorphosed into a Nature Spirit" is a rather strange image that seems rather fantastic at first. The "Rabbit" is changing its very nature; it is somehow "morphing" into a different being, a "Nature Spirit." The "Rabbit" has gone from using its baser, animal or sexual instincts into living as a more spiritual being. When something "Metamorphoses" there is usually a change of appearance and way of behaving or being, but it is still the same being at a core level, just operating on a different plane of expression.

Oracle: You may find yourself having a transformative realization that will take your focus away from your more basic animal instincts to a more spiritual level of perception. Your vital energies may remain constant, but the way in which these respond to the environment can change considerably. Issues such as battling for survival can become less important. Life takes on a different purpose and new and more liberating ways of acting in the world become available. In shifting from a focus on the lower chakras (physical and sexual) to the higher chakras (third eye and crown) we move closer to our relationship with the universal energy that motivates and inspires us. This transformation can lead to a calmer way of living or perhaps a more specialized state of being. This can happen through having some kind of religious experience, such as an epiphany, where we find that life changes on many levels, leaving us somehow different and unable to go back to our old ways of being and relating. Welcoming this new state of being can lead to incredible layers of perception unfolding, transforming life into a higher vibration and making life more worthwhile.

Keywords: Revelation of hidden talents. Vegetarianism. Changing one's lifestyle completely. Rapid and total transformation. Morphing. Giving up merely battling for survival. Ascension of consciousness. Elementals. Evolution. Moving into a new level of being. Raising one's vibration. Complete changes. Psychic attunement. Losing one's sexual charge.

The Caution: Being dissatisfied with transformation as not economically useful. Feeling ineffective or impotent, having one's sexual power taken away. Feeling desexed or "neutered." Losing one's drive or libido. Feeling alone and misunderstood. Dumbed-down energies. Neglecting body in favor of spirit or emotion.

What does this **SYMBOL** say to *you?*

We're born princes and the civilizing process turns us into frogs.
Eric Berne

Rabbits of the world—stop!
Anonymous

I'm not bad; I'm just drawn that way.
Jessica Rabbit

Don't go into Mr. McGregor's garden: your father had an accident there; he was put in a pie by Mrs. McGregor.
Beatrix Potter

Man is physically as well as metaphysically a thing of shreds and patches, borrowed unequally from good and bad ancestors, and a misfit from the start.
Ralph Waldo Emerson

The moment we indulge our affections, the earth is metamorphosed; there is no winter and no night; all tragedies, all ennuis vanish, all duties even.
Ralph Waldo Emerson

I am not now that which I have been.
Lord Byron

All things must change to something new, to something strange.
Henry Wadsworth Longfellow

Scorpio 24

The mountains are fountains of men as well as of rivers, of glaciers, and of fertile soil. The great poets, philosophers, prophets, able men whose thoughts and deeds have moved the world, have come down from the mountains.
John Muir

Talking much about oneself can also be a means to conceal oneself.
Friedrich Nietzsche

That person proves his worth who can make us want to listen when he is with us and think when he is gone.
Anonymous

The reason there are so few good talkers in public is that there are so few thinkers in private.
Anonymous

And he goes through life, his mouth open and his mind closed.
Oscar Wilde

CROWDS COMING DOWN THE MOUNTAIN TO LISTEN TO ONE INSPIRED MAN

Commentary: "Crowds" are "Coming Down the Mountain to Listen to One Inspired Man." There is a message that needs to be heard and people are making their way to the "One" who can deliver it. There must be a reason for them to come "Down the Mountain to Listen"—there is probably something important and stimulating that they come together to receive. This "One Inspired Man" most likely has some gift, certainly he'll have the gift of speech, knowledge and communication. There's no guarantee, however, that everyone is going to be receptive to what's being said; people will have many different responses to the messages being given. Although it's fairly clear that not all will be swayed, the message is likely to resonate with many.

Oracle: Whether you are one among the "Crowds" or you are, indeed, the "Inspired Man," you may feel that you have had some wonderful realizations and insights and now you need to bring these insights, these messages, "Down" from "the Mountain," and integrate them into your everyday life in some way. It's wonderful to be turned on by an inspired speaker or message, but what will be done with these revelations or new information? The truth may very well lie within yourself—listening to the positive messages from your higher self, or from others who can lift your focus. This can move you to take charge of your less positive thoughts and actions. However, there may need to be some kind of thoughtful discrimination about what's actually being said as blindly accepting what's being imparted can lead to a loss of one's individual mindset.

Keywords: Power to sway the feelings and thoughts of many. The ability to draw a large audience. The Jesus story. Giving one's power away to those who apparently have more authority. Charisma. Having a large audience. The minds and the ears of the many. Oratory skills. Gurus. Listening. Ascending the mountain to acheive a purer state of being. Lecturing.

The Caution: Naïveté, gullibility. Feeling like someone else holds all the answers, but you don't. Situations that smack of guru mentality. Idolatry and the manipulation that can result from it. Never knowing when to keep quiet. Forcing ideas on others when they don't really want to listen. Not letting anyone else get a word in. Demanding attention. Feeling above everyone. Snobbery.

What does this **SYMBOL** say to *you?*

AN X-RAY PHOTOGRAPH HELPS WITH THE DIAGNOSIS

Scorpio 25

A smart mother makes often a better diagnosis than a poor doctor.
August Bier

Commentary: "An X-Ray Photograph Helps with the Diagnosis" of some ailment, dilemma or situation. The "X-Ray Photograph" allows things to be revealed that otherwise would not be seen or understood. The American Heritage Dictionary defines "Diagnosis" as: "The act or process of identifying or determining the nature and cause of a disease or injury through evaluation of patient history, examination, and review of laboratory data." It pierces through external layers to the core of things to show what's really there or what's really going on. This can allow for remedies to be decided and healing to be set in motion.

Creativity is piercing the mundane to find the marvelous.
Bill Moyers

Life is uncharted territory. It reveals its story one moment at a time.
Leo Buscaglia

Oracle: You may be in need of a deeper understanding of your situation. There's quite possibly the impulse to peel away the layers of the situation, using the emotions or the intellect. What is needed or wanted to be known, and what is being done to reveal the reality or structure of the situation that is facing you? Talking to others may be necessary, as they can help reflect to you what is really going on from an uninvolved perspective. Looking somewhere "inside" for clues can bring issues to light that otherwise would have gone undetected. An "X-Ray" is able to see through layers into the structures of things, it cuts through extraneous, or unnecessary, details to get to the heart of the matter to find out what's going on. We can use our minds to the same effect; with a clever "Diagnosis" we can delve into things to find solutions and remedies. Likewise, a "Photograph" can freeze life in one moment of time. These "snapshots" can show us many things and can answer questions that may have otherwise long gone unanswered. Someone in this story can be feeling that it is impossible to hide anything as someone is scrutinizing every move that's made. Look deeply, you'll come up with a "Diagnosis."

To him that watches, everything is revealed.
Italian Proverb

DIAGNOSIS, n. A physician's forecast of the disease by the patient's pulse and purse.
Ambrose Bierce

If you don't ask the right questions, you don't get the right answers. A question asked in the right way often points to its own answer. Asking questions is the ABC of diagnosis. Only the inquiring mind solves problems.
Edward Hodnett

Keywords: Penetrating insight. Piercing through external appearances. Pure understanding. Incredible insight and revelations. Having the eyes to see. X-ray machines, spying, detective work. Reaching conclusions. Evaluations. Photographs. Negatives. Radiation. X-ray vision. Expensive and up-to-date equipment. Chemotherapy. Mammograms. Scanning equipment. Finding causes. Paparazzi.

If your pictures aren't good enough, you aren't close enough.
Robert Capa

The Caution: Disregarding the flesh on the outside—the humanity of people. Invading other people's psychic or intellectual space. Undressing or revealing people through subtle manipulation. Always being intense and dissatisfied with the easy, or obvious, answers.

What does this **SYMBOL** say to *you?*

Scorpio 26

We are the land. To the best of my understanding, that is the fundamental idea that permeates American Indian life.
Paula Gunn Allen

Illegal aliens have always been a problem in the United States. Ask an Indian.
Robert Orben

A hundred men may make an encampment, but it takes a woman to make a home.
Chinese Proverb

Some national parks have long waiting lists for camping reservations. When you have to wait a year to sleep next to a tree, something is wrong.
George Carlin

The Puritans gave thanks for being preserved from the Indians, and we give thanks for being preserved from the Puritans.
Finley Peter Dunne

Life is uncharted territory. It reveals its story one moment at a time.
Leo Buscaglia

AMERICAN INDIANS MAKING CAMP IN NEW TERRITORY

Commentary: "American Indians Making Camp in New Territory" shows people seeking out and finding somewhere "New" to set up their lives. They've found somewhere suitable to make "Camp" and are probably busy going about their business to ensure they'll be comfortable and their needs will be met as best they can. Perhaps it's intended that they'll stay long term in this "New Territory" but it could also be that they're just there for the short term and will be moving on before long.

Oracle: Someone—perhaps many people—has found "New Territory" and there is a need to acclimate, assess the environment and get their life in order. There is also the need to adjust quickly on a psychological level to the environment they are settling into. Whether it's the actual moving of home, or settling into a new job, you need to feel at home in both an inner and outer sense. This "New Territory" doesn't necessarily have to be about actual encampments; its "newness" can be represented in an emotional or spiritual framework. However, if someone doesn't feel at home, there may be a creeping sense of unease as you or others find it hard to relax and feel safe and accepted in this new environment. If there is no real conflict over this "Territory" and no stepping on other people's toes, this can be a very enriching experience that can lead to all sorts of new experiences, relationships and possibilities. However, people sometimes merely inhabit a space and then depart, leaving a mess all around them. How can you and others help in making an effort to ensure that everyone's territory, living and personal space, and even emotional space, is not overcrowded, compromised or damaged in some way?

Keywords: Settling in. Walk-ins. Having to learn the rules of being in a new environment. The need for freedom to live one's life as one wants. Concerns with territory. Immigration. Migration across countries. Gathering things together for family and community needs. Tents. Shelter. Cohabitation. Revering and protecting the environment. Setting up camp. Going on a walk. Squatters. Respecting boundaries. Reservations.

The Caution: Moving into or invading other's territory. Putting up with things when one should move on. Feeling invaded. Kicking people out because they don't fit in or don't belong. Segregation on grounds of color, race or religion. Compromising other's living space. Arriving unannounced. Barging in. Attack and invasion.

What does this **SYMBOL** say to *you?*

A MILITARY BAND MARCHES NOISILY ON THROUGH THE CITY STREETS

Commentary: "A Military Band" is shown. It "Marches Noisily on through the City Streets." As it makes its way along the streets it draws attention to itself through its music and the loud banging of drums. The "Military Band" can inspire national pride among the onlookers, or it can arouse suspicion and distrust as people are left wondering just what the real agenda is. Is the "Military Band" rallying people together or is it just flexing "Military" muscles to show the common folk who's in charge?

Oracle: There is occasionally a need to make a show for society to remind us of our own or our country's successes and achievements. You may find that this will take up a great deal of your time possibly for no real return, but the morale of those around you will benefit and that should be the true goal. Sometimes there's a perceived need to impress others with one's existence, so that they don't forget that you exist. However, this Symbol can also show people who make enormous amounts of noise and demand attention, drowning out all that is going on around them. These people are often hard to ignore and can be irritating and downright disruptive. Perhaps they have a "drum that they need to bang" in order to wake up others who are not paying attention to their needs, wants or desires. Perhaps they are trying to wake people from their apathy. Sometimes the mere act of showing attention, appreciation and admiration can stop the need for such noisy displays and bring everything back to a more peaceful space.

Keywords: Making music to rouse people from complacency. Noisy announcements. Demanding attention. Trumpeting achievements. Reminders from the authorities that individuals are often not in charge. Celebrations of past battles. Corporate advertising. Peace rallies or war marches. Marching and drills. Precision movements. Baton twirling. Drums and trumpets. Spit and polish.

The Caution: A lot of volume that can be too pompous. So much volume that the true message gets lost. Demanding to be heard. Banging one's drum, even when others might be unresponsive or not want to hear. Blaring announcements. Warnings to others to follow orders or to be complicit. Big ego displays. Propaganda. Threats to peace. Momentary disruptions.

If a man does not keep pace with his companions, perhaps it is because he hears a different drummer. Let him step to the music which he hears, however measured or far away.
Henry David Thoreau

Love is not a victory march.
Leonard Cohen

The intellectual man requires a fine bait; the sots are easily amused. But everybody is drugged with his own frenzy, and the pageant marches at all hours, with music and banner and badge.
Ralph Waldo Emerson

Once vigorous measures appear to be the only means left of bringing the Americans to a due submission to the mother country, the colonies will submit.
King George III

Military justice is to justice what military music is to music.
Groucho Marx

Military intelligence is a contradiction in terms.
Groucho Marx

What does this **SYMBOL** say to *you?*

Scorpio 28

Lord, what fools these mortals be!
William Shakespeare

The king is the man who can.
Thomas Carlyle

*A little kingdom I possess,
Where thoughts and feelings dwell;
And very hard the task I find
Of governing it well.*
Louisa May Alcott

I could be bound in a nutshell and count myself a king of infinite space.
William Shakespeare

But above all things I strive to train them to be useful to the Holy Church of God and for the glory of your kingdom.
Alcuin of York

I am, indeed, a king, for I know how to rule myself.
Pietro Aretino

Obsessed by a fairytale, we spend our lives searching for a magic door and a lost kingdom of peace.
Eugene O'Neill

Unfortunately this earth is not …a fairyland, but a struggle for life, perfectly natural and therefore extremely harsh.
Martin Bormann

Not what I have, but what I do is my kingdom.
Thomas Carlyle

THE KING OF THE FAIRIES APPROACHING HIS DOMAIN

Commentary: "The King of the Fairies" is seen "Approaching His Domain." He understands, or has a sense of, where he belongs and his place in the overall scheme of things. He is approaching or reclaiming what somehow "belongs" to him. He may have been away from his true place for a long time, he may have had some reason to leave temporarily or he may never have known (or found) where his true place was. Whatever, he is now coming closer and closer to his "Domain," his "realm."

Oracle: This pictures a situation of someone who needs to feel in charge, or that they are an authority figure or they are in their own element. "His Domain," in this situation, is not necessarily a place that would be broadly seen as a "kingdom," but it can appear to be so in one's mind. There can be the feeling that there is a nice, calm and spiritual place to be found. You may feel that you, or someone else, are finally finding the place where one can belong or feel comfortable. This may have been after a long period of being somewhere alien, or in a place that didn't resonate with your true self. A new sense of claiming one's power, being a "King," someone "in charge," may arise. As this is said to be the "King's Domain," this place may be outside of or disconnected from the normal rules and expectations of society. Hence, it can show someone living in a world of his or her own creation or imagination. There can also be the feeling of having some form of power over others. Power and leadership should be accepted and embraced with humility and gratitude, not merely by throwing around the ego. People will then show respect and gratitude. Being a prominent "leader" can be fine as long as there's no exploitation or demands made upon the people around. Some probably have, after all, kindly agreed to be the "Fairies."

Keywords: Imaginary worlds. Finding a place. Feeling comfortable. Taking command of life. Leadership and its responsibilities. Feeling like a dominant leader and that one has a doting populace. Being welcomed. *A Midsummer Night's Dream.* Returning home. Web domains. Finding one's true vocation or purpose.

The Caution: Imaginary worlds and dependence on trickery. Ridicule aimed at those who don't have their feet on the ground. Someone acting like a "hot shot." Feelings of superiority which alienate others. The fear of approaching the unknown. Never finding a real place to settle down. Fairytales about how life could or should be. Lording it over others. Being bossy and commanding. Being impotent. The fear and loathing of having to accept one's true place. Not taking command of one's life. Loneliness. Feeling locked out.

What does this **SYMBOL** say to *you?*

AN INDIAN WOMAN PLEADING TO THE CHIEF FOR THE LIVES OF HER CHILDREN

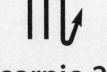

Scorpio 29

Commentary: "An Indian Woman" is "Pleading to the Chief for the Lives of Her Children." Something that the children have done, or are suspected of doing, has led to the "Children" needing the "Woman" to stand up for them, state their case clearly and ask for mercy or leniency. It could be that the "Children" are not really children, but are something merely seen as being useless, expendable or to be sacrificed for other causes.

Oracle: You may find a need to stand up for those in your care, whether it is your "Children," your ideals, creative pursuits or other people. Even if they might somehow draw or deserve rejection, punishment or judgment, there is a need for you to act as a go-between, or an advocate. It needs to be remembered, though, that being "deserving of punishment" is often a perception of society, and quite probably prejudice, and not always something that's grounded in reality. On the other hand, you may need someone else to be an advocate or to translate your feelings or actions so that others may understand. The solution will probably best be found not so much in being defensive as in simply asking for leniency, or that attention be paid to the matter at hand. Apologies may need to be made. When people understand what is truly going on they often relax and this serves to take a lot of the emotional "charge" out of the proceedings. As the situation is brought more into the light, and people see what's really happening, there is usually a lot of the pain, distrust and fear taken away. People will be more forgiving or accepting if they understand the full picture.

Keywords: Patterns of family dominance. Pleading one's cause. Seeking love, mercy or forgiveness. Asking higher powers to step in, help or heal. Intercession. Counseling. Protecting the younger ones. Family law courts, magistrates, lawyers. Divorce. Young people taken seriously. Guilt and innocence. Weaving words to a desired outcome. Intervention. Schools. Juvenile delinquents. Being nailed for an offence. Speaking on behalf of others. Tribunals. Begging for mercy. Custody battles. Sexual discrimination. Advocates.

The Caution: Being dominated. Sacrificing one's self for peace and quiet. Making a spectacle. Ramming one's opinions. Going on the defensive. Bullying and browbeating. Harping on and on about things that should be forgiven or forgotten. Disruptive elements that get away with anything. Being expelled. Being made an example of.

What does this **SYMBOL** say to *you?*

All humanity is one undivided and indivisible family, and each one of us is responsible for the misdeeds of all the others. I cannot detach myself from the wickedest soul.
Mahatma Gandhi

Blessed are the merciful, for they shall obtain mercy.
The Bible

Children need love, especially when they don't deserve it.
Harold Hulbert

Children wish fathers looked but with their eyes; fathers that children with their judgment looked; and either may be wrong.
William Shakespeare

In the early days of the Indian Territory, there were no such things as birth certificates. You being there was certificate enough.
Will Rogers

Few parents nowadays pay any regard to what their children say to them. The old-fashioned respect for the young is fast dying out.
Oscar Wilde

Pretty much all the honest truth telling there is in the world is done by children.
Oliver Wendell Holmes

God could not be everywhere and therefore he made mothers.
Jewish Proverb

Scorpio 30

It is a double pleasure to trick the trickster.
Jean de la Fontaine

Alas! That such affected tricks should flourish in a child of six!
Hilaire Belloc

If there was a trick, there must be a trickster.
Dorothy Miller Richardson

There's no trick to being a humorist when you have the whole government working for you.
Will Rogers

You can't teach an old dogma new tricks.
Dorothy Parker

But man, proud man, drest in a little brief authority, most ignorant of what he's most assured, his glassy essence like an angry ape, plays such fantastic tricks before high heaven as make the angels weep.
William Shakespeare

Curses are like processions: they return to whence they set out.
Italian Proverb

One thing vampire children have to be taught early on is, don't run with a wooden stake.
Jack Handy

CHILDREN IN HALLOWEEN COSTUMES INDULGING IN VARIOUS PRANKS

Commentary: "Children in Halloween Costumes" are seen "Indulging in Various Pranks." They are most likely having a wonderful time, playing around in the streets, going door to door and watching the reactions of the people they encounter. Sometimes they wear lots of makeup and masks in their endeavor to win people over or to convince them that they deserve their treats. If they don't receive a treat, or reward, sometimes they get very mischievous and play "Pranks" on people. This Symbol can show the "Prankster" in all of us, in some measure. "Halloween" is said to be a time when the veil between the living and the dead becomes an illusion, nebulous or very thin.

Oracle: You may feel that the trickster is out and around at the moment, or you may be the focus of pranks. Whichever, it should be acknowledged that there needs to be an occasional outlet for immature or fun-loving energies. Often, though, it's hard to relax when this energy is around. It can be difficult to know when to take things at face value or to see, or realize, a deeper meaning when it can be loaded with illusions. Not knowing what's going to happen next can lead to a feeling of unease. What ghoulish emotion or reality may emerge next? Are these tricks or is this more about things getting blown up and out of control? What's important here is to play the game, or to go along with it, and to know that it's basically harmless. This can picture somebody who just can't take anything seriously. In the true sense of "Halloween," the "Prankster" is not really malicious in any way and is really looking for a reward. Gifts, small trinkets or the fun of seeing someone's shock and reaction, whether this is superficial or real, is probably enough. In the end, it's often really only about play.

Keywords: The madman inside all of us. Astro-drama. The lifting of the veil between the living and the dead. Unintegrated energies playing tricks on the unwary. Tricksters. Creative surprises. Halloween. Trick or treat. Practical jokes played on the unwary. Roaming the streets. Dressing up. Ghouls and ghosts.

The Caution: Being unable to connect with real and immediate emotions. Contempt for the establishment. "Mucking around" and not getting to the core of things. Evading one's responsibilities through being silly or madcap. Not respecting other people's boundaries.

What does this **SYMBOL** say to *you?*

RETIRED ARMY VETERANS GATHER TO REAWAKEN OLD MEMORIES

Sagittarius
1

Commentary: "Retired Army Veterans Gather to Reawaken Old Memories" is an image of a gathering or reunion of people who have shared some kind of companionship, struggle or history. In this "Gathering," comrades reminisce about tales of the "old days," "Reawakening Old Memories." Gathering together can ignite old feelings of camaraderie and great passions, even among people who they may not remember or know so well. This can evoke many emotions, all the way from sadness to laughter and amazement.

Oracle: In the situation facing you, going over the memories of "old battles" may bring clues to how you can handle any current ones. You may be drawn to those who have shared your struggle or have gone through similar battles in life. Perhaps you haven't seen each other for a very long time. Through sharing these "Old Memories," old wounds can be healed as new insights are gleaned. There's a need to be cautious, though, as this "Gathering" can often exclude those who don't measure up or fit in. This Symbol can point to a feeling of "being in the club," with those who don't share these memories or feel as though they're on the outside, looking in. Are there people who feel that they are left out of sharing these experiences? Having not had the same history, experiences or the woes of battle that the others have, can make them feel that they are on the other side of the fence, and, in extreme cases, they may seem like "the enemy." Also, the "Gathering to Reawaken Old Memories" can reinforce injuries, wounds and hurts and these can be brought up, so that they're rehashed over and over. This can cause difficulties in healing, recovery, forgiving and forgetting, all of which may be necessary in order to move on. As these are "Retired Army Veterans," it's through the passing of time and with the hindsight of age that many things can be laid to rest.

Keywords: Masculine domains. Understanding the individual's needs and idealistic struggles. Moratoriums and calls for peace. Past life memories of fellowship. Prisoners of war. Memorials to war. Bringing up painful memories in the hope of sharing understanding and healing. Tears of the past. Being confronted by memories. School and other reunions. Talking over strategies. Finding comrades. Brothers and sisters.

The Caution: Being unable to let go of the past. Exaggerating past successes to justify current strategies. Excluding others as being "unworthy," having not experienced the struggle or pain. Going over things from the past and never letting them go. Boasting and glorifying. Identities that belong in the past.

What does this **SYMBOL** say to *you?*

I like to reminisce with people I don't know.
Steven Wright

Great perils have this beauty, that they bring to light the fraternity of strangers.
Victor Hugo

Forsake not an old friend, for the new is not comparable unto him. A new friend is as new wine: when it is old thou shalt drink it with pleasure.
Ecclesiasticus

There is no stronger bond of friendship than a mutual enemy.
Frankfort Moore

The so-called lessons of history are for the most part the rationalizations of the victors. History is written by the survivors.
Max Lerner

Those who cannot remember the past are condemned to repeat it.
George Santayana

Sagittarius
2

Thou shalt not separate thy being from BEING, and the rest, but merge the Ocean in the deep, the drop within the Ocean.
H.P. Blavatsky

Don't think there are no crocodiles because the water is calm.
Malayan Proverb

The winds and the waves are always on the side of the ablest navigators.
Edward Gibbon

Always behave like a duck— keep calm and unruffled on the surface but paddle like the devil underneath.
Jacob Braude

Still waters run deep.
Proverb

Below raging waves, the depths of the ocean do not churn as does its surface. Down there, temperature, depth and salinity create the hydrodynamics.
Philip Sedgwick

The populace is like the sea, motionless in itself, but stirred by every wind, even the lightest breeze.
Titus Livius

THE OCEAN COVERED WITH WHITECAPS

Commentary: "The Ocean Covered with Whitecaps" shows what happens when the wind whips up the surface of the "Ocean," turning the water to froth. The wind can sometimes quickly bring up a storm, coming seemingly from out of nowhere. What appears on the surface is often very different from what's happening just below it. Things are, or are going to be, much calmer and quieter than you would imagine from looking at the whipped up "Whitecaps."

Oracle: The day-to-day experiences of life can create a "quick wind" which can blow out of control if things get overheated or overstated. Because these experiences take up a lot of space in our current thoughts, they seem to be more important than they really are. In essence, they are really only passing by, just so much "froth and bubble" or "monkey chatter" and will soon be replaced by other considerations. The effect, however, can play havoc with your emotions and can create some storms of their own. At this time there seems to be a lot going on and you may feel that your emotions are on a really bumpy ride. You may find that surface emotions have been whipped up and this has led to a concern that is disproportionate to the depth of the real issue before you. Things have a deeper sense of strength and permanence than they seem on the surface. Whether your situation contains difficult components, or whipped up and excited ones, the truth of the matter is that the foundations of your life are much more settled and the surface emotional distress is probably just misleading matters. Staying anchored to what is true, permanent and stable in your life can help you get through whatever has been churned up. If you understand that the wind will die down, or at least change, then you can simply ride out this time secure in the strength of your deeper stability. Getting below the surface where things are calmer and more reliable could alter your perspective.

Keywords: Mobilization of energy and emotions. Safety in more secure emotions. Blustery days. Churning thoughts. Being flighty and changeable. Overblown reactions. Energy that needs an outlet for expression. The need for stillness and meditation.

The Caution: Getting fussed and irritable over nothing, or at least very little. Nervousness. Whipping up emotions and reactions. Overdoing things. Not knowing how to rest. Responding too readily to external conditions. Gathering gloom.

What does this **SYMBOL** say to *you?*

TWO MEN PLAYING CHESS

Sagittarius
3

Commentary: "Two Men Playing Chess" is an image of people concentrating and planning moves in order to defeat their opponent in a game. They have to be quiet, focused and attuned to what it is they're doing if they want to succeed. The theme of a "Chess" game is to knock the opponent out, to literally kill the king, and to take his position and his territory. There can be a certain degree of tension in the air as each tries to "checkmate" the other. First, one may appear to be "winning," and then the other may make a sudden move, sometimes completely unexpected or unforeseen, get the upper hand and take the whole game. Alternatively, it could be an all-out slaughter if one person is more practiced or efficient at the game than the other.

Oracle: In the current situation you may need to be very thoughtful and cautious about the moves you make and the risks that you are prepared to take. It's important to take into account the wider picture and all the possible outcomes of any actions taken. Impulsive acts with no forward planning will probably be risky and may lead to others taking advantage of the situation. The same can happen if you show your weak side. There can be a lot at stake here if you lose, but there may be much to be gained if you win. Effective strategies and forward-thinking maneuvers are needed. Take some time to compose yourself and assess what's really going on: you may then find the way forward or out of the maze or conflict. However, it can be very difficult to relax in this type of competitive environment—one often feels that they can't let their guard down for one moment in case they are taken advantage of, or overtaken, in some way. Keep your concentration focused on the main aim and outcome. Take one step at a time, thinking all the while, and move with purpose and forethought.

Keywords: Strategic competition. Seeing the picture several moves ahead. Arguments that can go on and on. Finding justification for being combative. Throwing down the gauntlet to the other. Taking lives. The need for peacekeeping. War strategies. Matching wits. Facing each other head on. Being royalty or being a mere pawn. Tactical maneuvers. Lawsuits. Custody. Having the bigger stick. Divorce. Disputes. Wit against wit.

The Caution: Depending on pure luck. Underestimating the opponent's skill or strategy. Arguments and arguing for the sake of it. Bickering and trying to get the better of the other. Always taking an opposing side, no matter what is really happening.

What does this **SYMBOL** say to *you?*

A quarrel is quickly settled when deserted by one party: there is no battle unless there be two.
Seneca

Once the game is over, the king and the pawn go back into the same box.
Italian Proverb

It is one of man's curious idiosyncrasies to create difficulties for the pleasure of resolving them.
Joseph Marie De Maistre

What a strange game. The only winning move is not to play.
Anonymous, on war games

Victory goes to the player who makes the next-to-last mistake.
Savielly Grigorievitch Tartakower, chess master

Daring ideas are like chessmen moved forward. They may be beaten, but they may start a winning game.
Goethe

I feel as if I were a piece in a game of chess when my opponent says of it: that piece cannot be moved.
Søren Kierkegaard

Sagittarius
4

A toddling little girl is a center of common feeling which makes the most dissimilar people understand each other.
George Eliot

Life is just a short walk from the cradle to the grave—and it sure behooves us to be kind to one another along the way.
Alice Childress

We are all novices. Only the dead have nothing left to learn.
Anonymous

One step at a time is good walking.
Chinese Proverb

We spend the first twelve months of our children's lives teaching them to walk and talk and the next twelve telling them to sit down and shut up.
Phyllis Diller

*Children, you are very little,
And your bones are very brittle;
If you would grow great and stately,
You must try to walk sedately.*
Robert Louis Stevenson

Parents who are afraid to put their foot down usually have children who step on their toes.
Chinese Proverb

A LITTLE CHILD LEARNING TO WALK WITH THE ENCOURAGEMENT OF PARENTS

Commentary: "A Little Child" is shown "Learning to Walk with the Encouragement of Parents." The "Child" needs the support of the "Parents" in order to learn how to do many of the most basic things. The "Child" needs guidance, love and encouragement in order to grow and have faith in his or her own abilities. Sometimes we have the "Encouragement" and support of our elders, other times not. The "Parents" can't be there all the time to catch the "Little Child" if he or she falls, so the "Little Child" must learn to master the steps that are needed in order to become an independent and confident grownup.

Oracle: You may be moving into a new phase of learning that, despite all your previous experience, is surprisingly difficult. Patience and step-by-step progress is needed now. There may be those around you who don't take your difficulties seriously, but the struggles to make progress will finally pay off, enabling the situation to move forward. This Symbol pictures a new situation that has to be tackled in a new way. You may feel nervous about taking your first steps toward what you want to accomplish. This may have something to do with the need for increased independence and while it may be exciting, it can also be nervewracking. Adopting creative methods and having an open mind and heart will help guarantee progress, even if it's not always easy. "Encouragement" and praise from others often helps to bolster the persistence that's needed to move past this "Learning" phase. True independence from outer circumstances takes time to learn and achieve. Being patient and not judgmental or demanding in this situation will bring rewards.

Keywords: Making genuine progress or always tripping over. Instinctive determination to get on with the job. People taking delight in the smallest progress. Baby steps leading to big things. Trying out and accepting one's individuality. Help from authorities. Seeking guidance and advice. Feeling mother earth under your feet. Parental assistance. Walking on new ground.

The Caution: Relying on skills not yet mastered. Not taking the initiative to put one's self forward. Putting yourself at risk rather than accepting help. Acting like one is incompetent in order to draw sympathy and/or help. Meddling and "assisting" when one should be on the sidelines, encouraging. Knowing that someone is going to "trip over" and not offering help.

What does this **SYMBOL** say to *you?*

AN OLD OWL PERCHED HIGH UP IN A TREE

Commentary: "An Old Owl" is "Perched High Up in a Tree." With the ability to twist his head right around, the wise "Old Owl" sees all, seeing what others miss, and keeps very quiet while digesting all that is going on. Even though it appears to sit quietly, the "Owl" is able to quickly snare its prey in the flash of a moment. The "Old Owl" pictured here is "Perched High Up in a Tree"; he is far from the tumult at ground level and is out of reach from most predators. He can observe wide vistas below him and watch for prey. Owls also have an incredible sense of hearing, pinpointing sounds accurately.

Oracle: This Symbol can indicate a degree of insomnia caused by an active mind and thinking too much at bedtime. What are the hidden elements of the situation facing you? If you sit quietly apart from things for a while and really endeavor to see "in the dark," you'll reveal things that previously only lurked in the shadows. You may need to consult with aged wisdom, either from within yourself or from the outside world. Knowledge of any type, but particularly knowledge garnered from books, can lead you to seeing further into very difficult situations where everything seems dark, and sometimes forbidding. The "Owl" may look sleepy and sedate but it can move very fast the minute it sees what it wants—it can move with surprising swiftness to catch its objective. Emulating this behavior can bring a certain solitude, but this may be just what is needed. However, a feeling of being seperate, high and remote can cause alienation, so be watchful for when it's time to start actively participating in life again.

Keywords: Wisdom and strength. Evening contemplation. Keeping thoughts to oneself. A wise "sage" type of person. Nocturnal vision. Exalted wisdom. "Night owls." Heightened sight and seeing. Being silent and alert for the slightest movement. The ability to see all around. The spirit of birds. Silent flight. Having acute hearing. Lofty ideals.

The Caution: Smug denial of available wisdom. Someone thinking they know it all. Not wanting to join in with others in fun activities. Acting old before one's time. Excluding others as being frivolous and unknowing. Waiting for one's prey. Black magic. Being old before one's time. Always being alone. Remote and cut off. Sitting isolated. Saying nothing when one should be saying something. Inability to sleep soundly.

What does this **SYMBOL** say to *you?*

A wise old owl sat on an oak;
The more he saw the less he spoke;
The less he spoke the more he heard;
Why aren't we like that wise old bird?
Edward Hersey Richards

Think first and speak afterward.
Proverb

The barn owl's left ear is higher than the right and points down to catch sounds from below. His right points up to hear above.
365 Amazing Trivia Facts

Alone and warming his five wits, The white owl in the belfry sits.
Lord Alfred Tennyson

Nature has given us two ears, two eyes, and but one tongue— to the end that we should hear and see more than we speak.
Socrates

The world is governed more by appearances than by realities, so that it is fully as necessary to seem to know something as to know it.
Daniel Webster

The quality of decision is like the well-timed swoop of a falcon which enables it to strike and destroy its victim.
Sun Tzu

Sagittarius
6

Only mad dogs and Englishmen go out in the noonday sun.
Indian Proverb

Always keep your composure. You can't score from the penalty box; and to win, you have to score.
Bobby Hull

How a man plays the game shows something of his character, how he loses shows all of it.
Anonymous

Please don't ask me what the score is, I'm not even sure what the game is.
Ashleigh Brilliant

Baseball, like cricket, is an elegant and leisurely summer game during which tension builds up slowly.
U.S. Department of Commerce

Cricket ... you have two sides: one out in the field and one in. Each man that's in the side that's in goes out and when he's out he comes in and the next man goes in until he's out.
Anonymous

If you must play, decide on three things at the start: the rules of the game, the stakes, and the quitting time.
Chinese Proverb

A GAME OF CRICKET

Commentary: "A Game of Cricket" is seen. "Cricket" is a "Game" that is associated with gentility, gamesmanship and decorum. It is a bat-and-ball game played on green fields with "gentlemen" players, all dressed in their "whites." There are two teams, with 11 players each. It is a game of skill, fairness and peaceful cooperation among its players. In days of old, particularly in England, people would gather from around the district to play on the field or on the pitch and the "Game" was usually one of friendliness and good-humored sportsmanship.

Oracle: This reflects a time when it is not necessarily the game that is important, but how it is played. You may find that integrity is vital in this situation and your honesty and ability to "play by the rules of the game" will give you just rewards, even if there is some initial sacrifice. Careful teamwork is probably needed to stop things getting through the gaps. Although the situation may take some time, everyone must keep on their toes, ready for something that may come out of "left field." It is important in this situation for everyone to understand the expectations required of them. Honesty and integrity are important, and also highly regarded. Behaving against these expectations can receive a harsh reaction and treatment and possibly even rejection from others on the playing field. This is not the time for anyone to be pushing the envelope to test what is acceptable to the rules of society. The rules and guidelines for operating in this situation are, or should be, made very clear—there will be some form of punishment for dishonesty. There is a need to remember everyone's position in the game: your own and others. Also, every game has its rules.

Keywords: Playing by the rules. Stiff-upper-lip responses. Seeing through the illusions of what constitutes "polite society." Having a role to play in the game of life. Sportsmanship. Being the "batsman" or the "bowler." Running and playing. Fair play. Impeccable behavior. Moving at will around the field. Scoring runs. People in the outfield. Holding the bat. Winning the toss. Opposing teams. Games that go on day after day. Patience. Summer games. Going by the umpire's decision. Everyone having a go.

The Caution: Difficulty in showing one's true feelings and emotions. Going against the rules of the game. Something that simply "is just not cricket" (not fair play). Curve balls. Being caught out. Games that are boring and long-winded. Being the thirteenth man. Silly rules that don't make sense.

What does this **SYMBOL** say to *you?*

CUPID KNOCKING AT THE DOOR OF A HUMAN HEART

Sagittarius
7

Commentary: "Cupid Knocking at the Door of a Human Heart" is an image of love asking to be let in. Barriers and defenses may be keeping him from coming inside, but how long will the "Heart" be able to resist? Opening the door to one's "Heart" can lead to new opportunities and possibilities around the issue of relationships. Finding "the key" to the "Heart" can lead to big realizations about one's self and others.

Oracle: It is particularly important to allow your heart center to open when you are in caring company as this can lead to amazing new things happening in your life now. By releasing your emotions and letting your guard down you open up the possibility for romantic love. However, do look out for any unrealistic projections put onto others and the need for seeking love, salvation or joy only through the other. We must find it in ourselves first before finding it in someone else, if that is what we really want. Having your consciousness overwhelmed with the thought, love or presence of another can be uplifting, but it can also become a burden. Being consumed with the love of a person can be quite stifling, whether you are on the giving or the receiving end. This is especially so if your affections are not reciprocated. If the other person doesn't respond in the same way, it can lead to sadness, bitterness and obsessive tendencies. Certain relationships can feel fated or impossible to ignore. Another aspect of this Symbol is that you may already be in a relationship with someone and a new love pops up unexpectedly. Is someone tapping you on the shoulder while you're busy not taking any notice? What is the true depth of your relationship? Regardless, as "Cupid Is Knocking," it appears that something wonderful is trying to get into your life. Are you resisting "Cupid's Knock"?

Keywords: Respectful invitation of love. Seeing purity of motive. Fear of commitment. Fear of romance. A key or an arrow. Cupids and cherubs. Unlocking the heart. One-pointed, focused energy, which can become obsessive. Softening one's boundaries. Cupid's bow. The need to lighten up one's approach to others.

The Caution: Waiting instead of taking the initiative. Rejecting love or emotion for fear of losing independence. Keeping up a strong, brave, severe face when one could be loosening up and enjoying another. Barriers and defenses around the heart. Seeing potential lovers in everyone. Being attracted to those you wouldn't normally notice. Frigid responses.

What does this **SYMBOL** say to *you?*

Gravitation cannot be held responsible for people falling in love.
Albert Einstein

Two friends, two bodies with one soul inspired.
Homer

Those that go searching for love only make manifest their own lovelessness, and the loveless never find love, only the loving find love, and they never have to seek for it.
D.H. Lawrence

It's a little bit the fiddle, but lots more who holds the bow.
Wilburn Wilson

The bow kept taut will quickly break, kept loosely strung, it will serve you when you need it.
Plato

Friendship is love without his wings!
Lord Byron

You kiss my lips and then it's done.
Leonard Cohen

I am not the one who loves—it's love that chooses me.
Leonard Cohen

Sagittarius
8

No pressure, no diamonds.
Thomas Carlyle

Crystals grew inside rock like arithmetic flowers. They lengthened and spread, added plane to plane in an awed and perfect obedience to an absolute geometry that even stones—maybe only the stones—understood.
Annie Dillard

I prefer to explore the most intimate moments, the smaller, crystallized details we all hinge our lives on.
Rita Dove

In the attitude of silence the soul finds the path in a clearer light, and what is elusive and deceptive resolves itself into crystal clearness. Our life is a long and arduous quest after truth.
Mahatma Gandhi

I see where we are starting to pay some attention to our neigbors to the south. We could never understand why Mexico wasn't just crazy about us; for we have always had their good will, and oil and minerals, at heart.
Will Rogers

DEEP WITHIN THE DEPTHS OF THE EARTH, NEW ELEMENTS ARE BEING FORMED

Commentary: "Deep within the Depths of the Earth, New Elements Are Being Formed" indicates that deep, organic changes are occurring. While these shifts may be big, significant and extremely life-changing, they may not be all that obvious on the surface. It seems certain that "Deep" down and "within," there is a lot going on, regardless of one's external demeanor.

Oracle: You may find new responses to life coming from deep within your mind and soul. This creation of new and essential levels of awareness is part of the natural result of inner changes and growth. "Within the Depths" of our lives and our very being there are extraordinary layers of possibilities, complications and divergent "Elements." Psychology and astrology can reveal these "Depths," through which the personality can be seen more clearly in its many elements. The way these "Elements" of our lives and our natures are combined results in the complex nature of our being. These "Elements" can be enriched by the experiences of life, the lessons being learned, and, as a result, new ways of being can be embraced and accepted. It is almost inevitable that this development will occur, but living a shallow existence or stubbornly refusing to accept the inevitable changes that happen within and around us can restrict energy. Allowing your inner "Depths" to be transformed and enriched by life is part of what this Symbol is about. This Symbol also reflects the imminent, or inevitable, rising of these "New Elements" to the surface, and the need for you to look "within" to benefit from this inner shift. Know that, by the very nature of having experiences in life, we are intuitively creating new potential, greater possibility and deeper wisdom in our lives.

Keywords: Deep elemental processes and change. Shifting of conservative values. Mining in its many forms. Crystal healings. Minerals, mining, colloidal minerals. Organic changes and shifts. Volcanoes and earthquakes. Earth rumblings. Reaching maturity. Earth, wind, fire and water. Mud and steam. Alchemical shifts.

The Caution: Moving forward while elements are still forming. Denying inner processes as unimportant. Not showing any change on the surface. Clinging stubbornly to old and outworn ways. Being afraid of change, particularly that which can't be seen. Unhealthy growths. Tumors.

What does this **SYMBOL** say to *you?*

A MOTHER LEADS HER SMALL CHILD STEP BY STEP UP THE STAIRS

Sagittarius 9

Commentary: "A Mother Leads Her Small Child Step by Step up the Stairs" pictures a situation where one needs to assist someone less experienced or indeed, possibly less evolved, to overcome difficulties and to rise up and learn to cope, to learn about life or to understand. The "Mother" is there to guide and encourage the "Small Child" in taking these rather unfamiliar "Steps." Even if the "Child" stumbles, trips or falls, the "Mother" should be there to protect, guide and facilitate these new experiences.

Oracle: You may find yourself in this situation as either the experienced or the inexperienced one, or possibly finding the "Mother" within you guiding your own "inner child." This Symbol is also about the way we develop the innocent elements of the inner self. Our inner qualities, as well as our outer ones, mature through experience, but it is important to remain aware of the protection we need to give to this growth. It is also important to remember to take your time, and to allow development to occur "Step by Step." To rush because there is a fear of some danger or failure is more likely to cause a problem than taking it easy. Mistakes are easily made when we're approaching something that we're unfamiliar with—something that we, or others, haven't yet learned the "Steps" of. Patience and guidance are extremely necessary in order not to discourage the "Small Child" who's learning very important lessons here. There may be a need to "hang back" while everyone else is charging forward; quick moves and harsh attitudes can be offputting to those in a vulnerable or less powerful position. Watching and observing the progress of this situation will reveal how best to deal with it as various issues arise.

Keywords: The inner child. Guidance and acceptance of those not so "upwardly mobile." Training. Careful consideration of other's immaturity or failings. Staying with the family in order to bring up the children. Guardianship and stewardship. Reversals of roles. Supervising parents. Looking after the younger or the elder. Taking things one by one. Alzheimer's disease. Handicaps. Step-by-step progress.

The Caution: Future vision and hope obscured. Exhausted by constant parental obligation. Not getting, or giving, the help that one needs. Being bossy and judgmental, thereby missing the joy inherent in the moment. Lack of supervision or training. Refusing to grow up. Wanting to be looked after.

What does this **SYMBOL** say to *you?*

The best thing about the future is that it comes one day at a time.
Abraham Lincoln

What an elder sees sitting; the young can't see standing.
Ibo Proverb

No matter how high one's aspirations may be, it must be achieved step-by-step.
Buddyo Dendo Kyokai

Children, taught either years beneath their intelligence or miles wide of relevance to it, or both: their intellect becomes hopelessly bewildered, drawn off its centers, bored, or atrophied.
James Agee

Every time you don't follow your inner guidance, you feel a loss of energy, loss of power, a sense of spiritual deadness ... we need to be willing to let our intuition guide us, and then be willing to follow that guidance directly and fearlessly.
Shakti Gawain

My mother had a great deal of trouble with me, but I think she enjoyed it.
Mark Twain

Sagittarius
10

A golden key can open any door.
Proverb

Personality is the glitter that sends your little gleam across the footlights and the orchestra pit into that big black space where the audience is.
Mae West

All the world's a stage and most of us are desperately unrehearsed.
Sean O'Casey

It's one of the tragic ironies of the theater that only one man in it can count on steady work—the night watchman.
Tallulah Bankhead

Ability is of little account without opportunity.
Napoleon Bonaparte

The bigger the information media, the less courage and freedom they allow. Bigness means weakness.
Eric Sevareid

Vulgarity is, in reality, nothing but a modern, chic, pert descendant of the goddess Dullness.
Dame Edith Sitwell

A THEATRICAL REPRESENTATION OF A GOLDEN-HAIRED GODDESS OF OPPORTUNITY

Commentary: "A Theatrical Representation of a Golden-Haired Goddess of Opportunity" is a wonderful image of promise, talent and possibility. The "Theater" traditionally represents "escape and fantasy" for the people in the populace. The audience expects to be entertained and they hope for something marvelous to happen. Whether the "storyline" of the play or presentation is fact or fiction, they will often hang onto every word or movement made.

Oracle: This Symbol can represent an offer that seems too good to refuse. It is probably only a reasonable reward for your efforts. You may want to respond quickly, almost impulsively, but there may be a need for caution. The temptation may be hard to resist, and it is most likely an opportunity that is worthwhile, but having a good, hard look at what's being "Represented" is probably necessary. You can still think the situation through if you act quickly. Let down any barriers or self-critical restrictions and listen to your heart as well. Try not to overestimate the rewards or outcomes as these may cloud your consideration. There may indeed be a great "Opportunity" before you that will have a positive outcome. Just how grand it is, isn't really important. This Symbol is also about presenting something you believe to be a wonderful opportunity to others. There probably needs to be some form of performance or presentation made. This may not be a time for a quiet chat or waiting for others to come to you. You need to present your idea, and yourself, for an audience. You need to touch their emotions and show confidence. The best way is to be honest and clear and come straight from the heart. How can you advertise or promote yourself or your product so that it gets the best possible response?

Keywords: Distinguishing reality from theater. Feeling that the "world is your stage." Playing out a story. Seeing others as a gateway to riches or fulfillment. Being "the talent." Being an "overnight success." Glamour and the allure of the media. The Academy Awards. Autographs of the noted. Seeing opportunity ahead of its time. Auditions. Promotions.

The Caution: Propaganda. Constantly chasing "things" that come to nothing. Being exploited or exploiting others for personal gain. Giving a deliberate false impression regarding opportunity and good fortune. Shallow adoration.

What does this **SYMBOL** say to *you?*

IN THE LEFT SECTION OF AN ARCHAIC TEMPLE, A LAMP BURNS IN A CONTAINER SHAPED LIKE A HUMAN BODY

Sagittarius
11

Commentary: "In the Left Section of an Archaic Temple, a Lamp Burns in a Container Shaped Like a Human Body" pictures a need for linking the spirit and the "Body." Sometimes we need to remember to be "in our bodies" and this Symbol shows the reward that can come from regarding our body as our "Temple." Logic is not always involved in this equation; it speaks more of emotions, spirit and physicality.

Oracle: Watching bodily rhythms can teach us something about the timing of our biology. There's a need to eat when we need to; to sleep and exercise when we need to; to be alive and happy. The spirit within us can shine out to enliven the spirits in others. We can somehow amplify light ourselves, like the "Lamp" that "Burns," shining outward, projecting our spirit and personality. To provide clues to your current situation, it may be a good idea to light a "Lamp" or a candle and place it to "the Left" of where you're sleeping, working, eating or exercising. The "Temple" of this Symbol implies that there may be a need for peace and quiet and respect. There may be a feeling that one somehow doesn't "belong" in their body. Is someone losing the plot and "leaving their body" in this situation? Is there a need for grounding your physical energy? How are you regarding your body and feeding yourself? Having faith and belief in one's self can lead to knowledge and enlightenment. Rituals of many kinds can help link mind and body so that a healthier you can emerge. This period may mark an incredible leap forward in understanding and consciousness.

Keywords: Connecting the left and right sides. Working out, physical fitness and exercise. Yoga. Grounding reality. Sexuality. Realizing that body is the same as spirit. Remembering to be in the body. Light workers. The acceptance of the body and its functions. Sport and its physical rewards. Metabolic rates. Oil burners. Gas lamps. Aladdin's lamp.

The Caution: Worshiping the body at the expense of the intellect, psyche or spirit. Concentrating exclusively on physical desires and needs. Needing actual physical evidence to accept anything. Being caught up in the illusion of the body, the "physical self."

What does this **SYMBOL** say to *you?*

Every man is the builder of a temple, called his body, to the god he worships, after a style purely his own, nor can he get off by hammering marble instead. We are all sculptors and painters, and our material is our own flesh and blood and bones.
Henry David Thoreau

A bodily disease may be but a symptom of some ailment in the spiritual past.
Nathaniel Hawthorne

He who knoweth the precepts by heart, but faileth to practice them, is like unto one who lighteth a lamp and then shutteth his eyes.
Nagarjuna

If anything is sacred the human body is sacred.
Walt Whitman

Sometimes our light goes out but is blown again into flame by an encounter with another human being.
Albert Schweitzer

For this is the great error of our day in the treatment of the human body. That physicians first separate the soul from the body.
Plato

Sagittarius
12

Thoughts and emotions are only momentary. Stand upright, speak thy thoughts, declare the truth thou hast, that all may share; Be bold, proclaim it everywhere: They only live who dare.
Lewis Morris

Vision without action is a daydream. Action without vision is a nightmare.
Japanese Proverb

Freedom is the sure possession of those alone who have the courage to defend it.
Pericles

There should be an Emperor Fabulous, don't you think?
Eddie Izzard

Success is a personal standard—reaching for the highest that is in us—becoming all that we can be.
Zig Ziglar

The chasm between the principles upon which this government was founded, in which it still professes to believe, and those which are daily practiced under the protection of the flag, yawn wide and deep.
Mary Church Terrell

A FLAG TURNS INTO AN EAGLE; THE EAGLE INTO A CHANTICLEER SALUTING THE DAWN

Commentary: "A Flag Turns into an Eagle; the Eagle into a Chanticleer Saluting the Dawn." Although symbols stretch across time and space with their own vibrations, this image is a particularly American one. To quote Dane Rudhyar from his book *An Astrological Mandala:* "The flag is the abstract symbol of the nation; it becomes an eagle—another U.S. symbol—when the concept is made alive by bold and transcendent action. The eagle symbolizes spiritual will and the power to rise to the highest possible altitude of consciousness and purpose. Flying at such an altitude, the eagle is the first living creature to perceive the rising sun. Having perceived it, it heralds it—and by so doing is identified with the crowing chanticleer, who had convinced himself that his resonant cry was responsible for the rise of the sun and the coming of the new day."

Oracle: This is a time when our highest ideals can be felt deeply and proudly and as an expression of spiritual purity all the way to pride in our selves and our nation. You may find that you are moved to burst forth with expressions or declarations of your higher self. Any issue that is really worthwhile and "centered" will be seen and heard in the clear light of day. However, you may need to be wary of forcing your opinions on others—especially on those who disagree or have a different view of things. Although it may be difficult to restrain the forward momentum contained here, there's a need to be cautious of going overboard with enthusiasm in the company of others. This can alienate people and cause distrust. Having said that, if there has been something you've wanted to do or say but have felt held back, now's the time to go for it. The "Dawn" reveals that a new day and the possibility of a new life is coming, and with it ideals that have to be allowed for, spoken about and expressed in life.

Keywords: Declared idealism. Trumpeting ideals. National pride. Peak experiences. Flags. Symbols of strength, unity and power. Truths. The pomp and ceremony of big political displays. Issues of nationhood. Issues of world domination. Elevated views and perspectives. Forceful voices. Reaching for the highest plane. Nobility and pride. Successful outcomes. National anthems. New empires. Messages from the president.

The Caution: Assuming one is right only because of might or power or because one can say it the loudest. Propaganda. Lording it over others. Seeing other "nations" as being lesser. Loud voices. Bullying.

What does this **SYMBOL** say to *you?*

A WIDOW'S PAST IS BROUGHT TO LIGHT

Commentary: "A Widow's Past Is Brought to Light" speaks of things coming out of the "Past" for people to see and learn about. There's a story or a situation from the "Past" that is finally being revealed. Something may have been known to exist but exactly what it was hasn't been made clear. Now, there's been an event, and something has been revealed; a story or situation from the "Past."

Oracle: You may find that the "Past" catches up with you, or someone you know, at this time. Although there may be sympathetic feelings in the hearts and minds of those around, somebody may not like what is being shown or revealed. This needs to be handled with care. Somebody's issues, history, deeds or personality have now, or will soon, come "to Light." This may be rather confronting or upsetting and it can take time to adjust to this new information. It often causes us to have to look at something, or someone, or a relationship, in a new "Light." As this Symbol pictures a "Widow," often there's a feeling that the situation is one with a long history or is rather old, even possibly outworn, in some way. Issues were probably previously left in the dark or "in the closet," suppressed by someone or at the very least forgotten about. Some may think it would have been better if these things had been left undisturbed and not "Brought to Light." Dwelling on issues from the "Past" can lead to the loss of joy in the present, so there needs to be careful thought about just where you direct your attention. However, a healing is often made possible by things being revealed. Try lighting a candle, or a special "Light," and allow illumination to pour over the situation. This can cast new "Light" and understanding and allow you, and others, to banish the shadows of the "Past." Further, often what was considered a "scandal" in former times is now nothing much of consequence and can be washed away rather easily.

Keywords: Unveiling and exposing—or creating a new and vibrant beginning. Getting rid of yesterday's darkness. Looking back to revision attitudes. Being freed for new opportunities. The "scales" falling from one's eyes. Reasons as to why relationships have failed. Remembering. Past life memories. Things being found or discovered. Wills. Inheritances. Death certificates. Burying the past. Pensions. Insurance policies.

The Caution: Old stories best forgotten. Dead-end feelings hanging around. Gossip and family secrets that hurt and otherwise cause harm. Feelings rehashed detrimental to stability. Someone being caught out. Bearing the weight of secrets.

What does this **SYMBOL** say to *you?*

Sagittarius 13

I wept not, so to stone within I grew.
Dante

"Widow" is a harsh and hurtful word. It comes from the Sanskrit and it means "empty." I have been empty too long.
Lynn Caine

The secret to life is that there is no secret.
Anonymous

None are so fond of secrets as those who do not mean to keep them.
Charles Caleb Colton

Truth, when not sought after, rarely comes to light.
Oliver Wendell Holmes

What the eye doesn't see, the heart doesn't grieve over.
Anonymous

Make it a rule of life never to regret and never to look back. Regret is an appalling waste of energy; you can't build on it; it's only good for wallowing in.
Katherine Mansfield

Every family has a skeleton in the cupboard.
Traditional Proverb

Sagittarius
14

History, although sometimes made up of the few acts of the great, is more often shaped by the many acts of the small.
Mark Twain

History is the version of past events that people have decided to agree upon.
Napoleon

When Moses was alive, the pyramids were a thousand years old ... Here people learned to measure time by a calendar, to plot the stars by astronomy ... Here they developed that most awesome of all ideas—the idea of eternity.
Walter Cronkite

All we know is still infinitely less than all that remains unknown.
William Harvey

Nobody even knows what a "henge" is.
Eddie Izzard, on Stonehenge

Order and simplification are the first steps toward the mastery of a subject.
Thomas Mann

The hallmark of our age is the tension between aspirations and sluggish institutions.
John W. Gardner

A VAST PANORAMA OF SAND AND TIME IS UNFOLDING; THE PYRAMIDS AND SPHINX IN THEIR GLORY RISE BEFORE THE EYE

Commentary: The "Pyramids and Sphinx" are a picture of grandeur and history. They stand as testimonials to days long gone. The Pyramids were built some 4,500 years ago, but probably not, as many believe, by slaves. Evidence suggests that social organization built the "Pyramids." The "Pyramids" at Giza were the foundation of the first nation state and the beginning of modern civilization. To participate in the building of the king's "Pyramid" was an honor that was sought by families right across Egypt. People, goods and livestock came from all corners of the country. The workers were respected, educated and healed if they were injured. This Symbol can speak of any large edifice, especially those that seem to hold some mystery as to how or why they were built. Ancient history is full of such human and spiritual wonders: Stonehenge, the great stone walls of Macchu Picchu and the Great Wall of China. They provide intriguing puzzles into the human mind and just how vast human accomplishment can be.

Oracle: There may be a feeling of the need to establish some type of monument. It can be something that makes a huge impression, something that won't easily be forgotten. Organization of people and labor toward a common goal on any scale can lead to great accomplishments. You may need an architect or a tour guide, and inner wisdom, as this will guide you. The resources that are available can bring reevaluations to current dilemmas. However, slave labor has very few real rewards. Be wary of merely being used for someone's grand agendas. Further, matters could have a lack of clarity about them. Is something in this situation so big or so difficult, it can hardly be approached? Is it really becoming outworn or outlived? Are you seeing the huge gulfs between the haves and the have nots?

Keywords: Ancient histories and mysteries. The power of the past affecting today's world. Spiritual ancestry. Mysteries that enrich. Decoding. Magicians and prophets. Secret messages or tricks of perception? Majestic properties. Riddles. Ingenuity. Plans and the executing of them. Egyptian things. Levels of power. Pyramid marketing. Taxes. The rich vs. the poor. The American monetary system. World finances. Masonic mysteries. Cement, sand, plaster. Tools. Architects. Builders.

The Caution: Treasures robbed by the greedy. Monuments that belittle other, lesser achievements. Aloofness through perceived superiority. Proclaiming treasures from the past more worthy, or grander, than present perceptions allow. Slave labor. Anonymity of the masses.

What does this **SYMBOL** say to *you?*

THE GROUNDHOG LOOKING FOR ITS SHADOW ON GROUNDHOG DAY

Sagittarius 15

Commentary: "The Groundhog Looking for Its Shadow on Groundhog Day," by its reactions and movements, provides clues as to whether winter will continue or spring will come with its warmth and rewards. As "Groundhog Day" is in February in the northern hemisphere, it symbolizes a time of cold, snow and the stiff breezes of winter. Although more fable than real, the "Groundhog" is said to be able to sense whether there's a change in the air. If he feels spring approaching, he gives a sign so others may know and anticipate it themselves. The "Groundhog" is somewhat of a "star" on "Groundhog Day," as people are watching him, wondering what he will signal. There is a lot of projection happening here as the animal is not consciously doing anything.

Oracle: You may need some sign to give you insight into the future. The solution to your question is close by and easy to perceive. It is based in your normal environment and relationships. Don't focus on things continuing to be hard or difficult, as this can lead to it actually happening. Don't read too much into things, as they may not be as they seem. However, acknowledging your "Shadow," and your projections and perceptions, will bring the clarity that's sought. Reading books, watching movies or television, hearing the words of a song, observing everyday life and the people around can remind you of things that have happened in your life. However, continually or compulsively looking for signs of assurance when they can be readily available on the physical plane can lead to losing your way, and worrying too much about what you cause in your life. There can be difficulty in finding rest, or sleep, when one looks continually at one's life and the effects that one creates. Are you relying on messages from the past? People may be with you, or this may be a lonely journey. Welcome the spring, and don't look back!

Keywords: Looking back, reading the signs. Divination and other systems of inquiry. Seeing society as being to blame. People having a good look at how they seem to others. Wondering how others perceive you and picture you. Prophets who can tell the "weather" ahead of time. Predictions. Prognosticating. Welcoming an early spring. Scrutinizing objectives and possible outcomes. Looking to nature for clues.

The Caution: Being scared to act without some message of confirmation. People (or society) looking for someone else to blame for conditions. Relying on the same solutions without consideration of changes. Blizzards and the cold.

What does this **SYMBOL** say to *you?*

Nice going boys, you're playing yesterday's tape.
Groundhog Day

Life can only be understood backwards; but it must be lived forwards.
Søren Kierkegaard

The measure of a man's real character is what he would do if he knew he would never be found out.
Thomas B. Macaulay

If you hate a person, you hate something in him that is part of yourself. What isn't part of ourselves doesn't disturb us.
Hermann Hesse

The life that is unexamined is not worth living.
Plato

A little man often casts a long shadow.
Italian Proverb

If you stand straight do not fear a crooked shadow.
Chinese Proverb

He has great tranquility of heart who cares neither for the praises nor the fault-finding in men.
Honore de Balzac

Sagittarius
16

We need to learn to set our course by the stars, not by the lights of every passing ship.
Omar Nelson Bradley

Where the carcass is, there shall the eagles be.
Proverb

I eat like a vulture. Unfortunately the resemblance doesn't end there.
Groucho Marx

A man with a surplus can control circumstances, but a man without a surplus is controlled by them, and often has no opportunity to exercise judgment.
Harvey S. Firestone

A pessimist is one who makes difficulties of his opportunities; an optimist is one who makes opportunities of his difficulties.
Reginald B. Mansell

A wise man will make more opportunities than he finds.
Sir Francis Bacon

SEAGULLS FLY AROUND A SHIP LOOKING FOR FOOD

Commentary: "Seagulls Fly around a Ship Looking for Food" symbolizes the search for sustenance in the form of handouts from the sailors, or the fish that get stirred up in the wash of the "Ship". The "Seagull" often has no need of loyalty to anyone but to him- or herself, although there may be young ones who need to share what food or other nourishment can be found.

Oracle: This pictures a situation of dependence, sometimes codependence. Don't look to others or have others look to you for opportunities and nourishment, for someone may miss the chance of being creative and truly independent. Continually looking and waiting for one's ship to come in, in order to be fed or otherwise looked after and sheltered, can be a tiring responsibility and one that isn't always appreciated by others. Look carefully, is someone using someone else? If there is no nourishment, food or resources such as money to be found where one is looking, there may be a need to seek elsewhere. There may also be the need to watch the situation very closely to see what is really going on. If you are a "Seagull," hovering around waiting to see what you can easily find or get for nothing, you will probably need to move fast in order to take advantage of opportunities when they pop up. For one thing, they may not last long; for another, there may be others who are on the lookout for the same things. If you are the "Ship" the "Seagulls" are circling, be wary of the motives of others wanting things from you. It can seem as if people are waiting for things to be "thrown overboard," or for things to fall off the "Ship." Who's looking for scraps? Are they worth it? People who settle for very little often find that very little is what they end up getting.

Keywords: Losing sight of alternative possibilities and going for the easy "feed." Issues of dependence. Diminishing one's essential worth while trying to please a specific need. Being opportunistic. Settling for the small things in life. Scalpers. Jettisoning scraps. Leftovers. The rewards and pitfalls of "meal tickets." Issues of social security. The homeless.

The Caution: Waiting for scraps that may not even be worth it or may never come. Losing the opportunity to care for one's self in an independent manner. Giving away one's power. Being opportunistic at the expense of others. Being ripped off. People "kissing and running." Users and abusers. Having satellites. Hovering for scraps.

What does this **SYMBOL** say to *you?*

AN EASTER SUNRISE SERVICE DRAWS A LARGE CROWD

Commentary: "An Easter Sunrise Service Draws a Large Crowd" is an image of people coming together in the early hours of the morning, at "Sunrise," to celebrate the joy of the resurrection of Jesus Christ. Our souls are renewed with the beauty of spring and the celebration of the resurrection of the Savior, Jesus. We can find hope and our faith deepened during this significant event in the life of Christ. Although "Easter" is a Christian festival, this situation can apply to any creed where rebirth and redemption is the path.

Oracle: Whatever the situation facing you, this is a time of spiritual rebirth where you, and others, can rise above the failings of the past into a whole new beginning. Coming out of doubt and despair will enable everyone to concentrate on what is possible in this new era. As this "Easter Sunrise Service Draws a Large Crowd," it seems that there is, or needs to be, an unwavering faith in communal spiritual values, although there can be a feeling of society offering up something or someone to sacrifice or to purge the guilt or the sins of the past. We need to move past the more difficult issues or the problems of our histories, particularly issues where someone felt a sense of failure, loss, despair, betrayal or unfaithfulness. Forgetting past hurts and insults in favor of enjoying the reality of life in the here and now will lift everyone's spirits. However, it may indeed be possible to resurrect ideas, situations or people that long since felt lost, or indeed, bring them back from "the dead." The present needs to be seen in the light of a new era, with the difficulties of the past being laid to rest for good. Join with others in expressions of joy as this can lift everyone's spirits. Rituals performed with ceremony, or going to a church or temple can reconnect you spiritually.

Keywords: Performing deeds with reverence, respect and a sense of celebration. Cohesive communal expressions of faith. The dawning of a new era. Church services. Dawn services. The community gathering for a common purpose. Resurrections and rebirths. Revivals. The need for faith in a bright future. Devotion. Worship.

The Caution: Obsession with the ceremony rather than the true purpose or ideal. Feeling unable to lift one's spirit. Loss and shame of the past clouding the possibilities of today's reality. Disillusionment around issues to do with the Church.

What does this **SYMBOL** say to *you?*

Sagittarius
17

Do not abandon yourselves to despair. We are the Easter people and hallelujah is our song.
Pope John Paul II

I come not to entertain you with worldly festivities but to arouse your sleeping memory of immortality.
Paramahansa Yogananda

The act of divine worship is the inestimable privilege of man, the only created being who bows in humility and adoration.
Hosea Ballou

But every act in consequence of our faith, strengthens faith.
Anna Letitia Barbauld

Do not let your deeds belie your words, lest when you speak in church someone may say to himself, "Why do you not practice what you preach?"
Saint Jerome

Everyone ought to worship God according to his own inclinations, and not to be constrained by force.
Flavius Josephus

Every day people are straying away from the church and going back to God.
Lenny Bruce

Sagittarius
18

Once you bring life into the world, you must protect it. We must protect it by changing the world.
Elie Wiesel

With each passage of human growth we must shed a protective structure [like a hardy crustacean]. We are left exposed and vulnerable—but also yeasty and embryonic again, capable of stretching in ways we hadn't known before.
Gail Sheehy

Goals too clearly defined can become blinders.
Mary Catherine Bateson

Let children read whatever they want and then talk about it with them. If parents and kids can talk together, we won't have as much censorship because we won't have as much fear.
Judy Blume

We all live in the protection of certain cowardices which we call our principles.
Mark Twain

TINY CHILDREN PLAYING IN SUNBONNETS

Commentary: "Tiny Children Playing in Sunbonnets" is an image that brings to mind childlike, carefree fun in a protective, caring environment. The "Children" are protected from the strong and sometimes fierce rays of the sun by wearing "Sunbonnets." We can assume that their mothers or other caregivers have put them on for them. They don't have to worry about sunburn and being exposed to the elements, all they need to do is "Play." Although they may interact with the other "Children," some may just play their own individual games side by side with each other.

Oracle: In your situation, someone may be in need of protection at the moment, and it is most likely for their own good, as long as there is not the sense of being "overprotected" and insulated from having to be responsible for themselves. Without having to worry about complicated details and difficult consequences, the feeling of a sense of security and safety can lead to more carefree and playful moments. Don't be distracted by efforts being made by others on your behalf, sometimes we need to be shielded by others from harmful elements. However, sometimes we also need to feel or intuit our way through the surface appearance of what's really going on. There can be a sense of having to keep some emotion or anger away, so as not to disturb or frighten others, or ourselves, but this may lead to having the "blinkers" or "blinders" on and not seeing life as it truly is. Is there a sense of naïveté here and of missing the real point of life? Is someone being kept in the dark, or kept from seeing reality? On the other hand, you may need to look after others and ensure that their wellbeing is at the top of the list of priorities. Approaching this question with a childlike, carefree attitude, while all the while keeping a true eye on the situation, will probably bring the message that's needed. Whatever, there's a need to remember to play and have fun.

Keywords: Care taken with small beginnings. Protection or blinkering? Propaganda that hides more severe life realities. Censorship. Innocence. Being treated like a child. Mollycoddling. Sunblocks and sunscreens. Screens that filter.

The Caution: Overprotection by institutionalized procedures that can lead to not being able to see the whole picture. "Organized religion" and its blinding of society to the true joy within and without. Infantile behavior. Being left in the dark without a clue as to what's going on. Naïveté. Being overshadowed by ego. Abuse and neglect.

What does this **SYMBOL** say to *you?*

PELICANS DISTURBED BY THE GARBAGE OF PEOPLE MOVE THEIR YOUNG TO A NEW HABITAT

Sagittarius 19

Commentary: "Pelicans Disturbed by the Garbage of People Move Their Young to a New Habitat." "Pelicans" in Christian art are a symbol of charity; they are also an emblem of Jesus Christ by "whose blood we are healed." This comes from the myth that "Pelicans" feed their young with their blood which arose from the fact that the parent "Pelican" transfers softened food from the large bag under its bill to its "Young."

Oracle: This Symbol often pictures the realization that conditions are changing and you, your family (and sometimes friends) don't feel safe and secure in your environment. You may need to move to a new situation that can provide a better way of life with more nourishment and less danger. This can also refer to an inner withdrawal from situations that feel threatening or unsure. It can be a case of having to leave homes, places or people that have outlived their usefulness or relevance in your life. A change of heart and mind can lead to new beginnings, with the past being left behind. Pollution or "Garbage" on any level can lead to a sense of unease in one's environment and the fear of how one can cope in the future. There may be a need to actually pick up one's possessions and move out of the path of some form of danger. If your environment is "polluted" by negative people, attitudes or some other form of debilitation or "Garbage," is it worth staying there? Are threats being taken seriously enough? This "danger" can manifest on any level; physical, emotional or spiritual. It can erupt as psychic or emotional outbursts that can be threatening or toxic; rubbish that is difficult to contain, manage or maneuver around. If you don't feel safe in your environment, how can you expect you and yours to grow and flourish?

Keywords: Concerns with survival. The endeavor to achieve mental, physical or emotional wellbeing or peace. Noise and other irritants that make life difficult. Looking out for the safety and security of one's children, home or creative ventures. Feeling unsafe. Conditions being insecure and unpredictable. Having nowhere to rest.

The Caution: Mess and rubbish left around. Not being prepared to compromise or cohabit. People not being able to live together. Fouling of one's nest. Things are being done "for your own good," regardless of what you want. Noise driving people out. Leases running out.

What does this **SYMBOL** say to *you?*

Young people everywhere have been allowed to choose between love and a garbage disposal unit. Everywhere they have chosen the garbage disposal unit.
Guy Debord

It is an ill bird that fouls its own nest.
Romanian Proverb

SYLPH, n. An immaterial but visible being that inhabited the air when the air was an element and before it was fatally polluted with factory smoke, sewer gas and similar products of civilization.
Ambrose Bierce

You must not lose faith in humanity. Humanity is an ocean; if a few drops of the ocean are dirty, the ocean does not become dirty.
Mahatma Gandhi

Lies, injustice, and hypocrisy are a part of every ordinary community. Most people achieve a sort of protective immunity, a kind of callousness, toward them. If they didn't, they couldn't endure.
Nella Larsen

Sagittarius
20

It wasn't raining when Noah built the ark.
Howard Ruff

The rich man has his ice in the summer and the poor man gets his in the winter.
Scottish Proverb

Some people are making such thorough plans for rainy days that they aren't enjoying today's sunshine.
William Feather

Discover a well before you are thirsty.
Chinese Proverb

A penny saved is a penny earned.
Proverb

For age and want save while you may: no morning sun lasts a whole day.
Romanian Proverb

They that have got a good store of butter may lay it thick on their bread.
Romanian Proverb

If I had eight hours to chop down a tree, I'd spend six sharpening my axe.
Abraham Lincoln

In the depth of winter, I finally learned that within me there lay an invincible summer.
Albert Camus

IN WINTER PEOPLE ARE CUTTING ICE FROM A FROZEN POND FOR SUMMER USE

Commentary: "In Winter People Are Cutting Ice from a Frozen Pond for Summer Use" speaks of the value of planning ahead so people can have their needs provided for. Food, water, materials, all kinds of provisions may be more available sometimes than others and it is sensible to ensure supply of what will be needed in the future.

Oracle: It may be necessary to take into account the reality of seasonal fluctuations and the resulting times of scarcity. This Symbol shows the importance of thinking about what will be needed or useful in the future, or at least making the best possible use of available materials to provide what is needed when it is needed. Storage of things, or adaptations of available materials for a "rainy day" can ensure that life will be easier to manage. This can point to storing food, water, money, or other types of goods. Money can be saved by having a savings plan for retirement. Things such as pension funds and savings can be a good idea as there is no way of knowing exactly what your resources will be later in life. By saving some kind of resource, and allowing for shifts in time and seasonal variations, you'll have what you need. Also, making building repairs and renovations to allow for fluctuations in the weather or for varying atmospheric changes can also lead to an increased level of safety and comfort. Watch to see if you have lost touch with your emotions by creating an icy barrier to future possibilities or eventualities. Also, someone may be working toward appropriating or plundering someone else's resources or savings. Any threats to future happiness or success can be overcome without great difficulty, just a little awareness, planning and action.

Keywords: Overcoming difficulties ahead of time through creative solutions to problems. Strategies for survival in harder times. Stocking up and storing supplies. Savings and funds. Pension plans. Retirement plans. Work and renovation. Planning for changes in external or internal realities. Seeing shortages ahead of time. Snow. Ice. Freezing conditions. Divorce settlements.

The Caution: Stoic acceptance of difficulties. Not seeing ahead of the times. Failing to plan for the future and just hoping that it will work out. Sitting on your hands instead of working for future possibilities. People storing up hurts or insults for later. Extortion.

What does this **SYMBOL** say to *you?*

A CHILD AND A DOG WEARING BORROWED EYEGLASSES

Commentary: "A Child and a Dog Wearing Borrowed Eyeglasses" shows play, impersonations and free-flowing perceptions of fun and enjoyment with others. The "Eyeglasses" can symbolize intelligence or a thoughtful nature and by wearing them one can give the impression of having these attributes. "A Child and a Dog" wearing the "Eyeglasses" shows that the "Child," who may be you or someone else in the situation, does not care what the "Eyeglasses" are all about. By giving the "Eyeglasses" to the "Dog," the "Child" shows that he doesn't know, or worry about, what intelligence or wisdom truly are. For the moment, he wants them to act like grownups, seemingly smart and in control of their lives.

Oracle: Perhaps someone is pretending to be more in control or smarter than they are, or is this a situation of innocent play? Whatever the situation, this can work to make a consciousness shift. By changing both your appearance and your perceptions, you can create some new understanding of your dreams, or understanding of how life can be, and it can help you to grow into it. People in this situation may have no idea where they are headed in life, or what they are doing with it now, but, with some play, some fun and light relief can be had in the process. Look to see whether someone is trying to fool you with appearances or by inappropriate action or confusing behavior. Make sure that everyone is looking at things through the right "lenses" in order to be able to see what's really going on. "Looking through" and into things can reveal layers of meaning that you wouldn't otherwise observe. Eyestrain can occur, especially if one doesn't want to see what's actually going on, or desires a pretend scenario rather than to face reality.

Keywords: Emulation leading to actualization. The rewards of make believe. Dog obedience classes and training. Pantomimes. Dealing with life through play or fantasy. Difficulty in understanding each other. The perception each has of the other. Spontaneous and carefree creativity. Cartooning and clowning. Having the "eyes" to see. Glasses of all kinds.

The Caution: Deliberately fooling with false impressions. Taking on masks to hide real intentions. The "blind leading the blind." Pretending to be something that one isn't. Not seeing people or things for who, what or how they really are. Getting lost in abstractions. Goofing around too much. Play acting to avoid the truth.

What does this **SYMBOL** say to *you?*

Rose-colored glasses are never made in bifocals. Nobody wants to read the small print in dreams.
Ann Landers

The dog is a yes animal. Very popular with people who can't afford a yes man.
Robertson Davies

In their sympathies, children feel nearer animals than adults.
Jessamyn West

Man is the only animal that learns by being hypocritical. He pretends to be polite and then, eventually, he becomes polite.
Jean Kerr

In our society those who are in reality superior in intelligence can be accepted by their fellows only if they pretend they are not.
Marya Mannes

The only good in pretending is the fun we get out of fooling ourselves that we fool somebody.
Booth Tarkington

There's none so blind as those who won't see.
Old Saying

Sagittarius
22

I believe you are your work. Don't trade the stuff of your life, time, for nothing more than dollars. That's a rotten bargain.
Rita Mae Brown

Big jobs usually go to the men who prove their ability to outgrow small ones.
Ralph Waldo Emerson

To open a business is very easy; to keep it open is very difficult.
Chinese Proverb

Work is not the curse, but drudgery is.
Henry Ward Beecher

Among poor people, there's not any question about women being strong—even stronger than men—they work in the fields right along with the men. When your survival is at stake, you don't have these questions about yourself like middle-class women do.
Dolores Huerta

The test of a vocation is the love of the drudgery it involves.
Logan Pearsall Smith

A CHINESE LAUNDRY

Commentary: "A Chinese Laundry" is pictured. The "Chinese Laundry" was once a place where a lot of the work was done laboriously by hand in cramped and difficult conditions, and for long hours. The Chinese did the work that other people did not want to do, indeed, would often refuse to do. There was often a sense of alienation which was made worse by language and cultural barriers. Although the wages were low, people would work hard side by side, not asking for much, but being glad of the opportunity to make an honest day's wage for a good day's work. There was also the opportunity to make a life in the "new world," in America. In those early days, and even today, discrimination was often directed toward foreign people who worked in menial occupations. However, if they withdrew their labor, whole sections of the community would collapse

Oracle: You may find that you are not being taken seriously and are expected to perform in a stereotypical way. You may also have closed your own mind to other options for employment, or your life's work, that could be more rewarding to you and your community. Be careful not to shut yourself away in a situation that will end up binding you to it. Make sure that you aren't putting yourself, or others, in a box that one can't escape from. This Symbol can bring all sorts of prejudices to the surface, be they social, racial or otherwise. This can also picture a situation where a few people are working closely together, speaking the same language. Even in this there can be alienation and loneliness. Remember to perform everyday tasks with reverence and see how this can transform your feelings and experience of life. Assessing how "clean" your act is may bring surprising results. Further, how much do you need to clean up for everyone around you?

Keywords: Restrictive expectations. Relations with others because of social duty. Performing tasks. Mediocrity, or the fear of it. Washing machines and dryers. Money and other laundering. Laws and legislation based on social and racial inequality. Issues of belonging. Cleaning up for others. The search for purity. Institutions that inhibit individuality. Convents. Stereotyping people. Work and the rewards it should bring.

The Caution: Giving in to prejudice. Self-inflicted sense of inferiority that can lead to missed opportunities for relating. Feeling trapped with no way out. Not being taken seriously. Doing menial jobs with little reward or real return. Slave labor. Lack of individual identity. Shutters to keep the world out.

What does this **SYMBOL** say to *you?*

A GROUP OF IMMIGRANTS FULFILLING THE REQUIREMENTS FOR ENTERING A NEW COUNTRY

Sagittarius
23

Commentary: "A Group of Immigrants Fulfilling the Requirements for Entering a New Country" shows people who are leaving the old behind in order to pursue a new life in a new place. They may be happy, hopeful and jubilant about this voyage to the unfamiliar or they may be somewhat sad, bedraggled and lost, it all depends on their individual circumstances. They may find themselves being assessed by others to see how "worthy" they are of being accepted into this "New Country"; just what are their qualifications for acceptance?

Oracle: This is a time of new possibility, the hope for better things and a new way of life. You may find yourself preparing to venture into new territory for the promise that is offered. There may need to be adjustments about the way you communicate your thoughts and ideas. Be receptive to this new way of life, as you'll learn a lot. Learning how to communicate will help you to succeed in this new territory, whether this be a new home, new country, new job, new relationship, etc., and can help dispel any feelings of alienation and loneliness. Perhaps there is a need to let go of past experiences or people in order to move on in life. Letting go of the hindering and stifling elements of the past will help transport hope into the "new world" that is opening up. How do you feel in this new environment? Do you feel strangely yet completely at home, or do you feel like a fish out of water? Give thanks for what is being released from the past and prepare for the new to come. It's bound to be challenging, yet rewarding!

Keywords: Reorientation of selfhood. Needing to change things in order to accept a new reality. The necessity of learning new languages or customs to fit in. Visas, passports, papers. Illegal immigrants. Boat people. Customs officials and regulations. Baggage and luggage. Shipping. Qualifications and certifications. Identification. Asylum. Immigration officers. Papers and qualifications that include or exclude. Refugees. Laws. Borders. Ellis Island. Throwing away the known in pursuit of the unknown.

The Caution: Entering new situations with inflexible traditions. Issues of social or racial prejudice, or the suspicion of it. Red tape getting in the way of enjoying life. Those not living up to requirements. Not getting successfully through the paperwork. Being untrue to one's self in order to be accepted. Being rejected or sent back.

What does this **SYMBOL** say to *you?*

Remember that happiness is a way of travel, not a destination.
Roy Goodman

Give me your tired, your poor, your huddled masses yearning to breathe free.
Emma Lazarus, from the verse inscribed on the Statue of Liberty.

I would place all the Indians of Nevada on ships in our harbor, take them to New York and land them there as immigrants, that they might be received with open arms ... and thus placed beyond the necessity of reservation help.
Sarah Winnemucca

A map of the world that does not include Utopia is not worth even glancing at, for it leaves out the one country at which Humanity is always landing.
Oscar Wilde

Sagittarius
24

No money is better spent than what is laid out for domestic satisfaction.
Samuel Johnson

Spread love everywhere you go: first of all in your own house. Give love to your children, to your wife or husband, to a next-door neighbor... Let no one ever come to you without leaving better or happier.
Mother Teresa

When one door of happiness closes, another door opens, but often we look so long at the closed door that we don't see the one that has opened.
Helen Keller

True love is not a bargain made, and not a thing to deal or trade.
For love's a gift that has no strings,
as free as songs the bluebird sings.
Michael Star

Good fences make good neighbors.
American Proverb

I am a marvelous housekeeper. Every time I leave a man I keep his house.
Zsa Zsa Gabor

A BLUEBIRD, A SIGN OF GOOD LUCK AND HAPPINESS, IS STANDING AT THE DOOR OF THE HOUSE

Commentary: "A Bluebird, a Sign of Good Luck and Happiness, Is Standing at the Door of the House." The "Bluebird" is often seen as an omen of good fortune and "Happiness," and it is pictured "Standing at the Door of the House," which shows "Good Luck" is coming into "the House" or headed your way in some sense.

Oracle: You may soon feel that you are in a time of natural, positive, good luck. Can you see and feel it? Responding with your higher hopes for a happy and productive life will ensure that the "Bluebird of Good Luck and Happiness" knows where to settle. Positive attitudes and hope for the future will see you moving forward unhindered, and your hopes becoming reality. Observing birds in nature or in your own environment can bring a reminder of how wonderful life can be. Birds are seen to be agents of spiritual messages and watching them go about their lives and hearing their calls can bring a sense of stronger connectedness to our everyday lives. Do you see or hear the "Bluebird"? If you have not paid much attention or noticed them before you may be surprised by just how many birds are around you. Are you allowing happiness to come knocking at your "Door"? If you can't feel it yet, meditate on the Symbol of the "Bluebird" bringing "Good Luck and Happiness" as life is sure to shift in some way. You could hang up a picture of a "Bluebird," or some other bird, as a token of your willingness to receive this "Good Luck and Happiness." This "Bluebird" may actually be a person who turns up in your life, or is already known to you. How lucky do you feel? How content with your life are you? Bring happiness into your home, take a moment to count your blessings—see how blessed you truly are.

Keywords: Calmness and rewards. Promise (or promises) of "Happiness." Love and happiness available by acknowledging its presence. Real estate, house boundaries. Reminders of joy. Cottages and picket fences. Waiting for invitations to enter. Omens of good luck. Blessings. Front doors and back doors.

The Caution: Denying happiness or good news. Feeling that the grass is always greener somewhere else. Putting on false shows of happiness for all to see. Thinking that buying things will make one's life happier. Wanting what's not available.

What does this **SYMBOL** say to *you?*

A CHUBBY LITTLE RICH BOY RIDES UPON A HOBBYHORSE

Sagittarius
25

Commentary: "A Chubby Little Rich Boy Rides upon a Hobbyhorse." Webster's dictionary defines a "Hobbyhorse" as "(1) a strong active horse, of middle size; (2) A stick, often with the head or figure of a horse, on which boys make believe to ride; (3) A subject or plan upon which one is constantly setting off; a favorite and ever-recurring theme of discourse, thought, or effort; that which occupies one's attention unduly, or to the weariness of others; a ruling passion." "A Chubby Little Rich Boy" shows a young child who has all his material needs met; he's well fed and looked after. He "Rides Upon his Hobbyhorse," which could be anything from a real horse to a stick horse. Presumably he enjoys the fun and the motion—perhaps it soothes him or keeps him occupied when he has nothing else to do. Perhaps there are other things he could be doing, such as school lessons or domestic chores, but he's probably not thinking about those right now. Does he enjoy what he's doing or is it that he's gotten into the habit of being on his "Hobbyhorse"? If he's just started playing, he may soon discover that he can't actually go anywhere with this "toy" as it's very limited in its range or motion. Indeed, if it is a "rocking horse," it has no real forward motion, rather it continually goes over the same ground, backward and forward.

Oracle: Somebody in this situation may feel that they are doing what is necessary, however it is probably not the real thing, but more of a training session, perhaps a practice run. Are you, or is someone else, doing something over and over? Perhaps there's a feeling of being bored with all the big plans and big endeavors that go nowhere and largely come to nothing. Still, this may be a time of learning. Looking upon life's experiences as a lesson will help you to move on to the next stage of the situation. Keep up the practice and the play, one day you'll probably have to prove yourself in a more rigorous, demanding situation.

Keywords: Hobbies and their pleasures. Unrestrained, imaginative play that can lead to truly wonderful creations, physically, emotionally and spiritually. Protected practice. Having to have one's sexual needs fulfilled before one loses energy. Exercise, doing something because one can. Constantly going off on distracting schemes. Boys and their toys. Unrestrained passion.

The Caution: Someone spoiled and shallow. Feeling that one can take on anything without thought of the actual consequences. Playing when one should be more serious about life. Not doing one's work, avoiding it by doing "fun" things instead. Having no friends to play with.

What does this **SYMBOL** say to *you?*

Do not handicap your children by making their lives easy.
Lazarus Long

Nothing is so hard as for those who abound in riches to conceive how others can be in want.
Jonathan Swift

It is amazing how quickly the kids learn to drive a car, yet are unable to understand the lawnmower, snow blower, or vacuum cleaner.
Ben Bergor

In this era of affluence and of permissiveness, we have, in all but cultural areas, bred a nation of overprivileged youngsters, saturated with vitamins, television and plastic toys.
Judith Crist

Well, you know when you're rocking in a rocking chair, and you go so far that you almost fall over backwards, but at the last instant you catch yourself? That's how I feel all the time.
Stephen Wright

Say not, when I have leisure I will study; you may not have leisure.
The Mishnah

Sagittarius
26

*It is better to die on your feet
than to live on your knees.*
Euripides

*Usually when people are sad,
they don't do anything. They
just cry over their condition. But
when they get angry, they bring
about a change.*
Malcolm X

*Courage is resistance to fear,
mastery of fear—not absence
of fear.*
Mark Twain

*Real courage is when you know
you're licked before you begin,
but you begin anyway and
see it through no matter what.*
Harper Lee

*Not the glittering weapon fights
the fight, but rather the hero's
heart.*
Proverb

*Those who are prepared to
die for any cause are seldom
defeated.*
Jawaharlal Nehru

*"Dying for an idea," again,
sounds well enough, but why
not let the idea die instead of
you?*
Wyndham Lewis

A FLAG BEARER IN A BATTLE

Commentary: "A Flag Bearer in a Battle" is seen. "Flag Bearers in Battle," in the old days, were the ones who were at the front of an advancing troop of soldiers, "Bearing" the "Flag" of their country or regiment. They were unarmed, therefore defenseless, and they were "up front" and obvious, and as such, were an easy target for those "on the other side." Taking the others' "Flag" was seen as a victory; hence the "Flag Bearer" was particularly vulnerable to attack. However, having the responsibility of being the "Flag Bearer" was seen as an honored and well-respected position.

Oracle: Nowadays, the "Flag Bearer" can be anybody with an issue to stand up for, to represent or promote. This issue can be anything from a worthy cause, such as the homeless or the disadvantaged, to political issues right through to wanting to promote or advertise something. All of these may attract some flack from outside pressure. You may feel that achievements have been made that should be acknowledged or respected in some way. It could be that duties and responsibilities have been piling up on you lately, and the struggle has not been easy. Don't worry, although the people around you are probably busy, they are most likely noticing your leadership abilities. You could be the linchpin of the whole situation. It takes guts to get out front, putting yourself directly in the firing line, but it may be time for you, or somebody near you, to go for it and stand up for what you believe. Being willing to be up front and "out there" in the line of fire can bring its own kind of rewards. However, it may be that you are more familiar with being the one "up front," rather than being an actual fighter or warrior and one day you may have to drop your standard (your "Flag") and pick up a tool or a weapon. Look to any consequences of what it is that you're taking on and see how they stack up. Are things likely to work out, or are you pushing others to have to defend themselves.

Keywords: Having the courage of convictions. Standing up for ideals. Representing one's collective in a worthy cause. Carrying the standard or the "Flag." David and Goliath. Being the messenger. Advocates. Ensigns. Leadership. Self sacrifice. Fighting for political ideals. Flag waving.

The Caution: The sacrificial lamb. Overzealous idealism. Empty shows of courage. The scapegoat. Always being ready to go into battle. Violence. Fanaticism. Stepping out of line. An inability to keep quiet. Not knowing when to back off.

What does this **SYMBOL** say to *you?*

THE SCULPTOR'S VISION IS SLOWLY BUT SURELY TAKING FORM

Sagittarius
27

Commentary: "The Sculptor's Vision" shows an image of some desired shape or outcome, a picture that is projected out onto the world through creative work. The fact that the "Vision Is Slowly but Surely Taking Form" shows that slow and sometimes painstaking detail is needed to work toward something that is truly worth the time and effort.

Oracle: You are in a situation where you are able to manipulate things or events into something of value and lasting integrity. There is the ability, or the need, to project shape and "Form" onto materials or situations to have a desired outcome; to have the "Vision" actually be allowed to "Take Form." Who and what we are in our more private moments right through to our public lives is largely shown through the life we manifest, the reality we see before us and create. This Symbol can indicate the changing of one's body shape or gaining or losing weight so the appearance can fit the vision that one has in mind. Whatever the "Vision" is, it is "Surely Taking Form," and you'll be able to see clues to how it's shaping up in the situation facing you. The work that needs to be done, or the desired outcome, is finally able to take shape. However, it is a good idea to observe and decide whether the "Form" that you want is actually what is eventuating or in the pipeline. Attention and work on the situation at hand will ensure a final outcome of one's objectives. Be especially careful to ask for what you truly want or need. Is the "Form" that is evolving truly resonant with who you are? Concentrate on what you want and don't deviate from the "Vision" as your work could be spoiled with one wrong stroke of the brush. Follow the "Vision" and be creative; picture an outcome and watch it materialize.

Keywords: Concrete creative manifestation. The Godhead. This is the Symbol of the Galactic Center. Creating the "Vision." Evolution. Things going from crude beginnings all the way up to concrete outcomes. Sculptors and sculptures. Molding shapes and forms. Seeing and visualizing things ahead of their time. Sticking with the creation.

The Caution: Disregard of others' needs. Unnatural focus on the goal. Being one-eyed about the outcome. Watching a situation, or one's life "crystallize" into unbending shapes. Having one's designs set in stone. Sitting back and thinking that things will just magically happen without any effort being made. Others believing they know what you should do or be.

What does this **SYMBOL** say to *you?*

It may be that our role on this planet is not to worship God but to create him.
Arthur C. Clarke

Art is not a mirror to reflect the world, but a hammer with which to shape it.
Vladimir Mayakovsky

A man paints with his brains and not with his hands.
Michelangelo

Every separate thought takes shape and becomes visible in color and form.
Liu Hua-Yang

The universe is one of God's thoughts.
Johann Christoph Friedrich von Schiller

If you do not find yourself beautiful yet, act as does the creator of a statue that is to be made beautiful: he cuts away here, he smoothes there, he makes this line lighter, this other purer, until a lovely face has grown upon his work.
Plotinus

We must become the change we want to see.
Mahatma Gandhi

Sagittarius
28

There is nothing that makes its way more directly to the soul than beauty.
Joseph Addison

We are told never to cross a bridge till we come to it, but this world is owned by men who have "crossed bridges" in their imagination far ahead of the crowd.
Anonymous

The bridges you cross before you come to them are over rivers that aren't there.
Gene Brown

Pass the bridge that your kinsmen have passed.
Azerbaijani Proverb

My mother, religious Negro, proud of having waded through a storm, is, very obviously, a sturdy bridge that I have crossed over on.
Toni Cade Bambara

If you destroy a bridge, be sure you can swim.
Swahili Proverb

We cross our bridges when we come to them and burn them behind us, with nothing to show for our progress except a memory of the smell of smoke, and a presumption that once our eyes watered.
Tom Stoppard

A SPLENDIDLY BUILT BRIDGE, A HERITAGE OF UNKNOWN AGES, STILL SPANS THE BEAUTIFUL AND WILDLY PRIMITIVE STREAM

Commentary: "A Splendidly Built Bridge" is shown. It is a "Heritage of Unknown Ages." The "Bridge" implies strength, dependability; and passages, links and shortcuts across things that would otherwise divide and keep people and places apart. This Symbol represents a "Bridge" that was "Built" long ago, but is still of use and benefit to all who use it.

Oracle: You may need to find "a Bridge" between your fresh, energetic aspirations, thoughts and emotions and constructive thought and activity. Traditional ways of approaching things may lead to the best solutions now. It may be that the "Bridge" was developed by the experiences of many generations. It could also reflect inherent qualities carried through from history, perhaps past lives. Whatever, you are able to span different levels of awareness with a "Splendidly Built Bridge." If you feel disconnected, know that you can be confident, resting in the reassurance that the "Bridge" is still there. The "Bridge" is an ever-present capacity that is a gift to you from the universe. However, there may be a "toll" to be paid for going across the "Bridge." If so, is this journey (this event, conversation or habit) an outworn one? Is there a continual reversing of direction or position—or is there movement and links being forged in one sure direction? If you don't know how to raise your level of awareness or intuition into the conscious realm, be confident that you really do know intuitively. Thoughts or emotions can act as a link or a barrier between our soul-centered inspiration and the source of higher awareness. The "Wildly Primitive Stream" is a symbol of those emotions, but no matter how far back or deeply active our emotional landscape is, the "Bridge" can take us safely across.

Keywords: Enduring elements from past traditions providing links with the modern day. Reverence for things of worth that stand as reminders of yesterday. Linking people, places and things with clarity. Connections with the "old country," or past lives. Beautiful and inspiring landscapes. Getting in touch with people. Ever repeating journeys. Passages across the water. Permanence.

The Caution: Sticking with old, outworn methods, with no new ideas. Themes of "buying the Brooklyn Bridge." Continually having to tread the tried-and-true path without deviating.

What does this **SYMBOL** say to *you?*

A FAT BOY MOWING THE LAWN

Sagittarius 29

Commentary: "A Fat Boy Mowing the Lawn" shows someone getting up and doing the necessary chores to improve the appearance around the home. The "Fat Boy" can be the "kid" who has everything available to him, but still, for the moment at least, has to do what his family and society says rather than what he may prefer to be doing. As he is said to be a "Fat Boy," perhaps he's not used to having to do or contribute very much, mostly laying around watching television or playing computer games. The "Fat Boy" here has to learn how to use machinery, to deal with things such as oil, petrol and spark plugs. It may be that he's not had to dirty his hands very often with jobs or menial chores.

Oracle: In order to remain socially acceptable among the people and in the neighborhood where we live, we regularly have to trim and clean up our environment. For whatever reason, it has to be accepted that everyday chores are important and necessary. Taken to extremes, however, this can lead to having to keep up with the Joneses. How well does the "appearance" of this situation look? Is there a need for maintenance and care to put on a better show and impress everybody for society's sake? You may be paying more attention to appearances than you are to those things that others don't see. The "front yard" may be all cleaned up and looking neat and tidy, but how does the "backyard" look? Many people are fooled by how things appear, but there is usually an unsettling feeling that everything is not quite right. Perhaps someone has to pay some price by proving themselves? There can be a feeling of having to do chores that don't truly reflect what one is capable of or desires to do. Is there something that you've been going to do for years, but haven't gotten around to? Jobs, chores, tasks and duties need to be done by someone. Have people been asking and asking for these things to be done? There may be an upside; with all the exercise there may be a possibility of losing a little weight and getting fit.

Keywords: Superficial show. Things looking respectable, and "right". Trying to lose weight through physical activity. Coming to grips with mechanical tools. Perspiring through effort. Training the youngsters to do the chores. Maintenance. Spare parts. Spark plugs. Doing odd jobs. Signs of affluence. Laborers. Hired hands.

The Caution: Pushing social respectability, avoiding something. Not wanting to help around the house. The "lounge lizard." Not dealing with the reality of life. Having too many jobs. Not getting off one's backside. Ignoring the nagging. Barging into others' space. Making a lot of noise. Incompetent helpers.

What does this **SYMBOL** say to *you?*

A perfect summer day is when the sun is shining, the breeze is blowing, the birds are singing, and the lawnmower is broken.
James Dent

The lazy man who goes to borrow a spade says, "I hope I will not find one."
Malagasy Proverb

The grass is always greener over the septic tank.
Erma Bombeck

It is amazing how quickly the kids learn to drive a car, yet are unable to understand the lawnmower, snow blower, or vacuum cleaner.
Ben Bergor

There are two kinds of men who never amount to much—those who cannot do what they are told and those who can do nothing else.
Cyrus H. K. Curtis

The fellow that owns his own home is always coming out of a hardware store.
Kin Hubbard

Laziness travels so slowly that poverty soon overtakes him.
Benjamin Franklin

Sagittarius
30

A single conversation with a wise man is better than ten years of study.
Chinese Proverb

What I'm looking for is a blessing that's not in disguise.
Kitty O'Neill Collins

It is one of the blessings of old friends that you can afford to be stupid with them.
Ralph Waldo Emerson

You must pay the price if you wish to secure the blessing.
Andrew Jackson

I would have made a good pope.
Richard Nixon

To err is human, to forgive, divine.
Alexander Pope

See everything, overlook a great deal, correct a little.
Pope John XXIII

A faithful friend is a strong defense; and he that hath found him hath found a treasure.
Louisa May Alcott

A true friend is the greatest of all blessings, and that which we take the least care of all to acquire.
François de La Rochefoucauld

THE POPE BLESSING THE FAITHFUL

Commentary: "The Pope" is an image of someone who has an exalted position and operates with a high sense of authority, hopefully with spiritual awareness and love. The word "Pope" comes from the Latin *papa* and the Greek *pappas*. He is dispensing "Blessings" on his people, those who believe in him, his position and his cause. "Blessings" can also come from worshipping a higher power with people of like mind. Dispensing the rewards of faith upon people who are committed and eager leads to an enlightening of those who receive, and also those who do the "Blessing." A major voice will be heard—who is the spokesperson who will be heard by the collective?

Oracle: There is often a need to create or assign someone as the physical representation of what is believed on the spiritual plane. This person of authority performs actions that give our beliefs a feeling of reality and draw the community together. When you do things that are true to your inner self there is a feeling of connection to a higher power. This feeling is like a "Blessing" and is a reminder of the spiritual purpose of life. The situation or event that is the center of your question may be in need of just such a "Blessing." If you are one of the "worthy ones," you will probably receive a sign that you are on the true path. If the question relates to a group situation, it may be that you or someone in the group needs to take on the role of spiritual representative, be a "Pope," and reward the group with your words of wisdom and experience. That will help maintain their focus, motivation and faith in what they are trying to achieve. It may be important to show reverence and respect to others, as this will lead to rewards of their own. This can also represent someone having a powerful memory. A noble or regal person will remember the faces and names of huge numbers of people who surround them. It can feel like a "Blessing" to be in their company.

Keywords: Rituals of reverence, blessings and worship. Sincere interest in others. Being on the inside looking out or being on the outside looking in. Recognizing the source of enormous inner riches. Rewards for loyalty. Seeking support or recognition. Eye-to-eye contact. Being remembered. Charisma and presence. Having an audience with someone.

The Caution: Overwhelming political or spiritual rituals. Lust for power. Negating, projecting and transferring one's shadow onto others. Not taking responsibility for one's actions. Begging people to dispense favors. Sucking up to be accepted or recognized. Manipulating for desired ends. Nervous reaction to power or position. Demanding obedience. Lording it over people. Leaving people out that don't measure up or conform. Having people at one's beck and call.

What does this **SYMBOL** say to *you?*

AN INDIAN CHIEF CLAIMS RECOGNITION AND POWER FROM THE ASSEMBLED TRIBE

Capricorn 1

Self-reverence, self-knowledge, self-control. These three alone lead life to sovereign power.
Alfred Tennyson

Commentary: "An Indian Chief Claims Recognition and Power from the Assembled Tribe" shows someone in a position of authority, standing strong, staking their "Claim" and place among the people that he or she leads or represents. This is a Symbol associated with the Jesus story. Jesus' karmic lesson was to rise above the crowd; to claim power in situations, places and with people; and to accept any consequences that such a "Claim" could lead to.

Oracle: There are leadership issues here. Sometimes we need to rise to the occasion and take charge, and this is most likely one of those times. This can lead to a struggle for control. You may be challenged to remind those around you of your leadership qualities and your ability to be strong, reliable and accountable. There's the need to stand up in front of others and be counted as someone who has what it takes. As long as nobody is "lording it over" others, life can operate in a smoother manner, with everyone understanding their place in the scheme of things. We all have to find the courage to stand up and exhibit a show of strength now and then. However, there can be the flip side: are those above you reminding you of the lesser position you occupy in the scheme of things? You can find your own internal authority by believing in yourself, by "Claiming Recognition and Power" and acknowledging your nobility and courage. There can be challenging events happening in the external world, a battle of wills perhaps, but if you stand strong and firm in your inner belief in yourself, you can come out victorious with a greater sense of authority radiating out to those around you. People will take you more seriously. Always know when to listen to and give way to the rights of others and you'll be given a stronger position in society.

Keywords: Assuming authority and the need for it. Benevolence bestowed. Winning by charisma and strength of numbers. Finding a true sense of place. Signs that one should be in charge. Staking one's claim. The "Claim of Recognition." Respect. Having to stand up or stand out in the crowd. Having the charisma of leadership. Consolidating power. Popularity contests.

The Caution: Power tripping and struggles. Overinflated views of one's self. The continual need to quieten power battles. Being challenged by those left and right. Demanding attention and that others follow orders. Taking over. Selfish and ego-driven. Too many chiefs.

What does this **SYMBOL** say to *you?*

To lead the people, walk behind them.
Lao-Tzu

A lot of young girls have looked to their career paths and have said they'd like to be chief. There's been a change in the limits people see.
Wilma Pearl Mankiller

There are two things people want more than sex and money—recognition and praise.
Mary Kay Ash

If your actions inspire others to dream more, learn more, do more and become more, you are a leader.
John Quincy Adams

He is not fit to command others that cannot command himself.
Proverb

There are too many chiefs and not enough Indians.
Proverb

There are no small parts, only small actors.
Proverb

Power corrupts; absolute power corrupts absolutely.
Proverb

Capricorn 2

As a vessel is known by the sound, whether it be cracked or not, so men are proved by their speeches whether they be wise or foolish.
Demosthenes

People are like stained-glass windows. They sparkle and shine when the sun is out, but when the darkness sets in, their true beauty is revealed only if there is a light from within.
Elizabeth Kübler-Ross

There is nothing fiercer than a failed artist. The energy remains, but, having no outlet, it implodes in a great black fart of rage which smokes up all the inner windows of the soul.
Erica Jong

Beautiful light is born of darkness, so the faith that springs from conflict is often the strongest and the best.
Robert James Turnbull

Events unfold so unpredictably, so unfairly, human happiness does not seem to have been included in the design of creation. It is only we, with our capacity to love, that give meaning to the indifferent universe.
Woody Allen

There is a crack, a crack in everything. That's how the light gets in.
Leonard Cohen

THREE STAINED-GLASS WINDOWS IN A GOTHIC CHURCH, ONE DAMAGED BY WAR

Commentary: "Three Stained-Glass Windows in a Gothic Church, One Damaged by War" pictures the need to stay strong on every level under the barrage of some type of bombardment. A "Church" is normally a place of safety and refuge, but "War" has broken through its divine barrier and caused "Damage," or some injury, that is much bigger than just a broken "Window." One of the three corners of unity, in this case the one of love, is "Damaged" and compromised by the aggressive warring nature of mankind.

Oracle: With the shattering of the "Window," there is often a loss of faith, hope and trust. Someone may have previously felt safe in the confines of their life and suddenly a "bomb hits," breaking and demolishing some aspect of their usually safe and secure life. This situation may take considerable time to heal, although if the structure is sound, fixing the "Window" (the place where the light gets in) can be done relatively quickly. Still, even with the best of thoughts, emotions and intentions, it might take months or years to truly heal the devastating effect that's been unleashed. In fact, the actual "Damage" that this Symbol implies may have started long ago. There is a need to get it repaired and things often need healing on the emotional and physical levels. Hypnotherapy, psychoanalysis and past life regression may reveal pain, injury and trauma that are holding one back from being able to accept or give love. Acceptance of love can lead to healing on many levels. Love is often the main issue that needs to be projected outward as well as accepted inward.

Keywords: Seeking sanctuary. Careless aggression where love should be. Religious or philosophical differences that spark off problems. Fears of being "under attack" while in the spotlight. Sorrow and despair over losses. Loss of faith. "Windows" that are cracked, broken or smashed. Cracks and shattering. Rescue of endangered holy places. Loss of love through harsh circumstance. The need for repair.

The Caution: Feeling disconnected from the reality of what's going on. Fearfulness or fearlessness, when one should be careful. Signs of rubble all around. Aggression between people. Burning down churches. A lack of safe places. Being shell-shocked and ravaged. Cold breezes entering sacred spaces. Psychological and emotional scars. Nowhere to run, nowhere to hide.

What does this **SYMBOL** say to *you?*

THE HUMAN SOUL, IN ITS EAGERNESS FOR NEW EXPERIENCES, SEEKS EMBODIMENT

Capricorn 3

Commentary: "The Human Soul, in Its Eagerness for New Experiences, Seeks Embodiment" is a Symbol of the soul's longing for self-expression. In our western calendar, this Symbol is highlighted on December 25 each year, on Christ's birthday. It reflects the Jesus story in many ways.

Oracle: This Symbol shows that a new level of consciousness is about to reveal and express itself. Many parts of yourself are seeking expression and "Embodiment" and there may be a sense of "Eagerness" or urgency in the process. Something "New" is being born, particularly something that's coming from deep inside of you, and it can feel like nothing is going to stop it from achieving this "Embodiment." You may feel very open to the messages of the world around you, as clues come through to show you how to go about "Embodying" these "New Experiences." There can be unbounded enthusiasm, but it may take some time before what you want can be brought into reality. At first, this is likely to be a quiet time of inner contemplation and outer observance. Regardless of your more immediate physical circumstances, there is an evolution of understanding going on. This Symbol can point to children wanting to come through into this life, along with an unfurling of one's creativity and projects into physical form. Whatever it represents, a new beginning of life or hope is wanting to come into conscious manifestation now. This Symbol often brings up issues to do with writing and self-expression. It may be a good idea to keep a diary or to write things down, as ideas will often just pour out. This situation may have a fated quality, with some extraordinary outcome just waiting to happen.

Keywords: Inner motivation leading to expansion. Jesus and his disciples. Being "born" quickly. Manifesting one's desires without concern for consequences. Being "born again." Feeling like a changed person. The need to drop into the body. Religious and spiritual rebirth. Reincarnation. The urge to create. Writers and writing.

The Caution: Denying the growth that's beckoning in favor of social responsibility. Not leaving when perhaps one should. Having to seek permission to come through any "new gateway." A loss of faith. Being obsessed about an ideal or idea. Feeling cast adrift from one's reality.

We must be the epitome, the embodiment of success. We must radiate success before it will come to us. We must first become mentally, from an attitude standpoint, the people we wish to become.
Earl Nightingale

I count life just a stuff to try the soul's strength on.
Robert Browning

God does not ask about our ability, but our availability.
Anonymous

The act of writing is the act of making soul, alchemy.
Gloria Evangelina Anzaldua

The greatest human quest is to know what one must do in order to become a human being.
Immanuel Kant

Variety is the soul of pleasure.
Aphra Behn

To know what you prefer instead of humbly saying amen to what the world tells you you ought to prefer is to keep your soul alive.
Robert Louis Stevenson

What does this **SYMBOL** say to *you?*

Capricorn 4

No member of a crew is praised for the rugged individuality of his rowing.
Ralph Waldo Emerson

Only the guy who isn't rowing has time to rock the boat.
Jean-Paul Sartre

...as one goes through life one learns that if you don't paddle your own canoe, you don't move.
Katharine Hepburn

A canoe does not know who is king. When it turns over, everyone gets wet.
Malagasy Proverb

Plenty of folks are so contrary that if they should fall into the river, they would insist upon floating upstream.
Josh Billings

Everyone must row with the oars he has.
Proverb

We may have all come on different ships, but we're in the same boat now.
Martin Luther King, Jr.

If there is no wind, row.
Latin Proverb

We are not human beings on a spiritual journey. We are spiritual beings on a human journey.
Stephen Covey

A GROUP OF PEOPLE ENTERING A CANOE FOR A JOURNEY BY WATER

Commentary: "A Group of People Entering a Canoe" is a Symbol of people coming together to set off on a "Journey." They may already know each other or they may come from many different places, or from overseas. Regardless of where they've come from, they are all "Entering" this "Canoe" for a "Journey by Water."

Oracle: To embark on a "Journey by Water" with a "Group of People" is to embark on a "Journey" of emotional discovery. People may have differing views of what's going on and everyone has to fully agree with where they're going. In a "Canoe," some people put in the effort of "paddling" while others are passengers, enjoying the ride in their various ways. If every person participates to the success of this endeavor, the "Journey" can be swift and strong. If all the effort is left to just a few, there can be an imbalance of energy that could lead to resentment and even the failure of the mission. Hence, there can be issues over "who does what." Depending on the sharing of the responsibilities, some members may be fatigued by the process whereas others will remain fresh. This may not be fair, as some will have an advantage over others, which can lead to emotional problems, especially jealousy, impatience, bickering or dissatisfaction. However, with cooperation, there can be great success. If this is a personal "Journey," then it is important that you remain balanced and don't overexert yourself on the emotional or physical level. This may also be a time when divergent aspects of your personality come together to explore an emotional situation. Getting everybody "in the same boat" can be a challenge here, whether it's real people, or the various parts of your own thought processes. Cooperation, compromise and common goals will win the day.

Keywords: Cohesive effort, cooperation and coordination. People coming together with a shared goal in sight. Being continually on the move. Feeling like one's on a "Journey" of destiny. People all pulling together. Canoes. Boats. Vehicles of discovery. Setting off on an adventure. Entering the unknown. Workshops. Unknown destinations. Setting sail. Observing the weather. Yacht races.

The Caution: Uncoordinated energies. Not going along with anybody. Rocking the boat. The urge to get off midstream. Being bored with close company. A lack of privacy or quiet time. Backseat drivers. No one navigating. Lack of a realistic itinerary.

What does this **SYMBOL** say to *you?*

INDIANS—SOME ROWING A CANOE WHILE OTHERS ARE DANCING A WAR DANCE

Vß

Capricorn 5

Commentary: "Indians—Some Rowing a Canoe" is an image of people pulling and working together in a communal effort to do something or to get somewhere. The fact that some are "Dancing a War Dance" may be the reason some are "Rowing a Canoe" in the first place. Perhaps they need to make a show of strength and define their boundaries. My friend Dale O'Brien says of this Symbol, "The purpose of the 'War Dance' is not merely to evoke frenzied anger, but to see a vision of the battle yet to come, a mystical warrior's preparation. It is as if the consciousness of the 'in trance' dancing warrior is also at once in the warrior's activity (e.g., rowing a canoe)." Maybe they have to "row" through enemy territory and are confronted by the prospect of an attack.

Oracle: In the situation facing you, some people will just want to get on with the job and get somewhere fruitful while others are seeking to act with aggression. It may be necessary to solve things with a firm determination and vigilant approach to others. Aggression isn't ever really the answer. However, to make a show of one's intentions and position, and the effort that one will go to defend it, may ultimately win the respect of those around. Who's doing the "War Dance" in this situation? Is it you or another? Perhaps you take turns with each other, with everyone ending up either "Rowing" or "Dancing a War Dance." There may be an element of the enjoyment of drama and getting people whipped up. This can be exciting for a while, but can quickly become tiring or boring. As they say, "Keep rowing, but row away from the rocks."

Keywords: Some getting on with their lives while others are not. Vehicles of discovery vs. arguing and bickering. Threats and intimidation. Making a show of power and mobility. Cooperation bringing release from difficulties. Mobilizing forces. Psyching one's self up. Group efforts. Traffic.

The Caution: Making one's case while having to be continually on the move. Being emotionally charged. Arguments and bickering that halt forward movement or growth. Intimidation. Moving targets. Superficial shows of strength for display purposes. Making a lot of noise. Pulling faces. Gestures that threaten. Accepting no opposition to progress. Aggression. Divergent motivations leading to confusion. Road rage.

What does this **SYMBOL** say to *you?*

He who rocks the boat seldom has time to row it.
Bryan Munro

There will never be an army of perfectly nonviolent people. It will be formed of those who will honestly endeavor to observe nonviolence.
Mohandas Gandhi

Don't insult the alligator until you've crossed the river.
Haitian Proverb

No man can paddle two canoes at the same time.
Bantu Proverb

Like watermen that row one way and look another.
Robert Burton

I think it much better that… every man paddle his own canoe.
Frederick Marryat

He alone is free who lives with free consent under the entire guidance of reason.
Benedict Spinoza

Paddle your own canoe.
Proverb

Capricorn 6

The oldest and strongest emotion of mankind is fear, and the oldest and strongest kind of fear is fear of the unknown.
H. P. Lovecraft

The block of granite which is an obstacle in the pathway of the weak, becomes a steppingstone in the pathway of the strong.
Thomas Carlyle

The road of life can only reveal itself as it is traveled; each turn in the road reveals a surprise. Man's future is hidden.
Anonymous

Man can learn nothing except by going from the known to the unknown.
Claude Bernard

As long as a man stands in his own way, everything seems to be in his way.
Ralph Waldo Emerson

TEN LOGS LIE UNDER AN ARCHWAY LEADING TO DARKER WOODS

Commentary: "Ten Logs Lie under an Archway Leading to Darker Woods" is an image of remnants of the past having fallen. The "Ten Logs" were previously trees, now they "Lie under an Archway," blocking the entrance to somewhere deeper in the "Woods." The "Ten Logs" may be smack in the way of the entrance to these "Darker Woods," blocking the possibility of the journey forward, or they may provide a bridge to venture deeper.

Oracle: Throughout life we develop skills and resources that enhance our ability to cope with the present and help us in the future. These things, represented by the "Ten Logs," often need to be stored somewhere. We usually store things out of the way and in a place that is least used. When it is time to move on, you come across all the things that have accumulated over time, and are waiting for use. Perhaps these things are not relevant to your path now. The thing is, you may have to let them go. This can cause some grief, as you may not wish to let them go. However, the skills, talents and memories that developed while creating these resources remain with you on your journey. You may feel there is a difficult and mysterious period ahead of you and that you need to prepare. This marks a time to make any preparations and create the necessary safeguards before continuing on your journey into the unknown. You are on an important journey, perhaps one of destiny, but you won't know for a while what, or where, this journey is really leading to. Let go of obstructions from the past before you venture into the future. See this as an opportunity for further growth. Look to see what's standing in your way. What could block your path now that you're at the "Archway Leading to Darker Woods"? The trip may be very rewarding; only time will tell.

Keywords: Journeys into the unknown. Getting past the past. Tenacity, stamina and energy preservation. Things to consider before moving deeper. Thresholds, "Archways," entrances. Dark forests. The unknown and the "unknowable." Delving into the subconscious. Memories that lead into deep or strange places. Gateways. Fallen trees.

The Caution: Fear of the untrodden path. Being afraid to make a move. Things blocked or obstructed. Getting lost in something and not knowing how to get out. Looking for directions that are obscure or concealed.

What does this **SYMBOL** say to *you?*

A VEILED PROPHET SPEAKS, SEIZED BY THE POWER OF A GOD

Capricorn 7

Commentary: "A Veiled Prophet Speaks, Seized by the Power of a God." The "Veiled Prophet Speaks" can picture anyone, or anything, that can bring information or knowledge through to others who are willing to listen. The "Veiled Prophet" may be someone who holds the key to questions that need to be answered. They can be a mouthpiece for the agendas of others.

Oracle: Information is coming through someone, or something, and it may be difficult to know whether to fully trust it. With our modern age of communications, we can receive incredible amounts of information. This can include all sorts of theories and wonders. Some will be useful while some stretch the truth. With such power contained in words, we have to be careful about what we say as well as what we hear. As this is a "Veiled Prophet," there can be complications associated with the "message" that's being spoken. As the "Prophet" is "Seized by the Power of a God," it can be very powerful and useful knowledge that is being bestowed. Sometimes these messages have fabulous revelations and kernels of truth that can lead you on a quest for more insight into how the world operates. There are often words and insights that we can live our lives by, although not everyone will be swayed or influenced by this "Prophet." However he or she can have an immense "Power" of attraction and persuasion. Remember to be careful to sift through the real meaning of what's being said. Look carefully for the signs—is it truth that you are being fed? This powerful energy can be used for the good of all involved, or it can just lead people astray. The old saying goes that words are like a "sword," they can cut deeply and leave a vast impression, for good and for bad.

Keywords: Hypnotherapy or hypnotic suggestion. Manipulation of lesser beings. Having insights that transport to other levels. Channelling and mediumship. Translations. Prophets and bringers of messages. Empowerment. Messages erupting. Speaking. Announcing. Bearing important news. Power. Charisma. Veils. Background voices.

The Caution: Conscious manipulation and propaganda. Not owning up to all the elements of one's personality. Denying expression. Blurting out things that hurt or alienate. Barging into others' conversations. Leading people astray with exaggeration or lies. False impressions.

Talking and eloquence are not the same: to speak and to speak well are two things. A fool may talk, but a wise man speaks.
Heinrich Heine

But words are things, and a small drop of ink falling like dew upon a thought, produces that which makes thousands, perhaps millions, think.
Lord Byron

In medieval times, people thought that evil spirits could enter a person through an open mouth. These days they more often leave that way.
David Deckert

The devil can cite scripture for his purpose.
William Shakespeare

When God wants to speak and deal with us, he does not avail himself of an angel but of parents, or the pastor, or of our neighbor.
Martin Luther

The great masses of the people … will more easily fall victims to a great lie than to a small one.
Adolf Hitler

What does this **SYMBOL** say to *you?*

Capricorn 8

If I keep a green bough in my heart, the singing bird will come.
Chinese Proverb

A forest bird never wants a cage.
Henrik Ibsen

We think caged birds sing, when indeed they cry.
John Webster

A bird does not sing because it has an answer. It sings because it has a song.
Chinese Proverb

A guest sees more in an hour than the host in a year.
Polish Proverb

How easy to be amiable in the midst of happiness and success.
Anne Sophie Swetchine

"Hope" is the thing with feathers That perches in the soul And sings the tunes without the words And never stops at all.
Emily Dickinson

A good laugh is sunshine in a house.
William Makepeace Thackeray

BIRDS IN THE HOUSE SINGING HAPPILY

Commentary: "Birds in the House" are "Singing Happily." This is a beautiful image of lightness and happiness. To hear "Birds Singing Happily" is like a blessing, and if their sounds are ringing through your "House," it can feel like a double blessing. The "Birds Singing Happily" can be echoed in the sounds of our loved ones' voices, as they go about their daily lives with a sunny and cheerful attitude. It may be music that's played in the home.

Oracle: You may feel a sense of uncomplicated contentment. Even though there are a number of social rules to obey, they probably don't bother you or those around you. This is a time for sharing good feelings and "Happiness" with all who enter your sphere of operations. Feelings of safety and protection are spontaneously shared by the act of "Singing," which can be actual "Singing," but can also be laughter or animated conversation. To enjoy the moment can often depend on you having faith that the good things of life will not fade, but will continue. In your situation it is important to hold to this faith and enjoy your life. It is wise to remember to be "in the moment." This Symbol is also about the contagious nature of displays of happiness and celebrations of joy and contentment. By expressing your pleasure you can lift the feelings of others and they will most likely join in the chorus, in some way. The question is: Are people as "Happy" and secure in this situation as they look? A fairly quick glance around will bring the message you probably need. Perhaps someone is walking around singing, bringing joy. Alternatively, they may be continually "singing the blues." Remember to have music playing often in your "House" as it can dispel stress and help everyone unwind.

Keywords: Being at one with everything. Tunes sung or whistled. The promise of contentment. Communal sharing and fun. Faith in the good things of life. Music. Instruments. Playing the piano. Singing. The radio. Chattering in the background. Entertaining others. Seeing the beauty in life. Reminding others of how life can be rewarding. The sound of voices. Birds. Positive thinking.

The Caution: Idle chatter. Smug superiority and the feeling that one has it all. Not seeing the happiness inherent in one's everyday life. Whining and complaining. Making noise for the sake of it. Looking only at the difficulties one faces. Feeling caged in. Unable to fly when and where one wants to. Loneliness. Feeling abandoned by the good things.

What does this **SYMBOL** say to *you?*

AN ANGEL COMES CARRYING A HARP

Commentary: "An Angel Comes Carrying a Harp." The "Angel" is an image of beauty, serenity, salvation and peace. As the "Angel Comes Carrying a Harp" there is the feeling of music, harmony and enchantment. People who play music can transport our minds, emotions and bodies through their beautiful melodies and remind us of simple pleasures. The music that this "Angel" plays is probably very soothing and reassuring. "Harps" are more common around us than most people probably realize. Pianos have "Harps" inside them, and harmonicas (mouth organs) are often called "Harps." Things such as wind chimes can radiate these harmonies as well.

Oracle: In the situation facing you, somebody is able to "tune in" and radiate harmony around him or her. This pictures a situation of caring for others, of generosity of spirit and a fulfilled selfhood. The "Angel" may come to inspire people to do their best. This Symbol implies that someone will come bringing themes of the hope and trust in all that's good in life. They can, indeed, offer joy and salvation, especially when it's most needed. Having said that, the "Angel Carrying a Harp" can also soothe your mind to the point where you can be persuaded to accept or do things that may not always be in your best interests. So, do be aware of the shadowy side of this Symbol: somebody trying to trick you, or someone else, into thinking a certain way, or believing something. Positively seen, this Symbol assures that there is an indication of the possibility of absolute serenity (and the need for it). It is a Symbol of being relaxed and reassured.

Keywords: Demons driven away by music. Lifting faith and hope. Messages of peace from the other side. Having a message to spin. Being in tune, spiritually. Having an elevated view of humanity. Creating harmony. Blowing the whistle. Advertising. Salvation that arrives when most needed. Harmonics. Music and musical instruments. Visitations of spirit. Messages of love and hope arriving. Pulling on the heartstrings. Heavenly attunement. Beautiful tunes. Promises of redemption. Revelations. Plucking strings.

The Caution: Having a holier-than-thou attitude. Losing oneself in fantasy. Promising more than can be delivered. "Melodies" that deceive or lead astray. "Harping" on things (dwelling on issues). Messages that deceive or lead astray. Playing a tune and expecting all to follow.

What does this **SYMBOL** say to *you?*

Capricorn 9

Fools rush in where angels fear to tread.
Alexander Pope

Angels rush in when fools are almost dead.
Rudolph Fisher

Music is the harmonious voice of creation; an echo of the invisible world.
Giuseppe Mazzini

Chords that were broken will vibrate once more.
Francis J. Crosby

When the angels present themselves, the devils abscond.
Egyptian Proverb

Music is well said to be the speech of angels.
Thomas Carlyle

Orpheus with his lute made trees,
And the mountain tops that freeze,
Bow themselves when he did sing.
William Shakespeare

For thou art my harp, and pipe, and temple—a harp for harmony—a pipe by reason of the Spirit a temple by reason of the word; so that the first may sound, the second breathe, the third contain the Lord.
The Bible

Harp not on that string, madam, that is past.
William Shakespeare

Capricorn 10

Courage is not the absence of fear, but rather the judgment that something else is more important than fear.
Ambrose Redmoon

Dangers bring fears, and fears more dangers bring.
Richard Baxter

Who sees all beings in his own Self, and his own Self in all beings, loses all fear.
Upanishad

I must not fear. Fear is the mind-killer. Fear is the little death that brings total obliteration. I will face my fear. I will permit it to pass over me and through me. And when it has gone past I will turn the inner eye to see its path. Where the fear has gone there will be nothing. Only I will remain.
Frank Herbert

The only thing we have to fear is fear itself.
Franklin D. Roosevelt

I once had a sparrow alight upon my shoulder for a moment while I was hoeing in a village garden, and I felt that I was more distinguished by that circumstance than I should have been by any epaulet I could have worn.
Henry Thoreau

Do not speak of a rhinoceros if there is no tree nearby.
African Proverb

AN ALBATROSS FEEDING FROM THE HAND OF A SAILOR

Commentary: "An Albatross Feeding from the Hand of a Sailor" is an image that implies the necessity of being able to overcome the perceived separation between humans and other living beings. Feelings of separation are usually the case when we don't really understand or trust each other in some way. The "Albatross" has to overcome the fear it experiences from being in such close contact with a human and the "Sailor" has to fight his superstitions about the "Albatross." In *The Rhyme of the Ancient Mariner*, a sailor is condemned to eternally sail the world, after killing an albatross that had helped rescue his ship.

Oracle: This is a time for overcoming fears through gentleness. Even seemingly natural "enemies" can realize the possibility of interaction and the joys it can bring. You may have to deal with someone, or something, from whom you have usually kept a distance. Trusting in the goodness of people and other living beings—rather than projecting negative thoughts and connotations onto them—can lead to experiences that few have. There can be a reward, tangible or otherwise, in calling all kinds of animals and people to you in the endeavor to have some kind of exchange or communication. You may end up helping each other in some way. Call out to those who appear to be different, far away or alien to you, as there's a good chance they will respond. Fears that inhibit communication and communion with others can be dispelled with simple and often spontaneous acts of kindness and gentleness. Large leaps of faith can develop out of the smallest efforts of overcoming fear, distance and superstition. Being receptive, outreaching and caring can shorten or even completely dispel the separation between you. Extending a hand to others without concern for the consequences can lead to fear and alienation being overcome. It often just takes the simple act of reaching out.

Keywords: Feeding one's higher nature with good nourishment. Banishing worries, so that one can fly ever higher. Overcoming superstitions or beliefs. Travelers who put themselves at risk in foreign lands or cultures. Talking to anybody anywhere. Sharing one's bounty. Sailors, boats. Birds. Empathy and sympathy for others. Restoring trust and hope.

The Caution: Manipulating events or people with false nourishment. Having alternative motives for wanting to draw others close. Being afraid of strangers or strange situations. The loss of independence. Fear of intimacy.

What does this **SYMBOL** say to *you?*

PHEASANTS DISPLAY THEIR BRILLIANT COLORS ON A PRIVATE ESTATE

Commentary: "Pheasants Display Their Brilliant Colors on a Private Estate" is an image of beauty, color and wealth. It pictures a situation of the enjoyment of life's luxuries. The "Pheasants" are beautiful as they "Display Their Brilliant Colors." They have long tails and brilliantly colored plumage. People are drawn to their beauty and can be awed by their presence. That they are on "a Private Estate" shows an environment of privilege and security.

Oracle: This can picture going after one's life goals. Riches, refinement and abundance are everywhere. However, just take care: "Pheasants" can be game birds, so there may be an element of underlying danger. Displays of wealth and beauty can inspire others, but they can also lead to jealousy and begrudging acknowledgments. That this place is pictured as a "Private Estate" signifies that it may need to be protected, and kept "Private." People who don't belong there may be able to come and visit, but it may be that they're really invading someone else's space or privacy. The visitors need to show respect and courtesy and not presume that they can move in and take over. On the other hand, being "Private," this place may not be truly welcoming to people; they may find it unwelcoming and forbidding in some way. There could be difficulty keeping up with the amount of work that goes into the maintenance of this "Private Estate"—it may take a lot of time to look after the house and grounds. Who does the work and who appreciates the luxury? Looking after the lawn and the garden can bring a feeling of improved wellbeing. Regardless of whether you're a visitor or an occupant, going out and looking at the beauty of the place, the plants and the wildlife, can heighten your day.

Keywords: Glorious houses and estates. Lawns and gardens. Statues and birdbaths. Peacocks, pheasants, swans, etc. Enjoying the riches the environment offers. Large plots of land. Nature reserves. Game birds. Aristocracy and the ruling elite. Beauty, elegance and grace. Fabulous displays of color. Parks.

The Caution: Foolish disregard of pending danger. Feeling that one has to be "on parade" or else they will be overlooked. Issues of standing out from the crowd. Jealousy and envy through things on display. Luxury and beauty or snobbery that excludes. Showing off. "Do Not Enter" and "Keep off the Grass" signs.

What does this **SYMBOL** say to *you?*

Capricorn 11

Fine feathers make fine birds.
Traditional Proverb

It is not only fine feathers that make fine birds.
Aesop

It is not that the French are not profound, but they all express themselves so well that we are led to take their geese for swans.
Van Wyck Brooks

Few rich men own their own property. The property owns them.
Robert Greene Ingersoll

The more things accumulate the more life is wasted because they have to be purchased at the cost of life.
Bhagwan Shree Rajneesh, a man with some 90 Rolls Royces

He enjoys true leisure who has time to improve his soul's estate.
Henry David Thoreau

*And as you consider the ways of surrender and which way the Buddah sat,
You're just trying on a hat.*
Paul Smyth

Some believe all that parents, tutors, and kindred believe. They take their principles by inheritance, and defend them as they would their estates, because they are born heirs to them.
Alan Watts

Capricorn 12

The study of Nature is intercourse with the Highest Mind. You should never trifle with Nature.
Louis Agassiz

It is not easy to describe the sea with the mouth.
Kokyu

The sun, with all the planets revolving around it, and depending on it, can still ripen a bunch of grapes as though it had nothing else in the universe to do.
Galileo Galilei

The happiness of the bee and the dolphin is to exist. For man it is to know that and to wonder at it.
Jacques Cousteau

Nature never says one thing and wisdom another.
Decimus Junius Juvenalis

Nature uses human imagination to lift her work of creation to even higher levels.
Luigi Pirandello

If you would thoroughly know anything, teach it to others.
Tryon Edwards

Nature that framed us of four elements, warring within our breasts for regiment, doth teach us all to have aspiring minds.
Christopher Marlowe

A STUDENT OF NATURE LECTURING, REVEALING LITTLE-KNOWN ASPECTS OF LIFE

Commentary: "A Student of Nature Lecturing, Revealing Little-Known Aspects of Life" is an image of someone who's studied the lessons that life teaches and is now giving that knowledge out to others so they can learn and benefit. This Symbol reflects the disconnection of modern thinking from "Nature" along with the disappearance and loss of the more holistic structure of life. The people who are listening to the "Student" may be in awe of how much he or she knows about the subject, especially as they are hearing about the "Little-Known Aspects of Life." The "Student" who's "Lecturing" may know a lot or perhaps they're sharing the rudimentary insights they have gleaned.

Oracle: Many have forgotten, or never learned, some important things about life and it's by reconnecting with "Nature" that we can start to redress the imbalance. It may be that too much weight has been given to the needs of modern society, to technology for instance, and now it is time to seek a more alternative viewpoint. We can teach or we can access knowledge through others who specialize in these subjects; they have done the footwork in gathering the relevant information. In other words, we can use the tools of intellectualism that have actually disconnected us from the world in order to reconnect our awareness. However, it may be that nobody much cares what the "Student" who is "Lecturing" has to say—it depends how the message is delivered and whether others really want to listen. In the situation facing you, you can be an example to others of somebody who understands the wonders of "Life." Practical certifications and applications of knowledge may or may not matter. Lecturing or telling stories of the wonders of life can inspire others to greater heights in their own lives. Revealing the truth of something can lead to wonder and awe, but it can also lead to disbelief; it really depends on how the message is received.

Keywords: Observing and translating so others may learn. Green politics. Issues the conservatives don't want revealed. Nature and natural remedies. Science and its rewards and drawbacks. Issues such as global warming. Whistle blowers. Natural healing methods. Documentaries. Conspiracy theories.

The Caution: Radical nonhumanistic views. Intellectual smugness. "Lecturing" and browbeating. Modern technological advances that stifle the environment. Lip service to conservation issues.

What does this **SYMBOL** say to *you?*

A FIRE WORSHIPPER MEDITATES ON THE ULTIMATE REALITIES OF EXISTENCE

Capricorn 13

Knowing trees, I understand the meaning of patience. Knowing grass, I can appreciate persistence.
Hal Boreland

The instinct to worship is hardly less strong than the instinct to eat.
Dorothy Thompson

Genius worship is the inevitable sign of an uncreative age.
Clive Bell

An egotist is a self-made man who worships his creator.
John Bright

We have become a generation of people who worship our work, who work at our play, and who play at our worship.
Charles Swindoll

The urge to know is inherent in each human being. The quest for the meaning of life, for self-knowledge, for eternity is timeless. It is not unique to any particular race, creed, culture, nor bound to any particular place. It is universal.
M.T.O. Shahmaghsoudi

The logic of words should yield to the logic of realities.
Louis Brandeis

Commentary: "A Fire Worshipper Meditates on the Ultimate Realities of Existence" pictures someone who's very focused on finding the core truths of "Reality" and the depth and breadth of what it really means to "Exist." "Fire Worshipping" comes from the religion of Zoroastrianism, and is a branch of Vedism. The term "Zoroastrianism" comes from the Persian prophet Zoroaster or Zarathustra who lived around 630 to 541 B.C. Whilst a young man, he began having conversations with Ahura Mazda, the "Lord of Wisdom." Fire was seen as the Creative God, as it was said to purify people, especially those whom it consumed. "Magian" is another word for "Fire Worshipper," and can be used to denote an astrologer. Many rituals were observed, among these the sacred "Fire" needed to be kept glowing in the home and also in the heart and mind.

Oracle: In your situation, you may find yourself very focused, with a great passion for getting to the core, or the truth, of the "Ultimate Realities of Existence." You may need to shut out extraneous sights, sounds and outside influences that distract or worry. By turning inward, examining your situation and being on the alert for any messages that come your way, either from God or from your higher self, you will see in a way you never have before. There can be a sense of danger, but also fascination as things are revealed to you. This can picture new beginnings. There may be a need to harness personal resources. This Symbol is often about creating magic. Look through appearances to get to the heart of things. Alternatively, it can picture someone who goes to fanatical lengths to understand or promote something. This Symbol often calls into question the true meaning of the material things of life; do they get too much or too little attention?

Keywords: Self-conquest. Kundalini energy. Playing with dangerous elements to reach a higher state of being. Philosophy. The stories of our lives. Examining life and its meaning. The buzz of being alive. Questions of our very existence. Finding the reasons behind everything. Contemplation and meditation. Incense. The hypnotic spell that fire can cast. Staring into the flames. Throwing oneself into the deep end. The search for core truths.

The Caution: Overestimation of personal power and abilities. Obsession to the point of self-obliteration. Being intense. Going too deeply. Exhausting oneself. Excluding family and friends because of philosophical or spiritual convictions. Not seeing the forest for the trees.

What does this **SYMBOL** say to *you?*

Capricorn 14

*Man's great powers of
thinking, remembering, and
communicating are responsible
for the evolution of civilization.*
Linus Pauling

*INSCRIPTION, n. Something
written on another thing—
mostly memorial, intended
to commemorate the fame of
some illustrious person and
be handed down to distant
ages … e.g., the name of
John Smith, penciled on the
Washington monument.*
Ambrose Bierce

*Write your injuries in dust, your
benefits in marble.*
Benjamin Franklin

*Memories are like stones, time
and distance erodes them like
acid.*
Ugo Betti

*History is the unrolled scroll of
prophecy.*
James A. Garfield

*Human history becomes more
and more a race between
education and catastrophe.*
H. G. Wells

*Either we make history or
remain a victim of it.*
Anonymous

*The ear is a less trustworthy
witness than the eye.*
Herodotus

AN ANCIENT BAS-RELIEF CARVED IN GRANITE REMAINS A WITNESS TO A LONG-FORGOTTEN CULTURE

Commentary: "Ancient Bas-reliefs Carved in Granite" often show gods or goddesses in scenes of life from the past. We see these icons in museums and books, portrayed in photographs, statues, carvings and other images. As it "Remains a Witness to a Long-Forgotten Culture," many things can be learned from this "Bas-relief" about history, cultures and the remains of cultures. An archeological dig can turn up incredible insights and answers to the way mankind lived long ago.

Oracle: Some things never fade. They stand as reminders of ancient eras, bringing messages, being "Witnesses," from the past. They remind us how life and civilization was in "Long-Forgotten Cultures." Messages may be found in these reminders about the stability and the longevity of the foundation of your society, or possibly that of some other culture, however distant in time and space. It could be something that resonates with you or draws you. Spiritual messages may be coming out of the past (or out of time and space), perhaps speaking through "Granite," concrete or things "written in stone." This can be very enriching and rewarding as these things can be beautiful remnants of the past, reminders of how life used to be. However, they can also be beliefs and self-defeating attitudes that have etched themselves into our very lives and are now difficult to erase. Therefore, sometimes we must be careful not to look back too much as we can lose the beauty and the reward inherent in the present and in the everyday things that are around us. We can feel stuck and frozen if we're not able to move on in the life we live in the here and now. This can also apply to the rules of our culture or the common practices of an individual's heritage, family history or even past-life experiences. These can be an undertone to current realities and times.

Keywords: Anonymous immortality. Things written or carved in stone, or concrete. Permanent records. Clues from the past. Things that should be shaped and changed with the times. Pieces of art or sculpture. Things that belong in a museum. Inscriptions and carvings. Ancient civilizations and their relics. History.

The Caution: Limitations that don't allow for changes. Old and outworn situations. Things that can not, or will not, ever change. Memories frozen in time. Feeling stuck, like no growth is possible. Frigidity of feelings.

What does this **SYMBOL** say to *you?*

IN A HOSPITAL, THE CHILDREN'S WARD IS FILLED WITH TOYS

Commentary: "In a Hospital, the Children's Ward Is Filled with Toys" brings to mind an image of children in varying states of health. They are in need of care, with doctors and nurses going about their business. There's the need for vigilant duty for the physical and emotional needs of "the Children." Some "Children" will be playing with the "Toys," while others may be sleeping or too ill to respond with much energy or enthusiasm.

Oracle: There may be a need for caring shows of affectionate concern, either for yourself or others. Simple things done to promote healing can bring great relief to all concerned. The fact that "the Children's Ward Is Filled with Toys" reflects a generosity of spirit. Service and the gift of healing are given, especially to those who are younger or less able to look after themselves without any expectation of reciprocal giving. The purpose of the "Toys" is to give the "Children" a special treat and is an acknowledgment of their value in society along with the community's concern for their welfare and good health. In times of healing there is a need for simple pleasures and rewards to raise one's spirit. Showing kindness and nurturance to those who are in need can lead to faster healing and allow people to take their place back out in the world again. Listening to the needs of "the Children" is very important, as they can provide clues as to what is really causing problems or happening in their lives. This can picture a situation where many kinds of healing methods can be employed, anything from "Toys" and gadgets all the way up to state-of-the-art, up-to-date technology. However, sometimes a simple smile, a special treat and some soothing words of encouragement are more healing than one can at first imagine.

Keywords: Bringing simple gifts to the sick or disadvantaged. Looking after one's responsibilities. Nurturing people of younger years or those who've had less growth. Workshops held to improve one's health, be it physical, mental, emotional or spiritual. Drugs, crutches, cots, doctors, nurses. Waiting for and needing individual attention. Waiting rooms. Magazines. Toys. Gadgets. Puzzles. Games.

The Caution: Making a large generous show when one doesn't really care. Being dogmatic. Feeling in charge of healing and not listening to what others have to say. Using gadgets instead of simple human caring. Fear of things such as needles, etc. Being greedy and wanting all the toys.

What does this **SYMBOL** say to *you?*

Capricorn 15

A hospital is no place to be sick.
Samuel Goldwyn

Society is a hospital of incurables.
Ralph Waldo Emerson

Do not mistake a child for his symptom.
Erik Erikson

We are so fond of one another because our ailments are the same.
Jonathan Swift

I found in you a holy place apart,
Sublime endurance, God in man revealed
Where mending broken bodies slowly healed
My broken heart.
Vera Brittain

One of the most difficult things to contend with in a hospital is the assumption on the part of the staff that because you have lost your gall bladder you have also lost your mind.
Jean Kerr

In this era of affluence and of permissiveness, we have, in all but cultural areas, bred a nation of overprivileged youngsters, saturated with vitamins, television and plastic toys.
Judith Crist

Capricorn 16

They call it physical education, but it feels like gym to me.
Lisa Simpson

Anatomy is destiny.
Sigmund Freud

The only reason I would take up jogging is so I could hear heavy breathing again.
Erma Bombeck

ACADEME, n. An ancient school where morality and philosophy were taught. ACADEMY, n. [from ACADEME] A modern school where football is taught.
Ambrose Bierce

Champions aren't made in gyms. Champions are made from something they have deep inside them—a desire, a dream, a vision. They have to have the skill, and the will. But the will must be stronger than the skill.
Muhammad Ali

A school without football is in danger of deteriorating into a medieval study hall.
Frank Leahy

Before the child ever gets to school it will have received crucial, almost irrevocable sex education and this will have been taught by the parents, who are not aware of what they are doing.
Mary Steichen Calderone

SCHOOL GROUNDS FILLED WITH BOYS AND GIRLS IN GYMNASIUM SUITS

Commentary: "School Grounds Filled with Boys and Girls in Gymnasium Suits" brings to mind images of youthful people, doing their exercises, playing with and enjoying each other on a physical level. The "Boys and Girls" learn how to interact with each other in the "School Grounds." There is the sense that they are having fun, regardless of their individual level of fitness. Some will be very good at sports and be the stars in the "Gym," while others are there because they want to join in the fun or because they are instructed to be there and have no choice. Many of their relationship lessons are first learned here.

Oracle: This Symbol asks whether you've been neglecting your physical wellbeing of late. Now is a good time to reestablish an affinity with your body and your vitality. Spontaneous enthusiasm and the joy of being truly "alive" and youthful can regenerate and revive and bring about carefree contact with like-minded people. Nourishing the body with good nutrition, being outdoors, enjoying the company of others and the competition of sport can enliven everyone's spirits. Physical exercise is a necessary part of the education of young people's minds and bodies. Giving youth the opportunity to learn how to play sports and the benefits of the concepts of "fair play" among their peers leads to a healthy society. However, discipline may need to be brought into this situation. Children picking on others for things such as not being clever physically, or not having a perfect body, etc., should be discouraged as everyone has their own special talents and needs. With this Symbol, there can be a form of "conscription" where one has to wear a uniform when one may not want to.

Keywords: Developing muscular coordination. Sexual energy, attraction or satisfaction. Playing, marching, competition, rivalry. Singing songs of unity. New anthems for the young. The search for identity. Being able to accomplish things on the physical level. Physical fitness. Uniforms and uniformity. Gymnasiums. Exercise equipment. Conscription. Being one of many. Learning how to get along with the opposite sex. Bodybuilding. Level playing fields.

The Caution: Physical showing off for sexual attention. Relationships based on purely physical or sexual attraction. Having to do things that one isn't capable of physically doing. Not joining in.

What does this **SYMBOL** say to *you?*

A YOUNG WOMAN SURREPTITIOUSLY BATHING IN THE NUDE

Capricorn 17

Commentary: "A Young Woman" is shown. She is "Surreptitiously Bathing in the Nude." Whether she's lying in the sun, or "Bathing" in a pool, she's letting her body soak up the energy of the elements without worrying about the constraints of clothing or the fear of someone seeing her. She may be enjoying the delicious feeling that comes from allowing her body to be caressed by the sun, the wind or the water. Perhaps she's surrendering to the impulse of independence and freedom as she employs the right to enjoy her body without worrying about what others may think or how they will react.

Oracle: You may feel the need to be rid of the restraints that have been imposed by social conditioning and its inhibitions. Although there may be some feelings of being "exposed," really letting go and not worrying about being "seen" can lead to feelings of freedom. This Symbol also speaks about the desire to break the "prudish" rules of society. The restrictions set on us by society are often against enjoying the physical body, and therefore prohibit openness and the resulting fun. The inhibitions that society imposes are often based on expressions of shame and criticism. This Symbol can also bring up issues to do with one's privacy and the desire to enjoy personal freedom and independence. There should be a sense of comfort within yourself, but without the desire to impose on others. It can also show the drive to reveal the real truth about yourself to others. Be wary of really exposing yourself too readily or too much to others, in the things you say or do, as you may do better to keep things more to yourself. What is it that's really being revealed, and what is it that needs to be revealed? Getting the outer layers of the situation off can show core realities that have so far been avoided. Try swimming, or getting out in the sun, as this will help ease up any tensions that are around.

Keywords: Confrontations with one's self. Reconnecting with nature. A desire to "reveal" one's self mentally, physically or emotionally. Issues with weight. The manipulation of the female form in the media. Exhibitionism. Learning to let go of extraneous things. Confronting puritanism. Being at one with the environment. Releasing inhibitions. Stripping. Streaking. Sun lotions.

The Caution: Suppression of natural attitudes. Bondage to social inhibitions. Feeling "indecent" about one's bodily responses. Hiding one's self away or being an exhibitionist. Showing off with no concern for other's feelings. Shocking and surprising behavior.

What does this **SYMBOL** say to *you?*

There is nothing so dangerous for anyone who has something to hide as conversation! A human being, Hastings, cannot resist the opportunity to reveal himself and express his personality which conversation gives him. Every time he will give himself away.
Agatha Christie

How much has to be explored and discarded before reaching the naked flesh of feeling.
Claude Debussy

What spirit is so empty and blind, that it cannot recognize the fact that the foot is more noble than the shoe, and skin more beautiful than the garment with which it is clothed?
Michelangelo Buonarroti

A bare assertion is not necessarily the naked truth.
George D. Prentice

From the American newspapers you'd think America was populated solely by naked women and cinema stars.
Nancy Astor

Clothes make the man. Naked people have little or no influence in society.
Mark Twain

Capricorn 18

Use power to curb power.
Chinese Proverb

I must study politics and war that
my sons may have liberty to study
mathematics and philosophy.
John Adams

Sail on, O Ship of State!
Sail on, O Union, strong and
    great! Humanity with all its
    fears,
With all the hopes of future years,
Is hanging breathless on thy
    fate!
Henry Wadsworth Longfellow

Councils of war never fight.
Proverb

FLAG, n. A colored rag borne
above troops and hoisted on
forts and ships. It appears to
serve the same purpose as
certain signs that one sees
on vacant lots in London—
"Rubbish may be shot here."
Ambrose Bierce

I went to a very militantly
Republican grammar school
and, under its influence,
began to revolt against the
establishment, on the simple
rule of thumb, highly satisfying
to a ten-year-old, that Irish
equals good, English equals bad.
Bernadette Devlin

Britain is not a country that is
easily rocked by revolution ... In
Britain our institutions evolve. We
are a Fabian Society writ large.
William Hamilton

THE UNION JACK FLIES FROM A NEW BRITISH WARSHIP

Commentary: "The Union Jack Flies from a New British Warship" is an image of the need for protection and control. It pictures having to oversee and protect a large "empire" where reliability and leadership are vital to the welfare of the people. Having to make one's presence felt and to guard one's territory can be a tiring responsibility, but there is an awareness of the guidance and protection of "all who went before." Effective supervision needs to be employed to protect what's been won, sometimes at great cost, from others who might want to take it away. Countries, and things such as social and political constructs, all the way down to the individual, need this surveillance and protection from those who might invade, attack or threaten. We invest the "armed forces' with this responsibility, so that we, as individuals in society, may enjoy our secure lives.

Oracle: This Symbol is about the need to defend our ideals, lifestyle or culture from outside influences. It is important to show one's power, but also to continually renew strength. This can be a show put on for others, but also an affirmation of safety for yourself and those who are in your circle of influence or protection. If there is a threat from outside your boundaries, or from within, there needs to be a swift response to snuff it out. However, if anarchy erupts within the ranks, political ploys may be used, such as the concept of "divide and rule"—the political rule that government is more easily maintained if factions are set against each other and not allowed to unite against the ruler. Distrust or disrespect for "authority" can lead to problems with people branded traitors. Having confidence in your ability to hold, maintain and protect your own "turf" will ensure others do as well.

Keywords: Colonialism. Protectionism. The government, big business and the media. Class consciousness. Power and political displays. Displays of "law and order." Border patrols and protection. Strength and might. Nationalism. Royalty. The ruling elite. Supervision. The armed forces. Patrols. Pitting people against each other. Empires. Victory bringing riches. The mother country. The struggle against decline. Flags. Imperialism. The commonwealth. The rule of law.

The Caution: Artificial shows of strength. Bullying from the "big guys." Being armed "to the teeth." Strong-arm tactics. Disrespect for authority. People or institutions that throw their weight around. Anarchy. Traitors. Being antiestablishment. Social disintegration. War games. Civil wars. Feeling squeezed by authority. Rebellion. Civilian lives lost for political causes. Governing forces that deny individual rights. Invasions. Being defensive.

What does this **SYMBOL** say to *you?*

A CHILD OF ABOUT FIVE CARRYING A HUGE SHOPPING BAG FILLED WITH GROCERIES

Capricorn 19

Commentary: "A Child of About Five" is seen. He is "Carrying a Huge Shopping Bag Filled with Groceries." Although the "Child" is only young, he has to act like a grownup, or at the very least like someone much older than his tender years. He probably has to carry many other responsibilities as well. Perhaps his parents aren't able to physically or mentally carry the load themselves. It may be that nobody else wants to. It could be that this young person is mature for his age and feels the need, the necessity or the desire to act above the usual expectations. Further, it could be that his parents want him to grow up with a strong sense of responsibility.

Oracle: You may feel that you have been lumbered with responsibilities beyond the normal dictates of your experience and possibly beyond your safe or comfortable capabilities. Despite being keen and enthusiastic, you should be mindful not to try to do too much, too quickly. There can be a feeling of having so much to carry in life that fears of your physical or mental health can arise. Whatever your situation, there's the need to play, be creative and rest as well. If you can find a balance between having fun and being youthful, and shouldering chores and jobs, you will achieve a lot and not wear yourself out in the process. Being the one who has to do things can crowd the consciousness and drum out your sense of youth and creativity. Having to always spring to attention and do the chores can lead to feelings of being used and "used up" before one's time. If someone in your environment is carrying too much of the load, perhaps you could lend a hand and relieve them.

Keywords: Being the one everyone counts on to do the job. Feeling weighed down. Having to carry the "bag." Lifting heavy weights and bearing the consequences. Taking on things above and beyond what one should. Acting the grownup. Maturing quickly. Looking after paperwork. Running errands. Providing food and sustenance for everyone.

The Caution: Overloading the innocent and the inexperienced without thought of the consequences. Taking on too much. Not allowing for fun and carefree activities. Never being "off duty." Joint, back and shoulder problems. Growing up too fast. Having a serious attitude. Lack of childhood. Dropping the bundle. Carrying the family's responsibilities.

What does this **SYMBOL** say to *you?*

Capricorn 20

Let us be silent that we may hear the whispers of the gods.
Ralph Waldo Emerson

Music expresses that which cannot be said and on which it is impossible to be silent.
Victor Hugo

The hidden harmony is better than the obvious.
Alexander Pope

Of course the music is a great difficulty. You see, if one plays good music, people don't listen, and if one plays bad music people don't talk.
Oscar Wilde

I like the silent church before the service begins, better than any preaching.
Ralph Waldo Emerson

Religion's in the heart, not in the knees.
Douglas William Jerrold

Let us go singing as far as we go: the road will be less tedious.
Virgil

A HIDDEN CHOIR SINGING DURING A RELIGIOUS SERVICE

Commentary: "A Hidden Choir Singing during a Religious Service" pictures the voices, music, celebration and worship of a group of people, the "Choir." They come together to celebrate a sense of unity and community. As they are a "Hidden Choir," they are the often unseen support that helps us to celebrate the spiritual or communal rituals and celebrations. Music raises the spirits, and the sounds of voices can be very uplifting. Songs are sung with or without music. Done well, they can sound almost "heavenly" to the ears, hearts and minds of those who are present to hear, as well as to those who participate.

Oracle: In the celebration of spiritual unity we are never truly isolated, separate or alone. Be receptive to your feminine, intuitive side; there are messages to be heard even though they may not, at first, be apparent. There is a voice, or voices, to be heard in moments of reverence, meditation, worship and giving thanks. The "Hidden Choir" can be "voices" that remind us of our history, our genetic background, even our past lives. Realize that you are not alone, there are other people who feel the same things. Everyone should feel that their voice can be heard. Women were long kept from having a voice in "the Church." Now the voices of women are being heard more and more through orthodox halls. Do you hear the "Choir" and do you want to contribute? It helps if we keep "in tune" with others as this allows us to either enthusiastically join in the chorus or remain a little quieter and reserved without feelings of embarrassment or discomfort. This Symbol can show both the community support for the positive celebration of life and the mindless chatter that goes on about issues to do with ethics, morals, beliefs, ways of life, etc. The faces of the people, the "Hidden Choir," may not necessarily be recognized, but their songs, words, opinions or voices can still be heard.

Keywords: Background messages. Voices not heard or noticed before. Men, women and the church. Sensitivity to spirituality. Speaking behind closed doors. Voices from "nowhere." Melodies from the past. Choirs, organs and organ music. Channeled voices. Songs, sheet music. Hidden speakers. Clairvoyance.

The Caution: Taking undue credit for group qualities. Keeping the feminine out of the picture. Discriminating against people as not being "spiritual" or finding that some just plain aren't! Background voices telling people how they should live. Using hidden messages to manipulate people, sometimes through guilt. Gossip. Messages that don't make sense. Being afraid to sing.

What does this **SYMBOL** say to *you?*

A RELAY RACE

Capricorn 21

Commentary: "A Relay Race" is an image of people working together as a team. They are endeavoring to finish a "Race" and to win a victory, often for some higher cause other than their own personal glory. This can be for their school, nation or ideals. As this is a "Relay Race," they take turns running, and pass the baton to another when the moment is right.

Oracle: You may sense that the end is in sight and the victory achievable, but you'll probably realize that you are only one member of a team, with your own special task to perform. A level of trust is required when you work with a team. It is vital that everyone gives their best and doesn't hold back. If someone endeavors to run the whole race alone, even if they think it's the right thing to do, it can be seen as a form of selfishness where everything is put at risk because of the inability to share or act cooperatively. The aim of each should be for the team to reach the finish line, or the goal, regardless of individual performances. In fact, it may almost be impossible to complete the course on your own. For the best results, people should work together in this situation, each taking their turn and their due rewards. Criticism should be kept to a minimum. As long as each member of the team has tried his or her best it is unwise to compare. You may not be the one who actually crosses the "finish line," but you will, eventually, share in the glory of the group effort. However, if you don't know where the "finish line" is, it can lead to confusion as you just keep running (or going for it), with no end in sight. The interconnectedness of people in a shared endeavor leads to the task being achieved. Just be watchful for when you should both take on and pass the responsibility.

Keywords: Shared endeavor. Knowing when to hand on responsibilities. Teamwork. Knowing when to finish. Encouragement and trust. Sharing and cooperation. Inheritances. Timing. Being competitive. Taking turns. Handing on responsibilities. Split-second timing. Hand-eye coordination. Having an on-off switch.

The Caution: Not giving control to another. Feeling defeated through feeling that you don't have the necessary resources to win. Criticism and competitiveness. Acting only for one's best interests. Competitiveness in interreactions and conversation. Butting in when others are talking. Expecting others to do all the work or carry responsibilities. Not sharing the glory or the rewards.

What does this **SYMBOL** say to *you?*

Sharing is sometimes more demanding than giving.
Mary Catherine Bateson

If you can't win, make the fellow ahead of you break the record.
Anonymous

The few who do are the envy of the many who only watch.
Jim Rohn

Life begins when you get out of the grandstand and into the game.
P. L. Debevoise

Great discoveries and improvements invariably involve the cooperation of many minds.
Alexander Graham Bell

One man alone can be pretty dumb sometimes, but for real bona fide stupidity, there ain't nothing to beat teamwork.
Edward Abbey

Talent wins games, but teamwork and intelligence win championships.
Michael Jordan

Conversation is an art in which man has all mankind for competitors.
Ralph Waldo Emerson

Capricorn 22

*The greatness of a man's power
is the measure of his surrender.*
William Booth

*There are some defeats more
triumphant than victories.*
Michel de Montaigne

*A proud heart can survive a
general failure because such a
failure does not prick its pride.*
Chinese Proverb

*An unjust peace is better than a
just war.*
Cicero

*Failure is nature's plan to prepare
you for great responsibilities.*
Napoleon

*Always imitate the behavior of
winners when you lose.*
Anonymous

*The surrender of life is
nothing to sinking down into
acknowledgment of inferiority.*
John C. Calhoun

*You don't always win your battles,
but it's good to know you fought.*
Marjorie Holmes

*But man is not made for defeat.
A man can be destroyed but not
defeated.*
Ernest Hemingway

*Part of the happiness of life
consists not in fighting battles,
but in avoiding them. A masterly
retreat is in itself a victory.*
Norman Vincent Peale

A GENERAL ACCEPTING DEFEAT GRACEFULLY

Commentary: "A General" is seen "Accepting Defeat Gracefully." He has to acknowledge a "Defeat" of some kind and respond without losing face. Being a "General," this person is obviously often a "winner," respected for being in charge and in command. Now there's the need for acknowledgment of a loss or a "Defeat," or a backing down of some kind.

Oracle: There's an old saying: Winning or losing doesn't matter as much as how you play the game. Through the acceptance of "Defeat," one can often discover important and valuable life lessons. Merely making excuses can lead to the same mistakes being made again and again, when there is no longer any point in pushing matters. At a time of "surrender," it is the way the situation is handled that will be remembered the most. It is how "Gracefully" you handle "Defeat" that will be the measure of your inner worth both to yourself and others. Sometimes it is wise to concede when the "victory" or the "prize" is more valuable for your opponent than yourself. Admitting that one has lost or is prepared to give up can free you up to get on with your life and more rewarding adventures. Learning from "Defeat" can bring strength of character. On a deeper level, "Defeat" shows us that we are neither perfect, nor indestructible. Is the objective, battle or conflict really worth winning or pursuing? Going for revenge, greed or glory can often prove to end up badly as things can turn sour. Sometimes pushing your agenda can hurt your cause and it's better to back off and hold your tongue. Struggling to have your point made or accepted may be self-defeating. This can happen in simple everyday situations such as conversation with others not understanding what you're saying or doing. Realizing that you're not going to change others can lead to being able to "Accept" things in a better light.

Keywords: True inner worth. Being a "good loser." Learning that every minor skirmish in life is not a major "Defeat." Being prepared to start again. Sacrificing things for the benefit of others. Nobility of character. Letting go of the "charge" around anger. Surrendering. Knowing when to let go.

The Caution: Being a "bad loser." Feeling everything is going to come out badly. Reliance on self-limitations. Seeing the negative in everything. Losing what's been worked for. Making excuses to get out of tight situations. Betrayal and loss. Loss of support. Surrendering too early. Giving up on life.

What does this **SYMBOL** say to *you?*

A SOLDIER RECEIVING TWO AWARDS FOR BRAVERY IN COMBAT

Capricorn 23

Commentary: "A Soldier" is seen "Receiving Two Awards for Bravery in Combat." The "Soldier" has been through a struggle or ordeal and has come out in some way victorious. "Awards" are given to the "Soldier" for "Bravery in Combat," with his courage and skill being recognized and rewarded. Indeed, true deeds of service, valor and "Bravery" should be rewarded and acknowledged in some way.

Oracle: We often need to be acknowledged for the issues or causes we've fought for and the battles we've endured, whether we come out on top, or not. In your situation, your efforts may be recognized with some show of appreciation or compensation. It may be that you need to recognize another's achievement, behavior, or "Bravery." Perhaps someone actually made it through by admitting defeat and pulling out when the time was right. If we've been wronged by society in some way, and shown ourselves to be strong and able to stand up to difficult or threatening situations, there may need to be reparations paid, money or rewards of some kind to make up for any trauma, lost opportunities or loss of family or social life. There's a warning though, of the feeling of being desperate to win, regardless of the cost. Sometimes people will fight over who is the most deserving for being battle-scarred and who's the braver or the stronger or there's a struggle over who deserves the "Award"—who put in the most effort, and who has come out the victor in a situation. It can be discouraging and disappointing if we feel we have to go into "Combat" to prove the merit of our deeds, our life or our beliefs. Sometimes we have to cut our losses before we end up plunging into "Combat" once again. Was the outcome worth what went into it? If you can see the "Awards" in a rewarding light, however they manifest, you can turn your life into a victory showing your power, strength and bravery.

Keywords: Desperate striving for recognition. Rewards for involvement in tough situations. Medals and trophies. Tributes, acknowledgments and benefits given or showered. Award ceremonies. Posthumous awards. Giving thanks. Compensation. Insurance and legal claims. Recompense for taking action.

The Caution: "Awards" as Band-Aids to assuage guilt produced in war. Expecting money or other rewards for doing anything that one doesn't want to. The ills, social and otherwise, of combat fighting. Neurotic seeking of praise or acknowledgment. Rejection lines. Bribery.

What does this **SYMBOL** say to *you?*

Try to get all of your posthumous medals in advance.
Anonymous

When I stand before thee at the day's end, thou shalt see my scars and know that I had my wounds and also my healing.
Rabindranath Tagore

Fortune favors the brave.
Virgil

To refuse awards is another way of accepting them with more noise than is normal.
Peter Ustinov

Courage is resistance to fear, mastery of fear—not absence of fear.
Mark Twain

One should use praise to recognize what one is not.
Elias Canetti

Courage—a perfect sensibility of the measure of danger, and a mental willingness to endure it.
William T. Sherman

Don't worry when you are not recognized, but strive to be worthy of recognition.
Abraham Lincoln

Capricorn 24

In confession ... we open our lives to the healing, reconciling, restoring, uplifting grace of Him who loves us in spite of what we are.
Louis Cassels

Sometimes the answer to prayer is not that it changes life, but that it changes you.
Rev. James Dillet Freeman

Every age has a keyhole to which its eye is pasted.
Mary McCarthy

When you're not feeling holy your loneliness tells you you've sinned.
Leonard Cohen

It is not easy to be a nun. It is a life of sacrifice and self-abnegation. It is a life against nature. Poverty, chastity and obedience are extremely difficult. But there are always the graces if you will pray for them.
Kathryn Hulme

I have been studying how I may compare the prison where I live unto the world.
William Shakespeare

The man who has begun to live more seriously within begins to live more simply without.
Ernest Hemingway

A WOMAN ENTERING A CONVENT

Commentary: "A Woman" is seen "Entering a Convent." She needs to spend time contemplating her inner thoughts and values away from the pressures of society. This may be a lonely passage and she may be disenchanted with the hassles, pressures and complications of society. There need to be times of inner work, just as for outer work. Sacrificing one's own needs for a time in order to dedicate one's life to the "big picture" can lead to an understanding of how one fits into the scheme of things.

Oracle: There may be the urge, or the need, to go into a period of silence or self-negation. Gathering in one's thoughts in a quiet place can lead to renewed faith and commitment to spiritual values and therefore better experiences with friends, family and relationships. For now, life may require you to go within and examine issues without the noise, clamor and problems of everyday life. Solitude can be self-affirming and life strengthening. You can learn a lot about yourself by observing how you spend your time. Spiritual practice can lead you to new and heightened states of awareness. Just be careful not to shut yourself away to such an extent that you feel resentful, lonely and unfulfilled. Watch out that you're not suppressing joy and spontaneity. Your physical needs are very important, as are your spiritual and emotional needs. Are you looking after the needs of your body? Are you caring for your physical needs or do you perhaps feel, if you're alone, that you're not worth the effort? Periods of silence and chastity can be good as these can heal, inspire and caress you until it comes time to return back into the fold of the reality of the everyday world again. The question is: How long can you stay secluded from others and relationships? Are you going into the "Convent" or coming out?

Keywords: Spiritual retreat. Sexual retreat. Losing the libido. Withdrawing without thought of the future. Vows. Renouncing things. Going within to find answers. Contact with higher sources. Faith renewed. Giving up things for a greater cause. Losing identity. Taking on new identities. Sacrifice. Opting out. The rejection of marriage. Marriage with God. Longing for love of a higher kind. Maintaining faith. Intense sexual experiences.

The Caution: Self-sacrifice to win sympathy. Neglect of self and hiding away. Nosedives into obscurity. Crisis of faith. Feeling let down by the world. Bad episodes again and again. Feeling devoid of emotion. Escaping war. Losing all and seeking sanctuary. Self denial. Forgetting how to enjoy life.

What does this **SYMBOL** say to *you?*

AN ORIENTAL RUG DEALER IN A STORE FILLED WITH PRECIOUS ORNAMENTAL RUGS

Capricorn 25

Commentary: "An Oriental Rug Dealer in a Store Filled with Precious Ornamental Rugs" is an image of the allure and the beauty of fine things and the appreciation of fine craftsmanship. "Precious Ornamental Rugs" can inspire awe with their beauty and the fine work, dedication and time that went into making them. The "Oriental Rug Dealer" should believe in the true worth and value of the "Precious Ornamental Rugs" he is selling, as these things are socially and culturally very valuable and useful. If he doesn't really believe in what he's doing, others won't respond to his "sales pitch" and his customers will wander off leaving him alone in the shop. His words and actions may be seen as a sham of some kind, like a bogus or shifty "used-car salesman." Honoring one's work or input into society is a necessary part of feeling that one contributes to the social whole.

Oracle: This Symbol shows the beautiful and yet practical products that society produces that protect and cushion us from hard reality and give a sense of safety, warmth and security. Taking pride in the products of our culture and selling useful and beautiful things is a responsible position, and the claims that are made about the products have to be tried and true. Having the knack of buying and selling things is very useful in this situation, but do you believe in what you're buying or selling? Not taking somebody seriously because of what they do as a profession or how they conduct their business can be alienating for all concerned. There may be the feeling of needing to reassess one's real attitudes and ideals. Further, you may feel the need to work with the physical and mental practices of oriental traditions that are available.

Keywords: Refinement of cultural understanding and values. Appreciating excellence of quality. Always looking for a bargain. Buying things at bargain prices and selling them at higher prices. Bartering and trading. Charging a fair price. The sales pitch. Secondhand goods. Marketing. Promotions. Sales. Discounts. Closing the sale. Being able to think on your feet.

The Caution: Bargaining only to personal advantage. Giving undue significance to unworthy goods. The archetypal "used-car salesman." Talking to others merely to gain advantage. Not appreciating the value of one's goods.

What does this **SYMBOL** say to *you?*

What is a man if he is not a thief who openly charges as much as he can for the goods he sells?
Mahatma Gandhi

The buyer has need of a hundred eyes, the seller of but one.
Proverb

Junk is the ideal product ... the ultimate merchandise. No sales talk necessary. The client will crawl through a sewer and beg to buy.
William S. Burroughs

There are very honest people who do not think that they have had a bargain unless they have cheated a merchant.
Anatole France

Advertising may be described as the science of arresting the human intelligence long enough to get money from it.
Stephen Leacock

All virtue is summed up in dealing justly.
Aristotle

Everyone lives by selling something.
Robert Louis Stevenson

Here's the rule for bargains: "Do other men. For they would do you." That's the true business precept.
Charles Dickens

Capricorn 26

SYLPH, n. An immaterial but visible being that inhabited the air when the air was an element and before it was fatally polluted with factory smoke, sewer gas and similar products of civilization.
Ambrose Bierce

*Dance like no one is watching,
Love like you'll never be hurt,
Sing like no one is listening,
Live like it's heaven on earth.*
Anonymous

The universe is full of magical things patiently waiting for our wits to grow sharper.
Eden Phillpotts

Discourse on virtue and they pass by in droves. Whistle and dance the shimmy, and you've got an audience.
Diogenes

Light be the earth upon you, lightly rest.
Euripides

Let your life lightly dance on the edges of Time like dew on the tip of a leaf.
Rabindranath Tagore

One must still have chaos in oneself to give birth to a dancing star.
Friedrich Nietzsche

A NATURE SPIRIT DANCING IN THE MIST OF A WATERFALL

Commentary: "A Nature Spirit" is seen "Dancing in the Mist of a Waterfall." The "Nature Spirit" is a carefree and beautiful image of effervescence and fun. Nymphs are "Nature Spirits" that live in water; they are divine manifestations of nature: of woods, groves, springs, streams, rivers, etc. The "Nature Spirits" dance in the "Mist" because they know to avoid the areas of heavy pressure in the "Waterfall." Even though the strength and power of emotional flow is in the middle of the "Waterfall," it is not possible to survive under such a torrent for very long. It is not always good to assault one's self with the full brunt of pressure from life.

Oracle: This Symbol can represent feelings of emotional lightness and almost mischievous intentions. The deeper parts of feelings are sometimes ignored, or rejected, as the "Spirit" flits over the surface of any troubles. "Nature Spirits" should be carefree and able to express themselves as they want. Go with your feelings and don't worry too much about social restrictions. Finding a comfortable and safe place in a situation or place may be necessary. "Dancing" and going with your gut feelings can lift your spirits to new heights. Be aware, however, that some people may not take your actions seriously. If you feel like "Dancing," there's no need to worry that people might see you. Indeed, it may be a really good idea for people to see your light side, the one that can throw caution to the wind. While this is, essentially, a beautiful Symbol of a "lightness of being," there may be an element of feeling cut off from one's body, or reality. Whatever, your worries or burdens can lift, leaving you feeling lighter and happier. Dance in "the Mist," in the gentle mysteries that arise even in the midst of life's struggles. That is the true way of the "Nature Spirit"; they're not concerned with the inane problems of life.

Keywords: Effervescent spirits or escapism. Dancing in a carefree manner. Water and fun. Peter Pan characters. Mountains, mists, fog. Reveling in nature. Picking up subtle energies. Being healed because of the heightened atmosphere (altitude). Celebrations of the natural world. Waterfalls. Water spraying and dripping. Finding one's habitat. Chinese water torture. Water nymphs, fairies and nature spirits, devas and angels.

The Caution: Irresponsibility, avoidance of real situations. Not taking anything seriously. Flitting off. Being held down and repressed when one is longing for light relief. Feeling abused by pressure. Being subjugated by cold, icy elements, thoughts or emotions. Tricks or perceptions of the light. Fear of dark places.

What does this **SYMBOL** say to *you?*

A MOUNTAIN PILGRIMAGE

Capricorn 27

Commentary: "A Mountain Pilgrimage" shows the human need to strive further, to go places that few people go and to take risks in the hope of reaching a somewhat "exalted" place. Taken literally, a "Mountain Pilgrimage" can be difficult, risky and even downright life-threatening, especially to those who are old, frail, in ill health or simply unfit. However, the "Pilgrimage" can manifest on many levels, from wanting to reach and attain the "highest office" in a company or a country, all the way to desiring and striving for ascension to higher levels of otherworldly or spiritual attainment.

Oracle: In the situation facing you, there may be a need to strive and to learn more on your path to understanding and fulfillment. You may feel the desire to follow those who have gone before you in order to achieve a true sense of inner fulfillment and achievement. The effort that you have to expend is sometimes great, but, then, so can be the rewards. A keen sense of ambition knows few limitations or boundaries and can lead to the top, even though it might be a steep climb. This "Pilgrimage" can signal the need to get back to the purer elements of life and finding one's spiritual grounding. The effort involved in the "Mountain Pilgrimage" can take you away from friends and family, and those things that have been familiar and comforting to you. However, you may be surrounded, sometimes above and sometimes below, by people who share the same hopes and visions. These aren't necessarily the friends and family whom you are used to sharing your life with, but people you meet up with on the journey. Still, this may be a lonely journey, whether you are with others or not. Regardless, keep striving—it may be well worth the time and effort as you work to reach your own "Mountain" top.

Keywords: Ascent in consciousness. Spiritual, material, corporate or political striving. Having an entourage of people (or wanting one). Aloneness and separation. Setting off to somewhere else. Going on a mission. Finding one's spiritual grounding. Getting back to the purer elements of life. Ambitions to get to the top. Wanting the highest office in the land.

The Caution: High moral stands with no depth of feeling. Feeling "high above" others. Feelings of being, or acting like, an ascended being. Haughtiness. Intellectual snobbery. People scrambling for the top. The "tall poppy" syndrome. Ambitions that know no bounds. People ridiculing others for their lesser positions. Spiritual or corporate struggling for position.

What does this **SYMBOL** say to *you?*

Climb mountains to see lowlands.
Chinese Proverb

The man who removes a mountain begins by carrying away small stones.
Anonymous

Mahomet made the people believe that he would call a hill to him … when the hill stood still, he was never a whit abashed, but said, "If the hill will not come to Mahomet, Mahomet will go to the hill."
Francis Bacon

It is the ultimate wisdom of the mountains that a man is never more a man than when he is striving for what is beyond his grasp.
James Ramsey Ullman

Do not seek to follow in the footsteps of the wise. Seek what they sought.
Matsuo Basho

If you wish to know the road up the mountain, ask the man who goes back and forth on it.
Zenrin

First there is a mountain, then there is no mountain, then there is.
Zen Aphorism

Life at the top is financially rewarding, spiritually draining, physically exhausting, and short.
Peter C. Newman

Capricorn 28

You cannot prevent the birds of sorrow from flying over your head, but you can prevent them from building nests in your hair.
Chinese Proverb

In almost everything that touches our everyday life on earth, God is pleased when we're pleased. He wills that we be as free as birds to soar and sing our maker's praise without anxiety.
A. W. Tozer

We are involved in a life that passes understanding and our highest business is our daily life.
John Cage

I know why the caged bird sings, ah me,
When his wing is bruised and his bosom sore,
When he beats his bars and he would be free;
It is not a carol of joy or glee,
But a prayer that he sends from his heart's deep core.
Paul Laurence Dunbar

The heart of a woman falls back with the night,
And enters some alien cage in its plight,
And tries to forget it has dreamed of the stars,
While it breaks, breaks, breaks on the sheltering bars.
Georgia Douglas Johnson

A LARGE AVIARY

Commentary: "A Large Aviary" is shown. As it is "Large," we can assume that there are many birds living in it. During the day, the "Aviary" is a hive of activity, with the birds jumping around and chirping and being generally busy. The birds hardly stop, they jump from one spot to another, while communicating with each other and eating and drinking. The "Aviary" can almost be like a beehive, with lots of noise and high energy. At night, it falls silent with all the birds sitting asleep on their perches.

Oracle: In the situation facing you, there is likely to be a lot of chattering, twittering and flitting around going on. While there is no harm being done, there's probably nothing much really being achieved. Is this because there is a level of mental confusion happening? Perhaps this is because things change constantly, and there's a lot of noise and distraction. Many "voices" can be heard in the "Large Aviary," but it can be hard to discern just one particular voice, that is unless that one voice comes from someone who is much larger or very different from the others. At least there is likely to be a feeling of brotherhood and not being alone in your situation. This Symbol can point to situations with many people; like "birds on perches" everywhere, all speaking at once and having lots to say. Also, although you are able to wander a little, you are actually caged into a particular reality. This Symbol can picture the ways of bureaucracy, government or big business. Sometimes the telephone and the Internet can feel like the "Large Aviary," especially if you never get to talk to a real live person!

Keywords: Clairaudience. Hearing many inner voices. Having a huge entourage or crowd. Tinnitus. Enormous activity. Many people living their individual lives in one space. Blocks of flats and units. Housing estates. Birds, aviaries, bird seed. Perches. People chattering. Girls sharing. Lots to say. Little true content. Confined living spaces. Communicating solely with those in the immediate environment. Living in a world of one's own with no thought of the realities of how other people live. Having to get along with others. Caged birds.

The Caution: Mental confusion bringing a lack of discernment. Too much chatter with not much being achieved. False sense of freedom. Chattering more than doing. Finding it hard to find peace, harmony or privacy. Lonely existences. Abandoned living spaces. Dependence on external sources of nourishment or other provisions.

What does this **SYMBOL** say to *you?*

A WOMAN READING TEA LEAVES

Commentary: "A Woman Reading Tea Leaves" shows someone looking into a cup and being able to see and "Read" signs and meaning in things that most people would never stop to notice or know how to make sense of. The patterns in the cup "speak" to the woman. There's no way of knowing how good she is at interpreting what she sees—she may be a very experienced reader, with a great depth of clairvoyance or intuition, or she may be trying to see how much she can "Read" into the "Tea Leaves" in a simpler, or experimental way.

Oracle: You may be open to the ability, or the need, for seeing meaning through the catalyst of the simplest of everyday events. It seems clear that you will receive messages about your situation if you are open to "seeing" the signs. The Symbol of the "Woman Reading Tea Leaves" shows that such simple things as the "Tea Leaves" in the bottom of your cup are able to give indicators and clues as to what's coming up in the future or in your life right now. One has to put aside skepticism and be able to embrace trust and an intuitive knowing in order to be able to listen to the messages that are all around you. Just be aware that this situation doesn't lead to looking for clues to things everywhere. You can lose the gift of enjoyment and spontaneity if there is no discrimination about where, and how often, you look for guidance and answers. Don't take everything verbatim, as the answers that are given in this situation are often rather symbolic and may need thoughtful interpretation. This may picture a situation where you are able to see these meanings, or it can show that another will perform this for you. Whatever, looking at things from a different perspective can reveal previously hidden information and truths, often in the simple things around you in the everyday world.

Keywords: Symbolism opening pathways to the spiritual center. Seeing the signs. Seeing signatures in small things that others miss. Intuition and clairvoyance. Creative visualization. Tea leaves and coffee grinds. Nonverbal cues. Rituals. Tea and sympathy. Fathoming the depths of simple things. Predicting the future. Seeking guidance and changes of fortune.

The Caution: Reliance on superstition or esoteric advice. Constantly seeking assurance. Taking things literally, not symbolically. Looking for answers or significance everywhere. Small rewards for talents that should be more respected.

Methods for predicting the future: (1) read horoscopes, tea leaves, tarot cards, or crystal balls... collectively known as "nutty methods"; (2) put well-researched facts into sophisticated computer... commonly referred to as "a complete waste of time."
Scott Adams

In tea the host is simplicity and the guest elegance.
Matsudaira Naritada

Tea pot is on, the cups are waiting, favorite chairs anticipating. No matter what I have to do, my friend, there's always time for you. And there is no trouble so great and grave that cannot be much diminished by a nice cup of tea.
Anonymous

Tea is a cup of life.
Great-Grandma Jewel

Where there is tea there is hope.
Sir Arthur Pinero

The art of tea is a spiritual one for us to share.
Alexandra Stoddart

Matrons, who toss the cup and see the grounds of fate in grounds of tea.
Alexander Pope

What does this **SYMBOL** say to *you?*

Capricorn 30

Immense power is acquired by assuring yourself in your secret reveries that you were born to control affairs.
Andrew Carnegie

Problems can become opportunities when the right people come together.
Robert Redford

Determine that the thing can and shall be done, and then we shall find the way.
Abraham Lincoln

Every thing secret degenerates, even the administration of justice; nothing is safe that does not show how it can bear discussion and publicity.
John Dalberg Acton

A meeting is an event where minutes are taken and hours wasted.
Anonymous

CORPORATION, n. An ingenious device for obtaining individual profit without individual responsibility.
Ambrose Bierce

Equal opportunity is good, but special privilege is better.
Anna Chennault

You people are telling me what you think I want to know. I want to know what is actually happening.
Creighton Abrams

DIRECTORS OF A LARGE FIRM MEET IN SECRET CONFERENCE

Commentary: "Directors of a Large Firm" are seen "Meeting in Secret Conference." The "Directors" come together as there are decisions to be made and plans to be discussed and pursued. Wherever those in authority gather, they rule and govern outcomes for themselves and others. A "Large Firm" can manifest in any area of life—on an emotional, spiritual or physical level.

Oracle: There can be a feeling of being out of direct control of the decisions being made by the "Directors of a Large Firm." No matter how much you are on the "inside," you may not be hearing all that is being said. Hence, there's a need to be cautious about what you presume, or imagine, to be really going on. Are you involved in a process without really knowing the bigger picture? You may be excluded because you don't really have enough knowledge of the system, or have the authority, to make an informed decision or to call the shots. However, you, or others, may just be "shut out." Things kept from others can be very painful, especially when the truth comes to light. The belief that someone is spying on others, or talking about them, can lead to a sense of paranoia with suspicion of the motives pervading the atmosphere. Information may be deliberately withheld as a way of maintaining power by secrecy. Call on the appropriate knowledgable friends or authorities; with them you may be able to iron out the details. Some may not want others to know what's going on, or is that just how it looks from the outside? This Symbol can also be about the processing of inner issues and thoughts. Things may feel out of your control and influenced by unknown forces. Be aware of what's happening, although you may feel as though you are being shut out, you can still make an effort to be heard or at least make your presence felt. Strategies may need to be made and carried out in the best way for all involved.

Keywords: Sharing innermost secrets. Confidential information. Masterly control. Big guys calling the shots. Being too busy to see people of "lesser" importance in your life. Rationing time. Governments and secrets. Spies. Privy Councils. Planning and plotting. Having a say in things. Doors. Whispers. Records of meetings. Important meetings. Boards of directors and secretaries. Conspiracies.

The Caution: Excluding some. Exploiting people or situations. Elitism. Being controlled by those above. Decisions made behind closed doors. Dark rooms and huddled people talking. Concealing the truth from others. Cliques and committees. Suspicions of motives.

What does this **SYMBOL** say to *you?*

AN OLD ADOBE MISSION IN CALIFORNIA

Commentary: "An Old Adobe Mission in California" is a symbol of man's ability to take natural materials from the environment to build something lasting and enduring that protects, sustains and nourishes the community on every level. The "Old Adobe Missions" were built in the early days of California in an attempt to bring civilization to this wild area. Although these "Missions" hold a certain romance in history, people have polarized perspectives of their actual significance. There's the traditional colonial version of altruistic Spanish missionaries and soldiers laboring to bring religion and European culture to the native peoples; and then there's the more contemporary version: white intruders subjugating and persecuting the Indians, indoctrinating them with religion, killing them off with strange new diseases and obliterating their culture. Somewhere in the middle, the truth can most likely be found.

Oracle: Sometimes it's easy to assume that one's beliefs are right and that others need to be shown the "real truth" or a better way to live their life. Efforts sometimes need to be turned toward creating the infrastructure to pursue our beliefs and way of life and this can enrich everyone's lives. There is a need for the provision of faith, love and shelter to those who require it. However, the effort may be too big for some and may leave them feeling "homesick," "homeless" or without a cause. It may be a case of someone trying to change or dominate the core beliefs of someone else, causing emotional restriction and pain. The truth to be remembered is that contributing to other's lives and caring about people in a community is not about control, but acceptance of, and reverence for, each person's divinity. There's no need for strict conformity, manipulation or pretension here.

Keywords: Spiritual retreats in natural surroundings. Finding new areas to work with spirit. Creating civilization out of natural elements. Hard work to create places of sanctuary and learning. Places once revered now tourist attractions. Forging links to new worlds. Missions and missionaries. Bringing faith to the "new world." Brotherhoods. Places that house and protect.

The Caution: Dogmatism. Pushing beliefs and ideas on others. Believing one's spiritual and religious beliefs contain all the answers. Taking over others' lives. Moving in and taking control. Monuments to the past sagging and fading. People moving in on others. Cults. Indoctrination.

What does this **SYMBOL** say to *you?*

Aquarius 1

A pile of rocks ceases to be a rock when somebody contemplates it with the idea of a cathedral in mind.
Antoine de Saint-Exupéry

If a man cannot be a Christian in the place where he is, he cannot be a Christian anywhere.
Henry Ward Beecher

When the missionaries came to Africa they had the Bible and we had the land. They said, "Let us pray." We closed our eyes. When we opened them we had the Bible and they had the land.
Desmond Tutu

The belief that there is only one truth and that oneself is in possession of it seems to me the deepest root of all evil that is in the world.
Max Born

It is easier to pull down than to build up.
Proverb

In the beginning was the word and it was misunderstood.
Native American Saying

Claim the vicinity in the name of divinity.
Steve Tripp

Aquarius 2

*The cosmos comes forth from
The Eternal, and moves In Him.
With His power it reverberates,
like thunder crashing in the sky.
Those who realize Him pass
beyond the sway of death.*
Upanishads

*Lightning is the shorthand of a
storm, and tells of chaos.*
Eric Mackay

*Clouds that thunder do not
always rain.*
Armenian Proverb

*Truly nothing is to be expected
but the unexpected.*
Alice James

*Times of general calamity and
confusion create great minds.
The purest ore is produced
from the hottest furnace, and
the brightest thunderbolt is
elicited from the darkest storms.*
Charles Caleb Colton

*Quiet minds cannot be
perplexed or frightened but go
on in fortune or misfortune at
their own private pace, like a
clock during a thunderstorm.*
Robert Louis Stevenson

*It is the flash which appears, the
thunderbolt will follow.*
Voltaire

AN UNEXPECTED THUNDERSTORM

Commentary: "An Unexpected Thunderstorm" symbolizes something coming out of the blue. It may be sudden, confronting, overwhelming and somewhat frightening. "Thunderstorms," especially those that are "Unexpected," are awesome powerhouses of energy that can unleash incredible levels of tension and release. However, "Thunderstorms" often clear the air after an extreme buildup of energy, and can leave us with a sense of awe and wonder at the extreme power, majesty and beauty of natural events. Flashes of clarity often come like bolts of lightning that shoot through one's mind, spirit and body. When the air clears, there can be a purging or clearing up of issues through incredible states of illumination.

Oracle: You may find that you are suddenly tested or taken by surprise, or that something shattering arises. This can overtake and overawe your sense of stability, and can happen when you least expect it. Perhaps you saw signs of something big coming, but didn't quite know what to expect, or what was going to be unleashed. Your inner strength and stability is likely to be put to the test however you can learn a lot from the experience, especially if you strive to stay at the center of the "Storm" and not get swept up and away by it. In fact, the effect can be quite liberating, after the initial shock. The best course of action to take is to not panic, but to see your true place in the scheme of things and help others cope with what's going on. You may need to let go of control in this situation, as trying to be in charge of what's happening may well be impossible. Endeavor to be a conduit for the unleashed energy in some way; let the energy run through you and into the ground. Stay with the feeling of grounding the energy as much as possible. When the "Storm" passes, assess what you can fix up.

Keywords: Sudden visitations of natural wonder. Something that drops on you, seemingly from out of nowhere. Things erupting and happening fast. Tempests in a teacup. Shocks and confrontations with raw energy. Thunder, lightning and electricity. The Tower card of the tarot. Being a lightning rod. Water and rain that quenches and revives. Things being unleashed.

The Caution: Losing control without warning. Emotional instability. A "backdraft" of emotions. Bottling up and blowing up. Confused by sudden outbursts. Loud bangs and crashes that shock and stun. Seizing up with fear. Sudden unleashing of emotions. Hurricanes of messy energy.

What does this **SYMBOL** say to *you?*

A DESERTER FROM THE NAVY STANDS SUDDENLY AWARE OF A DAWNING TRUTH: FREEDOM IS NEVER THE RESULT OF COMPROMISE

Aquarius 3

Commentary: "A Deserter from the Navy Stands Suddenly Aware of a Dawning Truth: Freedom is Never the Result of Compromise" shows someone who's come to the conclusion that staying in a situation that stretches, tests or "Compromises" his needs, desires and values in some way is not worth the energy that has to go into it. As with being in the "Navy," perhaps he had signed up for something for the long haul. He was expected to fulfill some employment, destiny, mission or perhaps stay committed to a relationship. Now there's been a realization that the mold cast for him just doesn't work. It doesn't satisfy his inner desires and longings. He may have been able to adjust to the situation for a while, but the time has come when he has to leave, bail out or jump ship.

Oracle: A decision to opt out may be based on moral or ethical grounds, where someone doesn't want to perform some duty or act because it is against their principles or in order to maintain a sense of free spirit, mobility or independence. You may find that the rigorous restraints and rules of the situation are no longer comfortable, bearable or tolerable. This can be about you, or it can be about someone (or something) else. Being "signed up" to some commitment can be restricting, limiting and sometimes confronting. There can be a feeling of being taken away from loved ones, home and family for a reason you don't really understand and of not wanting to accept the pressures of separation. However, it could be the exact opposite—home and family life can be too constricting and there may be a desire to leave to pursue another, more independent life. However, there are always consequences for opting out, running away or not playing the game. Are you prepared for them? Is there a "Sudden" realization, "a Dawning Truth" that what you've been doing is not necessarily what you want to be doing?

Keywords: Rebellion. Leaving, although allegiance had been pledged. Opting out because of pressure, harassment or bullying. Taking risks to get out of a dangerous/destructive/alienating situation. Being left behind by someone who's "jumped ship." Going AWOL. Standing by personal truths. Refusing compromise.

The Caution: Not playing by the rules of socially structured games. Self-ruin. Refusal to face social consequences. Not turning up. Withdrawing support in a physical, emotional or spiritual way. Blowing security. Rats deserting the sinking ship.

What does this **SYMBOL** say to *you?*

I had examined myself pretty thoroughly and discovered that I was unfit for military service.
Joseph Heller, Catch 22

A man must consider what rich realm he abdicates when he becomes a conformist.
Ralph Waldo Emerson

His secret realization of his physical cowardice led him to underrate his exceptional moral courage.
Vera Brittain

COWARD, n. One who, in a perilous emergency, thinks with his legs.
Ambrose Bierce

I was court martialed in my absence, and sentenced to death in my absence, so I said they could shoot me in my absence.
Brendan F. Behan

There are two freedoms—the false, where a man is free to do what he likes; and the true, where he is free to do what he ought.
Charles Kingsley

The brave man inattentive to his duty is worth little more to his country than the coward who deserts in the hour of danger.
Andrew Jackson

Aquarius 4

The doctor is to be feared more than the disease.
Latin Proverb

Just because your doctor has a name for your condition doesn't mean he knows what it is.
Anonymous

Physician heal thyself.
The Bible

You already have the precious mixture that will make you well. Use it.
Rumi

Prayer, like radium, is a luminous and self-generating form of energy.
Alexis Carrel

It requires a great deal of faith for a man to be cured by his own placebos.
John L. McClenahan

Natural forces within us are the true healers of disease.
Hippocrates

Medicine can only cure curable diseases, and then not always.
Chinese Proverb

It takes a wise doctor to know when not to prescribe.
Baltasar Gracian

Nature is better than a middling doctor.
Chinese Proverb

A HINDU HEALER GLOWS WITH A MYSTIC HEALING POWER

Commentary: "A Hindu Healer" is someone capable of natural, alternative and sometimes miraculous "Healing." He "Glows" with "a Mystic Healing Power" and inspires others to greater heights of "Healing," understanding and "Power" within themselves. A "Hindu Healer" channels the energy of God to manifest the "Healing" process. There may be a need to heal wounds, illness, trauma or some other affected part of the body or mind. There is often the sense of having to sacrifice for another. It can feel as though the "Healer" has a cleansed and enlightened soul together with a sense of purity.

Oracle: This pictures being "Healed" by someone who has undertaken the rituals of learning, self-sacrifice and self-knowledge. The "Hindu Healer" can pass on the benefits of this knowledge to the unwell through "Healing" and purification. You may not be having much success in solving problems logically and rationally at the moment. The message is to look to your spiritual center for genuine, lasting solutions. This requires focus, practice and determination. You can heal yourself or others in some way by using traditional spiritual methods. It could be that someone can offer these methods to you, and this person could have a special aura about them. Natural "Healing" methods of any kind are likely to work well in this situation as this "Hindu Healer Glows with a Mystic Healing Power." "Healers" of any type are likely to enter your life at this time. Indeed, your own healing ability may be revealed to you. This is true especially if you concentrate your energies on the issue that needs solving. There may be a need to leave the pressures of modern society for spaces that are much calmer, more spiritual or self-focused. Take some time and effort to tune in as the "Healing" experience is occurring. Indeed, a "Mystic Healing" experience could descend over you and change your life forever.

Keywords: Divine healing potency. Natural healing methods. Going on faith. Humility in the face of greatness. Yogis and fakirs. Finding one's center. Healers of all kinds. Glowing health. Radiating love, spirit and calm. Tapping vast reservoirs of healing forces. Reverence for simple methods. Auras that radiate. Urine therapy. Pranic energy. Reiki healing

The Caution: False claims of powers. Charlatans. Claims of healing that are just manipulation. Snake-oil salesmen. Tricks with smoke and mirrors. What to trust, what to believe? Orthodox healing methods failing to cure. Feeling invincible.

What does this **SYMBOL** say to *you?*

A COUNCIL OF ANCESTORS HAS BEEN CALLED TO GUIDE A MAN

Aquarius 5

Commentary: "A Council of Ancestors Has Been Called to Guide a Man" implies faith, trust and hope in the wisdom and understanding of those who have gone before. The wisdom of the "Council of Ancestors" is often invoked in tribal spiritual practice. With this Symbol, whenever there is a need for guidance, wisdom or knowledge, whether it is in the present or from the spirit world, the energy of the elders can "Guide" us. This "Guidance" often comes from the "Ancestors" who have passed on, but can also originate from the knowledgable ones who are still among us.

Oracle: This Symbol reflects the energy and influence that is always available to us through spiritual practice, meditation and the willingness to seek help. You will find you are strengthened by the wisdom of precedent; that which has gone before. There is so much understanding available through the experienced elders and this is what needs to be tapped, experienced, followed and honored in some way. The "Council of Ancestors" holds a storehouse of knowledge and experience and this image suggests that they are being called on to lead and "Guide" you. An issue out of the past may need to be brought to the present day and this can secure much-needed guidance and protection. Those who are older and probably wiser in some measure have something valuable to teach us and the time is probably right for this to come through now. However, sometimes things from the past really belong in the past. What the truth of the matter really is needs to be assessed by those involved. Whatever, getting the "authorities" on your side will help you achieve what you want. Listening and learning from those above will lead, one day, to you being able to take charge in your own good time. Sooner or later, you may find yourself invited to join this "Council," taking your own place of authority.

Keywords: Inner knowledge. Instruction. Direct roots to deep sources of energy. Karmic connections with the past. The place one comes from. Ancient wisdom vs. "old fogies." Parents and grandparents. Families and family lineage. Proving bloodlines. Committees, boards and councils. Memories of those who've gone before. The Akashic records.

The Caution: Reliance on conservatism. Obsolete boards of authority. Not being able to move with the times. Needing the nod of approval from others to validate what one's doing. Not being free to do what one wants. Having to please the elders in some way. Bound by family or past-life karma. Nagging negativity. Old-fashioned views that limit expansion.

What does this **SYMBOL** say to *you?*

We do not inherit the land from our ancestors; we borrow it from our children.
Native American Proverb

It is indeed a desirable thing to be well descended, but the glory belongs to our ancestors.
Plutarch

Others have done it before me. I can, too.
Corporal John Faunce

Behind every able man, there are always other able men.
Chinese Proverb

I write to keep in contact with our ancestors and to spread truth to people.
Sonia Sanchez

One cool judgment is worth a thousand hasty councils. The thing is to supply light and not heat.
Woodrow Wilson

Humans are not proud of their ancestors, and rarely invite them round to dinner.
Douglas Adams

Some families can trace their ancestors back three hundred years, but can't tell you where their children were last night.
Anonymous

Aquarius 6

My life has a superb cast but I can't figure out the plot.
Ashleigh Brilliant

My life has a brilliant plot but I can't figure out the cast.
Lynda Hill

All the world's a stage,
And all the men and women merely players:
They have their exits and their entrances;
And one man in his time plays many parts.
William Shakespeare

Life is not a dress rehearsal.
Sheri Rose Shepard

We wear the mask that grins and lies,
It hides our cheeks and shades our eyes,
This debt we pay to human guile …
But let the world dream otherwise,
We wear the mask!
Paul Laurence Dunbar

Real life seems to have no plots.
Ivy Compton Burnett

We are not human beings having a spiritual experience, we are spiritual beings having a human experience.
Pierre Teilhard de Chardin

I liked myself better when I wasn't me.
Carol Burnett

A MASKED FIGURE PERFORMS RITUALISTIC ACTS IN A MYSTERY PLAY

Commentary: "A Masked Figure Performs Ritualistic Acts in a Mystery Play" shows someone playing a role in some kind of "Act" or drama. This can be for the sake of "Ritual," or it can convey a story or message to those observing. Church men on church premises performed the original "Mystery Plays" in Latin. They depicted such subjects as the Creation, Adam and Eve, the murder of Abel, and the Last Judgment. As time went on, the "Plays" left the Church and took to the cities and the once strictly religious themes changed into less reverent themes. Nowadays, "Mystery Plays" are rather different.

Oracle: In the situation facing you it seems there are "Mysteries" in the themes that are being played out, perhaps to the point where it's not clear exactly what's going on and who, or what, the actors, the "Masked Figures" truly are. However, it may be that the audience, and this can be you or someone else, is not really supposed to know the ins and outs of what's really going on. It can feel that everything and everyone is not quite how they seem. Issues of faith and trust may come up. There could be the sense that you are not being shown the true face of the situation. Look to see who the performers are in this "Mystery." Are you part of the "Play" or are you in the audience? Sometimes people have a need or desire to be cautious in what they reveal of themselves to others. Does someone in this situation find it necessary to put on an "Act" in order to cover up their real intentions, emotions or reactions? It's quite likely that false motives will eventually be uncovered, so be wary of what actions are taken, and be cautious with what's said. There may be a desire to perform some kind of "Ritual" or "Act," even if you're not sure what you're doing or where it will lead you. This can picture someone living out his or her life in a type of "Mystery" or charade and not really knowing what turn life is going to take next. There may be concerns about how one truly fits into the story that's being played out.

Keywords: Rituals. Shamanism. Archetypes of personality. Putting on a show. Portrayals of performances that don't always add up. The unmasking of someone. Comedy. Banditry. Mystery. Drama. Acting. Rituals. Executioners' masks. Smoke screens. Doing the technical but not the emotional. Saying or doing things because they "should." Having alternate personalities.

The Caution: Neurotic performances. Putting on superficial acts. Carrying out "rituals" without being aware of why. Sticking to tradition. Unwilling to admit to changing times. Not knowing who the players are or what the plot is. Being unsure of direction. Lying. Coverups. Deceptions. Tricks. Ploys to manipulate.

What does this **SYMBOL** say to *you?*

A CHILD BORN OUT OF AN EGGSHELL

Commentary: "A Child Born out of an Eggshell" shows something being "Born" in a way that was probably never expected; it is "Born out of an Eggshell." Alchemists saw the "Egg" as the container for both matter and thought. This led to the concept of the Cosmic Egg or World Egg, a cosmic symbol in many traditions. The vault of space came to be seen as an "Egg," and this "Egg" consisted of seven layers, each enfolding the other, showing the seven heavens or spheres. The Chinese believed that the first man sprung from an "Egg." This image is around us in many ways, from in-vitro fertilization to human cloning.

Oracle: This Symbol signifies innovative ways of doing things, with new directions and new solutions. You need to find a unique approach that will give you the ability to follow unusual and original paths leading to a new emergence. There's the possibility of unleashing rebellious energy, so make sure that this beginning doesn't start off with any precocious or "spoiled" attitudes. It is important to provide nourishing environments in order to grow and learn, and nourishment must be provided to last through the course of the development. There can be an uneasy or unsure feeling about the viability of your situation. Many ideas or projects die because they don't have enough initial capital or support or dedication to last the distance. It may be something out of the ordinary or slightly odd. Don't let this scare you; try to recognize the potential rewards and see what you can learn from them. This Symbol can also show prejudice or fear of things that are different. There may be the need to be more consciously tolerant toward people or situations no matter their origins or backgrounds. This can also represent the gestation of an idea, process or project that's outside your direct influence.

Keywords: Transmutation. The birth of a new creative original impulse. Incubated ideas coming to fruition. Genetic engineering. In-vitro fertilization. People beyond their time. Mutations. Seeking the unusual. The unexpected birth. The desire to have children. The nurturing egg. Emerging in a unique way. The matrix and the casket. The struggle to break free. Genetic engineering. Indigo children. Children who seem unrelated to their parents. Adoption.

The Caution: Being different only to follow fashion. Afraid of new ideas. Lack of support. Spoiled and naïve attitudes. Rebellion. Uneasiness. Prejudice and racial stereotypes. Refusing to believe even what the eyes can see.

What does this **SYMBOL** say to *you?*

Aquarius 7

In the beginning, all the universe was non-being. It became being. It grew and formed an egg, which remained unbroken for a year. Then it broke open. Of the two halves of the shell, one was of silver and the other of gold.
Upanishads

First there was the Great Cosmic Egg. Inside the egg was chaos. Floating in the chaos was P'an Ku, the undeveloped divine embryo.
Huai-nan Tzu

The creator, Awonawilona, thought himself into being.
Zuni Indian Saying

"Ex ovo omnia." Everything from an egg.
William Harvey

Man's main task in life is to give birth to himself, to become what he potentially is.
Erich Fromm

We are all cells in the same body of humanity.
Peace Pilgrim

The shell must break before the bird can fly.
Lord Alfred Tennyson

Do not compute the totality of your poultry population until all the manifestations of incubation have been entirely completed.
William Jennings Bryan

Aquarius 8

In order to be irreplaceable one must always be different.
Coco Chanel

One should either be a work of art, or wear a work of art.
Oscar Wilde

Fashion is a potency in art, making it hard to judge between the temporary and the lasting.
E. C. Stedman

Nothing's beautiful from every point of view.
Horace

Clothes make the man.
Latin Proverb

It is an interesting question how far men would retain their relative rank if they were divested of their clothes.
Henry David Thoreau

Clothes make the man. Naked people have little or no influence in society.
Mark Twain

You may turn into an archangel, a fool, or a criminal; no one will see it. But when a button is missing, everyone sees that.
Erich M. Remarque

BEAUTIFULLY GOWNED WAX FIGURES ON DISPLAY

Commentary: "Beautifully Gowned Wax Figures on Display" pictures a situation of the enjoyment, even the glorifying, of physical beauty, shape and form. When we see "Beautifully Gowned Wax Figures" it can be rather startling; we may get caught for a moment, thinking they are real flesh and blood. These "Wax Figures" can be like "mannequins" in a store window or they can be people who fuss and care about how they look more than care how they relate as real human beings.

Oracle: It is not enough to just look and play a part; we must know and live that part as well. Although there may be the desire to present one's self in a beautiful and manicured way, it is also necessary to know how to "walk your talk." Being well rehearsed and fully aware of fulfilling one's role can lead to people being pleased and impressed with this "Display." This Symbol can also show elements of a situation that are too superficial, driven externally by society or events, or have only been allowed to have a shallow influence. Something, or someone, may look good on the outside for some time, but what's truly going on inside? Are issues of "Beauty" involved here? Or "heartlessness"? There's often the choice of hiding one's internal feelings in a display of elegance, beauty or fashion, however, being stiff, uncaring and robotic can lead to people being alienated or disillusioned. External appearances need the heart's warmth to give life; is warmth missing in this situation? If there's plenty of substance involved, the display of "Beauty" will bring nothing but good.

Keywords: Setting standards. Exemplars of social ritual. Superficial values on display. Superficial beauty or avatars of fashion? Not showing true feelings. Beauty salons, modeling. Judging a book by its cover. No substance. Pretty on the outside. Positions of power and privilege that seem unreal. Models. Beauty and its allure. Store dummies. Money spent on appearances. Always having to look good. The need for real flesh-and-blood responses.

The Caution: Putting on a false front. Expecting to be noticed. Acting "wooden" about something. Not contributing anything of real value. Beauty that has no "voice." Lack of depth and integrity. Fake responses. Acting only for social acceptance. Bloodless realities. Lifeless figures. Obsession with beauty and fashion. Judging others without regard for their humanity. Emotionless realities. Being a "handbag" wife or husband.

What does this **SYMBOL** say to *you?*

A FLAG IS SEEN TURNING INTO AN EAGLE

Aquarius 9

Commentary: A "Flag Turning into an Eagle" represents nationalistic ideals and values being taken to their highest level. The "Flag" and the "Eagle" are both symbolic representations of these strong ideals. The "Flag" is a pictorial representation of a nation or a country's spirit, and the "Eagle" is the physical manifestation of that spirit. As the "Flag" turns into the "Eagle," the feeling of spirit is transformed into a physical expression of that ideal; they are made physical and become more realistic.

Oracle: This Symbol reflects the need or desire for our inner thoughts to become manifest into daily life practice. Your core beliefs can be seen as your "Flag" and your announcements of and allegiance to them is like the "Eagle." You may find that you are being asked to no longer just project an image, but to own your own true power. In more dramatic situations, one may feel like they have been reborn, or suddenly become more motivated or inspired to carry through actions that they have previously only thought about. However, not everybody will agree with or believe in the ideals behind one's actions and words. Someone may be "blowing their horn" about issues that others might not want to salute. Be aware that although you may have experienced a personal transformation, not everyone will be keen to hear about it in great detail. Others may be thrilled at your successes and want to hear all about them. On the other hand, you may be doing a lot more talking than action, but that will most likely change soon. Be sure to retain your modesty and gauge others' reactions accordingly. With a positive focus you can watch your ideas take flight.

Keywords: Turning away from having to prove one's self. Rising above the commonplace. Ascension. Rebirth. Homespun truth. Ideals that uplift and free. Shouting joy from the treetops. Boosts in self-esteem. Strength. Transformation. Plans taking shape. Power and might. Conveying images of strength and fidelity. Declaring visions and dreams. Totems. Strong displays of independence and freedom. Announcements. High flight.

The Caution: Forcefully displaying private beliefs. Swallowing advertising or propaganda. Believing the party line. Blowing your own horn. Bragging. Sudden mood swings. Arrogance. Throwing one's weight around. Threatening others with loud displays of might. Bullying. Talking over the top of others. Not listening because of righteousness.

What does this **SYMBOL** say to *you?*

It is not good enough for things to be planned, they still have to be done; for the intention to become a reality, energy has to be launched into operation.
Pir Vilayat Khan

Let us raise a standard to which the wise and honest can repair; the rest is in the hands of God.
George Washington

Aim for the highest.
Andrew Carnegie

*If I have freedom in my love,
And in my soul am free,
Angels alone that soar above,
Enjoy such liberty.*
Richard Lovelace

The chasm between the principles upon which this government was founded, in which it still professes to believe, and those which are daily practiced under the protection of the flag, yawn wide and deep.
Mary Church Terrell

This is an important announcement. This is flight 121 to Los Angeles. If your travel plans today do not include Los Angeles, now would be a perfect time to disembark.
Douglas Adams

Aquarius 10

Every great work, every big accomplishment, has been brought into manifestation through holding to the vision, and often just before the big achievement, comes apparent failure and discouragement.
Florence Scovel Shinn

Better be ill spoken of by one before all than by all before one.
Scottish Proverb

A free society is a place where it's safe to be unpopular.
Adlai Stevenson

Those whom the gods would destroy they first call "promising."
Cyril Connolly

Glory is fleeting, but obscurity is forever.
Napoleon Bonaparte

Shun praise. Praise leads to self-delusion. Thy body is not Self, thy SELF is in itself without a body, and either praise or blame affects it not.
H.P. Blavatsky

Do not trust the cheering, for those persons would shout as much if you or I were going to be hanged.
Oliver Cromwell

Everything is an illusion, including this notion.
Stanislaw J. Lec

A MAN WHO HAD FOR A TIME BECOME THE EMBODIMENT OF AN IDEAL IS MADE TO REALIZE THAT AS A PERSON HE IS NOT THIS IDEAL

Commentary: "A Man Who Had for a Time Become the Embodiment of an Ideal is Made to Realize That as a Person He Is Not This Ideal" shows the dawning of the understanding that one cannot always live up to one's own expectations, let alone the expectations of others. The "Person" involved in this issue may have been put on a pedestal, looked up to in some way and thought very highly of. On the other hand, he may have been putting on a false show to get some kind of response from others. Now there's been a "Realization"—something has happened and there's an adjustment of beliefs, feelings, responses and expectations.

Oracle: You may be looking at yourself, or someone else, and discovering that things are not as "Ideal" as you perhaps thought. The important thing to "Realize," or remember, is that true depth of character and self-worth does not always equate with having the popular support of others. Also, we often project what we want to see onto both ourselves and others and this may not have much to do with the actual core of the real person. Having said that, there can be immense disappointment and disillusionment when someone doesn't live up to their promises or responsibilities. It's important not to get disheartened by the "Realization" that someone isn't as perfect as was once thought; instead, consider ways to restore faith. Staying true to one's own "Ideals" is the aim here. On a personal level, there can be periods of feeling worthless, unloved and falling into depression with feelings of failure and despair. However, there are often wonderful opportunities for "self-disclosure" here. Read the signs and learn more about yourself as well as others. This Symbol can also show opportunities that are merely fleeting, like being idolized or famous for "fifteen minutes" and then falling from grace.

Keywords: Staying true to one's self. Ideas that look great for a time, but lose their gloss. Lost opportunities. Waking up just in time. Depression. Self-esteem issues. Projections of personality. Not clearly seeing people. Realizing that people have changed. False expectations. Falling off the pedestal. Finding one's core identity.

The Caution: Clinging to false feelings of fame. Not accepting that things have moved on or changed. Disillusionment and disappointment. Losing one's faith. Religious questions and doubts. Aiming too high. Reversals of fortune. Idols and idolizing. Self pity. Giving up. Being slammed by others.

What does this **SYMBOL** say to *you?*

DURING A SILENT HOUR, A MAN RECEIVES A NEW INSPIRATION WHICH MAY CHANGE HIS LIFE

Aquarius 11

Commentary: "During a Silent Hour, a Man Receives a New Inspiration" shows someone taking some time out to contemplate, meditate, or just be by themselves. He "Receives a New Inspiration": he has a thought, an idea or an "Inspiration" that is the answer to a dilemma or provides clues of how to proceed with something. This "New Inspiration May Change His Life"—he's had some deep understanding and it is likely to turn his life around.

Oracle: This Symbol shows the benefits of "getting away from it all" in order to reassess your life and goals. This "Silent Hour" could be a short minute, a few hours, or a period of days, etc. What the Symbol shows is that a "New Inspiration" will be "Received." You may have found that despite racking your brain there's been no rational guidance available. It's important to realize that a lot of internal as well as external noise needs to be quieted. The rational mind can be noisy and tends to interfere with the flow of the imagination or intuition. You need to slow down and open up to the messages of your inner "Inspiration." By reducing the external noise, clutter and distraction, your mind can focus on what is essential, rather than what may just be convenient. This Symbol shows that there is an answer coming, which will probably change many things, or at least change what most needs to be changed. This can also imply the need for a shift of some kind, and this may have been forgotten, or neglected, because of preoccupations with social matters, or being too busy. Listen for clues: it may not be external voices that bring this "New Inspiration" but the voices within. If there is difficulty blocking out the hustle and bustle of everyday life, meditation or delving into your dreams or fantasies may lead to the solution.

Keywords: Welling creative power. Inspiration = breathing in the spirit. Coming to terms with one's reality. Visionary people and events. Being reborn. Spiritual awakenings. Meditation and reflective thought. Intuitive awareness rising up into conscious awareness. Spending time alone, thinking. Contemplation. Reversals. Flashes of insight.

The Caution: Exclusion of others. Obsession with one's objectives. Being a hermit. Hearing voices. Feeling trapped. Shooting off in all directions. Dropping things without resolution. Cutting off from life. Constantly changing directions. Regretting the past. Not moving on.

What does this **SYMBOL** say to *you?*

It is in your moments of decision that your destiny is shaped.
Anthony Robbins

They are never alone who are accompanied by noble thoughts.
Philip Sidney

Silence at the proper season is wisdom, and better than any speech.
Plutarch

Those who dream by day are cognizant of many things which escape those who dream only by night.
Edgar Allen Poe

Imagination is the outreaching of mind ... the bombardment of the conscious mind with ideas, impulses, images and every sort of psychic phenomena welling up from the preconscious. It is the capacity to "dream dreams and see visions ..."
Rollo May

God is the friend of silence. See how nature—trees, flowers, grass—grows in silence; see the stars, the moon and the sun, how they move in silence ... We need silence to be able to touch souls.
Mother Teresa

The universe is full of magical things patiently waiting for our wits to grow sharper.
Eden Phillpots

Aquarius 12

Stairs are climbed step by step.
Kurdish Proverb

You cannot push anyone up the ladder unless he is willing to climb himself.
Andrew Carnegie

Never look down on anybody unless you're helping him up.
Rev. Jesse Jackson

Don't bother just to be better than your contemporaries or predecessors. Try to be better than yourself.
William Faulkner

The rung of a ladder was never meant to rest upon, but only to hold a man's foot long enough to enable him to put the other somewhat higher.
Thomas Henry Huxley

The higher one climbs on the spiritual ladder, the more they will grant others their own freedom, and give less interference to another's state of consciousness.
Paul Twitchell

Always be nice to people on the way up; because you'll meet the same people on the way down.
Wilson Mizner

PEOPLE ON A VAST STAIRCASE, GRADUATED UPWARD

Commentary: "People on a Vast Staircase, Graduated Upward" is a Symbol of people operating or standing at different levels. As they are "Graduated Upward" some are higher up while some are lower down the ladder, or "Staircase." The "People" pictured here may be looking up at those above, peering down at those below, or just observing their place in the scheme of things. The "Staircase" in the movie *Titanic* is a good example of how this Symbol can operate, with those with wealth and power going off in one direction and those in a lesser position going in another.

Oracle: You may be seeking to find your place in the scheme of things. Striving for the top is wonderful, and achieving your own successes is admirable, and the climb up will probably bring the rewards you need. Be careful not to concern yourself with thoughts of "who's in front" or "who's behind." It's probably of no real consequence. Concentrating on your own position and where you want to go will bring happiness and success. No matter what your status, and regardless of what others are doing, be patient and trust that you and yours are heading in the right direction. This Symbol doesn't always involve outright competition, although it can. It can show the consequence of the layers of the class system, which can be rewarding to some, but alienating to others. Be careful of the "rungs" you are climbing, one that isn't secure can have you in a risky or compromising situation. Being at the bottom, or even at the top can lead to problems. It's not useful to consider your present position unimportant. Being expendable is not a good thing. Accept your position as it is now and work toward and look forward to a promotion to both your place and the wisdom that is yet to come.

Keywords: Observing life from different levels. Social gradations and graduations. Working class to aristocracy. Orders from above, in any sense of the meaning. Waiting for one's turn at the top. Politics. Big business. Multilevel marketing. Gradual upward climbs. Competitiveness. Stairs and ladders. Taking life step by step. Admiring success. Promotions. Corporate ladders.

The Caution: Nervous worry about social position. Snobbery because of monetary, intellectual or social status. Can imply class, creed or racial prejudice. Climbing the ladder of success without care for those who are supplanted. Unsafe heights. Falling from grace. Denigrating or undermining others. Snakes and ladders. Rarefied atmospheres.

What does this **SYMBOL** say to *you?*

A BAROMETER

Commentary: "A Barometer" is shown. The word "Barometer" comes from the Greek *baros*, meaning weight. It measures atmospheric pressure by responding to fluctuations. In weather forecasting, the "Barometer" is used to signify and help the analysis of weather-producing pressure systems. A storm is generally anticipated when the "Barometer" is falling rapidly; when the "Barometer" is rising, fair weather may usually be expected.

Oracle: You may feel the need to plan for future action and to know what to expect or at least anticipate. This can picture a situation where there's the task of being a "translator" of what's going on in the environment. You will find in your own sensitivity to the environment, and to the people around you, the very instrument that can sense how they're feeling or what's coming up next. Watching, waiting and feeling out the atmosphere before taking any action will lead to the best answer. Observing others' reactions will provide clues, as well. Once you know which way to move with this situation, you'll be able to go straight for the objective, so take a little time to sniff things out. Perhaps someone else is doing this, watching and waiting. It may be that they also don't want to commit to anything without the benefit of further information. Opening yourself up to the signals around you may lead to increased psychic ability with people turning to you for advice or instruction. It can indicate a need to live day by day and not make any major decisions until things become clear. Checking the "weather" and how the prevailing conditions "feel" will help you to proceed with your plans or dreams. Whether these things are emotionally, physically or mentally important, you'll know in good time. If something doesn't feel quite right, and a change in the environment seems imminent, taking precautions ahead of time can save a lot of problems.

Keywords: Staying ahead of the weather. Feeling changes ahead of time. Measured responses. Measurements. Perceiving subtle changes. Insight. Indicators. Knowing when rain or storms are coming. Stilling one's self for answers. Talking about the weather. Putting out one's feelers. Anticipating shifts. Opinion polls. Anticipating what's going to happen. Being on guard for inclement weather.

The Caution: Fear of change. Constant looking to fashions or fads. Not knowing how to react because of shifts in the atmosphere. Watching and waiting to see how other people act, seemingly with no will of one's own. Being changeable. Having no anchor. Constant looking. Not being able to read the environment accurately.

What does this **SYMBOL** say to *you?*

Aquarius 13

BAROMETER, n. An ingenious instrument which indicates what kind of weather we are having.
Ambrose Bierce

Sudden resolutions, like the sudden rise of mercury in a barometer, indicate little else than the variability of the weather.
David Hare

It doesn't matter what temperature the room is; it's always room temperature.
Stephen Wright

No mind is much employed upon the present; recollection and anticipation fill up almost all our moments.
Samuel Johnson

Some are weather-wise, some are otherwise.
Benjamin Franklin

Observe due measure, for right timing is in all things the most important factor.
Hesiod

Those who speak most of progress measure it by quantity and not by quality.
George Santayana

Aquarius 14

The only way round is through.
Dietrich Bonhoeffer

No steam or gas ever drives anything until it is confined. No Niagara is ever turned into light and power until it is tunneled. No life ever grows until it is focused, dedicated, disciplined.
Harry Emerson Fosdick

Due to the current economic climate, the light at the end of the tunnel will be turned off until further notice.
Anonymous

The best way out is always through.
Robert Frost

The most common of all antagonisms arises from a man's taking a seat beside you on the train, a seat to which he is completely entitled.
Robert Benchley

If you board the wrong train, it is no use running along the corridor in the other direction.
Dietrich Bonhoeffer

RAILROAD, n. The chief of many mechanical devices enabling us to get away from where we are to where we are no better off.
Ambrose Bierce

A TRAIN ENTERING A TUNNEL

Commentary: "A Train Entering a Tunnel" shows the ability to take the shortest and most direct route to a destination or outcome. Years ago, we would have had to go the long way around a mountain, but now we can use many pathways, methods and "shortcuts" to get where we want to go quickly and expediently. Often, though, going into a "Train Tunnel" can be a weird experience; the sunlight suddenly disappears, and it can feel as though we are hurtling through the earth to some unknown destination. This can be exciting, but also often rather disconcerting as the "Train" speeds toward its destination or goal.

Oracle: You may feel the need to cut through any obstacles you encounter and to go straight ahead, regardless of any unseen hazards on your way. It may be necessary to examine whether you are operating at cross purposes with someone. There may be a need to check the "Train's" signals, to make sure that there's not a collision with people, or complications, coming the other way. This can be particularly true if this feels like a "one-track" journey. Perhaps the situation feels like it's never going to end, as though you're stuck in a "Tunnel," but it's certain that it will. You are likely to have a great deal of drive and it's probable that others are with you, or people may be depending on you, so plough on through. However, this can be a lonely journey that you're on. It may feel like you're going through a dark "Tunnel" all by yourself, and there can be a sense of isolation. Whatever the situation, there's a need to cut to the heart of the problem, without stopping to consider every single detail. Quickly adjusting, changing or making up your mind about some issue or problem can lead to swift conclusions and solutions. Getting stuck in the details of the situation will probably just add to a much longer outcome than is needed. You, or someone close to you, may need to just go for it. Look to ensure that you're not missing out on the joy in the journey though. Perhaps you'd really rather go the long way than through the "Tunnel"?

Keywords: Deep penetration. Cutting through extraneous or stifling detail. Persistence. Shortcuts to a desired end. Heart bypasses—physical, emotional, spiritual, etc. Cutting to the chase. Going for the objective regardless of side issues. Working at getting something finished or done. Near-death experiences. The need for track maintenance. Dropping all distracting considerations. Fallopian tubes. Hurried sex.

The Caution: Being overcautious. Taking the long way around. Shortcuts that inhibit deep penetration. Cutting through the crap. Tunnel vision. Cutting people off. Not listening to others. Having a one-track mind that doesn't allow for detours or deviations. Severe changes in pressure. Railroading and bulldozing.

What does this **SYMBOL** say to *you?*

TWO LOVEBIRDS SITTING ON A FENCE AND SINGING HAPPILY

Aquarius 15

Commentary: "Two Lovebirds Sitting on a Fence and Singing Happily" is an image that brings to mind togetherness, friendship, happiness, love and the rejoicing of relationship. The "Lovebirds" may be "Singing Happily," but as they are "Sitting on a Fence," this could be masking a reality; perhaps they are not exactly happy; perhaps they are not so together. If, indeed, the "Two" are "Singing Happily," this is cause for joy and celebration about issues relating to love, partnership, being together and the sharing of lives.

Oracle: "Singing" and making statements about love out loud can bring happiness to those nearby and lift the spirits of all involved. However, this Symbol can also point to dividing lines between people, like having a "Fence" of some kind between them. Although there may be superficial feelings of contentment and pleasure, this can be based on someone having a noncommitted, tenuous or shaky position. To go one way or another with conviction in a relationship can invite the risk of separation, but commitment eventually needs to be chosen or rejected. How long can people sit on the "Fence"? The "Fence" can represent actual physical divisions between people, where they can see each other, but can't actually connect or be with each other. Is that what's happening? Is one "Lovebird Singing Happily" and the other one wanting to escape? Divisions of hearts and minds can lead to sorrow. See if you can look to love and happiness. It may take time for people to relax into a relationship, especially if they've learned to distrust each other or relationships in general. Is there a pledging of commitment to each other? This Symbol can also indicate problems with fertility and getting pregnant. If people are always "on the Fence," how can they commit to the lives of their offspring—whether the "offspring" are their young, their creative ideas or their future.

Keywords: Faith in love. Waiting for signs. Friendship and companionship. Issues of "that's them and this is us." Fences, borders and barriers. Showing love for all to see. Commitment to relationship. Mating for life. The need for honest communications. Singing. Speaking one's truth.

The Caution: Sitting on the fence. Complaining about relationships. Waiting to see what the others do. Being stuck when one would rather fly off and be free. Having a fixed position. Not wanting to comply with the other. Neighborhood disputes. Noises from next door. Boasting of happiness.

What does this **SYMBOL** say to *you?*

Do not wrong or hate your neighbor for it is not he that you wrong but yourself.
Native American Proverb

Throw your heart over the fence and the rest will follow.
Norman Vincent Peale

Sometimes I wonder if men and women really suit each other. Perhaps they should live next door and just visit now and then.
Katharine Hepburn

There is room in the smallest cottage for a happy loving pair.
Johann Friedrich Von Schiller

The wavering multitude is divided into opposite factions.
Virgil

A hedge between keeps friendship green.
Traditional Proverb

A long dispute means both parties are wrong.
Voltaire

Good fences make good neighbors.
Proverb

The same fence that shuts others out shuts you in.
William Taylor Copeland

Aquarius 16

A desk is a dangerous place from which to watch the world.
John LeCarre

What the world really needs is more love and less paperwork.
Pearl Bailey

A billion here and a billion there and pretty soon you're talking big money.
Everett M. Dirksen, U.S. politician

I hate being a grown-up. Having to learn things I don't want to know really pisses me off.
Barbara Sher

Having more money does not ensure happiness. People with ten million dollars are no happier than people with nine million dollars.
Hobart Brown

Life's been nothing but paperwork.
Gustav Mahler

Ever notice that even the busiest people are never too busy to tell you just how busy they are?
Anonymous

A BIG BUSINESSMAN AT HIS DESK

Commentary: "A Big Businessman at His Desk" reflects the need for organization, power and leadership. As the "Businessman" is seen as being "Big," he probably has much to look after; details, finances, paperwork, possibly for a large business or group. He can't truly be successful if he doesn't have control over the various aspects of his work life. "His Desk" must be in order and he needs a healthy command of his sphere of operations.

Oracle: This Symbol implies the need to feel confident and able to operate efficiently in the "Business" world. Sometimes "Business" takes up so much time in our lives that we forget to unwind and talk and think about anything else. How often and for how long does one have to be "at His Desk"? Are "Business" considerations more important than home and family or health? Someone in this situation may be unable to get directly involved in life, but have to stay behind and attend to details and do the organizing. Feeling "Big," confident, assured and proud of one's achievements can lead to expanded feelings about what one is capable of doing and contributing. Someone may have to stand up and declare what is and isn't desirable, ethical or possible. Emotional reactions may be out of place here; employing a rational manner may be what's needed to resolve things. Then again, emotions may not be playing any part and maybe that's the issue. Perhaps someone is being rather cold and possibly cut off in the pursuit of their objectives. This Symbol asks: Are you organized, or do you have a huge mess piling up in your life? Are you taking notice of necessary details? Are you living your life the way you think is best for your future, your relationships and physical well-being? Perhaps there's a need for more creativity, more time for your emotional and spiritual life. After all, allowing creative and emotional energy to flow will most likely increase your business success.

Keywords: Issues of being happy in one's career. Making decisions. Management. Being in charge and in control. Calling the shots. The head rules the heart. Delegating duties or jobs. Economic rationalism. Sorting paperwork. Corporations. Keeping a diary. Striking a balance between having a life and doing all that needs to be done. Desks, telephones, computers, faxes, etc. Details and more details.

The Caution: Taking advantage. Bossing others. Shoving people around. Getting depressed about work. Always being "on the job." Talking about money and business constantly. Greediness. Exploiting people and events for personal gain. Having difficulty retiring. The removal of the "little people." Not doing the paperwork. Brushes with the law.

What does this **SYMBOL** say to *you?*

A WATCHDOG STANDING GUARD, PROTECTING HIS MASTER AND HIS POSSESSIONS

Aquarius 17

Commentary: "A Watchdog Standing Guard, Protecting His Master and His Possessions." The "Watchdog" needs to stay alert for possible intrusion, robbery or someone stepping over their boundaries and into his territory. The "Watchdog" can't truly relax as there's the need to be constantly "on guard" in case of trouble. If the "Watchdog" lets down his "Guard" for even a short time, problems may occur when he's not looking. This can end up being a tiring responsibility, especially if he is the only one who is taking the situation seriously.

Oracle: In the situation facing you, you may feel unsafe and sense the need to be alert for signs of trouble. Enlisting the support of trusted and loyal helpers may be necessary, as there are likely to be others who also have a vested interest in everything going smoothly or continuing to be okay. There is probably the need for some form of reassurance, self-assurance or confidence that all is safe in your environment. Relaxation may be an issue: is a lack of sleep impinging on your life? Alternatively, somebody may be prying, or watching for someone to slip up. However, sometimes we imagine all sorts of intrusions or threats that aren't there in reality. This can lead to the distrust of others, even those close to you. Any small noise or sudden movement can set off a chain reaction of suspicion and paranoia. However, one needs to be able to feel that it's possible to let down one's "Guard" now and then. There can be sense of "Protection" discovered from being able to discern what's real and what's not.

Keywords: Guardianship. Things that stand guard and protect. Being on the alert against invasion or other trouble. Loyalty, possessiveness. Jealousy. The worry of loss. Alarm and security systems. Locks. Watchdogs. Being afraid of intrusion. Survival instincts. Bouncers and musclemen. Security guards. Constantly checking up. Sudden responses. Having one's ear to the ground for danger.

The Caution: Suspicion and paranoia that rob the joy of ownership. Being unable to let down one's guard because of the possibility of invasion or attack. Feelings of being exposed. Possible betrayal. Greed. Envy. Lust for power. Having others do "the dirty work." Stool pigeons. Spying. Stooges. Being the fall guy. Worrying endlessly about loss. Resenting intrusion. Jealousy.

What does this **SYMBOL** say to *you?*

CERBERUS, n. The watchdog of Hades, whose duty it was to guard the entrance—against whom or what does not clearly appear; everybody, sooner or later, had to go there, and nobody wanted to carry off the entrance.
Ambrose Bierce

There is no rule more invariable than that we are paid for our suspicions by finding what we suspect.
Henry David Thoreau

I loathe people who keep dogs. They are cowards who haven't got the guts to bite people themselves.
August Strindberg

There's nothing so comfortable as a small bankroll. A big one is always in danger.
Wilson Mizner

Gold will be slave or master.
Horace

A barking dog is often more useful than a sleeping lion.
Washington Irving

Liberals feel unworthy of their possessions. Conservatives feel they deserve everything they've stolen.
Mort Sahl

Possession is nine tenths of the law.
Proverb

Aquarius 18

Alas, fortune does not change men; it unmasks them.
Stephen T. Steve

The greatest way to live with honor in this world is to be what we pretend to be.
Socrates

Man is least himself when he talks in his own person. Give him a mask, and he will tell you the truth.
Oscar Wilde

Whoever is detected in a shameful fraud is ever after not believed even if they speak the truth.
Phaedrus

It is only the superficial qualities that last. Man's deeper nature is soon found out.
Oscar Wilde

People that seem so glorious are all show; underneath they are like everyone else.
Euripides

One may sometimes tell a lie, but the grimace that accompanies it tells the truth.
Friedrich Nietzsche

Who are you going to believe, me or your own eyes?
Groucho Marx

A MAN BEING UNMASKED AT A MASQUERADE

Commentary: "A Man Being Unmasked at a Masquerade" shows the inevitable outcome for anyone who is participating in a "Masquerade." He can get away with wearing the "Mask" for a period of time, but eventually circumstances will lead him to have to reveal himself sooner or later. This could happen voluntarily or involuntarily. He may decide when it's time to reveal who he truly is, or he may be forced to lift the "Mask" against his own wishes.

Oracle: Sometimes life uncovers "Masks," intrigues, coverups and mysteries so that the truth may be revealed. Things may look better or worse in their true light. What is revealed may be beyond most people's expectations with a very happy result. On the other hand, there can be real disappointment as one's true identity, and even the way one looks, becomes unveiled. Secret motives may have some kind of purpose, but they almost invariably become known in time and pretending to be something or someone that one isn't can lead to painful realizations when the truth comes out. Lies or coverups being revealed can lead to big changes in relationships. You may find that this confronts you now. The first concern may be for the embarrassment and difficulties that can arise, but it's probably too late to worry about that. With this Symbol, the truth will be revealed and exposed sooner or later. The question is: are people being true to the truth themselves? Are things being covered up? If they are, sooner than later it will begin to come to light that things aren't as they've seemed. Is it possible in this situation to forgive and forget? If needed, psychotherapy and other forms of healing can bring issues to the surface so they can be faced.

Keywords: Secret motives exposed. Having to face one's self. Facing the truth about another. Coming to terms with judgments about one's true worth. Owning up to who one truly is. Being able to see through characters and trickery. Wearing a "Mask" that suits the situation. Insights into people. Dropping pretense. Stripping away coverups. Aliases. Finding or revealing one's true self. The desire for authenticity.

The Caution: Detrimentally revealing yourself too quickly or too early. Being found out to be a fraud. Finding answers that aren't welcome. Layers of deception discovered. Charades, pretense and ploys to manipulate. Lies. Assumed identities.

What does this **SYMBOL** say to *you?*

A FOREST FIRE FINALLY QUENCHED

Aquarius 19

What is to give light must endure burning.
Viktor Frankl

Commentary: "A Forest Fire Finally Quenched" pictures a situation where enthusiastic drive and zeal can set off an uncontrollable, exciting and sometimes destructive chain of events. The "Forest Fire" can cause a lot of damage and burn up anything that happens to be in its path. There has been no choice but to fight for control and minimize the destruction to the "Forest" and those things in the path of the fire—animals, humans, houses, etc.

Oracle: In this situation "a Fire" is "Finally Quenched." Any efforts to contain the damage will at last be successful, and some people will find the challenge to have been exhilarating. Regaining control of the environment will lead to things coming back to normal again, but everything, or at least many things, may be changed. Major transformations may have taken place on many levels. It is said that a "Forest Fire" is actually good for the forest as a whole, as it makes room for new growth by removing old and dead matter. Farmers burn off their dead crops on a regular basis to recycle the nutrients into the soil so as to nourish the new growth. The "Fire" also destroys the taller plants and trees which crowd out the shorter ones and block the sun from reaching them (just as our illusions can block us from "seeing the light" of the truth). However, much can be lost in a "Forest Fire"; there can be threats to life and property. You may find that you have been caught up in a situation, fighting for emotional or physical control. Something that was raging in its intensity has "Finally" been extinguished or satisfied. This may have left you somewhat exhausted, but the exhilaration that can come from surviving such a struggle can leave you transformed and jubilant.

Keywords: Exuberant feelings that come after struggles. Coming out of an experience with a new sense of commitment or a new understanding of consequences. Getting a bee in your bonnet. Spot fires. Jubilation and release after hard labor. Fighting for control. Sparks getting out of control. Events taking off in all directions. Sexual energy and the containment of it. Ideas that get whipped up and take off at high speed. The ferocity of nature. The calm after the storm. Smouldering passions. Smoke. One-eyed focus.

The Caution: Giving up too soon and losing it all. Self-defeating delight in drama. Looking back on a situation that got out of control and produced a lot of rubble. Destructive passions. Losing one's spark. Running out of fuel. Feeling burnt out. Exhaustion and despair at what's lost.

What does this **SYMBOL** say to *you?*

A little fire is quickly trodden out, which being suffered, rivers cannot quench.
William Shakespeare

It is with our passions as it is with fire and water; they are good servants, but bad masters.
Aesop

Get excited and enthusiastic about you own dream. This excitement is like a forest fire—you can smell it, taste it, and see it from a mile away.
Denis Waitley

Do not quench your inspiration and your imagination; do not become the slave of your model.
Vincent van Gogh

Genius is the power of lighting one's own fire.
John Foster

Contentment consisteth not in adding more fuel, but in taking away some fire.
Thomas Fuller

I've seen public opinion shift like the wind and put out the very fire it lighted.
Rachel Field

Aquarius 20

Our soul is escaped as a bird from the snare of the hunters, the snare is broken and we are delivered.
Catholic Encyclopedia

Something was dead in each of us, and what was dead was Hope.
Oscar Wilde

We must accept finite disappointment, but never lose infinite hope.
Martin Luther King, Jr.

Lift me like an olive branch, be my homeward dove.
Leonard Cohen

A secret is like a dove, when it leaves my hand it takes wing.
Saudi Arabian Proverb

Censure pardons the ravens but rebukes the doves.
Latin Proverb

I got the message. All of us get the message, sooner or later. If you get it before it's too late or before you're too old, you'll pull through all right.
Nat King Cole

A LARGE WHITE DOVE BEARING A MESSAGE

Commentary: "A Large White Dove Bearing a Message" shows messages of peace and love. The "Dove" is a symbol of innocence, gentleness and affection; also, in art and in the Scriptures, it is the typical symbol of the Holy Ghost. When Jesus was baptized, the Holy Ghost descended in the shape of a "Dove." It also symbolizes the soul and as such is sometimes represented coming out of the mouths of saints at death. "Doves" are a symbol of inspiration and divine guidance. A caged "Dove" signifies the human soul imprisoned in the flesh and held captive during the period of mortal life. They can represent peace and in this Symbol the "Large White Dove Is Bearing a Message." The "Dove" brought to Noah a bough of an olive tree as a sign that the deluge of wrath that was unleashed by the flood was over. Further "Doves" are said to be able to perform miracles with their "Messages." Mahomet's miracle from the Koran speaks of a white "Dove" whispering a "Message" from God into Mahomet's ear.

Oracle: You may need to solve your situation by relying on peaceful messages that come from either outside or inside of yourself. A "Message" is very likely to be on its way, one that you may have been waiting to hear for some time. This "Message" can reassure your spiritual center and will probably be offered with gentleness and without malice. Further, someone could say or reveal something that changes the whole situation, turning it around. However, it could be that the "Message" is not an easy one for someone to deliver. It may cause you to have to face something you'd rather not. Whatever, the "Large White Dove" can be quietly reassuring that everything will be okay in the end. Healing rifts between people with promises of improvements, faith and trust will uplift the spirit. Miracles are known to happen, so it's best to hold to positive outcomes. After all, Noah had to do that on his Ark. Listen intently for "Messages," as they will be around you, in one way or another.

Keywords: Being seen as a savior or one who needs saving. Blessings delivered—all will be well. Celebration. Somebody who brings blessed relief. Issues of hope and salvation. The Covenant. News. Announcements. Peace movements. *The Rainbow Warrior.* Utopian idealism. Olive branches.

The Caution: Staying with the assumption that things will never improve. Refusing solace. Shooting the messenger. Not trusting the good things in life. Not being content with any message that's relayed. Insincere messages caused by the pain of not facing the real truth.

What does this **SYMBOL** say to *you?*

A WOMAN DISAPPOINTED AND DISILLUSIONED, COURAGEOUSLY FACING A SEEMINGLY EMPTY LIFE

Aquarius 21

Commentary: "A Woman Disappointed and Disillusioned" is an image of apparent sadness and loss. As she's "Courageously Facing a Seemingly Empty Life," she's putting on a brave face, even though it may feel to her that she doesn't have much of a future. This could really be just a matter of perception and expectations. Perhaps there are some, or indeed many, things that she could be grateful for, but some areas of her life are unfulfilled and not working. Perhaps there are no children, there is no relationship or something has been lost.

Oracle: There can be feelings of wasted energy, trying to achieve something against the odds, while creating only failure. However, it is always important to look on "Disappointment" and loss as a teacher. The feeling, or belief, that one will never have the life one wants can lead to exactly that outcome. Trying to be objective can help, as things could improve far beyond your expectations or dreams in the future. As they say, while there is life there is hope and we always have something to strive for and achieve, if only we can have faith in it. "Courage" is a key to recognizing the fullness and beauty of life, regardless of how others see it. The biggest barrier to overcome is the bitterness and barriers that can arise. There may be someone else who really needs your support. Reconnect with what is available and possible in your situation. Although it requires courage and faith to get back on track, we always return to life with greater wisdom and understanding. Realizing one's limitations, but doing so with a sense of purpose and hope, will help ease matters. Try turning doom and gloom into faith, inspiration and thanks for what *is* possible and *is* available, and watch how things improve.

Keywords: Breaking through illusions. Facing stark reality with hope. Loneliness and depression overcome. Positive outlooks. Counting one's blessings. Looking toward the future. Having to battle through relationship losses while maintaining a sense of self and purpose. Turning points reached. Having a belief in miracles. Choosing joy.

The Caution: Wallowing in failure. Not seeing the joy and beauty of one's life. Accepting defeat. Feeling like all is lost. Bitterness. Walling one's self off from others. Not trusting people. Finding nothing to be happy about. Feeling deserted and alone. Not letting go of the past. Injuries. Infertility. Incurable "diseases." Unrequited love. The loss of a partner. Staring into space. Being a sad, old person.

What does this **SYMBOL** say to *you?*

Life is what we make it, and the world is what we make it. The eyes of the cheerful and of the melancholy man are fixed upon the same creation; but very different are the aspects which it bears to them.
Albert Pike

Just think how happy you would be if you lost everything you have right now, and then got it back again.
Frances Rodman

Remember that too many people who faithfully follow the prescription to work hard, sacrifice, achieve, accomplish, create and get ahead either "crack up" in the process or find an emotional vacuum at the end of it all.
Arnold Lazarus

Some people are sympathetic; others are just pathetic.
Peter Wastholm

Doubt is the vestibule through which all must pass before they can enter into the temple of wisdom.
Charles Caleb Colton

We consume our tomorrows fretting about our yesterdays.
Persius

Even when I'm sick and depressed, I love life.
Arthur Rubenstein

Aquarius 22

Here Skugg,
Lies snug,
As a bug,
In a rug.
Benjamin Franklin

If you let everyone walk over you,
you become a carpet.
Bulgarian Proverb

My husband and I are either
going to buy a dog or have a
child. We can't decide whether to
ruin our carpet or ruin our lives.
Rita Rudner

It's easier to put on slippers than
to carpet the whole world.
Al Franken

BOUNDARY, n. In political
geography, an imaginary line
between two nations, separating
the imaginary rights of one from
the imaginary rights of the other.
Ambrose Bierce

There is a boundary to men's
passions when they act from
feelings; but none when they
are under the influence of
imagination.
Edmund Burke

Life is like a blanket too short.
You pull it up and your toes
rebel, you yank it down and
shivers meander about your
shoulder; but cheerful folks
manage to draw their knees up
and pass a very comfortable
night.
Marion Howard

A RUG PLACED ON THE FLOOR FOR CHILDREN TO PLAY ON

Commentary: "A Rug Placed on the Floor for Children to Play on" is an image of cushioning, comfort, safety, and fun places for activity and play. The "Rug" has been "Placed on the Floor" because it is safe for "the Children" to "Play" there, they can enjoy themselves and each other. People need times of "Play," at any age. Taking care of the "inner child," one's own or another's, can lead to a new sense of security and comfort.

Oracle: It's human nature to want to feel safe, loved and comfortable in our lives. You may feel as though you are struggling as you seek to grow and develop, but even if you are not aware of it, there are cushions, safeguards and protection all around. Higher forces may be looking after you in your search for safety and security. The "Rug" can picture a space where you can be creative, play and relate with others. However, the "Rug" can also be like a border or boundary that restricts activity. The "Rug" can be put in place by those who believe they are acting in others' best interests, or through issues of control. When someone wanders off the "Rug," whose decision is it to have them return to the same place? If you are one of the "Children," having fun and being carefree, then the "Rug" is quite probably a good thing. This can be like a safety net for your activities. If you are merely being treated like a "Child," the "Rug" can be a form of control, of others letting you know how much "space" you can take up. There may be a need to look after "Children" or those younger than you, to provide somewhere safe for them to live and grow —even if it proves to be difficult. If we allow a sense of security and love into our lives we can lift our fun and enjoyment and put up with any difficulties more easily.

Keywords: Comfort and care provided. The caring and longing for children. Having a place of belonging. A sense of security. Rugs, carpets, cribs and cots. Defining areas of possible activity. Being aware of the needs of the young. Adoption. Sleeping on the floor or the sofa. Fun, joy, toys. Playing with others. Nurseries. Day care. Cribs. Play pens.

The Caution: Being overprotected. Not growing up. Insulation from reality. Self-indulgence. Limits of activity. Having the rug pulled. Expecting to be looked after vs. self-reliance. Assuming the young and inexperienced can look after themselves. Lines that shouldn't be crossed. Territorial attitudes. Always having to watch the young ones. Inability to relax. Infertility.

What does this **SYMBOL** say to *you?*

A BIG TRAINED BEAR SITTING DOWN AND WAVING ALL ITS PAWS

Aquarius 23

Commentary: "A Big Trained Bear Sitting Down and Waving All Its Paws" paints a picture of a performing animal, and a big one at that, going through its tricks. "Bears" are easily "Trained," taught and sometimes forced into performing many actions that are alien to their natural behaviors and habits. By having "All Its Paws" off the ground, the "Bear" has symbolically given up the ability to be able to run away or fight. It may be that it is receptive to friendly or playful interaction. The "Bear" is revealing its soft underbelly, which can also be a sign of feeling safe and unthreatened, at least for the moment. The "Bear" may watch for cues from its trainer or it may be able to perform the tricks all by itself.

Oracle: Perhaps there are things you don't want to do, but it seems your duty to do, act out or perform. There is a need to develop responses above and beyond the normal expected level. Perhaps you are indeed excelling in your level of performance, only you can really tell, although others may also judge this. Look to your situation and see if you are compromising yourself or merely acting out conditioned responses for the sake of others. Is someone waving their arms around when they should just get on with the job at hand? Having to play out an act for the sake of social protocol against one's natural instincts may lead to compromises that lower your self-esteem. Is someone acting a certain way and claiming they have no choice but to act that way? This image can also reflect a feeling of safety, or having no sense of threat, which allows for playful antics or experimentation with unusual behaviors.

Keywords: Developing skills. Making excuses. Performing rote responses. Expecting others to perform. Entertaining people. Being theatrical. Stomach rubs. Big, tall, brute energies. Sitting down or standing up. Fur and fuzzy hair. Playing instruments. Dancing. Performances. Arm waving. Animal training. Bears. Training. Learning by example. Fun vs. drudgery.

The Caution: Being unable to recover one's feet. Instinctive and creative performances for the crowd. Fatuous need to be the center of attention. Defying authority. Vulnerable. Working against normal instincts or desires. Flapping one's arms. Sitting things out. Making a big noise, but doing nothing. Being cranky, ill tempered. Crazy behavior. Not having a mind of one's own. Giving up control of one's destiny. Mindless and brainless. Drugs and dope. Loss of spontaneity.

What does this **SYMBOL** say to *you?*

If animals had reason, they would act just as ridiculous as we men folks do.
Josh Billings

If an animal does something, we call it instinct; if we do the same thing for the same reason, we call it intelligence.
Will Cuppy

Every animal knows more than you do.
American Proverb

Our expression and our words never coincide, which is why the animals don't understand us.
Malcolm de Chazal

If animals play, this is because play is useful in the struggle for survival; because play practices and so perfects the skills needed in adult life.
Susanna Miller

It's all to do with the training: You can do a lot if you're properly trained.
Queen Elizabeth II

You can't teach an old dog new tricks.
Proverb

Everything pays for growing tame.
Maxine Kumin

Aquarius 24

Man is a creation of desire, not a creation of need.
Gaston Bachelard

It is with our passions as it is with fire and water; they are good servants, but bad masters.
Sir Roger L'Estrange

It is in vain to hope to please all alike. Let a man stand with his face in what direction he will, he must necessarily turn his back on one half of the world.
George Dennison Prentice

The heart is wiser than the intellect.
Josiah Gilbert Holland

Been there, done that, got the T-shirt.
Anonymous

To understand the world one must not be worrying about one's self.
Albert Einstein

Life must be lived and curiosity kept alive. One must never, for whatever reason, turn his back on life.
Eleanor Roosevelt

Man is only truly great when he acts from his passions.
Benjamin Disraeli

A MAN TURNING HIS BACK ON HIS PASSIONS TEACHES DEEP WISDOM FROM HIS EXPERIENCE

Commentary: "A Man Turning His Back on His Passions Teaches Deep Wisdom from His Experience" shows someone turning away from something that's been important in the past, but has now lost its value or relevance. The "Man" has had to "Turn His Back on His Passions"—he has most likely had valuable lessons in the letting go of desire. This can show a "Turning" away from many things; a lover, a job, a belief, some of the very things he's wanted or worked hard for. Perhaps he sees there is now a more important job or mission to be pursued. As he "Teaches Deep Wisdom from His Experience," he has some knowledge or insight to transmit, "Teach" or pass on to others.

Oracle: Going through difficult circumstances and coming out with new realizations and codes for life is implied by this Symbol. By controlling your "Passions," and making conscious and wise decisions about your life, you can find an objective position that allows you to understand what's happening. You may feel that you can no longer survive the roller-coaster ride of your emotions. You can benefit others by "Teaching" the new "Wisdom" and the understanding that come after having gone through some hard lessons. The question is: Can you sublimate your thoughts, desires and "Passions"? You may be in the process of going after more tangible, real or worthwhile spiritual or material concerns. Living life true to your path and giving up things that can lead you astray will allow more and more "Deep Wisdom" to come through. "Teaching" or setting a good example for others can bring its own rewards. These "Teachings" will develop out of a deep resonance that has come from the trials of "Experience." It can feel like a case of "been there, done that."

Keywords: Conquering one's base nature. Changing through maturing realizations. Learning lessons the hard way. Realizing it's time to let go of things that once mattered. Being an example so others may learn. Reforming one's ways. Dignity. Guidance. Turning around. Dropping the lower ego or society. Leading a monastic life. Showing what you've learned.

The Caution: Giving up on emotional growth. Being dissatisfied with life. Being forced to perform for another's benefit. Sticking to things that are no longer worthwhile. Stubborn refusal to move forward. Misguiding others. Severe reactions.

What does this **SYMBOL** say to *you*?

A BUTTERFLY WITH THE RIGHT WING MORE PERFECTLY FORMED

Aquarius 25

The bird that would soar above the plain of tradition and prejudice must have strong wings.
Kate Chopin

You cannot fly with wings made of butter.
Netherlands Antillean Proverb

A bird never flew on one wing.
Proverb

Is he alone who has courage on his right hand and faith on his left hand?
Charles A. Lindbergh

All of us failed to match our dreams of perfection. So I rate us on the basis of our splendid failure to do the impossible.
William Faulkner

Let us take things as we find them: let us not attempt to distort them into what they are not. We cannot make facts. All our wishing cannot change them. We must use them.
John Henry Cardinal Newman

I thank God for my handicaps, for through them, I have found myself, my work and my God.
Helen Keller

Commentary: "A Butterfly with the Right Wing More Perfectly Formed" shows a situation of imbalance, lopsidedness and sometimes physical distortions. The "Butterfly" may have difficulty flying and therefore its very life is compromised because of this "handicap." However, perhaps this "Right Wing More Perfectly Formed" is only a problem in how things look and not how they perform. It could be that the "Butterfly" has learned how to cope with this imbalance and can still live its life unhindered by the defect.

Oracle: In your situation, you may find that you are applying your rational logical mind out of balance to your intuition and creative wisdom. It is often harder to understand your intuitive messages, but reliance on logic can limit your possibilities. On the other hand, it could be that life is swamped with a lack of rational thought and responses, relying more heavily on the emotional, creative and spiritual. This would have to be accessed by the individual that has this situation or problem in their life. This Symbol can show problems or issues to do with language or the ability to verbally express feelings. It can also show someone or a situation where the emotional aspects get the upper hand before the rational mind really understands or "gets it." With this Symbol around, it may be necessary to not only learn to trust your intuitive feelings, but also to be careful not to overreact emotionally and take the extra effort to bring your thoughts and rational awareness up to speed. It can show emotional, mental or physical handicaps that prevent one from doing what one truly wants, or imbalances or mutations on the spiritual level. The main issue here is about balance. Balance can still be achieved, but only if there is a genuine acceptance of the problems inherent.

Keywords: Rising above life's distortions. A need to bring some type of balance to situations. Injuries or problems with hands or arms. One side being more "Perfect" than the other. The "Right" being better than the left. Mutations. Handicaps. Challenges. Disabilities. Impediments.

The Caution: Imbalances and physical distortions. Asymmetry. An imbalance of functions leading to involuntary flapping around. Distortions of reactions or of the truth. Lopsidedness. Hindrances. Being at a disadvantage. Feeling incapacitated.

What does this **SYMBOL** say to *you?*

Aquarius 26

The expectations of life depend upon diligence; the mechanic that would perfect his work must first sharpen his tools.
Confucius

I do not forget that I am a mechanic. I am proud to own it. Neither do I forget that the apostle Paul was a tentmaker; Socrates was a sculptor; and Archimedes was a mechanic.
Andrew Jackson

On mechanical slavery, on the slavery of the machine, the future of the world depends.
Oscar Wilde

A creative economy is the fuel of magnificence.
Ralph Waldo Emerson

The great happiness of life, I find, after all, to consist in the regular discharge of some mechanical duty.
Friedrich von Schiller

We boil at different degrees.
Ralph Waldo Emerson

Humanity is moving in a circle. The progress in mechanical things of the past hundred years has proceeded at the cost of losing many other things which perhaps were much more important for it.
George Gurdjieff

A GARAGE MAN TESTING A CAR'S BATTERY WITH A HYDROMETER

Commentary: "A Garage Man Testing a Car's Battery with a Hydrometer" is an image of a mechanic "Testing" the running efficiency of a "Car." He's checking to see if any mechanical problems or repairs are needed. Most specifically, he's checking the water in the "Car's Battery" in order to ensure that things will run well. A "Hydrometer" is capable of measuring many things; alcohol, salt, sugar, anything that may be held or suspended in water.

Oracle: This Symbol reflects the need for a mechanical approach to the issue at hand or the calling in of a "mechanically minded" person. There is a need to take a more objective or inventive view that is relative to modern society. Performing necessary checks and balances to ensure the smooth running of our lives is part of the everyday maintenance of society, our appliances and ourselves. The "Garage Man" could be "Testing the Battery" because there is a problem he needs to analyze or he could be performing routine preventative maintenance. Certainly it is better to keep an eye on things before they go wrong. Figuring out any malfunctions so that life can proceed in a smoother, more efficient manner will help keep everything running smoothly. Perhaps there's a need for someone of authority, someone removed from your situation, to give some assistance, repairs or feedback. An interesting aspect of the "Car's Battery" is that the water (the emotional element) when combined with the positive and negative elements of the battery is a self-empowering system. In this situation, it is the level of water or the emotional dependability of the situation that is being measured because that is what is important. Ideally, water that is used in a "Car's Battery" should be pure. You may need to use some type of gauge on the health of your emotional reactions. This Symbol can reflect the need to keep an eye on the mechanics of the body and to be careful of dehydration or drinking enough water.

Keywords: Testing the earthly vehicle for its roadworthiness. Situations that have "boiled over," bringing all to a stop. Breakdowns and the need for repair. Checking water levels. Anticipating future problems. The need for good batteries. Cars being serviced. Oil, petrol and grease. Checkups and tuneups. Bringing forward movement to a halt.

The Caution: Causing distress by constantly analyzing people or situations. Bad breath or dry skin. Not taking time for repairs or tuneups. Running on empty.

What does this **SYMBOL** say to *you?*

AN ANCIENT POTTERY BOWL FILLED WITH FRESH VIOLETS

Aquarius 27

Commentary: The image of "An Ancient Pottery Bowl Filled with Fresh Violets" is a reminder of the delicacy and beauty of nature. It can picture flowers in earthenware bowls, mortar and pestles for the preparation of herbs, and things such as flower essences and homeopathy. There is a feeling here of purity of motive and contentment. The simpler, more natural responses to problems and society can often bring a sense of refreshment and realignment with what is beautiful. Honest expressions of simplicity and respect for beauty and purity can bring joy. These can be simple gifts given with a sense of giving from the heart.

Oracle: In the situation facing you, there may be a need to remember to employ love, peace, beauty and simplicity. This could be in relationship to you, with yourself, to others or to the environment. Complications and difficulties are much more easily solved if a fresh and simple approach is taken, rather than more complicated, intellectual or highly-charged emotional responses. Place a "Bowl" filled with fresh flowers somewhere where it can remind you of the good things in life. Even a simple display of flowers picked from around your neighborhood can bring joy and settle feelings back to a more even keel and can remind you of the true beauty of life in a very simple way. Also, picture yourself as the open vessel, the "Bowl," and allow yourself to receive the blessings of the "Fresh Violets." Soon, things will get better and those things that you need will come to you. It can be a question of asking yourself, "What do I need, really?" Simplifying one's life on some level will lead to more charm and beauty.

Keywords: Returning to ancient sources. Flower and herbal remedies. Beauty. Setting standards for society. Slowing down the tempo to get to the purity of something. Watering the garden. The mortar and pestle. Homeopathy and pharmacopoeia. Stains and dyes. Flowers. African violets. Dainty, small and lacy things. Antiques and curios. Beautiful reminders of yesterday. Valentine's Day flowers, roses. Things that remind you of your grandmother. The old supporting and nourishing the new.

The Caution: Lack of subtlety. Insensitivity. Being dried up and withered from lack of water or emotion. Stagnant water. Being shy and unresponsive. "Shrinking violets." Neglecting the small things. Being so accomodating that one's needs are neglected or trodden on.

What does this **SYMBOL** say to *you?*

Big doesn't necessarily mean better. Sunflowers aren't better than violets.
Edna Ferber

Forgiveness is the fragrance the violet sheds on the heel that has crushed it.
Mark Twain

Flowers always make people better, happier and more helpful; they are sunshine, food and medicine to the soul.
Luther Burbank

We should let our godliness exhale like the odor of flowers. We should live for the good of our kind, and strive for the salvation of the world.
Alexander Crummell

Fair flowers that are not gather'd in their prime
Rot and consume themselves in little time.
William Shakespeare

Music, when soft voices die, Vibrates in the memory— Odors, when sweet Violets sicken, Live within the sense they quicken.
Percy Bysshe Shelley

Arranging a bowl of flowers in the morning can give a sense of quiet in a crowded day—like writing a poem, or saying a prayer.
Anne Morrow Lindbergh

Aquarius 28

When the oak is felled the whole forest echoes with its fall, but a hundred acorns are sown in silence by an unnoticed breeze.
Thomas Carlyle

If I had eight hours to chop down a tree, I'd spend six sharpening my axe.
Abraham Lincoln

Chop your own wood and it will warm you twice.
Henry David Thoreau

The pioneers cleared the forests from Jamestown to the Mississippi with fewer tools than are stored in the typical modern garage.
Dwayne Laws

From a fallen tree, all make kindling.
Spanish Proverb

Some men go through a forest and see no firewood.
English Proverb

Write without pay until somebody offers to pay you. If nobody offers within three years, sawing wood is what you were intended for.
Mark Twain

A TREE FELLED AND SAWED TO ENSURE A SUPPLY OF WOOD FOR THE WINTER

Commentary: "A Tree Felled and Sawed to Ensure a Supply of Wood for the Winter" represents the sacrifice of one thing for the benefit of another. This Symbol pictures the shifting and changing values we place on our environment and the tools we use. A "Tree" begins as a fragile life that may need our attention, care, concern and, in time, our gratitude. It develops into something that provides us with beauty and shade and is a haven for many birds and animals. In time, whether the "Tree" completes its growing cycle and dies or is cut down in its prime; it still has much to offer. The energy that has been stored in the timber can be used to fuel our need for warmth and comfort in hard times.

Oracle: This Symbol shows there is energy stored in everything and that many things we may think are of no real value can be helpful on an entirely different level. "The Tree Felled and Sawed" by being used as fuel, or made into paper, is released to rejoin the universal flow in many useful ways and forms. There are many things that grow around us during life. Sometimes there can be other uses that are of greater benefit than just to let things stand like monuments or memories. You may feel a need to sacrifice something old to find its current usefulness. There's a need for putting in time and effort to ensure comfort, security and hope for the future. Gather your resources when you can, don't wait for the last minute when supply might not be so readily available, or harder to put your hands on. Ensuring that things are in order for the "Winter" can allow you, and yours, to be sure of warmth and love during more difficult times.

Keywords: Gathering resources. Being prepared for harder times. Stocking up and stockpiling. Log cabins. Open fires. Care and reverence for things of wood and the earth. The making of paper. The publishing of books. Renewable resources. Christmas trees. Axes and tools. Stores and provisions. Logging. Timber. Wood for burning. Oil, petrol, fuel of all kinds. Woodchips. Storage.

The Caution: Hoarding supplies—not wanting anyone to get them. Destroying the old for modern advances. Feeling cut off at the knees. Being chopped down and stacked away somewhere. Fearing that there won't be enough fuel, money, etc. for harder times. Nonrenewable resources. Wanton destruction and logging of the forests. Waste.

What does this **SYMBOL** say to *you?*

A BUTTERFLY EMERGING FROM A CHRYSALIS

Aquarius 29

I do not know whether I was then a man dreaming I was a butterfly, or whether I am now a butterfly dreaming I am a man.
Chuang Tse

With each passage of human growth we must shed a protective structure [like a hardy crustacean]. We are left exposed and vulnerable—but also yeasty and embryonic again, capable of stretching in ways we hadn't known before.
Gail Sheehy

The butterfly becomes only when it's entirely ready.
Chinese Proverb

There is nothing in a caterpillar that tells you it's going to be a butterfly.
Sarah Margaret Fuller

It takes courage to push yourself to places that you have never been before … to test your limits … to break through barriers. And the day came when the risk it took to remain tight inside the bud was more painful than the risk it took to blossom.
Anais Nin

So long as a person is capable of self-renewal they are a living being.
Henri Frederic Amiel

Commentary: "A Butterfly Emerging from a Chrysalis" is nothing less than a complete emergence into a new life and total transformation. It's facing a whole new beginning and an entirely new life from what it has previously known. The "Butterfly," after it struggles to "Emerge" from its "Chrysalis," takes a moment to stretch its wings and orient itself. It has shrugged off its "Chrysalis" and is free to take flight when the moment is right.

Oracle: Like an awakening, you may feel that you are suddenly able to do something that truly reflects your inner self and what you've always wanted or meant to become. Things have been developing within you that reflect who you truly want to be. Care will need to be taken with this great effort of birth and rebirth to ensure a smooth transition into another dimension of life. With this brand-new start you will be able to realize many more of your talents and potentials, even the "latent" ones. What have you been storing up and learning and what do you assess your life's purpose to be? There is likely to be an awakening to a whole new field of opportunity, and this can be very exciting, although it can be somewhat confusing and confronting. A cautious but hopeful attitude at first will help you to ease into it. There can be nervousness here, a feeling of having to "find one's feet." It may be a good idea to take a moment to adjust to any new developments before taking flight. There can be some pain involved in the birth of the new, but if one has faith in the new beginning, this is soon forgotten and life takes on a whole new meaning. Events often happen to us to help us come out of ourselves in a more meaningful and beautiful way. Seeing each event as an opportunity for rebirth can lead to new depths of life that you've possibly only previously imagined. Imagine the beauty that is coming through in the birthing of your new wings and this new life.

Keywords: Slow building of confidence. Coming out into a fuller participation in the bigger picture. Growing up and out. Emerging from the dark. Leaving yesterday behind. Becoming more and more beautiful. Finding one's feet or wings. Metamorphosis. Huge changes in the works. Giving up struggling. The drama of new life unfolding.

The Caution: Failing to allow changes to be experienced. Feeling like one will never "arrive." Struggling to emerge ahead of time. Feeling confined. Being tied to the past. Rushing, leading to disorientation or injury.

What does this **SYMBOL** say to *you?*

Aquarius 30

We are like ignorant shepherds living on a site where great civilizations once flourished. The shepherds play with the fragments that pop up to the surface, having no notion of the beautiful structures of which they were once a part.
Allan Bloom

By the waters of Babylon we sit down and weep, when we think of thee, O America!
 Horace Walpole

More than any time in history mankind faces a crossroads. One path leads to despair and utter hopelessness, the other to total extinction. Let us pray that we have the wisdom to choose correctly.
Woody Allen

If it should turn out that we have mishandled our own lives as several civilizations before us have done, it seems a pity that we should involve the violet and the tree frog in our departure.
Loren Eiseley

The earth laughs in flowers.
Ralph Waldo Emerson

MOONLIT FIELDS, ONCE BABYLON, ARE BLOOMING WHITE

Commentary: "Moonlit Fields, Once Babylon, Are Blooming White" is an expression of purity, innocence and the fruits of the past. The Hanging Gardens of Babylon were a magnificent structure that long ago celebrated the rule of human culture. The Gardens were said to be enormous structures with incredibly intricate watering systems. They are one of the Wonders of the Ancient World. Whether real or not, these gardens appeal to the human desire to return to the simple and exquisite life of the Garden of Eden, a life of earthly paradise. The myth of an original garden with perfumed trees and luscious fruits, birds and animal life, and rivers of life-giving waters is common to many faiths including Christianity, Judaism and Islam. Many great advances come out of this region, including language, astronomy and mathematics. Long after Babylon's fall and the manmade structures disappeared, mere remnants of the garden that was "Once Babylon" remain.

Oracle: Even though the grandeur of the past may be lost, changed or damaged by war or time, the energy and power of a place remains. This Symbol reflects the permanence of the natural essence of a place, a person, an idea or a civilization. The essence will long remain and the seeds will sprout forth anew as these "Moonlit Fields Are Now Blooming White." Rewards come from nature's bounty for all the work that's been done even among the devastation and ruin that has been endured. No matter what is thrown at something, the resilience and beauty of its spirit will continue to push through the odds. There may be a feeling that you are in the right place at the right time. All in all, your best qualities or your talents will be recognized and appreciated. When you are following a true path, you are able to rely on the support of the universe in its flow. This is the degree of the beginning of the Age of Aquarius. As the energy of the Age of Pisces wanes, the Age of Aquarius sprouts forth like a "flower" from the ruins of the old.

Keywords: Rewards coming through from past generations. The feeling of ancestors surrounding one's present deeds. Alchemy. Loss of ancient civilizations. Reverence for things from the past. The Middle East and all things middle eastern. Belly dancing. Rebirths of old civilizations. Grandeur. Seeds of the past becoming flowers and fruits of the present. Records. Fields that were once Avalon.

The Caution: Disbelieving because there are no rational structures or support. Destroying ancient lands or monuments because of religious beliefs or greed. The devastation and ruin of Iraq in order for the modern world to succeed. Projecting the sins of the world onto people or places that are foreign.

What does this **SYMBOL** say to *you?*

A CROWDED PUBLIC MARKETPLACE

Pisces 1

Commentary: "A Crowded Public Marketplace" brings to mind images of people bargaining, buying, selling and looking at the products for sale and exchanging thoughts and pleasantries. In a "Public Marketplace" many different things are on display, depending on the current economy and how well people's needs can be met. As the "Market" is "Crowded," there are many people bustling as they move around. People come together, meet each other, and learn about life in their community. They keep up with the news of what's going on while bargaining or buying food, clothing and other necessities.

Oracle: This pictures products being available for sale, barter or investment. Depending on how you see things, the best—and possibly also the worst—aspects of the products available to the community are on display. You may be able to contribute as well as benefit from this. Getting yourself or your products "out there" where they can be appreciated will get you into the game—or is it just the rat race? What can you do to ensure that you can get a fair share of the rewards or the money changing hands? If you are a salesperson, are you prepared to have your "wares" out in the open where they can be criticized and evaluated? If you are a buyer, it is likely that you will find what you're looking for, and possibly more, if you look long enough. Do you know how to bargain, close the sale and get the best deal? There may be questions as to whether things are worth the price placed on them. Ensuring that whatever you have to sell or buy is worthwhile, on all levels—the emotional, mental, physical or spiritual—will protect your good name, reputation or financial status. Are gains and investments equally balanced?

Keywords: Human interchange. Bartering. Commercialism. Shopping centers, markets. The Internet. People fulfilling each other's desires. Buyers and sellers. Classifieds. Consumables. Money changing hands. Products of all kinds. Globalization—its rewards and trappings. Shops and landlords. Storage, stockpiles and stock taking. Bargains and bargaining. The rules of fair trade. Competition. Public opinion. The economy. Trade embargoes. Big business. The stock market. Advertising.

The Caution: Being too stingy or greedy to share benefits. Airing ones "laundry," emotions or possessions in public. Panicking from feeling "crowded in." Exploiting for greed. Disputes over costs. Monopolies. Not letting anything get in the way of making a buck. Always bargaining for one's own advantage. Ripoffs. Sweatshops. Being too busy to enjoy people.

What does this **SYMBOL** say to *you?*

Civilization consists in the multiplication and refinement of human wants.
Robert Millikan

Strategy should evolve out of the mud of the marketplace, not in the antiseptic environment of an ivory tower.
Al Ries

He that does not ask will never get a bargain.
French Proverb

Call someone your lord and he'll sell you in the slave market.
Saudi Arabian Proverb

Everything is worth what its purchaser will pay for it.
Syrus Publilius

The market came with the dawn of civilization and it is not an invention of capitalism … If it leads to improving the wellbeing of the people there is no contradiction with socialism.
Mikhail Gorbachev

The market is a place set apart where men may deceive each other.
Diogenes Laertius

Pisces 2

Why not go out on a limb? Isn't that where the fruit is?
Frank Scully

God gives the nuts but he does not crack them.
German Proverb

Of all the thirty-six alternatives, running away is best.
Chinese Proverb

There is perhaps nothing so bad and so dangerous in life as fear.
Jawaharlal Nehru

Giving advice to a stupid man is like giving salt to a squirrel.
Kashmiri Proverb

A sly rabbit will have three openings to its den.
Chinese Saying

The fox has many tricks. The hedgehog has but one. But that is the best of all.
Desiderius Erasmus

One of the rules of caution is not to be too cautious.
Bahya ibn Paquda

Fear defeats more people than any other one thing in the world.
Ralph Waldo Emerson

Never feel self-pity, the most destructive emotion there is. How awful to be caught up in the terrible squirrel cage of self.
Millicent Fenwick

A SQUIRREL HIDING FROM HUNTERS

Commentary: "A Squirrel Hiding from Hunters" is an image of fear, worry and apprehension. The "Squirrel" senses it is somehow threatened, or that its very survival is at risk. The "Squirrel" is afraid to come out into the open because of a perception that something is out to get it, whether it is true or not. There's a need, or an instinct, to hide from the threatening or aggressive elements in life.

Oracle: Is someone fretting about their position or future? There may be a sense of aggression in the air where you, or someone you know, may be one of the smaller players. Sometimes the "enemy" is actually not really there, and we make it up through fear or paranoia. To be cautious is wise, but hiding oneself away can lead to missed opportunities for any kind of nourishment and the possibility of freedom, sunshine and basking in the light. The provision of nourishment and sustenance may be difficult if one feels somehow threatened. This feeling of "threat" can happen on any level. It may have been a necessary process to go through the fright, care and worry facing you, but the time has to eventually come when you can feel safe and able to enjoy life. Is your neighborhood threatening or unsafe in some way? Although we may not like to admit it, sometimes "Hiding" away is the best option, whether your fears are real or merely imagined. This can give you time to sort things through in your heart and mind to decide what your next move will be. This Symbol can bring nervousness and a lack of sleep. If you feel victimized and "holed up" in this matter, perhaps a safer home or living environment would make things easier. It is true that if we project fear out into our environment, it will most likely manifest in a reaction or event somewhere. What creative solutions can you employ to ensure a safe outcome for all concerned? After all, do the "Hunters" really want to shoot a "Squirrel"?

Keywords: Using tactics to ensure survival. "Hiding" one's self away. Not stepping out into the big wide world for fear of making the wrong move. Security systems. Caution and reserve. Using common sense. Things or people that feel tiny, uncertain or insecure. Refuges and the need for them. Staying out of people's way. Staying home. Locks and keys. Stockpiling for harder times.

The Caution: People picking on each other. Being bullied out of what you deserve. Giving those "out there" more power than they warrant. Not trusting life. Paranoia. Running away from things. Not wanting to go out and socialize. Truancy. Not speaking up for fear of being shot down. Threats of terrorism. Having to lie about one's whereabouts. Not answering the door. Being caged in. Agoraphobia. Claustrophobia.

What does this **SYMBOL** say to *you?*

A PETRIFIED FOREST, AN ETERNAL RECORD OF A LIFE LIVED LONG AGO

Pisces 3

Commentary: "A Petrified Forest" brings to mind fossils and insects stuck in amber and other remnants of ages past. They are "Records" that have long been around to remind us of how life was in more ancient times. That it is "an Eternal Record of a Life Lived Long Ago" shows that the achievements of life do not necessarily disappear when we move on, or go through major change or the death of the old. Things continue to exist such as records, memories, art, literature, photographs, letters, e-mails, etc.

Oracle: There's a need to retrieve, sort through, or go over "Records" from the past in some way. This may be the time to look to these histories or to appreciate their value and relevance to life today. However, memories from the past can freeze up life in the present and hold us in an unmovable state. Sometimes difficult or painful memories from childhood can inhibit and stop the processes of new growth in the present. Is the past stopping you from growth or are worries about age freezing you? Is the situation facing you stuck in time without a clear understanding of how to proceed? Therapies can act to reawaken memories or knowledge from out of the past, even when it looks like everything has dried up or died. Perhaps you're learning about the importance of keeping records; the past can so easily be lost and it can be difficult, if not impossible, to accurately remember or recall it. Try looking at your "Records," your memories and things such as photographs and diaries from years gone by. New life can be found as long as one is willing to look. Getting the "dead wood" out of your life, whether it is clogging up your cupboards, your relationships, your emotional life, even the garden, etc., can clear the way for the growth of new life.

Keywords: Remnants from the past. Stillness. Agelessness. Plastic surgery. Being able to withstand life's storms. Resilience. Crystals, diamonds, gemstones. Beauty that remains ageless. Wood and lacquered wood. Coal, oil and petrochemicals. Diets. Dependability. Family histories. Keeping records. Amber. Fossils. Geology. Archeology. Ancient remnants. Mental and emotional filing cabinets. Lingering evidence. Petrified wood. Photographs and photography. Stones. Stone monuments. Diaries.

The Caution: Rigidity, immobility, inflexibility. Being frozen. Not letting go of difficulties. Hanging on for grim death. Feeling stuck. Destroying the old. Severing links to the past. Keeping tabs. Memories that destroy the present.

What does this **SYMBOL** say to *you?*

The tendency of old age to the body, say the physiologists, is to form bone. It is as rare as it is pleasant to meet with an old man whose opinions are not ossified.
J. F. Boyse

A photograph never grows old. You and I change, people change all through the months and years, but a photograph always remains the same. How nice to look at a photograph of mother or father taken many years ago. You see them as you remember them. But as people live on, they change completely. That is why I think a photograph can be kind.
Albert Einstein

Every scientific truth goes through three states: first, people say it conflicts with the Bible; next, they say it has been discovered before. Lastly, they say they always believed it.
Louis Agassiz

Keep some souvenirs of your past, or how will you ever prove it wasn't all a dream?
Ashleigh Brilliant

Language is the amber in which a thousand precious and subtle thoughts have been safely embedded and preserved.
Richard C. Trench

Pisces 4

I'm astounded by people who want to "know" the universe when it's hard enough to find your way around Chinatown.
Woody Allen

When everything's coming your way, you're in the wrong lane.
Stephen Wright

Maybe I'm lucky to be going so slowly, because I may be going in the wrong direction.
Ashleigh Brilliant

When you come to a roadblock, take a detour.
Mary Kay Ash

In between goals is a thing called life, that has to be lived and enjoyed.
Sid Caesar

All men should strive to learn before they die, what they are running from, and to, and why.
James Thurber

Every road has two directions.
Russian Proverb

To know the road ahead, ask those coming back.
Chinese Proverb

I'm wanted at the traffic jam, they're saving me a seat.
Leonard Cohen

HEAVY CAR TRAFFIC LINKING TWO SEASIDE RESORTS

Commentary: "Heavy Car Traffic Linking Two Seaside Resorts" pictures "Traffic" streaming along a road or thoroughfare. The journey to and from desirable places like "Seaside Resorts" can be difficult and frustrating as many people may be in the same area, having the same destination. When the situation is "Linking Two Seaside Resorts," it can be even more difficult with traffic backups, delays and accidents, particularly at peak hour. If the "drivers" don't follow the codes of good driving by merging politely and allowing people to come into the flow of "Traffic," there can be "road rage," impatience and intolerance.

Oracle: This can show communications and linkages between separate worlds leading to increased pleasure or frustration, confusion or psychic indigestion. There's a need for patience and give and take as there is a lot going on and confusion can set in if one doesn't follow the rules of the game. Abiding by acceptable rules and procedures along with common sense will ensure a smooth flow of operations. You may feel like you are getting stuck in a pattern that continually bounces back and forth, never arriving at any final or desirable destination. This can be very tiring. It is important to realize that although being "squeezed in" can bring on a sense of panic or discomfort, the chances are that it will not be permanent and there is probably something better and more pleasurable waiting for you once you get out of the current situation. See if you can get some time out from running around, mentally, emotionally or physically. This Symbol can show someone who loves pleasure being easily bored or distracted by what seem to be better offers or opportunities, and continually on the lookout for better places or people. Much time can be lost on the journey only to find that you are in the same sort of position you were in in the first place.

Keywords: Going with the flow. Running back and forth. Having to move continually. Pollution and car exhaust. Rush hour and road rage. Plans for arrivals and departures. Public holidays. Traffic jams. Traffic backing up. Having trouble making left-hand turns. Detours. Packing and unpacking. Luggage. Travel itineraries. Impasses. Nervous systems. Urine therapy. Constant phone calls. Switchboard jams. Heat and smog.

The Caution: Creating barriers. Constant traffic stopping the possibility of real human interchange. Claustrophobia. Feeling like there is no escape. Exhaustion due to everyday hustle and bustle. Running out of fuel. Accidents. Taking the long way around. Blockages.

What does this **SYMBOL** say to *you?*

A CHURCH BAZAAR

Commentary: "A Church Bazaar" is an image of people in a community coming together to have fun, have something to eat and drink, get a bargain, and possibly make some new friends. This "Bazaar" could be something that the community has long been anticipating, or it could be a more regular event. Either way, there are things bought and sold, fun and gossip to be had and new relationships forged. For some, there is a considerable amount of work to be done. Money from the "Bazaar" often goes to the "Church" or to help people in need in the community.

Oracle: This Symbol shows the pooling of talents and resources to help people or create uplifting experiences for others. It also represents old-fashioned values brought to the community through simple commerce and the warmth of sharing. This is primarily a time for group cooperation to benefit the people of the community. People cooperate and get involved in activities that have a people-centered outcome rather than a purely economic one. In this situation, you may be unable to achieve your goals on your own, so a certain amount of trust must be bestowed on those around you. Altruistic and selfless attitudes should be employed. The community can be enriched in many ways from displays of togetherness, giving and sharing, and through charitable works. There can, however, be a tendency to use faith or communal goodwill to extract money or services from people. Be sure that the benefits go to the correct causes, not simply for one's own gain. However, someone may need to give up always doing or giving for others, in order to receive. There are often small rewards here, but they can be bigger or better than you first realized or prove to be more important than they first appeared. For the "Bazaar" to be successful, people need to gather together the bits and pieces for the sale, bring the jars of jam, organize the stalls and ensure that the community knows about it.

Keywords: Overcoming loneliness and alienation. Selling things. The issue of real worth. A lot of effort for small rewards. Small-scale commercial bartering and interchange. The collection plate. Generosity and charitable community attitudes. Jars of jam and things handmade. Bric-a-brac. Bargains. Practical spirituality. Volunteers. People sharing the load. Charity work. Money raising. Garage or yard sales. Secondhand clothes.

The Caution: Spiritual or social exclusivity. Giving things smaller worth than they deserve. Using people. Deception on the grounds of faith. Fussing about small details. Fighting over "position." Issues of territory. Pushy people. Social boundaries that exclude some.

What does this **SYMBOL** say to *you?*

Sharing is sometimes more demanding than giving.
Mary Bateson

One man gives freely, yet grows all the richer; another withholds what he should give, and only suffers want.
The Bible

He who bestows his goods upon the poor shall have as much again, and ten times more.
John Bunyan

If you have great wealth, give alms out of your abundance; if you have but little, distribute even some of that. But do not hesitate to give alms.
Apocrypha

Charity has its own rewards.
Anonymous

Never let your zeal outrun your charity. The former is but human, the latter is divine.
Hosea Ballou

In necessary things, unity; in doubtful things, liberty; in all things, charity.
Richard Baxter

Pisces 6

What a curious phenomenon it is that you can get men to die for the liberty of the world who will not make the little sacrifice that is needed to free themselves from their own individual bondage.
Bruce Barton

Duty is the sublimest word in our language. Do your duty in all things. You cannot do more. You should never do less.
Robert E. Lee

Pressed into service means pressed out of shape.
Robert Frost

Every generation of Americans needs to know that freedom consists not in doing what we like, but in having the right to do what we ought.
Pope John Paul

Parades should be classed as a nuisance and participants should be subject to a term in prison.
Will Rogers

Eternal nothingness is fine if you happen to be dressed for it.
Woody Allen

If you look good and dress well, you don't need a purpose in life.
Robert Pante

A PARADE OF ARMY OFFICERS IN FULL DRESS

Commentary: "A Parade of Army Officers in Full Dress." They have smartened themselves up, put on their uniforms and gathered together in a display put on for the sake of the community. There's a need for them to follow protocol and show a brave, cohesive face for the sake of the "Parade." Their morale needs to be high and upbeat.

Oracle: There is a need to be aware of duty, honor and the protection of higher ideals. You may be a part of something big and worthwhile. Wearing some kind of "uniform" may be required to show allegiance to a particular cause, country, relationship or other area of life. Wearing the "right clothes" and presenting the "right image" can lead to feelings of acceptance, respect and belonging. Dedication, discipline and duty bring their own kinds of rewards. However, sometimes people would rather not have to put in all the effort for little apparent return. Whatever, showing pride and solidarity will help this situation move forward. There are issues of having to show one's "authority" in public. One may have to learn to withstand criticism or feelings of just being "one of the crowd." Maybe there's a desire for, or a fear of, typecasting: being cast in a stereotypical mold. Do you really belong in this situation, or would you really rather go AWOL? Are you being bullied and told what to do and how to live your life? Perhaps you feel like you've signed up for a commitment and, at times, you do not want to put in the work. What procedures must be followed here? This "Parade" is something that will eventually pass by. Putting on your best face and joining with others will ensure success.

Keywords: National pride on display. Reminders of those putting life and limb on the line for kin and country. Uniforms, hats. People seeking recognition from the community, regardless of what they've personally achieved. Patriotism. Memories of war. Being committed to service. Medals. Stripes. Uniformity. Grinning and bearing it. Projecting the "right image." Drills and routines. Displays of courage. Assembling together. Braiding and piping. Spit and polish. Parades and marching. Police and law enforcement. Guns and bayonets. The importance of looking good.

The Caution: "Stiff" and unfeeling displays. Having special privileges that others don't. Doing what one must do. Hiding behind a façade. Not being prepared, or able, to show one's true self. "Drill sergeants" who scream and shout. People parading their importance. False courage. Taking the glory away from the little people. Wearing anything.

What does this **SYMBOL** say to *you?*

ILLUMINATED BY A SHAFT OF LIGHT, A LARGE CROSS LIES ON ROCKS SURROUNDED BY SEA AND MIST

Pisces 7

Commentary: "Illuminated by a Shaft of Light, a Large Cross Lies on Rocks Surrounded by Sea and Mist" is an image that inspires feelings of chaos and misplaced loyalties. It can feel as though something has been unjustly sacrificed and things have come to nothing. Christ was forsaken on "a Large Cross." The "Cross" can indicate a crucifix and can show the shouldering of trouble and misfortune or faith and hope. The "Shaft of Light" indicates that spiritual and creative help is at hand.

Oracle: There could be a feeling that life has not been "good" enough. Thoughts of helplessness can come from feeling as though one's life is finished and that all is lost. Perhaps one's aim was too high and things have come crashing down. Feeling forsaken or used in relationships can lead to a sense of loss of belonging or identity. It may indeed seem that much has been lost, but do we really have to continue to suffer so much? Seeing the positive or the spiritual messages that come in dark moments can shed new understandings that transcend even the most difficult times. With faith and a positive outcome in mind, you may experience a true awakening, or a reconnection with your spiritual ideals and hope for the future. A sign may come soon to show that you are on the right track to recovery of life and love. Letting go of outworn relationships, allegiances or beliefs will assist you to move on with a stronger sense of self. However, are there still some worthwhile and wonderful things that can be salvaged or things to be grateful for? Concentrate on "the Shaft of Light" as this can lead you to see that "Light" is indeed all around you.

Keywords: Renewed dedication after loss. Looking for signs of hope and recovery. Coming to terms with loss or failure. Rocks, mist, howling winds on coasts. Crosses of faith. Important and substantial sacrifices. Being devastated by events. Being in the "spotlight" in difficult times. Finding the way through the dark. The need for sacrifice. Alternative religions. Stepping outside religious boundaries.

The Caution: Lost faith. Hopes dashed. Giving up. Being shattered by the constraints of life. Depression. Feeling like one is being sacrificed, sometimes for nothing. Unable to see through the fog. Scorn, persecution and attack because of religious or social reasons. Hopelessness. Things grim, dark and foreboding.

What does this **SYMBOL** say to *you?*

Crosses are ladders that lead to heaven.
Proverb

In order for the light to shine so brightly, the darkness must be present.
Francis Bacon

No pain, no palm; no thorns, no throne; no gall, no glory; no cross, no crown.
William Penn

Call on God, but row away from the rocks.
Indian Proverb

When things are at the worst they begin to mend.
Proverb

I don't believe in miracles because it's been a long time since we've had any.
Joseph Heller

We see but dimly through the mists and vapors;
Amid these earthly damps
What seem to us but sad, funeral tapers
May be heaven's distant lamps.
Henry Wadsworth Longfellow

Faith is one of the forces by which men live, and the total absence of it means collapse.
William James

Pisces 8

If you wish in this world to advance,
Your merits you're bound to enhance;
You must stir it and stump it,
And blow your own trumpet,
Or trust me, you haven't a chance.
William Gilbert

The very essence of leadership is that you have to have a vision. You can't blow an uncertain trumpet.
Theodore Hesburgh

He seems determined to make a trumpet sound like a tin whistle.
Aneurin Bevan

If the trumpet gives an uncertain sound, who shall prepare himself for the battle?
The Bible

No trumpets sound when the important decisions of our life are made. Destiny is made known silently.
Agnes George DeMille

Stay we no longer, dreaming of renown, but sound the trumpets, and about our task.
William Shakespeare

Trumpet in a herd of elephants; crow in the company of cocks; bleat in a flock of goats.
Malayan Proverb

Ambition is like love, impatient both of delays and rivals.
Sir John Denham

A GIRL BLOWING A BUGLE

Commentary: "A Girl Blowing a Bugle" brings to mind someone performing reveille; the "Bugle" call used in the armed forces announcing that it is time to "rise and shine." The "Bugle" is a brass-wind instrument, somewhat like a trumpet, but usually without keys or valves. It has been used mostly for military calls and signals, but it's also sometimes used as a hunting horn. Its chief function is to sound, to summon, to signal by blowing a "Bugle" call. In dream imagery, the "Blowing of a Bugle" foretells fortunate things coming your way.

Oracle: You may need to sound the call to wake up those around you, or perhaps be woken yourself. The situation facing you may be bogged down in irrational complexity, when everybody needs to have a central focus and be rallying and going for the objective. There may be unexpected revelations and something may take you by shock. If somebody is "sounding off" loudly, it can cause irritation and upset. Is it you, or another, who's making all the noise? There may need to be a balance around exactly how much noise one should make. Having a cause to loudly "trumpet" can make people respond by pulling back or being disinterested. Keeping a balance between excited enthusiasm, forward momentum and just plain making noise will bring rewards of some kind—even if it only wakes up those around you. "Blowing the Bugle" too early or too forcefully can put people off, which can be the exact opposite of what's desired. This can lead to people not listening, indeed even running away, instead of being aroused to their duty. Does everyone around want to hear the message that's being trumpeted, or are they trying, or fighting, to cover their ears? Using simple, receptive innocence will get the situation on track.

Keywords: Sounding the call. Awakening all to action. Going on and on about something. Loudspeakers, telephones, announcements. Being prepared to state one's case. Calling attention to one's self. Blowing your own trumpet. Whistleblowers. Heralding and proclaiming the dawn. Rise and shine! Girls in a man's world. Leading the charge. Resurrection. Mass announcements. Advertising campaigns. Alarm clocks. Ear plugs. Blindfolds. Break the fast. Proclamations.

The Caution: Making unwarranted and disturbing noise. Showing off. Unbalanced messages. Evangelists and politicians. Sounding the call but not making the grade. Being annoying. Trumpeting about one's achievements. Not listening to people.

What does this **SYMBOL** say to *you?*

THE RACE BEGINS: INTENT ON OUTDISTANCING HIS RIVALS, A JOCKEY SPURS HIS HORSE TO GREAT SPEED

Commentary: "The Race Begins: Intent on Outdistancing His Rivals, a Jockey Spurs His Horse to Great Speed" is an image of competition, speed and excitement. The "Jockey" has one goal in mind; he is "Intent on Outdistancing His Rivals."

Oracle: The race is on and you may feel that you are near the finish, but there is no guarantee of victory. Although it is time to extract all available energy possible into the situation, make sure you're not expending it too quickly and not really getting anywhere or achieving anything of lasting value. Be careful not to bolt out of the gate without thought of the ramifications. Watching your competitors brings some reassurance regarding your position, but you can't always be looking around, you have to get on with the job at hand. What can you do in this situation to ensure "the win"? Wanting to be better and faster and wanting the prize can lead to incredible feats and accomplishments, and this is to be admired and praised. What efforts will push you further, faster, than the rest of the field? Having a one-sighted goal of winning the race can lead to a wonderful victory. However, it can also bring a kind of addiction to outdoing others. It can lead to wanting, and needing, to win regardless of the cost. This can alienate you from others, especially if attention is always solely on the goal of winning. Be wary of expending your energy too soon as it can lead to running out of steam before the finish line. Being "Intent on Outdistancing" one's "Rivals" can also lead to feelings of wanting to outdo your own efforts again and again. Seeing your goal and heading straight toward it can see you taking first place but how's your training for this situation? Have you done the groundwork in order to compete?

Keywords: Competitiveness and high ambitions. Wanting to win, sometimes against the odds. Losing and gaining weight. Weightlessness. Racing to be first at things. Demanding quick flight. Bolting out of the gate. Aggressive desires. Exhilaration. Wanting to better oneself. Being on the home run. Speed and the need for it. Facing forward with great intensity. Rivals and competitors. The value of training. Horsemanship. Discipline. Energy poured into the drive to succeed. Starting whistles, pistols or lights.

The Caution: Galloping at full speed prematurely. Being too ambitious. Ruthless measures. Jumping the gun. Doing anything to win or succeed. Being pushy or single minded. Running out of steam before the finish line. Weight dropping off too quickly. Sabotage or blocking other's efforts. Reigning in energy at the last moment.

What does this **SYMBOL** say to *you?*

You were born to win, but to be a winner, you must plan to win, prepare to win, and expect to win.
Zig Ziglar

Courage is being scared to death but saddling up anyway.
John Wayne

Half the failures in life arise from pulling in one's horse as he is leaping.
A. W. Hare

When my horse is running good, I don't stop to give him sugar.
William Faulkner

Seize the day.
Horace

I began to suggest that thought, which I had always before looked on as a cart-horse to be driven, whipped and plodding between shafts, might be really a Pegasus, so suddenly did it alight beside me from places I had no knowledge of.
Joanna Field

We tolerate shapes in human beings that would horrify us if we saw them in a horse.
William Ralph Inge

Pisces 10

Here's a riddle for our age: when the sky's the limit, how can you tell you've gone too far?
Rita Dove

No bird soars too high if he soars with his own wings.
William Blake

Flying might not be all plain sailing, but the fun of it is worth the price.
Amelia Earhart

No flying machine will ever fly from New York to Paris … [because] no known motor can run at the requisite speed for four days without stopping.
Orville Wright

As we do at such times, I turned on my automatic pilot and went through the motions of normalcy on the outside, so that I could concentrate all my powers on surviving the near-mortal wound inside.
Sonia Johnson

Don't "over control" like a novice pilot. Stay loose enough from the flow that you can observe it, modify, and improve it.
Donald Rumsfeld

Ah, Hope! what would life be, stripped of thy encouraging smiles, that teach us to look behind the dark clouds of to-day, for the golden beams that are to gild the morrow.
Susanna Moodie

AN AVIATOR IN THE CLOUDS

Commentary: "An Aviator in the Clouds" is an image of a pilot in his plane flying at such a high altitude that he is among the "Clouds." It must be exhilarating to be up so high and observing this wonderful other realm. However, flying high can lead to feelings of being cut off and separate from reality and the real world and it is only a matter of time before the "Aviator" must come down out of the "Clouds" as the constraints of his more earth-bound existence eventually kick in.

Oracle: There may be a need to transcend what's going on and to rise above difficulties. You may find that you have to rely on your intellectual or emotional skills to take you above and beyond your current situation. Just be aware that you may not be seeing the complete picture very clearly at the moment. Alternatively, you may be actively evading the real truth. If you take special notice, you will be able to see through illusions, to see through surface appearances and observe things that others may miss. Where are you sailing in the sky? Is it too high up to be able to really "see" anything? Do you feel the need to disconnect with what's going on and to simply observe instead of becoming involved? What will happen if you keep flying without watching how much fuel you have at your disposal, and you run out? Whatever the situation, put your energy into enjoying the journey. Watch, observe and learn about your life from a heightened perspective. Are you the "pilot" or a copilot?

Keywords: Elevated views. Always seeing the best in people and things. Peace and tranquility. The longing for transcendence. Not seeing limitations. Being in a refined "head space." Mastery. Flight, planes, pilots. Avoidance of time constraints. Pollyanna attitudes. Free flights of fantasy and escapism. The need for accurate navigation. Being in charge of the controls. Seeking higher truths. Maps. Compasses. Global satellite positioning. Clouds. Mist and fog. Hang-gliding.

The Caution: Sailing through difficulties or missing what's really going on. Escapist use of alcohol and drugs, etc. Lack of grounded energy or reality. Being unearthed. Escaping responsibilities. Isolating oneself. Completely missing the point. Feeling high and mighty and above everyone else, particularly with intellectual skills. Wrong turns. Missing the signs. Feeling like you're living in a fog. Disconnecting from others, leading to isolation. Losing the plot. Taking huge risks. One's head being separate from the body.

What does this **SYMBOL** say to *you?*

MEN TRAVELING A NARROW PATH, SEEKING ILLUMINATION

Pisces 11

The difficulties you meet will resolve themselves as you advance. Proceed, and light will dawn, and shine with increasing clearness on your path.
D'Alembert

There are two mistakes one can make along the road to truth—not going all the way, and not starting.
Buddha

On a long journey of human life, faith is the best of companions; it is the best refreshment on the journey; and it is the greatest property.
Buddha

Awake, arise! Strive for the Highest, and be in the Light! Sages say the path is narrow and difficult to tread, narrow as the edge of a razor.
Upanishads

If you follow your bliss, you put yourself on a kind of track, which has been there all the while waiting for you, and the life that you ought to be living is the one you are living.
Joseph Campbell

Commentary: "Men Traveling a Narrow Path, Seeking Illumination" is an image of people on a mission, seeking to find some knowledge or truth. They are on a journey of discovery, endeavoring to find the answers to questions that may have eluded them until now. They are "Traveling a Narrow Path," one that probably has deep meaning, regardless of the perceived outcome in terms of society's expectations. This journey is likely to be a very personal one for each participant, even though there may be many who are "Seeking" the same things.

Oracle: Sometimes the search for "Illumination," with its high levels of understanding and idealism, places us at odds with more conservative social expectations. It is the ability to persevere with the search, regardless of the cost, that marks the sincerity of a journey. Most often this quest is "Illuminating," although it can sometimes be confusing, as new information comes flooding into the as yet unformed, or uninformed, conscious awareness. You will need to reject that which is unworthy on the "Path" as it could lead to disillusionment about values and what is truly worth pursuing. This Symbol can indicate the need to go without many things or to stick to a strict agenda in order to accomplish a task, goal or education. It may have taken some time to find this particular direction in life. Disregarding one's more mundane physical needs and emotions may be necessary in the quest for getting to the place of ambition or attainment. You may have to leave others behind when you set out. As this is a "Narrow Path," not all can share the same endeavor or, indeed, would want to. The rewards are usually rich in some measure as one moves toward the light, the "Illumination." Maybe you should ask yourself—are you on "a Path" or a treadmill? Be wary of taking shortcuts, as these may not lead to the thing that's intended.

Keywords: People "on the Path." Sticking to one mindset, diet, regimen or habit. Having a cause to follow. Not looking sideways. Awakening one's base senses in order to progress. Physical ecstasy. Being in the now. Going toward the light. Staying true to self. The promise of light at the end of the journey.

The Caution: Blinded by the light. Not knowing where you're really going. Disillusionment about what's been chosen. Being one-eyed about goals and beliefs. The denial of physical pleasure. Puritanical behavior. Distractions that stop forward movement. Narrow mindedness.

What does this **SYMBOL** say to *you?*

Pisces 12

To avoid criticism, do nothing, say nothing, be nothing.
Elbert Hubbard

Don't wait for the last judgment; it takes place every day.
Albert Camus

Great Spirit, help me never to judge another until I have walked in his moccasins for two weeks.
Sioux Indian Prayer

The sage, who is living outside the routine of the world, contemplates his own character, not as an isolated ego manifestation, but in relation to the laws of life. He judges freedom from blame to be the highest good.
I Ching

I was thrown out of college for cheating on the metaphysics exam; I looked into the soul of the boy sitting next to me.
Woody Allen

Life is a classroom in which each of us is being tested, tried, and passed.
Robert Thibodeau

These are the times that try men's souls.
Thomas Paine

Don't judge a book by it's cover.
Old Saying

AN EXAMINATION OF INITIATES IN THE SANCTUARY OF AN OCCULT BROTHERHOOD

Commentary: "An Examination of Initiates in the Sanctuary of an Occult Brotherhood" pictures students, "Initiates," doing their "Examinations," and being judged or evaluated by their elders. They are "In the Sanctuary of an Occult Brotherhood" which suggests that they are somehow "cloistered" or closed off from the prying eyes of the external world. This may have been through their own choice or it could have been forced on them by society.

Oracle: You may find that those above or around you are judging or testing you. It is difficult to know just what their qualifications to judge you are, but this is often the nature of progression through the ranks. Sometimes we need to let others make their own practical assessments of our individual worth and "Examinations" of any kind can show others the stuff we're made of. If you feel that you, or someone else, are being tested and examined, remember that if you perform at your best that is really the best that can be done. People being critical of one another can lead to better behavior, better performances or the like, or it can lead to feeling judged, violated and intruded upon. There might be a desire to pull someone down, particularly someone who seems to be getting "too big for their boots." Sometimes it seems that our lives are like lessons, and we are periodically "Examined" to see how we are doing on our "path." Does everyone want to stay on the same track or are some people wondering what they're doing or where they're going?

Keywords: The ordeal that comes to any initiate for entrance into higher realms of being. Hermits. Tests, examinations, having to prove one's self. Being judged or being judgmental. Being cross-examined. Rarefied atmospheres that demand personal sacrifice. Initiations. Proving courage and purity. Trials. The attainment of knowledge. Apprenticeships. Being a candidate. Finding out how and where one fits in. One-eyed dedication. Trial by media. Cults. Rituals.

The Caution: Refusing advice. Arrogance. People saying "I told you so." Invading others' private space. Hiding away because of fear or social ridicule. Severe trials and tests that strip the joy of life. People assuming they know the truth about others. Fear of failure. Not living up to other's expectations. Narrow mindedness. Harsh treatment. Going without.

What does this **SYMBOL** say to *you?*

A SWORD, USED IN MANY BATTLES, IS NOW IN A MUSEUM

Pisces 13

Commentary: "A Sword" that has been "Used in Many Battles" is "Now in a Museum." It has most likely seen many struggles, battles and conflicts. It may have had to defend the honor of someone or something, and now it is placed in a "Museum" where people can come and look at it and wonder at its history. The "Sword" is such a masculine image, strong, heroic, metallic, sharp, hard and forbidding. The "Sword" has done its job and now needs to be put away somewhere where it won't need to fight or defend. That it is in "a Museum" points to the fact that it is a reminder of the battles of days gone by.

Oracle: When reminded of the "Battles" of the past, hopefully we are influenced toward peace, but we are also uplifted by the memory of the strength of the participants, their bravery and valor. You may be faced with the choice of fighting for something or reasoning with the intellect. This can be confusing if you lack training or experience in the ways of doing "Battle." The obvious message is that it's time to lay down one's "Sword," not in order to necessarily surrender, but to stop "the warring." Perhaps this pictures someone who doesn't know when to give up taking others on and fighting. This Symbol shows it's time to give up "Battling," to aim now for more peaceful solutions. There may have been a lot learned in the "Battles" you've experienced, but the thing that's best learned is that continuing to fight may lead to a bitter end, with no one being a true winner. Now's the time to lay down the "Sword" and accept love and peace back into your life. Putting the "Sword" away in a "Museum" can allow others to benefit from the struggles that have been undertaken, without worrying about how this weapon will be used in the future. How long can one go on battling, fighting and defending?

Keywords: Willpower. Martial arts. Putting aside thoughts of vengeance and revenge. Hanging up or laying down one's "Sword." Trophies of conquest that remind us of the past. History. Aging and maturing. Retirement. Remnants of battles. Souvenirs of the past. "Words as swords." The Spear of Destiny. The sword Excalibur. Disarming weapons. The search for truth and justice. Suits of armor. Peace at last. Sexual impotence.

The Caution: A lack of sensitivity. A pretense of one's abilities. Giving up and "falling on one's sword" from defeat. Grudges. Wanting to go into "Battle" at the slightest excuse. Selfish agendas. Weapons of mass destruction or weapons of mass distraction? Preemptive strikes. Defensive behavior. Domestic violence.

What does this **SYMBOL** say to *you?*

Yet each man kills the thing he loves,
By each let this be heard,
Some do it with a bitter look,
Some with a flattering word,
The coward does it with a kiss,
The brave man with a sword!
Oscar Wilde

If we could read the secret history of our enemies we should find in each man's life sorrow and suffering enough to disarm all hostility.
Henry Wadsworth Longfellow

The basic difference between an ordinary man and a warrior is that a warrior takes everything as a challenge, while an ordinary man takes everything as either a blessing or a curse.
Don Juan

Logic is like the sword—those who appeal to it shall perish by it.
Samuel Butler

We are going to have peace even if we have to fight for it.
Dwight D. Eisenhower

The writer, making every effort to appear innocent and noble, takes his revenge with the pen; while the murderer, less hypocritical, takes it with the sword.
Christopher Spranger

All who take the sword will perish by the sword.
The Bible

Pisces 14

BEAUTY, n. That power by which a woman charms a lover and terrifies a husband.
Ambrose Bierce

Plain women know more about men than beautiful women do.
Katharine Hepburn

Instinct is untaught ability.
Alexander Bain

Feminine virtue is nothing but a convenient masculine invention.
Ninon de Lenclos

Money is better than poverty, if only for financial reasons.
Woody Allen

There is nothing so agonizing to the fine skin of vanity as the application of a rough truth.
Edward G. Bulwer-Lytton

In our society those who are in reality superior in intelligence can be accepted by their fellows only if they pretend they are not.
Marya Mannes

The common practice of keeping up appearances with society is a mere selfish struggle of the vain with the vain.
John Ruskin

A WOMAN WRAPPED IN FOX FUR

Commentary: "A Woman" is "Wrapped in Fox Fur." She presents a beautiful image and one has the sense that she radiates intelligence, grace and wealth. The "Fox Fur" carries the feeling of protection being given through the use of wit, tact, diplomacy, glamour and intellect. There is an aura of "street smarts" about the "Woman Wrapped in Fox Fur," like she could get out of (or into) any situation that she chooses.

Oracle: Someone is trying to present an image that will enhance their position. Whether this is you or another, using intelligence and wit will probably see one through. If, however, the guise, or disguise, were to be stripped away, would the same qualities be expressed? You may find that you have to display your capabilities because you suffer negative prejudice or chauvinism, or are underestimated. It may be that you are not being listened to. Difficulties can arise when others misunderstand what it is that you are projecting and over- or underestimate your message. In any case, there's a need to be quick-witted and perceptive. Also, there may be occasion to have to change strategies quickly. This can show proof of your intelligence and your ability to "think on your feet." The display of elegance has to come not only from your appearance and your demeanor but also through the things you say. It is important to be able to deliver and follow through on the image you portray. Any artificial attempts to try to fool others about how smart you are may lead to unwarranted reactions. However, do be wary of focusing solely on others' perceptions of you. This Symbol can also represent the desire to show off one's wealth, as though possessions and material gains are an example of class and intelligence. You may lose track of what you truly feel about yourself.

Keywords: Outer expressions of real inner worth. Animal magnetism and attraction. Intelligence and its display. Cloaks of feminine wit and sexuality. Beguiling minds. Animal totems and furs. Perceived beauty. The sense of having class and money. Beauty, fashion and talent. Being forward and upfront. Sense of personal style. Grace and composure. Elegance. Knowing what to say and when. Dressing up. Money spent on beauty. Tempting others with sexual signals. Perfumes. Pheromones. Taxidermy.

The Caution: False fronts and expressions of wealth. Selling out for momentary, or monetary, gain. Wrapped in intellectual superficiality. The fatal allure of beauty. Scoring points solely through charisma. Being so caught up in fashion and glamor that one loses a true sense of self. Being overdressed.

What does this **SYMBOL** say to *you*?

AN OFFICER DRILLING HIS MEN IN A SIMULATED ATTACK

Pisces 15

Commentary: "An Officer Drilling His Men in a Simulated Attack." Sometimes in life, the danger of things is overstated, exaggerated and overestimated and it looks like all hell is going to break lose at any minute. However, there is wisdom in practicing being on the alert to reduce the chance of error or failure when a real "Attack" comes along. Putting on a show of strength in order to put off threats from the outside can help promote feelings of safety and solidarity.

Oracle: You may need to rehearse or prepare for a difficult upcoming situation. It's true that if we stay alert to the possibility of "Attack" or confrontation, it helps us to respond when it's really necessary. However, often the expected "Attack" never eventuates. Sometimes there is more energy expended in the "Drilling" of tactical maneuvers than exists in the actual threat itself. The trick is to be able keep on one's guard, and to relax at the same time. People can be yelled at and commanded to respond in a certain way to the point where they lose their sense of natural spontaneity, fun and lightheartedness of being. There could be provocation and possibly downright bullying, but it probably doesn't have much substance, especially if you don't allow it any. Keeping a strong sense of your own authority will ensure a better outcome for all. How prepared are you for what might happen? Are you going over the possible outcomes a little too much, thereby losing the joy that can be found in relaxing or letting down your guard? Is there someone picking on you or telling you what to do, or are you the perpetrator yourself? One exercise for disciplining the mind is to make up some positive commands and apply them to your everyday thoughts. Try allowing only positive thoughts. Witnessing the mind for negative, self-defeating or annoying messages can stop them dead in their tracks.

Keywords: Taking orders to better respond to situations. The higher self training the lower self. Exercises. Marching and going through the motions. The need for defense. Seeing ahead. Planning strategies. Fire drills. Smoke alarms. Being prepared. Issuing orders and expecting them to be followed through. Discipline. Martial arts of all kinds. Going over and over possible outcomes. Safeguards put in place. Gas masks and bomb shelters.

The Caution: Rigid routine for no real or valuable purpose. Feeling that one has always to be on the defensive. Being under attack, whether real or imagined. Overreacting to things. Feelings of unworthiness in the face of battle or confrontation. Victim consciousness. Fearful responses. Getting others to respond through spreading fear. Scare tactics.

What does this **SYMBOL** say to *you?*

It is hard to fight an enemy who has outposts in your head.
Sally Kempton

It takes 15,000 casualties to train a major general.
Ferdinand Foch

Do not touch anything unnecessarily. Beware of pretty girls in dance halls and parks who may be spies, as well as bicycles, revolvers, uniforms, arms, dead horses, and men lying on roads—they are not there accidentally.
Soviet infantry manual, issued in the 1930s

A frightened captain makes a frightened crew.
Lister Sinclair

Military intelligence is a contradiction in terms.
Groucho Marx

To be prepared against surprise is to be trained. To be prepared for surprise is to be educated.
James Carse

You have to be fast on your feet and adaptive or else a strategy is useless.
Charles de Gaulle

Pisces 16

There never was a great soul that did not have some divine inspiration.
Marcus Tullius Cicero

Whatever is your best time in the day, give that to communion with God.
Hudson Taylor

Inspiration never arrived when you were searching for it.
Lisa Alther

Cease trying to work everything out with your minds. It will get you nowhere. Live by intuition and inspiration and let your whole life be Revelation.
Eileen Caddy

Wonders will never cease.
Proverb

What to do when inspiration doesn't come: Be careful not to spook, get the wind up, force things into position. You must wait around until the idea comes.
John Huston

In life you need either inspiration or desperation.
Anthony Robbins

IN A QUIET MOMENT, A CREATIVE INDIVIDUAL EXPERIENCES THE FLOW OF INSPIRATION

Commentary: "A Quiet Moment" is pictured in which "a Creative Individual Experiences the Flow of Inspiration." The "Creative Individual" can experience rushes of energy, thought and "Inspiration" through finding some "Quiet" time or through meditation.

Oracle: The "Flow of Inspiration" will come if you allow it through and the more creative you allow yourself to be, the more "Inspiration" there will be. Taking time out for things such as meditation, looking at art or the beauty of nature will allow for the peace that's needed to stop any hurrying thoughts. One's whole life can be changed, in a "Moment," when the mind is stilled and creative solutions are allowed to come through. You may find that with each idea or "Creative Inspiration" there follows another and another. This is a great time to relax and go with the flow, neither fighting against anything nor pushing forward. If things have been hectic in your life and you're looking for guidance, hope and inspiration, try spending a "Quiet Moment" by yourself and allow your intuition to come through. This Symbol shows that no matter what the problem, it will be resolved in time spent contemplating it with the right attitude. Negative thoughts can keep one locked in a cycle of negativity. Closed minds and fixed attitudes will not help in this situation. You may find that answers to questions or situations come when you're least expecting them, e.g., when you're in the bath or going for a walk. Creative projects that you have had difficulty starting (or completing) may indeed begin to find form. Hold on to any impressions you get and before long you'll start to see the solution to your problem or situation.

Keywords: Creativity inspired from above. Openness to higher forces and ideals. Realizations. Dreams. Channeling thoughts and feelings. Messages from one's higher self. Finding solutions. Moments of calm leading to resolutions. Free flowing thoughts. The gift of inspiration. Turning on the tap of creativity. Blockages unblocked.

The Caution: Being too tired to meditate. Choosing to be unaware or to sleep instead of thinking purposefully. Not talking about what needs to be said. Having a lot of ideas that don't translate into reality. Shutting off from others. Loud voices in the head. Schizophrenia.

What does this **SYMBOL** say to *you?*

AN EASTER PROMENADE

Commentary: "An Easter Promenade" is seen. A "Promenade" is defined as a "leisurely walk taken for pleasure, to display one's finery, etc." The "Easter Promenade" is a celebration of bright clothes, fancy hats and competitions, with appearances by such things as the Easter bunny. This is a tradition born more out of the older celebrations of the spring solstice than the Christian festival of Easter not celebrating the crucifixion, but these separate festivals long ago became combined and they now complement each other. In the northern hemisphere our souls are renewed with the beauty of spring approaching and the celebration of the resurrection of Jesus. Feelings of hope and faith are deepened during this very significant event in the Christian calendar.

Oracle: There is regularly a need to share with others the celebration of your community's religious or spiritual aspirations and ideals. It doesn't matter whether there is a feeling of actual religious cohesion amongst the people in this "Easter Promenade," it's more about sharing strong community values. Often, the actual meaning behind the celebration is completely ignored. New traditions can build on old traditions until, sometimes, the origins can seem lost, blurred or forgotten. This is not really a problem as long as it brings people together in an atmosphere of peace and joy. On a deeper level, there may be other layers of meaning to these celebrations that have also been lost completely, but nevertheless leave a vibration or resonance that is in our unconscious awareness. The "Easter Promenade" is about the layering of traditions and to some extent the superimposing of new traditions on the old. No matter how structured or organized this celebration is, if it's done with joy and warmth of feeling, it will inspire the group, infusing them with a sense of emotional unity. It is the combination of celebrations of rebirth, fertility and the communal renewal of faith in the good things of life.

Keywords: Renewed faith in one's life circumstances. Rising up from doubt, fear and loss. Public holidays and their celebrations. Dressing up. Easter bonnets. Easter eggs, chickens and the fertility rites of spring. Rebirth. Forgiveness. Joy. Spiritual unity. Religious holidays. Worship. Renewal. Parades. Transformation.

The Caution: Superficial shows of unity. Craving for attention. Always needing an excuse to get together and unite. Empty displays of faith or joy. Doing things only because everyone else is doing them. Feeling lost, alone and forsaken in the crowd. Guilt trips. Exclusion of other faiths. Religious domination.

What does this **SYMBOL** say to *you?*

Do not abandon yourselves to despair … We are the Easter people and hallelujah is our song.
Pope John Paul II

I come not to entertain you with worldly festivities but arouse your sleeping memory of immortality.
Paramahansa Yogananda

Any ritual is an opportunity for transformation.
Starhawk

The Easter feeling does not end. It signals a new beginning, Of nature, spring, and brand new life, And friendship, peace, and giving. The spirit of Easter is all about Hope, love, and joyful living.
Anonymous

Easter is the gift of hope. Easter is the gift of peace. Easter is the gift of love. Let us rejoice in Him, Who gives them all.
Anonymous

And when it rains on your parade, look up rather than down. Without the rain, there would be no rainbow.
Jerry Chin

Pisces 18

One filled with joy preaches without preaching.
Mother Teresa

A man must have a good deal of vanity who believes, and a good deal of boldness who affirms, that all the doctrines he holds are true, and all he rejects are false.
Benjamin Franklin

What is true preaching like? Instead of preaching to others, if one worships God all the time, that is enough preaching. He who strives to make himself free is the real preacher. Hundreds come from all sides, no one knows whence, to him who is free, and are taught by him. When a rosebud blooms, the bees come from all sides uninvited and unasked.
Sri Ramakrishna

A fool always finds some greater fool to admire him.
Nicholas Boileau

Condense some daily experience into a glowing symbol, and the audience is electrified.
Ralph Waldo Emerson

Good teaching is one-fourth preparation and three-fourths theater.
Gail Godwin

IN A HUGE TENT A FAMOUS REVIVALIST CONDUCTS HIS MEETING WITH A SPECTACULAR PERFORMANCE

Commentary: "In a Huge Tent a Famous Revivalist Conducts His Meeting with a Spectacular Performance." This pictures somebody who has the ability to get people up and going on a spiritual, emotional and physical level. Words of hope and redemption and the giving of one's self to higher purposes and goals are delivered. He works hard to ensure that his words strike the minds and hearts of those listening. Singing and dancing can erupt out of people in celebration. This is largely the result of the passion of the "Famous Revivalist" and the audience may be very inspired by the occasion with people joining in, in some way.

Oracle: You may find there is a need to organize and stage a display of the situation, bringing the community together in a common goal. The symbolism of the "Huge Tent" can represent many things; it can be a school hall, a church, a circus tent, an outdoor arena all the way up to something such as the World Wide Web. It indicates anywhere people come together to experience a lecture or a performance, or, as this Symbol pictures, "a Famous Revivalist." They gather to listen to inspired and inspiring messages being delivered. There is a need for caution, though, as sometimes this can picture situations of hysteria, overstating one's case, or having the audience get out of control. With the power to influence or sway groups of people, there needs to be some feeling of care and moderation. People are often prepared to listen, but for how long? Is the audience listening? Is the cause just? The person "Conducting His Meeting" may be arrogant and believe that only he has the true answers. Sometimes the "Revivalist" may need to top up his own knowledge, feelings and understanding about life and spirituality by listening to those around him.

Keywords: Energy and inspiration. Evangelism. Whipped-up emotions. Having a lot to say. Being instructional and dogmatic about how things should be. Being in charge. Ecstasy. Loud voices. Conversations that are said out loud. Acoustics affecting sounds. Preaching. Mind control. Performing. Political, religious and spiritual activism. Showmanship. Transformative experiences. Captivated audiences. The media circus.

The Caution: Using spiritualism for greedy financial gain. Overblown feelings of one's abilities. Big egos. Hysteria. People whipped up and manipulated by those in charge. Having the agenda of controlling others. Feeling that one has all the answers. Getting worked up about ideals and beliefs. Manipulation and exploitation. Bigotry.

What does this **SYMBOL** say to *you?*

A MASTER INSTRUCTING HIS DISCIPLE

Pisces 19

Commentary: "A Master" is "Instructing His Disciple." He is giving his "Disciple Instruction" on how to handle life in the spiritual, intellectual and emotional realms. The "Disciple" must listen to all the "Master" says and teaches and must learn from his example. There's an old saying, "When the student is ready, the teacher appears." It could easily also be, "When the student is ready, the lesson appears"—there are many ways to learn life's lessons.

Oracle: This is a time for the transfer of higher knowledge and wisdom. In this situation you may find that you are the teacher, the "Master," or the pupil, the "Disciple." Remember that it is often the teacher who learns and the pupil who teaches. Perhaps it's time for listening to your own higher wisdom. The teacher can inspire great personal achievements through teaching the wisdom that the "Disciple" is ready and willing to learn. These lessons can be on many levels, from the purest of teaching and education all the way to downright emotional manipulation—the teachings that are being passed on can be used to elevate or manipulate the thoughts and emotions of the "Disciple." People will sometimes believe the message coming from the "Master" without questioning, merely because of his charisma and presence. The "Master" may have an alternate agenda that he wants to fulfill. There is sometimes a need to separate the actual person of the "Master" from that which he is teaching, as they are not necessarily the same. The "Master" is only human, after all. Someone having something worthwhile to say will find someone who will listen to it.

Keywords: To give and to receive. Lessons that need to be well learned. The transfer of knowledge. Taking time to instruct others. Being willing to both teach and learn. Step-by-step lessons. Passing on information. Instructions and directions. Laying down the law with someone. Manuscripts and lessons. Masters. Gurus. Guiding lights. Reinforcement of knowledge, wisdom and spirituality. Listening and learning. Knowing what questions to ask. Doing homework. Being or setting a good example.

The Caution: Dogmatic instruction by rote. Talking down to others, thinking they know less. Someone having a "know it all" attitude. Manipulating people for one's personal agenda. Using knowledge as power over people. Feeling above everyone else. Codependant behavior. One-eyed attitudes. Losing one's self in another.

What does this **SYMBOL** say to *you?*

Knowledge increases in proportion to its use—that is, the more we teach the more we learn.
H.P. Blavatsky

Teach thy tongue to say I do not know and thou shalt progress.
Maimonides

By learning you will teach; by teaching you will learn.
Latin Proverb

The true teacher defends his pupils against his own personal influence. He inspires self-distrust. He guides their eyes from himself to the spirit that quickens him. He will have no disciple.
Amos Bronson Alcott

A master can tell you what he expects of you. A teacher, though, awakens your own expectations.
Patricia Neal

I can tell you, honest friend, what to believe: believe life; it teaches better than book or orator.
Goethe

Do not believe what your teacher tells you merely out of respect for the teacher.
Buddha

Pisces 20

There is no sincerer love than the love of food.
George Bernard Shaw

The reflections on a day well spent furnish us with joys more pleasing than ten thousand triumphs.
Thomas A. Kempis

It is a good thing that life is not as serious as it seems to a waiter.
Don Herold

Sometimes you struggle so hard to feed your family one way, you forget to feed them the other way, with spiritual nourishment. Everybody needs that.
James Brown

God gave teeth; He will give bread.
Lithuanian Proverb

Man who waits for roast duck to fly into mouth must wait a very, very long time.
Chinese Proverb

My doctor told me to stop having intimate dinners for four. Unless there are three other people.
Orson Welles

A TABLE SET FOR AN EVENING MEAL

Commentary: "A Table" is "Set for an Evening Meal." This image brings to mind "a Table" having been prepared, the food cooked and the hospitality served up for those who come together to share. There's no mention of how many people are to be at this "Meal," but attention has been, or should be, given to the proper nourishment of body, mind and soul.

Oracle: The "Table" may be set for a celebration, a family, a couple or just for one. It could be that everything is in place other than the substance, which may be still in preparation, and those to sit at the "Table" to appreciate it. If the "Table" is not only "Set," but also the food ready and the people enjoying the "Meal," there's the need for a calm state of mind and a quiet and receptive heart. Having said that, it's not always possible to have peace and quiet at the dinner table. Issues of the day may be brought to the "Table" to be discussed, and these may disturb the atmosphere or need resolution. Still, it's important to have a calm and quiet enjoyment while eating, as this ensures a healthy mind and body. This Symbol is often an assurance of that. Having worked hard and long, you may need to realize that your needs will be met. You may find that you have prepared the situation well. What you need will come. Those already at home, as well as those returning home, will find comfort, safety and sustenance. Remember to attend to these everyday tasks with a sense of reverence. Try to remember to say Grace in thanks for the good things that you have.

Keywords: Provision of life's necessities. Being well nourished. Having to prepare for others. Issues of "who will serve and who will eat." Dinner and dinner parties. Issues of nourishment and having a roof over one's head. Food allergies. Food technology. Breaking bread with others. People bringing a plate to share. Cutlery, plates, glasses. Wine and water. Diets. Groceries. Doing the dishes. Making a meal of something. Obesity. Attention to detail. Hired hands. Catering. Candles. Sharing life's bounty.

The Caution: Making preparations with no ability to nourish or satisfy. Devouring things or people. Banging on the table and asking for more. Guilt around issues of providing. Feasts or famines. Eating syndromes. Empty spaces at the table. Arguing at meal times. Indigestion and heartburn. People not turning up for dinner. Overindulging. Consuming people. Not appreciating life's bounty. Continually having to provide for others. Always having to come up with what's for dinner.

What does this **SYMBOL** say to *you?*

A LITTLE WHITE LAMB, A CHILD AND A CHINESE SERVANT

Pisces 21

Commentary: "A Little White Lamb, a Child and a Chinese Servant" is a Symbol that shows the innocence and purity of both childhood and the animal realm. The "Child" is symbolic of potential and curiosity and the need for care and supervision; and the "Chinese Servant" shows the freedom for self-development apart from family influence or dominance. The "Little White Lamb" is of no threat to the "Child" even if things get out of control. The "Chinese Servant" shows that the safety concerns of the "Child" and, indeed, also of the "Lamb," will be watched over and monitored. Being a "Chinese Servant," the care will probably be more lenient than if a parent were involved. There is likely to be more consideration of the value of life experience and lessons rather than domination and discipline. The "Child" pictured may need the guidance, help and nurturing of the "Chinese Servant" because of special needs or because the parents are too busy with their own lives to provide childcare.

Oracle: Children can be fascinated by small, young animals, but can be rough as they test the boundaries of the animals' tolerance. A parent may not like to see the "Child" hurting the "Lamb" at all, whereas the "Chinese Servant" is more likely to give some latitude in order for the "Child" to learn some lessons. It is natural to try and gain a physical awareness of one's situation first. In our earliest years it was the feeling (or tactile) sense that was initially satisfied. You may need to get back to the basic understanding of your situation. By looking at your situation from a kind, caring and considerate perspective, it will be possible to deal with it or solve it in an efficient manner, rather than becoming flustered and reacting harshly or unjustly. This Symbol may show the instinct to judge others by what they look like. Obviously, in this situation, stereotypical images are conjured up, not only with the "Servant," but the "Child" and the "Lamb." It is important to avoid falling into this trap; instead, try to look under the surface of things. You may be surprised by what you find.

Keywords: Being protected by higher, more aware, energies. The privileges money and social status bring. Awareness of the different levels of situations. Differing perspectives. Helpers, servants. Care. Being watched over. Watchfulness. Pets and animals. The supervision of youngsters. Purity of vision. Caring for the child within.

The Caution: Social incompatibility. Purity merely by nature of wealth. Not having to grow up because of the social environment. Not taking responsibility for one's self. Acting like a brat and getting away with it.

What does this **SYMBOL** say to *you?*

Children in ordinary dress may always play with sand.
Hilaire Belloc

The moment the slave resolves that he will no longer be a slave, his fetters fall. He frees himself and shows the way to others. Freedom and slavery are mental states.
Mahatma Gandhi

In the master there is a servant, in the servant a master.
Marcus Tullius Cicero

To maintain a joyful family requires much from both the parents and the children. Each member of the family has to become, in a special way, the servant of the others.
Pope John Paul II

We teachers can only help the work going on, as servants wait upon a master.
Maria Montessori

If thou are a master, be sometimes blind; if a servant, sometimes deaf.
Thomas Fuller

Money is a terrible master but an excellent servant.
P.T. Barnum

Pisces 22

The words printed here are concepts. You must go through the experiences.
St. Augustine

Every age hath its book.
The Koran

The seven deadly sins are: wealth without work; pleasure without conscience; knowledge without character; business without morality; science without humanity; worship without sacrifice; politics without principle.
Mahatma Gandhi

The ideas I stand for aren't mine. I borrowed them from Socrates. I swiped them from Chesterfield. I stole them from Jesus. And I put them in a book. If you don't like their rules, whose would you use?
Dale Carnegie

Any fool can make a rule, and any fool will mind it.
Henry David Thoreau

Three things it is best to avoid: a strange dog, a flood, and a man who thinks he is wise.
Welsh Proverb

There is no such thing as a moral or an immoral book. Books are well written, or badly written.
Oscar Wilde

Only law can give us freedom.
Goethe

A PROPHET BRINGING DOWN THE NEW LAW FROM THE MOUNTAIN

Commentary: "A Prophet Bringing Down the New Law from the Mountain" pictures revelations concerning spirit and truth being delivered through the agency of a single individual, the "Prophet." This message, this "New Law" can be "brought down" orally or in written form in order to be given to the people. "Laws" relate to the culture of the time and will vary as technology and society change, but the "Prophet" is able to manifest "Laws" that will apply not just for his time, but also for times to come.

Oracle: There is a "New Law" being brought "Down from the Mountain" and it is important to make it manifest and integrated into everyday existence. This Symbol can show people watching and waiting for what someone has to say, as if it will change their lives in some way. However, in this day and age it is important not to take what people say as "gospel" without considering your own beliefs and thoughts and whether these "New Laws" ring true to your inner being. Beliefs are something that can bring people together, but they can also just as easily tear people apart. Being asked, or forced, to take on new beliefs or codes of living or being can be confronting. This Symbol can also indicate things being acted out in "biblical proportions," with huge fanfare and importance placed on them, and this may be a good thing, but only you will know whether these apply to you in your life. Misuse of messages for the personal gain of the one who's seen as the "Prophet" can lead to alienation and a loss of faith. Although the principles of "Law" may stay the same, it is the specifics that must vary in order to accommodate the changing perceptions of the times. It is wonderful if the message resonates with you, but if it doesn't you should be able to choose another code for living.

Keywords: Revelations and channeling of new information. Truths being revealed. Thoughts, ideas, guidelines. The Ten Commandments. Laying down the law. New resolutions. New pathways of living. Social justice messages. The Koran. The Torah. The Bible. Finding records. People of the book. The Ark of the Covenant. Newly codified laws. Amendments. The Testaments. Avatars and guides. Moses. Mt. Sinai. Legislation. Laws enacted.

The Caution: Being told what to do. Believing that one has all the answers or believing that someone else has all the answers. Disregarding the religious ways of the past. Rules set in stone. The statement "this is what's going to happen." Rigid application of dogmatic moral codes.

What does this **SYMBOL** say to *you?*

A MATERIALIZING MEDIUM GIVING A SÉANCE

Pisces 23

Commentary: "A Materializing Medium" has a sensitivity to and awareness of spiritual forces. She is "Giving a Séance," and can manifest messages from spirit that are given from the "other side." Roget's Thesaurus references "Medium" as meaning "That by which something is accomplished or some end achieved: agency, agent, instrument, instrumentality, instrumentation, intermediary." She is an "instrument" who is able to receive radiations, frequencies, or vibrations that cannot easily be sensed by most people.

Oracle: Many things can be "Materialized" in our lives; they can come seemingly out of nowhere. They may be messages, voices, noises, stories or episodes from one's life. Objects can be "Materialized" as well; we can conjure them up. Sometimes it can cause confusion, other times enlightenment. Realizing that one can create one's own reality and the responsibility implied in this can lead to the belief that just about anything is possible in one's life. The things that are "Materialized" can be tangible and rewarding things, however, there should be some caution as sometimes they can have more to do with drama and show rather than having any real or lasting substance. Sit with any new impressions you may be receiving until you understand the authenticity or depth. If you have to do something or perform in front of people, rest assured that with the right attitude and a little preparation there should be no problem. You may have the talent and the ability to make things up as you go along. Energy can feel as though it is coursing "through you." Notice the physical evidence that leads you to realize, see or "hear" messages. Certain words standing out in a newspaper or magazine, words of a song that bring messages, something special noticed in a photo or other image, etc. Pay attention to these messages and allow them to inspire you to connect with whatever and whoever is guiding you. Aspects of personality can erupt, at appropriate or sometimes inappropriate moments. How much is true in this situation and how much is made up or imagined?

Keywords: Spiritual channeling. A need to free up "stuck" or earthbound entities. Efforts to materialize things. Coming straight out with things. Giving voice to spirit. Tarot readings, clairvoyance and clairsentience. Things seen ahead of their time. Bringing messages from the other side. Contacting the dead.

The Caution: Putting on a false front. Merely doing a performance for others. Making things up. Using mind control over others to get a desired outcome. Using sensational methods to induce others to give up control over their own lives. Exorcisms performed by the inexperienced. Inviting weird energies or people.

What does this **SYMBOL** say to *you?*

Be careful of your thoughts;
they may become words at any
moment.
Anonymous

The act of contemplation
creates the thing contemplated.
Isaac D'Israeli

Only he who can see the
invisible can do the impossible.
Frank Gaines

I am an invisible man. No, I am
not a spook like those who
haunted Edgar Allen Poe nor
am I one of your Hollywood-
movie ectoplasms. I am a man
of substance, of flesh and bone,
fiber and liquids—and I might
even be said to possess a mind.
I am invisible, simply because
people refuse to see me.
Ralph Ellison

Faith is power to believe and
power to see.
Prentice Mulford

What does mysticism really
mean? It means the way to
attain knowledge. It's close
to philosophy, except in
philosophy you go horizontally
while in mysticism you go
vertically.
Elie Wiesel

Pisces 24

No man is an Island, entire of itself; every man is a piece of the Continent, a part of the main; if a clod be washed away by the sea, Europe is the less, as well as if a promontory were, as well as if a manor of thy friends or of thine own were; any man's death diminishes me, because I am involved in Mankind; And therefore never send to know for whom the bell tolls; It tolls for thee.
John Donne

How I wish that somewhere there existed an island for those who are wise and of good will.
Albert Einstein

In a sense, each of us is an island. In another sense, however, we are all one. For though islands appear separate, and may even be situated at great distances from one another, they are only extrusions of the same planet, earth.
J. Donald Walters

Why are they called apartments when they are all stuck together?
Anonymous

We may be a small island, but we are not a small people.
Edward Heath

THE TINY ISLAND SEEMS LOST IN THE BROAD OCEAN, BUT ITS HAPPY INHABITANTS HAVE CREATED A WORLD ALL THEIR OWN

Commentary: "The Tiny Island" shows a tiny speck of territory in the "Broad Ocean." It implies a small area of people living together. "Its Happy Inhabitants Have Created a World All Their Own"; they have created their own happiness on this somewhat isolated piece of turf. They have carved their life together, but as this is a "Tiny Island," there's a need for compromise in order to sustain good community relations.

Oracle: There are issues of having to learn to get along with people. Drawn together by similar circumstances, hopes or ambitions, it is ironic that sometimes compromise, for the sake of agreement, is the only way to successful coexistence. There is a clear boundary within which everyone concerned must be considered. This can lead to a lack of privacy or intimate exchanges between people. To leave anyone out can lead to divisions and problems of territory and/or possessions. To include others can bring other problems. Issues of territory and one's space will come up eventually. The positive aspect of the "Island" is that you can have clear boundaries and expand your energies into your space. This may be about family, a work situation, or it may take in your whole world. The key is to adapt, consider others and use the available energies in the situation to create something worthwhile. Celebrate each other rather than diminish each other for your individuality. However, too many people living closely together can lead to feeling like you're living on "main street," with some not being able to just hang out and let loose. Having people dropping in can be pleasurable and fun or it can be compromising, as time, space and privacy are lost. Do the same people turn up in your life again and again? Who are you comfortable sharing your space with? Who would you share your desert island with? What possessions would you take if you could only take a few?

Keywords: Adaptability and cohabitation. People jammed in. Seeking others of like mind. Knowing a lot of people. Always considering others. Noise and light pollution. Feeling like new blood is needed in order to grow and flourish. Coexistence. Apartments. Living together. People moving in.

The Caution: Cutting off from those around. Not having enough privacy—or space. Things being kept too "all in the family." No chance to be alone. Pollution and garbage. Crowding out people. Loneliness even among many. Being deserted and lost.

What does this **SYMBOL** say to *you?*

THE PURGING OF THE PRIESTHOOD

Pisces 25

Commentary: "The Purging of the Priesthood" is an image of people having to measure up to spiritual or moral values. Whoever upholds a position in the "Priesthood" should act in an appropriate manner and minister to the needs of people without any ulterior motives. When people don't live up to their duties or the expectations of others, it often leads to someone having to leave, retire, resign or be ejected. "Purging" means to get rid of and it can lead to scapegoats: those who are thrown into the desert, abandoned and forgotten.

Oracle: Periodically, there is a need to cleanse and purify motives, leading to a better representation of moral and spiritual values. Sometimes we need to reexamine moral and spiritual sincerity in a person, corporation, community or situation. Getting rid of people or ideals that hold one back can open up situations to more trust, sharing and enjoyment. You may have to dismiss someone, or a group of people, from their duties or from their ability to affect your life in some way. It is easy to lose sight of the ideal through the use of the rationalizing mind, the ego, security issues or emotive passion. However, if someone has not lived up to their responsibilities on some level, often it's best for the future, and one's peace of mind, to be free of them. It may lead to a breakthrough in the understanding of where they've gone "off the rails," as well. Sometimes there's a need to get clearly out of the reach of people's "influence." People who hold "Priestly" attitudes often have quite a lot of power and hold on others. People will often give them power, thereby forsaking their own powers in the process. What side of this "Purging" are you on? Are you the one with the "right" motives? There could be a fear of rejection at work. Whatever your situation, stating your truth and staying with it is the best option.

Keywords: Revealing the truth of people for who and what they truly are. Cutting people off. Throwing out things that don't measure up. Forced retirement and redundancies. Payouts at the end of employment. Dismissals. Opting out for moral reasons. Being fired. Holes left where someone took up a lot of space.

The Caution: Stressful battle over who's in charge. Blackmail. The threat of being thrown out. Something being revealed. Evicting people because they deceive, lie or mislead or just because they're not liked. Bringing somebody down. Scapegoating others. Corruption and scandal that threaten collapse. Wanting to appear to be doing the right thing. Coverups. The burning of books. Perversion.

What does this **SYMBOL** say to *you?*

Sometimes you've got to let everything go—purge yourself. If you are unhappy with anything ... whatever is bringing you down, get rid of it. Because you'll find that when you're free, your true creativity, your true self comes out.
Tina Turner

It has been my experience that folks who have no vices have very few virtues.
Abraham Lincoln

A priest is a man who is called Father by everyone except his own children who are obliged to call him Uncle.
Italian Proverb

Whoever undertakes to set himself up as a judge in the field of truth and knowledge is shipwrecked by the laughter of the Gods.
Albert Einstein

The heresies we should fear are those which can be confused with orthodoxy.
Jorge Luis Borges

Faith is not a thing which one "loses," we merely cease to shape our lives by it.
Georges Bernanos

He that serves at the altar ought to live by the altar.
Romanian Proverb

Pisces 26

A person needs at intervals to separate himself from family and companions and go to new places. He must go without his familiars in order to be open to influences, to change.
Katharine Butler Hathaway

O, swear not by the moon,
  th' inconstant moon,
That monthly changes in her
  circled orb,
Lest that thy love prove likewise
  variable.
William Shakespeare

Although the connections are not always obvious, personal change is inseparable from social and political change.
Harriet Lerner

Separation secures manifest friendship.
Indian Proverb

The difference between divorce and legal separation is that a legal separation gives a husband time to hide his money.
Johnny Carson

There is a star above us which unites souls of the first order, though worlds and ages separate them.
Christina of Sweden

We must change in order to survive.
Pearl Bailey

A NEW MOON REVEALS THAT IT'S TIME FOR PEOPLE TO GO AHEAD WITH THEIR DIFFERENT PROJECTS

Commentary: "A New Moon Reveals That It's Time for People to Go Ahead with Their Different Projects" shows the realization of a new time dawning; there's a new beginning. Each month, at the "New Moon," there is the necessary energy and impetus to get new things started. It is conventionally a time to put energy into anything new in your life, as it will have forward momentum.

Oracle: There's an image here of the emergence of new possibilities and new horizons. This Symbol can imply a moving away from or a splitting up of people, however this may not always be the case. There could be a call for a couple to split off from the rest of the family, or somebody might need some space to be alone or get on with something they want or need to do. Hence it doesn't always mean a split or separation, although it certainly can. People have their own responses to situations, so it is important not to expect everyone to react in the same way when something unexpected, or new, comes up. Periodically, there is a need to let go of things from the past. Relationships, jobs, friendships; in fact any situation at all might be coming to completion, or needing a break for a while. There can be the feeling of a dividing wall coming up between you and others. This situation may have been brewing for some time and now the consequences of it are coming to light. However, if people are given their own measure of freedom, they may come back together when the time and the energy is right. Perhaps it's a good idea to direct some energy into a new project at the time of the next "New Moon." Light a candle and state your intentions with honesty and feel the effects of the rewards that can come flooding in with this new beginning. Remember to honor "the other," the other person who may have their own "Project" or path to follow.

Keywords: Diversifying. Applying talents in a different direction. People splitting up and splitting off. New opportunities and potentials. The beginning of a new age. Letting go of the old and outworn. Separations. Embracing one's future without the need for others. Coming to a fork in the road. Divorces. New jobs, directions and destinies. The dawning of a new era.

The Caution: Not giving or receiving emotional support. Feeling split off and alone, even when one is with others. The fear and loathing of possible separation. Overthrowing the old too quickly. Changing direction unexpectedly. The fear of old age. Relationships that fail again and again.

What does this **SYMBOL** say to *you?*

A HARVEST MOON ILLUMINATES THE SKY

Pisces 27

Commentary: "A Harvest Moon Illuminates the Sky." This is an extraordinary Symbol, considering the fact that these Symbols came through the clairvoyant, Elsie Wheeler, in random order. It's extraordinary because the "Harvest Moon" can very easily fall on this degree, as the "Harvest Moon" is calculated as the full moon occurring nearest to the autumnal equinox in the northern hemisphere, about September 23. On several nights in succession, at this time of the year, the moonrise is at nearly the same time, because of the relation of the moon's path to the horizon. On these nights, there is full moonlight almost from sunset to sunrise if the sky is unclouded.

Oracle: This Symbol shows an abundant time of "Harvest." The "Harvest Moon" is a positive sign, with high energy abounding. The sky is clear and conditions are perfect. It's a time of fertility and abundance, but it is also a sign that there may still be much work to be done. For now, though, this can be an opportunity to relax, enjoy, and to conserve strength in anticipation of the tasks ahead. For the time being, you can reap the benefits of the work that's been accomplished so far. There can be strong feelings of culmination, fertility and fullness. You may feel that it has taken a while to get where you are, and this is a good chance to take some time out to celebrate and reconnect with family and loved ones. Capture this magical moment while it lasts, as the energy may start to wane before you know it. However, while it is great now to celebrate the achievements of the "Harvest," it is also a time of self-discipline because the task must be completed or the fruits of one's labors may go rotten or be wasted. Be sure not to get so carried away in the celebration that you neglect finishing the tasks before you. With all of this light "Illuminating" the night "Sky," take a look around with open eyes and see what can be seen.

Keywords: Situations that are very ripe and full of fruition. Celebrating what you have. Expanded perspective making everything clear. A sense of achievement. Seizing the moment to make the most of what's possible. Nature's bounty. The beauty of the moon in the night sky.

The Caution: Neglecting the tasks at hand because of the appearance of abundance. Achievements waning because of neglect. Wasting energy on inconsequential activities. "Lunatic" behavior. Not being able to sleep.

What does this **SYMBOL** say to *you?*

Sow a thought, reap an action; sow an action, reap a habit; sow a habit, reap a character; sow a character; reap a destiny.
Anonymous

Sow much, reap much; sow little, reap little.
Chinese Proverb

Give fools their gold, and knaves their power;
Let fortune's bubbles rise and fall;
Who sows a field, or trains a flower,
Or plants a tree, is more than all.
John Greenleaf Whittier

Under the harvest moon,
When the soft silver
Drips shimmering
Over the garden nights,
Death, the gray mocker,
Comes and whispers to you
As a beautiful friend
Who remembers.
Carl Sandburg

Write your wishes on the door and come in. Stand outside in the pools of the harvest moon.
Carl Sandburg

Talk unbelief, and you will have unbelief; but talk faith, and you will have faith. According to the seed sown will be the harvest.
Ellen G. White

Everyone is a moon, and has a dark side which he never shows anyone.
Mark Twain

Pisces 28

The first farmer was the first man, and all historic nobility rests on possession and use of land.
Ralph Waldo Emerson

A moon garden is one which is filled with white-flowering plants that catch the moonlight and awaken the moon faeries. Only white blossoms are able to capture and reflect the pale light cast by a moonbeam.
Dubh Sidhe

Ever since man began to till the soil and learned not to eat the seed grain but to plant it and wait for the harvest, the postponement of gratification has been the basis of a higher standard of living and civilization.
S. I. Hayakawa

It's the opinion of some that crops could be grown on the moon. Which raises the fear that it may not be long before we're paying somebody not to.
Franklin P. Jones

Ignorance is the night of the mind, but a night without moon and star.
Confucius

A mind without instruction can no more bear fruit than can a field, however fertile, without cultivation.
Cicero

A FERTILE GARDEN UNDER THE FULL MOON

Commentary: The symbol, "A Fertile Garden under the Full Moon" is a vital, alive and positive picture. This is a very powerful image of the Goddess energy. Not only is it the "Fertile Garden" of creativity and growing life, but also the gentle light and water energy of "the Full Moon" are radiating energy through it.

Oracle: The "tidal" effect of the "Full Moon" on the emotional "waters" in this moment are raising feelings high and creating a strong sense of satisfaction, all under the blessing of the "Moon's" strong feminine energy. There's a sense that one has all that's needed, and emotions are running at full tilt. The "Garden" is "Fertile" and full of produce, vegetables, apples, flowers and plants of all descriptions. It may be time for the harvesting of the fruits of your efforts and there may be a need for more fertilization soon, but right now you can enjoy the fullness of this time. As there's so much "Fertile" energy around, this is a situation brimming with rewards and opportunities for new life. Enjoy the moment and try to keep a sense of equilibrium, though, as soon the energy will be on the wane and you'll have to get back to more practical, everyday tasks. However, there can also be the sense that one is at the peak of some experience and at any moment it could all slide away. The time of the "Full Moon" is a time when the male and female energies are at their greatest polarity, with the sun, representing male energies, and the "Moon," the feminine aspect, being in opposition to each other in the sky. If there's a rift between people, it may be time to reflect on what's causing it. Don't feel that your opportunities for happiness have passed. "Fertile" periods come in cycles, and it is likely that another opportunity will come soon. In the meantime, carry on with everyday tasks and prepare for the next "Fertile" stage.

Keywords: Fullness and fertility. Peak of energy and experiences. Brilliantly active unconscious life. Cycles. Waiting for the right time to approach or handle a situation. The effect of the moon. Astrology and predictive practices. The time for harvesting the rewards of hard work. Nature sprites. Vegetables, herbs and nature's bounty.

The Caution: Jealous protection of possessions. Not being able to make one's mind up because of the number of possibilities. Missed opportunities. Difficulty shutting down the mind. Emotions that get out of hand.

What does this **SYMBOL** say to *you?*

LIGHT BREAKING INTO MANY COLORS AS IT PASSES THROUGH A PRISM

Pisces 29

Commentary: "Light Breaking into Many Colors as It Passes through a Prism" is an image of beauty and shape. A "Prism" in optics is a piece of translucent glass or crystal that is used to form a spectrum of light that is separated according to colors. The light becomes separated because different wavelengths or frequencies are bent by different amounts as they enter the prism and again as they leave it. The shorter wavelengths, toward the blue or violet end of the spectrum, are refracted by the greatest amount; the longer wavelengths, toward the red end, are refracted the least.

Oracle: You may need to break your situation down into its simpler components in order to see the full picture. Even though there are complex things that need to be broken down to their elemental parts, it is not as difficult as it might seem. This is vital to the success of the situation, and will lead to a greater understanding of the relationship between the many parts. Just be careful not to overanalyze, thereby losing the joy that's inherent. This Symbol can also indicate that you are of a curious nature, or perhaps just have a natural capacity for probing into complexities and learning about the makeup of an object, situation or person. This can, on one hand, make for a constant fascination with the connectedness and the larger questions of life. However, be aware that an emphasis on pulling things apart, and continual analysis can lead to disappointment; the various elements may be somehow less exciting than the whole. This Symbol is encouraging you to take a single vision and develop it into its many possible individual streams. Color may indeed have a part to play, as can symbols and images. Hang a crystal in the window to attract the rays of the sun. This can bring some glorious energy your way.

Keywords: Spectrum analysis. Color and crystal healing. Rainbows. Light refraction. Side effects. Considering many facets of a situation. Endless opportunities. Optics. Sight. Seeing. Copying and sharing ideas or things. Disseminating information. Auras and aura photography. Triangles. Polarization of light. Reflection. Laboratory tests. Diffracted personality.

The Caution: Locked in to a set of parameters. Over analyzing things. Being blinded by ambition. Daunted by the task ahead. Mirages. Using microscopes and binoculars but not seeing things as they really are.

What does this **SYMBOL** say to *you?*

An optimist is a person who sees a green light everywhere, while a pessimist sees only the red stoplight ... The truly wise person is colorblind.
Albert Schweitzer

Nothing has such power to broaden the mind as the ability to investigate systematically and truly all that comes under thy observation in life.
Marcus Aurelius

It's a good thing that when God created the rainbow, He didn't consult a decorator or He would still be picking colors.
Samuel Levenson

The purest and most thoughtful minds are those which love color the most.
John Ruskin

...daydreams, as it were... I look out the window sometimes to seek the color of the shadows and the different greens in the trees, but when I get ready to paint I just close my eyes and imagine a scene.
Grandma Moses

All colors are the friends of their neighbors and the lovers of their opposites.
Marc Chagall

Pisces 30

A MAJESTIC ROCK FORMATION RESEMBLING A FACE IS IDEALIZED BY A BOY WHO TAKES IT AS HIS IDEAL OF GREATNESS; AS HE GROWS UP, HE BEGINS TO LOOK LIKE IT

Commentary: "A Majestic Rock Formation Resembling a Face Is Idealized by a Boy Who Takes It as His Ideal of Greatness; as He Grows Up, He Begins to Look Like It" shows the ability that we have of projecting an ideal or an image into the future. This can be an image of what, or who, we'd like to become. We can then grow and emerge into that reality.

Oracle: Sometimes we see an image of ourselves that we'd like to emulate or aspire to or become. It's good to have a goal in life, something we can inspire us, and something to work toward. Truly in this life, we can set our sights high and aim for them, as did the "Boy" who looked on the "Majestic Rock Formation" as "His Ideal of Greatness." Having an "Ideal" of how we'd like to be can be great, as long as we aren't trying to be something that we naturally or intrinsically are not possible of being. What is it that you "Idealize"? What is it that you'd like to project? What image suits the real person inside of you? You may find that you are growing into the "Ideal" that you have imagined and it gives you a sense of pride and fulfillment, assuming you have imagined a positive image. Meditating on a goal or the projection of an ideal can lead to actuality, just be clear about what you really desire in the situation—you just might get it!

Keywords: Concrete manifestation of one's ideals. Enduring truths. Culmination of efforts. Projections of ideal images. Wanting to be "big" and successful. Tutankhamen's mask. Wanting a sense of immortality. Defining one's fate through conscious manifestation. Morphing reality to suit an objective. Ambition. The ability to see life in inanimate objects.

The Caution: Not being at all clear about whom one is or what one can be. Becoming a screen for the projection of others' ideals. Stony faces that show the hardships of life. Hardening of one's personality. Stony faces. Idealizing others therefore losing one's own identity.

What does this **SYMBOL** say to *you?*

	January			February			March			April
1	10–12 Cap		1	12–14 Aqu		1	10–12 Pis		1	11–13 Ari
2	11–13 Cap		2	13–15 Aqu		2	11–13 Pis		2	12–14 Ari
3	12–14 Cap		3	14–16 Aqu		3	12–14 Pis		3	13–15 Ari
4	13–15 Cap		4	15–17 Aqu		4	13–15 Pis		4	14–16 Ari
5	14–16 Cap		5	16–18 Aqu		5	14–16 Pis		5	15–17 Ari
6	15–17 Cap		6	17–19 Aqu		6	15–17 Pis		6	16–18 Ari
7	16–18 Cap		7	18–20 Aqu		7	16–18 Pis		7	17–19 Ari
8	17–19 Cap		8	19–21 Aqu		8	17–19 Pis		8	18–20 Ari
9	18–20 Cap		9	20–22 Aqu		9	18–20 Pis		9	19–21 Ari
10	19–21 Cap		10	21–23 Aqu		10	19–21 Pis		10	20–22 Ari
11	20–22 Cap		11	22–24 Aqu		11	20–22 Pis		11	21–23 Ari
12	21–23 Cap		12	23–25 Aqu		12	21–23 Pis		12	22–24 Ari
13	22–24 Cap		13	24–26 Aqu		13	22–24 Pis		13	23–25 Ari
14	23–25 Cap		14	25–27 Aqu		14	23–25 Pis		14	24–26 Ari
15	24–26 Cap		15	26–28 Aqu		15	24–26 Pis		15	25–27 Ari
16	25–27 Cap		16	27–29 Aqu		16	25–27 Pis		16	26–28 Ari
17	26–28 Cap		17	28–30 Aqu		17	26–28 Pis		17	27–29 Ari
18	27–29 Cap		18	29 Aqu–1 Pis		18	27–29 Pis		18	28–30 Ari
19	29 Cap–1 Aqu		19	30 Aqu–2 Pis		19	28–30 Pis		19	29 Ari–1 Tau
20	30 Cap–2 Aqu		20	1–3 Pis		20	29 Pis–1 Ari		20	30 Ari–2 Tau
21	1–3 Aqu		21	2–4 Pis		21	30 Pis–2 Ari		21	1–3 Tau
22	2–4 Aqu		22	3–5 Pis		22	1–3 Ari		22	1–3 Tau
23	3–5 Aqu		23	4–6 Pis		23	2–4 Ari		23	2–4 Tau
24	4–6 Aqu		24	5–7 Pis		24	3–5 Ari		24	3–5 Tau
25	5–7 Aqu		25	6–8 Pis		25	4–6 Ari		25	4–6 Tau
26	6–8 Aqu		26	7–9 Pis		26	5–7 Ari		26	5–7 Tau
27	7–9 Aqu		27	8–10 Pis		27	6–8 Ari		27	6–8 Tau
28	8–10 Aqu		28	9–11 Pis		28	7–9 Ari		28	7–9 Tau
29	9–11 Aqu					29	8–10 Ari		29	8–10 Tau
30	10–12 Aqu					30	9–11 Ari		30	9–11 Tau
31	11–13 Aqu					31	10–12 Ari			

	May			June			July			August
1	10–12 Tau		1	10–12 Gem		1	9–11 Can		1	8–10 Leo
2	11–13 Tau		2	11–13 Gem		2	10–12 Can		2	9–11 Leo
3	12–14 Tau		3	12–14 Gem		3	11–13 Can		3	10–12 Leo
4	13–15 Tau		4	13–15 Gem		4	12–14 Can		4	11–13 Leo
5	14–16 Tau		5	14–12 Gem		5	13–15 Can		5	12–14 Leo
6	15–17 Tau		6	15–16 Gem		6	14–16 Can		6	13–15 Leo
7	16–18 Tau		7	16–17 Gem		7	14–16 Can		7	14–16 Leo
8	17–19 Tau		8	17–18 Gem		8	15–17 Can		8	15–17 Leo
9	18–20 Tau		9	18–19 Gem		9	16–18 Can		9	16–18 Leo
10	19–21 Tau		10	19–20 Gem		10	17–19 Can		10	17–19 Leo
11	20–22 Tau		11	20–22 Gem		11	18–20 Can		11	18–20 Leo
12	21–23 Tau		12	21–23 Gem		12	19–21 Can		12	19–21 Leo
13	22–24 Tau		13	22–24 Gem		13	20–22 Can		13	20–22 Leo
14	23–25 Tau		14	23–25 Gem		14	21–23 Can		14	21–23 Leo
15	24–26 Tau		15	24–26 Gem		15	22–24 Can		15	22–24 Leo
16	25–27 Tau		16	24–26 Gem		16	23–25 Can		16	23–25 Leo
17	26–28 Tau		17	25–27 Gem		17	24–26 Can		17	24–26 Leo
18	27–29 Tau		18	26–28 Gem		18	25–27 Can		18	25–27 Leo
19	28–30 Tau		19	27–29 Gem		19	26–28 Can		19	26–28 Leo
20	29 Tau –1 Gem		20	28–30 Gem		20	27–29 Can		20	27–29 Leo
21	30 Tau –2 Gem		21	29 Gem–1 Can		21	28–30 Can		21	28–30 Leo
22	1–3 Gem		22	30 Gem –2 Can		22	29 Can–1 Leo		22	29 Leo–1 Vir
23	1–3 Gem		23	1–3 Can		23	30 Can–2 Leo		23	29 Leo–1 Vir
24	2–4 Gem		24	2–4 Can		24	1–3 Leo		24	30 Leo–2 Vir
25	3–5 Gem		25	3–5 Can		25	2–4 Leo		25	1–3 Vir
26	4–6 Gem		26	4–6 Can		26	3–5 Leo		26	2–4 Vir
27	5–7 Gem		27	5–7 Can		27	4–6 Leo		27	3–5 Vir
28	6–8 Gem		28	6–8 Can		28	5–7 Leo		28	4–6 Vir
29	7–9 Gem		29	7–9 Can		29	5–7 Leo		29	5–7 Vir
30	8–10 Gem		30	8–10 Can		30	6–8 Leo		30	6–8 Vir
31	9–11 Gem					31	7–9 Leo		31	7–9 Vir

	September			October			November			December
1	8–10 Vir		1	7–9 Lib		1	8–10 Sco		1	8–10 Sag
2	9–11 Vir		2	8–10 Lib		2	9–11 Sco		2	9–11 Sag
3	10–12 Vir		3	9–11 Lib		3	10–12 Sco		3	10–12 Sag
4	11–13 Vir		4	10–12 Lib		4	11–13 Sco		4	11–13 Sag
5	12–14 Vir		5	11–13 Lib		5	12–14 Sco		5	12–14 Sag
6	13–15 Vir		6	12–14 Lib		6	13–15 Sco		6	13–15 Sag
7	14–16 Vir		7	13–15 Lib		7	14–16 Sco		7	14–16 Sag
8	15–17 Vir		8	14–16 Lib		8	15–17 Sco		8	16–18 Sag
9	16–18 Vir		9	15–17 Lib		9	16–18 Sco		9	17–19 Sag
10	17–19 Vir		10	16–18 Lib		10	17–19 Sco		10	18–20 Sag
11	18–20 Vir		11	17–19 Lib		11	18–20 Sco		11	19–21 Sag
12	19–21 Vir		12	18–20 Lib		12	19–21 Sco		12	20–22 Sag
13	20–22 Vir		13	19–21 Lib		13	20–22 Sco		13	21–23 Sag
14	21–23 Vir		14	20–22 Lib		14	21–23 Sco		14	22–24 Sag
15	22–24 Vir		15	21–23 Lib		15	22–24 Sco		15	23–25 Sag
16	23–25 Vir		16	22–24 Lib		16	23–25 Sco		16	24–26 Sag
17	24–26 Vir		17	23–25 Lib		17	24–26 Sco		17	25–27 Sag
18	25–27 Vir		18	24–26 Lib		18	25–27 Sco		18	26–28 Sag
19	26–28 Vir		19	25–27 Lib		19	26–28 Sco		19	27–29 Sag
20	27–29 Vir		20	26–28 Lib		20	27–29 Sco		20	28–30 Sag
21	28–30 Vir		21	27–29 Lib		21	28–30 Sco		21	29 Sag–1 Cap
22	29 Vir–1 Lib		22	28–30 Lib		22	29 Sco–1 Sag		22	30 Sag–2 Cap
23	30 Vir–2 Lib		23	29 Lib–1 Sco		23	30 Sco–2 Sag		23	1–3 Cap
24	1–3 Lib		24	30 Lib–2 Sco		24	1–3 Sag		24	2–4 Cap
25	2–4 Lib		25	1–3 Sco		25	2–4 Sag		25	3–5 Cap
26	3–5 Lib		26	2–4 Sco		26	3–5 Sag		26	4–6 Cap
27	3–5 Lib		27	3–5 Sco		27	4–6 Sag		27	5–7 Cap
28	4–6 Lib		28	4–6 Sco		28	5–7 Sag		28	6–8 Cap
29	5–7 Lib		29	5–7 Sco		29	6–8 Sag		29	7–9 Cap
30	6–8 Lib		30	6–8 Sco		30	7–9 Sag		30	8–10 Cap
			31	7–9 Sco					31	9–11 Cap

Leap Year

	January			February			March			April
1	9–11 Cap		1	11–13 Aqu		1	10–12 Pis		1	11–13 Ari
2	10–12 Cap		2	12–14 Aqu		2	11–13 Pis		2	12–14 Ari
3	11–13 Cap		3	13–15 Aqu		3	12–14 Pis		3	13–15 Ari
4	12–14 Cap		4	14–16 Aqu		4	13–15 Pis		4	14–16 Ari
5	13–15 Cap		5	15–17 Aqu		5	14–16 Pis		5	15–17 Ari
6	14–16 Cap		6	16–18 Aqu		6	15–17 Pis		6	16–18 Ari
7	15–17 Cap		7	17–19 Aqu		7	16–18 Pis		7	17–19 Ari
8	16–18 Cap		8	18–20 Aqu		8	17–19 Pis		8	18–20 Ari
9	17–19 Cap		9	19–21 Aqu		9	18–20 Pis		9	19–21 Ari
10	18–20 Cap		10	20–22 Aqu		10	19–21 Pis		10	20–22 Ari
11	19–21 Cap		11	21–23 Aqu		11	20–22 Pis		11	21–23 Ari
12	20–22 Cap		12	22–24 Aqu		12	21–23 Pis		12	22–24 Ari
13	21–23 Cap		13	23–25 Aqu		13	22–24 Pis		13	23–25 Ari
14	22–24 Cap		14	24–26 Aqu		14	23–25 Pis		14	24–26 Ari
15	23–25 Cap		15	25–27 Aqu		15	24–26 Pis		15	25–27 Ari
16	24–26 Cap		16	26–28 Aqu		16	25–27 Pis		16	26–28 Ari
17	25–27 Cap		17	27–29 Aqu		17	26–28 Pis		17	27–29 Ari
18	26–28 Cap		18	28–30 Aqu		18	27–29 Pis		18	28–30 Ari
19	27–29 Cap		19	29 Aqu–1 Pis		19	28–30 Pis		19	29 Ari–1 Tau
20	29 Cap–1 Aqu		20	30 Aqu–2 Pis		20	29 Pis–1 Ari		20	30 Ari–2 Tau
21	30 Cap–2 Aqu		21	1–3 Pis		21	30 Pis–2 Ari		21	1–3 Tau
22	1–3 Aqu		22	2–4 Pis		22	1–3 Ari		22	2–4 Tau
23	2–4 Aqu		23	3–5 Pis		23	2–4 Ari		23	3–5 Tau
24	3–5 Aqu		24	4–6 Pis		24	3–5 Ari		24	4–6 Tau
25	4–6 Aqu		25	5–7 Pis		25	4–6 Ari		25	5–7 Tau
26	5–7 Aqu		26	6–8 Pis		26	5–7 Ari		26	6–8 Tau
27	6–8 Aqu		27	7–9 Pis		27	6–8 Ari		27	7–9 Tau
28	7–9 Aqu		28	8–10 Pis		28	7–9 Ari		28	8–10 Tau
29	8–10 Aqu		29	9–11 Pis		29	8–10 Ari		29	9–11 Tau
30	9–11 Aqu					30	9–11 Ari		30	9–11 Tau
31	10–12 Aqu					31	10–12 Ari			

	May			June			July			August
1	10–12 Tau		1	10–12 Gem		1	9–11 Can		1	9–11 Leo
2	11–13 Tau		2	11–13 Gem		2	10–12 Can		2	10–12 Leo
3	12–14 Tau		3	12–14 Gem		3	11–13 Can		3	11–13 Leo
4	13–15 Tau		4	13–15 Gem		4	12–14 Can		4	11–13 Leo
5	14–16 Tau		5	14–12 Gem		5	13–15 Can		5	12–14 Leo
6	15–17 Tau		6	15–16 Gem		6	14–16 Can		6	13–15 Leo
7	16–18 Tau		7	16–17 Gem		7	15–17 Can		7	14–16 Leo
8	17–19 Tau		8	17–18 Gem		8	16–18 Can		8	15–17 Leo
9	18–20 Tau		9	18–19 Gem		9	17–19 Can		9	16–18 Leo
10	19–21 Tau		10	19–20 Gem		10	18–20 Can		10	17–19 Leo
11	20–22 Tau		11	20–22 Gem		11	19–21 Can		11	18–20 Leo
12	21–23 Tau		12	21–23 Gem		12	19–21 Can		12	19–21 Leo
13	22–24 Tau		13	22–24 Gem		13	20–22 Can		13	20–22 Leo
14	23–25 Tau		14	23–25 Gem		14	21–23 Can		14	21–23 Leo
15	24–26 Tau		15	24–26 Gem		15	22–24 Can		15	22–24 Leo
16	25–27 Tau		16	25–27 Ccm		16	23–25 Can		16	23–25 Leo
17	26–28 Tau		17	26–28 Gem		17	24–26 Can		17	24–26 Leo
18	27–29 Tau		18	27–29 Gem		18	25–27 Can		18	25–27 Leo
19	28–30 Tau		19	28–30 Gem		19	26–28 Can		19	26–28 Leo
20	29 Tau –1 Gem		20	29 Gem–1 Can		20	27–29 Can		20	27–29 Leo
21	30 Tau –2 Gem		21	29 Gem–1 Can		21	28–30 Can		21	28–30 Leo
22	1–3 Gem		22	30 Gem –2 Can		22	29 Can–1 Leo		22	29 Leo–1 Vir
23	2–4 Gem		23	1–3 Can		23	30 Can–2 Leo		23	30 Leo–2 Vir
24	3–5 Gem		24	2–4 Can		24	1–3 Leo		24	1–3 Vir
25	4–6 Gem		25	3–5 Can		25	2–4 Leo		25	2–4 Vir
26	5–7 Gem		26	4–6 Can		26	3–5 Leo		26	3–5 Vir
27	6–8 Gem		27	5–7 Can		27	4–6 Leo		27	4–6 Vir
28	7–9 Gem		28	6–8 Can		28	5–7 Leo		28	5–7 Vir
29	7–9 Gem		29	7–9 Can		29	6–8 Leo		29	6–8 Vir
30	8–10 Gem		30	8–10 Can		30	7–9 Leo		30	6–8 Vir
31	9–11 Gem					31	8–9 Leo		31	7–9 Vir

	September			October			November			December
1	8–10 Vir		1	8–10 Lib		1	8–10 Sco		1	9–11 Sag
2	9–11 Vir		2	9–11 Lib		2	9–11 Sco		2	10–12 Sag
3	10–12 Vir		3	10–12 Lib		3	10–12 Sco		3	11–13 Sag
4	11–13 Vir		4	11–13 Lib		4	11–13 Sco		4	12–14 Sag
5	12–14 Vir		5	12–14 Lib		5	12–14 Sco		5	13–15 Sag
6	13–15 Vir		6	13–15 Lib		6	13–15 Sco		6	14–16 Sag
7	14–16 Vir		7	14–16 Lib		7	14–16 Sco		7	15–17 Sag
8	15–17 Vir		8	15–17 Lib		8	15–17 Sco		8	16–18 Sag
9	16–18 Vir		9	16–18 Lib		9	16–18 Sco		9	17–19 Sag
10	17–19 Vir		10	17–19 Lib		10	17–19 Sco		10	18–20 Sag
11	18–20 Vir		11	18–20 Lib		11	18–20 Sco		11	19–21 Sag
12	19–21 Vir		12	19–21 Lib		12	19–21 Sco		12	20–22 Sag
13	20–22 Vir		13	20–22 Lib		13	20–22 Sco		13	21–23 Sag
14	21–23 Vir		14	20–22 Lib		14	21–23 Sco		14	22–24 Sag
15	22–24 Vir		15	21–23 Lib		15	22–24 Sco		15	23–25 Sag
16	23–25 Vir		16	22–24 Lib		16	23–25 Sco		16	24–26 Sag
17	24–26 Vir		17	23–25 Lib		17	24–26 Sco		17	25–27 Sag
18	25–27 Vir		18	24–26 Lib		18	25–27 Sco		18	26–28 Sag
19	26–28 Vir		19	25–27 Lib		19	26–28 Sco		19	27–29 Sag
20	27–29 Vir		20	26–28 Lib		20	27–29 Sco		20	28–30 Sag
21	28–30 Vir		21	27–29 Lib		21	29 Sco–1 Sag		21	29 Sag–1 Cap
22	29 Vir–1 Lib		22	28–30 Lib		22	30 Sco–2 Sag		22	30 Sag–2 Cap
23	30 Vir–2 Lib		23	29 Lib–1 Sco		23	1–3 Sag		23	1–3 Cap
24	1–3 Lib		24	30 Lib–2 Sco		24	2–4 Sag		24	2–4 Cap
25	2–4 Lib		25	1–3 Sco		25	3–5 Sag		25	3–5 Cap
26	3–5 Lib		26	2–4 Sco		26	4–6 Sag		26	4–6 Cap
27	4–6 Lib		27	3–5 Sco		27	5–7 Sag		27	5–7 Cap
28	5–7 Lib		28	4–6 Sco		28	6–8 Sag		28	6–8 Cap
29	6–8 Lib		29	5–7 Sco		29	7–9 Sag		29	7–9 Cap
30	7–9 Lib		30	6–8 Sco		30	8–10 Sag		30	8–10 Cap
			31	7–9 Sco					31	9–11 Cap